3rd Edition
1994 North American
Coins & Prices

A GUIDE TO U.S., CANADIAN, AND MEXICAN COINS

edited by
David C. Harper
Editor of WORLD COIN NEWS
and BANK NOTE REPORTER

Published by

krause
publications

700 E. State Street • Iola, WI 54990-0001
Telephone: 715/445-2214

Library of Congress Catalog Number: 91-76402
ISBN: 0-87341-266-4
Printed in the United States of America

Contents

Preface... 4

Chapter 1: "A Small Beginning"............................... 5

Chapter 2: Making Money...................................... 15

Chapter 3: The Thrill of the Hunt........................... 25

Chapter 4: The Grading Factor............................... 36

Chapter 5: Get a Map 58

Chapter 6: Caring for Coins 75

Chapter 7: The Profit Motive................................. 83

Chapter 8: Join the Club....................................... 87

Chapter 9: What's Hot, What's Not 90

Glossary of Coin Terms 98

PRICING SECTION

Introduction to Pricing 107

UNITED STATES:

Colonial Coins.. 110

Issues of 1792 153

United States Coins.. 155

Commemoratives 266

American Eagle Bullion Coins 293

U.S. Minting Varieties and Errors 296

CANADA:

Canadian Coins... 318

MEXICO:

Mexican Coins.. 382

Bibliography 509

Preface

Providing coin collectors with accurate, independently produced pricing information on collectible coins has become a trademark of Krause Publications in its 40 years of publishing. We employ a full-time staff of market analysts who monitor auction results, trading on electronic networks connecting dealers across the United States, and trading at major coin shows.

This information is compiled by our analysts, and they determine what price most accurately reflects the trading that has occurred for each date and mintmark in each grade listed in *North American Coins & Prices*. By studying this information and referring back to it repeatedly, a collector can arm himself with the necessary knowledge to go out in the market and make wise purchasing decisions in adding pieces to his collection.

U.S. coins are perhaps the most popularly collected issues in the world. This is attributable in part to the popularity of coin collecting in the United States, but collectors in many other countries also covet collectible U.S. coins. After collecting U.S. coins for a while, many collectors in the United States branch out into issues of Canada and Mexico. These coins also enjoy a popular following in their countries of origin.

Thus, *North American Coins & Prices* brings together pricing information on all three of these countries. But this book also takes the price-guide concept a step further by providing information on the nuts and bolts of collecting coins: acquiring coins, grading them, organizing them into a collection, storing them properly, and much more. Novice collectors can gain the necessary knowledge to collect coins enjoyably; veterans can pick up some pointers to add to their knowledge.

1

"A small beginning"

The U.S. Mint grew from a modest start

By Robert R. Van Ryzin

It was a "small beginning" but a significant one. In July 1792, a site for the new U.S. Mint not yet having been secured, 1,500 silver half dismes were struck on a small screw press nestled in the cellar of a Philadelphia building owned by sawmaker John Harper. Though some have since categorized these early emissions of the fledgling U.S. Mint as patterns, it is clear that first President George Washington — who is said to have deposited the silver from which the coins were struck — considered this small batch of half dismes the first official U.S. coins.

It is true that this limited coinage, the first since passage of the act establishing the Mint on April 2, 1792, pales by comparison to modern U.S. Mint presses. Today's machines can churn out up to 750 coins a minute, striking as many as four coins at a time and boasting yearly mintages in the billions. But it is also true that these first small pieces — struck from silver and stamped with a plump Liberty on the obverse and a scrawny eagle in flight on the reverse — have tremendous historical importance.

For within what Washington would declare in his 1792 address to Congress as a "small beginning" were the seeds of a monetary system that has lasted more than 200 years and has become the study and admiration of many.

Before the U.S. Mint

Collectors today can trace much of the nation's development and learn of its struggles and growth through its coinage: from a cumbersome system first proposed by Robert Morris, a Revolutionary War financier and first

superintendent of finance, to the refinements tendered by Thomas Jefferson and Alexander Hamilton, which firmly placed the nation on an easily understood decimal system of coinage.

At first there was little coinage in circulation, except for foreign coins that arrived through trade or in the purses of the first settlers. Despite a dire need for coinage in the Colonies, Great Britain considered it a royal right and granted franchises sparingly. Much of the Colonial economy, therefore, revolved around barter, with food staples, crops, and goods serving as currency. Indian waupum or bead money also was used, first in the fur trade and later as a form of money for Colonial use.

Copper pieces were produced around 1616 for Sommer Islands (now Bermuda), but coinage within the American Colonies apparently didn't begin until 1652, when John Hull struck silver threepence, sixpence and shillings under authority of the General Court of Massachusetts. This coinage continued, with design changes (willow, oak and pine trees), through 1682. Most of the coins were dated 1652, apparently to avoid problems with England.

In 1658 Cecil Calvert, second Lord Baltimore, commissioned coins to be struck in England for use in Maryland. Other authorized and unauthorized coinages — including those of Mark Newby, John Holt, William Wood, and Dr. Samuel Higley — all became part of the landscape of circulating coins. In the 1780s this hodgepodge of coinage was augmented by influxes of counterfeit British halfpence and various state coinages.

In terms of the latter, the Articles of Confederation had granted individual states the right to produce copper coins. Many states found this to be appealing, and merchants in the mid-1780s traded copper coins of Vermont, Connecticut, Massachusetts, New Jersey, and New York. Not all were legal issues; various entrepreneurs used this as an invitation to strike imitation state coppers and British halfpence. Mutilated and worn foreign coins also circulated in abundance. Included among these were coins of Portugal, Great Britain and France, with the large majority of the silver arriving from Spain.

The accounting system used by the states was derived from the British system of pounds, shillings and pence. Each state was allowed to set its own rates at which foreign gold and silver coins would trade in relation to the British pound.

In 1782 Robert Morris, newly named superintendent of finance, was appointed to head a committee to determine the values and weights of the gold and silver coins in circulation. Asked simply to draw up a table of values, Morris took the opportunity to propose the establishment of a federal mint. In his Jan. 15, 1782, report (largely prepared by his assistant, Gouverneur Morris), Morris noted that the exchange rates between the states were complicated.

He observed that a farmer in New Hampshire would be hard-pressed if asked to determine the value of a bushel of wheat in South Carolina. Morris recorded that an amount of wheat worth four shillings in his home state of New Hampshire would be worth 21 shillings and eightpence under the

Robert Morris devised a complicated plan for a national coinage based on a common denominator of 1,440.

accounting system used in South Carolina.

Morris claimed these difficulties plagued not only farmers, but that "they are perplexing to most Men and troublesome to all." Morris further pressed for the adoption of an American coin to solve the problems of the need for small change and debased foreign coinages in circulation.

In essence, what he was advocating was a monometallic system based on silver. He said that gold and silver had fluctuated throughout history. Because these fluctuations resulted in the more valuable metal leaving the country, any nation that adopted a bimetallic coinage was doomed to have its gold or silver coins disappear from circulation.

Gouverneur Morris calculated the rate at which the Spanish dollar traded to the British pound in the various states. Leaving out South Carolina, because it threw off his calculations, Gouverneur Morris arrived at a common denominator of 1,440. Robert Morris, therefore, recommended a unit of value of 1/1,440, equivalent to a quarter grain of silver. He suggested the striking of a silver 100-unit coin, or cent; a silver 500-unit coin, or quint; a silver 1,000-unit coin, or mark; and two copper coins, one of eight units and the other of five units.

On Feb. 21, 1782, the Grand Committee of Congress approved the proposal and directed Morris to press forward and report with a plan to establish a mint. Morris had already done so. Apparently feeling confident that Congress would like his coinage ideas, Morris (as shown by his diary) began efforts at the physical establishment prior to his January 1782 report. He had already engaged Benjamin Dudley to acquire necessary equip-

ment for the mint and hoped to have sample coins available to submit with his original report to Congress.

Things went awry, however.

By Dec. 12, 1782, 10 months after Congress had approved his plan, Morris still could not show any samples of his coins. He was forced, ironically, to suggest that Congress draw up a table of rates for foreign coins to be used until his report was ready. It was not until April 2, 1783, that Morris was able to note in his diary that the first of his pattern coins were being struck.

"I sent for Mr. Dudley who delivered me a piece of Silver Coin," he wrote, "being the first that has been struck as an American Coin."

He also recorded that he had urged Dudley to go ahead with production of the silver patterns.

It wasn't until April 23, 1783, that Morris was able to send his Nova Constellatio patterns to Congress and suggest that he was ready to report on establishing a mint. Apparently nothing came of Morris' efforts. Several committees looked into the matter, but nothing was accomplished. Dudley was eventually discharged as Morris' hopes dimmed.

Thomas Jefferson was the next to offer a major plan. Jefferson liked the idea of a decimal system of coinage, but disliked Morris' basic unit of value. As chairman of the Currency Committee, Jefferson reviewed Morris' plan and formulated his own ideas.

To test public reaction, Jefferson gave his "Notes on Coinage" to *The Providence Gazette, and Country Journal*, which published his plan in its July 24, 1784, issue. Jefferson disagreed with Morris' suggestion for a 1/1,440 unit of value and instead proposed a decimal coinage based on the dollar, with the lowest unit of account being the mil, or 1/1,000.

"The most easy ratio of multiplication and division is that by ten," Jefferson wrote. "Every one knows the facility of Decimal Arithmetic."

Jefferson argued that although Morris' unit would have eliminated the unwanted fraction that occurred when merchants converted British farthings to dollars, this was of little significance. After all, the original idea of establishing a mint was to get rid of foreign currencies.

Morris' unit, Jefferson said, was too cumbersome for use in normal business transactions. According to Jefferson, under Morris' plan a horse valued at 80 Spanish dollars would require a notation of six figures and would be shown as 115,200 units.

Jefferson's coinage plan suggested the striking of a dollar, or unit; half dollar, or five-tenths; a double tenth, or fifth of a dollar, equivalent to a pistereen; a tenth, equivalent to a Spanish bit; and a one-fifth copper coin, relating to the British farthing. He also wanted a gold coin of $10, corresponding to the British double guinea; and a copper one-hundredth coin, relating to the British halfpence.

In reference to his coinage denominations, Jefferson said, it was important that the coins "coincide in value with some of the known coins so nearly, that the people may by quick reference in the mind, estimate their value."

Thomas Jefferson proposed that the United States adopt a decimal system of coinage.

More than a year, however, passed without any further action on his plan or that proposed by Morris. In a letter to William Grayson, a member of the Continental Congress, Washington expressed concern for the establishment of a national coinage system, terming it "indispensibly necessary." Washington also complained of the coinage in circulation: "A man must travel with a pair of scales in his pocket, or run the risk of receiving gold at one-fourth less than it counts."

A plan at last

On May 13, 1785, the 13-member Grand Committee, to whom Jefferson's plan had been submitted, filed its report, generally favoring Jefferson's coinage system. The committee did, however, make slight alterations, including the elimination of the gold $10 coin, the addition of a gold $5 coin, and the dropping of Jefferson's double tenth, which it replaced with a quarter dollar. The committee also added a coin equal to 1/200 of a dollar (half cent). On July 6, 1785, Congress unanimously approved the Grand Committee's plan. It failed, however, to set a standard weight for the silver dollar or to order plans drawn up for a mint. These two factors led to new proposals.

On April 8, 1786, the Board of Treasury, which had been reinstated after Morris' resignation as superintendent of finance two years prior, tendered three distinct coinage proposals based on varying weights and bimetallic ratios for the silver dollar. The first of these three plans (the one passed by Congress on Aug. 8, 1786) required the silver dollar to contain 375.64 grains of pure silver. The board's proposal varied from earlier coinage plans in that it advocated a higher bimetallic ratio of 15.256-to-1 and differing charges to depositors for coining of gold and silver. It called for minting of gold $5 and $10 coins, and silver denominations of the dime, double dime, half dollar, and dollar. In copper were a cent and half cent. The proposal came during the peak of state coinages and influxes of debased coppers, which, as the board reported, were being "Imported into or manufactured in the Several States."

Concerned over the need to control state coinages and foreign coppers, the board suggested that, within nine months of passage of its proposal, the legal-tender status of all foreign coppers be repealed and that values be set at which the state coppers would circulate. The board obviously expected immediate action and ordered a supply of copper that was being stored in Boston to be brought to New York in the hope that it might soon be coined. Their hopes, however, rested on the positive and quick action of Congress, something that hadn't occurred with the other proposals and would not occur this time.

Opposition to the mint was beginning to surface. Several members of Congress expressed their belief that the supply of foreign gold and silver coins in circulation was sufficient to preclude any need for a mint. They also argued that the problem with debased coppers could be solved by contracting with private individuals to strike the nation's cents and half cents.

Several proposals were offered for a contract coinage. On April 21, 1787, the board accepted a proposal by James Jarvis to strike 300 tons of copper coin at the federal standard. Jarvis, however, delivered slightly less than 9,000 pounds of his contract. The contract was voided the following year for his failure to meet scheduled delivery times, but helped to delay further action on a mint. Concerted action on a coinage system and a mint would wait until the formation of the new government.

Alexander Hamilton, named in September 1789 to head the new Treasury, offered three different methods by which the new nation could achieve economic stability, including the funding of the national debt, establishment of the Bank of North America, and the founding of the U.S. Mint. On Jan. 21, 1791, Hamilton submitted to Congress a "Report on the Establishment of a Mint." It was compiled through his study of European economic theories and the earlier works of Morris and Jefferson, along with the 1786 report of the Board of Treasury.

Hamilton agreed with Jefferson that the dollar seemed to be best suited to serve as the basic unit, but believed it necessary to establish a proper weight and fineness for the new coin. To do so, Hamilton had several Spanish coins assayed to determine the fine weight of the Spanish dollar. He also watched the rate at which Spanish dollars traded for fine gold (24 3/4 grains

per dollar) on the world market.

From his assays and observations he determined that the Spanish dollar contained 371 grains of silver. He then multiplied 24 3/4 by 15 (the gold value of silver times his suggested bimetallic ratio) and arrived at 371 1/4 as the proper fine silver weight for the new silver dollar.

In regard to his findings, Hamilton admitted that Morris had made similar assays and had arrived at a weight of 373 grains for the Spanish dollar. Hamilton attributed the discrepancy to the differing equipment used in making the assays. He failed, however, to observe that silver coins were traded in the world market at actual weight rather than the weight at time of issue. The Spanish dollar contained 376 grains of pure silver when new, 4 3/4 grains more than Hamilton's proposed silver dollar.

Hamilton also wanted a bimetallic ratio of 15-to-1, in contrast to the Board of Treasury's 15.6-to-1 ratio. Hamilton said his ratio was closer to Great Britain's, which would be important for trade, and Holland's, which would be important for repaying loans from that country.

His report suggested the striking of a gold $10; gold dollar; silver dollar; silver tenth, or disme; and copper one-hundredth and half-hundredth. Hamilton felt the last of these, the half cent, was necessary because it would enable merchants to lower their prices, which would help the poor.

Congress passed the act establishing the U.S. Mint in April 1792. It reinstated several coin denominations left out by Hamilton and dropped his gold dollar. In gold, the act authorized a $10 coin, or "eagle"; a $5 coin, or "half eagle"; and a $2.50 coin, or "quarter eagle". In silver were to be a dollar, half dollar, quarter dollar, disme, and half disme, and in copper a cent and half cent.

Though it established a sound system of U.S. coinage, the act failed to address the problem of foreign coins in circulation. It was amended in February 1793 to cancel their legal-tender status within three years of the Mint's opening.

Coinage begins

Coinage totals at the first mint were understandably low. Skilled coiners, assayers and others who could handle the mint's daily operations were in short supply in the United States. Also in want were adequate equipment and supplies of metal for coinage. Much of the former had to be built or imported. Much of the latter was also imported or salvaged from various domestic sources, including previously struck tokens and coins, and scrap metal.

Coinage began in earnest in 1793 with the striking of half cents and cents at the new mint located at Seventh Street between Market and Arch streets in Philadelphia. Silver coinage followed in 1794, with half dimes, half dollars and dollars. Gold coinage did not begin until 1795 with the minting of the first $5 and $10 coins. Silver dimes and quarters and gold $2.50

Production at the first U.S. mint, in Philadelphia, was minuscule by today's standards.

coins did not appear until 1796.

Under the bimetallic system of coinage by which gold and silver served as equal representations of the unit of value, much of the success and failure of the nation's coinage to enter and remain in circulation revolved around the supply and valuation of precious metals. One need only to gain a cursory knowledge of such movements to understand what role precious metals played in development of U.S. coinage. That role, to a large extent, determined why some coins today are rare and why some passed down from generation to generation are still plentiful and of lower value to collectors.

From the Mint's beginning, slight miscalculations in the proper weight for the silver dollar and a proper bimetallic ratio led gold and silver to disappear from circulation. The U.S. silver dollar traded at par with Spanish and Mexican dollars, but because the U.S. coin was lighter, it was doomed to export.

A depositor at the first mint could make a profit at the mint's expense by sending the coins to the West Indies. There they could be traded at par for the heavier Spanish or Mexican eight reales, which were then shipped back to the United States for recoinage. As a result, few early silver dollars entered domestic circulation; most failed to escape the melting pots.

Gold fared no better. Calculations of the bimetallic ratio by which silver traded for gold on the world market were also askew at first and were always subject to fluctuations. Gold coins either disappeared quickly after minting or never entered circulation, languishing in bank vaults. These problems led President Jefferson to halt coinage of the gold $10 and silver dollar.

The gold $10 reappeared in 1838 at a new, lower-weight standard. The silver dollar, not coined for circulation since 1803, returned in 1836 with a limited mintage. Full-scale coinage waited until 1840.

Nor was the coining of copper an easy matter for the first mint. Severe shortages of the metal led the Mint to explore various avenues of obtaining sufficient supplies for striking cents and half cents.

Witness, for example, the half-cent issues of 1795 and 1797 struck over privately issued tokens of the New York firm of Talbot, Allum & Lee

because of a shortage of copper for the federal issue. Rising copper prices and continued shortages forced the Mint to lower the cent's weight from 208 grains to 168 grains in 1795.

By that same year Congress had begun to investigate the Mint. Complaints about high costs and low production had been raised. Suggestions that a contract coinage might be more suitable for the new nation surfaced again, despite bad experiences with previous attempts.

The Mint survived this and another investigation, but the problems of fluctuating metal supplies continued to plague the nation. In 1798, because of the coinage shortage, the legal-tender status of foreign coins was restored. Several more extensions were given during the 1800s, ending with the withdrawal of legal-tender status for Spanish coins in 1857.

In the 1830s great influxes of silver from foreign mints raised the value of gold in relation to silver, which made it necessary for the Mint to lower the standard weight of all gold coins in 1834. It also led to the melting of great numbers of gold coins of the old specifications.

By the 1850s discovery of gold in California had again made silver the dearer metal. All silver quickly disappeared from circulation. Congress reacted in 1853 by lowering the weight of the silver half dime, dime, quarter, and half dollar, hoping to keep silver in circulation. A new gold coin of $20 value was introduced to absorb a great amount of the gold from Western mines.

Not long after, silver was discovered in Nevada. By the mid-1870s the various mines that made up what was known as the Comstock Lode (after its colorful early proprietor, Henry P. Comstock) had hit the mother lode. Large supplies of silver from the Comstock, combined with European demonetization, caused a severe drop in its value, which continued through the close of the 19th century.

It was believed that the introduction of a heavier, 420-grain silver dollar in 1873, known as the Trade dollar, would create a market for much of the Comstock silver, bolster its price, and at the same time wrest control from Great Britain of lucrative trade with the Orient. It didn't. Large numbers of Trade dollars eventually flooded back into the United States, where they were, ironically, accepted only at a discount to the lesser-weight Morgan dollars.

The latter had been introduced in 1878 as a panacea to the severe economic problems following the Civil War. Those who proudly carried the banner of free silver contended that by taking the rich output of the Comstock mines and turning it into silver dollars, a cheaper, more plentiful form of money would become available. In its wake, they believed, would be a much needed economic recovery.

The Free Silver Movement gained its greatest support during the late 19th century when William Jennings Bryan attempted to gain the White House on a plank largely based on restoration of the free and unlimited coinage of the standard 412.5-grain silver dollar. He failed. Silver failed. Shortly thereafter the United States officially adopted a gold standard.

Silver continued to be a primary coinage metal until 1964, when rising

prices led the Mint to remove it from the dime and quarter. Mintage of the silver dollar had ended in 1935. The half dollar continued to be coined through 1969 with a 40-percent-silver composition. It, too, was then debased.

Gold coinage ended in 1933 and exists today only in commemorative issues and American Eagle bullion coins with fictive face values. A clad composition of copper and nickel is now the primary coinage metal. Even the cent is no longer all copper; a copper-coated zinc composition has been used since 1982.

Precious-metal supplies were also linked to the opening of additional mints, which served the parent facility in Philadelphia. The impact of gold discoveries in the 1820s in the southern Appalachian Mountains was directly tied to the construction of branch mints in Dahlonega, Ga., and Charlotte, N.C., in 1838. These new mints struck only gold coins. New Orleans also became the site of a branch mint in the same year as Dahlonega and Charlotte. It took in some of the outflow of gold from Southern mines, but also struck silver coins.

Discovery of gold in California in the late 1840s created a gold rush, and from it sprang a great western migration. Private issues of gold coinage, often of debased quality, were prevalent, and the cost of shipping the metal eastward for coinage at Philadelphia was high. A call for an official branch mint was soon heard and heeded in 1852 with the authorization of the San Francisco Mint, which began taking deposits in 1854.

The discovery of silver in the Comstock Lode led to yet another mint. Located only a short distance via Virginia & Truckee Railroad from the fabulous Comstock Lode, the Carson City Mint began receiving bullion in early 1870. It struck only silver coins during its tenure.

Denver, also located in a mineral-rich region, became the site of an assay office in 1863 when the government purchased the Clark, Gruber & Co. private mint. It became a U.S. branch mint in 1906. In addition to the Denver and Philadelphia mints, San Francisco and a newly upgraded facility in West Point, N.Y., continue to serve as U.S. mints, but the others have left behind a rich legacy.

The collector taking a more extended journey into the history of U.S. coinage can find plenty of interesting tales — some as tall as the day is long and others factually based — all of which are part of the rich and ever-changing panoply of U.S. coinage history. There are stories of denominations that failed, great discoveries, great rarities, great collectors, and, for those with an artistic bent, a rich field of pattern coins to be explored and a wealth of much-heralded designs by famous sculptors such as Augustus Saint-Gaudens, Adolph Weinman, James Earle Fraser, and others.

For those who are drawn to the hobby by the allure of age-old relics of days gone by, or by coins handed down through the family, or even by dreams of great wealth, coin collecting has much to offer. The history of the U.S. Mint, with its small but ever so important beginning, is the starting point.

2

Making money

How coins are manufactured

By Alan Herbert

Just as printing is the process by which paper money is made, so is minting the method of manufacturing coins. The two are often confused by the public, but they are completely different.

The history of minting goes back several centuries before the birth of Christ. The Lydians are credited with making the first crude coins in the Middle East about 700 B.C., although the Chinese and Koreans trace their coinage back even further.

Some early coins were cast. That process continued in China into the 1900s, but only for low-value pieces. Here again the average person often assumes that all coins are cast, but as you will see, only a tiny fraction of a percent are — or were — actually made that way.

The methods developed by the Greeks and Romans centered on making dies that could be hammered by hand into the surface of a lump of metal, flattening it and impressing a design. Hammered coinage continued until after the end of the Middle Ages, about 1500. After that the first machines that could strike coins were invented. Today their successors can pound out 750 or more coins a minute.

From the early days when the fixed die was driven into a stump or a hole drilled in a rock, through fixing it in an anvil (the fixed die is still called the anvil die), to today's modern coin presses, the process is much the same. Force is applied to devices that impress or apply a design to a piece of material, which is transformed into a coin.

Early dies were made of wood. Then came copper, bronze, and finally iron as technology advanced. Today dies are made from exotic steels with special qualities that make them ideal for striking coins.

The history of coinage is fascinating. Interwoven into it are several familiar names: Leonardo da Vinci is credited with inventing one of the

first coin presses. James Watt, English inventor of the steam engine, was the first to incorporate steam power to drive the coin presses that earlier had depended on horses or human arms.

Whether the power comes from a hand holding a hammer or a mechanical ram, and whether it comes from above, below, or the side, the process is called "striking" a coin. Modern coin presses use a variety of methods in applying brute force to a piece of metal to turn it into a coin.

Another fable that traces to casting coins is the common belief that coins are made from liquid metal or at the least are red hot when they are struck. Neither is true. A coin's design is formed by the pressure that causes the metal to cold-flow into the pattern that you see on the coins in your pocket.

There are three basic parts of the minting process: (1) the making of the planchet, which is divided into the selection and processing of the metal and the preparation of the planchets, (2) the making of the dies, and (3) the use of the dies to strike the planchets. To help you remember these three parts, think of "P", "D" and "S" for planchet, die and striking.

Choosing a metal

Many different metals have and are being used for coins. The most popular coinage metals are those commonly found and relatively cheap, so they can be used for striking low-value coins. Precious metals — like silver, gold and platinum — are still used for commemorative coins.

A good coinage metal requires certain properties. The metal must be soft enough to be easily worked yet hard enough to withstand the wear and tear of a thousand pockets, a hundred thousand transactions. Few metals have all the right properties, so coin metals usually are an alloy, or mixture of two or more metals.

Copper is a favorite coin metal, either by itself or in an alloy. Zinc, nickel, iron, and aluminum are also found in coins struck by the United States and other countries. Silver and gold have to be alloyed with some metal, usually copper, to be hard enough to withstand commercial life. The so-called "pure" coins of silver or gold are known as "bullion coins," bought and sold primarily for their precious-metal content.

The metals chosen for a coin are melted and mixed together, and either poured into ingots or blocks, or extruded from furnaces that continuously cast a long strip of the metal. The ingots are passed several times between the big rolls in a rolling mill to reduce the ingot to the thickness of the blanks needed.

Once the strip is rolled to the correct thickness, it is sent to a blanking press. A gang of blunt-end punches are driven through the sheet, producing a dozen or more blanks with each stroke. The rough blanks are then ready to be processed.

Strips of coin metal stand ready to be cut into "blanks."

A binful of blanks are ready for the coin press.

Making the "blanks"

The piece of metal (occasionally some other material, so it isn't always metal) that becomes a coin is known as a "blank." This is a usually round, flat piece that usually has been punched or cut from a sheet or strip of coin metal.

Before a blank can become a coin it has to be processed, cleaned, softened, and given what is known as an "upset edge" — a raised ridge or rim around both sides. The blank then becomes a "planchet" and is ready to be struck into a coin by the dies.

First they go through what looks like a monstrous cement mixer. A huge cylinder revolves slowly as the planchets are fed in at one end and spiral their way through. This is an annealing oven, which heats the planchets to soften them. When they come out the end, they fall into a bath where they are cleaned with a diluted acid or soap solution.

As the final step, they go through the upsetting mill, the machine that puts the raised rim on the blank and turns it into a planchet, ready to be struck. In a different department the process of making the dies used to strike the coins has already begun.

Preparing the dies

For those who haven't studied metallurgy, the concept of hard metal flowing about is pretty hard to swallow, but this is actually what happens. It is basically the same process as the one used in an auto plant to turn a flat sheet of steel into a fender with multiple curves and sharp bends. The cold metal is moved about by the pressure applied.

To make the metal move into the desired design, there has to be a die. Actually there has to be two dies, because one of the laws of physics is that for every action there has to be an equal and opposite reaction. You cannot hold a piece of metal in midair and strike one side of it. Instead you make two dies, fix one, and drive the other one against it — with a piece of metal in between to accept the design from each die.

A die is a piece of hard metal, like steel, with a design on its face that helps to form a mirror image on the struck coin. Early dies were made by hand. Engravers used hand tools to laboriously cut each letter, each digit, and each owl or eagle or whatever design was being used into the face of the die. Notice that this is "into" the surface of the die. Each part of the die design is a hole or cavity of varying shape and depth.

This is because we want a mirror image on the coin, but we want it raised, or in "relief." To make a relief image on a coin, the image on the die has to be into the face of the die, or "incuse." Of course, if we want an incuse image on the coin, such as the gold $2.50 and $5 coins of 1908-1929, the design on the die face would have to be in relief.

To fully understand this, take a coin from your pocket and a piece of aluminum foil. Press the foil down over the coin design and rub it with an

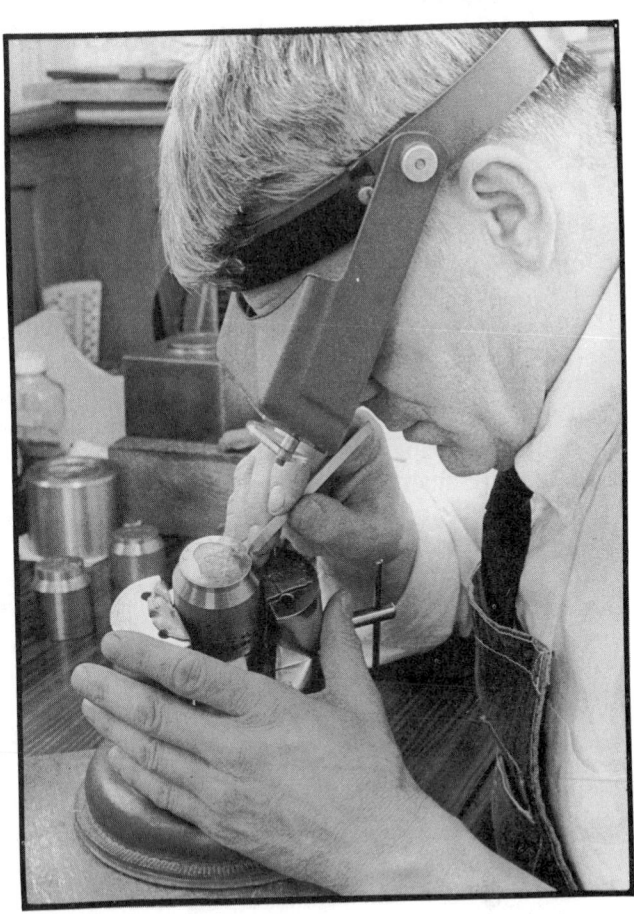

An engraver at the U.S. Mint puts the finishing touches on a die.

eraser. When you take the foil off and look at the side that was in contact with the coin, you have a perfect copy of a die. Everywhere there is a relief design on the coin there is an incuse design on your foil "die."

A galvano goes on the reducing lathe.

From sketchbook to coin

The design process begins with an artist's sketch. This is translated into a three-dimensional relief design that is hand-carved from plaster or, in recent years, from a form of plastic.

The plaster or plastic design is then transformed into a "galvano," which is an exact copy of the design that has been plated with a thin layer of copper. This is used as a template or pattern in a reducing lathe, which cuts the design into a die blank.

This die becomes the master die, from which all of the following steps descend. The process can be reversed so that the design will be cut in relief, forming a tool called a "hub," which is simply a piece of steel with the design in relief, exactly the same as the relief design on the intended coin.

To make working dies, pieces of special steel are prepared, with one end shaped with a slight cone. The die blank is softened by heating it. Then the hub is forced into the face of the die, forming the incuse, mirror-image design in the face of the die.

The process usually has to be repeated because the die metal will harden from the pressure. The die is removed, softened, and returned to the hubbing press for a second impression from the hub. As you can imagine, it takes several hundred tons per square inch to force the hub into the die. Logically, this process is called "hubbing" a die.

The advantage of hubbing a die is that thousands of working dies can be made from a single hub, each one for all practical purposes as identical as the proverbial peas in a pod. This enables, for example, U.S. mints to strike billions of one-cent coins each year, each with the identical design.

Die making has come a long way from the early days when it took a skilled engraver a full day to carve a single letter into a die. The use of punches with the digits, letters or even parts of the design on the end reduced the amount of time required for the process. Today, thanks to the use of hubs, a complete die can be finished in a matter of hours.

Striking the coin

Yesterday's die might strike only a few hundred coins. Today it is not unusual for a die to strike well over a million coins.

The coin press used to strike modern coins is a complicated piece of equipment that consists basically of a feed system to place the planchets in position for the stroke of the hammer die to form a coin. This process takes only a fraction of a second, so the press has to operate precisely to spew out the hundreds of coins that are struck every minute.

The end of the early hammered coinage came with the introduction of the collar, which often is called the "third" die. The collar is nothing more than a steel plate with a hole in it. This hole is the exact diameter of the intended coin and often is lined with carbide to prolong its life. It surrounds the lower, or fixed, die. Its sole purpose is to contain the coin metal

Rows of modern coin presses at the Philadelphia Mint turn out billions of coins a year.

A hopper is full of shiny new one-cent coins ready for shipment.

to keep it from spreading sideways under the force of the strike.

If the intended coin has serrations, or "reeds," on the edge, then the collar has the matching design. The strike forces the coin metal against the serrations in the collar, forming the reeded edge at the same time that the two dies form the front and back, or obverse and reverse, of the coin.

Lettered-edge coins are produced usually by running the planchets through an edge-lettering die, or by using a segmented collar that is forced against the edge of the planchet during the strike by hydraulic pressure.

Several hundred tons were required to drive a hub into a die. Not as much but still significant amounts of force are needed to strike coins. A cent, for example, requires about 30 tons per square inch. One of the silver dollars took 150 tons. The other denominations fall in between.

Modern coin presses apply pressure in a variety of ways. A ram, carrying the moving or "hammer" die, is forced against the planchet. Most commonly this is with the mechanical advantage of a "knuckle" or connected pieces to which pressure is applied from the side. When the joint straightens — like straightening your finger — the ram at the end of the piece is driven into the planchet.

Once the strike is complete, at the final impact of the die pair, the coin has been produced. It is officially a coin now, and it's complete and ready to be spent.

The making of proof coins

While the high-speed coining presses are turning out billions of coins for commerce, there are other presses working at much slower speeds to produce collector coins, such as "proof" coins.

Proof coins started out as special presentation pieces. They were and still are struck on specially prepared planchets with specially prepared dies. Today the definition of a proof coin also requires that it be struck two or more times.

To make a proof coin, the planchets go through much the same process, but with some special care and some extra steps. Currently all proof versions of circulating U.S. coins are struck at the San Francisco Mint, but some of the proof commemorative coins have been struck at the other mints, including West Point.

After the proof blanks are punched from the strip, they go through the annealing oven, but on a conveyor belt rather than being tumbled in the revolving drum. After cleaning and upsetting they go into a huge vibrating machine where they are mixed with steel pellets that look like tiny footballs. The movement of the steel pellets against the planchets burnishes, or smooths, the surface so any scratches and gouges the planchets pick up during processing are smoothed over.

Proof dies get an extra polishing before the hubbing process. Like all other dies, they are made at Philadelphia and shipped to the branch mints.

When the proof dies arrive at San Francisco, they are worked on by a

team of specialists who use diamond dust and other polishing agents to turn the fields of the proof dies into mirrorlike surfaces. The incuse design is sandblasted to make the surface rough, producing what is known as a "frosted" design.

Because collectors like the frosted proofs, the design is periodically swabbed with acid to keep the surface rough and increase the number of frosted proofs from each die. This is a relatively recent improvement, so frosted examples of earlier proofs are considerably scarcer.

The presses that strike proof coins usually are hand-operated rather than automatic. Some of the newer presses use equipment such as vacuum suction devices to pick up the planchets, place them in the coining chamber, and then remove the struck coins. This avoids handling the pieces any more than necessary.

On a hand-operated press, the operator takes a freshly washed and dried planchet and, using tongs, places it in the collar. The ram with the die descends two or more times before the finished coin is removed from the collar and carefully stored in a box for transport to storage or the packaging line. After each strike the operator wipes the dies to make sure that lint or other particles don't stick to the dies and damage the coins as they are struck.

Proof dies are used for only a short time before being discarded. Maximum die life is usually less than 10,000 coins, varying with the size of the coin and the alloy being struck.

Keeping up with demand

The minting process has come a long way from the first metal pellets that are barely recognizable as coins. Companies that manufacture equipment used in the world's mints are constantly researching to develop new methods of producing coins.

The purpose is to strike coins at as low a cost as possible and still retain the desired beauty in the design. Modern machines and new methods help the mints keep up with demand for coins.

The important point to remember is that the coins in your pocket are made no differently from the coins in the pocket of an English schoolchild or a Spanish police officer or an Italian opera singer. Mints around the world use the same methods, same equipment, and same common coin metals, with few if any variations from the basic methods. The minting process was shrouded in secrecy for centuries, but now has become common knowledge.

For the collector, knowing exactly how coins are minted can be some of the most valuable knowledge that can be learned. It often will make the difference between accepting a coin as a valuable addition to a collection or spotting it as a fake, counterfeit, or altered coin.

Because of the improvements in the making of coins, collecting the rare

misstrikes and defective coins that escape quality control has become an important segment of the numismatic hobby. For a detailed description of over 400 categories of minting varieties, see the "U.S. Minting Varieties and Errors" section in this book.

3

The thrill of the hunt

How to acquire coins for your collection

By Al Doyle

Among the many pleasures coin collecting offers is the satisfaction of acquiring that long-sought piece that fills an important hole in a set or completes a collection. Many collectors say half the fun of pursuing the hobby is the thrill of the hunt — trying to find that needed coin in the condition desired and for a good price. Following are the main sources from which collectors acquire coins.

Circulation finds

Once the most popular method of building a collection, hunting through pocket change has declined substantially since 1965, when silver dimes and quarters were replaced by clad (base-metal) coinage.

Most collectors from 1935 into the 1960s got started in numismatics by searching through circulating coinage. It was worth the effort, as scarce and interesting coins such as the 1909-S "VDB" and 1914-D Lincoln cents, Liberty and Buffalo nickels, 1916-D and 1921 Mercury dimes, and Barber and Standing Liberty quarters were often found. Hobbyists who searched bank rolls and bags obtained at face value had no downside risk, and entire date collections of Lincoln cents were obtained in this manner.

Other denominations were also pursued in the treasure hunt. One Midwestern dealer found dozens of 1939-D Jefferson nickels (worth $1 to $30 each at the time, depending on condition) by searching through change obtained from parking meters of a nearby city. Another well-known numismatist put together a complete date and mintmark set of Walking Liberty half dollars in one afternoon by searching through coins obtained at his bank. Needless to say, those days are gone forever.

What is available to pocket-change searchers today? Even the pre-1959

It's still possible to find collectible coins by searching large quantities of change, such as rolls.

cents, with the wheat-ears reverse, are rare sights, but some interesting coins remain undiscovered.

Jefferson nickels can provide plenty of collecting enjoyment for virtually no financial commitment. A recent sampling of five rolls (200 coins, or $10) turned up 58 different date and mintmark combinations. Some of the highlights were a 1938-S (mintage 4.1 million) in grade fine, a 1947 in very fine, and a 1953-S. Looking through Jeffersons on a regular basis should lead to building the better part of a date and mintmark set.

Half dollars are the other relatively untapped area in modern coinage. The 40-percent-silver pieces of 1965 to 1969 can sometimes be found in bank rolls. Half dollars seldom circulate, which means that older coins may be gathering dust in your local bank vault at this very moment.

Collecting Lincoln cents with the memorial reverse, from 1959 to date, makes an excellent starter set. Many of the dates can be found in circulation.

What else might turn up in pocket change? Modern proofs enter circulation from time to time, and foreign coins are found occasionally. Canadian and U.S. coins frequently cross their respective borders.

Collectors of error coins sometimes find unusual pieces in circulation. What may be scorned as a reject by the average person is a valuable item to the error and variety specialist.

Start examining your pocket change. It's an inexpensive and pleasant way to get involved in the coin hobby.

Coin shops

Most medium-sized or larger cities and suburbs have at least one coin shop within driving distance, and a surprising number of small towns also boast of having a store that caters to local numismatists. Living in or near a metropolitan area is an advantage for the coin-shop enthusiast. For example, more than 15 dealers live in or near Cincinnati, and southern Cal-

ifornia and the New York area are home to hundreds of numismatic firms.

In some ways, a coin shop is similar to a small museum. All kinds of items from early coppers to gold coinage and other collectibles such as paper currency, stock certificates, and historic curiosities can be seen. A visit to a well-stocked shop is a visual treat.

It is likely that some of those coins in the display cases will appeal to you, and that means some comparison shopping and determining the value of your favorite coin are desirable. Prices do fluctuate, although collector-oriented coins tend to maintain steadier values than coins sought by investors.

If you are a casual collector, consider a subscription to *Coins* magazine. A monthly publication, *Coins* offers articles on a wide range of topics as well as a Coin Value Guide of retail prices for U.S. coins in most grades.

Serious collectors and others who want more frequent information will find *Numismatic News* to be a timely source of knowledge. Published weekly, the *News* includes coverage of recent market trends and reports from major coin conventions. *World Coin News* is published every other week and covers non-U.S. issues. All three publications also carry display advertisements from dozens of coin dealers.

Prices are determined by supply and demand as well as the grade, or state of preservation. Grading is often described as a subjective art rather than an exact science, and it does take some study and experience to become a competent grader (see Chapter 4).

Numismatic education is a never-ending process. Getting to know an experienced dealer who is enthusiastic about his product will certainly increase your knowledge of coins. Most shops carry a wide assortment of items, but dealers (like anyone else) have their personal favorites. If you find a dealer who is especially knowledgeable about a certain series, it could be to your advantage to do business with him or her if that also happens to be your favorite area too.

Strangely enough, doing business with a dealer who does not share your particular interest could work in your favor. Learning about collectible coins is a massive undertaking, and no one knows everything. Collectors of large cents and Bust half dollars are willing to pay substantial premiums for coins that have minor differences from other specimens struck during the same year, and specialists in those areas frequently "cherrypick" rare varieties that are offered at common-date prices.

Never be embarrassed to ask questions about coins or the dealer's experience in the hobby. As the old saying goes, "There is no such thing as a dumb question." A question asked at the right time could save you plenty of grief and money.

Mail order

This is one area that generates a fair amount of emotion among collectors. Many hobbyists swear by the convenience of shopping at home; others

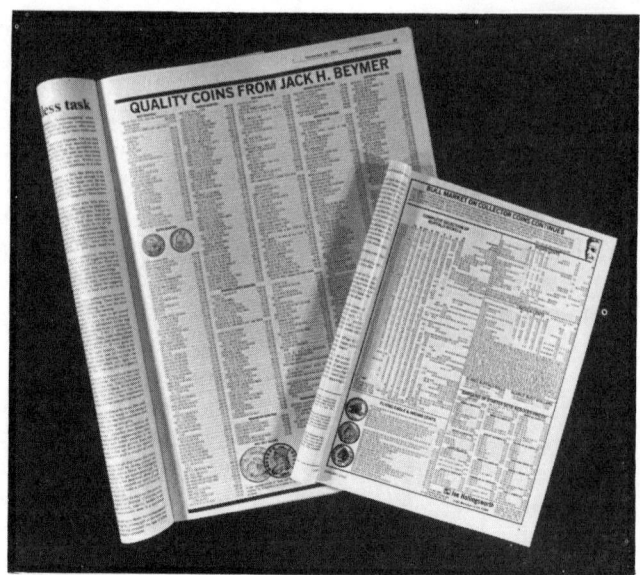

Advertisements in numismatic publications provide the convenience of shopping at home.

swear at mail-order firms that send overgraded and overpriced coins. Common sense and the same guidelines that apply to shopping for any other item should be used in selecting a mail-order coin dealer.

Look for someone who has a fair amount of experience in coins as well as enthusiasm for the hobby. Reputable dealers are willing to answer questions about their numismatic backgrounds and business practices. Word of mouth is often said to be one of the most effective forms of advertising, and it pays to ask other collectors about their favorite mail-order companies.

If several people agree that a firm provides accurately graded coins at fair prices, chances are excellent that you will also be a satisfied customer. How do you avoid being cheated? Collectors can be their own worst enemies and are often victimized by their own greed.

Take a coin that has a retail value in the $100 range in a particular grade. If that same coin is advertised at the same grade for $49.95, the savvy collector should immediately become suspicious. When a coin is offered at a price far under the going rate, remember these two sayings: "If it sounds too good to be true, it usually is," and "there is no Santa Claus in numismatics."

A dealer will generally pay $70 to $80 to acquire a popular coin with a retail value of $100. With that in mind, how can someone offer the same coin in the same grade at far less than wholesale cost? Wouldn't it be much easier to sell those coins to other dealers at a higher price and save on advertising expenses?

Obviously, the "underpriced" coins are not the same quality as their properly graded counterparts. It pays to keep up with current prices and grading standards. It is possible to find good deals at less than full retail cost, but don't expect to purchase decent coins for half price.

Does that mean all coins sold at real market prices are properly graded? Don't get complacent; overgraded coins are sometimes sold at full retail. But not everyone who sells an overgraded coin is intentionally fraudulent.

Grading standards are not carved in stone, which means that one person's MS-63 can be someone else's MS-64. Even though most dealers are extremely knowledgeable about coins, they can be fooled at times. The altered coin that a dealer bought as problem-free may be passed on to a collector in good faith, with no intention of deceit.

There is one important means of protection for consumers who buy through the mail: the return policy. Reputable firms allow buyers to return any unsatisfactory item for a full refund. The time allowed for returns varies widely from three working days to a month, but seven to ten days seems to be the most popular policy among mail-order dealers.

Most dealers list "terms of sale" in their ads. Always look for them and read them before placing your order.

If you don't like coins received through the mail for any reason, send them back within the alloted time for a full refund. Companies might extend the deadline by a day or two if you call and ask for extra time.

What happens if you don't receive a refund or cannot satisfactorily resolve a problem with a mail-order dealer? There are several options:

The first step is to file a written complaint with the advertising department of any publication in which the dealer advertises. Include copies of invoices and other documentation. The publication cannot act on verbal complaints.

Written complaints can also be filed with a local or state chapter of the Better Business Bureau as well as any hobby-related organizations (the American Numismatic Association, Professional Numismatists Guild, and so on) in which the dealer holds membership. If you do business with a reputable dealer, it is unlikely that you will ever have to endure such a drawn-out complaint process, but be ready to take the proper steps if necessary.

For those who live in rural areas or prefer to shop at home, buying coins through the mail can be a rewarding experience and a convenient way to build a collection.

Coin shows

Dozens of shows are held every weekend across the nation. These events range from simple one-day shows with 10 to 20 tables to nationally known events such as the annual American Numismatic Association convention, Florida United Numismatists convention, the three-times-a-year shows held in Long Beach, Calif., and the Central States Numismatic Society convention.

Admission to club-sponsored shows is usually free. Commercially sponsored shows oftentimes charge a small admission fee.

Shows big and small are held across the nation every weekend.

Somewhere between the show at the local VFW hall and Long Beach are state and regional conventions. Often sponsored by a club, these shows will have 40 to 150 dealer tables as compared to the 400 to 600 tables at a major convention. Tables at local and some regional conventions are often manned by part-time, or "vest pocket," dealers. Smaller shows tend to feature less expensive items; the larger shows will have a greater variety of scarce and expensive coins in addition to the more affordable pieces.

Major conventions will have a stunning array of merchandise ranging from coins of ancient Greece to major U.S. rarities. Even if you can't afford the expensive items, it doesn't cost anything to stroll the aisles and see some historic coins.

The big-ticket items are just part of the action at regional and major shows. A large assortment of affordable coins are available, and prices are often lower than at coin shops.

Dealers buy and sell thousands of coins among themselves at shows, and new purchases can often be had for a small markup. Good buys can sometimes be found later in the show when dealers are preparing to return

home. A reasonable offer will often result in a new addition to your collection.

Speaking of offers, negotiating and dickering are as much a part of coin shows as silver dollars, but be reasonable. Tossing out an offer of $50 on a $200 coin is not shrewd; it's insulting.

If you make an offer on a coin and it is accepted, the coin is yours. Backing out of a deal is considered bad form. The coin business tends to be informal, and verbal offers carry serious weight. Your word is your bond on the bourse floor.

Purchases at a coin show do not carry a return policy. Unlike a mail-order transaction, you have ample opportunity to carefully examine the coin firsthand before making a financial commitment.

Why attend a show when you can acquire coins through the mail or from a local shop? There are many reasons to give the show circuit a try:

Conventions are an educational experience. Touring the bourse floor and talking to dealers and other collectors will increase your knowledge of numismatics, but there are other learning opportunities as well.

Many shows offer educational forums featuring speakers and presentations on various topics. These seminars cover everything from little-known specialties to advice on obtaining the best buys in a particular area of numismatics.

Exhibits will also add to your knowledge. Most medium-sized and major shows reserve a section of the bourse for collectors to display some of their holdings and compete for awards based on the educational value of their exhibit. The exhibit section offers an excellent opportunity to view something new and different.

You might be motivated to put together an exhibit yourself after a visit to a show. Keep in mind that it does not require a major collection to create a decent exhibit. Some of the most interesting displays incorporate low-priced coins and other collectibles.

Shows are excellent places to search for key-date coins and other material that may not be in stock at your local shop. Dealers do much of their shopping at shows, which should tell you something about the opportunities at a good-sized convention.

Want to introduce a friend or relative to coin collecting? Take them to a show and let them look around. Chances are excellent that the newcomer will become a fellow collector.

Looking for something different to collect? Paper money, world coins, tokens, medals, and medieval coins are often found at shows. You could find a new area of interest, and shows provide collectors with a chance to meet dealers and well-known hobbyists from across the country.

Have a game plan when you attend a show. Decide beforehand what you want to buy and how much money you plan to spend. Buying whatever looks nice will soon deplete your funds.

Coin shows offer something for everyone, so consider bringing the family. Jewelry (usually for much less than jewelry-store prices), baseball cards, antiques, and arts and crafts are also sometimes found at bourse tables.

It's OK to bargain with a dealer at a show or shop, but collectors should be reasonable with their offers.

One final note on coin-show etiquette: If you don't agree with a dealer's prices or grading, do not tell him that you can buy the same coin for less at another table or call him a crook. Just move on to the next table, and enjoy the rest of the show.

Information on upcoming shows in your area can be found in *Coins* and *Numismatic News*. Shows that feature a significant number of world coins are also listed in *World Coin News*. Coin-show advertising sometimes appears in local newspapers during the week prior to a show or in the paper's free listings of community events.

Auctions

As in other collectible fields, auctions play an important role in the coin business. Prices realized at major auctions can indicate where the coin market is headed, as price fluctuations are a fact of life in numismatics. Important collections with major rarities are usually sold at auction.

However, affordable coins are often sold along with the heart-stopping pieces. A typical sale for a major auction firm will contain 1,000 to 4,000 lots, and most of those coins are not of the headline-grabbing variety.

A collector doesn't have to actually attend an auction to participate in it.

The vast number of coins offered at a typical coin auction can work in favor of the collector who has a limited budget. Typical low- to medium-priced coins are often overlooked, as dealers and collectors focus on the trophy items. That may allow you to pick up some coins at reasonable prices.

How can you participate in an auction that is being held thousands of miles from your home? Catalogs are produced by auction companies for each sale, and mail bids are encouraged.

A typical auction catalog is illustrated with black and white as well as color photos of hundreds of coins. Descriptions of each lot give you an idea of the appearance of any coins that might be of interest.

If you are located near an auction site, it pays to examine your potential purchases at the pre-auction viewing session. The process is simple: Just visit the auction location (usually a major hotel or convention center) prior to the sale. The auction company sets up a room where the lots can be viewed. Long rows of tables with good lighting are provided. All you have to do is tell one of the attendants the lot numbers of the coins you want to view.

You can place written bids before you leave the premises, but it might pay to hang around for the auction and bid on coins in person. The action can be fast and furious at a major auction. Bidding increments of thousands of dollars are the rule when an expensive coin is being sold. It's an unforgettable sight to watch five or six serious competitors run up the price on a truly rare coin.

Keep several things in mind before you get involved in buying through auctions:

■ You are legally responsible to honor all winning bids placed, so plan accordingly. It is unlikely that you will win every coin on which you bid, but placing too many bids could be hazardous to your financial health.

■ Return policies vary among the major firms. Generally, floor bidders (those who personally attend the sale) do not have return privileges, as it is assumed that an adequate opportunity was provided to examine coins during the pre-auction viewing session.

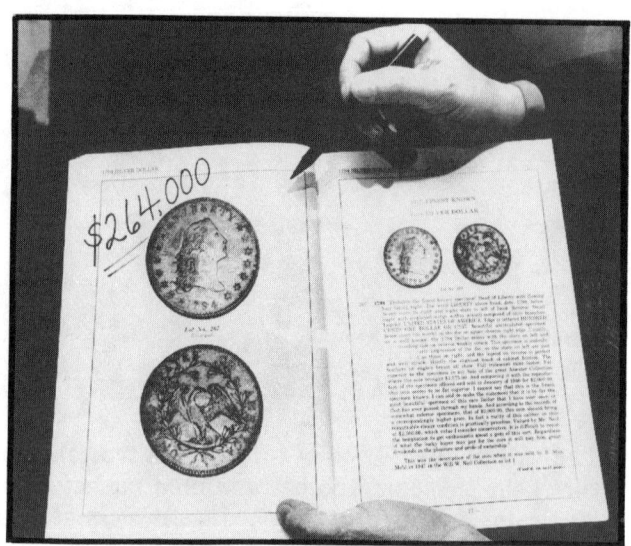

An auction catalog describes each lot offered.

One auction house does not allow any returns by mail bidders on certified coins, which are independently graded and encapsulated in a protective holder by an outside grading service. However, return privileges are the rule for all coins graded by the auction company's staff.

■ Winning bids are generally subject to a 10 percent premium, or buyer's fee. If you successfully bid $300 on a coin, your final cost will be $330 plus postage and handling. Consider the buyer's fee when deciding on bids.

Getting started in buying through auctions requires a catalog of an upcoming sale. Typically priced at $10 to $25, auction catalogs can be excellent buys even if you don't participate in the sale, as they provide a wealth of numismatic information.

Following are the four major U.S. auction houses:

■ Auctions by Bowers and Merena, P.O. Box 1224, Wolfeboro, NH 03894.

■ Heritage Numismatic Auctions, Heritage Plaza, Highland Park Village, Dallas, TX 75205.

■ Stack's, 123 W. 57th St., New York, NY 10019.

■ Superior Galleries, 9478 W. Olympic Blvd., Beverly Hills, CA 90212.

Smaller auctions will allow you to test the bidding process before you compete at a major sale. Local firms concentrate on less expensive coins, and a typical sale for these companies ranges from 250 to 1,000 lots. Catalogs are less elaborate, but they are also inexpensive. Prices range from free to $3, and mail bids are accepted.

Among the dozens of local companies that conduct coin auctions are the following:

■ Michael Aron, P.O. Box 4388, San Clemente, CA 92672.

■ Connecticut Numismatic Auctions, P.O. Box 471, Plantsville, CT 06479.

■ Sonny Henry's Auction Service, 1510 Illinois Ave., Mendota, IL 61342.

Buying coins through auctions appeals to many collectors. Where else can you set your own price?

Where to write for more information

Coins Magazine: 700 E. State St., Iola, WI 54990.

Numismatic News: 700 E. State St., Iola, WI 54990.

World Coin News: 700 E. State St., Iola, WI 54990.

American Numismatic Association: 818 N. Cascade Ave., Colorado Springs, CO 80903-3279.

Professional Numismatists Guild: P.O. Box 430, Van Nuys, CA 91408.

Florida United Numismatists: P.O. Box 1527, Gainesville, FL 32602-1527.

Long Beach Numismatic, Philatelic, & Baseball Card Exposition: c/o Sam Lopresto, 112 E. Broadway, Long Beach, CA 90802.

Central States Numismatic Society: c/o Robert E. Douglas, 58 Devonwood Ave. S.W., Cedar Rapids, IA 52404.

4

The grading factor
How to classify a coin's condition

By Arlyn G. Sieber

Grading is one of the most important factors in buying and selling coins as collectibles. Unfortunately, it's also one of the most controversial. Since the early days of coin collecting in the United States, buying through the mail has been a convenient way for collectors to acquire coins. As a result, there has always been a need in numismatics for a concise way to classify the amount of wear on a coin and its condition in general.

A look back

In September 1888, Dr. George Heath, a physician in Monroe, Mich., published a four-page pamphlet titled *The American Numismatist*. Publication of subsequent issues led to the founding of the American Numismatic Association, and *The Numismatist*, as it's known today, is the association's official journal. Heath's first issues were largely devoted to selling world coins from his collection. There were no formal grades listed with the coins and their prices, but the following statement by Heath indicates that condition was a consideration for early collectors:

"The coins are in above average condition," Heath wrote, "and so confident am I that they will give satisfaction, that I agree to refund the money in any unsatisfactory sales on the return of the coins."

As coin collecting became more popular and *The Numismatist* started accepting paid advertising from others, grading became more formal. The February 1892 issue listed seven "classes" for the condition of coins (from worst to best): mutilated, poor, fair, good, fine, uncirculated, and proof. Through the years, the hobby has struggled with developing a grading sys-

The first formal grading guide was Brown and Dunn's *A Guide to the Grading of United States Coins.*

tem that would be accepted by all and could apply to all coins. The hobby's growth was accompanied by a desire for more grades, or classifications, to more precisely define a coin's condition. The desire for more precision, however, was at odds with the basic concept of grading: to provide a *concise* method for classifying a coin's condition.

For example, even the conservatively few classifications of 1892 included fudge factors.

"To give flexibility to this classification," *The Numismatist* said, "such modification of fine, good and fair, as 'extremely,' 'very,' 'almost,' etc. are used to express slight variations from the general condition."

The debate over grading continued for decades in *The Numismatist*. A number of articles and letters prodded the ANA to write grading guidelines and endorse them as the association's official standards. Some submitted specific suggestions for terminology and accompanying standards for each grade. But grading remained a process of "instinct" gained through years of collecting or dealing experience.

A formal grading guide in book form finally appeared in 1958, but it was the work of two individuals rather than the ANA. *A Guide to the Grading of United States Coins* by Martin R. Brown and John W. Dunn was a breakthrough in the great grading debate. Now collectors had a reference that gave them specific guidelines for specific coins and could be studied and restudied at home.

The first editions of Brown and Dunn carried text only, no illustrations. For the fourth edition, in 1964, publication was assumed by Whitman Publishing Co. of Racine, Wis., and line drawings were added to illustrate the text.

The fourth edition listed six principal categories for circulated coins (from worst to best): good, very good, fine, very fine, extremely fine, and about uncirculated. But again, the desire for more precise categories was evidenced. In the book's introduction, Brown and Dunn wrote, "Dealers will sometimes advertise coins that are graded G-VG, VG-F, F-VF, VF-XF. Or the description may be ABT. G. or VG plus, etc. This means that the coin in question more than meets minimum standards for the lower grade but is not quite good enough for the higher grade."

When the fifth edition appeared, in 1969, the "New B & D Grading System" was introduced. The six principal categories for circulated coins were still intact, but variances within those categories were now designated by up to four letters: "A", "B", "C" or "D". For example, an EF-A coin was "almost about uncirculated." An EF-B was "normal extra fine" within the B & D standards. EF-C had a "normal extra fine" obverse, but the reverse was "obviously not as nice as obverse due to poor strike or excessive wear." EF-D had a "normal extra fine" reverse but a problem obverse.

But that wasn't the end. Brown and Dunn further listed 29 problem points that could appear on a coin — from No. 1 for an "edge bump" to No. 29 for "attempted re-engraving outside of the Mint." The number could be followed by the letter "O" or "R" to designate whether the problem appeared on the obverse or reverse and a Roman numeral corresponding to a clock face to designate where the problem appears on the obverse or reverse. For example, a coin described as "VG-B-9-O-X" would grade "VG-B"; the 9 designated a "single rim nick"; the "O" indicated the nick was on the obverse; and the "X" indicated it appeared at the 10 o'clock position, or upper left, of the obverse.

The authors' goal was noble — to create the perfect grading system. They again, however, fell victim to the age-old grading-system problem: Precision comes at the expense of brevity. Dealer Kurt Krueger wrote in the January 1976 issue of *The Numismatist*, ". . . under the new B & D system, the numismatist must contend with a minimum of 43,152 different grading combinations! Accuracy is apparent, but simplicity has been lost." As a result, the "new B & D system" never caught on in the marketplace.

The 1970s saw two important grading guides make their debut. The first was *Photograde* by James F. Ruddy. As the title implies, Ruddy uses photographs instead of line drawings to show how coins look in the various circulated grades. Simplicity is also a virtue of Ruddy's book. Only seven

Photograde was the first widely accepted grading guide to use photos to illustrate the amount of wear on circulated coins.

circulated grades are listed (about good, good, very good, fine, very fine, extremely fine, and about uncirculated), and the designations stop there.

In 1977 the longtime call for the ANA to issue grading standards was met with the release of *Official A.N.A. Grading Standards for United States Coins.* Like Brown and Dunn, the first editions of the ANA guide used line drawings to illustrate coins in various states of wear. But instead of using adjectival descriptions, the ANA guide adopted a numerical system for designating grades.

The numerical designations were based on a system used by Dr. William H. Sheldon in his book *Early American Cents,* first published in 1949. He used a scale of 1 to 70 to designate the grades of large cents.

"On this scale," Sheldon wrote, "1 means that the coin is identifiable and not mutilated — no more than that. A 70-coin is one in flawless Mint State, exactly as it left the dies, with perfect mint color and without a blemish or nick."

(Sheldon's scale also had its pragmatic side. At the time, a No. 2 large cent was worth about twice a No. 1 coin; a No. 4 was worth about twice a

Official A.N.A. Grading Standards for United States Coins **is now in its fourth edition.**

No. 2, and so on up the scale.)

With the first edition of its grading guide, the ANA adopted the 70-point scale for grading all U.S. coins. It designated 10 categories of circulated grades: AG-3, G-4, VG-8, F-12, VF-20, VF-30, EF-40, EF-45, AU-50, and AU-55. The third edition, released in 1987, replaced the line drawings with photographs, and another circulated grade was added: AU-58. A fourth edition was released in 1991.

Grading circulated U.S. coins

Dealers today generally use either the ANA guide or *Photograde* when grading circulated coins for their inventories. (Brown and Dunn is now out of print.) Many local coin shops sell both books. Advertisers in *Numismatic News*, *Coins*, and *Coin Prices* must indicate which standards they are using in grading their coins. If the standards are not listed, they must conform to ANA standards.

Following are some general guidelines, accompanied by photos, for grad-

ing circulated U.S. coins. Grading even circulated pieces can be subjective, particularly when attempting to draw the fine line between, for example, AU-55 and AU-58. Two longtime collectors or dealers can disagree in such a case.

But by studying some combination of the following guidelines, the ANA guide, and *Photograde*, and by looking at a lot of coins at shops and shows, collectors can gain enough grading knowledge to buy circulated coins confidently from dealers and other collectors. The more you study, the more knowledge and confidence you will gain. When you decide which series of coins you want to collect, focus on the guidelines for that particular series. Read them, reread them, and then refer back to them again and again.

AU-50

Indian cent

Lincoln cent

Buffalo nickel

Jefferson nickel

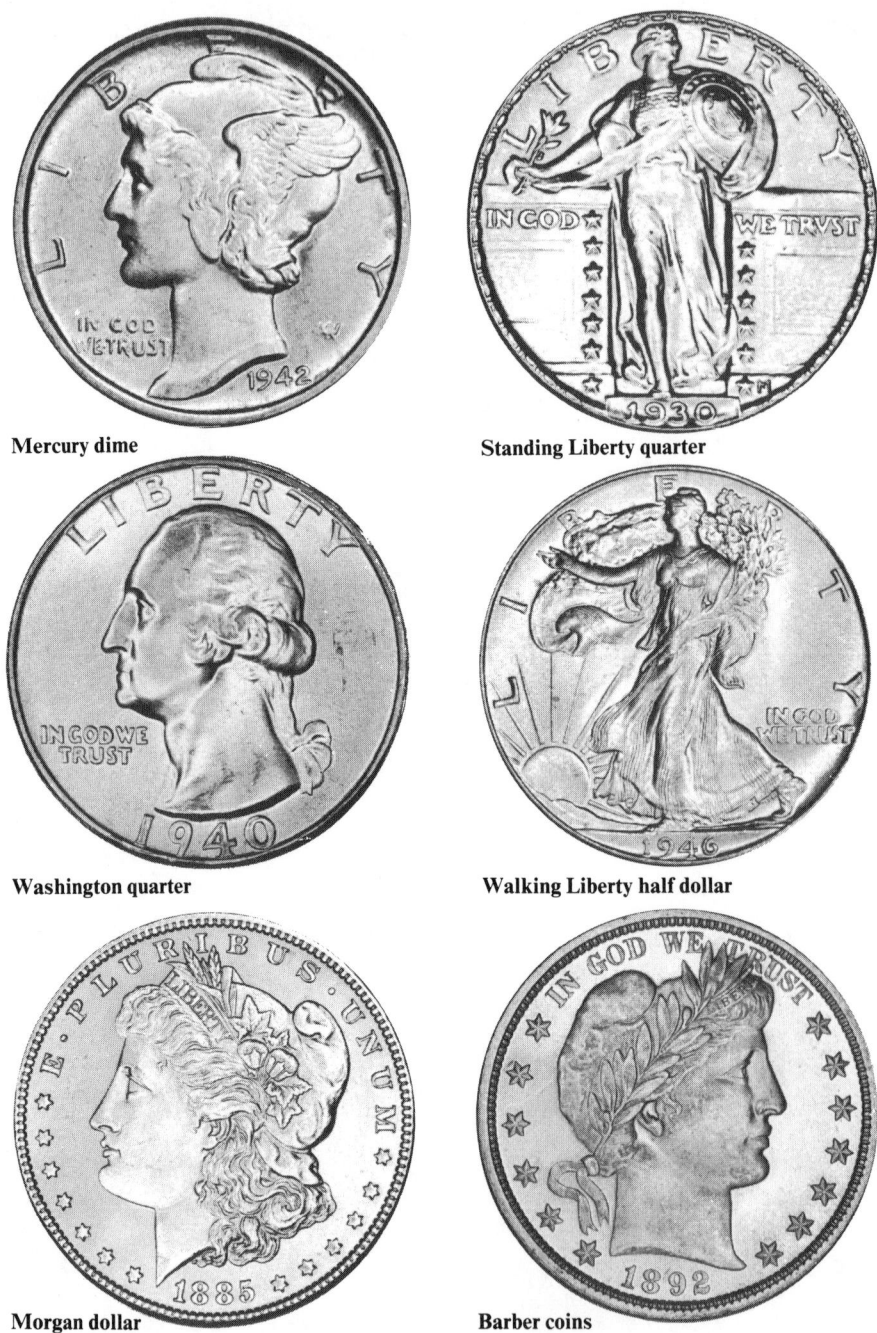

Mercury dime

Standing Liberty quarter

Washington quarter

Walking Liberty half dollar

Morgan dollar

Barber coins

AU-50 (about uncirculated): Just a slight trace of wear, the result of brief exposure to circulation or light rubbing from mishandling, may be evident on the elevated design areas. These imperfections may appear as scratches or dull spots, along with bag marks or edge nicks. At least half of the original mint luster generally is still evident.

XF-40

Indian cent

Lincoln cent

Buffalo nickel

Jefferson nickel

Mercury dime

Standing Liberty quarter

Washington quarter

Walking Liberty half dollar

Morgan dollar

Barber coins

XF-40 (extremely fine): The coin must show only slight evidence of wear on the highest points of the design, particularly in the hair lines of the portrait on the obverse. The same may be said for the eagle's feathers and wreath leaves on the reverse of most U.S. coins. A trace of mint luster may still show in protected areas of the coin's surface.

VF-20

Indian cent

Lincoln cent

Buffalo nickel

Jefferson nickel

Mercury dime

Standing Liberty quarter

Washington quarter

Walking Liberty half dollar

Morgan dollar

Barber coins

VF-20 (very fine): The coin will show light wear at the fine points in the design, though they may remain sharp overall. Although the details may be slightly smoothed, all lettering and major features must remain sharp.

Indian cent: All letters in "Liberty" are complete but worn. Headdress shows considerable flatness, with flat spots on the tips of the feathers.

Lincoln cent: Hair, cheek, jaw, and bow-tie details will be worn but clearly separated, and wheat stalks on the reverse will be full with no weak spots.

Buffalo nickel: High spots on hair braid and cheek will be flat but show some detail, and a full horn will remain on the buffalo.

Jefferson nickel: Well over half of the major hair detail will remain, and the pillars on Monticello will remain well defined, with the triangular roof partially visible.

Mercury dime: Hair braid will show some detail, and three-quarters of the detail will remain in the feathers. The two diagonal bands on the fasces will show completely but will be worn smooth at the middle, with the vertical lines sharp.

Standing Liberty quarter: Rounded contour of Liberty's right leg will be flattened, as will the high point of the shield.

Washington quarter: There will be considerable wear on the hair curls, with feathers on the right and left of the eagle's breast showing clearly.

Walking Liberty half dollar: All lines of the skirt will show but will be worn on the high points. Over half the feathers on the eagle will show.

Morgan dollar: Two-thirds of the hairlines from the forehead to the ear must show. Ear should be well defined. Feathers on the eagle's breast may be worn smooth.

Barber coins: All seven letters of "Liberty" on the headband must stand out sharply. Head wreath will be well outlined from top to bottom.

F-12

Indian cent

Lincoln cent

Buffalo nickel

Jefferson nickel

Mercury dime   **Standing Liberty quarter**

Washington quarter   **Walking Liberty half dollar**

Morgan dollar   **Barber coins**

F-12 (fine): Coins show evidence of moderate to considerable but generally even wear on all high points, though all elements of the design and lettering remain bold. Where the word "Liberty" appears in a headband, it must be fully visible. On 20th century coins, the rim must be fully raised and sharp.

VG-8

Indian cent

Lincoln cent

Buffalo nickel

Jefferson nickel

Mercury dime

Standing Liberty quarter

Washington quarter

Walking Liberty half dollar

Morgan dollar

Barber coins

VG-8 (very good): The coin will show considerable wear, with most detail points worn nearly smooth. Where the word "Liberty" appears in a headband, at least three letters must show. On 20th century coins, the rim will start to merge with the lettering.

G-4

Indian cent

Lincoln cent

Buffalo nickel

Jefferson nickel

Mercury dime

Standing Liberty quarter

Washington quarter

Walking Liberty half dollar

Morgan dollar

Barber coins

G-4 (good): Only the basic design remains distinguishable in outline form, with all points of detail worn smooth. The word "Liberty" has disappeared, and the rims are almost merging with the lettering.

About good or fair: The coin will be identifiable by date and mint but otherwise badly worn, with only parts of the lettering showing. Such coins are of value only as fillers in a collection until a better example of the date and mintmark can be obtained. The only exceptions would be rare coins.

Grading uncirculated U.S. coins

The subjectivity of grading and the trend toward more classifications becomes more acute when venturing into uncirculated, or mint-state, coins. A minute difference between one or two grade points can mean a difference in value of hundreds or even thousands of dollars. In addition, the standards are more difficult to articulate in writing and illustrate through drawings or photographs. Thus, the possibilities for differences of opinion on one or two grade points increase in uncirculated coins.

Coins graded and encapsulated by a third-party grading service are nicknamed "slabs." The Professional Coin Grading Service graded this Saint-Gaudens gold $20 coin.

Back in Dr. George Heath's day and continuing through the 1960s, a coin was either uncirculated or it wasn't. Little distinction was made between uncirculated coins of varying condition, largely because there was little if any difference in value. When *Numismatic News* introduced its value guide in 1962 (the forerunner of today's Coin Market section in the *News*), it listed only one grade of uncirculated for Morgan dollars.

But as collectible coins increased in value and buyers of uncirculated coins became more picky, distinctions within grade uncirculated started to surface. In 1975 *Numismatic News* still listed only one uncirculated grade in Coin Market, but added this note: "Uncirculated and proof specimens in especially choice condition will also command proportionately higher premiums than these listed."

The first edition of the ANA guide listed two grades of uncirculated, MS-60 and MS-65, in addition to the theoretical but non-existent MS-70 (a flawless coin). MS-60 was described as "typical uncirculated" and MS-65 as "choice uncirculated." *Numismatic News* adopted both designations for Coin Market. In 1981, when the second edition of the ANA grading guide was released, MS-67 and MS-63 were added. In 1985 *Numismatic News* started listing six grades of uncirculated for Morgan dollars: MS-60, MS-63, MS-65, MS-65+, and MS-63 prooflike.

Then in 1986, a new entity appeared that has changed the nature of grading and trading uncirculated coins ever since. A group of dealers led by David Hall of Newport Beach, Calif., formed the Professional Coin Grading Service. For a fee, collectors could submit a coin through an authorized PCGS dealer and receive back a professional opinion of its grade.

The concept was not new; the ANA had operated an authentication service since 1972 and a grading service since 1979. A collector or dealer could submit a coin directly to the service and receive a certificate giving the service's opinion on authenticity and grade. The grading service was the source of near constant debate among dealers and ANA officials. Dealers charged that ANA graders were too young and inexperienced, and

The Numismatic Guaranty Corp. is another major grading service.

that their grading was inconsistent.

Grading stability was a problem throughout the coin business in the early 1980s, not just with the ANA service. Standards among uncirculated grades would tighten during a bear market and loosen during a bull market. As a result, a coin graded MS-65 in a bull market may have commanded only MS-63 during a bear market.

PCGS created several innovations in the grading business in response to these problems:

1. Coins could be submitted through PCGS-authorized dealers only.

2. Each coin would be graded by at least three members of a panel of "top graders," all prominent dealers in the business. (Since then, however, PCGS does not allow its graders to also deal in coins.)

3. After grading, the coin would be encapsulated in an inert, hard-plastic holder with a serial number and the grade indicated on the holder.

4. PCGS-member dealers pledged to make a market in PCGS-graded coins and honor the grades assigned.

5. In one of the most far-reaching moves, PCGS said it would use all 11 increments of uncirculated on the 70-point numerical scale: MS-60, MS-61, MS-62, MS-63, MS-64, MS-65, MS-66, MS-67, MS-68, MS-69, and MS-70.

The evolution of more uncirculated grades had reached another milestone.

Purists bemoaned the entombment of classic coins in the plastic holders and denounced the 11 uncirculated grades as implausible. Nevertheless, PCGS was an immediate commercial success. The plastic holders were nicknamed "slabs," and dealers couldn't get coins through the system fast enough.

In subsequent years, a number of similar services have appeared. Among them, one of the original PCGS "top graders," John Albanese, left PCGS to found the Numismatic Guaranty Corp. The ANA grading service succumbed to "slab mania" and introduced its own encapsulated product.

Although there are still several other reputable grading services, PCGS

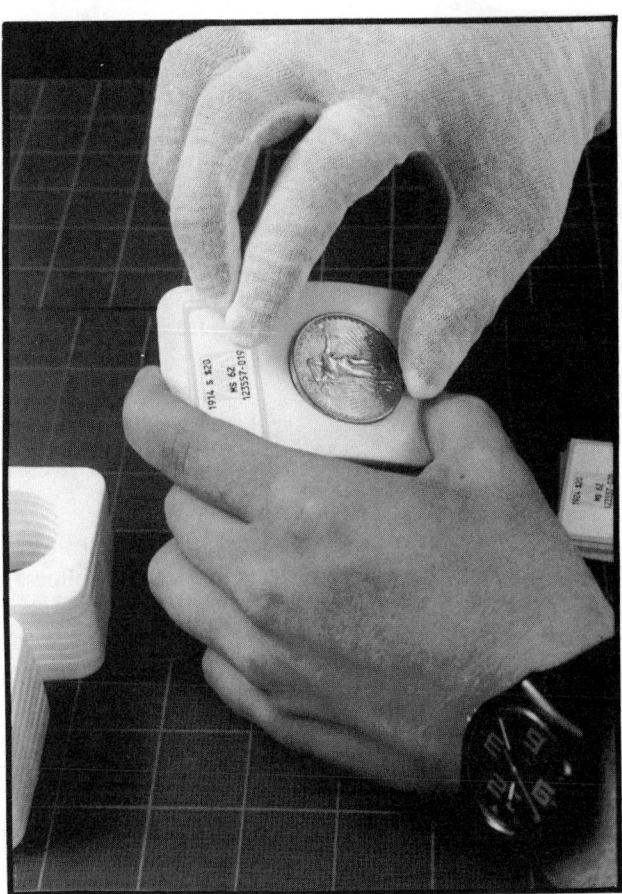

An NGC worker places a coin in its holder after it has been graded.

and NGC dominate market share. In 1990 the ANA sold its grading service to a private company. The association continues to authenticate coins.

How should a collector approach the buying and grading of uncirculated coins? Collecting uncirculated coins worth thousands of dollars implies a higher level of numismatic expertise by the buyer. Those buyers without that level of expertise should cut their teeth on more inexpensive coins, just as today's experienced collectors did. Inexperienced collectors can start toward that level by studying the guidelines for mint-state coins in the ANA grading guide and looking at lots of coins at shows and shops.

Study the condition and eye appeal of a coin and compare it to other coins of the same series. Then compare prices. Do the more expensive coins look better? If so, why? Start to make your own judgments concerning relationships between condition and value.

According to numismatic legend, a collector walked up to a crusty old dealer at a show one time and asked the dealer to grade a coin the collector had with him. The dealer looked at the coin and said, "I grade it a hundred dollars." Such is the bottom line to coin grading.

Grading U.S. proof coins

Because proof coins are struck by a special process (see Chapter 2), they receive their own grading designation. A coin does not start out being a proof and then become mint state if it becomes worn. Once a proof coin, always a proof coin.

In the ANA system, proof grades use the same numbers as circulated and uncirculated grades, and the amount of wear on the coin corresponds to those grades. But the number is preceded by the word "proof." For example, Proof-65, Proof-55, Proof-45, and so on. In addition, the ANA says a proof coin with many marks, scratches or other defects should be called an "impaired proof."

Grading world coins

The state of grading non-U.S. issues is similar to U.S. coin grading before Brown and Dunn. There is no detailed, illustrated guide that covers the enormous scope and variety of world coins; collectors and dealers rely on their experience in the field and knowledge of the marketplace.

The *Standard Catalog of World Coins* gives the following guidelines for grading world coins, which apply to the Canadian and Mexican value listings in this book:

In grading world coins, there are two elements to look for: (1) overall wear and (2) loss of design details, such as strands of hair, feathers on eagles, designs on coats of arms, and so on. Grade each coin by the weaker of the two sides. Age, rarity or type of coin should not be considered in grading.

Grade by the amount of overall wear and loss of detail evident in the main design on each side. On coins with a moderately small design element that is prone to early wear, grade by that design alone.

In the marketplace, adjectival grades are still used for Mexican coins. The numerical system for Canadian coins is now commonplace:

Uncirculated, MS-60: No visible signs of wear or handling, even under a 30X microscope. Bag marks may be present.

Almost uncirculated, AU-50: All detail will be visible. There will be wear on only the highest point of the coin. There will often be half or more of the original mint luster present.

Extremely fine, XF-40: About 95 percent of the original detail will be visible. Or, on a coin with a design that has no inner detail to wear down, there will be light wear over nearly the entire coin. If a small design is used as the grading area, about 90 percent of the original detail will be visible. This latter rule stems from the logic that a smaller amount of detail needs to be present because a small area is being used to grade the whole coin.

Very fine, VF-20: About 75 percent of the original detail will be visible. Or, on a coin with no inner detail, there will be moderate wear over the entire coin. Corners of letters and numbers may be weak. A small grading area will have about 60 percent of the original detail.

Fine, F-12: About 50 percent of the original detail will be visible. Or, on a coin with no inner detail, there will be fairly heavy wear over the entire coin. Sides of letters will be weak. A typically uncleaned coin will often appear dirty or dull. A small grading area will have just under 50 percent of the original detail.

Very good, VG-8: About 25 percent of the original detail will be visible. There will be heavy wear on the entire coin.

Good, G-4: Design will be clearly outlined but with substantial wear. Some of the larger detail may be visible. The rim may have a few weak spots of wear.

About good, AG-3: Typically only a silhouette of a large design will be visible. The rim will be worn down into the letters, if any.

Where to write for more information

Official A.N.A. Grading Standards for United States Coins: Western Publishing Co. Inc., P.O. Box 700, Racine, WI 53404.

Photograde: Bowers and Merena Galleries Inc., Books Department, Box 1224, Wolfeboro, NH 03894.

Professional Coin Grading Service: P.O. Box 9458, Newport Beach, CA 92658.

Numismatic Guaranty Corp.: P.O. Box 1776, Parsippany, NJ 07054.

American Numismatic Association Authentication Bureau: 818 N. Cascade Ave., Colorado Springs, CO 80903-3279.

5

Get a map

How to organize a collection

By David C. Harper

Do you have a jar full of old coins? Did a favorite relative give you a few silver dollars over the years? Or did you just come across something unusual that you set aside?

All three circumstances make good beginnings for collecting coins. It may surprise you, but this is how just about everybody starts in the hobby. It is a rare collector who decides to start down the hobby road without first having come into a few coins one way or another.

What these random groupings lack is organization. It is organization that makes a collection. But think about it another way: Organization is the map that tells you where you can go in coin collecting and how you can get there.

Have you ever been at a large fair or a huge office building and seen the maps that say "you are here"? Did you ever consider that, over time, thousands of other people have stood on the same spot? This is true in numismatics also. Figuratively, you are standing on the same spot on which the writers of this book stood at some point in their lives.

At a fair, the map helps you consider various ways of seeing all the sights. In coin collecting, too, there are different ways to organize a collection. The method you choose helps you see the hobby sights you want to see.

It should be something that suits you. Remember, do what you want to do. See what you want to see. But don't be afraid to make a mistake; there aren't any. Just as one can easily retrace steps at a fair, one can turn around and head in another direction in the coin-collecting hobby. Besides, when you start off for any given point, often you see something along the way that was unplanned but more interesting. That's numismatics.

There are two major ways to organize a collection: by type, and by date and mintmark. These approaches work in basically the same fashion for coins of the United States, Canada and Mexico. Naturally, there are differences. But to establish the concepts, let's focus first on U.S. coins.

United States

Let's take collecting by type first. Look at your jar of coins, or take the change out of your pocket. You find Abraham Lincoln and the Lincoln Memorial on current cents. You find Thomas Jefferson and his home, Monticello, on the nickel. Franklin D. Roosevelt and a torch share the dime. George Washington and an eagle appear on the quarter. John F. Kennedy and the presidential seal are featured on the half dollar.

Each design is called a "type." If you took one of each and put the five coins in a holder, you would have a type set of the coins that are currently being produced for circulation by the U.S. Mint.

With just these five coins, you can study various metallic compositions. You can evaluate their states of preservation and assign a grade to each. You can learn about the artists who designed the coins, and you can learn of the times in which these designs were created.

As you might have guessed, many different coin types have been used in the United States over the years. You may remember seeing some of them circulating. These designs reflect the hopes and aspirations of people over time. Putting all of them together forms a wonderful numismatic mosaic of American history.

George Washington did not mandate that his image appear on the quarter. Quite the contrary. He would have been horrified. When he was president, he headed off those individuals in Congress who thought the leader of the country should have his image on its coins. Washington said it smacked of monarchy and would have nothing of it.

Almost a century and a half later, during the bicentennial of Washington's birth in 1932, a nation searching for its roots during troubled economic times decided that it needed his portrait on its coins as a reminder of his great accomplishments and as reassurance that this nation was the same place it had been in more prosperous days.

In its broadest definition, collecting coins by type requires that you obtain an example of every design that was struck by the U.S. Mint since it was founded in 1792. That's a tall order. You would be looking for denominations like the half cent, two-cent piece, three-cent piece, and 20-cent piece, which have not been produced in over a century. You would be looking for gold coins ranging in face value from $1 to $50.

But even more important than odd-sounding denominations or high face values is the question of rarity. Some of the pieces in this two-century type set are rare and expensive. That's why type collectors often divide the challenge into more digestible units.

Type collecting can be divided into 18th, 19th and 20th century units. Starting type collectors can focus on 20th century coin designs, which are easily obtainable. The fun and satisfaction of putting the 20th century set together then creates the momentum to continue backward in time.

In the process of putting a 20th century type set together, one is also learning how to grade, learning hobby jargon, and discovering how to obtain coins from dealers, the U.S. Mint, and other collectors. All of this knowledge is then refined as the collector increases the challenge to himself.

This book is designed to help. How many dollar types were struck in the 20th century? Turn to the U.S. price-guide section and check it out. We see the Morgan dollar, Peace dollar, Eisenhower dollar, and Anthony dollar. Hobbyists could also add the Ike dollar with the Bicentennial design of 1976 and the silver American Eagle bullion coin struck since 1986. One can also find out their approximate retail prices from the listings.

The beauty of type collecting is that one can choose the most inexpensive example of each type. There is no need to select a 1903-O Morgan when the 1921 will do just as well. With the 20th century type set, hobbyists can dodge some truly big-league prices.

As a collector's hobby confidence grows, he can tailor goals to fit his desires. He can take the road less traveled if that is what suits him. Type sets can be divided by denomination. You can choose two centuries of one-cent coins. You can take just obsolete denominations or copper, silver or gold denominations.

You can even collect by size. Perhaps you would like to collect all coin types larger than 30 millimeters or all coins smaller than 20 millimeters. Many find this freedom of choice stimulating.

Type collecting has proven itself to be enduringly popular over the years. It provides a maximum amount of design variety while allowing collectors to set their own level of challenge.

The second popular method of collecting is by date and mintmark. What this means, quite simply, is that a collector picks a given type — Jefferson nickels, for example — and then goes after an example of every year, every mintmark, and every type of manufacture that was used with the Jefferson design.

Looking at this method of collecting brings up the subject of mintmarks. The "U.S. Mint" is about as specific as most non-collectors get in describing the government agency that provides everyday coins. Behind that label are the various production facilities that actually do the work.

In two centuries of U.S. coinage, there have been eight such facilities. Four are still in operation. Those eight in alphabetical order are Carson City, Nev., which used a "CC" mintmark to identify its work; Charlotte, N.C. ("C"); Dahlonega, Ga. ("D"); Denver (also uses a "D," but it opened long after the Dahlonega Mint closed, so there was never any confusion); New Orleans ("O"); Philadelphia (because it was the primary mint, it used no mintmark for much of its history, but currently uses a "P"); San Francisco ("S"); and West Point, N.Y. ("W").

A basic type set of 20th century dollar coins would consist of (from top), a Morgan type, Peace type, Eisenhower type, and Anthony type.

A person contemplating the collecting of Jefferson nickels by date and mintmark will find that three mints produced them: San Francisco, Denver and Philadelphia. Because the first two are branch mints serving smaller populations, their output has tended over time to be smaller than that of Philadelphia. This fact, repeated in other series, has helped give mintmarks quite an allure to collectors. It provides one of the major attractions in collecting coins by date and mintmark.

The key date for Jeffersons is the 1950-D when using mintages as a guide. In that year, production was just 2.6 million pieces. Because collectors of the time were aware of the coin's low mintage, many examples were saved. As a result, prices are reasonable.

Jefferson nickels have been produced at the (from top) Philadelphia, Denver and San Francisco mints. Note the Denver and San Francisco mintmarks to the right of Monticello.

The wartime nickels of 1942-45 marked the first time a "P" mintmark, for Philadelphia, was used.

The Depression-era 1939-D comes in as the most valuable regular-issue Jefferson nickel despite a mintage of 3.5 million — almost 1 million more than the 1950-D. The reason: Fewer were saved for later generations of coin collectors.

Date and mintmark collecting teaches hobbyists to use mintage figures as a guide but to take them with a grain of salt. Rarity, after all, is determined by the number of surviving coins, not the number initially created.

The Jefferson series is a good one to collect by date and mintmark, because the mintmarks have moved around, grown in size, and expanded in number.

When the series was first introduced, the Jefferson nickel was produced at the three mints previously mentioned. In 1942, because of a diversion of certain metals to wartime use, the coin's alloy of 75 percent copper and 25 percent nickel was changed. The new alloy was 35 percent silver, 56 percent copper, and 9 percent manganese.

To denote the change, the mintmarks were moved and greatly enlarged. The pre-1942 mintmarks were small and located to the right of Monticello; the wartime mintmarks were enlarged and placed over the dome. What's more, for the first time in American history, the Philadelphia Mint used a mintmark ("P").

The war's end restored the alloy and mintmarks to their previous status. The "P" disappeared. This lasted until the 1960s, when a national coin shortage saw all mintmarks removed for three years (1965-1967) and then returned, but in a different location. Mintmarks were placed on the obverse, to the right of Jefferson's portrait near the date in 1968. In 1980 the "P" came back in a smaller form and is still used.

Another consideration arises with date and mintmark collecting: Should the hobbyist include proof coins in the set? This can be argued both ways. Suffice to say that anyone who has the desire to add proof coins to the set will have a larger one. It is not necessary nor is it discouraged.

Some of the first proof coins to carry mintmarks were Jefferson nickels. When proof coins were made in 1968 after lapsing from 1965 to 1967, production occurred at San Francisco instead of Philadelphia. The "S" mintmark was placed on the proof coins of that year, including the Jefferson nickel, to denote the change. Since that time, mintmarks used on proof

In 1968 mintmarks reappeared on U.S. coins and production of proof coins resumed, this time at the San Francisco Mint. On the nickels, the mintmark moved from the reverse to the obverse below the date.

examples of various denominations have included the "P", "D", "S", and "W".

For all of the mintmark history that is embodied in the Jefferson series, prices are reasonable. For a first attempt at collecting coins by date and mintmark, it provides excellent background for going on to the more expensive and difficult types. After all, if you are ever going to get used to the proper handling of a coin, it is far better to experiment on a low-cost coin than a high-value rarity.

As one progresses in date and mintmark collecting and type collecting, it is important to remember that all of the coins should be of similar states of preservation. Sets look slapdash if one coin is VG and another is MS-65 and still another is VF. Take a look at the prices of all the coins in the series before you get too far, figure out what you can afford, and then stick to that grade or range of grades.

Sure, there is a time-honored practice of filling a spot with any old example until a better one comes along. That is how we got the term "filler." But if you get a few placeholders, don't stop there. By assembling a set of uniform quality, you end up with a more aesthetically pleasing collection.

The date and mintmark method used to be the overwhelmingly dominant form of collecting. It still has many adherents. Give it a try if you think it sounds right for you.

Before we leave the discussion of collecting U.S. coins, it should be pointed out that the two major methods of organizing a collection are simply guidelines. They are no hard-and-fast rules that must be followed without question. Collecting should be satisfying to the hobbyist. It should never be just one more item in the daily grind. Take the elements of these collecting approaches that you like or invent your own.

It should also be pointed out that U.S. coinage history does not start with 1792 nor do all of the coins struck since that time conform precisely to the two major organizational approaches. But these two areas are good places to start.

There are coins and tokens from the American Colonial period (1607-1776) that are just as fascinating and collectible as regular U.S. Mint issues. There are federal issues struck before the Mint was actually established. See the Colonial price-guide section in this book.

There are special coins called commemoratives, which have been struck by the U.S. Mint since 1892 to celebrate some aspect of American history or a contemporary event. They are not intended for circulation. There was a long interruption between 1954 and 1982, but currently numerous commemoratives are being offered for sale directly to collectors by the Mint.

Collecting commemoratives has always been considered something separate from collecting regular U.S. coinage. It is, however, organized the same way. Commemoratives can be collected by date and mintmark or by type.

Current commemoratives can be purchased from the U.S. Mint. To get on its mailing list, write U.S. Mint, Customer Service Center, 10001 Aerospace Drive, Lanham MD 20706. Once on the list, hobbyists will get the various solicitations for not only commemoratives, but regular proof sets and mint sets and American Eagle bullion coinage.

Buying coins from the Mint can be considered a hobby pursuit in its own right. Some collectors let the Mint organize their holdings for them. They buy complete sets and put them away. They never buy anything from anywhere else.

Admittedly, this is a passive form of collecting, but there are individuals around the world who enjoy collecting at this level without ever really going any deeper. They like acquiring every new issue as it comes off the Mint's presses.

Once done, there is a certain knowledge that one has all the examples of the current year. Obviously, too, collectors by date and mintmark of the current types would have to buy the new coins each year, but, of course, they do not stop there.

Varieties and errors make up another area. Under this heading come the coins the Mint did not intend to make. There are all kinds of errors. Many of them are inexpensive. Check out the U.S. Minting Varieties and Errors section in the price guide. If you want to pursue it further, there are specialty books that deal with the topic in more detail.

Canada

Starting point for the national coinage of Canada is popularly fixed at 1858. In that year a large cent was first produced for use in Upper and Lower Canada (Ontario and Quebec). These pieces were intended to supplant local copper coinage, which in turn had been attempts to give various regions a medium of exchange.

What was circulating in Canada at the time was a hodgepodge of world issues. The large cent predates a unified national government by nine years, but it is considered the beginning of national issues nevertheless.

There are many similarities between the United States and Canada and their respective monetary systems. Both continent-sized nations thought in terms of taming the frontier, new settlements, and growth. Both came to use the dollar as the unit of account because of the pervasiveness of the Spanish milled dollar in trade. For each, the dollar divides into 100 cents.

Canadian coins have depicted (from top) Queen Victoria, King Edward VII, King George V, King George VI, and Queen Elizabeth II.

However, Canada had a far longer colonial history. Many of its residents resisted the tide that carried the United States to independence and worked to preserve their loyalties to the British crown. As a result, Canada was firmly a part of the British Empire. So even today with its constitution (the British North America Act transferred from Westminster to Ottawa in 1982), parliamentary democracy, and a national consciousness perhaps best symbolized by the maple leaf, Canada retains a loyalty to the crown in the person of Queen Elizabeth II of the United Kingdom. Canada is a member of the British Commonwealth of Nations.

The effect of this on coins is obvious. Current issues carry the queen's effigy. How Canada got its coins in the past was also influenced. The fledgling U.S. government set about creating its own mint as one of its earliest goals, despite that better-quality pieces could be purchased abroad at lower cost. Canada found that ties to mints located in England were logical and comfortable.

The Royal Canadian Mint was not established until 1908, when it was called the Ottawa branch of the British Royal Mint, and it was not given its present name until 1931. Both events are within living memory. Canadian coins, therefore, have a unique mixture of qualities. They are tantalizingly familiar to U.S. citizens yet distinctly different.

The coinage of a monarchy brings its own logic to the organization of a collection. Type collecting is delineated by the monarch. United Canada has had six. The first was Queen Victoria, whose image appeared on those large cents of 1858. Her reign began in 1837 and lasted until 1901.

She was followed by Edward VII, 1901-1910; George V, 1910-1936; Edward VIII, 1936; George VI, 1936-1952; and Queen Elizabeth II, 1952-present. All but Edward VIII had coins struck for circulation in Canada. The collectible monarchs, therefore, number five, but the longer reigns inspired changes of portraits over time to show the aging process at work. Legends also changed. When George VI ceased being emperor of India, Canada's coins were modified to recognize the change.

Like U.S. coins, sizes and alloys were altered to meet new demands placed on the coinage. However, the separateness of each nation might best be summed up this way: Though the United States abolished its large cent in 1857, Canada's was just getting under way in 1858. The United States put an end to the silver dollar in 1935, the very year Canada finally got its series going.

And Canada, the nickel-mining giant, used a small-sized silver five-cent coin until 1921, almost 50 years after the half dime was abolished in the United States. But whereas the Civil War was the major cause of the emergence of modern U.S. coinage as specified by the Coinage Act of 1873, World War I influenced the alterations that made Canada's coins what they are today.

It might be assumed that change in the monarch also signaled a change in the reverse designs of the various denominations. A check of the Canadian price guide section shows this is not necessarily the case. Current

designs paired with Queen Elizabeth II basically date back to the beginning of her father's reign. The familiar maple-leaf cent, beaver five-cent piece, schooner 10-cent, caribou 25-cent, and coat-of-arms 50-cent have been running for over 50 years. Significant changes were made to the 50-cent coin in 1959, but the reverse design remains the coat of arms.

So where does that leave type collectors? It puts them in a situation similar to categorizing the various eagles on U.S. coins. They can be universalists and accept the broadest definitions of type, or they can narrow the bands to whatever degree suits them best.

By checking the price-guide section, date and mintmark collectors will quickly note that their method of organization more or less turns into collecting by date. Though currently there are three mints in Canada — Hull, Quebec; Ottawa, Ontario; and Winnipeg, Manitoba — they don't use mintmarks. Historically, few mintmarks were employed.

Ottawa used a "C" on gold sovereigns of 1908-1919 and on some exported colonial issues. The private Heaton Mint in Birmingham, England, used an "H" on coins it supplied to Canada from 1871 to 1907.

But the coins supplied to Canada by the British Royal Mint and later by its Ottawa branch did not carry any identifying mark. Collectors who confine their activities to the more recent issues need never think about a mintmark.

It would be easy to slant a presentation on Canadian issues to stress similarities or differences to U.S. issues. One should remember that the monetary structures of each evolved independently, but each was always having an impact on the other.

Common events, such as World War II, had a similar impact. For example, the Canadian five-cent coin changed in much the same way as the U.S. nickel. In Canada, nickel was removed and replaced first by a tombac (brass) alloy and then by chromium-plated steel. Peace brought with it a return to the prewar composition.

To see an example of differences between the United States and Canada, take the Canadian approach to the worldwide trend of removing silver from coinage. Canada made its move in 1968, three years after the United States. Instead of choosing a copper-nickel alloy as a substitute for silver, Canada looked to its own vast natural resources and employed pure nickel.

Canada also seems more comfortable with its coinage than the United States. Whereas the United States often feared confusion and counterfeiting from making the least little changes in its coins, Canada has long embraced coinage to communicate national events, celebrations and culture. Its silver-dollar series actually began as a celebration of George V's 25 years on the throne.

Succeeding years saw additional commemorative $1 designs interspersed with the regular voyageur design. When the centennial of national confederation was observed in 1967, all of the denominations were altered for one year. The United States only reluctantly tried out the idea on three of its denominations for the nation's Bicentennial.

Like the U.S. Mint, the Royal Canadian Mint offers sets of coins in a variety of finishes to the collector market.

Ultimately, Canada began an annual commemorative dollar series in 1971. It issued coins for the 1976 Montreal Olympic Games and again in 1988 for the Calgary Olympic Games. Bullion coins were created to market its gold, silver and platinum output. A commemorative series of gold $100 coins was also undertaken. Canada, too, issues special proof, prooflike and specimen sets, similar to the United States.

Hobbyists who would like to be informed of new issues should write Royal Canadian Mint, P.O. Box 473, Station "A," Ottawa, Ontario K1N 1A1, Canada. The mint also maintains special toll-free lines. In the United States, hobbyists may telephone the Royal Canadian Mint at 1-800-268-6468. In Canada the number is 1-800-267-1871. You can get on the mailing list by using these numbers and you can buy currently available coins.

When collecting Canada, another thing to remember is the importance varieties play in the nation's various series. Certainly, a type collector has no need to dwell on this information, but the date and mintmark collector may puzzle over the many extra identifying abbreviations in the price guide for certain coins. These varieties should not be confused with the U.S. variety-and-error category.

Here the varieties are not mistakes; they are deliberately created and issued variations of the standard design. We see voyageur dollars on which the number of water lines changes. Other dollars count the number of beads.

These differences are minor. Though they were deliberately done to meet varying mint needs, they were not intended to be set apart in the public mind. The hobby, however, likes to look at things under a microscope.

Some varieties were indeed intended to be deliberately and noticeably different. An example of this occurs with 1947-dated issues. A maple leaf was placed on the 1947-dated cent through 50-cent issues. This indicated

the coin was struck after George VI lost his title of emperor of India, as proclaimed in the Latin legend, but that the design had not yet been altered to reflect this. All of these varieties are considered integral parts of the Canadian series, and they are listed as such.

Do not construe any of this to mean there is no collecting of varieties and errors of the type common in the United States. There is. Collecting Royal Canadian Mint mistakes is just as active, just as interesting, and just as rewarding. After all, mint errors are universal. The methods of manufacture are the same. So the mistakes can be classified in the same manner.

Canada's numismatic listings also include items from various provinces issued before they were part of the confederation. The largest portion of this section is devoted to Newfoundland, because it retained a separate status far longer than the other provinces — until 1949 in fact.

Advice given to collectors of U.S. coins also applies to collectors of Canadian coins: Do what interests you. Do what you can afford. Create sets of uniform grade.

The rules of rarity transcend national boundaries. The only thing to keep in mind is the relative size of the collecting population. Because Canada has only a tenth of the U.S. population, it stands to reason that the number of collectors in that nation is but a fraction of the U.S. number. A mintage that seems to indicate scarcity for a U.S. coin, therefore, could indicate something quite common in Canada.

Don't forget that mintage is just a guide. The same factors that caused loss of available specimens or preserved unusually large quantities were at work in Canada, too.

Mexico

Coinage produced in Mexico dates to the establishment of a mint in Mexico City in 1536, over 250 years before a federal mint was set up in the United States and more than 300 years before Canada circulated its own coins. The output of those extra centuries alone would make organizing a Mexican coin collection more challenging than a collection of U.S. or Canadian coins. But there are numerous other factors involved.

You say you like the kings and queens on Canada's coins? Mexico has kings, too — nearly 300 years' worth, plus a couple of emperors. You say the ideals of liberty embodied by the great men and women on U.S. coins is more your cup of tea? Mexico's coins also feature men and women committed to liberty.

In addition, Mexico is the crossroads of civilizations and empires. The great pyramid-building society of southern Mexico and Central America met its end at the hands of the Spanish conquistadors led initially by Hernando Cortez. The great Aztec empire was looted and overturned in 1519-1521 in the name of Spain.

The great natural resources of the area then supported successive Spanish kings in their grand dreams of dominating Europe. Through the doors

One thousand of these equaled one new peso as 1993 began. The new peso is worth about 33 cents.

of the Mexico City Mint and later facilities scattered about the country passed legendary quantities of silver. Even today the country ranks at the top of the list of silver producers.

But while Spain could dominate Mexico for a long time, the basic ideals of liberty and human dignity eventually motivated the people to throw off the foreign yoke. Unfortunately, victory was often neither complete nor wisely led. And in more recent years, the scourge of inflation has exacted a high toll on the currency itself. The numismatic consequences of a long history punctuated by periods of turmoil are an abundance of denominations, metals and types.

It is tempting for a would-be collector of Mexican coins to forget about anything that happened in the country prior to its monetary reform of 1905. By starting at that point, a hobbyist can happily overlook anything other than a decimal monetary system in which 100 centavos equal 1 peso. That system is as modern as any. The coins' striking quality is high. Legends are easy to read and understand, and the variety of issues is wide but not overwhelming.

There always is a certain logic to begin the collecting of any country with recent issues. The costs of learning are minimized, and as one becomes comfortable, a level of confidence can be built up sufficient to prompt diving further into the past.

The issues of 1905 to date also more easily fit into the mold of type collecting and collecting by date and mintmark. To take type collecting, for example, let's look at the peso. In 1905 it was a silver-dollar-sized coin with a silver-dollar-sized quantity of bullion in it, 0.786 ounces. In 1918 it was reduced to 0.4663 ounces; in 1920, 0.3856 ounces; in 1947, 0.2250 ounces; 1950, 0.1285 ounces; 1957, 0.0514 ounces; and in 1970 silver was eliminated completely in favor of a copper-nickel alloy.

At almost every one of those steps, the design changed, too. After sinking to 3,300 to the U.S. dollar, monetary reform dropped three zeroes at the start of 1993. The new peso, equal to 1,000 old pesos, is three to the dollar.

By beginning with 1905, a date and mintmark collector misses out on issues of the various branch mints that were located around the country. Regular issues were all struck in Mexico City. Yearly output was reasonably regular for the various denominations, so date sets are extensive.

There have been rumblings since the early 1980s that Mexico would

Mexico also strikes commemorative coins for the collector market. They are available through private firms in the United States.

abandon the peso because of its greatly reduced value. The government, however, has been working hard to retain it. So far it has succeeded.

One thing the government cannot do, however, is turn the clock back to a time when the fractional denominations of 1, 2, 5, 10, 20, 25, and 50 centavos had sufficient face value to circulate. However, it is stimulating to assemble sets because they offer a range of rarities. They are neither so expensive that it would prevent a collector from acquiring them at some point, but neither are they so common that you can walk into a shop, write a check, and come away with all of the 20th century sets complete. Check out the price guide section and see.

Gold in the post-1905 era is basically so much bullion. There are some scarcer pieces and some strikingly beautiful designs, such as the centenario, a gold 50-peso coin containing 1.2 ounces of bullion. It was first struck in 1921 to mark 100 years of independence. Because Mexico actively restruck its gold coins, however, it is virtually impossible to tell an original issue from the newer version.

The result is a retail price structure based on metallic content. Gold, however, does not conjure up the images that silver does. Silver is the magic word for Mexico. That, of course, means the peso.

The modern Mexico City Mint also strikes commemoratives and collector sets from time to time. These are generally marketed to collectors through private firms, details of which are published in hobby newspapers like *World Coin News*. Mexico, like the United States and Canada, also issues gold and silver bullion coins.

These also are marketed through arrangements with private firms. Interestingly, Mexico's many gold-coin restrikes were the bullion coins of their day. They had the advantage of ready identification, and they were legally tradable according to gold-coin regulations that existed in the United States from 1933 through 1974.

It is appropriate that we conclude discussion of the modern period on the

concept of bullion, because bullion is at the root of Mexico's numismatic history. That is a period to which we now turn.

When Cortez toppled the Aztec Empire, for a time the wealth returning to Spain was merely that taken by the victors from the vanquished. But the business of permanently administering a vast area in the name of the Spanish king, exploiting its natural resources, and funneling the proceeds to Spain quite soon involved the establishment of a mint in Mexico City. This was undertaken in 1536, just 15 years after the end of Aztec dominion.

At first, the authorized coins were low denominations: silver quarter, half, 1, 2, 3, and 4 reales, and copper 2 and 4 maravedis. To understand their face values and how they related to each other, let's take the common reference point of a silver dollar. The silver dollar is 8 reales, and you might recognize the nickname for the denomination of "piece of eight" from pirate lore. The eighth part, the silver real, was divided into 34 copper maravedis. That means the 8 reales was worth 272 copper maravedis.

The copper coinage was hated and soon abolished, not to reappear until 1814. The silver coins were fine as far as they went. When the mines of Mexico began producing undreamed of quantities of metal, however, it was the 8 reales that took center stage. This occurred after 1572. The piece of eight became the standard form for shipping silver back to Spain.

Mexico City's output was prodigious. Minting standards were crude. All denominations produced are called "cobs," because they are basically little more than irregular-looking lumps of metal on which bits and pieces of design can be seen. The only constant was weight, fineness, and the appearance of assayer's initials (which guaranteed the weight and fineness). Not showing those initials was cause for severe punishment.

Designs showed the arms of the monarch on one side, a cross on the other, appropriate legends, and an indication of denomination. The period of cob issues lasted until 1732. Rulers of the period start with Charles and Johanna, 1516-1556; Philip II, 1556-1598; Philip III, 1598-1621; Philip IV, 1621-1665; Charles II, 1665-1700; Philip V, 1700-1724 and 1724-1746; and Luis I, 1724.

Modern mint machinery began turning out coins in 1732. Quality was similar to today. The arms design was continued. It was not until 1772 that the monarch's portrait began appearing. The honor of this numismatic debut belongs to Charles III. Kings of this period are Ferdinand VI, 1746-1759; Charles III, 1760-1788; Charles IV, 1788-1808; and Ferdinand VII, 1808-1821. The *Standard Catalog of Mexican Coins* by Colin R. Bruce II and Dr. George W. Vogt is recommended to those who want to study this period in greater depth.

The revolutionary period begins in 1810, when a parish priest, Miguel Hidalgo y Costilla, issued the call for independence. The first attempts to achieve this were violently suppressed. Hidalgo was executed, but independence did come in 1821.

With revolt against central authority came a dispersal of the right to

strike coins. Mexico City continued as the major facility, but other operations began. The list of these over the next century is lengthy. Mintmarks and assayer initials proliferated.

The old colonial coinage standard survived the period. The 8 reales and its parts carried on. A slight reduction in bullion content had been ordered by the king in 1760, but otherwise things continued as they were. Gold was coined during the colonial period beginning in 1679 based on an 8-escudo piece, which divided into eighths just like the 8 reales. Gold, however, was not as important as silver.

Mexico's first emperor came shortly after independence. He was a leader in the struggle that set Mexico free from Spain. Augustin de Iturbide, originally an officer in the service of Spain, was proclaimed emperor in 1822. He abdicated in 1823 and was executed in 1824.

The second emperor had a reign almost as short as the first. Maximilian I, emperor only because he had a French army to secure the throne, reigned from 1863 to 1867. He was shot by a firing squad when the French left.

He is remembered numismatically because he decided to decimalize the coinage. The centavo and peso were born. Soon afterward, the republic was re-established. Further monetary changes were minor thereafter until 1905.

Collectors focusing on Mexico can devote much time to the study of the quasi-official issues of rebels during the periods of instability. They can look at hacienda tokens, which were issued by large farms or ranches that employed hundreds or thousands of people. Or they can pick whichever period in Mexico's history that fascinates them most. Whatever collectors of Mexico eventually settle on, they will find it rewarding.

Where to write for more information

World Coin News: 700 E. State St., Iola, WI 54990.
Standard Catalog of Mexican Coins: 700 E. State St., Iola, WI 54990.

6

Caring for coins

How to store and preserve your collection

By Alan Herbert

From the day you acquire your first collectible coin, you have to consider where and how to store your collection. Often a shoebox or a small cardboard or plastic box of some kind will be the principal storage point as you start to gather coins, even before they can be considered a collection. Sooner or later you will outgrow that first box and need to think seriously about what to do with your coins to protect and preserve them.

All too often security takes precedence over preservation. We're more worried that the kids will dip into the coins for candy or ice cream or that burglars will somehow learn about your "valuable" collection and pay a visit. It often isn't until years later when you suddenly notice that your once beautiful coins are now dingy and dull, with spots and fingerprints all over them, that preservation becomes a primary consideration.

Learning good storage habits should be one of the first things to do right along with acquiring those first coins. There are a multitude of storage products on the market that are intended for more or less specific situations, so learning which to use and how to use them is vital to the health of your collection. Most if not all of the products mentioned here should be available at your nearest coin shop or hobby store.

Safe storage methods

The common impulse is to use what's available around the house; never allow that impulse to control your collecting. Plastic wrap, aluminum foil, cardboard, stationery envelopes, and other common household products are not designed for coin storage and never should be used for your collec-

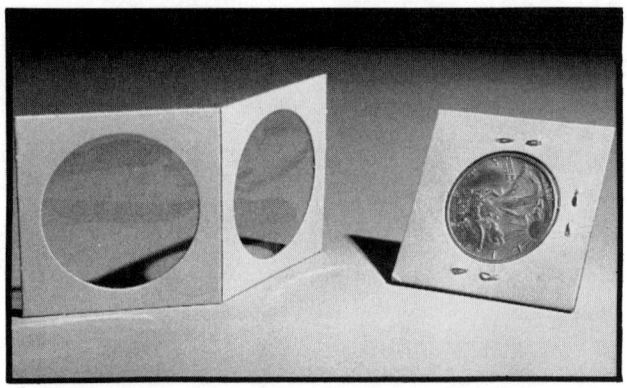

Two-by-two cardboard holders are a common form of short-term, inexpensive coin storage.

Many dealers sell coins in 2-by-2 plastic "flips," but they should not be used for long-term storage.

tion. The same goes for soaps and cleansers found around the home.

There are specific products that have been designed, tested and found safe to use for coins. These are the media your collection deserves. The slight added expense will pay a thousand dividends years from now when you sell your collection or pass it on to your heirs.

The most common storage media are 2-inch by 2-inch cardboard holders with Mylar windows, 2-by-2 plastic "flips," coin tubes, hard-plastic holders, coin boards, and coin albums.

The 2-by-2 cardboard holders are the cheapest and most commonly used storage method. They are usually folded and stapled around the coin. They are intended for short-term general storage. They are not airtight or watertight, and staples driven too close to the coin can ruin it.

The 2-by-2 plastic flips come in good and bad varieties. The old, usually soft flips are made of plastics that contain polyvinylchloride, a chemical found in many plastics. Over time it breaks down into substances that put a green slime on your coins, which attacks the surface and ruins them.

The good flips are made of Mylar, but they are brittle and prone to splitting. So they should not be used to mail coins or when the coins are moved about frequently. Mylar flips, too, are for short-term general storage.

Coin tubes are often used for bulk storage, but there is a proper technique to placing the coins in the tube.

Often you will find coins in PVC holders when you buy them from a dealer. Remove them immediately and put them in some better storage medium.

Coin tubes come in clear and cloudy, or translucent, plastic. These are made of an inert plastic that will not harm your coins. Tubes are intended for bulk, medium- to long-term storage, with one caution: Use care when inserting the coins. Merely dropping one coin onto another in a tube can damage both coins. The best technique is to make a stack or pile of the coins, then slide the pile carefully into the tube while holding it at an angle.

Hard-plastic holders are the elite items for storing your collection. There are a number of varieties, some of which come in three parts that are screwed together. Some come in two pieces that fit together. Some of these are airtight and watertight. They are more expensive, but they deserve to be used for any really valuable coins in your collection.

Coins processed by the third-party grading services come in hard-plastic holders, most of which are at least semiairtight. The hard-plastic holders used by the U.S. Mint for proof sets since 1968 are not airtight, so coins should be watched carefully for signs of problems. In recent years these holders have been improved, but you should check your proof sets periodically.

Any stored coins should be checked regularly, at least twice a year. Check coins for signs of spotting or discoloration. Check the storage media for any signs of deterioration, rust, mildew, or other problems.

The older mint sets and proof sets — issued from 1955 to 1964 — come in soft-plastic envelopes that are not intended for long-term storage. Coins

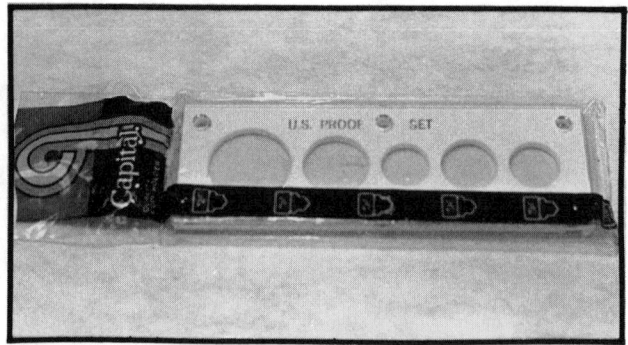

Hard-plastic holders are the top of the line in coin storage.

Coin folders are a low-cost and attractive way to store inexpensive circulated coins.

in these envelopes should be put in better storage media for the long term. In recent years the Mint has switched to an inert, stiffer plastic for the mint sets. This plastic is safe.

A coin folder is frequently the first piece of equipment the beginning collector buys. It is simply a piece of cardboard with holes to hold the coins. The holder folds up for storage. It is intended for inexpensive circulated coins only.

They give no protection from contamination or fingerprints. Worn coins will often fall out of the holes, which leads some novice collectors to tape the coins in the album. This is another example of misuse of a household

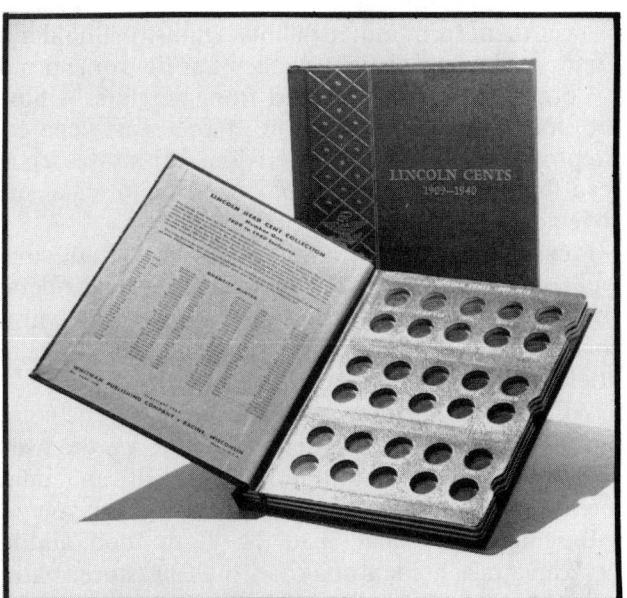

Coin albums also provide attractive storage for inexpensive circulated coins.

product; tape can permanently damage a coin's surface.

Pride of ownership and the desire to show off a collection are the moving forces behind the sale of thousands of coin albums. They should also be used for inexpensive circulated coins only, with a couple of exceptions.

Some albums are merely coin boards mounted between covers. Others have pages with sliding plastic strips on both sides of the page so both sides of the coin can be seen.

The open-face albums are subject to fingerprints and contamination. Sneezing on your coins can do as much damage as gouging them with a knife. The slides will rub on your coins, damaging the high points of the design over time. These two types of albums should never be used for expensive uncirculated or proof coins, although they are fine for circulated coins that you want to display.

Fairly new on the market are albums designed for coins in inert, airtight holders. This allows you to display your coins and still keep them safe from handling and contact with the atmosphere.

One more storage medium that deserves mention is the clear-plastic notebook page that has pockets for 2-by-2 holders or flips. Here again there are good and bad. Most old pocket sheets contain PVC, so they cannot be used to hold coins in non-airtight holders because the gases will migrate into the holders and damage the coins. The newer Mylar pages are brittle but will not generate damaging gases or liquids.

When buying storage media, make sure the dealer guarantees that his products are safe for coins. Many of the old albums, flips and pocket pages are still around, especially at flea markets. If you are in doubt, don't buy.

There are also thin, two-piece, inert plastic holders that many collectors use to protect coins put in flips or 2-by-2 cardboard holders, especially to

protect them from moving about against the holder and getting scratched. They are virtually airtight, so they do offer some protection.

Coins need to be protected from burglars. A box under the bed or in the closet offers no protection. If you must keep coins at home, a good, fireproof safe is a must. Otherwise, rent a safe-deposit box at a bank, but read the fine print on your box contract to make sure a coin collection is covered.

Most homeowner's insurance policies will not cover a coin collection or will cover only a fraction of its value. Special riders are expensive, but if you keep most of your coins at the bank, this will cut costs. For details, consult your insurance agent. The American Numismatic Association also offers collection insurance.

Where to store coins is often a problem. The commonest solution is to put them in the attic or basement. Those are the two worst places for your collection. Attics are notoriously hot. Heat can damage almost any storage media, and if there is the slightest hint of PVC, you've got trouble.

Basements are equally bad. They can flood, and humidity is high. Mildew can attack holders and other material stored with your coins.

So what's left? Ideally coins should be treated like a family member. They should be stored in some part of the house where temperature and humidity are relatively constant year round. If it's comfortable for you, it's probably much more comfortable for your coins than the basement or attic.

Protecting coins from humidity is always a good idea, even in areas where it is not a major health problem. For your coins, too much dampness can become a serious problem, often before you realize it. A good solution is to get several good-sized packets of silica gel and store them with your coins in your safe or a container of some kind that will isolate them from the general climate in the home.

To clean or not to clean

Before you store your coins, you should be aware that coins are like dishes: They should never be put away dirty. Ah, but you've probably already heard or read that you should never clean a coin. If you haven't, I'll say it now: Never clean a coin.

OK, so there are exceptions, but be careful of those exceptions and for good reason. Ignoring the exceptions can be excruciatingly and embarassingly expensive.

Coins get dirty, just like anything else. The impulse is to shine them up — polish them to a brilliance that will dazzle the viewer. If you've already succumbed to the temptation to clean even a single coin, stand up, kick yourself, then sit back down and read on. The one exception is loose dirt, grease, oil, or something similar, and there are even exceptions to that rule.

Use a neutral solvent to dissolve the grease and oils that usually coat uncirculated coins as they come from the mint. Follow the instructions on the container exactly, and if the directions say to use the product outdoors, they mean it.

For circulated coins, lighter fluid will often dissolve the accumulated "gunk" that sticks to them, but I don't recommend it for uncirculated coins, especially copper alloy coins. Air dry the coins; don't rub or wipe them. Even the softest cloth or paper towel can pick up sharp-edged particles that will ruin a coin's surface. Proof coins are clean when they are packaged, so this should not be necessary and should be done only as a last resort if they have somehow picked up oil in handling.

Using dips, household cleansers, metal polish, and even soap can permanently damage a coin. Avoid acid-based cleaners at all costs. They work by eating away the coin's surface to remove the embedded dirt or discoloration. Cleaning a coin with any of these products will sharply reduce its collectible value. To put it simply, collectors do not want cleaned coins, so they are heavily discounted.

One of the reasons for this is that once a coin has been cleaned, it will discolor much more quickly, requiring fresh cleaning. Each time it is cleaned, the surface is further dulled, reducing the coin's appeal and reducing its value.

Obviously this advice applies especially to uncirculated and proof coins, but it applies to any coin that is or has the potential to become valuable. But if you clean it, its career ends right there.

There are products specifically designed for removing the green PVC slime from coins. They do not contain acid, so they are safe. They will stop but cannot reverse the damage that the PVC has already done to the coin. Read the label, and use exactly as directed.

I frequently am asked about ultrasonic cleaners. They fall under the same heading as the various cleaning products I've described. In other words, the apparatus should not be used for uncirculated, proof, or other valuable coins. If you do use one, do one coin at a time so there is no chance for the vibration to rub two coins together. Change or filter the cleaning solution frequently to keep abrasive particles from coming in contact with the vibrating coin.

Like anything else, cleaning can be carried to an extreme, so I'll give you one horror story of just such a mistake: Years ago I had a collector fly several hundred miles to bring his collection for me to sell for him. When he laid out the coins on the table, I was shocked to discover that the hundreds of coins had all been harshly cleaned.

When I questioned him he calmly recounted that he had decided that the coins needed cleaning, so he dumped them all into a rock tumbler and left it on for several hours. It ruined all his coins, reducing them to face value. With his passion for cleanliness he had destroyed several thousand dollars worth of collectible value, plus air fare, a rental car, and a motel bill.

The key to a long-term collection that might appreciate in value is to learn what not to do to your coins and what care they need to survive years

of waiting in the wings. Learning to protect your coins with the best available storage methods and media is a key first step toward enjoying your collection for years to come.

Where to write for more information

American Numismatic Association: 818 N. Cascade Ave., Colorado Springs, CO 80903-3279.

7

The profit motive

Some comments on coins as investments

By Robert E. Wilhite

When gold and silver bullion prices reached all-time highs in 1980, prices for many U.S. gold and silver coins hit record highs too. Double-digit inflation prompted many investors to seek refuge in tangible assets. Companies touting coins as investments popped up all over. Many of those investors, however, became disenchanted when coin prices crashed along with precious-metals prices just a few months later.

Also, as mentioned in Chapter 4, grading standards for uncirculated coins were loose during the boom but tightened during the bust in these pre-slab days. Investors who bought coins billed as MS-65 or higher during the boom tried to sell during the bust and oftentimes were offered only MS-63 or lower money.

The investment aspect of coins was not new in 1980. Articles in early coin publications often addressed the subject. Those collectors who fancy themselves as traditionalists generally scorn the thought of coins as investments. To them, the reasons to collect coins are the joy and educational benefits of pursuing a hobby.

In reality, though, few collectors purchase coins with the expectation that they will go down in value. There is no guarantee that their coins will increase in value, but collectors who do their homework before buying help their chances. They check the value guides — such as those appearing in *Numismatic News*, *Coins* and *Coin Prices* — and shop their local dealers, shows and advertisements in the aforementioned publications to try to get the best value for their money.

There are many financial success stories in numismatics, as evidenced by auction results. Some common themes keep reappearing in profiles of the people whose collections have provided major sales: These people collected

coins over a long time — 10, 20, 30 years or more — and they knew their stuff. They knew what was rare and what was common, and they knew the going rates for each. They formed collections of coins; they didn't just accumulate a mishmash of pieces.

Many had an advantage from the beginning: They were wealthy and could afford some of the top rarities. But their methods carry lessons for collectors of all means.

The financial failure stories also have common themes: There are coin sellers who operate on the fringe of numismatics and prey upon people who know nothing about coins. A slick salesman calls on the telephone and overstates the rarity of the coins he has for sale. He sells them for several times what they could be purchased for from a mainstream numismatic dealer. Several years later the buyer takes them to a mainstream dealer and finds out his coins are worth a fraction of what he paid for them. A person who studies coins and the market for them before jumping in, however, avoids such a scenario.

The value guide for U.S. coins in this book includes charts showing the price performance of selected key dates. As can be seen, coins are subject to price fluctuations just like any investment that carries risk. Some coins experienced a great increase in value in the early 1980s and then dropped toward the middle of the decade. Others have been less volatile, showing little if any fluctuation over the time studied.

Generally the volatile areas are the more popularly collected coins in high grades — series like Morgan dollars, Walking Liberty half dollars, and some gold coins. The less volatile areas usually have a smaller universe of collectors — series like the early silver and copper coins, and obsolete denominations (3 cents and 20 cents, for example).

In the latter case, the rarity of these coins sometimes works against them. To have a successful promotion, a dealer selling coins as investments needs a certain quantity to fill all his orders. The earlier issues are usually not available in the quantities needed for a profitable promotion. Demand for these earlier issues comes mostly from a relatively small but avid group of collectors, and as a result, they're less subject to sharp price fluctuations.

In 1979 *Numismatic News* began publishing a weekly Coin Market Index. The index charts the composite performance of the market's more expensive coins, similar to the stock market's Dow Jones industrial average. It provides a means for comparing the state of the market at various points in the index's 14-year history.

A chart of the index from 1979 through 1993 shows a number of peaks and valleys in the market. After its inception in May 1979, the index jumped over 4,000 points to 6,062 on July 5, 1980, during the precious metals boom. It then crashed to 3,540 on Sept. 11, 1982. Over the next six years the index enjoyed a steady climb to 6,311 on Sept. 27, 1988.

Shortly thereafter, several Wall Street investment firms announced that they would offer limited partnerships that invested in coins. This set off speculation that coins would increase in value because of the new demand. The index climbed to an all-time high of 10,190 on June 18, 1989, but

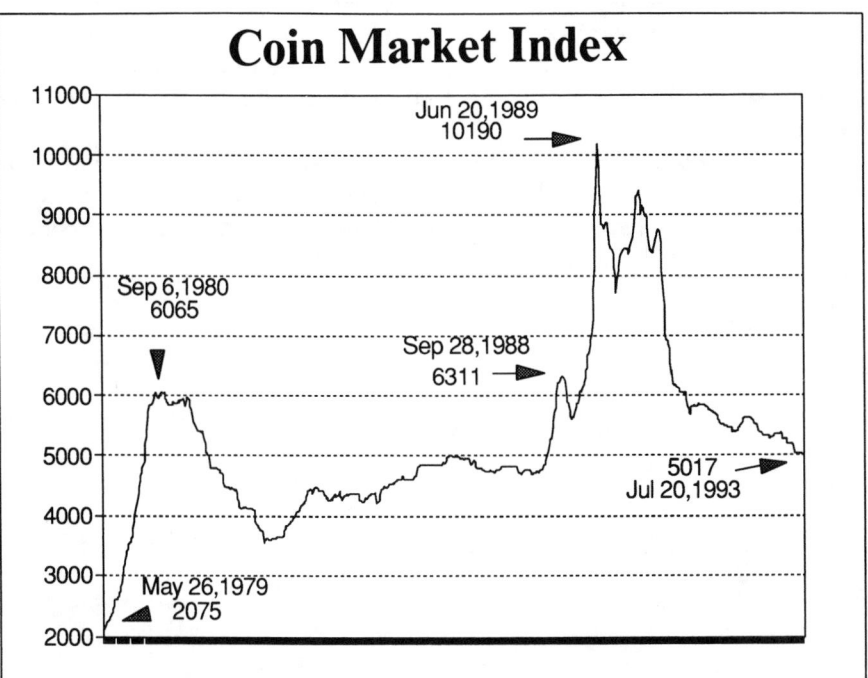

Coin Market Index

when the demand did not turn out to be great enough to support the widespread speculation, the index crashed to 6,160 on Dec. 18, 1990. It enjoyed a bit of a spurt in early 1991, before dropping steadily to close the year at 5,482. The index recovered slightly in the first two quarters of 1992, but by July 1993 its descent took it to just over 5,000.

The lesson the index teaches is, to be a successful coin investor, think like a collector. That means forming a "set" of coins (see Chapter 5) and holding for the long term — 10, 15, 20 years or more. Those who bought high-grade coins at the June 18, 1989, peak are hurting right now, but maybe they won't be in 10 years. Those who bought in May 1979 and didn't sell on June 18, 1989, probably wished they had, but they're still ahead of prices from 14 years ago.

There is no guarantee that high-grade coins will continue to increase in value over time, but market history shows that the odds favor those collectors who stick it out for the long term. Remember, too, that the index is slanted toward high-grade coins. Because the index is down, it does not mean that every coin decreased in value. In fact, as high-grade investment coins experienced a slump in 1991, some traditional collectible series — such as Indian cents, Lincoln cents, and Buffalo nickels — saw a resurgence of trading activity.

Whether your motivation for buying collectible coins is purely investment or purely collecting pleasure or somewhere in between, keep good rec-

ords of your purchases. You'll need them after you sell your coins for figuring your gain or loss on your taxes. Record the date of purchase, seller, and purchase price. To make sure your records are adequate, consult a certified public accountant.

Also, advise your heirs on the disposal of your collection in the event of your death. Make sure they know where your records stored, approximately how much your collection is worth, and possible purchasers of your coins.

8

Join the club

Coin collecting has lots of organizations

By David C. Harper

More than 150 years ago, Alexis de Tocqueville noted in his *Democracy in America* the penchant of people in the United States to create and voluntarily join public groups for a multitude of purposes. This urge to join carries over into coin collecting.

Whether it be a national organization or local coin club, groups have been organized in the United States, Canada and Mexico to help collectors enhance their hobby knowledge and enjoyment. They serve as clearinghouses for new information, maintain libraries, and bring collectors together in meetings to share their hobby experiences with each other. Clubs are so well defined that collectors can find one to serve any activity level and any degree of personal interaction with other collectors.

At the extreme, you can join a national organization by mail, spend a hobby lifetime utilizing its services, and yet never leave the privacy and comfort of home. At the other end, some areas offer such a multitude of clubs that you can find a meeting to attend on many nights of the week.

There are many ways to find a club. Some hobbyists inquire at the local coin shop to identify the organization nearest them. *Numismatic News* publishes news about clubs. Also, watch your local newspaper for listings of community events.

How does a collector match his needs with an appropriate club? The closest thing to a one-stop shopping place for an answer is the American Numismatic Association.

It is the United States' national coin-collecting organization and was granted a perpetual charter by Congress with a mission of education. It can be reached at 818 N. Cascade Ave., Colorado Springs, CO 80903-3279. It offers a wide array of personal hobby services, and its benefits cross

national boundaries. In fact, when it was founded in 1891, it was expected that Canadians and Mexicans would be just as likely to join as U.S. citizens.

The most obvious benefit to an ANA member is a subscription to *The Numismatist*, the association's monthly magazine. In it you find news, historical features, membership information, and advertisements placed by dealers who are ready to fill every collector's want list.

More than 30,000 titles are available in the ANA library, and you don't have to walk into the ANA building to check them out. Any member anywhere can do that by mail. The ANA has called upon renowned numismatic authorities to create a correspondence course, which distills into 29 separate readings information that has taken many people a lifetime to learn. There are ANA educational seminars held in Colorado Springs and other sites across the United States.

The ANA sponsors two conventions annually. The early spring convention is usually held in March at locations across the country, selected and announced well in advance. The summer convention, which is so huge that it's billed as the "World's Fair of Money," is a tradition that dates back almost to the organization's founding.

Members also are offered a variety of optional services, ranging from coin-collection insurance to credit cards and car rental discounts. And if you do go to Colorado Springs, the ANA maintains its Money Museum at its headquarters. In it are some of the rarest and most famous coins in history.

Joining the ANA is easy. The membership fee is $32 the first year and $26 thereafter. Members over 65 years old get a $4 discount, and junior members (those under 18) are charged $11.

Beyond simply belonging to the ANA, though, are the doors that open to members. If you want to find a regional, state or local club, you can get help from the ANA. The important thing to remember is that you set your own level of involvement. If your profession is so hectic that you don't need another meeting to go to, the ANA is the place for you. If your hours are so regular that joining in the fun and camaraderie of a local club is just what you are looking for, the ANA can help you find that, too.

And just because the American Numismatic Association has "American" in its name, it doesn't mean that members are focused only on U.S. coins. Far from it. It is more accurate to say that if a coin was struck at any time anywhere in the world in the last 2,600 years, there are ANA members who collect it.

The ANA, if it connotes any exclusivity at all, is basically a regional designation based on where its members live. The farther one gets from the United States, the longer correspondence takes and the greater the possibility of a language barrier between the ANA staff and a potential member. It is therefore not surprising to find that the 31,000 members are predominantly located in the United States.

The Canadian Numismatic Association dates to 1950. It publishes *The Canadian Numismatic Journal*, published 11 times a year, and it also spon-

sors an annual summer convention. Membership is considerably smaller than the ANA's, in line with the population difference between the United States and Canada. Membership fee is $25 a year. The mailing address is Executive Secretary, Canadian Numismatic Association, P.O. Box 226, Barrie, Ontario L4M 4T2, Canada.

The Sociedad Numismatica de Mexico A.C. was established in 1952. Basically it oversees a convention in Mexico City once a year. It may be contacted at Eugenia 13-301, Mexico 18, D.F., Mexico.

That covers the national hobby umbrella groups. There are many more organizations of a national character that have somewhat narrower purposes. Among these is the American Numismatic Society in New York City. It is older than the ANA, having been established in 1858. It also maintains a superb museum of U.S. and world coins, and a world-class library. Emphasis in the ANS is on scholarly research.

Numismatics would be nothing if it were not for its research pioneers. If that is what appeals to you, you can write the ANS at Broadway and 155th St., New York, NY 10032, for information regarding its structure and various classes of membership.

Other national organizations focus on specific collectible areas, such as Seated Liberty coinage or tokens and medals. These are popular and active. Many are member organizations of the ANA and hold meetings in conjunction with the ANA's conventions.

Coin dealers have organizations of their own. The Professional Numismatists Guild Inc. maintains high standards of membership qualification and conduct. Members are a who's who of the commercial sector of the hobby. All are ready to serve you in furthering your collecting goals. For a membership roster, contact Paul L. Koppenhaver, Executive Director, P.O. Box 430, Van Nuys, CA 91408.

This brief review merely puts you on the threshold of the organized numismatic world. It is up to you to open that door or walk away. Over the years, many collectors have found membership to be the most rewarding aspect of the hobby. They have benefited from working with others with a common interest to further their own knowledge and advance their collecting goals in an environment of mutual support and friendship.

9
What's hot, what's not
Collectors dealt winning hands
By Christopher Batio

What's hot? Collectors always want to know where the action is in the coin market. This past year, the average collector was dealt some winning hands.

The White House commemorative dollar sold out in a month and the price almost quadrupled to $100 after orders were delivered. It then backed off, but White House buyers still have pleasantly higher prices to look at when compared to the $23 and $28 issue prices for uncirculated and proof versions, respectively.

Another coin that got hot was the USO dollar. Like the White House coin, anyone could have ordered it from the U.S. Mint. Like the White House coin, it shot higher before coming back toward earth.

Gold is up, too. Many market forecasters say the bullion market finally bottomed out at approximately $326 a troy ounce in March 1993 and the trend is now upward through 1994. Sales of American Eagle gold bullion coins have jumped along with higher prices as people put more gold aside.

Canada issued its 12-piece Canada 125 series in 1992 at face value, and the popularity of the quarter set just continues to boom. Buyers have to pay around triple the $3 face value now to get the full uncirculated set. No one can say the sky is the limit, but the Royal Canadian Mint was staggered by its success.

Mexican coin collectors have been showered with gorgeous new silver bullion issues. Interest in them his risen with silver prices. The silver American Eagle has also participated in this rally.

As you can see, there have been many reasons to for excitement in the past year. Coin prices are moving up. Although many items are still much lower than levels achieved during the 1980s bull market, there have been definite increases in U.S. gold, commemorative half dollars and high-grade Morgan and Peace dollars. More gains seem to be in the offing.

For all of 1994, collector tastes are expected to move the market. Stronger bullion is expected to add a kicker. Watch the U.S. Mint as it releases commemoratives, American Eagles, proof sets and mint sets. With collector activity rising, there might be a sleeper among them.

In the meantime, to discover some of the background behind where the market is now and where it is going, let's take a look at the highlights of the year that has passed since the last edition of this book was published.

The year that was

September 1992: News of the sellout of the White House dollar swept the hobby. Collectors wanted almost 100,000 coins more than were available. The issue had a mintage limit of 500,000. Approximate sales figures totaled 376,000 proofs and 124,000 uncirculated coins. Within six months, the White House dollar nearly quadrupled its value and dealers scrambled to find them.

Another U.S. Mint commemorative program that was released in September, did not do nearly as well. Consisting of a gold $5 coin, a silver dollar and a clad half dollar, the coin set marked the 500th anniversary of the voyage of Christopher Columbus to the New World. With mintage limits ranging from 500,000 for the gold coin to six million for the half dollar, collectors did not rush out to buy them.

The 1992 Olympic commemoratives also experienced slow sales. By September, after a few months on the market, only 1.4 million total coins had been sold.

The Coin Market Index published weekly by *Numismatic News* continued to fall, dropping to 5335 by the end of the month. But gold and silver ended the month on an up note, rising slightly to $349.80 and $3.82 a troy ounce, respectively.

The Royal Canadian Mint adopted a policy to allow coins from its numismatic and bullion programs to be redeemed at face value as payment for new issues or for cash at any Royal Canadian Bank branch. Coins commemorating the 1976 Olympic Games in Montreal have, at times, had their commercial value fall below their face value. This cleared up questions collectors raised from time to time as to whether their Canadian commemoratives were "real money."

The Royal Canadian Mint also introduced the ninth coin in its program commemorating the 125th anniversary of the Canadian Confederation. The coin, a 25-cent piece depicting a lighthouse on the coast of Nova Scotia, was one of 12 coins to be released one each month at face value throughout 1992. Coins that had already been issued depict scenes from New Brunswick, Northwest Territories, Newfoundland, Manitoba, Yukon, Alberta, Prince Edward Island, and Ontario. Each was struck in pure nickel. A silver proof version of each quarter was also available.

Another Canadian coin that was released in September was a $200 gold coin showing two children catching maple leaves with Niagara Falls in the background. The coin is the third in a continuing annual series of gold coins designed to celebrate the spirit and promise of Canadian youth.

Mexico introduced 1991-dated fractional silver Libertads in 1/20th-, 1/10th-, ¼-, ½- and 1-ounce sizes.

October 1992: Congress approved a bill authorizing commemorative coins to be struck marking the 50th anniversary of World War II. The three-coin set, consisting of a gold $5 coin, a silver dollar, and a clad half dollar, was to be released in 1993 following an open design contest.

Two other numismatic bills were also approved by Congress. One autho-rized the striking of 1.5 million silver medals to honor American fire fight-ers; the other approved a medal to commemorate the 250th anniversary of the founding of the American Philosophical Society by Thomas Jefferson.

The Coin Market Index rose to 5342. Gold and silver dropped to $347.80 and $3.74, respectively.

The U.S. Mint announced the lowest annual mintage limits ever for proof American Eagle gold bullion coins. The mintage limits were 50,000 each for the one-ounce, half-ounce, and quarter-ounce coins, and 70,000 for the tenth-ounce coins. By contrast, the 1991 mintage limits were as high as 110,000 coins. The maximum mintage for the proof American Eagle silver bullion coin was 500,000, down 200,000 from 1991.

The Casa de Moneda de Mexico announced that, beginning in 1993, it would strike a bimetallic circulating 10-peso coin with an outer rim of alumi-num-bronze and a center containing five grams of silver. The coins were to be issued in conjunction with a planned currency reform.

The Royal Canadian Mint issued a quarter representing Quebec as the tenth coin in the 125 series. It shows Perce Rock, a picturesque stone out-crop near the province's Atlantic coast.

November 1992: Gov. Bill Clinton of Arkansas was elected President and American coin dealers voiced mixed expectations of how his administration would affect their businesses. Some said Clinton's economic policies would lead to a weaker dollar, a boost in interest rates and higher gold prices, which then would bring U.S. collectors back into the coin market. Others saw a countervailing problem where stricter government regulation in the United States, Canada, but especially Europe, was threatening the coin business.

Gold coins indeed were the first numismatic winners of the Clinton Administration, with prices for type coins and rare-date U.S. gold rising steadily in the days following the election.

Gold moved lower, dropping to $337.10 in mid-November, while silver moved up slightly to $3.84. Despite the gains in gold, the Coin Market Index declined sharply, dropping to 5296.

The U.S. Mint reported that fewer 1991 USO silver dollars had been sold than any other modern commemorative silver dollar. Final figures showed a total of 446,233 dollars sold. Almost immediately, dealers were looking to buy the scarce coins and their price began to rise.

The Royal Canadian Mint released the 11th coin in its successful Canada 125 program. The new quarter honored Saskatchewan by depicting a freight train rolling by a towering grain elevator and a field of wheat. The RCM also announced that, because of unexpected demand, it was increasing its pro-duction of the Canada 125 commemorative quarters. It had planned to pro-duce about 10 million of each type of coin in the 12-coin series. However, public and collector demand caused that number to rise to about 13 million each. In addition, mint officials decided to increase the number of silver 125 proof sets from 5,000 to 50,000.

December 1992: The U.S. Mint announced that sales of proof sets were at the highest point since 1982. A total of 3.8 million proof sets were sold in 1992, spurred on by the re-introduction of .900 fine silver in the dime, quarter and half dollar in a special silver proof set. These accounted for 1.2 million of all the sets sold.

There were signs that the coin market was turning around and prices were beginning to rise. Collector issues were in demand. Mail order showed strength.

Gold hovered near $335. Silver dropped slightly to $3.74. The Coin Market Index rose slightly to 5321.

The Royal Canadian Mint released the 12th and final design in the Canada 125 commemorative quarter series. The final coin, honoring British Columbia, depicts a group of whales breaking the ocean's surface with mountains in the background. The 125 program was hailed as one of the most innovative coin programs in recent history. Demand for the coins was very high. After being distributed at face value, each quarter quickly rose in price until they were routinely being sold for almost $1 each.

January 1993: Designs were unveiled for the new 1993 James Madison/ Bill of Rights commemorative coin program. The six winning designs for obverse and reverse were chosen from 815 entries. Each obverse for the three-coin set depicts James Madison in a variety of portraits. The reverses show his home, Montpelier, a torch symbolizing the Bill of Rights, and a quote from that document.

The uncirculated silver half dollar that is part of the Madison/Bill of Rights commemorative coin program was struck at the West Point Mint. It was the first commemorative half dollar to be struck there since commemoratives were re-introduced in 1982.

The traditionally slow period for the coin market following the holidays was not as slow as expected. There was a push in the market for older commemoratives in MS-64 and MS-65. Prices for popular modern commemoratives, such as the USO and White House silver dollars, rose.

Gold fell to $332.50 and silver to $3.65. The Coin Market Index moved higher to 5354.

Hopes of a sellout for 1992 proof American Eagle bullion coins were dashed despite the lowest maximum mintages ever. Final figures were released in April.

Numismatic News reported that common-date AU and BU Eisenhower clad dollars were earning small premiums in the coin market. With some effort, the coins can still be obtained at face value through banks, but can earn a 20 percent premium when sold as promotional items, coin jewelry, or to collectors.

Mexico instituted a currency reform designed to curb inflation and bring its monetary values closer in line with the Canadian and American governments it hopes to join in the North American Free Trade Agreement. The reform cut three zeroes off current denominations, meaning a new peso is worth 1,000 old ones. Coinage will reflect these changes, being issued in denominations of 5, 10, 20 and 50 centavos and 1, 2, 5 and 10 pesos.

February 1993: For the presidential inauguration, a flood of Clinton-related memorabilia was released. Some of the items included the official inaugural medal, an unofficial inaugural medal, several issues from countries such as Liberia and Hutt River Province, elongates, novelty dollars and trading cards.

The legendary King of Siam proof set containing an 1804 dollar sold at auction for $1.65 million — a price that represents a sharp decline from its last sale for $3.19 million in 1990. The nine-coin set was purchased by Dwight Manley of Spectrum Numismatics International of Santa Ana, Calif. The set, first assembled in 1836 resurfaced in 1962 when Spink & Son Ltd. of Great Britain purchased it from an unknown source.

The U.S. Mint announced Feb. 16 that the Young Collector's Set from the Madison/Bill of Rights commemorative coin program sold out, and a special coin and medal set was nearing a sellout. The Young Collector's Set, which was limited to 50,000 examples, was designed to introduce numismatics to children 10 and under. It contained an uncirculated 1993 silver Madison half dollar and educational information on the Bill of Rights and Madison. The coin and medal set also contained a bronze restrike of an Indian Peace Medal from Madison's presidency.

The Coin Market Index took a sharp drop. A seldom-traded MS-65 1893-S Morgan dollar was sold at a Bowers & Merena auction for $110,000 — more than $130,000 less than its last recorded sale of $242,000. The sale caused a 96-point drop in the index, taking it down to 5277.

Gold dipped below $330 to $329.30, while silver remained stable at a low price of $3.65 per ounce.

The U.S. government's once-huge strategic stockpile of silver bullion has been cut in half through coin sales, according to a Silver Institute report. Since 1986 more than 66 million troy ounces of silver have been used for production of commemorative and bullion coins.

The Royal Canadian Mint released a .925 fine silver dollar commemorating the 100th anniversary of professional hockey's Stanley Cup. The Cup was donated by Canada's Governor-General Lord Stanley. The coin depicts a modern hockey player and one from 100 years ago flanked by the original Cup and how it appears today.

The Casa de Moneda de Mexico without fanfare or even a press release began distribution of four new silver bullion coins. The coins first appeared at this month's Long Beach Expo and are dated 1992. They contain from one-quarter to five ounces of silver bullion, and are denominated under the old monetary system in figures ranging from 25 pesos to 10,000 pesos. The quarter-ounce, half-ounce, and one-ounce coins share the same design of an Aztec eagle warrior on the reverse and the Mexican eagle and snake emblem on the obverse. The five-ounce coin shows two stylized Aztec warriors on the reverse, with the Mexican emblem on the obverse.

March 1993: Demand for the 1992 U.S. proof set exceeded supply by about 35,000 sets. As of March 1, the Mint sold 2.7 million 1992 proof sets and could not fill additional orders.

The bullion markets remained sluggish. Gold fell to almost $326 and sil-

Before turning around, silver dropped so low that 40-percent silver half dollars almost saw the point where face value exceeded bullion content.

ver dipped lower to $3.56. The Coin Market Index also dropped, moving to 5268.

A multi-tiered trading system took shape among dealers. Prices were set for sight-unseen coins that are white, encapsulated and graded MS-65; sight-unseen MS-65 coins that are toned and encapsulated; raw coins; coins that are encapsulated and graded MS-65 but must be viewed before purchase; and several other combinations.

The U.S. General Accounting Office released a study recommending the replacement of the $1 bill with a new dollar coin.

A sale in Los Angeles by Heritage Numismatic Auctions Inc. realized more than $1.4 million. Included in the sale were an MS-65 1892-S Barber dime sold for $3,200, a VF 1918/7-S Buffalo nickel for $1,600, and an AU 1859-S Liberty $5 gold piece, hammered down for $9,750.

The Royal Canadian Mint offered a new $100 gold and silver coin that shows Canada's first electric car, the Featherstonehaugh. The .5833 fine gold and .4167 fine silver coin marks the evolution of the car during the turn of the century. The Canadian car is shown surrounded by other cars of that era from Germany, France and the United States.

Prices for the 1991 Canadian quarter went through the roof. Advertised prices (in Canadian dollars) for the coins ranged from $4-$5 for an average uncirculated example to $14 for a high-grade piece. And 1991 quarter rolls sold for $150 and up. The reason for this boost was simply low mintage. Only 459,000 1991 quarters were struck.

April 1993: The U.S. Mint released its final mintage figures for the 1992 American Eagle bullion coins. The gold half-ounce was definitely the scarcest, with only 54,404 business strikes and 40,982 proofs. The other mintages were as follows: gold one-ounce, 275,000 BU, 44,835 proof; gold quarter-ounce, 59,546 BU, 46,290 proof; gold tenth-ounce, 209,300 BU, 64,902 proof; silver one-ounce, 5,540,068 BU, 498,552 proof. Although American Eagle sales were down from last year, they were rescued from even lower numbers by a sales boost in the last quarter of 1992.

Gold and silver bullion began rebounding. Gold was $342.50 and silver traded for $3.86 an ounce.

Unfortunately, the Coin Market Index did not follow the bullion trend. It dropped to 5195.

The U.S. Mint earned $5.1 million in profits from sales of 1992 Columbus commemorative coins. As of April 1, a total of 1,086,002 Columbus coins were sold, breaking down to 102,438 gold $5 coins, 476,949 silver dollars, and 506,615 clad half dollars.

Sales of U.S. 1992 Olympic comemmoratives ended April 30. The program raised $9.1 million in surcharges that were used to train American Olympians. Final mintages for the coins are as follows: clad half dollar proof, 524,533; clad half dollar uncirculated, 160,781; silver dollar proof, 501,098; silver dollar uncirculated, 185,081; gold $5 proof, 76,356; gold $5 uncirculated, 27,675.

There was significant interest in Canadian silver Maple Leaf coins — specifically the 1992 issue. Rumors later confirmed had it that the official mintage would be less than 350,000. Up until then, the 1991 issue was considered the key date, with a mintage of 644,300.

American Eagle gold bullion coins are growing in popularity again due to rising gold prices.

The second part of the Mexican pre-Columbian bullion series was released. Gold coins in quarter-ounce, half-ounce, and one-ounce sizes were introduced. The gold coins share an identical Aztec-inspired design depicting a stylized jaguar head. The coins are dated 1992 and denominated as 250, 500 and 1,000 pesos, respectively.

May 1993: Gold broke through $350 and continued to rise. Similarly, silver neared $4.20 and kept climbing. The rising metals trend boosted bourse and coin shop traffic around the United States and had people saying that $400 gold and $5 silver was not far away.

The Coin Market Index dove to 5053. Bob Wilhite, who compiles the index wrote that the upper end of the dollar market, upon which so much of the index is based, was "a confusing mess," registering larger and larger price disparities between sight-seen and sight-unseen coins.

U.S. Mint officials reported that sales of 1993-S proof sets passed the 1.2 million sales mark during their first month on the market.

The Casa de Moneda de Mexico struck a 20-peso coin based on the composition of its earlier 10-peso coin — a quarter ounce of .925 fine silver center surrounded by an aluminum-bronze ring. The coin depicts Mexican priest and revolutionary Miguel Hidalgo on the reverse and the country's eagle and snake emblem on the obverse.

Mintages for Canada's 1992 Loon dollar and 1992 Caribou 25-cent coin were the lowest numbers ever reported for both series. A total of 4,242,085 Loon dollars were struck in 1992, whereas only 238,371 Caribou quarters were produced. This is because the Canada 125 coins used up much of the Royal Canadian Mint's production capacity in 1992. The 1992 Caribou quarters were only produced for inclusion in uncirculated and specimen sets. The 1992 Canadian 50-cent coin also had a very low mintage of 248,000 — the third lowest for this series.

June 1993: The U.S. Mint began selling its World War II 50th anniversary commemorative coins.

Reports said that the Susan B. Anthony dollar, long thought to be laying useless in Federal Reserve and Mint vaults, is sneaking into circulation. According to the Coin Coalition, a lobbying group agitating for a new dollar coin, the number of Susie B's in the vaults has declined from almost 500 million to 385 million. The coins are mainly used in mass-transit systems, toll booths, and vending machines. However, the U.S. Postal Service recently introduced new change machines that will accept the coin at 4,200 post offices.

The Coin Market Index slipped to 5040. More high-priced coins sold for less, establishing lower levels for the index. Still, coins sold briskly. Gold and silver continued to rise. Gold was $371.50. Silver was $4.34.

The Royal Canadian Mint began evaluating the future of the Canadian cent. The coin, composed of copper, tin and zinc costs more to produced than its face value. The RCM is looking at changing the coin's composition as the United States did with its cent in 1982, eliminating it, or finding some way to bring idle cents back into the economic stream.

Glossary of coin terms

Adjustment marks: Marks made by use of a file to correct the weight of overweight coinage planchets prior to striking. Adjusting the weight of planchets was a common practice at the first U.S. mint in Philadelphia and was often carried out by women hired to weigh planchets and do any necessary filing.

Altered coin: A coin that has been changed after it left the mint. Such changes are often to the date or mintmark of a common coin in an attempt to increase its value by passing to an unsuspecting buyer as a rare date or mint.

Alloy: A metal or mixture of metals added to the primary metal in the coinage composition, often as a means of facilitating hardness during striking. For example, most U.S. silver coins contain an alloy of 10-percent copper.

Anneal: To heat in order to soften. In the minting process planchets are annealed prior to striking.

Authentication: The act of determining whether a coin, medal, token or other related item is a genuine product of the issuing authority.

Bag marks: Scrapes and impairments to a coin's surface obtained after minting by contact with other coins. The term originates from the storage of coins in bags, but such marks can occur as coins leave the presses and enter hoppers. A larger coin is more susceptible to marks, which affect its grade and, therefore, its value.

Base metal: A metal with low intrinsic value.

Beading: A form of design around the edge of a coin. Beading once served a functional purpose of deterring clipping or shaving parts of the metal by those looking to make a profit and then return the debased coin to circulation.

Blank: Often used in reference to the coinage planchet or disc of metal from which the actual coin is struck. Planchets or blanks are punched out of a sheet of metal by what is known as a blanking press.

Business strike: A coin produced for circulation.

Beading

Cast copy: A copy of a coin or medal made by a casting process in which molds are used to produce the finished product. Casting imparts a different surface texture to the finished product than striking and often leaves traces of a seam where the molds came together.

Center dot: A raised dot at the center of a coin caused by use of a compass to aid the engraver in the circular positioning of die devices, such as stars, letters and dates. Center dots are prevalent on early U.S. coinage.

Chop mark

Chop mark: A mark used by Oriental merchants as a means of guaranteeing the silver content of coins paid out. The merchants' chop marks, or stamped insignia, often obliterated the original design of the host coin. U.S. Trade dollars, struck from 1873 through 1878 and intended for use in trade with China, are sometimes found bearing multiple marks.

Clash marks: Marks impressed in the coinage dies when they come together without a planchet between them. Such marks will affect coins struck subsequently by causing portions of the obverse design to appear in raised form on the reverse, and vice versa.

Clipping: The practice of shaving or cutting small pieces of metal from a coin in circulation. Clipping was prevalent in Colonial times as a means of surreptitiously extracting precious metal from a coin before placing it back into circulation. The introduction of beading and a raised border helped to alleviate the problem.

Coin alignment: U.S. coins are normally struck with an alignment by which, when a coin is held by the top and bottom edge and rotated from side-to-side, the reverse will appear upside down.

Collar: A ring-shaped die between which the obverse and reverse coinage dies are held during striking. The collar contains the outward flow during striking and can be used to produce edge reeding.

Commemorative: A coin issued to honor a special event or person. U.S. commemoratives are generally produced for sale to collectors and are not placed in circulation.

Copy: A replica of an original issue. Copies often vary in quality and metallic composition to the original. Since passage of the Hobby Protection Act (Public Law 93-167) of Nov. 29, 1973, it has been illegal to produce or import copies of coins or other numismatic items that are not clearly and permanently marked with the word "Copy."

Counterfeit: A coin or medal or other numismatic item made fraudulently, either for entry into circulation or sale to collectors.

Denticles: The toothlike pattern found around a coin's obverse or reverse border.

Die: A cylindrical piece of metal containing an incuse image that imparts a raised image when stamped into a planchet.

Die crack: A crack that develops in a coinage die after extensive usage, or if the die is defective or is used to strike harder metals. Die cracks, which often run through border lettering, appear as raised lines on the finished coin.

Device: The principal design element.

Double eagle: Name adopted by the Act of March 3, 1849, for the gold coin valued at 20 units or $20.

Rim

Field

Mintmark

Exergue

Obverse

Legend

Reverse

Eagle: Name adopted by the Coinage Act of 1792 for a gold coin valued at 10 units or $10.

Edge: The cylindrical surface of a coin between the two sides. The edge can be plain, reeded, ornamented, or lettered.

Electrotype: A copy of a coin, medal or token made by electroplating.

Exergue: The lower segment of a coin, below the main design, generally separated by a line and often containing the date, designer initials and mintmark.

Face value: The nominal legal-tender value assigned to a given coin by the governing authority.

Fasces: A Roman symbol of authority consisting of a bound bundle of rods and an ax.

Field: The flat area of a coin's obverse or reverse, devoid of devices or inscriptions.

Galvano: A reproduction of a proposed design from an artist's original model produced in plaster or other substance and then electroplated with metal. The galvano is then used in a reducing lathe to make a die or hub.

Glory: A heraldic term for stars, rays or other devices placed as if in the sky or luminous.

Grading: The largely subjective practice of providing a numerical or adjectival ranking of the condition of a coin, token or medal. The grade is often a major determinant of value.

Gresham's law: The name for the observation made by Sir Thomas Gresham, 16th century English financier, that when two coins with the same face value but different intrinsic values are in circulation at the same time, the one with the lesser intrinsic value will remain in circulation while the other is hoarded.

Half eagle: Name adopted by the Coinage Act of 1792 for a gold coin valued at five units or $5.

Hub: A piece of die steel showing the coinage devices in relief. The hub is used to produce a die that, in contrast, has the relief details incuse. The die is then used to produce the final coin, which looks much the same as the hub. Hubs may be reused to make new dies.

These Canadian Olympic commemoratives have lettered edges.

Legend: A coin's principal lettering, generally shown along its outer perimeter.

Lettered edge: Incuse or raised lettering on a coin's edge.

Matte proof: A proof coin on which the surface is granular or dull. On U.S. coins this type of surface was used on proofs of the early 20th century. The process has since been abandoned.

Magician's coin: A term sometimes used to describe a coin with two heads or two tails. Such a coin is impossible in normal production, and all are products made outside the Mint as novelty pieces.

Medal: Made to commemorate an event or person. Medals differ from coins in that a medal is not legal tender and, in general, is not produced with the intent of circulating as money.

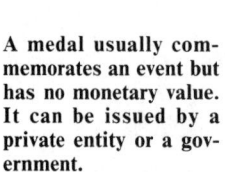

A medal usually commemorates an event but has no monetary value. It can be issued by a private entity or a government.

Medal alignment: Medals are generally struck with the coinage dies facing the same direction during striking. When held by the top and bottom edge and rotated from side-to-side, a piece struck in this manner will show both the obverse and reverse right side up.

Mintage: The total number of coins struck during a given time frame, generally one year.

Mintmark: A letter or other marking on a coin's surface to identify the mint at which the coin was struck.

Mule: The combination of two coinage dies not intended for use together.

Numismatics: The science, study or collecting of coins, tokens, medals, paper money, and related items.

Obverse: The front or "heads" side of a coin, medal or token.

Overdate: Variety produced when one or more digits of the date are re-engraved over an old date on a die at the Mint, generally to save on dies or correct an error. Portions of the old date can still be seen under the new one.

Overmintmark: Variety created at the Mint when a different mintmark is punched over an already existing mintmark, generally done to make a coinage die already punched for one mint usable at another. Portions of the old mintmark can still be seen under the new one.

Overstrike: A coin, token or medal struck over another coin, token or medal.

Pattern: A trial strike of a proposed coin design, issued by the Mint or authorized agent of a governing authority. Patterns can be in a variety of metals, thicknesses and sizes.

This U.S. Trade dollar has a reeded edge.

Phrygian cap: A close-fitting, egg-shell-shaped hat placed on the head of a freed slave when Rome was in its ascendancy. Hung from a pole, it was a popular symbol of freedom during the French Revolution and in 18th century United States.

Planchet: A disc of metal or other material on which the image of the dies are impressed, resulting in a finished coin. Also sometimes called a blank.

Proof: A coin struck twice or more from specially polished dies and polished planchets. Modern proofs are prepared with a mirror finish. Early 20th century proofs were prepared with a matte surface.

Prooflike: A prooflike coin exhibits some of the characteristics of a proof despite having been struck by regular production processes. Many Morgan dollars are found with prooflike surfaces. The field will have a mirror background similar to that of a proof, and design details are frosted like some proofs.

Quarter eagle: Name adopted by the Coinage Act of 1792 for a gold coin valued at 2.5 units or $2.50.

Reeding: Serrated (toothlike) ornamentation applied to the coin's edge during striking.

Relief: The portion of a design raised above the surface of a coin, medal or token.

A token is issued by a private entity and can be redeemed for its face value in trade or service.

Restrike: A coin, medal or token produced from original dies at a later date, often with the purpose of sale to collectors.

Reverse: The backside or "tails" side of a coin, medal or token, opposite from the principal figure of the design or obverse.

Rim: The raised area bordering the edge and surrounding the field.

Series: The complete group of coins of the same denomination and design and representing all issuing mints.

Token: A privately issued piece, generally in metal, with a represented value in trade or offer of service. Tokens are also produced for advertising purposes.

Type coin: A coin from a given series representing the basic design. A type coin is collected as an example of a particular design rather than for its date and mintmark.

Variety: Any coin noticeably different in dies from another of the same design, date and mint. Overdates and overmintmarks are examples of varieties.

Wire edge: Created when coinage metal flows between the coinage die and collar, producing a thin flange of coin metal at the outside edge or edges of a coin.

PRICING SECTION

Introduction to pricing

The following value guide is divided into six sections:

1. Colonial coins, issued prior to the establishment of the United States.
2. U.S. issues of 1792.
3. U.S. issues of 1793-present.
4. U.S. minting varieties and errors.
5. Canadian coins.
6. Mexican coins.

Value listings

Values listed in the following price guide are average retail prices. These are the approximate prices collectors can expect to pay when purchasing coins from dealers. They are not offers to buy or sell. The pricing section should be considered a guide only; actual selling prices will vary.

The values were compiled by Krause Publications' independent staff of market analysts. They derived the values listed by monitoring auction results, business on electronic dealer trading networks, and business at major shows, and in consultation with a panel of dealers. For rare coins, when only a few specimens of a particular date and mintmark are known, a confirmed transaction may occur only once every several years. In those instances, the most recent auction result is listed.

Grading

Values are listed for coins in various states of preservation, or grades. Standards used in determining grades for U.S. coins are those set by the American Numismatic Association. See Chapter 4 for more on grading.

Dates and mintmarks

The dates listed are the individual dates that appear on each coin. The letter that follows the date is the mintmark and indicates where the coin was struck: "C" — Charlotte, N.C. (1838-1861); "CC" — Carson City, Nev. (1870-1893); "D" — Dahlonega, Ga. (1838-1861), and Denver (1906-present); "O" — New Orleans (1838-1909); "P" — Philadelphia (1793-present); "S" — San Francisco (1854-present); and "W" — West Point, N.Y. (1984-present). Coins without mintmarks were struck at Philadelphia.

A slash mark in a date indicates an overdate. This means a new date was engraved on a die over an old date. For example, if the date is listed as "1899/8," an 1898 die had a 9 engraved over the last 8 in the date. Portions of the old numeral are still visible on the coin.

A slash mark in a mintmark listing indicates an overmintmark (example: "1922-P/D"). The same process as above occurred, but this time a new mintmark was engraved over an old.

See the "U.S. Minting Varieties and Errors" section for more information on overdates and overmintmarks.

Price charts

Pricing data for the selected charts in the U.S. section were taken from the January issues of "Coin Prices" for the years indicated.

Mexican coin mintages

Quantities minted of each date are indicated when that information is available, generally stated in millions and rounded off to the nearest 10,000 pieces. The following mintage conversion formulas are used:

10,000,000 — 10,000.
1,000,000 — 1.000.
100,000 — .100.
10,000 — .010.
9,999 — 9,999.
1,000 — 1,000.
842 — 842 pcs. (pieces).
27 — 27 pcs.

Precious-metal content

Throughout this book precious-metal content is indicated in troy ounces. One troy ounce equals 480 grains, or 31.103 grams.

Abbreviations

AGW. Actual gold weight.

APW. Actual platinum weight.

ASW. Actual silver weight.

BV. Bullion value. This indicates the coin's current value is based on the amount of its precious-metal content and the current price for that metal.

Est. Indicates the exact mintage is not known and the figure listed is an estimate.

G. Grams.

Inc. Abv. Indicates the mintage for the date and mintmark listed is included in the previous listing.

KM#. In the Canadian and Mexican price sections, indicates "Krause-Mishler number." This sequential cataloging numbering system originated with the "Standard Catalog of World Coins" by Chester L. Krause and Clifford Mishler, and provides collectors with a means for identifying world issues.

Leg. Legend.

Mkt value. Market value.

MM. Millimeters.

Obv. Obverse.

P/L. Indicates "prooflike," a type of finish used on some Canadian coins.

Rev. Reverse.

Spec. Indicates "specimen," a type of finish used on some Canadian coins.

Colonial coins

Massachusetts

"New England" Coinage

NE/III Threepence

(1652)   Only Two Examples Known

NE/VI Sixpence
Garrett 75,000.

(1652)   Only Seven examples Known

NE/XII Shilling

Date	AG	Good	VG	Fine	VF
(1652)	1,250.	3,500.	5,500.	10,000.	22,500.

Willow Tree Coinage

Threepence

Date					
1652					Only Three Examples Known

Sixpence

1652	3,500.	7,500.	10,000.	15,000.	20,000.

Shilling

Date	AG	Good	VG	Fine	VF
1652	4,000.	10,000.	12,500.	18,000.	25,000.

Oak Tree Coinage

Twopence

	AG	Good	VG	Fine	VF
1662	150.00	300.00	500.00	700.00	1,200.

Threepence

	AG	Good	VG	Fine	VF
1652 (Two Types of Legends.)	200.00	400.00	600.00	850.00	1,750.

Sixpence

	AG	Good	VG	Fine	VF
1652 (Three Types of Legends.)	200.00	400.00	600.00	1,150.	2,200.

Shilling

	AG	Good	VG	Fine	VF
1652 (Two Types of Legends.)	180.00	350.00	625.00	850.00	2,000.

Pine Tree Coinage

Threepence

Date	AG	Good	VG	Fine	VF
1652 Tree Without Berries	150.00	320.00	400.00	500.00	900.00

1652 Tree With Berries (Two Types of Legends.)	180.00	360.00	450.00	600.00	1,000.

Sixpence

	AG	Good	VG	Fine	VF
1652 Tree Without Berries ("Spiney Tree".)	525.00	900.00	1,400.	1,800.	2,650.

1652 Tree With Berries	160.00	350.00	625.00	850.00	1,200.

Shilling, Large Planchet

Date	AG	Good	VG	Fine	VF
1652 (Many Varieties; Some Very Rare)	160.00	350.00	550.00	850.00	1,600.

Small Planchet, Large Dies

1652 (Struck With Large Dies, All Examples Are Thought To Be Contemporary Fabrications.)

Small Planchet, Small Dies

Date	AG	Good	VG	Fine	VF
1652 (Many Varieties; Some Very Rare)	150.00	220.00	320.00	550.00	1,150.

Maryland

Lord Baltimore's Coinage

Penny (denarium)

(1659)				Only Four Examples Known	

Fourpence (groat)

	AG	Good	VG	Fine	VF
(1659) Large Bust and Shield	500.00	1,000.	1,850.	4,250.	7,000.
(1659) Small Bust and Shield		Norweb 26,400			Unique

Sixpence

	AG	Good	VG	Fine	VF
(1659) Small Bust	450.00	850.00	1,500.	2,500.	4,250.

(Known in Two Other Rare Small Bust Varieties, Plus Two Rare Large Bust Varieties.)

Date	AG	Shilling Good	VG	Fine	VF
(1659) (Varieties, One Very Rare)	500.00	1,000.	1,750.	3,000.	5,500.

New Jersey

St. Patrick or Mark Newby Coinage

Date	AG	Farthing Good	VG	Fine	VF
(1682) (Also Rare Varieties)	20.00	40.00	60.00	100.00	150.00
(1682) Struck of Silver	300.00	500.00	1,000.	1,500.	2,650.

		Halfpenny			
(1682)	50.00	75.00	100.00	200.00	350.00

Coinage of William Wood

"Rosa Americana" Coinage

Date	Good	Halfpenny VG	Fine	VF	XF
1722 D.G. REX	40.00	60.00	80.00	200.00	450.00

Date	Good	VG	Fine	VF	XF
1722 DEI GRATIA REX (Several Varieties)	30.00	50.00	70.00	120.00	300.00

| 1722 VTILE DVLCI | — | — | 1,045. | — | — |

| 1723 Crowned Rose | 35.00 | 60.00 | 85.00 | 165.00 | 275.00 |

| 1723 Uncrowned Rose | — | — | 660.00 | — | — |

Penny

| 1722 UTILE DULCI (Several Varieties) | 30.00 | 50.00 | 85.00 | 135.00 | 250.00 |

Date	Good	VG	Fine	VF	XF
1722 VTILE DVLCI (Several Varieties)	30.00	50.00	100.00	150.00	275.00

(Also Known In Two Rare Pattern Types With Long Hair Ribbons, One With V's for U's on Obverse.)

1723 (Several Varieties)	30.00	50.00	100.00	150.00	275.00

1724 (Pattern)   Only Two Examples Known

(1724) Undated.   Norweb 2,035.   Only Five Examples Known
1727 Pattern, George II   Only Two Examples Known

Twopence

	Good	VG	Fine	VF	XF
(1722) Undated, Motto With Scroll	60.00	100.00	190.00	300.00	450.00

Date	Good	VG	Fine	VF	XF
(1722) No Scroll				Only Three Examples Known	

1722 Dated, period After Rex	40.00	60.00	90.00	165.00	370.00
1722 No Period	40.00	60.00	90.00	165.00	370.00

1723 (Several Varieties)	40.00	65.00	100.00	175.00	350.00

1724 Patterns; Two Types	Garrett 6,000.	Both Extremely Rare

Date	Good	VG	Fine	VF	XF
1733 Pattern	Norweb 19,800.			Only Four Examples Known	

Hibernia Coinage

Farthing

	Good	VG	Fine	VF	XF
1722 Pattern	50.00	125.00	220.00	325.00	700.00
1723 D:G:REX. (1722 Obverse)	40.00	60.00	90.00	150.00	300.00

	Good	VG	Fine	VF	XF
1723 DEI.GRATIA.REX.	20.00	40.00	65.00	100.00	170.00
1723 Silver	—	—	—	1,000.	2,000.
1723 Silver	—	—	—	Proof	3,500.
1724	25.00	45.00	75.00	125.00	200.00

Halfpenny

	Good	VG	Fine	VF	XF
1722 Harp Left. Head Right	15.00	30.00	55.00	115.00	220.00

	Good	VG	Fine	VF	XF
1722 Harp Left. Head Right	—	—	1,800.	2,350.	3,200.

Date	Good	VG	Fine	VF	XF
1722 Harp Right	15.00	30.00	55.00	115.00	220.00
1722 Legend DEII Error	90.00	180.00	300.00	500.00	750.00
1723/22 Three Varieties	20.00	35.00	80.00	145.00	250.00

	Good	VG	Fine	VF	XF
1723 Many Varieties	15.00	25.00	50.00	90.00	165.00
1723 Large Head. Rare, Generally Mint State Only. Probably a Pattern					Rare

	Good	VG	Fine	VF	XF
1724 Varieties	15.00	25.00	50.00	110.00	220.00
1724 Continuous Legend Over Head	65.00	150.00	300.00	475.00	750.00

Pitt tokens

Farthing

1766	—	—	1,500.	2,500.	4,750.

Halfpenny

1766	60.00	100.00	225.00	375.00	900.00

States of the Confederation
Connecticut

Date	Good	VG	Fine	VF	XF
1785 Bust Right	30.00	50.00	80.00	165.00	375.00

	Good	VG	Fine	VF	XF
1785 African Head	45.00	65.00	175.00	400.00	1,250.

	Good	VG	Fine	VF	XF
1785 Bust Left	120.00	160.00	250.00	385.00	725.00

Small Mailed Bust Right

	Good	VG	Fine	VF	XF
1786 ETLIB INDE	35.00	55.00	85.00	160.00	400.00
1786 INDE ET LIB	55.00	75.00	115.00	225.00	450.00

Date	Good	VG	Fine	VF	XF
1786 Large Mailed Bust right	45.00	85.00	155.00	325.00	750.00

1786 Mailed Bust Left	30.00	50.00	90.00	200.00	500.00

1786 Hercules Head	40.00	75.00	120.00	280.00	550.00

1786 Draped Bust	35.00	65.00	115.00	250.00	525.00

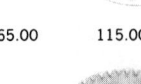

1787 Small Head, ETLIB INDE	40.00	80.00	145.00	275.00	500.00
1787 Small Head, INDE ET LIB	125.00	165.00	245.00	375.00	650.00
1787 Medium Bust, Two Rev. Legend Types	80.00	140.00	200.00	325.00	550.00

Date	Good	VG	Fine	VF	XF
1787 Muttonhead Variety (Extremely Rare With Legend: INDE ET LIB.)	50.00	125.00	250.00	700.00	1,450.

1787 Mailed Bust Left	25.00	40.00	80.00	140.00	300.00
1787 Perfect Date. Legend: IN DE ET	65.00	85.00	125.00	225.00	550.00

1787 Laughing Head	25.00	40.00	65.00	150.00	475.00
1787 Horned Bust	25.00	40.00	65.00	150.00	475.00
1787/8 IND ET LIB	40.00	75.00	130.00	250.00	600.00
1787/1887 INDE ET LIB	30.00	55.00	95.00	190.00	500.00
1787 CONNECT / INDE ET LIB	37.50	60.00	115.00	200.00	525.00

(Also Two Additional Scarce Reverse Legend Types)

1787 Draped Bust, Many Varieties	20.00	35.00	75.00	135.00	275.00
1787 AUCIORI Variety	25.00	40.00	85.00	175.00	475.00
1787 AUCTOPI Variety	30.00	50.00	100.00	200.00	500.00
1787 AUCTOBI Variety	30.00	50.00	90.00	160.00	450.00
1787 CONNFC Variety	25.00	40.00	85.00	175.00	475.00
1787 CONNLC Variety	30.00	60.00	120.00	250.00	550.00
1787 FNDE Variety	25.00	40.00	85.00	160.00	450.00
1787 ETLIR Variety	25.00	40.00	85.00	160.00	450.00
1787 ETIIB Variety	30.00	50.00	100.00	175.00	475.00

Date	Good	VG	Fine	VF	XF
1788 Mailed Bust Right	25.00	40.00	65.00	150.00	325.00
1788 Small Mailed Bust right	125.00	250.00	500.00	900.00	2,250.

	Good	VG	Fine	VF	XF
1788 Mailed Bust Left	25.00	50.00	100.00	260.00	475.00

Date	Good	VG	Fine	VF	XF
1788 Legend: CONNLC	25.00	40.00	65.00	150.00	325.00
1788 Draped Bust Left, INDE ET LIB	20.00	35.00	50.00	115.00	265.00
1788 Similar, INDLET LIB	30.00	55.00	75.00	150.00	335.00
1788 Similar, CONNLC/INDE ET LIB	35.00	60.00	90.00	160.00	350.00
1788 Similar, CONNLC/INDL ET LIB	35.00	60.00	90.00	160.00	350.00

Massachusetts

Halfpenny
Garrett 40,000.

1776   Unique

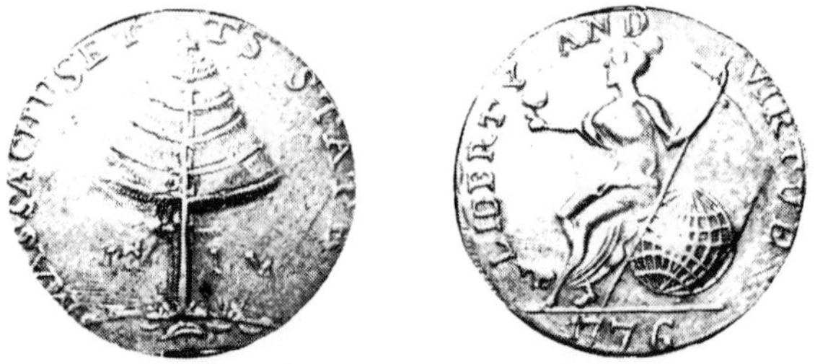

Penny

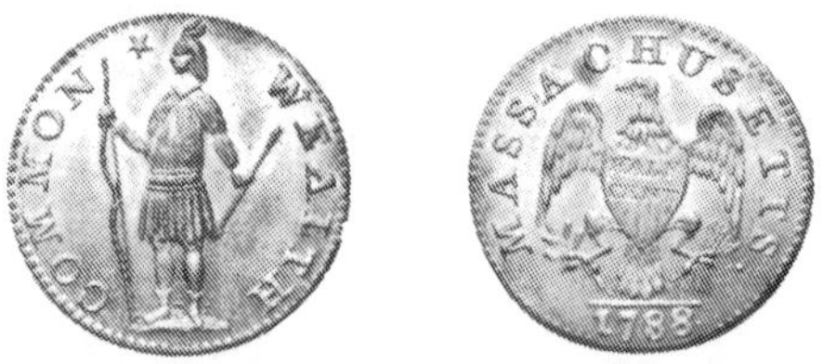

Date	Good	VG	Fine	VF	XF
1776					Unique

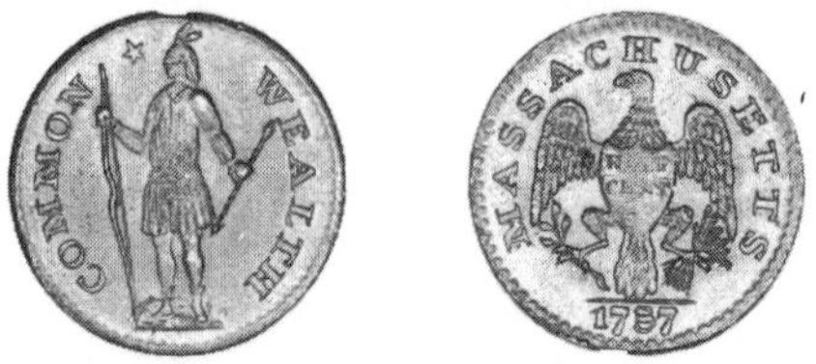

Half Cent

	Good	VG	Fine	VF	XF
1787 (Varieties — some Rare)	45.00	60.00	95.00	250.00	450.00

	Good	VG	Fine	VF	XF
1788 (Two Varieties — One Rare)	50.00	90.00	130.00	275.00	550.00

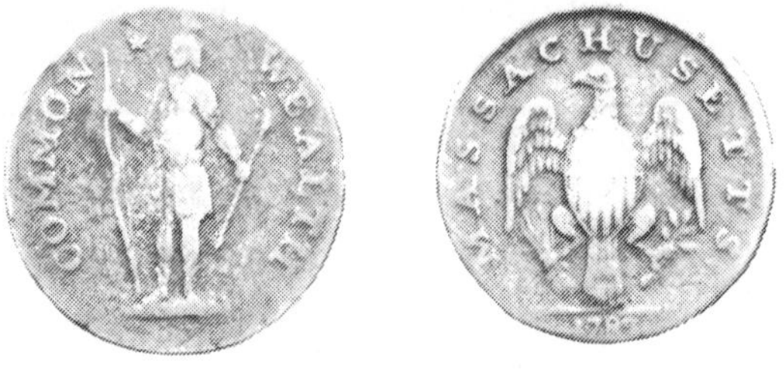

Cent

1787 Arrows in Right Talon		Garrett 5,500.			Rare

	Good	VG	Fine	VF	XF
1787 Arrows in Left Talon	35.00	60.00	90.00	220.00	450.00

Date	Good	VG	Fine	VF	XF
1787 "Horned Eagle" Die Break	35.00	55.00	95.00	250.00	475.00

	Good	VG	Fine	VF	XF
1788 No Period After Massachusetts	40.00	65.00	90.00	250.00	475.00
1788 Period. Normals S's	35.00	55.00	80.00	235.00	450.00

	Good	VG	Fine	VF	XF
1788 Period. S's Like 8's	35.00	55.00	80.00	235.00	450.00

New Hampshire

1776	Garrett 13,000	Extremely Rare

New Jersey

Date	Good	VG	Fine	VF	XF
(1786) Washington Obverse	Garrett 50,000 Steinberg 12,650			Only Three Examples Known	

1786 Eagle obverse | Garrett 37,500. | Unique
1786 Washington Obv., Eagle Rev. | | Only Two Examples Known

1786 Immunis Columbia Obverse | Rescigno, AU 33,000. Steinberg VF 11,000. | Extremely Rare

1786 Immunis Columbia/Eagle | Only Three Examples Known

1786 Date Below Draw Bar | Garrett 52,000. | Extremely Rare

Date	Good	VG	Fine	VF	XF
1786 Large Horse Head, Date Below Plow. No Coulter On Plow	125.00	250.00	425.00	950.00	3,200.
1786 Narrow Shield, Straight Beam	35.00	50.00	100.00	250.00	825.00
1786 Wide Shield, Curved Beam (Varieties)	45.00	65.00	120.00	260.00	850.00
1786 Bridle Variety (Die Break) (Other Reverse Varieties)	45.00	70.00	125.00	285.00	900.00
1787 Small Planchet, Plain Shield (Varieties)	30.00	50.00	90.00	160.00	375.00
1787 Small Planchet, Shield Heavily Outlined	30.00	50.00	90.00	160.00	375.00
1787 "Serpent Head" Variety	50.00	75.00	125.00	265.00	675.00
1787 Large Planchet, Plain Shield (Varieties)	30.00	50.00	90.00	185.00	400.00

Date	Good	VG	Fine	VF	XF
1787 "PLURBIS" Variety	60.00	120.00	170.00	425.00	675.00
1788 Horse's Head Right (Varieties)	30.00	60.00	100.00	225.00	450.00

	Good	VG	Fine	VF	XF
1788 Fox Before Reverse Legend (Varieties)	60.00	120.00	180.00	450.00	1,000.

	Good	VG	Fine	VF	XF
1788 Horse's Head Left (Varieties)	135.00	225.00	385.00	650.00	1,500.

New York

Date	Good	VG	Fine	VF	XF
1786 NON VI Virtute VICI	1,800.	2,800.	3,750.	5,850.	10,000.

	Good	VG	Fine	VF	XF
1787 Obv.: Eagle On Glove Faces Right	650.00	950.00	1,750.	4,000.	9,000.

Date	Good	VG	Fine	VF	XF
1787 Obv.: Eagle On Glove Faces Left	600.00	925.00	1,350.	3,600.	8,500.

| 1787 Rev.: Large Eagle, Arrows in Right Talon | Norweb 18,700. | | | Only Two Examples Known | |

| 1787 George Clint | 3,500. | 4,500. | 7,500. | 19,500. | — |

| 1787 Indian/N.Y. Arms | 1,750. | 3,250. | 5,000. | 10,500. | 20,900. |

| 1787 Indian/Eagle On Glove | 2,250. | 5,000. | 9,750. | 20,000. | 30,000. |

Date	Good	VG	Fine	VF	XF
1787 IMMUNIS COLUMBIA	200.00	325.00	450.00	750.00	2,250.

| 1787 NOVA EBORAC/Rev. Figure Seated Right | | | | | |
| | 75.00 | 120.00 | 225.00 | 350.00 | 750.00 |

| 1787 Rev. Figure Seated Left | 50.00 | 85.00 | 170.00 | 275.00 | 550.00 |

| 1787 NOVA EBORAC/Obv. Small Head, Star Above | | | | | |
| | 600.00 | 1,750. | 3,000. | 4,500. | 6,500. |

| 1787 NOVA EBORAC/Obv. Large Head, Two Quatrefoils Left | | | | | |
| | 300.00 | 400.00 | 600.00 | 1,100. | 2,450. |

Machin's Mill Coppers

Date	Good	VG	Fine	VF	XF
	50.00	90.00	160.00	275.00	750.00

Crude, lightweight imitations of the British Halfpenny were struck at Machin's Mill in large quantities bearing the obverse legends: GEORGIVS II REX, GEORGIVS III REX, and GEORGIUS III REX, with the BRITANNIA reverse, and dates of: 1747, 1771, 1772, 1774, 1775, 1776, 1777, 1778, 1784, 1785, 1786, 1787 and 1788. Other dates may exist. There are many different mulings. These pieces, which have plain crosses in the shield of Britannia, are not to be confused with the very common British made imitations, which usually have outlined crosses in the shield. Some varieties are very rare.

Vermont

(1785) IMMUNE COLUMBIA	1,750.	2,650.	3,750.	—	—

| 1785 VERMONTIS | 175.00 | 225.00 | 375.00 | 950.00 | 2,150. |

| 1785 VERMONTS | 100.00 | 185.00 | 325.00 | 850.00 | 1,950. |

| 1786 VERMONTENSIUM | 75.00 | 150.00 | 300.00 | 750.00 | 1,750. |

Date	Good	VG	Fine	VF	XF
1786 AUCTORI: VERMON:/Baby Head	110.00	190.00	350.00	900.00	3,000.
1786 VERMON: AUCTORI:/Head Left	70.00	160.00	290.00	450.00	1,250.
1787 Bust Left			Extremely Rare		
1787 Bust Right. Several Varieties	45.00	85.00	200.00	450.00	1,000.
1787 BRITANNIA Mule	40.00	60.00	120.00	385.00	950.00
1788 Rev. INDE ET LIB. Several Varieties	45.00	75.00	180.00	400.00	1,000.
1788 "C" backward in AUCTORI			Extremely Rare		
1788 ET LIB INDE	120.00	225.00	350.00	700.00	—
1788 GEORGE III REX Mule	120.00	275.00	400.00	800.00	1,750.

Federal issues
of the confederation

Continental dollar

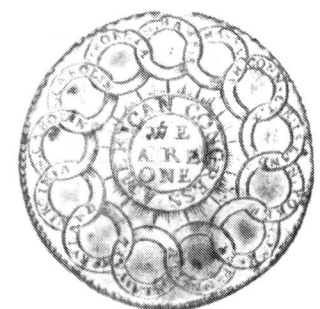

Date	Good	VG	Fine	VF	XF
1776 CURRENCY, Pewter	1,250.	1,600.	2,450.	2,850.	5,750.
1776 CURRENCY, EG FECIT, Pewter	1,200.	1,500.	2,250.	2,750.	5,500.
1776 CURRENCY, EG FECIT, Silver				Only Two Examples Known	
1776 CURRENCY, Pewter					Extremely Rare
1776 CURRENCY, Pewter Floral Cross		Norweb 50,600.			Two Recorded

	Good	VG	Fine	VF	XF
1776 CURENCY, Pewter	1,200.	1,500.	2,250.	2,900.	5,500.
1776 CURENCY, Brass (2 Vars.)	—	—	—	12,000.	15,500.
1776 CURENCY, Silver		Romano 99,000.			Unique

Nova Constellatio coppers

1783 CONSTELLATIO, Pointed Rays, Small US				
25.00	50.00	70.00	175.00	385.00

Date	Good	VG	Fine	VF	XF
1783 CONSTELLATIO, Pointed Rays, Large US					
	28.00	55.00	80.00	185.00	395.00

| 1783 CONSTELATIO, Blunt Rays | 28.00 | 55.00 | 95.00 | 200.00 | 425.00 |

| 1785 CONSTELATIO, Blunt Rays | 35.00 | 65.00 | 110.00 | 225.00 | 450.00 |

| 1785 CONSTELLATIO, Pointed Rays | 25.00 | 75.00 | 150.00 | 260.00 | 475.00 |
| 1786 Similar. Contemporary Circulating Counterfeit | | | | | Extremely Rare |

Nova Constellatio silver

BIT-100
Garrett 97,500.
Stack's auction, May 1991, 72,500

1783 leaf edge
1783 plain edge

2 known
Unique

QUINT-500

Date	Good	VG	Fine	VF	XF
1783 Type 1		Garrett 165,000.			Unique

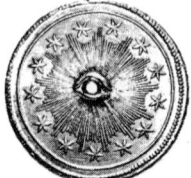 

1783 Type 2		Garrett 55,000.			Unique

MARK-1000

1783		Garrett 190,000.			Unique

Immune Columbia coppers

Date	Good	VG	Fine	VF	XF
1785 CONSTELLATIO, Copper	—	—	—	—	13,750.
1785 CONSTELLATIO, Silver	—	—	—	—	17,600.

1785 CONSTELLATIO, Copper, Extra Star in Border	Caldwell 4,675.

Date	Good	VG	Fine	VF	XF
1785 CONSTELATIO, Copper, Blunt Rays	Norweb 22,000.				
1785 CONSTELATIO, Gold				Only Two Examples Known	Unique

	Good	VG	Fine	VF	XF
1785 George III Obverse	1,250.	1,850.	2,250.	5,000.	9,000.
1785 Vermon Obverse	1,000.	1,650.	2,000.	4,750.	8,500.

Confederatio coppers

Date	Good	VG	Fine	VF	XF
1785 Small Circle of Stars (Laird U. park VF 47.00)					Norweb 16,500.

1785 Large Circle of Stars   Extremely Rare
NOTE: The Confederatio dies were struck in combination with thirteen other dies of the period. All surviving examples of these combinations are extremely rare.

Fugio cents

Date	Good	VG	Fine	VF	XF
1787 Club Rays, Round Ends	50.00	100.00	220.00	450.00	900.00
1787 Club Rays, Concave Ends	500.00	1,000.	2,000.	4,000.	—
1787 Similar, FUCIO Error	550.00	1,200.	2,250.	4,850.	—

	Good	VG	Fine	VF	XF
1787 Pointed Rays, UNITED above, STATES below	200.00	500.00	900.00	1,350.	3,000.
1787 Similar, UNITED STATES, at sides of Ring	40.00	65.00	115.00	175.00	400.00
1787 Similar, STATES UNITED at sides of Ring	45.00	90.00	150.00	220.00	500.00
1787 Similar, 8-pointed Stars on ring	60.00	100.00	150.00	275.00	550.00
1787 Similar, Raised Rims on Ring, Large Lettering in Center	65.00	120.00	185.00	400.00	750.00
1787 Obv: No Cinquefoils. Cross after Date. Rev: UNITED STATES	100.00	200.00	425.00	575.00	950.00
1787 Same Obv., Rev: STATES UNITED	125.00	225.00	450.00	650.00	1,250.
1787 Same Obv., Rev: Raised Rims on Ring	—	—	—	2,600.	—

1787 Same Obv.: Rev. with Rays and AMERICAN CONGRESS	Norweb 63,800.	Extremely Rare

 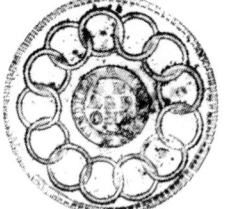

New Haven Restrikes (1858): Brass		Unc 325.00
Copper		325.00
Silver		825.00
Gold	Norweb 1,430. (Holed)	Only Two Examples Known

Colonial tokens

New Yorke token

Date	Good	VG	Fine	VF	XF
C.1700 Brass	1,250.	2,750.	4,000.	6,500.	—
White Metal				Only Four Examples Known	

American plantations 1/24th-real

Date	Good	VG	Fine	VF	XF
(1688) Legend: ET HIB REX	125.00	165.00	220.00	300.00	425.00
(1828) Restrike. Two obverse dies rider's head left of "B" in legend	90.00	120.00	180.00	250.00	350.00
(1688) Reverse. Horizontal 4	325.00	400.00	475.00	550.00	
(1688) Legend: ET HB REX					Extremely Rare
(1688) Reverse. Arm of Scotland left, Ireland right	750.00	1,250.	2,000.	2,500.	—

Elephant tokens

Date	Good	VG	Fine	VF	XF
(1664) Thick Planchet	80.00	100.00	150.00	300.00	550.00
(1664) Thin Planchet	100.00	150.00	225.00	450.00	850.00
(1664) Diagonals Tie Shield	140.00	175.00	300.00	550.00	950.00
(1664) Sword Right Side of Shield		Norweb 1,320.		Only Three Examples Known	

	Good	VG	Fine	VF	XF
(1684) Legend: LON DON	300.00	500.00	1,000.	1,450.	2,300.

Date	Good	VG	Fine	VF	XF
1694 NEW ENGLAND	Norweb 25,300.			Only Two Examples Known	

| 1694 CAROLINA (PROPRIETERS) | Norweb 35,200. | | | Only Five Examples Known | |

| 1694 CAROLINA (PROPRIETORS, O over E) | 1,000. | 1,600.
Norweb 17,600. | 2,250. | 4,500. | 10,000. |

Gloucester token

| (1714) | Garrett 36,000. | | | Only Two Examples Known | |

Higley or Granby coppers

Date	Good	VG	Fine	VF	XF
1737 THE VALVE OF THREE PENCE/ CONNECTICVT		Garrett 16,000.			
1737 THE VALVE OF THE THREE PENCE/ I AM GOOD COPPER	Ex-Norweb 6,875.			Only Two Examples Known	

Date		Good	VG	Fine	VF	XF
1737 VALUE ME AS YOU PLEASE/I AM GOOD COPPER				Garrett 8,000.		
1737 Similar Except Legend: VALVE						Only Two Examples Known

(1737) Broad Axe Reverse
1739 Similar

Garrett 45,000; Stack's auction, May 1991, 6,500
Oechsner 9,900.   Only Five Examples Known
Roper 7,700
Steinberg (holed) 4,400.

(1737) THE WHEELE GOES ROUND/
J CUT MY WAY THROUGH

Roper 60,500.   Unique

Hibernia-Voce Populi coppers

Farthing

		Good	VG	Fine	VF	XF
1760 Large Letters		120.00	225.00	350.00	525.00	1,150.
1760 Small Letters			Norweb 5,940.			Extremely Rare

Halfpenny

		Good	VG	Fine	VF	XF
1700 Date is Error			Norweb 577.50			Extremely Rare
1760 Varieties		25.00	45.00	75.00	115.00	240.00

Date	Good	VG	Fine	VF	XF
1760 Legend VOOE POPULI	30.00	50.00	75.00	125.00	320.00

Virginia halfpenny

Date	VG	Fine	VF	XF	Unc.
1773 Small 7's in date, struck on Irish Halfpenny Planchets					Proof 5,000.
1773 Period After GEORGIVS Varieties with 7 to 8 strings in harp	25.00	50.00	100.00	150.00	350.00
1773 No Period After GEORGIVS Varieties with 6, 7 or 8 strings in harp	30.00	60.00	120.00	185.00	465.00
NOTE: 1773 No Period 8 harp strings variety Unc.					Steinberg 1,210.

1774 So-called "Shilling." Silver proofs

Garrett 23,000. Only Six Examples Known

Early American tokens

Rhode Island ship tokens

Date	Good	VG	Fine	VF	XF
1779 No wreath below ship	60.00	150.00	255.00	450.00	900.00

(Specimens known in Brass and Copper and Pewter.)

	Good	VG	Fine	VF	XF
1779 Wreath below ship	100.00	220.00	350.00	650.00	1,150.
	(Extremely rare in pewter.)				
1779 "VLUGTENDE" below ship, brass		Garrett 16,000.			Unique

North American token

Date	Good	VG	Fine	VF	XF
1781 Halfpenny	10.00	20.00	50.00	120.00	450.00

Chalmers' silver tokens

Threepence

1783					
	500.00	900.00	1,250.	1,850.	3,400.

Sixpence

Date	Good	VG	Fine	VF	XF
1783 Small Date	650.00	1,250.	1,850.	4,000.	10,000.
1783 Large date	500.00	1,000.	1,600.	2,500.	8,000.

Shilling

1783 Birds with long worm	350.00	500.00	900.00	1,600.	2,800.
1783 Birds with short worm	250.00	425.00	800.00	1,500.	2,500.

1783 Rings and Stars Reverse	Garrett 75,000.	Only Four Examples Known

Bar "cent"

Date	Good	VG	Fine	VF	XF
(1785)	150.00	275.00	650.00	1,000.	1,750.

Auctori Plebis token

Date	Good	VG	Fine	VF	XF
1787	35.00	50.00	125.00	200.00	350.00

Brasher's doubloon

Date	Good	VG	Fine	VF	XF
1787 E.B. on Wing	Garrett 725,000.			Only Six Examples Known	

| 1787 EB on Breast | Garrett 625,000. | | | Unique | |

Mott token

Date	Good	VG	Fine	VF	XF
1789 Thin Planchet	60.00	120.00	200.00	380.00	725.00
1789 Thick Planchet (Weight generally about 170 grs.)	50.00	100.00	160.00	300.00	475.00
1789 Fully Engrailed Edge	85.00	160.00	325.00	600.00	1,200.

(Specimens of the above struck with perfect dies are scarcer and generally command higher prices.)

Albany church penny

(1790) No "D" above CHURCH
(1790) With "D" above CHURCH

Bowers Sale 11,550.

Only Five Examples Known
Extremely Rare

Standish Barry threepence

Date	Good	VG	Fine	VF	XF
1790	1,200.	1,850.	2,750.	5,000.	9,000.

Kentucky token

Date	VG	Fine	VF	XF	Unc.
(c.1793) Plain Edge	45.00	60.00	75.00	250.00	500.00
Engrailed edge	125.00	200.00	300.00	500.00	1,200.
Lettered Edge	45.00	65.00	85.00	275.00	600.00
PAYABLE AT BEDWORTH		Norweb 1,760.			Unique
PAYABLE AT LANCASTER	45.00	65.00	85.00	270.00	480.00
PAYABLE AT I. FIELDING					Unique
Branch with two leaves on edge					Unique

Talbot, Allum & Lee cents

With NEW YORK above ship

Date	Good	VG	Fine	VF	XF
1794 Edge: PAYABLE AT THE STORE OF	40.00	65.00	125.00	250.00	725.00
1794 Edge: Plain				Only Three Examples Known	

(Size of ampersand varies on obverse and reverse dies)

Without NEW YORK

Date	Good	VG	Fine	VF	XF
1794 Edge: PAYABLE AT THE STORE OF	300.00	600.00	900.00	1,850.	—

Date	VG	Fine	VF	XF	Unc.
1795 Edge: WE PROMISE TO PAY THE BEARER ONE CENT	25.00	50.00	120.00	280.00	800.00
1795 Edge: CURRENT EVERYWHERE					Unique
1795 Edge: Oliva Leaf		Norweb 4,400.			Unique
1795 Plain Edge					Two Known
1795 Edge: Cambridge Bedford Huntingdon. X.X.		Norweb 3,960.			Unique

Franklin press token

Date	VG	Fine	VF	XF	Unc.
1794 Plain edge	45.00	75.00	115.00	225.00	500.00

Myddelton tokens

1796 Copper
1796 Silver

Proof 6,500.
Proof 5,500.

Copper Company of Upper Canada

1796 Copper/Copper Company Rev.

Proof 2,650.

Castorland "Half Dollar"

Date		Unc.
1796 Silver, Reeded Edge		4,500.
1796 Copper, Reeded Edge		Only Three Examples Known
1796 Brass, Reeded Edge		Unique
1796 Copper, Plain Edge. Thin Planchet	Norweb 467.50	Unique
1796 Silver, Same Dies. Reeded Edge. Thin Planchet Restrike		Proof 250.00
1796 Silver, Same but ARGENT on Plain Edge		Proof 50.00
1796 Copper, Same. Restrike on Thin Planchet		Proof 150.00
1796 Copper, Same but CUIVRE on Plain Edge		Proof 30.00

Modern Restrikes with large and small lettering on the reverse have been produced in Gold, Silver, Copper and Bronze.
Original dies distinguished by wavy die breaks about the upper right corner of pot on the reverse.

New York Theatre token

Date	VG	Fine	VF	XF	Unc.
(c.1796)	250.00	850.00	1,750.	2,750.	6,000.

Washington pieces

Date	Good	VG	Fine	VF	XF
1782 GEORGIVS TRIUMPHO	35.00	50.00	115.00	225.00	600.00

	Good	VG	Fine	VF	XF
1782 Large military bust, several varieties	12.00	20.00	40.00	85.00	190.00
1783 Small military bust, plain edge	18.00	25.00	45.00	100.00	210.00
Note: One Proof is known. Value $12,500.					
1783 Similar, engrailed edge	30.00	45.00	65.00	125.00	275.00

	Good	VG	Fine	VF	XF
1783 Draped Bust, no button on drapery. Sm. Let.	15.00	30.00	50.00	85.00	200.00
1783 Draped Bust, button on drapery. Lg. Let.	25.00	40.00	80.00	150.00	265.00
1783 Similar, copper restrike, large modern lettering, plain edge					Proof 500.00
1783 Similar, but Engrailed edge					Proof 300.00
1783 Similar, Bronzed					
1783 Similar, Silver					
1783 Similar, Gold					

Date	Good	VG	Fine	VF	XF
1783 UNITY STATES	15.00	30.00	50.00	100.00	200.00

(1783) Double Head Cent	15.00	30.00	50.00	100.00	210.00

Date	VG	Fine	VF	XF	Unc.
1784 Ugly Head	Roper 14,850.			3 Known Copper, 1 White Metal	

	Good	VG	Fine	VF	XF
1791 LIVERPOOL HALFPENNY	450.00	550.00	750.00	—	—

	Good	VG	Fine	VF	XF
1791 Small Eagle Cent	60.00	125.00	250.00	375.00	950.00

Date	VG	Fine	VF	XF	Unc.
1791 Large Eagle Cent	60.00	125.00	250.00	375.00	950.00

Date	Good	VG	Fine	VF	XF
1792 "Half Dollar" Copper, Lettered Edge		Roper 2,860.		Only Two Examples Known	
1792 Similar, Plain Edge				Only Three Examples Known	
1792 Similar, Silver, Lettered Edge			Roper 35,200.		Rare
1792 Similar, Plain Edge					Rare
1792 Similar, Gold					Unique

Date	VG	Fine	VF	XF	Unc.
1792 WASHINGTON PRESIDENT Cent. Plain Edge	Steinberg 12,650. 1,450.	3,250. Garrett 15,500.	5,000.	7,500.	—
1792 Similar. Lettered Edge Est.	2,250.	4,500.	7,500.	12,500.	—

Date	Good	VG	Fine	VF	XF
(1792) BORN VIRGINIA. Varieties	450.00	850.00	1,350.	2,250.	6,500.
Silver, Lettered Edge				Only Two Examples Known	
Silver, Plain Edge		Roper 16,500.		Only Four Examples Known	
Mule, Heraldic Eagle 1792 Half Dollar Reverse				Only Three Examples Known	

	Good	VG	Fine	VF	XF
1792 Half Dollar, Silver, Small Eagle, Plain Edge Garrett 24,500.		Roper 17,050.			
1792 Half Dollar, Similar, Circle and Squares Ornamented Edge				Levinson 6,160.	Rare
1792 Half Dollar, Similar, Copper		Garrett 34,000.		Only Five Examples Known	
1792 Half Dollar, Copper, Plain Edge	1,450.	2,000.	3,500.	Roper 24,200. —	Rare —
1792 Half Dollar, Silver, Twin Olive Leaves on Edge		Garrett 32,000.			Unique

1792 Half Dollar, Silver, Large Heraldic Eagle   Garrett 16,500.   Unique

1792 Roman Head Cent   Proof 11,000.

	Good	VG	Fine	VF	XF
1793 Ship Halfpenny. Lettered Edge	30.00	60.00	100.00	200.00	500.00
1793 Ship Halfpenny. Plain Edge					Extremely Rare

Date	VG	Fine	VF	XF	Unc.
1795 "Grate" Halfpenny, Large Coat Buttons, Reeded Edge	30.00	60.00	110.00	220.00	525.00
1795 Similar, Lettered Edge	180.00	250.00	320.00	650.00	1,200.
1795 Similar, Small Coat Buttons, Reeded Edge	60.00	100.00	150.00	300.00	750.00

Date	Good	VG	Fine	VF	XF
(1795) LIBERTY AND SECURITY Halfpenny, Plain Edge	60.00	100.00	180.00	350.00	490.00
(1795) Similar, Edge Lettered: PAYABLE AT LONDON etc.	30.00	50.00	85.00	135.00	325.00
(1795) Similar, Edge Lettered: BIRMINGHAM etc.	35.00	55.00	95.00	145.00	425.00
1795 Similar, Edge Lettered: An ASYLUM etc.	50.00	80.00	150.00	325.00	650.00
1795 Similar, Edge Lettered: PAYABLE AT LIVERPOOL etc.					Unique
1795 Similar, Edge Lettered: PAYABLE AT LONDON-LIVERPOOL					Unique

Date	VG	Fine	VF	XF	Unc.
(1795) LIBERTY AND SECURITY Penny, Lettered Edge	60.00	120.00	200.00	450.00	1,100.
(1795) Similar, Plain Edge					Extremely Rare
(1795) Similar, Engine Turned Borders		EX-Garrett 2,750.			Very Rare
1795 Date on Reverse, Design Similar to Halfpenny		Roper 6,600.			Very Rare

Date	Good	VG	Fine	VF	XF
(c.1795) Small Success Medal, Plain or Reeded Edge	60.00	90.00	135.00	245.00	500.00
(c.1795) Large Success Medal, Plain or Reeded Edge	60.00	90.00	135.00	245.00	480.00

	Good	VG	Fine	VF	XF
(1795) NORTH WALES Halfpenny, Plain Edge	75.00	115.00	185.00	450.00	1,250.
(1795) Similar, Lettered Edge	325.00	450.00	725.00	1,400.	2,950.
(1795 Four Stars at Bottom of Reverse	600.00	1,250.	2,250.	4,000.	—

Issues of 1792

Half disme

Date	Good	Fine	VF
1792	1,000.	3,000.	5,000.
1792 copper, unique	2,000.	3,500.	6,000.

Disme

1792 silver (3 known)
1792 copper (2 reeded edge, about 10 plain right)   Garrett 54,000.

Silver-center cent

1792 silver center (about 8 known)   Norweb, MS-60, 143,000.
1792 no silver center (copper or billon, 4 known)   Norweb, EF-40, 35,200.

Birch cent

1792 copper known with plain and two types of lettered edges,
  about 15 known combined.   Garrett 200,000.
1792 "G.W.Pt." on reverse below wreath tie,
  white metal, unique   Garrett 90,000.

Wright quarter

Date	Good	Fine	VF
1792 copper, reeded edge (2 known)			
1792 white metal, die trial			Garrett 12,000.

Half cents

Liberty Cap

Head facing left

Designer: Adam Eckfeldt. **Size:** 22 millimeters. **Weight:** 6.74 grams. **Composition:** 100% copper.

Date	Mintage	G-4	VG-8	F-12	VF-20	XF-40	MS-60
1793	35,334	1600.	2250.	4500.	6500.	11,000.	—

Head facing right

Designers: Robert Scot (1794) and John Smith Gardner (1795). **Size:** 23.5 millimeters. **Weight:** 6.74 grams (1794-1795) and 5.44 grams (1795-1797). **Composition:** 100% copper. **Notes:** The "lettered edge" varieties have "Two Hundred for a Dollar" inscribed around the edge. The "pole" varieties have a pole, upon which the cap is hanging, resting on Liberty's shoulder. The "punctuated date" varieties have a comma after the 1 in the date. The 1797 "1 above 1" variety has a second 1 above the 1 in the date.

Date	Mintage	G-4	VG-8	F-12	VF-20	XF-40	MS-60
1794	81,600	265.	375.	750.	1400.	2450.	—
1795 lettered edge, pole	25,600	245.	350.	550.	1000.	1900.	—
1795 plain edge, no pole	109,000	225.	285.	540.	915.	1700.	—
1795 lettered edge, punctuated date	Inc. Ab.	245.	350.	550.	1000.	2100.	—
1795 plain edge, punctuated date	Inc. Ab.	240.	335.	535.	900.	1800.	—
1796 pole	5,090	5500.	6900.	9500.	12,500.	20,000.	—
1796 no pole	1,390	—	—	—	Rare	—	—
1797 pl. edge	119,215	265.	375.	575.	1000.	1900.	—
1797 let. edge	Inc. Ab.	1000.	1600.	2500.	5000.	—	—
1797 1 above 1	Inc. Ab.	225.	285.	540.	915.	1700.	—

Draped Bust

  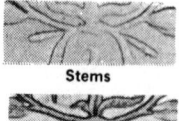

Stems

Stemless

Designer: Robert Scot. **Size:** 23.5 millimeters. **Weight:** 5.44 grams. **Composition:** 100% copper. **Notes:** The wreath on the reverse was redesigned slightly in 1802, resulting in "reverse of 1800" and "reverse of 1802" varieties. The "stems" varieties have stems extending from the wreath above and on both sides of the fraction on the reverse. On the "crosslet 4" variety, a serif appears at the far right of the crossbar on the 4 in the date. The "spiked chin" variety appears to have a spike extending from Liberty's chin, the result of a damaged die. Varieties of the 1805 strikes are distinguished by the size of the 5 in the date. Varieties of the 1806 strikes are distinguished by the size of the 6 in the date.

Date	Mintage	G-4	VG-8	F-12	VF-20	XF-40	MS-60
1800	211,530	30.00	42.50	65.00	150.	325.	—
1802/0 rev. 1800	14,366	5000.	8500.	12,000.	—	—	—
1802/0 rev. 1802	Inc. Ab.	440.	975.	2350.	4000.	9800.	—
1803	97,900	33.00	44.00	65.00	125.	325.	—
1804 plain 4, stemless wreath	1,055,312	28.00	32.00	44.00	63.00	140.	1050.
1804 plain 4, stems	Inc. Ab.	30.00	40.00	52.00	75.00	175.	1050.
1804 crosslet 4, stemless	Inc. Ab.	30.00	40.00	52.00	75.00	175.	1050.
1804 crosslet 4, stems	Inc. Ab.	30.00	40.00	52.00	75.00	175.	1050.
1804 spiked chin	Inc.Ab.	28.00	32.00	44.00	63.00	175.	1050.
1805 small 5, stemless	814,464	29.00	37.00	50.00	77.00	200.	—
1805 small 5, stems	Inc. Ab.	475.	995.	2250.	3000.	3800.	—
1805 large 5, stems	Inc. Ab.	29.00	37.00	50.00	77.00	200.	—
1806 small 6, stems	356,000	185.	295.	450.	775.	1650.	—
1806 small 6, stemless	Inc. Ab.	28.00	32.00	44.00	63.00	185.	1040.
1806 large 6, stems	Inc. Ab.	28.00	32.00	44.00	63.00	185.	—
1807	476,000	28.00	32.00	50.00	77.00	325.	1500.
1808/7	400,000	60.00	105.	200.	625.	—	—
1808	Inc. Ab.	29.00	37.00	50.00	77.00	330.	1050.

Classic Head

Designer: John Reich. **Size:** 23.5 millimeters. **Weight:** 5.44 grams. **Composition:** 100% copper. **Notes:** Restrikes listed were produced privately in the mid-1800s. The two varieties of the 1831 restrikes are distinguished by the size of the berries in the wreath on the reverse. The 1828 strikes have either 12 or 13 stars on the obverse.

Date	Mintage	G-4	VG-8	F-12	VF-20	XF-40	MS-60
1809/6	1,154,572	26.00	32.00	36.00	56.00	80.00	500.
1809	Inc. Ab.	21.00	30.00	36.00	53.00	75.00	475.
1810	215,000	31.00	36.00	45.00	105.	200.	1750.
1811	63,140	80.00	175.	550.	1100.	1950.	—

1825 Half Cent
Grade F-12

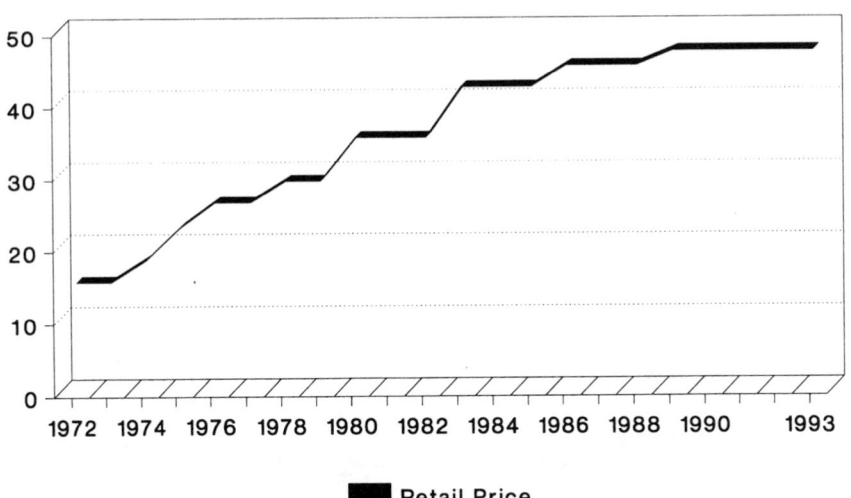

Retail Price

Source: COIN PRICES

Date	Mintage	G-4	VG-8	F-12	VF-20	XF-40	MS-60
1811 restrike, reverse of 1802, uncirculated						—	6500.
1825	63,000	33.00	39.00	47.00	67.00	225.	1000.
1826	234,000	28.00	35.00	40.00	56.00	110.	675.
1828 13 stars	606,000	21.00	30.00	35.00	44.00	57.00	220.
1828 12 stars	Inc. Ab.	25.00	35.00	40.00	56.00	80.00	500.
1829	487,000	25.00	32.00	35.00	46.00	69.00	600.
1831 original	2,200	—	—	—	4000.	5000.	7500.
1831 restrike, lg. berries, reverse of 1836, proof						—	6000.
1831 restrike, sm. berries, reverse of 1852, proof						—	7000.
1832	154,000	21.00	30.00	35.00	44.00	57.00	220.
1833	120,000	21.00	30.00	35.00	44.00	57.00	220.
1834	141,000	21.00	30.00	35.00	44.00	57.00	220.
1835	398,000	21.00	30.00	35.00	44.00	57.00	350.
1836 original	—	—		Proof only	—	—	6500.
1836 restrike, reverse of 1852, proof only						—	6500.

Coronet

Designer: Christian Gobrecht. **Size:** 23 millimeters. **Weight:** 5.44 grams. **Composition:** 100% copper. **Notes:** 1840-1848 strikes, both originals and restrikes, are known in proof only; mintages are unknown. The small-date varieties of the 1849, both originals and restrikes, are known in proof only. Restrikes were produced clandestinely by Philadelphia Mint personnel in the mid-1800s.

Date	Mintage	G-4	VG-8	F-12	VF-20	XF-40	MS-60	Prf-60
1840 original	—	—	—		Proof only	—	—	3800.
1840 restrike	—	—	—		Proof only	—	—	3200.
1841 original	—	—	—		Proof only	—	—	3800.
1841 restrike	—	—	—		Proof only	—	—	3000.
1842 original	—	—	—		Proof only	—	—	3800.
1842 restrike	—	—	—		Proof only	—	—	3200.
1843 original	—	—	—		Proof only	—	—	3800.
1843 restrike	—	—	—		Proof only	—	—	3200.
1844 original	—	—	—		Proof only	—	—	3800.
1844 restrike	—	—	—		Proof only	—	—	3200.
1845 restrike	—	—	—		Proof only	—	—	3800.
1845 restrike	—	—	—		Proof only	—	—	3200.
1846 original	—	—	—		Proof only	—	—	3800.
1846 restrike	—	—	—		Proof only	—	—	3200.
1847 original	—	—	—		Proof only	—	—	3800.
1847 restrike	—	—	—		Proof only	—	—	3200.
1848 original	—	—	—		Proof only	—	—	3800.
1848 restrike	—	—	—		Proof only	—	—	3200.
1849 original, small date		—	—		Proof only	—	—	3800.
1849 restrike small date		—	—		Proof only	—	—	3200.

Date	Mintage	G-4	VG-8	F-12	VF-20	XF-40	MS-60
1849 lg. date	39,864	39.00	43.00	50.00	58.00	80.00	400.
1850	39,812	36.00	40.00	48.00	55.00	80.00	400.
1851	147,672	27.00	34.00	43.00	50.00	63.00	160.
1852	—	—	—		Proof only	—	4250.
1853	129,694	27.00	34.00	43.00	50.00	63.00	160.
1854	55,358	29.00	37.00	44.00	52.00	75.00	160.
1855	56,500	29.00	37.00	44.00	52.00	75.00	160.
1856	40,430	35.00	39.00	50.00	60.00	85.00	275.
1857	35,180	50.00	55.00	65.00	80.00	110.	275.

Large cents

Flowing Hair

Chain reverse

Designer: Henry Voigt. **Size:** 26-27 millimeters. **Weight:** 13.48 grams. **Composition:** 100% copper.

Date	Mintage	G-4	VG-8	F-12	VF-20	XF-40	MS-60
1793 chain	36,103	2500.	4850.	6650.	9750.	25,000	—

Wreath reverse

Designer: Adam Eckfeldt. **Size:** 26-28 millimeters. **Weight:** 13.48 grams. **Composition:** 100% copper.

Date	Mintage	G-4	VG-8	F-12	VF-20	XF-40	MS-60
1793 wreath	63,353	975.	1450.	1950.	3750.	6950.	—

Liberty Cap

Designers: Joseph Wright (1793-1795) and John Smith Gardner (1795-1796). **Size:** 29 millimeters. **Weight:** 13.48 grams (1793-1795) and 10.89 grams (1795-1796). **Notes:** The heavier pieces were struck on thicker planchets. The Liberty design on the obverse was revised slightly in 1794, but the 1793 design was used on some 1794 strikes. The 1795 "lettered edge" variety has "One Hundred for a Dollar" and a leaf inscribed on the edge.

Date	Mintage	G-4	VG-8	F-12	VF-20	XF-40	MS-60
1793 cap	11,056	1850.	2800.	4500.	6000.	—	—
1794	918,521	165.	250.	440.	825.	1450.	—
1794 head '93	Inc. Ab.	325.	500.	1100.	2000.	—	—
1795	501,500	160.	200.	415.	725.	1400.	—
1795 lettered edge, "One Cent" high in wreath							
	37,000	180.	275.	450.	750.	1375.	—
1796 Lib. Cap	109,825	175.	260.	415.	900.	1650.	—

Draped Bust

Designer: Robert Scot. **Size:** 29 millimeters. **Weight:** 10.98 grams. **Composition:** 100% copper. **Notes:** The "stemless" variety does not have stems extending from the wreath above and on both sides of the fraction on the reverse. The 1801 "3 errors" variety has the fraction on the reverse reading "1/000", has only one stem extending from the wreath above and on both sides of the fraction on the reverse, and "United" in "United States of America" appears as "linited."

Date	Mintage	G-4	VG-8	F-12	VF-20	XF-40	MS-60
1796	363,375	70.00	90.00	165.	335.	750.	—
1797	897,510	40.00	60.00	125.	325.	750.	—
1797 stemless	Inc. Ab.	60.00	100.	200.	1500.	2250.	—
1798	1,841,745	30.00	50.00	125.	325.	700.	—
1798/97	Inc. Ab.	70.00	115.	185.	450.	800.	—
1799	42,540	900.	1650.	4000.	5900.	—	—
1800	2,822,175	37.00	45.00	110.	425.	700.	—
1801	1,362,837	37.00	45.00	110.	375.	690.	—
1801 3 errors	Inc. Ab.	37.00	65.00	170.	425.	700.	—
1802	3,435,100	35.00	42.00	95.00	285.	700.	2000.
1803	2,471,353	35.00	42.00	95.00	285.	665.	2000.
1804	756,838	600.	1000.	1800.	3250.	5000.	—
1805	941,116	35.00	42.00	100.	290.	665.	—
1806	348,000	40.00	65.00	125.	475.	750.	—
1807	727,221	30.00	42.00	120.	350.	665.	—

1804 Cent
Grade F-12

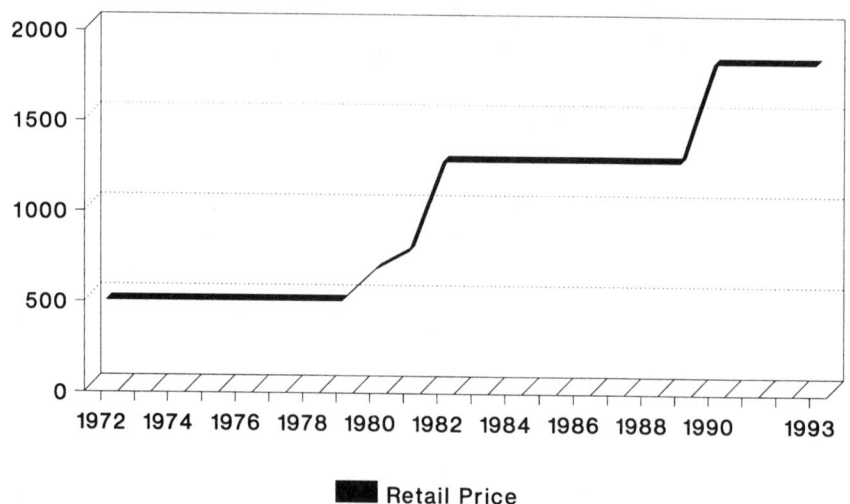

Retail Price

Source: COIN PRICES

Classic Head

Designer: John Reich. **Size:** 29 millimeters. **Weight:** 10.89 grams. **Composition:** 100% copper.

Date	Mintage	G-4	VG-8	F-12	VF-20	XF-40	MS-60
1808	1,109,000	33.00	65.00	195.	510.	1075.	3150.
1809	222,867	70.00	135.	250.	800.	1500.	—
1810	1,458,500	32.00	38.00	190.	500.	1075.	3150.
1811	218,025	65.00	105.	250.	695.	1070.	—
1812	1,075,500	33.00	42.00	190.	510.	1075.	3150.
1813	418,000	45.00	72.00	200.	600.	1200.	—
1814	357,830	32.00	38.00	190.	530.	1100.	3150.

Coronet

Designer: Robert Scot. **Size:** 28-29 millimeters. **Weight:** 10.89 grams. **Composition:** 100% copper. **Notes:** The 1817 strikes have either 13 or 15 stars on the obverse.

Date	Mintage	G-4	VG-8	F-12	VF-20	XF-40	MS-60
1816	2,820,982	12.50	17.00	30.00	70.00	120.	300.
1817 13 stars	3,948,400	11.00	13.00	21.00	40.00	100.	225.
1817 15 stars	Inc. Ab.	12.00	20.00	30.00	60.00	155.	450.
1818	3,167,000	10.00	13.00	21.00	40.00	100.	350.
1819	2,671,000	11.00	13.00	21.00	40.00	100.	315.
1820	4,407,550	11.00	13.00	21.00	40.00	100.	225.
1821	389,000	17.50	30.00	45.00	100.	250.	—
1822	2,072,339	11.00	15.00	24.00	46.00	135.	350.
1823	Inc. 1824	30.00	55.00	90.00	235.	650.	—
1823/22	Inc. 1824	27.00	45.00	65.00	175.	350.	1750.
1824	1,262,000	11.50	16.00	28.00	60.00	80.00	575.
1824/22	Inc. Ab.	20.00	95.00	220.	295.	—	1500.
1825	1,461,100	10.50	14.00	24.00	55.00	150.	350.
1826	1,517,425	10.50	14.00	24.00	50.00	130.	600.
1826/25	Inc. Ab.	18.00	30.00	60.00	115.	250.	800.
1827	2,357,732	10.50	12.50	20.00	45.00	115.	600.
1828	2,260,624	10.00	12.50	20.00	50.00	115.	300.
1829	1,414,500	10.50	13.00	21.00	45.00	120.	350.
1830	1,711,500	10.50	13.00	20.00	40.00	110.	325.
1831	3,359,260	9.50	10.50	16.50	35.00	100.	325.
1832	2,362,000	9.50	10.50	16.50	40.00	100.	325.
1833	2,739,000	9.50	10.50	16.50	35.00	100.	325.
1834	1,855,100	9.50	10.50	16.50	40.00	100.	350.
1835	3,878,400	9.50	10.50	16.50	40.00	100.	325.
1836	2,111,000	9.50	10.50	16.50	40.00	95.00	300.

Braided Hair

Designer: Christian Gobrecht. **Size:** 27.5 millimeters. **Weight:** 10.89 grams. **Composition:** 100% copper. **Notes:** 1840 and 1842 strikes have either small or large dates, with little difference in value. 1855 and 1856 strikes have either slanting or upright 5s in the date, with little difference in value. A slightly larger Liberty head and larger reverse lettering were used beginning in 1843. One 1843 variety uses the old obverse with the new reverse.

Date	Mintage	G-4	VG-8	F-12	VF-20	XF-40	MS-60
1837	5,558,300	9.50	10.50	16.50	33.00	90.00	300.
1838	6,370,200	9.50	10.50	16.50	33.00	80.00	225.
1839	3,128,661	9.50	10.50	16.50	42.00	100.	350.
1839/36	Inc. Ab.	175.	350.	750.	1500.	—	—
1840	2,462,700	9.50	10.50	11.50	19.00	58.00	265.
1841	1,597,367	10.00	12.00	15.00	23.00	68.00	300.
1842	2,383,390	9.50	10.50	11.50	18.00	55.00	265.
1843	2,425,342	9.50	10.50	17.00	25.00	65.00	225.
1843 obverse 1842 with reverse of 1844							
	Inc. Ab.	10.00	13.00	19.00	38.00	80.00	350.

Date	Mintage	G-4	VG-8	F-12	VF-20	XF-40	MS-60
1844	2,398,752	9.75	10.50	12.00	17.00	49.00	160.
1844/81	Inc. Ab.	12.00	20.00	28.00	60.00	130.	450.
1845	3,894,804	9.50	10.50	12.00	14.00	40.00	160.
1846	4,120,800	9.50	10.50	12.00	14.00	40.00	160.
1847	6,183,669	9.50	10.50	12.00	14.00	40.00	160.
1848	6,415,799	9.50	10.50	12.00	14.00	40.00	160.
1849	4,178,500	9.50	10.50	12.00	14.00	40.00	160.
1850	4,426,844	9.50	10.50	12.00	14.00	40.00	160.
1851	9,889,707	9.50	10.50	12.00	14.00	40.00	160.
1851/81	Inc. Ab.	10.00	12.50	18.00	35.00	95.00	400.
1852	5,063,094	9.50	10.50	12.00	14.00	40.00	160.
1853	6,641,131	9.50	10.50	12.00	14.00	40.00	160.
1854	4,236,156	9.50	10.50	12.00	14.00	40.00	160.
1855	1,574,829	9.75	11.00	14.00	17.00	45.00	170.
1856	2,690,463	9.50	10.50	12.00	14.00	40.00	160.
1857	333,456	25.00	28.00	35.00	55.00	85.00	300.

Small cents

Flying Eagle

Large letters; "AM" connected   Small letters; "AM" separated

Designer: James B. Longacre. **Size:** 19 millimeters. **Weight:** 4.67 grams. **Composition:** 88% copper, 12% nickel. **Notes:** On the large-letter variety of 1858, the "A" and "M" in "America" are connected at their bases; on the small-letter variety, the two letters are separated.

Date	Mintage	G-4	VG-8	F-12	VF-20	XF-40	AU-50	MS-60	MS-65	Prf-65
1856	Est. 1,000	2600.	3000.	3500.	3850.	4200.	4600.	5250.	16,000.	21,000.
1857	17,450,000	14.00	15.00	20.00	36.00	70.00	150.	225.	2600.	17,500.
1858 LL	24,600,000	14.00	15.00	24.00	40.00	105.	160.	225.	2600.	19,500.
1858 SL	Inc. Ab.	14.00	15.00	24.00	40.00	105.	160.	225.	2600.	13,000.

Indian Head

1859   1860-1909   1864 "L"

Copper-nickel composition

Designer: James B. Longacre. **Size:** 19 millimeters. **Weight:** 4.67 grams. **Composition:** 88% copper, 12% nickel.

Date	Mintage	G-4	VG-8	F-12	VF-20	XF-40	AU-50	MS-60	MS-65	Prf-65
1859	36,400,000	6.00	7.75	11.00	31.00	75.00	125.	145.	2200.	4900.
1860	20,566,000	4.50	6.75	9.50	15.00	42.00	60.00	140.	975.	1950.
1861	10,100,000	11.00	18.00	23.00	37.00	75.00	145.	200.	975.	1955.
1862	28,075,000	3.75	5.00	7.50	14.50	25.00	55.00	100.	950.	1850.
1863	49,840,000	3.00	4.00	6.00	11.50	22.00	40.00	55.00	950.	1950.
1864	13,740,000	9.00	14.00	19.50	25.00	42.00	70.00	140.	950.	2100.

1857 Cent
Grade XF-40

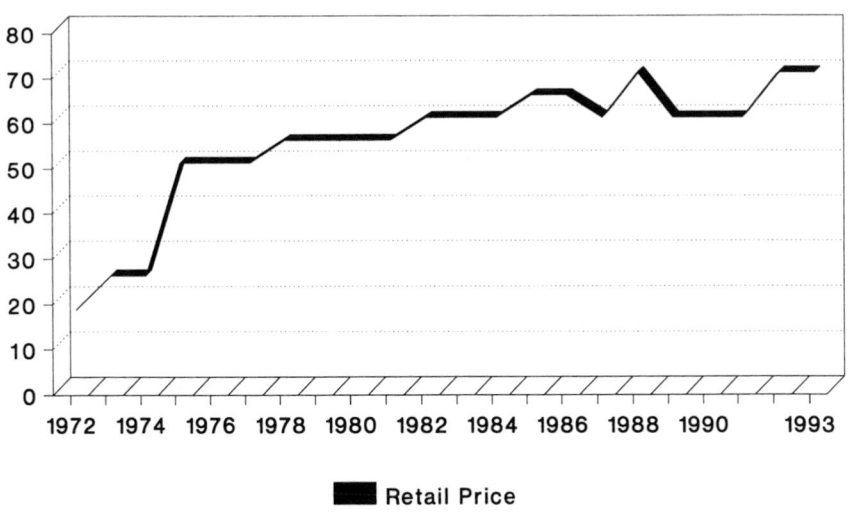

■ Retail Price

Source: COIN PRICES

Bronze composition

Weight: 3.11 grams. **Composition:** 95% copper, 5% tin and zinc. **Notes:** The 1864 "L" variety has the designer's initial in Liberty's hair to the right of her neck.

Date	Mintage	G-4	VG-8	F-12	VF-20	XF-40	AU-50	MS-60	MS-65	Prf-65
1864	39,233,714	4.00	8.50	13.00	22.00	37.00	50.00	77.00	450.	1850.
1864 L	Inc. Ab.	35.00	48.00	62.00	105.	180.	210.	315.	1150.	35,000.
1865	35,429,286	4.00	7.00	9.50	19.50	30.00	42.00	76.00	400.	630.
1866	9,826,500	29.00	33.00	45.00	74.00	135.	175.	240.	840.	725.
1867	9,821,000	29.00	33.00	45.00	74.00	135.	175.	250.	945.	1000.
1868	10,266,500	29.00	33.00	45.00	74.00	135.	175.	240.	850.	600.
1869/8	6,420,000	115.	175.	275.	375.	495.	595.	975.	2400.	—
1869	Inc. Ab.	40.00	63.00	150.	235.	265.	295.	420.	1100.	1150.
1870	5,275,000	32.00	57.00	155.	220.	260.	350.	470.	1100.	950.
1871	3,929,500	42.00	70.00	168.	230.	265.	350.	470.	1200.	1050.
1872	4,042,000	55.00	85.00	210.	280.	350.	370.	490.	1675.	1400.
1873	11,676,500	13.00	18.00	38.00	45.00	75.00	85.00	170.	595.	560.
1874	14,187,500	10.00	13.00	22.00	39.00	65.00	77.00	170.	500.	490.
1875	13,528,000	10.00	13.00	22.00	39.00	65.00	77.00	170.	595.	595.
1876	7,944,000	19.00	24.00	37.00	55.00	87.50	115.	190.	630.	600.
1877	852,500	265.	325.	475.	675.	1150.	1450.	2200.	4900.	4150.
1878	5,799,850	23.00	32.00	40.00	67.00	110.	125.	190.	595.	450.
1879	16,231,200	3.50	4.75	8.00	14.00	30.00	40.00	63.00	385.	450.
1880	38,964,955	2.00	3.75	5.50	7.50	20.00	30.00	63.00	350.	450.
1881	39,211,575	2.00	3.75	5.50	7.50	18.50	25.00	35.00	280.	440.
1882	38,581,100	2.00	3.75	5.50	7.50	16.00	25.00	35.00	280.	440.
1883	45,589,109	2.00	3.75	5.50	7.50	16.00	25.00	35.00	280.	440.
1884	23,261,742	2.50	4.00	6.00	10.00	20.00	30.00	50.00	335.	440.
1885	11,765,384	4.00	6.50	12.00	19.50	32.00	39.00	100.	490.	465.
1886	17,654,290	3.00	5.00	10.00	28.00	42.50	57.00	105.	490.	465.
1887	45,226,483	1.30	1.80	3.00	4.95	13.50	25.00	35.00	245.	465.
1888	37,494,414	1.30	1.80	3.00	4.95	13.50	25.00	35.00	350.	465.
1889	48,869,361	1.30	1.65	2.75	4.50	12.00	25.00	35.00	250.	430.
1890	57,182,854	1.30	1.65	2.50	4.50	10.00	23.00	35.00	250.	490.
1891	47,072,350	1.30	1.65	2.50	4.50	10.00	23.00	35.00	250.	440.
1892	37,649,832	1.30	1.65	2.50	4.50	10.00	23.00	35.00	250.	500.
1893	46,642,195	1.30	1.65	2.50	4.50	10.00	23.00	35.00	250.	630.
1894	16,752,132	1.75	3.00	6.50	10.00	18.00	32.00	48.00	375.	575.
1895	38,343,636	1.00	1.75	2.50	4.00	10.00	19.00	30.00	165.	500.

1864-L Cent
Grade F-12

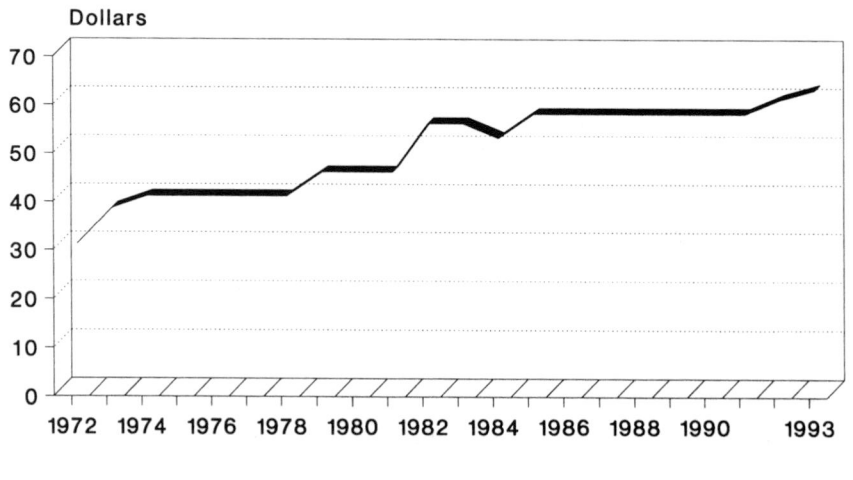

Dollars

Retail Price

Source: COIN PRICES

Date	Mintage	G-4	VG-8	F-12	VF-20	XF-40	AU-50	MS-60	MS-65	Prf-65
1896	39,057,293	1.00	1.75	2.50	4.00	10.00	17.00	30.00	160.	525.
1897	50,466,330	1.00	1.75	2.50	4.00	10.00	17.00	30.00	160.	440.
1898	49,823,079	1.00	1.75	2.50	4.00	10.00	17.00	30.00	160.	440.
1899	53,600,031	.90	1.30	2.00	3.50	9.50	17.00	30.00	160.	440.
1900	66,833,764	.90	1.20	2.00	3.50	9.50	15.00	22.00	135.	430.
1901	79,611,143	.80	.95	1.25	2.25	7.50	15.00	22.00	135.	430.
1902	87,376,722	.80	.95	1.25	2.25	7.50	15.00	22.00	135.	430.
1903	85,094,493	.80	.95	1.25	2.25	7.50	15.00	22.00	135.	440.
1904	61,328,015	.80	.95	1.25	2.25	7.50	15.00	22.00	135.	430.
1905	80,719,163	.80	.95	1.25	2.25	7.50	15.00	22.00	135.	430.
1906	96,022,255	.80	.95	1.25	2.25	7.50	15.00	22.00	135.	430.
1907	108,138,618	.80	.95	1.25	2.25	7.50	15.00	22.00	135.	440.
1908	32,327,987	.80	.95	1.50	2.50	7.50	15.00	22.00	135.	430.
1908S	1,115,000	25.00	27.00	30.00	35.00	72.00	115.	160.	420.	—
1909	14,370,645	1.50	2.00	2.65	4.50	9.00	19.00	31.00	135.	450.
1909S	309,000	170.	175.	195.	210.	275.	325.	385.	675.	—

Lincoln

"V.D.B."

Wheat reverse, bronze composition

Designer: Victor D. Brenner. **Size:** 19 millimeters. **Weight:** 3.11 grams. **Composition:** 95% copper, 5% tin and zinc. **Notes:** The 1909 "V.D.B." varieties have the designer's initials inscribed at the 6 o'clock position on the reverse. Later in 1909 the initials were removed until 1918, when they were placed on the obverse.

PRICING SECTION

1914-D Cent
Grade F-12

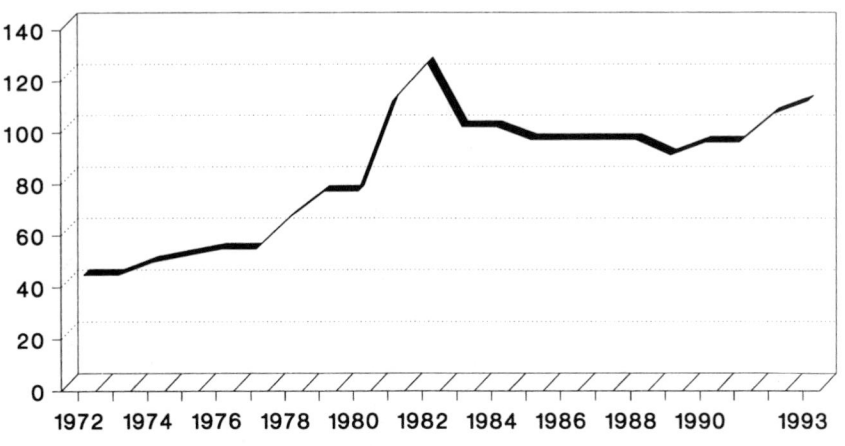

■ Retail Price

Source: COIN PRICES

Date	Mintage	G-4	VG-8	F-12	VF-20	XF-40	AU-50	MS-60	MS-65	Prf-65
1909	72,702,618	.50	.55	.85	1.35	2.25	5.50	15.00	85.00	450.
1909VDB	27,995,000	2.10	2.30	2.40	2.75	3.50	6.00	10.00	65.00	2800.
1909S	1,825,000	42.00	46.00	53.00	60.00	95.00	120.	155.	300.	—
1909SVDB	484,000	325.	365.	420.	435.	450.	475.	510.	1600.	—
1910	146,801,218	.15	.20	.25	.60	2.50	4.75	15.00	91.00	530.
1910S	6,045,000	7.00	7.75	8.50	12.00	22.00	49.00	87.00	230.	—
1911	101,177,787	.25	.30	.50	1.95	4.90	7.00	18.00	170.	775.
1911D	12,672,000	4.25	5.50	6.10	11.50	30.00	50.00	77.00	700.	—
1911S	4,026,000	16.50	19.50	21.00	22.00	31.00	65.00	120.	770.	—
1912	68,153,060	.50	.85	1.85	3.90	12.00	18.00	25.00	155.	380.
1912D	10,411,000	4.50	5.60	7.85	15.00	39.50	54.00	120.	840.	—
1912S	4,431,000	12.00	12.75	14.25	17.25	40.00	52.00	105.	975.	—
1913	76,532,352	.35	.50	1.25	3.50	9.50	11.00	23.00	210.	380.
1913D	15,804,000	2.00	2.50	3.00	7.00	24.00	40.00	84.00	875.	—
1913S	6,101,000	6.00	6.75	7.75	12.00	30.00	51.00	110.	1250.	—
1914	75,238,432	.35	.40	1.50	3.75	10.00	18.50	40.00	210.	380.
1914D	1,193,000	84.00	91.00	110.	170.	400.	595.	840.	4300.	—
1914S	4,137,000	8.00	10.50	12.00	19.50	40.00	63.00	175.	3900.	—
1915	29,092,120	1.10	1.35	3.90	10.75	41.00	60.00	91.00	335.	380.
1915D	22,050,000	1.00	1.25	2.20	3.50	10.00	22.00	49.00	350.	—
1915S	4,833,000	7.00	8.50	9.00	11.50	31.00	46.00	100.	1550.	—
1916	131,833,677	.15	.20	.45	1.50	4.50	5.00	10.00	85.00	650.
1916D	35,956,000	.25	.35	1.25	2.50	9.50	28.00	53.00	980.	—
1916S	22,510,000	.60	1.00	1.50	2.50	9.00	26.00	60.00	2800.	—
1917	196,429,785	.10	.15	.25	.50	2.75	5.00	11.00	120.	—
1917D	55,120,000	.30	.40	1.00	2.20	7.50	24.00	56.00	560.	—
1917S	32,620,000	.35	.55	.80	2.20	6.75	32.50	60.00	1475.	—
1918	288,104,634	.10	.15	.35	.60	2.50	7.25	11.00	125.	—
1918D	47,830,000	.25	.35	1.00	2.00	7.00	15.00	51.00	840.	—
1918S	34,680,000	.35	.50	.80	2.00	6.50	18.50	59.00	2800.	—
1919	392,021,000	.10	.15	.20	.50	2.00	5.00	8.50	63.00	—
1919D	57,154,000	.20	.30	.60	2.20	7.50	11.00	45.00	450.	—
1919S	139,760,000	.20	.25	.50	.85	2.00	7.00	30.00	735.	—
1920	310,165,000	.10	.15	.20	.45	2.50	5.00	9.75	77.00	—
1920D	49,280,000	.20	.35	.75	2.00	8.00	13.00	53.00	560.	—
1920S	46,220,000	.20	.30	.40	1.25	4.00	14.00	77.00	2800.	—
1921	39,157,000	.25	.35	.60	2.00	5.75	12.00	39.00	180.	—
1921S	15,274,000	.75	.85	1.50	3.50	12.00	50.00	125.	2500.	—
1922D	7,160,000	5.85	6.75	7.00	10.50	18.00	42.00	70.00	490.	—
1922	Inc. Ab.	175.	240.	335.	540.	2100.	3350.	5600.	23,500.	—
1923	74,723,000	.20	.30	.35	1.80	6.00	7.00	9.75	155.	—

Date	Mintage	G-4	VG-8	F-12	VF-20	XF-40	AU-50	MS-60	MS-65	Prf-65
1923S	8,700,000	1.70	1.90	3.00	5.00	20.00	70.00	190.	2450.	—
1924	75,178,000	.20	.25	.30	1.50	5.75	7.00	22.00	170.	—
1924D	2,520,000	9.00	10.50	12.00	19.00	48.00	100.	235.	2800.	—
1924S	11,696,000	.75	1.10	1.50	3.75	16.00	28.00	120.	2500.	—
1925	139,949,000	.10	.15	.20	.85	2.50	4.50	8.50	63.00	—
1925D	22,580,000	.40	.45	.70	2.90	7.50	12.00	47.00	1100.	—
1925S	26,380,000	.30	.35	.45	1.25	6.75	14.00	61.00	2500.	—
1926	157,088,000	.10	.15	.20	.85	2.00	3.50	7.00	35.00	—
1926D	28,020,000	.30	.35	.65	1.75	4.00	10.00	45.00	1050.	—
1926S	4,550,000	3.50	3.75	4.00	4.75	11.00	50.00	100.	3000.	—
1927	144,440,000	.10	.15	.25	.85	2.00	3.75	7.25	70.00	—
1927D	27,170,000	.25	.30	.45	1.00	3.25	9.50	35.00	735.	—
1927S	14,276,000	.60	.70	1.60	3.00	9.50	16.00	65.00	1200.	—
1928	134,116,000	.10	.15	.20	.80	2.00	3.75	7.00	63.00	—
1928D	31,170,000	.25	.30	.35	.75	2.25	7.00	20.00	295.	—
1928S	17,266,000	.45	.50	.70	1.75	3.50	9.00	46.00	560.	—
1929	185,262,000	.15	.20	.25	.80	1.50	3.75	5.50	70.00	—
1929D	41,730,000	.15	.20	.25	.45	2.00	5.00	16.00	135.	—
1929S	50,148,000	.15	.20	.25	1.00	2.25	3.75	7.75	135.	—
1930	157,415,000	.15	.20	.30	.45	1.50	2.50	4.25	35.00	—
1930D	40,100,000	.15	.20	.30	.50	1.75	5.75	12.00	70.00	—
1930S	24,286,000	.20	.25	.35	.70	1.60	4.00	7.00	49.00	—
1931	19,396,000	.40	.50	.65	1.00	2.50	6.00	16.50	91.00	—
1931D	4,480,000	2.85	2.95	3.50	4.00	7.00	24.00	45.00	300.	—
1931S	866,000	32.00	35.00	37.00	39.00	42.00	49.00	59.00	245.	—
1932	9,062,000	1.95	2.10	2.15	2.25	3.50	9.00	17.50	56.00	—
1932D	10,500,000	.90	1.00	1.10	1.35	3.75	9.00	14.00	56.00	—
1933	14,360,000	1.15	1.25	1.50	1.80	3.75	9.00	16.00	63.00	—
1933D	6,200,000	2.00	2.10	2.25	2.50	4.50	11.00	17.00	36.00	—
1934	219,080,000	—	.10	.15	.20	.75	1.50	3.00	15.00	—
1934D	28,446,000	.10	.15	.20	.25	2.00	6.50	18.00	35.00	—
1935	245,338,000	—	.10	.15	.20	.75	1.00	1.50	7.75	—
1935D	47,000,000	—	.10	.15	.20	.75	3.00	4.50	15.00	—
1935S	38,702,000	—	.20	.25	.30	2.25	5.00	10.00	42.00	—
1936	309,637,569	—	.10	.15	.20	.75	1.00	1.50	6.25	700.
1936D	40,620,000	—	.10	.15	.25	.75	1.50	1.75	9.00	—
1936S	29,130,000	.10	.15	.25	.30	.75	1.75	2.25	10.00	—
1937	309,179,320	—	.10	.15	.20	.70	.90	1.00	6.25	275.
1937D	50,430,000	—	.10	.15	.25	.70	1.00	1.90	7.70	—
1937S	34,500,000	—	.10	.15	.25	.60	1.50	1.75	10.50	—
1938	156,696,734	—	.10	.15	.20	.50	1.00	1.60	7.00	175.
1938D	20,010,000	.15	.15	.25	.30	.75	1.50	2.00	9.00	—
1938S	15,180,000	.30	.35	.45	.60	.80	1.25	1.80	11.00	—
1939	316,479,520	—	.10	.15	.20	.25	.40	.65	4.25	165.
1939D	15,160,000	.35	.40	.50	.60	.85	1.90	2.25	12.50	—
1939S	52,070,000	—	.15	.20	.25	.45	.90	1.15	15.00	—
1940	586,825,872	—	—	.15	.20	.25	.40	.85	4.25	150.
1940D	81,390,000	—	.10	.15	.20	.25	.50	.90	5.25	—
1940S	112,940,000	—	.10	.15	.20	.25	.75	1.00	7.00	—
1941	887,039,100	—	—	—	—	.15	.30	.85	4.25	150.
1941D	128,700,000	—	—	—	.10	.15	1.00	1.75	8.50	—
1941S	92,360,000	—	—	—	.10	.15	1.25	2.00	9.00	—
1942	657,828,600	—	—	—	—	.15	.25	.50	2.75	150.
1942D	206,698,000	—	—	—	.10	.15	.25	.50	4.25	—
1942S	85,590,000	—	—	—	.15	.25	1.50	4.00	24.00	—

Steel composition

Weight: 2.7 grams. **Composition:** steel coated with zinc.

Date	Mintage	G-4	VG-8	F-12	VF-20	XF-40	AU-50	MS-60	MS-65	Prf-65
1943	684,628,670	—	—	—	—	.40	.60	.70	2.80	—
1943D	217,660,000	—	—	—	—	.45	.65	1.00	5.00	—
1943S	191,550,000	—	—	—	—	.45	.70	1.50	8.50	—

Copper-zinc composition

Weight: 3.11 grams. **Composition:** 95% copper, 5% zinc. **Notes:** The 1955 "doubled die" has distinct doubling of the date and lettering on the obverse.

Date	Mintage	XF-40	MS-60	Prf-65	Date	Mintage	XF-40	MS-60	Prf-65
1944	1,435,400,000	.10	.40	—	1946S	198,100,000	.15	.50	—
1944D	430,578,000	.10	.45	—	1947	190,555,000	.15	1.00	—
1944D/S	—	150.	375.	—	1947D	194,750,000	.10	.40	—
1944S	282,760,000	.15	.45	—	1947S	99,000,000	.15	.45	—
1945	1,040,515,000	.10	.50	—	1948	317,570,000	.10	.50	—
1945D	226,268,000	.10	.70	—	1948D	172,637,000	.10	.45	—
1945S	181,770,000	.15	.45	—	1948S	81,735,000	.15	.50	—
1946	991,655,000	.10	.30	—	1949	217,775,000	.10	.40	—
1946D	315,690,000	.10	.45	—	1949D	153,132,000	.10	.40	—

Date	Mintage	XF-40	MS-60	Prf-65
1949S	64,290,000	.20	1.00	—
1950	272,686,386	.10	.50	35.00
1950D	334,950,000	.10	.50	—
1950S	118,505,000	.15	.80	—
1951	295,633,500	.10	.90	35.00
1951D	625,355,000	.10	.50	—
1951S	136,010,000	.15	.75	—
1952	186,856,980	.10	.50	33.00
1952D	746,130,000	.10	.50	—
1952S	137,800,004	.15	.75	—
1953	256,883,800	.10	.50	23.00
1953D	700,515,000	.10	.50	—
1953S	181,835,000	.15	.45	—

Date	Mintage	XF-40	MS-60	Prf-65
1954	71,873,350	.15	.75	11.50
1954D	251,552,500	.10	.25	—
1954S	96,190,000	.15	.35	—
1955	330,958,000	.10	.20	10.00
1955 doubled die	—	440.	700.	—
1955D	563,257,500	.10	.20	—
1955S	44,610,000	.25	.60	—
1956	421,414,384	—	.15	1.95
1956D	1,098,201,100	—	.15	—
1957	283,787,952	—	.15	.95
1957D	1,051,342,000	—	.15	—
1958	253,400,652	—	.15	1.40
1958D	800,953,300	—	.15	—

Lincoln Memorial reverse

Reverse designer: Frank Gasparro. **Weight:** 3.11 grams (1959-82) and 2.5 grams (1982-present). **Composition:** 95% copper, 5% tin and zinc (1959-62); 95% copper, 5% zinc (1962-82); and 97.6% zinc, 2.4% copper (1982-present). **Notes:** The dates were modified in 1960, 1970 and 1982, resulting in large-date and small-date varieties for those years. The 1972 "doubled die" shows doubling of "In God We Trust." The 1979-S Type II proof has a clearer mintmark than the Type I proof. Some 1982 cents have the predominantly copper composition; others have the predominantly zinc composition. They can be distinguished by weight. The 1983 "doubled die reverse" shows doubling of "United States of America." The 1984 "doubled die" shows doubling of Lincoln's ear on the obverse.

Date	Mintage	XF-40	MS-65	Prf-65
1959	610,864,291	—	.20	.70
1959D	1,279,760,000	—	.20	—
1960 small date	588,096,602	1.60	4.50	15.00
1960 large date	Inc. Ab.	—	.15	.50
1960D small date	1,580,884,000	—	.25	—
1960D large date	Inc. Ab.	—	.15	—
1961	756,373,244	—	.15	.40
1961D	1,753,266,700	—	.15	—
1962	609,263,019	—	.15	.40
1962D	1,793,148,400	—	.15	—
1963	757,185,645	—	.15	.40
1963D	1,774,020,400	—	.15	—
1964	2,652,525,762	—	.15	.40
1964D	3,799,071,500	—	.15	—
1965	1,497,224,900	—	.15	—
1966	2,188,147,783	—	.15	—
1967	3,048,667,100	—	.15	—
1968	1,707,880,970	—	.15	—
1968D	2,886,269,600	—	.15	—
1968S	261,311,510	—	.15	1.10
1969	1,136,910,000	—	.25	—
1969D	4,002,832,200	—	.15	—
1969S	547,309,631	—	.15	.95
1970	1,898,315,000	—	.15	—
1970D	2,891,438,900	—	.15	—
1970S	693,192,814	—	.15	.65
1970S small date	—	—	42.00	—
1971	1,919,490,000	—	.25	—
1971D	2,911,045,600	—	.25	—
1971S	528,354,192	—	.15	.85
1972	2,933,255,000	—	.15	—
1972 doubled die	—	120.	250.	—
1972D	2,665,071,400	—	.15	—
1972S	380,200,104	—	.15	.80
1973	3,728,245,000	—	.10	—
1973D	3,549,576,588	—	.10	—
1973S	319,937,634	—	.15	.70
1974	4,232,140,523	—	.10	—
1974D	4,235,098,000	—	.10	—
1974S	412,039,228	—	.15	.75
1975	5,451,476,142	—	.10	—
1975D	4,505,245,300	—	.10	—
1975S	(2,845,450)	—	—	4.50

Date	Mintage	XF-40	MS-65	Prf-65
1976	4,674,292,426	—	.10	—
1976D	4,221,592,455	—	.10	—
1976S	(4,149,730)	—	—	3.00
1977	4,469,930,000	—	.10	—
1977D	4,149,062,300	—	.10	—
1977S	(3,251,152)	—	—	1.95
1978	5,558,605,000	—	.10	—
1978D	4,280,233,400	—	.10	—
1978S	(3,127,781)	—	—	1.90
1979	6,018,515,000	—	.10	—
1979D	4,139,357,254	—	.10	—
1979S T-I	(3,677,175)	—	—	2.30
1979S T-II	(Inc. Ab.)	—	—	2.20
1980	7,414,705,000	—	.10	—
1980D	5,140,098,660	—	.10	—
1980S	(3,554,806)	—	—	1.35
1981	7,491,750,000	—	.10	—
1981D	5,373,235,677	—	.10	—
1981S T-I	(4,063,083)	—	—	1.00
1981S T-II	(Inc. Ab.)	—	—	7.50
1982 copper large date	10,712,525,000	—	.10	—
1982 copper small date		—	.15	—
1982 zinc large date		—	.35	—
1982 zinc small date		—	.75	—
1982D copper large date	6,012,979,368	—	.10	—
1982D zinc large date		—	.20	—
1982D zinc small date		—	.10	—
1982S	(3,857,479)	—	.10	1.65
1983	7,752,355,000	—	.10	—
1983 doubled die rev.	—	—	195.	—
1983D	6,467,199,428	—	.10	—
1983S	(3,279,126)	—	—	4.00
1984	8,151,079,000	—	.10	—
1984 doubled die	—	—	130.	—
1984D	5,569,238,906	—	.25	—
1984S	(3,065,110)	—	—	4.25
1985	5,648,489,887	—	.10	—
1985D	5,287,399,926	—	.10	—
1985S	(3,362,821)	—	—	3.95
1986	4,491,395,493	—	.15	—
1986D	4,442,866,698	—	.10	—
1986S	(3,010,497)	—	—	7.95
1987	4,682,466,931	—	.10	—
1987D	4,879,389,514	—	.10	—
1987S	(4,227,728)	—	—	3.95

1955 doubled die

1972 doubled die

1983 doubled die

Small date

Large date

Large date

Small date

Large date

Small date

Date	Mintage	XF-40	MS-65	Prf-65	Date	Mintage	XF-40	MS-65	Prf-65
1988	6,092,810,000	—	.10	—	1991	—	—	.10	—
1988D	5,253,740,443	—	.10	—	1991D	—	—	.10	—
1988S	(3,262,948)	—	—	4.50	1991S	Proof only	—	—	5.00
1989	7,261,535,000	—	.10	—	1992	—	—	.10	—
1989D	5,345,467,111	—	.10	—	1992D	—	—	.10	—
1989S	(3,220,194)	—	—	6.25	1992S	Proof only	—	—	6.00
1990	6,851,765,000	—	.10	—	1993	—	—	—	—
1990D	4,922,894,533	—	.10	—	1993D	—	—	—	—
1990S	Proof only	—	—	6.75	1993S	Proof only	—	—	6.00
1990 no S	—	—	—	1800.					

Two-cent

Small motto

Large motto

Designer: James B. Longacre. **Size:** 23 millimeters. **Weight:** 6.22 grams. **Composition:** 95% copper, 5% tin and zinc. **Notes:** The motto "In God We Trust" was modified in 1864, resulting in small-motto and large-motto varieties for that year.

Date	Mintage	G-4	VG-8	F-12	VF-20	XF-40	AU-50	MS-60	MS-65	Prf-65
1864 SM	19,847,500.	50.00	66.00	85.00	135.	220.	325.	550.	1700.	30,000.
1864 LM	Inc. Ab.	6.50	10.00	18.00	19.50	27.00	45.00	100.	400.	1350.
1865	13,640,000	6.50	10.00	18.00	19.50	27.00	45.00	100.	400.	1350.
1866	3,177,000	6.50	10.00	18.00	19.50	27.00	45.00	100.	510.	1350.
1867	2,938,750	6.50	10.00	18.00	19.50	27.00	60.00	110.	400.	1400.
1868	2,803,750	6.50	10.00	18.00	21.00	33.00	65.00	145.	440.	1375.
1869	1,546,000	7.00	11.00	18.00	22.00	36.00	75.00	135.	410.	1375.
1870	861,250	8.00	12.00	18.50	32.50	57.00	90.00	210.	630.	1375.
1871	721,250	10.00	15.00	21.00	40.00	75.00	120.	235.	690.	1400.
1872	65,000	65.00	95.00	150.	210.	325.	450.	720.	2750.	1350.
1873	Est. 1100	—	—	Proof only				—	—	2000.
		Impaired proof		750.	800.	850.	900.			

Silver three-cent

Type I

Designer: James B. Longacre. **Size:** 14 millimeters. **Weight:** 0.8 grams. **Composition:** 75% silver (0.0193 ounces), 25% copper. **Notes:** The Type I design has no outlines in the star.

Date	Mintage	G-4	VG-8	F-12	VF-20	XF-40	AU-50	MS-60	MS-65	Prf-65
1851	5,447,400	10.00	12.00	15.00	23.00	65.00	120.	145.	1350.	—
1851O	720,000	16.00	19.00	33.00	54.00	130.	225.	375.	4200.	—
1852	18,663,500	9.00	12.00	15.00	23.00	60.00	130.	165.	1350.	—
1853	11,400,000	9.00	12.00	15.00	23.00	50.00	130.	145.	1350.	—

Type II

Weight: 0.75 grams. **Composition:** 90% silver (0.0218 ounces), 10% copper. **Notes:** The Type II design has three lines outlining the star.

1851-O Silver Three-Cent
Grade XF-40

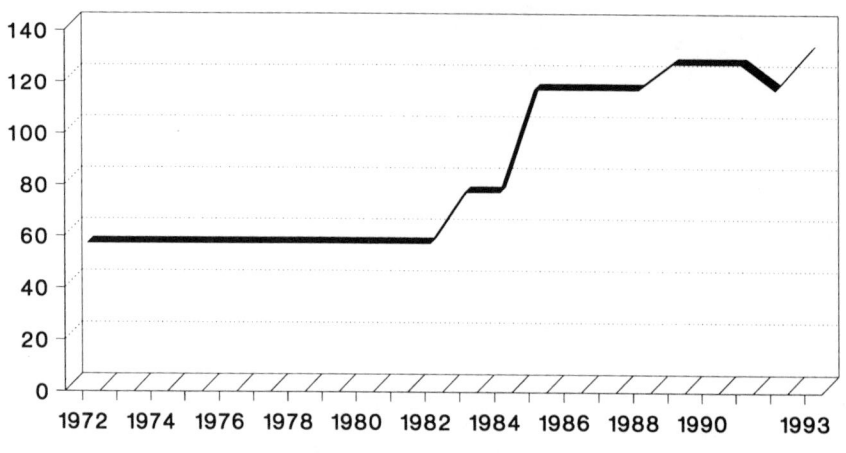

■ Retail Price

Source: COIN PRICES

Date	Mintage	G-4	VG-8	F-12	VF-20	XF-40	AU-50	MS-60	MS-65	Prf-65
1854	671,000	12.00	14.50	23.00	37.50	110.	230.	310.	7000.	25,000.
1855	139,000	16.50	24.00	42.00	85.00	250.	440.	14,500.	15,000.
1856	1,458,000	11.50	14.00	19.00	35.00	95.00	210.	230.	8400.	—
1857	1,042,000	11.50	14.00	19.00	35.00	85.00	225.	310.	7000.	8000.
1858	1,604,000	11.50	14.00	22.00	40.00	95.00	210.	230.	7000.	8000.

Type III

Notes: The Type III design has two lines outlining the star.

Date	Mintage	G-4	VG-8	F-12	VF-20	XF-40	AU-50	MS-60	MS-65	Prf-65
1859	365,000	11.50	14.00	19.00	32.00	55.00	125.	140.	1250.	3250.
1860	287,000	11.50	14.00	19.00	32.00	55.00	125.	140.	1250.	7500.
1861	498,000	11.50	14.00	19.00	32.00	68.00	125.	140.	1250.	2850.
1862	343,550	11.50	14.00	19.00	32.00	55.00	125.	140.	1250.	3000.
1863	21,460	200.	225.	280.	315.	350.	375.	565.	2750.	2750.
1864	12,470	250.	275.	325.	375.	425.	465.	565.	2550.	2750.
1865	8,500	260.	300.	350.	375.	400.	450.	565.	3125.	2750.
1866	22,725	225.	250.	280.	325.	375.	450.	600.	2750.	2750.
1867	4,625	285.	325.	350.	375.	400.	485.	625.	5050.	2250.
1868	4,100	285.	325.	350.	375.	400.	440.	625.	7200.	2250.
1869	5,100	285.	325.	350.	375.	460.	525.	625.	5200.	2750.
1870	4,000	285.	325.	350.	375.	400.	440.	625.	6400.	2750.
1871	4,360	285.	325.	350.	375.	400.	595.	750.	2500.	2750.
1872	1,950	325.	375.	450.	550.	650.	750.	950.	6400.	2250.
1873	600	—	—	Proof only		—	—	—	—	2850.
		Impaired proof		750.	850.	950.	1200.	—	—	—

Nickel three-cent

Designer: James B. Longacre. **Size:** 17.9 millimeters. **Weight:** 1.94 grams. **Composition:** 75% copper, 25% nickel.

Date	Mintage	G-4	VG-8	F-12	VF-20	XF-40	AU-50	MS-60	MS-65	Prf-65
1865	11,382,000	5.00	6.25	6.75	7.50	15.00	37.50	95.00	900.	1700.
1866	4,801,000	5.00	6.25	6.75	7.50	15.00	37.50	95.00	9000.	1075.
1867	3,915,000	5.00	6.25	6.75	7.50	15.00	37.50	95.00	900.	1000.
1868	3,252,000	5.00	6.25	6.75	7.50	15.00	37.50	95.00	900.	1025.
1869	1,604,000	5.50	6.50	7.00	7.75	15.00	40.00	95.00	900.	950.
1870	1,335,000	6.25	6.75	7.50	8.50	16.00	42.00	100.	900.	1025.
1871	604,000	6.25	6.75	8.00	11.00	18.00	45.00	100.	900.	950.
1872	862,000	6.00	6.50	7.25	10.00	17.00	43.00	100.	1250.	875.
1873	1,173,000	6.00	6.25	7.50	8.50	16.00	42.00	100.	2400.	900.
1874	790,000	6.25	7.00	7.50	9.00	17.00	43.00	110.	2000.	875.
1875	228,000	7.50	8.00	10.50	16.00	25.00	63.00	160.	900.	1125.
1876	162,000	10.00	12.50	17.00	24.00	38.00	100.	175.	2150.	875.
1877	Est. 900	—	—		Proof only	—	—	—	—	1625.
		Impaired proof		875.	900.	950.	975.	—	—	—
1878	2,350	—	—		Proof only	—	—	—	—	800.
		Impaired proof		375.	400.	425.	450.	—	—	—
1879	41,200	45.00	50.00	60.00	70.00	80.00	120.	240.	900.	750.
1880	24,955	63.00	70.00	80.00	100.	130.	150.	265.	900.	750.
1881	1,080,575	5.00	6.25	6.75	7.50	14.00	38.00	65.00	900.	750.
1882	25,300	63.00	70.00	80.00	90.00	110.	145.	250.	1000.	750.
1883	10,609	125.	145.	175.	200.	240.	270.	375.	2900.	750.
1884	5,642	290.	330.	350.	380.	425.	450.	550.	4800.	750.
1885	4,790	350.	380.	425.	460.	500.	600.	725.	1950.	825.
1886	4,290	—	—		Proof only	—	—	—	—	750.
		Impaired proof		—	—	—	—	—	—	—
1887/6	7,961	—	—		Proof only	—	—	—	—	700.
		Impaired proof		—	—	—	—	—	—	—
1887	Inc. Ab.	240.	250.	275.	300.	325.	425.	500.	1175.	725.
1888	41,083	35.00	40.00	45.00	50.00	70.00	110.	270.	900.	700.
1889	21,561	63.00	70.00	90.00	105.	125.	150.	260.	900.	700.

Half dimes

Flowing Hair

Designer: Robert Scot. **Size:** 16.5 millimeters. **Weight:** 1.35 grams. **Composition:** 89.24% silver (0.0388 ounces), 10.76% copper.

Date	Mintage	G-4	VG-8	F-12	VF-20	XF-40	MS-60
1794	86,416	1075.	1250.	1850.	2650.	4500.	8500.
1795	Inc. Ab.	595.	700.	950.	1350.	2650.	5050.

Draped Bust

Small-eagle reverse

Designer: Robert Scot. **Size:** 16.5 millimeters. **Weight:** 1.35 grams. **Composition:** 89.24% silver (0.0388 ounces), 10.76% copper. **Notes:** Some 1796 strikes have "Liberty" spelled as "Libekty." The 1797 strikes have either 13, 15 or 16 stars on the obverse.

Date	Mintage	G-4	VG-8	F-12	VF-20	XF-40	MS-60
1796	10,230	950.	1000.	1350.	2150.	3350.	5650.
1796 "Liberty"	Inc. Ab.	950.	1000.	1350.	2150.	3350.	—
1796/5	Inc. Ab.	1200.	1400.	1600.	2400.	3400.	9000.
1797 13 stars	44,527	900.	975.	1400.	2200.	3350.	11,500.
1797 15 stars	Inc. Ab.	850.	925.	1350.	2150.	3350.	5650.
1797 16 stars	Inc. Ab.	875.	950.	1375.	2150.	3350.	5650.

Heraldic-eagle reverse

Notes: Some 1800 strikes have "Liberty" spelled as "Likerty."

Date	Mintage	G-4	VG-8	F-12	VF-20	XF-40	MS-60
1800	24,000	575.	750.	875.	1400.	2400.	5050.
1800 "Likebty"	Inc. Ab.	575.	750.	875.	1400.	2650.	5050.
1801	33,910	750.	975.	1100.	1500.	2750.	10,000.
1802	13,010	10,500.	13,000.	23,000.	32,000.	45,000.	—
1803	37,850	625.	700.	1050.	1400.	2400.	5050.
1805	15,600	975.	1175.	1500.	1900.	3250.	—

Liberty Cap

Designer: William Kneass. **Size:** 15.5 millimeters. **Weight:** 1.35 grams. **Composition:** 89.24% silver (0.0388 ounces), 10.76% copper. **Notes:** Design modifications in 1835, 1836 and 1837 resulted in variety combinations with large and small dates, and large and small "5C." inscriptions on the reverse.

Date	Mintage	G-4	VG-8	F-12	VF-20	XF-40	AU-50	MS-60	MS-65
1829	1,230,000	12.00	18.00	25.00	50.00	125.	225.	290.	3500.
1830	1,240,000	12.00	18.00	25.00	50.00	125.	225.	290.	3500.
1831	1,242,700	12.00	18.00	25.00	50.00	125.	225.	290.	3500.
1832	965,000	12.00	18.00	25.00	50.00	125.	300.	450.	7000.
1833	1,370,000	12.00	18.00	25.00	50.00	125.	230.	325.	3500.
1834	1,480,000	12.00	18.00	25.00	50.00	125.	230.	290.	3500.
1835 large date, large "5C."	2,760,000	12.00	18.00	25.00	50.00	110.	250.	290.	3500.
1835 large date, small "5C."	Inc. Ab.	12.00	18.00	25.00	50.00	125.	230.	290.	3500.

1802 Half Dime
Grade F-12

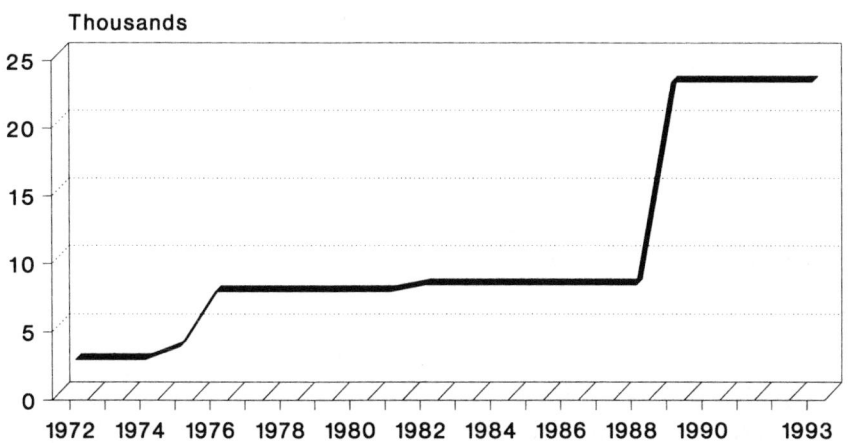

Thousands

Retail Price

Source: COIN PRICES

Date	Mintage	G-4	VG-8	F-12	VF-20	XF-40	AU-50	MS-60	MS-65
1835 small date, large "5C."									
	Inc. Ab.	12.00	18.00	25.00	50.00	125.	225.	290.	3500.
1835 small date, small "5C."									
	Inc. Ab.	12.00	18.00	25.00	50.00	125.	225.	290.	3500.
1836 large "5C."									
	1,900,000	12.00	18.00	25.00	50.00	125.	225.	290.	3500.
1836 small "5C."									
	Inc. Ab.	12.00	18.00	25.00	50.00	125.	225.	290.	3500.
1837 large "5C."									
	2,276,000	12.00	18.00	25.00	50.00	125.	225.	290.	3500.
1837 small "5C."									
	Inc. Ab.	25.00	40.00	60.00	85.00	150.	350.	1250.	8500.

Seated Liberty

No stars around rim

Designer: Christian Gobrecht. **Size:** 15.5 millimeters. **Weight:** 1.34 grams. **Composition:** 90% silver (0.0388 ounces), 10% copper. **Notes:** A design modification in 1837 resulted in small-date and large-date varieties for that year.

Date	Mintage	G-4	VG-8	F-12	VF-20	XF-40	AU-50	MS-60	MS-65
1837 sm. date	Inc. Ab.	25.00	35.00	53.00	100.	210.	435.	600.	4500.
1837 lg. date	Inc. Ab.	25.00	35.00	53.00	100.	210.	435.	600.	4500.
1838O	70,000	100.	150.	225.	400.	750.	5000.	—	—

1846 Half Dime
Grade XF-40

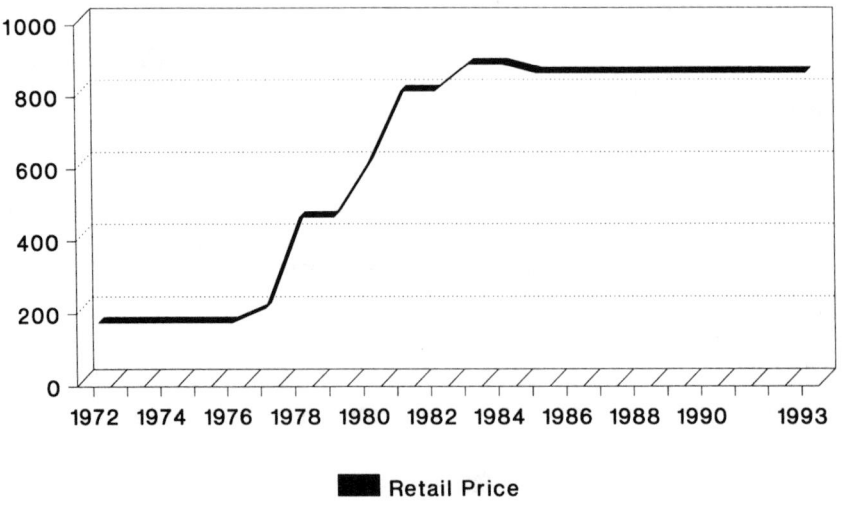

Retail Price

Source: COIN PRICES

Stars around rim

Notes: The two varieties of 1838 are distinguished by the size of the stars on the obverse. The 1839-O with reverse of 1838-O was struck from rusted reverse dies. The result is a bumpy surface on this variety's reverse.

Date	Mintage	G-4	VG-8	F-12	VF-20	XF-40	AU-50	MS-60	MS-65
1838 lg.stars	2,255,000	5.00	6.25	10.00	25.00	65.00	135.	250.	3150.
1838 sm.stars	Inc. Ab.	25.00	35.00	50.00	100.	185.	285.	750.	10,500.
1839	1,069,150	8.00	10.00	13.00	29.00	70.00	170.	250.	3150.
1839O	1,034,039	9.00	12.00	16.00	31.00	75.00	200.	300.	3150.
1839O rev. 1838O	—	75.00	100.	175.	250.	500.	—	—	—
1840	1,344,085	5.00	6.25	13.00	21.00	65.00	135.	450.	3150.
1840O	935,000	10.00	13.00	18.00	35.00	85.00	200.	600.	10,500.

Drapery added to Liberty

Notes: In 1840 drapery was added to Liberty's left elbow. Varieties for the 1848 Philadelphia strikes are distinguished by the size of the numerals in the date.

Date	Mintage	G-4	VG-8	F-12	VF-20	XF-40	AU-50	MS-60	MS-65
1840	Inc. Ab.	20.00	32.50	50.00	75.00	150.	250.	700.	6500.
1840O	Inc. Ab.	30.00	50.00	80.00	120.	200.	1500.	—	—
1841	1,150,000	5.00	6.25	8.75	22.00	55.00	95.00	160.	2450.
1841O	815,000	10.00	15.00	22.50	40.00	85.00	200.	650.	—
1842	815,000	5.00	6.25	8.75	22.00	55.00	95.00	160.	2450.
1842O	350,000	28.00	45.00	65.00	140.	375.	1800.	—	—
1843	1,165,000	5.00	6.25	8.75	18.00	41.00	95.00	160.	2450.
1844	430,000	6.50	8.50	11.00	24.00	60.00	110.	225.	2450.
1844O	220,000	60.00	100.	175.	350.	950.	2800.	—	15,000.
1845	1,564,000	5.00	6.25	8.75	22.00	44.00	95.00	160.	2450.
1845/1845	Inc. Ab.	8.00	11.00	15.00	30.00	75.00	200.	225.	5000.
1846	27,000	150.	200.	275.	450.	850.	3200.	7000.	—
1847	1,274,000	6.00	7.00	8.00	18.00	55.00	95.00	225.	2450.
1848 med. date	668,000	7.00	8.50	11.00	32.00	60.00	125.	225.	2450.
1848 lg. date	Inc. Ab.	20.00	26.00	35.00	75.00	175.	375.	425.	2450.
1848O	600,000	12.00	17.50	25.00	42.50	90.00	225.	600.	5000.
1849/8	1,309,000	12.00	17.50	25.00	45.00	100.	180.	500.	5000.
1849/6	Inc. Ab.	10.00	14.00	20.00	35.00	75.00	175.	425.	5000.
1849	Inc. Ab.	6.00	8.00	11.00	18.00	45.00	95.00	600.	5000.
1849O	140,000	22.00	40.00	75.00	180.	450.	800.	1200.	16,000.
1850	955,000	5.00	6.25	8.75	18.00	41.00	175.	250.	2750.
1850O	690,000	11.00	16.00	22.50	40.00	80.00	350.	800.	4000.
1851	781,000	5.00	6.25	8.75	18.00	50.00	115.	300.	2450.
1851O	860,000	10.00	15.00	25.00	35.00	75.00	165.	800.	2450.
1852	1,000,500	6.00	7.00	12.50	18.00	41.00	115.	160.	2450.
1852O	260,000	30.00	48.00	70.00	150.	400.	1400.	—	11,000.
1853	135,000	25.00	38.00	55.00	85.00	150.	350.	500.	8500.
1853O	160,000	145.	210.	325.	425.	850.	3000.	—	—

Arrows at date

Weight: 1.24 grams. **Composition:** 90% silver (0.0362 ounces), 10% copper.

Date	Mintage	G-4	VG-8	F-12	VF-20	XF-40	AU-50	MS-60	MS-65	Prf-65
1853	13,210,020	5.00	6.25	8.75	17.00	50.00	100.	160.	4550.	20,000.
1853O	2,200,000	6.00	8.00	11.00	24.00	60.00	125.	325.	—	—
1854	5,740,000	5.00	6.50	8.75	17.00	50.00	135.	250.	4550.	20,000.
1854O	1,560,000	7.00	9.00	12.00	20.00	55.00	175.	700.	—	—
1855	1,750,000	5.50	7.00	12.00	20.00	55.00	135.	250.	5000.	20,000.
1855O	600,000	12.00	17.00	25.00	45.00	100.	275.	1000.	—	—

Arrows at date removed

Notes: On the 1858/inverted date variety, the date was engraved into the die upside down and then re-engraved right side up. Another 1858 variety has the date doubled.

Date	Mintage	G-4	VG-8	F-12	VF-20	XF-40	AU-50	MS-60	MS-65	Prf-65
1856	4,880,000	5.00	6.25	9.00	18.00	41.00	95.00	225.	2750.	22,500.
1856O	1,100,000	8.00	10.00	12.00	27.00	70.00	200.	600.	—	—
1857	7,280,000	5.00	6.25	8.75	15.00	45.00	95.00	225.	2300.	5000.
1857O	1,380,000	7.00	9.00	11.00	25.00	65.00	200.	450.	—	—
1858	3,500,000	5.00	6.25	8.75	18.00	45.00	85.00	160.	2300.	9000.
1858 inverted date										
	Inc. Ab.	35.00	48.00	75.00	115.	200.	350.	700.	—	—
1858 doubled date										
	Inc. Ab.	45.00	60.00	90.00	140.	240.	500.	1200.	—	—
1858O	1,660,000	7.00	9.00	12.00	26.00	65.00	190.	265.	—	—
1859	340,000	9.00	12.00	15.00	33.00	85.00	175.	250.	3000.	5000.
1859O	560,000	8.00	10.00	13.00	30.00	80.00	165.	350.	—	—

Transitional patterns

Notes: These non-circulation pieces were struck as experiments in transferring the legend "United States of America" from the reverse to the obverse.

Date	Mintage	G-4	VG-8	F-12	VF-20	XF-40	AU-50	MS-60	MS-65	Prf-65
1859 obverse of 1859, reverse 1860						—	—	—	—	17,500.
1860 obverse of 1859, reverse 1860						—	—	4000.	8500.	—

Obverse legend

Notes: In 1860 the legend "United States of America" replaced the stars on the obverse.

Date	Mintage	G-4	VG-8	F-12	VF-20	XF-40	AU-50	MS-60	MS-65	Prf-65
1860	799,000	6.00	7.50	12.50	25.00	40.00	70.00	140.	1800.	2150.
1860O	1,060,000	6.00	7.50	12.50	25.00	40.00	85.00	350.	3550.	—
1861	3,361,000	5.00	6.25	8.00	14.00	28.00	57.00	140.	1800.	2150.
1861/0	Inc. Ab.	20.00	35.00	60.00	120.	250.	500.	800.	—	—
1862	1,492,550	5.00	6.25	8.00	16.00	30.00	57.00	140.	1800.	2150.
1863	18,460	135.	165.	200.	260.	375.	500.	800.	3250.	3500.
1863S	100,000	15.00	23.00	35.00	65.00	125.	250.	900.	—	—
1864	48,470	225.	290.	350.	450.	625.	700.	950.	4500.	3500.
1864S	90,000	22.50	34.00	50.00	80.00	250.	500.	1000.	—	—
1865	13,500	225.	275.	350.	450.	625.	850.	1300.	4700.	3500.
1865S	120,000	12.50	18.00	25.00	50.00	100.	300.	975.	—	—
1866	10,725	185.	225.	285.	375.	550.	750.	1000.	4700.	3500.
1866S	120,000	12.50	18.00	25.00	50.00	100.	375.	950.	6000.	—
1867	8,625	365.	425.	475.	550.	675.	850.	1300.	4700.	3500.
1867S	120,000	12.50	18.00	25.00	55.00	100.	375.	900.	—	—
1868	89,200	40.00	60.00	85.00	115.	175.	350.	600.	5000.	3500.
1868S	280,000	10.00	14.00	20.00	33.00	60.00	150.	500.	—	—
1869	208,600	6.50	8.00	20.00	33.00	60.00	175.	475.	4900.	3500.
1869S	230,000	10.00	14.00	20.00	33.00	60.00	150.	500.	—	—
1870	536,600	6.00	7.50	9.00	17.00	35.00	125.	275.	4400.	2150.
1870S	Unique, Superior Galleries, July 1986, B.U., $253,000.									
1871	1,873,960	5.00	6.25	8.00	14.00	28.00	65.00	160.	4400.	2150.
1871S	161,000	15.00	19.00	25.00	40.00	65.00	175.	450.	3800.	—
1872	2,947,950	5.00	6.25	8.00	13.00	25.00	65.00	160.	4400.	2150.
1872S mint mark in wreath										
	837,000	5.00	6.50	8.00	15.00	30.00	65.00	425.	4400.	—
1872S mint mark below wreath										
	Inc. Ab.	5.00	6.50	8.00	15.00	30.00	125.	450.	2400.	—
1873	712,600	8.00	10.00	12.50	18.00	32.00	125.	350.	4450.	3500.
1873S	324,000	8.00	10.00	14.00	22.00	38.00	65.00	200.	4000.	—

Nickel five-cent

Shield

With rays   Without rays

Designer: James B. Longacre. **Size:** 20.5 millimeters. **Weight:** 5 grams. **Composition:** 75% copper, 25% nickel. **Notes:** In 1867 the rays between the stars on the reverse were eliminated, resulting in varieties with and without rays for that year.

Date	Mintage	G-4	VG-8	F-12	VF-20	XF-40	AU-50	MS-60	MS-65	Prf-65
1866	14,742,500	11.00	13.00	20.00	31.00	95.00	140.	160.	3900.	4950.
1867 with rays										
	2,019,000	13.00	16.00	25.00	50.00	125.	250.	290.	4200.	37,500.
1867 without rays										
	28,890,500	7.00	9.50	10.00	14.00	26.00	56.00	100.	850.	1200.
1868	28,817,000	7.00	9.50	10.00	14.00	26.00	50.00	100.	850.	1150.
1869	16,395,000	7.00	9.50	10.00	14.00	31.00	52.00	100.	850.	940.
1870	4,806,000	9.50	10.00	11.00	17.50	45.00	56.00	100.	1050.	1200.
1871	561,000	25.00	30.00	45.00	75.00	95.00	160.	270.	1550.	1000.
1872	6,036,000	9.50	10.00	11.00	17.50	40.00	70.00	115.	780.	820.
1873	4,550,000	9.50	10.00	12.00	19.00	34.00	65.00	125.	780.	1000.
1874	3,538,000	10.00	11.50	12.50	19.00	38.00	70.00	125.	1100.	800.
1875	2,097,000	10.00	12.50	17.50	40.00	65.00	85.00	150.	2600.	1125.
1876	2,530,000	10.00	12.00	16.50	32.00	55.00	90.00	125.	1250.	1000.
1877	Est. 900	—	—	Proof only		—	—	—	—	1875.
		Impaired proof		—	1000.	—	1050.	1100.	—	—	—
1878	2,350	—	—	Proof only		—	—	—	—	1000.
		Impaired proof		550.	600.	650.	675.	—	—	—
1879	29,100	240.	280.	330.	415.	480.	550.	625.	2000.	820.
1880	19,995	265.	325.	350.	400.	550.	600.	650.	4000.	1000.
1881	72,375	150.	180.	250.	300.	400.	430.	530.	1250.	800.
1882	11,476,600	8.75	9.50	11.00	16.00	30.00	50.00	100.	850.	800.
1883	1,456,919	12.00	14.00	17.50	22.50	32.50	60.00	100.	850.	800.
1883/2	—	—	50.00	75.00	180.	225.	275.	325.	3000.	—

Liberty

With "Cents"   No "Cents"

Designer: Charles E. Barber. **Size:** 21.2 millimeters. **Weight:** 5 grams. **Composition:** 75% copper, 25% nickel. **Notes:** In 1883 the word "Cents" was added to the reverse, resulting in varieties with "Cents" and without "Cents" for that year.

Date	Mintage	G-4	VG-8	F-12	VF-20	XF-40	AU-50	MS-60	MS-65	Prf-65
1883 NC	5,479,519	2.60	3.25	3.60	5.00	6.75	11.50	32.00	450.	1000.
1883 WC	16,032,983	5.00	7.00	12.00	20.00	36.00	68.00	94.00	650.	650.
1884	11,273,942	7.00	9.00	13.00	22.00	42.00	68.00	120.	775.	650.
1885	1,476,490	180.	250.	315.	390.	600.	650.	850.	1800.	875.
1886	3,330,290	44.00	56.00	115.	175.	220.	325.	470.	1900.	700.
1887	15,263,652	5.40	6.25	11.00	14.00	29.00	60.00	90.00	700.	650.
1888	10,720,483	7.50	9.00	14.00	23.00	40.00	80.00	115.	675.	650.
1889	15,881,361	3.75	5.00	9.25	13.50	29.00	60.00	94.00	650.	650.
1890	16,259,272	4.25	5.50	11.00	17.00	31.00	66.00	100.	825.	650.
1891	16,834,350	3.50	4.50	9.50	13.00	28.00	60.00	94.00	800.	650.
1892	11,699,642	3.50	4.00	9.50	14.50	31.00	66.00	100.	690.	650.
1893	13,370,195	3.50	4.00	10.00	14.50	28.00	60.00	95.00	775.	650.
1894	5,413,132	5.25	7.00	26.00	56.00	120.	150.	170.	1100.	650.
1895	9,979,884	2.25	2.75	7.00	12.00	28.00	60.00	87.00	1075.	780.
1896	8,842,920	3.00	4.00	9.50	15.00	32.00	69.00	94.00	1075.	650.
1897	20,428,735	1.50	2.00	3.75	6.50	19.00	55.00	80.00	950.	650.
1898	12,532,087	1.50	2.00	4.50	6.50	20.00	57.00	80.00	650.	650.
1899	26,029,031	.65	1.10	4.00	5.50	16.00	50.00	80.00	650.	650.
1900	27,255,995	.65	1.00	3.75	5.00	15.00	41.00	75.00	650.	650.
1901	26,480,213	.65	1.00	3.75	5.00	15.00	41.00	75.00	650.	650.
1902	31,480,579	.65	1.00	3.75	5.00	15.00	41.00	75.00	650.	650.
1903	28,006,725	.65	1.00	3.75	5.00	15.00	41.00	75.00	650.	650.
1904	21,404,984	.65	1.00	3.75	5.00	15.00	41.00	75.00	650.	725.
1905	29,827,276	.65	1.00	3.75	5.00	15.00	41.00	75.00	650.	650.
1906	38,613,725	.65	1.00	3.75	5.00	15.00	41.00	75.00	650.	650.
1907	39,214,800	.65	1.00	3.75	5.00	15.00	41.00	75.00	650.	650.
1908	22,686,177	.65	1.00	3.75	5.00	15.00	41.00	75.00	775.	650.
1909	11,590,526	.80	1.30	5.00	6.00	17.00	60.00	80.00	725.	650.
1910	30,169,353	.65	1.00	3.75	5.00	15.00	41.00	75.00	680.	650.
1911	39,559,372	.65	1.00	3.75	5.00	15.00	41.00	75.00	650.	650.
1912	26,236,714	.65	1.00	3.75	5.00	15.00	41.00	75.00	650.	650.
1912D	8,474,000	1.00	1.25	4.25	7.50	36.00	95.00	145.	800.	—
1912S	238,000	38.00	41.00	65.00	220.	400.	530.	595.	2300.	—

1913 Only 5 known, Buss Sale, Jan.1985, Prf-63, $385,000.

1884 Nickel Five-Cent
Grade F-12

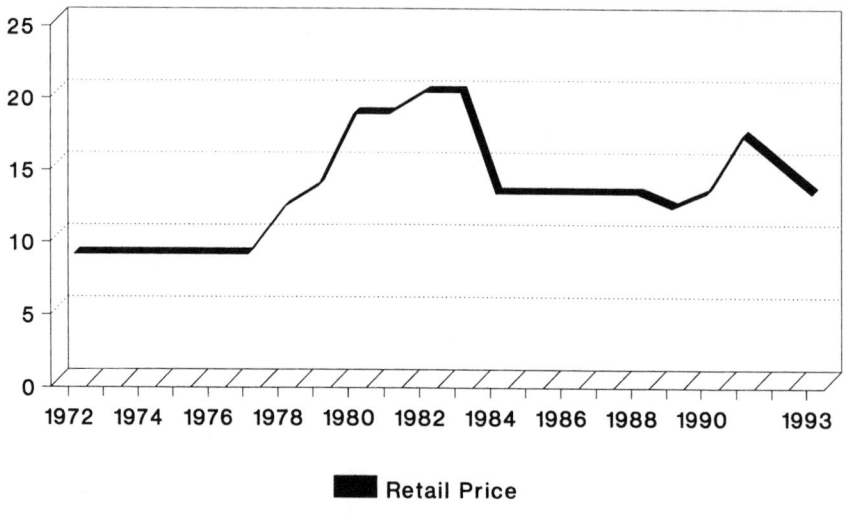

■ Retail Price

Source: COIN PRICES

Buffalo

Mound type

Designer: James Earle Fraser. **Size:** 21.2 millimeters. **Weight:** 5 grams. **Composition:** 75% copper, 25% nickel.

Date	Mintage	G-4	VG-8	F-12	VF-20	XF-40	AU-50	MS-60	MS-65	Prf-65
1913	30,993,520	4.25	4.90	5.50	7.00	12.00	21.00	32.00	90.00	1950.
1913D	5,337,000	7.00	8.50	10.00	14.00	23.00	41.00	56.00	250.	—
1913S	2,105,000	11.00	12.50	17.00	25.00	41.00	53.00	63.00	680.	—

Line type

Notes: In 1913 the reverse design was modified so the ground under the buffalo was represented as a line rather than a mound. On the 1937-D 3-legged variety, the buffalo's right front leg is missing, the result of a damaged die.

1921-S Nickel Five-Cent
Grade F-12

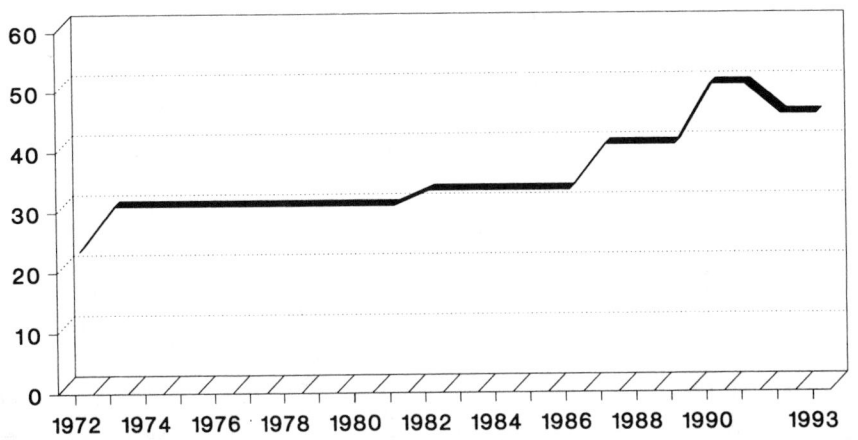

◼ Retail Price

Source: COIN PRICES

Date	Mintage	G-4	VG-8	F-12	VF-20	XF-40	AU-50	MS-60	MS-65	Prf-65
1913	29,858,700	5.00	5.75	7.00	9.00	13.50	20.00	29.00	260.	1350.
1913D	4,156,000	34.00	40.00	46.00	56.00	70.00	115.	170.	850.	—
1913S	1,209,000	77.00	100.	135.	140.	195.	280.	335.	2500.	—
1914	20,665,738	4.35	5.60	6.25	8.00	17.00	27.00	45.00	310.	1100.
1914D	3,912,000	29.00	39.00	50.00	67.00	105.	140.	210.	1225.	—
1914S	3,470,000	6.00	7.00	11.00	18.00	35.00	50.00	110.	2450.	—
1915	20,987,270	2.10	2.75	5.00	6.00	12.00	26.00	45.00	245.	1100.
1915D	7,569,500	5.75	7.00	17.00	35.00	55.00	75.00	170.	2650.	—
1915S	1,505,000	12.00	14.00	25.00	63.00	125.	210.	420.	2450.	—
1916	63,498,066	.80	.90	1.60	2.50	4.90	15.00	38.00	215.	2000.
1916/16	Inc. Ab.	1500.	3350.	5300.	8400.	11,000.	14,000.	16,000.	53,000.	—
1916D	13,333,000	5.00	6.25	9.00	25.00	50.00	77.00	140.	2800.	—
1916S	11,860,000	3.15	4.00	6.50	19.00	43.00	74.00	155.	2100.	—
1917	51,424,029	.70	1.00	1.75	2.95	9.00	26.00	42.00	450.	—
1917D	9,910,800	4.00	6.00	13.00	41.00	84.00	120.	275.	2800.	—
1917S	4,193,000	4.50	6.50	14.00	45.00	105.	195.	280.	2800.	—
1918	32,086,314	1.10	1.25	2.10	5.60	17.00	35.00	56.00	1125.	—

1918/17-D

Date	Mintage	G-4	VG-8	F-12	VF-20	XF-40	AU-50	MS-60	MS-65	Prf-65
1918/17D	8,362,314	385.	500.	775.	2175.	4000.	5950.	12,000.	56,000.	—
1918D	Inc. Ab.	4.50	6.00	16.00	67.00	160.	245.	330.	3100.	—
1918S	4,882,000	4.00	5.25	13.00	59.00	150.	210.	280.	8400.	—
1919	60,868,000	.90	1.05	1.20	2.45	7.50	22.00	42.00	360.	—
1919D	8,006,000	4.00	6.50	15.00	70.00	170.	265.	420.	3400.	—
1919S	7,521,000	2.90	3.65	9.00	63.00	160.	250.	435.	7150.	—
1920	63,093,000	.70	.80	1.20	2.45	7.75	24.00	45.00	550.	—
1920D	9,418,000	2.00	4.70	11.00	70.00	210.	280.	385.	4900.	—
1920S	9,689,000	1.85	2.75	6.65	49.00	140.	195.	230.	13,250.	—

Date	Mintage	G-4	VG-8	F-12	VF-20	XF-40	AU-50	MS-60	MS-65	Prf-65
1921	10,663,000	1.05	1.20	1.80	6.00	20.00	42.00	84.00	460.	—
1921S	1,557,000	15.00	20.00	45.00	315.	665.	875.	1050.	4400.	—
1923	35,715,000	.70	.80	1.00	2.10	6.75	17.00	35.00	390.	—
1923S	6,142,000	1.60	2.60	4.75	91.00	175.	230.	295.	8550.	—
1924	21,620,000	.70	.80	1.05	2.95	8.75	28.00	49.00	460.	—
1924D	5,258,000	2.50	3.30	7.00	53.00	140.	220.	280.	2650.	—
1924S	1,437,000	4.85	6.50	25.00	420.	1075.	1250.	1675.	4600.	—
1925	35,565,100	.90	1.00	1.25	2.25	7.00	21.00	31.00	250.	—
1925D	4,450,000	4.00	6.65	15.00	60.00	125.	200.	350.	3650.	—
1925S	6,256,000	1.25	3.50	7.00	53.00	140.	225.	390.	22,500.	—
1926	44,693,000	.45	.50	.65	1.40	4.50	17.00	28.00	100.	—
1926D	5,638,000	2.25	3.25	14.00	63.00	120.	160.	210.	2300.	—
1926S	970,000	6.00	6.75	13.00	300.	840.	1085.	2200.	21,000.	—
1927	37,981,000	.45	.50	.65	1.40	4.50	18.00	25.00	155.	—
1927D	5,730,000	1.00	1.75	3.00	11.00	39.00	65.00	120.	2350.	—
1927S	3,430,000	.90	1.50	1.75	17.00	65.00	105.	375.	14,000.	—
1928	23,411,000	.45	.50	.65	1.40	4.75	18.00	27.00	210.	—
1928D	6,436,000	.85	1.00	1.80	4.35	14.00	25.00	31.00	740.	—
1928S	6,936,000	.70	.80	1.35	3.15	10.00	30.00	175.	3150.	—
1929	36,446,000	.45	.50	.65	1.20	3.50	15.00	25.00	210.	—
1929D	8,370,000	.70	1.00	1.50	3.75	12.50	28.00	42.00	880.	—
1929S	7,754,000	.60	.75	1.00	1.50	8.75	21.00	36.00	265.	—
1930	22,849,000	.45	.50	.65	1.25	3.75	15.00	23.00	100.	—
1930S	5,435,000	.55	.65	1.00	1.55	7.50	25.00	34.00	415.	—
1931S	1,200,000	3.00	3.50	4.25	5.00	11.00	28.00	38.00	180.	—
1934	20,213,003	.35	.45	.50	1.40	3.50	13.00	21.00	250.	—
1934D	7,480,000	.40	.55	.75	1.75	5.50	18.00	36.00	1125.	—
1935	58,264,000	.35	.45	.50	1.05	3.50	8.50	18.00	71.00	—
1935D	12,092,000	.35	.45	.50	3.15	7.00	21.00	27.00	400.	—
1935S	10,300,000	.35	.45	.50	1.05	3.65	13.00	24.00	180.	—
1936	119,001,420	.35	.45	.50	1.05	3.50	7.50	14.00	38.00	950.
1936D	24,814,000	.35	.45	.50	1.05	3.50	10.50	17.50	56.00	—
1936S	14,930,000	.35	.45	.50	1.05	3.50	12.00	16.00	56.00	—
1937	79,485,769	.35	.45	.50	1.05	3.50	7.00	13.00	34.00	950.
1937D	17,826,000	.35	.45	.50	1.05	3.50	9.00	14.00	35.00	—
1937D 3 Leg.	Inc. Ab.	150.	210.	280.	325.	490.	750.	1375.	13,000.	—

1937-D three-legged

Date	Mintage	G-4	VG-8	F-12	VF-20	XF-40	AU-50	MS-60	MS-65	Prf-65
1937S	5,635,000	.35	.45	.50	1.05	3.15	9.00	14.00	38.00	—
1938D	7,020,000	.35	.45	.50	1.05	2.80	8.50	13.00	30.00	—
1938 D/D	—	1.00	2.00	3.00	4.00	5.00	10.00	16.00	90.00	—
1938D/S	Inc. Ab.	4.90	7.00	7.75	8.50	10.00	21.00	35.00	140.	—

Jefferson

Prewar composition

Designer: Felix Schlag. **Size:** 21.2 millimeters. **Weight:** 5 grams. **Composition:** 75% copper, 25% nickel. **Notes:** Some 1939 strikes have doubling of the word "Monticello" on the reverse.

Date	Mintage	G-4	VG-8	F-12	VF-20	XF-40	MS-60	MS-65	Prf-65
1938	19,515,365	—	.40	.50	1.00	1.50	3.50	7.00	45.00
1938D	5,376,000	.60	.90	1.00	1.25	1.75	4.25	7.50	—
1938S	4,105,000	1.25	1.50	1.75	2.00	2.50	5.00	8.00	—
1939	120,627,535	—	—	.15	.25	.30	1.75	2.00	57.00
Doubled Monticello			7.50	10.00	25.00	50.00	200.	—	—
1939D	3,514,000	2.50	3.00	3.50	4.50	6.75	29.00	50.00	—
1939S	6,630,000	.40	.45	.60	1.00	3.25	1.00	30.00	—
1940	176,499,158	—	—	—	—	.25	1.00	1.25	45.00
1940D	43,540,000	—	—	.15	.30	.40	2.50	2.75	—
1940S	39,690,000	—	—	.15	.20	.50	2.25	2.75	—
1941	203,283,720	—	—	—	—	.20	.75	1.00	45.00
1941D	53,432,000	—	—	.15	.25	.35	2.50	4.00	—
1941S	43,445,000	—	—	.15	.25	.40	3.75	5.75	—
1942	49,818,600	—	—	—	—	.40	1.50	1.75	30.00
1942D	13,938,000	—	.30	.40	.60	2.00	17.50	35.00	—

Wartime composition

Composition: 56% copper, 35% silver (0.0563 ounces), 9% manganese. **Notes:** Wartime-composition nickels have a large mintmark above Monticello on the reverse.

Date	Mintage	G-4	VG-8	F-12	VF-20	XF-40	MS-60	MS-65	Prf-65
1942P	57,900,600	.40	.65	.85	1.00	1.75	12.50	20.00	120.
1942S	32,900,000	.40	.70	1.00	1.10	1.75	9.00	15.00	—
1943P	271,165,000	.30	.50	.85	1.00	1.50	4.00	6.50	—
1943/2P	Inc. Ab.	20.00	30.00	45.00	70.00	110.	250.	600.	—
1943D	15,294,000	.55	.90	1.10	1.50	1.75	2.75	5.50	—
1943S	104,060,000	.40	.65	.85	1.00	1.50	3.50	5.75	—
1944P	119,150,000	.30	.50	.85	1.00	1.50	3.50	6.00	—
1944D	32,309,000	.40	.65	.85	1.00	1.75	7.25	12.00	—
1944S	21,640,000	.45	.85	.95	1.25	2.00	5.50	15.00	—
1945P	119,408,100	.30	.50	.85	1.00	1.75	4.00	7.50	—
1945D	37,158,000	.40	.65	.85	1.00	1.25	2.75	6.50	—
1945S	58,939,000	.30	.50	.70	.80	.90	1.90	7.50	—

Prewar composition resumed

Notes: The 1979-S Type II proof has a clearer mintmark than the Type I.

Date	Mintage	G-4	VG-8	F-12	VF-20	XF-40	MS-60	MS-65	Prf-65
1946	161,116,000	—	—	—	.15	.20	.40	.60	—
1946D	45,292,200	—	—	—	.25	.35	.75	.95	—
1946S	13,560,000	—	—	—	.30	.40	.60	.70	—
1947	95,000,000	—	—	—	.15	.20	.40	.55	—
1947D	37,822,000	—	—	—	.20	.30	.65	.75	—
1947S	24,720,000	—	—	—	.15	.20	.55	.65	—
1948	89,348,000	—	—	—	.15	.20	.35	.55	—
1948D	44,734,000	—	—	—	.25	.35	1.00	1.25	—
1948S	11,300,000	—	—	—	.25	.50	1.00	1.25	—
1949	60,652,000	—	—	—	.20	.25	.75	1.25	—
1949D	36,498,000	—	—	—	.30	.40	1.00	1.25	—
1949D/S	Inc. Ab.	—	—	20.00	40.00	75.00	175.	350.	—
1949S	9,716,000	—	.25	.35	.45	1.50	2.00	2.50	—
1950	9,847,386	—	.25	.45	.50	.75	1.90	2.25	38.00
1950D	2,630,030	—	5.00	5.00	5.25	5.50	6.50	9.00	—
1951	28,609,500	—	—	—	.40	.50	1.00	1.50	33.00
1951D	20,460,000	—	.25	.30	.40	.50	1.25	1.50	—
1951S	7,776,000	—	.30	.40	.50	.75	1.75	4.00	—
1952	64,069,980	—	—	—	.15	.20	.55	.65	32.00
1952D	30,638,000	—	—	—	.20	.35	.75	1.75	—
1952S	20,572,000	—	—	—	.15	.20	.65	.90	—
1953	46,772,800	—	—	—	.15	.25	.35	.45	30.00
1953D	59,878,600	—	—	—	.15	.20	.30	.40	—
1953S	19,210,900	—	—	—	.15	.20	.35	.50	—
1954	47,917,350	—	—	—	—	—	.20	.30	16.50
1954D	117,136,560	—	—	—	—	—	.30	.40	—
1954S	29,384,000	—	—	—	—	.15	.35	.45	—
1954S/D	Inc. Ab.	—	—	3.50	7.00	11.00	25.00	40.00	—
1955	8,266,200	—	.25	.35	.40	.45	.75	1.25	10.00
1955D	74,464,100	—	—	—	—	—	.20	.30	—
1956	35,885,384	—	—	—	—	—	.25	.35	1.90

Date	Mintage	G-4	VG-8	F-12	VF-20	XF-40	MS-60	MS-65	Prf-65
1956D	67,222,940	—	—	—	—	—	.20	.35	—
1957	39,655,952	—	—	—	—	—	.25	.35	—
1957D	136,828,900	—	—	—	—	—	.20	.40	.70
1958	17,963,652	—	—	—	.15	.20	.30	.55	1.70
1958D	168,249,120	—	—	—	—	—	.20	.35	—

Date	Mintage	MS-65	Prf-65	Date	Mintage	MS-65	Prf-65
1959	28,397,291	.35	.80	1979	463,188,000	.15	—
1959D	160,738,240	.25	—	1979D	325,867,672	.15	—
1960	57,107,602	.25	.50	1979S T-I	Proof only	—	.75
1960D	192,582,180	.25	—	1979S T-II	Proof only	—	1.25
1961	76,668,244	.25	.40	1980P	593,004,000	.15	—
1961D	229,342,760	.25	—	1980D	502,323,448	.15	—
1962	100,602,019	.25	.40	1980S	Proof only	—	.50
1962D	280,195,720	.25	—	1981P	657,504,000	.15	—
1963	178,851,645	.25	.40	1981D	364,801,843	.15	—
1963D	276,829,460	.25	—	1981S T-I	Proof only	—	.55
1964	1,028,622,762	.25	.40	1981S T-II	Proof only	—	1.25
1964D	1,787,297,160	.25	—	1982P	292,355,000	.20	—
1965	136,131,380	.25	—	1982D	373,726,544	.20	—
1966	156,208,283	.25	—	1982S	Proof only	—	1.00
1967	107,325,800	.25	—	1983P	561,615,000	.40	—
1968	None minted	—	—	1983D	536,726,276	.40	—
1968D	91,227,880	.25	—	1983S	Proof only	—	1.50
1968S	103,437,510	.25	.60	1984P	746,769,000	.20	—
1969	None minted	—	—	1984D	517,675,146	.20	—
1969D	202,807,500	.25	—	1984S	Proof only	—	2.75
1969S	123,099,631	.25	.55	1985P	647,114,962	.20	—
1970	None minted	—	—	1985D	459,747,446	.20	—
1970D	515,485,380	.25	—	1985S	Proof only	—	1.95
1970S	241,464,814	.25	.45	1986P	536,883,483	.25	—
1971	106,884,000	.60	—	1986D	361,819,140	.25	—
1971D	316,144,800	.25	—	1986S	Proof only	—	3.50
1971S	Proof only	—	1.15	1987P	371,499,481	.15	—
1972	202,036,000	.25	—	1987D	410,590,604	.15	—
1972D	351,694,600	.20	—	1987S	Proof only	—	1.75
1972S	Proof only	—	1.10	1988P	771,360,000	.15	—
1973	384,396,000	.15	—	1988D	663,771,652	.15	—
1973D	261,405,000	.15	—	1988S	Proof only	—	2.25
1973S	Proof only	—	1.05	1989P	898,812,000	.15	—
1974	601,752,000	.15	—	1989D	570,842,474	.15	—
1974D	277,373,000	.20	—	1989S	Proof only	—	1.85
1974S	Proof only	—	1.50	1990P	661,636,000	.15	—
1975	181,772,000	.35	—	1990D	663,938,503	.15	—
1975D	401,875,300	.15	—	1990S	Proof only	—	1.85
1975S	Proof only	—	1.00	1991P		.15	—
1976	367,124,000	.15	—	1991D		.15	—
1976D	563,964,147	.15	—	1991S	Proof only	—	2.25
1976S	Proof only	—	1.00	1992P		.15	—
1977	585,376,000	.15	—	1992D		.15	—
1977D	297,313,460	.35	—	1992S	Proof only	—	2.50
1977S	Proof only	—	.55	1993P		.15	—
1978	391,308,000	.15	—	1993D		.15	—
1978D	313,092,780	.15	—	1993S	Proof only	—	2.50
1978S	Proof only	—	.60				

Dimes

Draped Bust

Small-eagle reverse

Designer: Robert Scot. **Size:** 19 millimeters. **Weight:** 2.7 grams. **Composition:** 89.24% silver (0.0775 ounces), 10.76% copper. **Notes:** The 1797 strikes have either 13 or 16 stars on the obverse.

Date	Mintage	G-4	VG-8	F-12	VF-20	XF-40	MS-60
1796	22,135	900.	1250.	1650.	2400.	4000.	7000.
1797 13 stars	25,261	1050.	1300.	1850.	2500.	4500.	7000.
1797 16 stars	Inc. Ab.	1000.	1275.	1700.	2500.	4150.	7000.

Heraldic-eagle reverse

Notes: The 1798 overdates have either 13 or 16 stars on the obverse. Varieties of the regular 1798 strikes are distinguished by the size of the 8 in the date. The 1804 strikes have either 13 or 14 stars on the obverse. The 1805 strikes have either 4 or 5 berries on the olive branch held by the eagle.

Date	Mintage	G-4	VG-8	F-12	VF-20	XF-40	MS-60
1798	27,550	550.	675.	950.	1300.	1900.	6000.
1798/97 13 stars	Inc. Ab.	1800.	2500.	4000.	5500.	7500.	—
1798/97 16 stars	Inc. Ab.	550.	700.	900.	1300.	1900.	4050.
1798 small 8	Inc. Ab.	1200.	1650.	2200.	3500.	5500.	—
1800	21,760	550.	675.	900.	1250.	1800.	5400.
1801	34,640	525.	650.	875.	1200.	1750.	—
1802	10,975	700.	975.	1575.	2650.	4500.	—
1803	33,040	550.	675.	900.	1300.	1750.	5500.
1804 13 stars	8,265	1200.	1500.	2250.	3750.	6000.	—
1804 14 stars	Inc. Ab.	1100.	1375.	2150.	3500.	5550.	—
1805 4 berries	120,780	450.	575.	850.	1050.	1700.	4050.
1805 5 berries	Inc. Ab.	500.	600.	900.	1200.	1900.	4200.
1807	165,000	450.	575.	850.	1050.	1900.	4050.

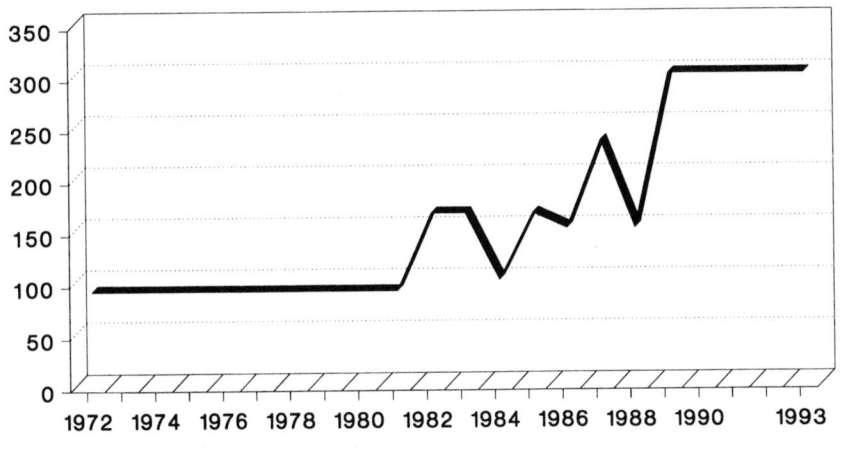

1809 Dime
Grade F-12

■ Retail Price

Liberty Cap

Designer: John Reich. **Size:** 18.8 millimeters. **Weight:** 2.7 grams. **Composition:** 89.24% silver (0.0775 ounces), 10.76% copper. **Notes:** Varieties of the 1814, 1821 and 1828 strikes are distinguished by the size of the numerals in the dates. The 1820 varieties are distinguished by the size of the 0 in the date. The 1823 overdates have either large "E's" or small "E's" in "United States of America" on the reverse.

Date	Mintage	G-4	VG-8	F-12	VF-20	XF-40	AU-50	MS-60	MS-65
1809	51,065	100.	180.	300.	475.	750.	900.	4200.	22,500.
1811/9	65,180	65.00	100.	140.	225.	550.	950.	4000.	22,500.
1814 sm. dt.	421,500	30.00	48.00	65.00	185.	425.	625.	900.	11,500.
1814 lg. dt.	Inc.Ab.	16.00	24.00	40.00	115.	335.	625.	900.	11,500.
1820 lg. O	942,587	17.00	24.00	35.00	105.	315.	625.	900.	11,500.
1820 sm. O	Inc.Ab.	17.00	24.00	35.00	105.	315.	625.	900.	11,500.
1821 lg. dt.	1,186,512	15.00	21.00	35.00	105.	315.	625.	750.	11,500.
1821 sm. dt.	Inc.Ab.	18.50	25.00	42.00	125.	350.	625.	900.	11,500.
1822	100,000	350.	560.	875.	1250.	2350.	4450.	6000.	—
1823/22 lg.E's	440,000	15.00	20.00	33.00	100.	285.	625.	900.	11,500.
1823/22 sm.E's	Inc.Ab.	17.50	25.00	45.00	125.	360.	625.	900.	11,500.
1824/22 Undetermined		30.00	40.00	60.00	165.	425.	625.	900.	11,500.
1825	510,000	14.00	20.00	32.00	90.00	310.	775.	900.	11,500.
1827	1,215,000	11.50	16.00	28.00	83.00	300.	625.	750.	11,500.
1828 lg.dt.	125,000	30.00	40.00	50.00	165.	425.	875.	3000.	38,000.

Reduced size

Size: 18.5 millimeters. **Notes:** The three varieties of 1829 strikes and two varieties of 1830 strikes are distinguished by the size of "10C." on the reverse. On the 1833 "high 3" variety, the last 3 in the date is higher than the first 3. The two varieties of the 1834 strikes are distinguished by the size of the 4 in the date.

Date	Mintage	G-4	VG-8	F-12	VF-20	XF-40	AU-50	MS-60	MS-65
1828 sm.dt.	Inc. Ab.	25.00	40.00	72.00	125.	340.	515.	1000.	—
1829 lg.10C.	770,000	27.00	38.00	50.00	75.00	180.	475.	625.	8000.
1829 med.10C.	Inc. Ab.	17.50	25.00	35.00	70.00	180.	425.	625.	8000.
1829 sm.10C.	Inc. Ab.	11.50	13.00	19.00	50.00	175.	415.	625.	8000.
1830 lg.10C.	510,000	11.50	13.00	19.00	50.00	175.	415.	625.	8000.
1830 sm.10C.	Inc. Ab.	13.50	18.00	25.00	63.00	180.	415.	625.	8000.
1830/29	Inc. Ab.	26.00	45.00	91.00	160.	360.	550.	1040.	—
1831	771,350	11.50	13.00	19.00	50.00	175.	350.	600.	7000.
1832	522,500	11.50	13.00	19.00	50.00	175.	350.	600.	7000.
1833	485,000	11.50	13.00	19.00	50.00	175.	350.	600.	7000.
1833 high 3	Inc. Ab.	11.50	13.00	19.00	50.00	175.	350.	600.	7000.
1834 lg. 4	635,000	11.50	13.00	19.00	50.00	175.	350.	600.	7000.
1834 sm. 4	Inc. Ab.	11.50	13.00	19.00	50.00	175.	350.	600.	7000.
1835	1,410,000	11.50	13.00	19.00	50.00	175.	350.	600.	9100.
1836	1,190,000	11.50	13.00	19.00	50.00	175.	350.	600.	7000.
1837	1,042,000	11.50	13.00	19.00	50.00	175.	350.	625.	7000.

Seated Liberty

No stars

Designer: Christian Gobrecht. **Size:** 17.9 millimeters. **Weight:** 2.67 grams. **Composition:** 90% silver (0.0773 ounces), 10% copper. **Notes:** The two 1837 varieties are distinguished by the size of the numerals in the date.

Date	Mintage	G-4	VG-8	F-12	VF-20	XF-40	AU-50	MS-60	MS-65
1837 sm.date	Inc. Ab.	29.00	40.00	55.00	275.	350.	665.	1100.	8000.
1837 lg.date	Inc. Ab.	29.00	40.00	75.00	300.	600.	850.	1100.	8000.
1838O	406,034	40.00	50.00	80.00	225.	675.	1000.	3500.	21,000.

Stars around rim

Notes: The two 1838 varieties are distinguished by the size of the stars on the obverse. The 1838 "partial drapery" variety has drapery on Liberty's left elbow. The 1839-O with reverse of 1838-O variety was struck from rusted dies. This variety has a bumpy surface on the reverse.

Date	Mintage	G-4	VG-8	F-12	VF-20	XF-40	AU-50	MS-60	MS-65
1838 sm.stars	1,992,500	20.00	30.00	45.00	75.00	150.	500.	2000.	—
1838 lg.stars	Inc. Ab.	8.00	11.00	15.00	25.00	60.00	170.	880.	8500.
1838 partial drapery									
	Inc. Ab.	40.00	65.00	100.	175.	400.	650.	1500.	—
1839	1,053,115	8.00	11.00	15.00	25.00	60.00	170.	265.	3500.
1839O	1,323,000	11.00	15.00	20.00	40.00	85.00	300.	950.	—
1839O rev. 18380	—	120.	300.	450.	600.	1500.	—	—	—
1840	1,358,580	8.00	11.00	15.00	25.00	60.00	170.	265.	3500.
1840O	1,175,000	11.00	15.00	20.00	40.00	85.00	250.	1500.	—

Drapery added to Liberty

Notes: In 1840 drapery was added to Liberty's left elbow.

Date	Mintage	G-4	VG-8	F-12	VF-20	XF-40	AU-50	MS-60	MS-65
1840	Inc. Ab.	25.00	45.00	75.00	135.	275.	1000.	—	—
1841	1,622,500	6.00	7.50	10.00	17.00	45.00	175.	260.	3450.
1841O	2,007,500	8.00	11.00	15.00	28.00	60.00	250.	1500.	—
1842	1,887,500	6.00	7.50	10.00	17.00	45.00	175.	260.	3450.
1842O	2,020,000	8.00	11.00	15.00	28.00	60.00	425.	2300.	—
1843	1,370,000	6.00	8.00	10.00	17.00	45.00	175.	260.	3450.
1843/1843	—	15.00	20.00	30.00	70.00	150.	250.	800.	—
1843O	150,000	45.00	85.00	125.	300.	650.	2000.	—	—
1844	72,500	50.00	60.00	110.	200.	300.	1200.	2000.	—
1845	1,755,000	6.00	7.50	10.00	25.00	65.00	175.	260.	3450.
1845/1845	Inc. Ab.	40.00	70.00	150.	250.	500.	—	—	—
1845O	230,000	15.00	30.00	50.00	125.	500.	2000.	—	—
1846	31,300	70.00	90.00	140.	250.	650.	1500.	—	—
1847	245,000	13.50	20.00	30.00	60.00	125.	350.	1200.	—
1848	451,500	9.00	12.00	17.00	30.00	65.00	140.	750.	7050.
1849	839,000	7.00	9.50	11.00	18.00	50.00	110.	725.	7050.

Date	Mintage	G-4	VG-8	F-12	VF-20	XF-40	MS-60	MS-65	Prf-65
1849/8	Inc. Ab.	30.00	70.00	125.	200.	350.	800.	—	—
1849O	300,000	12.50	18.00	25.00	75.00	175.	1200.	—	—
1850	1,931,500	6.00	7.00	9.00	25.00	60.00	180.	260.	3450.
1850O	510,000	10.00	14.00	20.00	40.00	80.00	200.	1000.	—
1851	1,026,500	6.00	7.00	9.00	15.00	40.00	120.	260.	3450.
1851O	400,000	10.00	15.00	25.00	45.00	90.00	150.	1500.	—
1852	1,535,500	6.00	7.00	9.00	15.00	40.00	120.	260.	3450.
1852O	430,000	14.00	22.00	30.00	85.00	225.	350.	1800.	—
1853	95,000	65.00	80.00	100.	180.	300.	450.	1000.	—

Arrows at date

Weight: 2.49 grams. **Composition:** 90% silver (0.0721 ounces), 10% copper.

Date	Mintage	G-4	VG-8	F-12	VF-20	XF-40	AU-50	MS-60	MS-65	Prf-65
1853	12,078,010	5.40	6.25	7.50	14.00	44.00	125.	330.	3800.	25,000.
1853O	1,100,000	6.00	7.00	10.00	30.00	90.00	325.	900.	—	—
1854	4,470,000	5.40	6.25	7.50	14.00	44.00	125.	330.	3800.	25,000.
1854O	1,770,000	5.50	6.50	9.00	25.00	75.00	175.	650.	—	—
1855	2,075,000	5.40	6.25	7.50	15.00	48.00	250.	350.	3800.	25,000.

Arrows at date removed

Notes: The two 1856 varieties are distinguished by the size of the numerals in the date.

Date	Mintage	G-4	VG-8	F-12	VF-20	XF-40	AU-50	MS-60	MS-65	Prf-65
1856 small date	5,780,000	5.40	6.50	8.25	12.50	32.00	115.	350.	7050.	25,000.
1856 large date	Inc. Ab.	10.00	12.00	15.00	25.00	65.00	150.	350.	—	—
1856O	1,180,000	7.00	9.00	12.00	25.00	60.00	150.	350.	—	—
1856S	70,000	120.	145.	200.	300.	450.	1400.	—	—	—
1857	5,580,000	5.40	6.25	8.25	12.50	32.00	100.	260.	3450.	5500.
1857O	1,540,000	6.00	7.25	9.00	18.00	50.00	200.	350.	—	—
1858	1,540,000	5.40	6.25	8.25	12.50	32.00	115.	260.	3450.	5500.
1858O	290,000	15.00	19.00	25.00	45.00	125.	275.	800.	—	—
1858S	60,000	95.00	125.	150.	250.	400.	550.	1300.	—	—
1859	430,000	6.00	7.00	9.00	17.00	50.00	140.	350.	—	5500.
1859O	480,000	7.50	9.50	12.50	25.00	70.00	225.	550.	—	—
1859S	60,000	100.	130.	175.	275.	425.	1500.	—	—	—
1860S	140,000	20.00	24.00	33.00	68.00	150.	800.	—	—	—

Transitional patterns

Notes: These non-circulation strikes were struck as experiments in transferring the legend "United States of America" from the reverse to the obverse.

Date	Mintage	G-4	VG-8	F-12	VF-20	XF-40	AU-50	MS-60	MS-65	Prf-65
1859 obverse of 1859, reverse of 1860			—		—	—	—	—	—	25,000.

1866-S Dime
Grade F-12

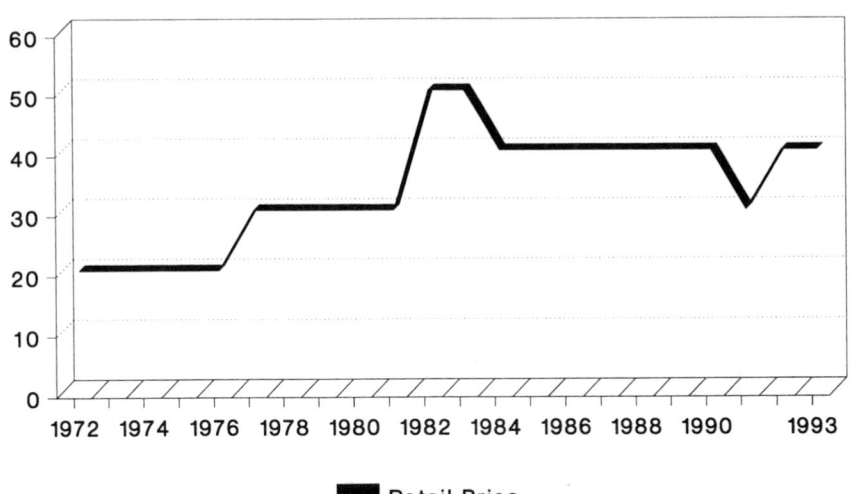

■ Retail Price

Source: COIN PRICES

Obverse legend

Notes: In 1860 the legend "United States of America" replaced the stars on the obverse. The 1873 "closed-3" and "open-3" varieties are distinguished by the amount of space between the upper left and lower left serifs of the 3 in the date.

Date	Mintage	G-4	VG-8	F-12	VF-20	XF-40	AU-50	MS-60	MS-65	Prf-65
1860	607,000	6.00	7.50	9.00	15.00	40.00	115.	525.	—	2150.
1860O	40,000	300.	425.	650.	950.	2000.	6500.	—	—	—
1861	1,884,000	4.50	5.50	7.00	12.00	28.00	100.	325.	—	2150.
1861S	172,500	30.00	35.00	50.00	75.00	175.	900.	—	—	—
1862	847,550	5.50	7.00	8.50	14.00	35.00	110.	500.	—	2150.
1862S	180,750	22.00	28.00	36.00	60.00	125.	800.	—	—	—
1863	14,460	300.	360.	450.	525.	650.	850.	1200.	—	2150.
1863S	157,500	20.00	26.00	35.00	70.00	150.	350.	1200.	—	—
1864	11,470	325.	400.	500.	575.	650.	1000.	1650.	—	2150.
1864S	230,000	12.50	19.00	28.00	50.00	100.	240.	1200.	—	—
1865	10,500	350.	450.	525.	600.	700.	1050.	1250.	—	2150.
1865S	175,000	15.00	22.00	30.00	60.00	125.	700.	—	—	—
1866	8,725	375.	450.	575.	675.	925.	1100.	1500.	—	4400.
1866S	135,000	28.00	34.00	50.00	75.00	150.	300.	1500.	—	—
1867	6,625	475.	575.	700.	825.	1000.	1350.	1800.	—	4400.
1867S	140,000	22.00	32.00	44.00	80.00	160.	325.	1200.	—	—
1868	464,600	7.00	8.00	10.00	18.00	50.00	—	—	—	2150.
1868S	260,000	10.00	14.00	20.00	33.00	85.00	—	1000.	—	—
1869	256,600	12.00	16.00	28.00	40.00	85.00	170.	725.	—	2150.
1869S	450,000	8.00	10.00	13.00	25.00	70.00	175.	825.	—	—
1870	471,500	7.00	8.00	10.00	18.00	50.00	150.	450.	—	2150.
1870S	50,000	140.	160.	210.	320.	475.	800.	2500.	—	—
1871	907,710	5.50	7.00	9.00	14.00	35.00	—	350.	—	2150.
1871CC	20,100	500.	700.	975.	1250.	2500.	3000.	—	—	—

Date	Mintage	G-4	VG-8	F-12	VF-20	XF-40	AU-50	MS-60	MS-65	Prf-65
1871S	320,000	13.00	20.00	30.00	60.00	125.	—	1000.	—	—
1872	2,396,450	5.40	6.25	7.50	11.00	25.00	—	350.	—	2150.
1872CC	35,480	300.	450.	675.	950.	2250.	3000.	—	—	—
1872S	190,000	25.00	38.00	55.00	85.00	175.	—	1100.	—	—
1873 closed 3	1,568,600	7.00	8.50	10.00	18.00	50.00	200.	350.	—	2150.
1873 open 3	Inc. Ab.	15.00	18.00	23.00	40.00	100.	—	—	—	—
1873CC	12,400	—	—			Unique	—	—	—	—

Arrows at date

Weight: 2.5 grams. **Composition:** 90% silver (0.0724 ounces), 10% copper.

Date	Mintage	G-4	VG-8	F-12	VF-20	XF-40	AU-50	MS-60	MS-65	Prf-65
1873	2,378,500	8.00	13.00	25.00	50.00	125.	350.	500.	6000.	8000.
1873CC	18,791	500.	800.	1000.	1500.	2750.	3500.	13,000.	—	—
1873S	455,000	10.00	16.00	27.00	60.00	180.	320.	1500.	—	—
1874	2,940,700	8.00	13.00	25.00	50.00	150.	315.	500.	6000.	8000.
1874CC	10,817	1000.	1400.	2000.	2500.	4300.	6000.	—	—	—
1874S	240,000	20.00	29.00	40.00	95.00	250.	450.	1500.	—	—

Arrows at date removed

Notes: On the 1876-CC doubled-obverse variety, doubling appears in the words "of America" in the legend.

Date	Mintage	G-4	VG-8	F-12	VF-20	XF-40	AU-50	MS-60	MS-65	Prf-65
1875	10,350,700	5.50	6.50	7.50	11.00	22.00	60.00	125.	2250.	4600.
1875CC mint mark in wreath	4,645,000	5.50	6.50	8.00	11.00	25.00		150.	160.	2700.	—
1875CC mint mark under wreath	Inc. Ab.	5.50	6.50	8.00	14.00	35.00	125.	160.	3000.	—
1875S mint mark in wreath	9,070,000	5.50	6.25	7.50	12.50	25.00	300.	500.	3100.	—
1875S mint mark under wreath	Inc. Ab.	5.50	6.25	7.50	11.50	22.00	60.00	125.	1800.	—
1876	11,461,150	5.40	6.25	7.50	11.00	24.00	60.00	125.	1800.	2150.
1876CC	8,270,000	5.50	6.50	7.50	11.00	25.00	60.00	125.	—	—
1876CC (doubled obverse)	Inc. Ab.	15.00	25.00	60.00	250.	400.	—	—	—	—
1876S	10,420,000	5.40	6.50	8.00	12.00	22.00	60.00	125.	1800.	—
1877	7,310,510	5.40	6.25	7.50	11.00	22.00	60.00	125.	1800.	2150.
1877CC	7,700,000	5.50	6.50	7.75	11.50	25.00	60.00	125.	—	—
1877S	2,340,000	5.50	6.50	8.00	15.00	39.00	90.00	150.	—	—
1878	1,678,800	5.50	6.50	8.00	13.00	30.00	60.00	125.	1800.	2150.
1878CC	200,000	65.00	90.00	125.	175.	250.	375.	775.	3500.	—
1879	15,100	175.	210.	250.	310.	400.	550.	750.	4300.	4400.
1880	37,335	125.	165.	190.	240.	300.	425.	650.	4300.	4400.
1881	24,975	150.	175.	215.	265.	350.	425.	675.	4300.	4400.
1882	3,911,100	5.40	6.25	7.50	11.00	22.00	60.00	125.	1800.	2050.
1883	7,675,712	5.40	6.25	7.50	11.00	22.00	60.00	125.	1800.	2050.
1884	3,366,380	5.40	6.25	7.50	11.00	22.00	60.00	125.	1800.	2050.
1884S	564,969	14.00	17.00	23.00	33.00	65.00	110.	450.	—	—
1885	2,533,427	5.40	6.25	7.50	11.00	22.00	60.00	125.	1800.	2050.
1885S	43,690	300.	375.	425.	550.	675.	1000.	3000.	—	—
1886	6,377,570	5.40	6.25	7.50	11.00	22.00	60.00	125.	1800.	2050.
1886S	206,524	22.00	30.00	40.00	70.00	90.00	150.	500.	—	—
1887	11,283,939	5.40	6.25	7.50	11.00	22.00	60.00	125.	1800.	2050.
1887S	4,454,450	5.40	6.25	7.50	11.00	22.00	60.00	125.	1800.	—
1888	5,496,487	5.40	6.25	7.50	11.00	24.00	60.00	125.	1800.	2050.
1888S	1,720,000	6.00	6.75	8.00	14.00	35.00	60.00	125.	1800.	—
1889	7,380,711	5.40	6.25	7.50	11.00	22.00	60.00	125.	1800.	2050.

Date	Mintage	G-4	VG-8	F-12	VF-20	XF-40	AU-50	MS-60	MS-65	Prf-65
1889S	972,678	7.00	9.00	15.00	25.00	50.00	125.	475.	4500.	—
1890	9,911,541	5.40	6.25	7.50	11.00	22.00	60.00	125.	1800.	2050.
1890S	1,423,076	8.00	10.00	13.50	25.00	45.00	100.	475.	4900.	—
1890S/S	Inc. Ab.	75.00	100.	130.	185.	275.	450.	—	—	—
1891	15,310,600	5.40	6.25	7.50	11.00	22.00	60.00	125.	1800.	2050.
1891O	4,540,000	5.50	6.50	7.75	11.50	22.00	70.00	475.	2250.	—
1891O/horz. O										
	Inc. Ab.	72.00	95.00	125.	175.	250.	400.	—	—	—
1891S	3,196,116	5.50	6.25	7.50	12.00	28.00	70.00	500.	4400.	—

Barber

Designer: Charles E. Barber. **Size:** 17.9 millimeters. **Weight:** 2.5 grams. **Composition:** 90% silver (0.0724 ounces), 10% copper.

Date	Mintage	G-4	VG-8	F-12	VF-20	XF-40	AU-50	MS-60	MS-65	Prf-65
1892	12,121,245	2.60	4.25	9.75	12.00	19.50	47.00	100.	1000.	1700.
1892O	3,841,700	4.00	6.00	14.00	19.50	29.00	59.00	145.	2050.	—
1892S	990,710	27.00	42.00	85.00	104.	120.	190.	325.	4800.	—
1893	3,340,792	4.00	6.00	14.00	20.00	27.00	65.00	165.	1000.	1700.
1893O	1,760,000	14.00	25.00	71.00	84.00	97.00	125.	260.	2600.	—
1893S	2,491,401	6.50	11.50	21.00	30.00	39.00	110.	230.	2400.	—
1894	1,330,972	7.00	14.00	65.00	85.00	91.00	110.	250.	1175.	1700.
1894O	720,000	32.00	52.00	125.	175.	290.	600.	945.	8300.	—
1894S	24			Stacks Sale, Jan. 1990, Ch. Proof $275,000.					—	—
1895	690,880	58.00	71.00	240.	300.	315.	410.	610.	1925.	2500.
1895O	440,000	160.	260.	570.	875.	1225.	1950.	2200.	10,000.	—
1895S	1,120,000	15.00	24.00	71.00	91.00	105.	180.	390.	6500.	—
1896	2,000,762	5.85	11.75	27.00	38.00	45.00	85.00	165.	1560.	1700.
1896O	610,000	41.00	62.00	155.	225.	330.	550.	725.	6300.	—
1896S	575,056	41.00	52.00	145.	180.	210.	410.	585.	6000.	—
1897	10,869,264	1.30	2.25	4.90	7.50	22.00	55.00	100.	1000.	1700.
1897O	666,000	36.00	47.00	150.	210.	305.	520.	725.	6600.	—
1897S	1,342,844	8.00	14.00	43.00	56.00	78.00	195.	325.	6600.	—
1898	16,320,735	1.30	1.45	4.75	8.00	19.50	46.00	100.	1000.	1700.
1898O	2,130,000	3.90	7.50	58.00	75.00	115.	165.	390.	4800.	—
1898S	1,702,507	3.90	6.20	15.00	23.00	35.00	95.00	250.	5700.	—
1899	19,580,846	1.30	1.45	4.00	7.00	19.50	46.00	100.	1150.	1700.
1899O	2,650,000	3.60	6.00	45.00	63.00	110.	200.	325.	5750.	—
1899S	1,867,493	2.90	6.50	11.00	18.00	30.00	85.00	275.	4800.	—
1900	17,600,912	1.35	1.65	4.90	7.75	19.50	46.00	90.00	1250.	1700.
1900O	2,010,000	4.90	8.45	57.00	78.00	155.	270.	565.	6000.	—
1900S	5,168,270	2.25	2.90	6.50	9.50	22.00	72.00	155.	1920.	—
1901	18,860,478	1.30	1.45	3.90	7.00	19.50	46.00	100.	1170.	1700.
1901O	5,620,000	2.25	3.25	8.50	14.00	42.00	115.	295.	2600.	—
1901S	593,022	35.00	45.00	175.	230.	370.	585.	775.	5150.	—
1902	21,380,777	1.30	1.45	3.50	6.50	19.50	46.00	120.	1000.	2600.
1902O	4,500,000	2.20	3.90	9.75	20.00	34.00	105.	300.	4600.	—
1902S	2,070,000	3.90	6.50	22.00	32.00	71.00	130.	295.	4080.	—
1903	19,500,755	1.30	1.45	3.65	6.25	19.00	46.00	120.	1325.	1700.
1903O	8,180,000	2.00	2.75	6.00	9.00	26.00	91.00	250.	7500.	—
1903S	613,300	26.00	39.00	210.	390.	550.	750.	775.	5100.	—
1904	14,601,027	1.30	1.45	5.00	8.25	20.00	46.00	100.	3700.	2600.
1904S	800,000	19.00	29.00	91.00	130.	250.	420.	525.	4400.	—
1905	14,552,350	1.30	1.45	3.90	6.25	19.00	46.00	100.	1000.	1700.
1905O	3,400,000	2.25	4.25	15.50	23.00	39.00	105.	215.	3250.	—
1905S	6,855,199	2.10	3.00	6.50	11.00	24.00	72.00	200.	1250.	—
1906	19,958,406	1.30	1.45	3.00	6.50	19.50	46.00	100.	1000.	2650.
1906D	4,060,000	2.10	3.00	6.50	11.00	24.00	72.00	150.	2650.	—
1906O	2,610,000	2.45	5.25	27.00	38.00	42.00	120.	210.	1300.	—
1906S	3,136,640	1.60	3.50	10.50	15.50	32.00	91.00	215.	1350.	—
1907	22,220,575	1.30	1.45	3.00	6.50	19.50	46.00	100.	1000.	2650.
1907D	4,080,000	1.45	2.60	6.50	10.00	32.00	85.00	225.	4800.	—
1907O	5,058,000	1.45	2.60	14.00	22.00	25.00	72.00	165.	1750.	—
1907S	3,178,470	1.90	3.90	7.75	13.00	35.00	100.	275.	4100.	—
1908	10,600,545	1.30	1.45	3.00	6.50	19.00	46.00	100.	1000.	2650.
1908D	7,490,000	1.30	1.80	5.50	9.50	21.00	55.00	140.	1800.	—
1908O	1,789,000	2.30	4.50	27.00	39.00	52.00	125.	250.	2100.	—
1908S	3,220,000	1.65	2.60	7.50	12.00	26.00	91.00	195.	2900.	—
1909	10,240,650	1.30	1.45	3.00	6.50	19.00	46.00	100.	1000.	2650.
1909D	954,000	2.95	6.75	32.00	45.00	76.00	150.	335.	3000.	—

1901-S Dime
Grade F-12

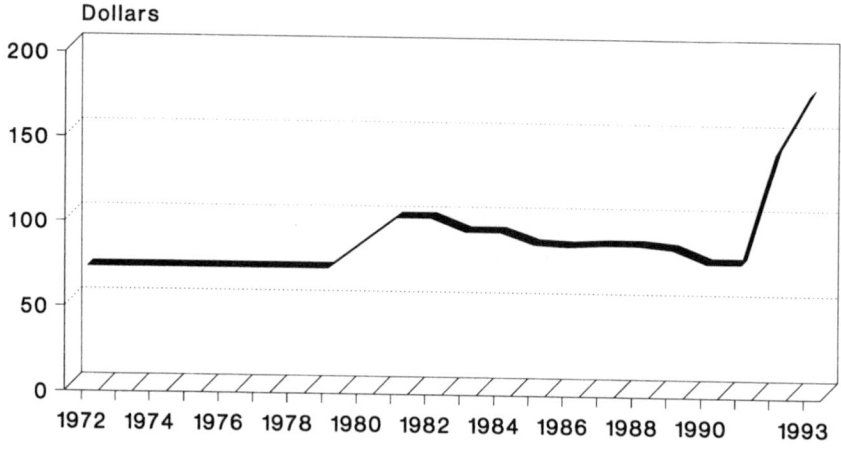

Dollars

■ Retail Price

Source: COIN PRICES

Date	Mintage	G-4	VG-8	F-12	VF-20	XF-40	AU-50	MS-60	MS-65	Prf-65
1909O	2,287,000	1.65	3.40	7.80	15.00	27.00	91.00	165.	1400.	—
1909S	1,000,000	3.00	6.50	45.00	58.00	135.	275.	390.	3400.	—
1910	11,520,551	1.30	1.45	4.50	7.50	19.00	46.00	100.	1000.	1700.
1910D	3,490,000	1.40	3.25	7.50	11.00	28.00	91.00	175.	3000.	—
1910S	1,240,000	1.50	4.50	26.00	35.00	55.00	150.	350.	1800.	—
1911	18,870,543	1.30	1.45	3.00	6.50	19.50	48.00	100.	1000.	2500.
1911D	11,209,000	1.30	1.45	3.90	7.00	19.00	46.00	100.	1000.	—
1911S	3,520,000	1.30	3.00	7.00	10.00	26.00	85.00	145.	1000.	—
1912	19,350,700	1.30	1.45	3.00	6.50	19.50	46.00	100.	1000.	2650.
1912D	11,760,000	1.30	1.45	4.00	6.50	19.00	46.00	100.	1000.	—
1912S	3,420,000	1.30	1.80	5.75	7.50	23.00	72.00	160.	1200.	—
1913	19,760,622	1.30	1.45	2.80	6.50	19.50	46.00	100.	1000.	1700.
1913S	510,000	6.50	11.50	52.00	98.00	175.	295.	360.	1450.	—
1914	17,360,655	1.30	1.45	2.80	6.50	19.50	46.00	100.	1000.	2650.
1914D	11,908,000	1.30	1.45	4.00	6.50	19.00	46.00	90.00	1000.	—
1914S	2,100,000	1.60	2.25	5.00	10.00	26.00	72.00	160.	1200.	—
1915	5,620,450	1.30	1.45	3.00	6.50	19.00	46.00	100.	1000.	3125.
1915S	960,000	1.75	3.50	17.00	23.00	43.00	120.	225.	2500.	—
1916	18,490,000	1.30	1.45	5.00	6.50	20.00	47.00	120.	1000.	—
1916S	5,820,000	1.30	1.45	4.00	6.00	20.00	47.00	100.	1000.	—

Mercury

Designer: Adolph A. Weinman. **Size:** 17.9 millimeters. **Weight:** 2.5 grams. **Composition:** 90% silver (0.0724 ounces), 10% copper. **Notes:** "-65FSB" values are for coins with fully split and rounded horizontal bands around the fasces on the reverse. The 1945-S "micro" variety has a smaller mintmark than the normal variety.

1916-D Dime
Grade F-12

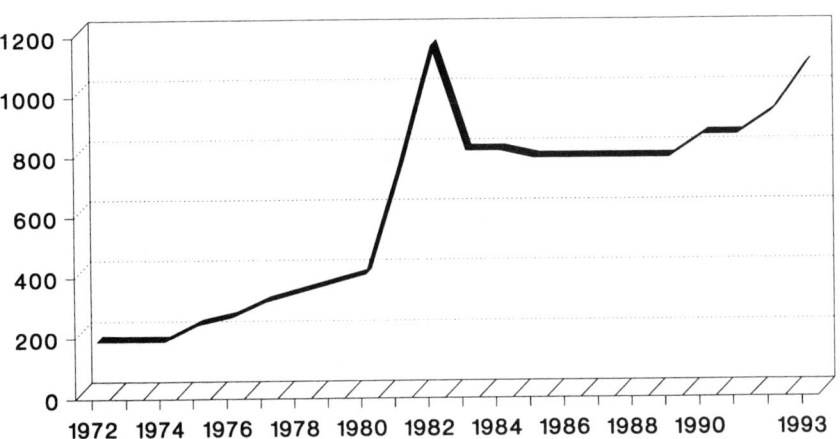

Retail Price

Source: COIN PRICES

Date	Mintage	G-4	VG-8	F-12	VF-20	XF-40	MS-60	MS-65	-65FSB	Prf-65
1916	22,180,080	2.25	3.50	4.75	7.25	11.00	25.00	100.	110.	—
1916D	264,000	390.	665.	1085.	1900.	2450.	4050.	11,750.	16,000.	—
1916S	10,450,000	3.50	4.50	5.75	9.75	16.50	34.00	195.	425.	—
1917	55,230,000	1.00	2.10	2.75	5.50	8.00	28.00	170.	325.	—
1917D	9,402,000	3.50	5.25	8.00	16.00	38.00	125.	1825.	5500.	—
1917S	27,330,000	1.25	2.35	3.25	6.00	9.50	49.00	775.	1825.	—
1918	26,680,000	1.25	3.00	4.25	11.00	25.00	70.00	390.	625.	—
1918D	22,674,800	2.25	3.00	4.00	9.50	23.00	105.	1100.	11,000.	—
1918S	19,300,000	2.00	2.50	3.50	6.50	14.00	85.00	1100.	5300.	—
1919	35,740,000	1.00	2.25	3.25	5.50	8.00	35.00	360.	520.	—
1919D	9,939,000	3.00	4.25	6.00	15.00	39.00	140.	1800.	5500.	—
1919S	8,850,000	2.50	3.60	5.00	13.00	29.00	175.	1275.	4350.	—
1920	59,030,000	1.00	2.10	2.75	5.00	7.00	27.00	230.	375.	—
1920D	19,171,000	2.25	3.25	4.25	7.00	15.00	100.	1250.	3000.	—
1920S	13,820,000	2.00	2.80	4.00	6.50	13.50	70.00	1175.	4475.	—
1921	1,230,000	19.50	30.00	70.00	175.	425.	1050.	2900.	4000.	—
1921D	1,080,000	30.00	41.00	110.	220.	500.	1150.	2850.	4000.	—
1923	50,130,000	1.00	2.10	2.75	4.25	7.00	25.00	115.	195.	—
1923S	6,440,000	2.25	3.50	4.25	9.50	29.00	135.	1700.	3775.	—
1924	24,010,000	1.00	2.10	2.75	5.00	9.00	38.00	170.	520.	—
1924D	6,810,000	2.25	3.25	5.50	10.00	29.00	155.	1275.	3100.	—
1924S	7,120,000	2.00	3.00	4.00	8.00	29.00	155.	1800.	5850.	—
1925	25,610,000	1.00	2.10	2.75	4.25	7.50	28.00	210.	495.	—
1925D	5,117,000	4.00	5.75	8.50	25.00	85.00	260.	1700.	5200.	—
1925S	5,850,000	2.00	2.80	4.00	8.00	30.00	140.	2200.	4000.	—
1926	32,160,000	1.00	1.85	2.25	4.25	6.50	28.00	285.	520.	—
1926D	6,828,000	1.95	3.00	4.00	7.50	15.00	70.00	550.	2200.	—
1926S	1,520,000	5.50	9.50	15.00	34.00	190.	770.	3000.	4900.	—
1927	28,080,000	1.00	1.80	2.25	4.25	6.50	21.00	180.	325.	—
1927D	4,812,000	2.75	3.75	5.00	12.00	42.00	175.	1550.	4700.	—
1927S	4,770,000	1.90	2.65	3.75	5.50	11.00	125.	1050.	4550.	—
1928	19,480,000	1.00	1.80	2.25	4.25	6.50	21.00	125.	250.	—
1928D	4,161,000	3.00	4.25	6.00	15.00	30.00	135.	975.	2200.	—
1928S	7,400,000	1.75	2.35	3.25	5.00	12.00	70.00	520.	1460.	—
1929	25,970,000	1.00	1.80	2.35	3.75	5.00	19.50	58.00	170.	—
1929D	5,034,000	2.65	3.60	5.00	8.00	12.00	28.00	100.	150.	—
1929S	4,730,000	1.65	1.90	2.25	4.25	5.50	34.00	155.	325.	—
1930	6,770,000	1.50	1.80	2.25	4.25	5.50	22.00	155.	275.	—
1930S	1,843,000	3.50	4.25	5.00	7.50	13.00	70.00	130.	250.	—
1931	3,150,000	2.00	2.75	3.50	5.00	11.00	35.00	155.	390.	—
1931D	1,260,000	5.50	7.50	11.00	18.00	30.00	77.00	210.	275.	—
1931S	1,800,000	3.50	4.00	5.00	7.50	13.00	63.00	210.	1100.	—

Date	Mintage	G-4	VG-8	F-12	VF-20	XF-40	MS-60	MS-65	-65FSB	Prf-65
1934	24,080,000	1.00	1.45	1.75	3.00	5.00	15.00	32.00	48.00	—
1934D	6,772,000	1.80	2.10	2.75	4.00	8.00	32.00	72.00	210.	—
1935	58,830,000	1.00	1.20	1.50	2.15	4.25	11.00	30.00	32.00	—
1935D	10,477,000	1.75	2.00	3.00	4.75	9.25	32.00	68.00	390.	—
1935S	15,840,000	1.35	1.50	1.75	3.00	5.50	24.00	35.00	145.	—
1936	87,504,130	1.00	1.25	1.50	2.25	3.50	8.50	24.00	28.00	1100.
1936D	16,132,000	1.25	1.50	2.00	3.25	6.75	22.00	42.00	110.	—
1936S	9,210,000	1.25	1.50	1.75	2.75	4.75	17.00	28.00	31.00	—
1937	56,865,756	1.00	1.25	1.50	2.00	3.25	10.00	24.00	28.00	385.
1937D	14,146,000	1.25	1.50	1.90	3.00	5.50	21.00	41.00	55.00	—
1937S	9,740,000	1.25	1.50	1.90	3.00	5.50	18.00	31.00	91.00	—
1938	22,198,728	1.00	1.25	1.50	2.25	3.50	14.00	23.00	28.00	280.
1938D	5,537,000	1.75	2.00	2.25	3.75	6.00	15.00	26.00	28.00	—
1938S	8,090,000	1.35	1.55	1.85	2.35	3.75	15.00	29.00	42.00	—
1939	67,749,321	1.00	1.25	1.50	2.00	3.25	10.00	19.00	78.00	265.
1939D	24,394,000	1.25	1.45	1.75	2.25	3.50	12.50	20.00	26.00	—
1939S	10,540,000	1.55	1.75	2.00	2.50	4.25	24.00	40.00	340.	—
1940	65,361,827	.50	.60	.70	1.00	2.50	6.50	19.00	26.00	250.
1940D	21,198,000	.50	.60	.70	1.00	1.50	8.50	20.00	28.00	—
1940S	21,560,000	.50	.60	.70	1.00	1.50	8.50	20.00	36.00	—
1941	175,106,557	.50	.60	.70	1.00	1.50	5.50	19.00	28.00	250.
1941D	45,634,000	.50	.60	.70	1.00	1.50	8.00	21.00	26.00	—
1941S	43,090,000	.50	.60	.70	1.00	1.50	10.00	19.00	32.00	—

Fully split bands

1942/41

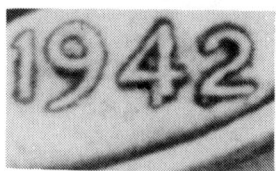

1942/41-D

1942	205,432,329	.50	.60	.70	1.00	1.50	5.50	20.00	26.00	250.
1942/41	Inc. Ab.	155.	180.	230.	250.	310.	1600.	6500.	9200.	—
1942D	60,740,000	.50	.60	.70	1.00	1.50	8.50	20.00	26.00	—
1942/41D	Inc. Ab.	165.	190.	240.	260.	400.	1400.	5000.	7150.	—
1942S	49,300,000	.50	.60	.70	1.00	1.50	10.00	20.00	49.00	—
1943	191,710,000	.50	.60	.70	1.00	1.50	6.50	19.00	26.00	—
1943D	71,949,000	.50	.60	.70	1.00	1.50	8.50	24.00	26.00	—
1943S	60,400,000	.50	.60	.70	1.00	1.50	10.00	20.00	34.00	—
1944	231,410,000	.50	.60	.70	1.00	1.50	5.50	20.00	58.00	—
1944D	62,224,000	.50	.60	.70	1.00	1.50	8.50	20.00	26.00	—
1944S	49,490,000	.50	.60	.70	1.00	1.50	10.00	20.00	31.00	—
1945	159,130,000	.50	.60	.70	1.00	1.50	5.50	22.00	2825.	—
1945D	40,245,000	.50	.60	.70	1.00	1.50	8.00	20.00	30.00	—
1945S	41,920,000	.50	.60	.70	1.00	1.50	8.50	20.00	65.00	—
1945S micro	Inc. Ab.	1.50	1.65	1.85	3.00	4.25	17.00	52.00	425.	—

Roosevelt

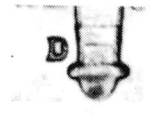

Reverse mintmark
(1946-64)

Obverse mintmark
(1968-present)

Silver composition

Designer: John R. Sinnock. **Size:** 17.9 millimeters. **Weight:** 2.5 grams. **Composition:** 90% silver (0.0724 ounces), 10% copper.

Date	Mintage	G-4	VG-8	F-12	VF-20	XF-40	AU-50	MS-60	MS-65	Prf-65
1946	225,250,000	—	—	—	.40	.80	.95	1.05	2.50	—
1946D	61,043,500	—	—	—	.40	.80	1.10	1.25	4.50	—
1946S	27,900,000	—	—	—	.40	.80	1.10	2.00	5.25	—
1947	121,520,000	—	—	—	.40	.80	.95	1.00	4.75	—
1947D	46,835,000	—	—	—	.40	.95	1.20	1.40	10.00	—
1947S	34,840,000	—	—	—	.40	.95	1.10	1.35	5.50	—
1948	74,950,000	—	—	—	.40	.95	1.10	1.75	11.00	—
1948D	52,841,000	—	—	—	.40	1.20	1.50	2.00	10.00	—
1948S	35,520,000	—	—	—	.40	.95	1.10	1.35	9.00	—
1949	30,940,000	—	—	—	1.00	1.50	4.50	6.00	29.00	—
1949D	26,034,000	—	—	.60	.80	1.25	2.00	3.50	12.50	—
1949S	13,510,000	—	1.00	1.25	1.50	2.75	7.50	9.00	55.00	—
1950	50,181,500	—	—	—	.40	.95	1.10	1.35	4.60	25.00
1950D	46,803,000	—	—	—	.40	.80	.95	1.00	4.60	—
1950S	20,440,000	—	.85	1.00	1.10	1.25	5.00	7.00	35.00	—
1951	102,937,602	—	—	—	.40	.85	1.00	1.00	3.30	23.00
1951D	56,529,000	—	—	—	.40	.80	.95	1.00	3.50	—
1951S	31,630,000	—	—	.95	1.00	1.05	2.75	3.25	24.00	—
1952	99,122,073	—	—	—	.40	.95	1.10	1.20	3.30	25.00
1952D	122,100,000	—	—	—	.40	.80	.95	1.00	3.80	—
1952S	44,419,500	—	—	.95	1.00	1.05	1.10	1.35	7.00	—
1953	53,618,920	—	—	—	.40	.90	1.00	1.10	3.60	23.00
1953D	136,433,000	—	—	—	.40	.80	.95	1.00	3.50	—
1953S	39,180,000	—	—	—	.40	.95	1.10	1.35	2.25	—
1954	114,243,503	—	—	—	.40	.75	.90	.95	2.15	10.00
1954D	106,397,000	—	—	—	.40	.80	.95	1.00	2.15	—
1954S	22,860,000	—	—	—	.40	.60	.65	.75	2.20	—
1955	12,828,381	—	—	—	.40	.60	.80	.90	3.00	9.00
1955D	13,959,000	—	—	—	.40	.60	.80	.90	2.25	—
1955S	18,510,000	—	—	—	.40	.60	.80	.90	2.00	—
1956	109,309,384	—	—	—	.35	.40	.50	.60	2.00	1.95
1956D	108,015,100	—	—	—	.35	.40	.50	.60	1.65	—
1957	161,407,952	—	—	—	.35	.40	.50	.60	1.60	1.25
1957D	113,354,330	—	—	—	.35	.40	.50	.60	3.00	—
1958	32,785,652	—	—	—	.35	.40	.50	.60	1.80	1.95
1958D	136,564,600	—	—	—	.35	.40	.50	.60	1.50	—
1959	86,929,291	—	—	—	.35	.40	.50	.60	1.50	1.25
1959D	164,919,790	—	—	—	.35	.40	.50	.60	1.35	—
1960	72,081,602	—	—	—	.35	.40	.50	.60	1.40	1.25
1960D	200,160,400	—	—	—	.35	.40	.50	.60	1.35	—
1961	96,758,244	—	—	—	.35	.40	.50	.60	1.35	1.10
1961D	209,146,550	—	—	—	.35	.40	.50	.60	1.35	—
1962	75,668,019	—	—	—	.35	.40	.50	.60	1.35	1.10
1962D	334,948,380	—	—	—	.35	.40	.50	.60	1.35	—
1963	126,725,645	—	—	—	.35	.40	.50	.60	1.35	1.10
1963D	421,476,530	—	—	—	.35	.40	.50	.60	1.35	—
1964	933,310,762	—	—	—	.35	.40	.50	.60	1.35	.95
1964D	1,357,517,180	—	—	—	.35	.40	.50	.60	1.35	—

Clad composition

Weight: 2.27 grams. **Composition:** clad layers of 75% copper and 25% nickel, bonded to a pure-copper core. **Notes:** The 1979-S Type II proof has a clearer mintmark than the Type I. On the 1982 no-mintmark variety, the mintmark was inadvertently left off.

Date	Mintage	G-4	F-12	VF-20	XF-40	AU-50	MS-60	MS-65	Prf-65
1965	1,652,140,570	—	—	—	—	—	—	.40	—
1966	1,382,734,540	—	—	—	—	—	—	.30	—
1967	2,244,007,320	—	—	—	—	—	—	.30	—
1968	424,470,000	—	—	—	—	—	—	.25	—
1968D	480,748,280	—	—	—	—	—	—	.25	—
1968S	Proof only	—	—	—	—	—	—	—	.75
1969	145,790,000	—	—	—	—	—	—	.45	—
1969D	563,323,870	—	—	—	—	—	—	.40	—
1969S	Proof only	—	—	—	—	—	—	—	.60
1970	345,570,000	—	—	—	—	—	—	.30	—
1970D	754,942,100	—	—	—	—	—	—	.30	—
1970S	Proof only	—	—	—	—	—	—	—	.50
1971	162,690,000	—	—	—	—	—	—	.35	—
1971D	377,914,240	—	—	—	—	—	—	.35	—
1971S	Proof only	—	—	—	—	—	—	—	.70
1972	431,540,000	—	—	—	—	—	—	.30	—
1972D	330,290,000	—	—	—	—	—	—	.25	—
1972S	Proof only	—	—	—	—	—	—	—	.70
1973	315,670,000	—	—	—	—	—	—	.25	—
1973D	455,032,426	—	—	—	—	—	—	.20	—
1973S	Proof only	—	—	—	—	—	—	—	.55
1974	470,248,000	—	—	—	—	—	—	.20	—
1974D	571,083,000	—	—	—	—	—	—	.20	—
1974S	Proof only	—	—	—	—	—	—	—	1.25
1975	585,673,900	—	—	—	—	—	—	.30	—

Date	Mintage	G-4	F-12	VF-20	XF-40	AU-50	MS-60	MS-65	Prf-65
1975D	313,705,300	—	—	—	—	—	—	.25	—
1975S	Proof only	—	—	—	—	—	—	—	.60
1976	568,760,000	—	—	—	—	—	—	.35	—
1976D	695,222,774	—	—	—	—	—	—	.35	—
1976S	Proof only	—	—	—	—	—	—	—	.75
1977	796,930,000	—	—	—	—	—	—	.20	—
1977D	376,607,228	—	—	—	—	—	—	.25	—
1977S	Proof only	—	—	—	—	—	—	—	.50
1978	663,980,000	—	—	—	—	—	—	.20	—
1978D	282,847,540	—	—	—	—	—	—	.20	—
1978S	Proof only	—	—	—	—	—	—	—	.50
1979	315,440,000	—	—	—	—	—	—	.20	—
1979D	390,921,184	—	—	—	—	—	—	.20	—
1979S T-I	Proof only	—	—	—	—	—	—	—	.55
1979S T-II	Proof only	—	—	—	—	—	—	—	1.25
1980P	735,170,000	—	—	—	—	—	—	.20	—
1980D	719,354,321	—	—	—	—	—	—	.20	—
1980S	Proof only	—	—	—	—	—	—	—	.45
1981P	676,650,000	—	—	—	—	—	—	.20	—
1981D	712,284,143	—	—	—	—	—	—	.20	—
1981S T-I	Proof only	—	—	—	—	—	—	—	.45
1981S T-II	Proof only	—	—	—	—	—	—	—	3.00
1982P	519,475,000	—	—	—	—	—	—	1.10	—
1982 no mint mark						100.	125.	190.	—
1982D	542,713,584	—	—	—	—	—	—	.30	—
1982S	Proof only	—	—	—	—	—	—	—	.50
1983P	647,025,000	—	—	—	—	—	—	.75	—
1983D	730,129,224	—	—	—	—	—	—	.60	—
1983S	Proof only	—	—	—	—	—	—	—	1.10
1984P	856,669,000	—	—	—	—	—	—	.25	—
1984D	704,803,976	—	—	—	—	—	—	.35	—
1984S	Proof only	—	—	—	—	—	—	—	1.60
1985P	705,200,962	—	—	—	—	—	—	.35	—
1985D	587,979,970	—	—	—	—	—	—	.30	—
1985S	Proof only	—	—	—	—	—	—	—	1.40
1986P	682,649,693	—	—	—	—	—	—	.35	—
1986D	473,326,970	—	—	—	—	—	—	.35	—
1986S	Proof only	—	—	—	—	—	—	—	2.25
1987P	762,709,481	—	—	—	—	—	—	.20	—
1987D	653,203,402	—	—	—	—	—	—	.20	—
1987S	Proof only	—	—	—	—	—	—	—	1.25
1988P	1,030,550,000	—	—	—	—	—	—	.20	—
1988D	962,385,488	—	—	—	—	—	—	.20	—
1988S	Proof only	—	—	—	—	—	—	—	1.50
1989P	1,298,400,000	—	—	—	—	—	—	.20	—
1989D	896,535,597	—	—	—	—	—	—	.20	—
1989S	Proof only	—	—	—	—	—	—	—	1.45
1990P	1,034,340,000	—	—	—	—	—	—	.20	—
1990D	839,995,824	—	—	—	—	—	—	.20	—
1990S	Proof only	—	—	—	—	—	—	—	1.40
1991P	—	—	—	—	—	—	—	.20	—
1991D	—	—	—	—	—	—	—	.20	—
1991S	Proof only	—	—	—	—	—	—	—	1.80
1992P	—	—	—	—	—	—	—	.20	—
1992D	—	—	—	—	—	—	—	.20	—
1992S	Proof only	—	—	—	—	—	—	—	1.80
1993P	—	—	—	—	—	—	—	.20	—
1993D	—	—	—	—	—	—	—	.20	—
1993S	Proof only	—	—	—	—	—	—	—	1.80

20-cent

Designer: William Barber. **Size:** 22 millimeters. **Weight:** 5 grams. **Composition:** 90% silver (0.1447 ounces), 10% copper.

Date	Mintage	G-4	VG-8	F-12	VF-20	XF-40	AU-50	MS-60	MS-65	Prf-65
1875	39,700	60.00	80.00	120.	130.	225.	400.	1300.	8400.	9500.
1875S	1,155,000	35.00	46.00	60.00	85.00	170.	380.	500.	7500.	—
1875CC	133,290	50.00	65.00	100.	150.	275.	525.	1450.	9500.	—
1876	15,900	85.00	100.	130.	260.	400.	600.	1500.	9500.	8000.
1876CC	10,000				Norweb Sale, Oct. 1987, MS-64, $69,300.				—	—
1877	510	—		Proof only					—	23,000.
Impaired proof					1850.	2100.	2450.	—	—	—
1878	600	—		Proof only	—	—	—	—	—	23,000.
Impaired proof				—	1175.	1575.	2000.	—	—	—

1876 20-Cent
Grade F-12

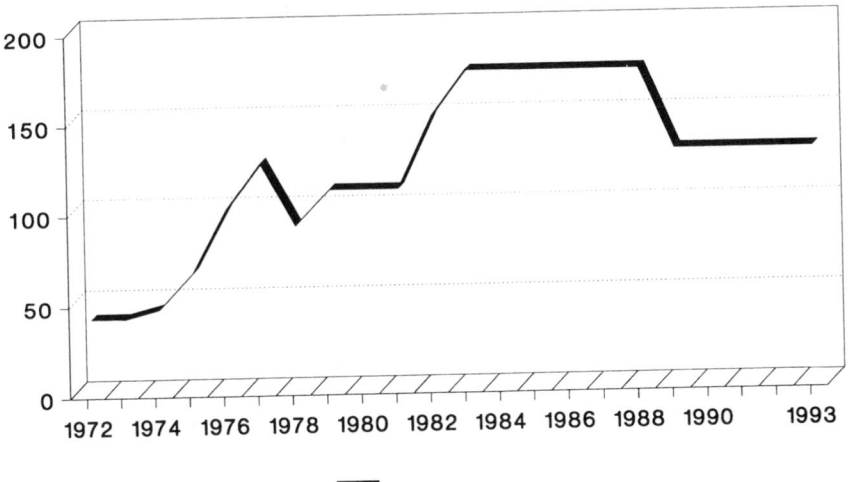

Retail Price

Source: COIN PRICES

1804 Quarter
Grade XF-40

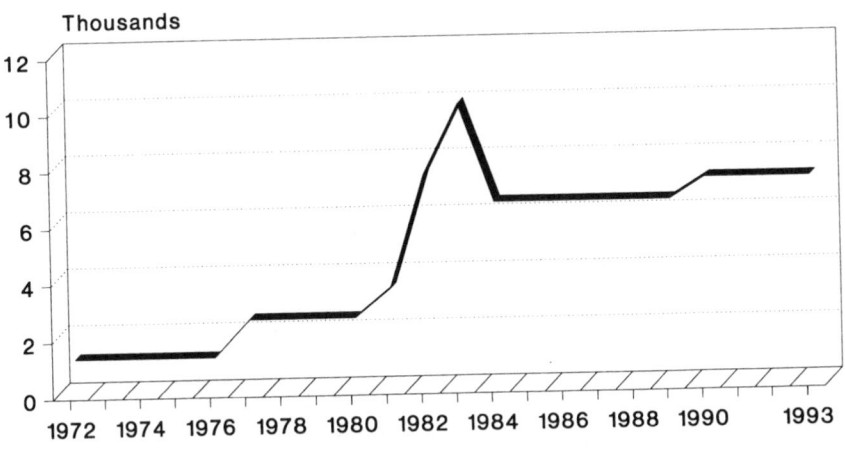

Retail Price

Source: COIN PRICES

Quarters

Draped Bust

Small-eagle reverse

Designer: Robert Scot. **Size:** 27.5 millimeters. **Weight:** 6.74 grams. **Composition:** 89.24% silver (0.1935 ounces), 10.76% copper.

Date	Mintage	G-4	VG-8	F-12	VF-20	XF-40	AU-50	MS-60	MS-65
1796	6,146	4150.	5400.	7300.	13,000.	18,500.	23,500.	28,000.	125,000.

Heraldic-eagle reverse

Date	Mintage	G-4	VG-8	F-12	VF-20	XF-40	AU-50	MS-60	MS-65
1804	6,738	1000.	1650.	2750.	4250.	7250.	16,500.	22,000.	116,000.
1805	121,394	225.	275.	500.	1000.	1900.	3250.	4400.	56,500.
1806	206,124	225.	275.	500.	1000.	1900.	3250.	4400.	56,500.
1806/5	Inc. Ab.	225.	325.	550.	1075.	1900.	3250.	4400.	56,500.
1807	220,643	225.	325.	550.	1075.	2000.	4150.	5650.	56,500.

Liberty Cap

Designer: John Reich. **Size:** 27 millimeters. **Weight:** 6.74 grams. **Composition:** 89.24% silver (0.1935 ounces), 10.76% copper. **Notes:** Varieties of the 1819 strikes are distinguished by the size of the 9 in the date. Varieties of the 1820 strikes are distinguished by the size of the 0 in the date. One 1822 variety and one 1828 variety have "25" engraved over "50" in the denomination. The 1827 restrikes were produced privately using dies sold as scrap by the U.S. Mint.

Date	Mintage	G-4	VG-8	F-12	VF-20	XF-40	AU-50	MS-60	MS-65
1815	89,235	60.00	80.00	100.	300.	725.	2000.	3100.	22,000.
1818	361,174	39.00	50.00	90.00	250.	525.	1300.	1550.	19,000.
1818/15	Inc. Ab.	65.00	95.00	150.	425.	950.	2000.	3100.	22,000.
1819 sm.9	144,000	44.00	55.00	100.	275.	600.	1350.	1550.	19,000.
1819 lg.9	Inc. Ab.	44.00	55.00	100.	275.	600.	1350.	1550.	19,000.
1820 sm.O	127,444	75.00	100.	165.	350.	750.	1500.	3000.	19,000.
1820 lg.O	Inc. Ab.	36.00	45.00	100.	250.	500.	1300.	1550.	19,000.
1821	216,851	36.00	45.00	100.	250.	500.	1300.	1550.	19,000.
1822	64,080	55.00	70.00	115.	350.	775.	1400.	1550.	19,000.
1822 25/50C.	I.A.	600.	850.	1400.	2750.	4500.	8000.	15,000.	25,000.
1823/22	17,800	5250.	6500.	9000.	13,000.	18,000.	—	—	—
			Superior, Aug. 1990, proof, $62,500.						
1824/2	Unrecorded	75.00	90.00	160.	425.	950.	1300.	1550.	19,000.
1825/22	168,000	70.00	85.00	125.	350.	800.	1500.	1550.	19,000.
1825/23	Inc. Ab.	40.00	50.00	100.	250.	550.	1500.	1550.	19,000.
1825/24	Inc. Ab.	44.00	55.00	100.	260.	575.	1500.	1550.	19,000.
1827 original	4,000			Superior, Aug. 1990, proof, $42,000.					—
1827 restrike	I.A.			Superior, Aug. 1990, proof, $23,000.				—	
1828	102,000	36.00	45.00	85.00	250.	550.	1500.	1550.	19,000.
1828 25/50C.	I.A.	110.	165.	225.	450.	900.	2000.	3100.	—

No motto

Designer: William Kneass. **Size:** 24.3 millimeters. **Notes:** In 1831 the motto "E Pluribus Unum" was removed from the reverse. Varieties of the 1831 strikes are distinguished by the size of the lettering on the reverse.

Date	Mintage	G-4	VG-8	F-12	VF-20	XF-40	AU-50	MS-60	MS-65
1831 small letters									
	398,000	35.00	38.00	50.00	100.	210.	750.	900.	15,500.
1831 lg.let.	Inc. Ab.	35.00	38.00	50.00	100.	210.	750.	900.	15,500.
1832	320,000	40.00	45.00	55.00	155.	210.	750.	900.	15,500.
1833	156,000	44.00	54.00	65.00	120.	350.	600.	1000.	17,000.
1834	286,000	40.00	45.00	55.00	100.	210.	750.	900.	15,500.
1835	1,952,000	35.00	38.00	50.00	100.	210.	750.	900.	15,500.
1836	472,000	35.00	38.00	50.00	100.	210.	750.	900.	15,500.
1837	252,400	37.00	42.00	50.00	100.	210.	750.	900.	15,500.
1838	832,000	35.00	38.00	50.00	100.	210.	750.	900.	15,500.

Seated Liberty

No drapery

Designer: Christian Gobrecht. **Size:** 24.3 millimeters. **Weight:** 6.68 grams. **Composition:** 90% silver (0.1934 ounces), 10% copper.

Date	Mintage	G-4	VG-8	F-12	VF-20	XF-40	AU-50	MS-60	MS-65
1838	Inc. Ab.	11.00	15.00	22.00	44.00	160.	400.	900.	25,000.
1839	491,146	9.50	15.00	22.00	44.00	160.	400.	900.	25,000.
1840O	425,200	9.50	15.00	22.00	44.00	160.	400.	900.	25,000.

Drapery added to Liberty

Notes: In 1840 drapery was added to Liberty's left elbow. Two varieties for 1842 and 1842-O are distinguished by the size of the numerals in the date. 1852 obverse dies were used to strike the 1853 no-arrows variety, with the 2 being recut to form a 3.

Date	Mintage	G-4	VG-8	F-12	VF-20	XF-40	AU-50	MS-60	MS-65
1840	188,127	45.00	65.00	100.	150.	250.	—	2500.	—
1840O	Inc. Ab.	30.00	50.00	75.00	110.	185.	—	1600.	—
1841	120,000	60.00	80.00	120.	200.	285.	—	1000.	—
1841O	452,000	25.00	40.00	60.00	100.	200.	—	1000.	—
1842 sm. dt.	88,000					Stacks, Jan. 1989, proof, $22,000.			—
1842 lg. dt.	Inc. Ab.	90.00	125.	150.	225.	425.	675.	2700.	—
1842O sm. dt.	769,000	475.	625.	850.	1350.	3000.	—	—	—
1842O lg. dt.	Inc. Ab.	10.00	16.00	30.00	50.00	100.	—	—	—
1843	645,600	9.50	10.00	12.50	40.00	80.00	—	290.	—
1843O	968,000	15.00	33.00	60.00	100.	200.	—	—	4500.
1844	421,200	12.50	16.00	26.00	43.00	80.00	185.	290.	4500.
1844O	740,000	12.50	21.00	37.50	64.00	125.	300.	1200.	—
1845	922,000	9.50	15.00	25.00	40.00	75.00	185.	290.	4500.
1846	510,000	8.00	16.00	25.00	50.00	90.00	185.	290.	4500.
1847	734,000	9.50	12.50	25.00	40.00	75.00	—	290.	4500.
1847O	368,000	22.00	30.00	50.00	90.00	250.	400.	725.	—
1848	146,000	30.00	42.00	70.00	95.00	175.	—	725.	—
1849	340,000	12.00	20.00	37.50	55.00	100.	—	600.	—
1849O	Unrecorded	350.	475.	750.	1350.	2500.	5000.	—	—
1850	190,800	23.00	45.00	55.00	85.00	150.	—	—	—
1850O	412,000	20.00	40.00	50.00	80.00	150.	—	1000.	—
1851	160,000	30.00	50.00	75.00	120.	250.	—	1100.	—
1851O	88,000	190.	280.	375.	625.	950.	2600.	1000.	—
1852	177,060	35.00	50.00	75.00	110.	210.	400.	—	—
1852O	96,000	185.	270.	350.	600.	900.	2500.	900.	—
1853 recut date	44,200	175.	225.	300.	400.	600.	1500.	—	—
								4500.	

Arrows at date, reverse rays

Weight: 6.22 grams. **Composition:** 90% silver (0.18 ounces), 10% copper.

Date	Mintage	G-4	VG-8	F-12	VF-20	XF-40	AU-50	MS-60	MS-65	Prf-65
1853 rays	15,210,020	7.25	14.00	20.00	38.00	170.	350.	900.	19,500.	—
1853/4	Inc. Ab.	75.00	100.	125.	210.	400.	900.	2000.	—	—
1853O rays	1,332,000	10.00	26.00	30.00	75.00	160.	—	3000.	—	—

Reverse rays removed

Notes: The 1854-O "huge O" variety has an oversized mintmark.

Date	Mintage	G-4	VG-8	F-12	VF-20	XF-40	AU-50	MS-60	MS-65	Prf-65
1854	12,380,000	7.50	14.00	21.00	32.00	115.	285.	410.	9500.	15,000.
1854O	1,484,000	8.00	14.00	23.00	35.00	115.	—	2500.	—	—
1854O huge O	Inc. Ab.	50.00	75.00	125.	185.	275.	—	—	—	—
1855	2,857,000	7.50	12.50	18.00	24.00	115.	285.	410.	9500.	15,000.
1855O	176,000	40.00	70.00	100.	175.	285.	—	1850.	—	—
1855S	396,400	25.00	45.00	65.00	100.	200.	—	1750.	—	—

Arrows at date removed

1856-S Quarter
Grade F-12

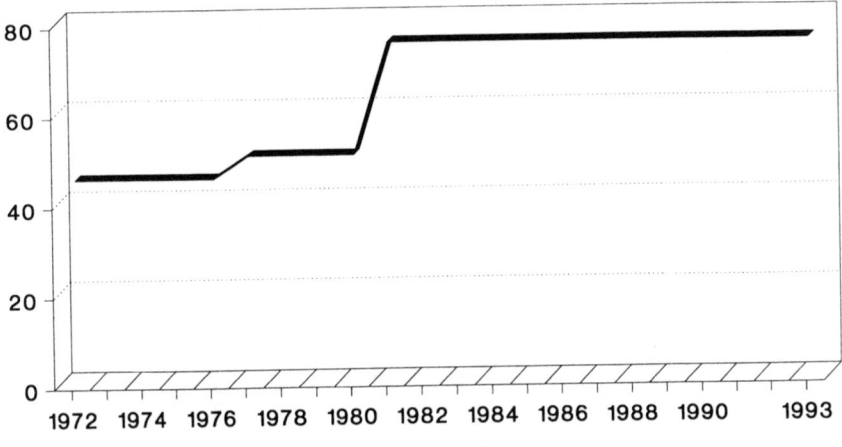

■ Retail Price

Source: COIN PRICES

Date	Mintage	G-4	VG-8	F-12	VF-20	XF-40	AU-50	MS-60	MS-65	Prf-65
1856	7,264,000	7.50	12.50	17.50	28.00	54.00	—	290.	4500.	15,000.
1856O	968,000	12.00	16.00	26.00	40.00	110.	—	850.	—	—
1856S	286,000	35.00	55.00	75.00	115.	225.	—	—	—	—
1856S/S	Inc. Ab.	75.00	100.	150.	300.	600.	—	—	—	—
1857	9,644,000	7.50	12.50	17.50	28.00	54.00	190.	290.	4500.	15,000.
1857O	1,180,000	13.00	17.00	25.00	40.00	80.00	—	900.	—	—
1857S	82,000	70.00	100.	140.	235.	385.	—	—	—	—
1858	7,368,000	7.50	12.50	21.00	28.00	54.00	190.	290.	4500.	11,500.
1858O	520,000	10.00	17.00	30.00	45.00	85.00	300.	900.	—	—
1858S	121,000	60.00	90.00	120.	180.	275.	—	—	—	—
1859	1,344,000	8.50	14.00	23.00	30.00	63.00	190.	700.	—	7000.
1859O	260,000	18.00	25.00	40.00	60.00	110.	—	900.	—	—
1859S	80,000	90.00	125.	175.	275.	400.	2500.	—	—	—
1860	805,400	9.50	13.00	23.00	30.00	64.00	250.	900.	11,500.	6000.
1860O	388,000	11.00	19.00	35.00	50.00	95.00	—	925.	—	—
1860S	56,000	145.	180.	275.	400.	600.	3000.	—	—	—
1861	4,854,600	7.50	12.50	17.50	28.00	54.00	190.	290.	4500.	6000.
1861S	96,000	65.00	100.	175.	225.	300.	—	2600.	—	—
1862	932,550	8.00	12.50	18.00	35.00	80.00	225.	290.	4500.	6000.
1862S	67,000	75.00	110.	160.	225.	375.	—	—	—	—
1863	192,060	25.00	35.00	45.00	75.00	150.	350.	750.	—	7000.
1864	94,070	50.00	60.00	90.00	125.	200.	400.	900.	11,500.	7000.
1864S	20,000	175.	240.	375.	500.	750.	1500.	1800.	—	7000.
1865	59,300	65.00	90.00	110.	150.	250.	—	1250.	11,500.	7000.
1865S	41,000	100.	125.	150.	225.	350.	—	2000.	—	—
1866	—		Unique	—	—	—	—	—	—	—

Motto above eagle

Notes: In 1866 the motto "In God We Trust" was added to the reverse. The 1873 closed-3 and open-3 varieties are distinguished by the amount of space between the upper left and lower left serifs in the 3.

Date	Mintage	G-4	VG-8	F-12	VF-20	XF-40	AU-50	MS-60	MS-65	Prf-65
1866	17,525	200.	260.	330.	450.	550.	—	1400.	—	6750.
1866S	28,000	185.	240.	310.	500.	700.	—	—	—	—
1867	20,625	175.	200.	225.	285.	500.	—	1300.	—	6750.
1867S	48,000	125.	175.	215.	300.	550.	—	3000.	—	—
1868	30,000	135.	165.	200.	275.	400.	—	1200.	—	6750.
1868S	96,000	60.00	70.00	100.	160.	250.	—	2300.	—	—
1869	16,600	200.	260.	325.	425.	550.	—	1400.	—	6750.
1869S	76,000	90.00	110.	150.	240.	400.	—	—	—	—
1870	87,400	40.00	48.00	65.00	80.00	125.	—	1000.	—	6550.
1870CC	8,340	1200.	1700.	2850.	3750.	5250.	—	—	—	—
1871	119,160	35.00	45.00	60.00	90.00	140.	—	1000.	—	6550.
1871CC	10,890	875.	1100.	1400.	2250.	4250.	—	—	—	—
1871S	30,900	165.	225.	285.	450.	700.	—	3000.	—	—
1872	182,950	30.00	40.00	60.00	90.00	135.	—	1000.	—	4050.
1872CC	22,850	375.	525.	750.	1250.	3000.	4000.	—	—	—
1872S	83,000	250.	325.	450.	600.	900.	—	4700.	—	—
1873 clsd.3	212,600	50.00	70.00	100.	160.	250.	—	—	—	8000.
1873 open 3	Inc. Ab.	40.00	45.00	60.00	80.00	125.	—	570.	—	—
1873CC	4,000					RARCOA, Aug. 1990, MS-65, $310,000.				

Arrows at date

Weight: 6.25 grams. **Composition:** 90% silver (0.1809 ounces), 10% copper.

Date	Mintage	G-4	VG-8	F-12	VF-20	XF-40	AU-50	MS-60	MS-65	Prf-65
1873	1,271,700	15.00	30.00	45.00	75.00	190.	380.	700.	4500.	8000.
1873CC	12,462	1100.	1550.	2250.	3500.	5500.	—	—	—	—
1873S	156,000	40.00	60.00	90.00	145.	275.	390.	700.	—	—
1874	471,900	15.00	30.00	45.00	75.00	200.	380.	700.	4500.	8000.
1874S	392,000	24.00	40.00	65.00	140.	225.	400.	700.	—	—

Arrows at date removed

Notes: The 1876-CC fine-reeding variety has a more finely reeded edge.

Date	Mintage	G-4	VG-8	F-12	VF-20	XF-40	AU-50	MS-60	MS-65	Prf-65
1875	4,293,500	7.50	12.50	19.50	28.00	70.00	115.	350.	4100.	4150.
1875CC	140,000	50.00	80.00	145.	250.	400.	700.	1400.	—	—
1875S	680,000	22.00	30.00	50.00	80.00	165.	300.	500.	—	—
1876	17,817,150	7.50	12.50	19.50	28.00	70.00	115.	350.	4100.	4150.
1876CC	4,944,000	9.00	15.00	22.50	35.00	70.00	200.	350.	3900.	—
1876CC fine reeding Inc. Ab.		15.00	25.00	40.00	60.00	100.	275.	450.	—	—
1876S	8,596,000	7.50	12.50	19.50	28.00	70.00	115.	220.	2350.	—
1877	10,911,710	7.50	12.50	19.50	28.00	70.00	115.	220.	2350.	2900.
1877CC	4,192,000	7.50	15.00	25.00	35.00	70.00	200.	825.	—	—
1877S	8,996,000	6.75	12.00	19.50	28.00	55.00	115.	220.	2350.	—
1877S/horizontal S Inc. Ab.		40.00	60.00	85.00	125.	225.	525.	1400.	—	—
1878	2,260,800	8.00	12.00	20.00	35.00	65.00	135.	360.	4100.	2900.
1878CC	996,000	16.00	30.00	38.00	55.00	100.	215.	360.	4100.	—
1878S	140,000	55.00	80.00	120.	150.	275.	500.	1500.	—	—
1879	14,700	115.	145.	190.	235.	300.	400.	600.	—	2900.
1880	14,955	115.	145.	190.	235.	300.	400.	600.	—	2900.
1881	12,975	125.	150.	195.	250.	300.	450.	600.	—	2900.
1882	16,300	125.	150.	195.	250.	300.	450.	600.	—	2900.
1883	15,439	125.	150.	195.	250.	300.	450.	600.	—	2900.
1884	8,875	165.	185.	200.	300.	375.	475.	650.	—	2900.
1885	14,530	125.	150.	190.	250.	400.	500.	600.	—	2900.
1886	5,886	300.	325.	400.	425.	525.	625.	750.	—	2900.
1887	10,710	210.	220.	240.	300.	400.	475.	650.	—	2900.
1888	10,833	125.	150.	175.	250.	300.	350.	600.	—	2900.
1888S	1,216,000	8.00	14.00	22.00	30.00	65.00	135.	220.	2350.	—
1889	12,711	140.	160.	195.	250.	325.	450.	600.	—	2900.
1890	80,590	50.00	75.00	90.00	120.	200.	300.	540.	—	2900.
1891	3,920,600	6.75	12.50	20.00	30.00	55.00	150.	220.	2350.	2900.
1891O	68,000	125.	165.	225.	350.	600.	—	—	—	—
1891S	2,216,000	6.75	12.00	20.00	30.00	60.00	135.	350.	4400.	—

Barber

Designer: Charles E. Barber. **Size:** 24.3 millimeters. **Weight:** 6.25 grams. **Composition:** 90% silver (0.1809 ounces), 10% copper.

Date	Mintage	G-4	VG-8	F-12	VF-20	XF-40	AU-50	MS-60	MS-65	Prf-65
1892	8,237,245	2.50	4.00	14.00	30.00	57.00	120.	205.	1900.	2350.
1892O	2,640,000	4.00	7.50	15.00	30.00	59.00	135.	250.	2100.	—

Date	Mintage	G-4	VG-8	F-12	VF-20	XF-40	AU-50	MS-60	MS-65	Prf-65
1892S	964,079	12.00	22.00	30.00	49.00	110.	245.	375.	7500.	—
1893	5,484,838	3.00	4.00	14.00	25.00	57.00	125.	205.	1900.	—
1893O	3,396,000	3.50	5.50	17.00	34.00	60.00	145.	245.	2900.	2350.
1893S	1,454,535	5.00	9.00	28.00	40.00	90.00	245.	380.	6700.	—
1894	3,432,972	2.75	3.75	14.00	29.00	57.00	120.	205.	2050.	2350.
1894O	2,852,000	3.50	6.00	17.00	31.00	60.00	180.	325.	6300.	—
1894S	2,648,821	3.50	5.50	15.50	30.00	60.00	160.	325.	6700.	—
1895	4,440,880	2.75	3.75	14.00	27.00	57.00	125.	205.	4900.	2350.
1895O	2,816,000	3.75	5.75	17.00	32.00	68.00	200.	340.	3100.	—
1895S	1,764,681	4.00	9.00	24.00	38.00	68.00	210.	345.	6000.	—
1896	3,874,762	2.75	4.00	14.00	26.00	57.00	125.	210.	2650.	2350.
1896O	1,484,000	3.75	8.75	38.00	180.	320.	580.	800.	8500.	—
1896S	188,039	195.	250.	510.	825.	1250.	2600.	3250.	24,500.	—
1897	8,140,731	2.00	3.00	14.00	26.00	55.00	120.	205.	2100.	2350.
1897O	1,414,800	6.00	10.00	50.00	150.	310.	550.	725.	5100.	—
1897S	542,229	11.00	22.00	60.00	135.	235.	525.	660.	6800.	—
1898	11,100,735	2.00	2.75	13.00	26.00	55.00	120.	205.	2050.	2350.
1898O	1,868,000	4.00	7.50	28.00	60.00	135.	350.	460.	7900.	—
1898S	1,020,592	3.75	7.75	19.00	35.00	60.00	165.	345.	3700.	—
1899	12,624,846	2.00	7.75	13.00	26.00	55.00	165.	205.	2000.	2350.
1899O	2,644,000	4.00	9.00	19.00	33.00	72.00	225.	350.	6300.	—
1899S	708,000	6.75	13.00	20.00	36.00	65.00	180.	345.	3600.	—
1900	10,016,912	2.10	2.75	14.00	26.00	55.00	120.	205.	2000.	2350.
1900O	3,416,000	4.50	8.00	23.00	36.00	78.00	225.	375.	4100.	—
1900S	1,858,585	4.25	6.50	16.00	31.00	60.00	120.	300.	5600.	—
1901	8,892,813	2.75	3.10	14.00	27.00	56.00	125.	205.	2300.	2350.
1901O	1,612,000	14.00	28.00	52.00	120.	260.	560.	700.	7400.	—
1901S	72,664	1050.	2100.	3000.	4500.	5700.	7100.	9000.	48,000.	—
1902	12,197,744	2.00	2.75	14.00	26.00	55.00	120.	205.	2000.	4150.
1902O	4,748,000	3.75	5.00	20.00	37.00	86.00	180.	360.	5800.	—
1902S	1,524,612	6.00	11.50	21.00	38.00	72.00	180.	360.	4400.	—
1903	9,670,064	2.20	3.00	14.00	27.00	57.00	120.	205.	2500.	2350.
1903O	3,500,000	3.75	5.00	20.00	36.00	73.00	180.	275.	7500.	—
1903S	1,036,000	7.00	11.50	23.00	42.00	85.00	220.	340.	3400.	—
1904	9,588,813	2.20	3.00	14.50	27.00	57.00	120.	205.	2400.	2350.
1904O	2,456,000	4.50	6.75	24.00	49.00	160.	325.	650.	3250.	—
1905	4,968,250	2.75	3.25	17.00	29.00	57.00	125.	205.	2200.	2350.
1905O	1,230,000	4.50	7.00	25.00	44.00	125.	275.	360.	6100.	—
1905S	1,884,000	4.50	7.00	15.00	32.00	75.00	185.	280.	6700.	—
1906	3,656,435	2.75	3.50	15.00	28.00	58.00	130.	205.	1700.	2350.
1906D	3,280,000	2.60	4.50	16.00	30.00	60.00	145.	210.	5400.	—

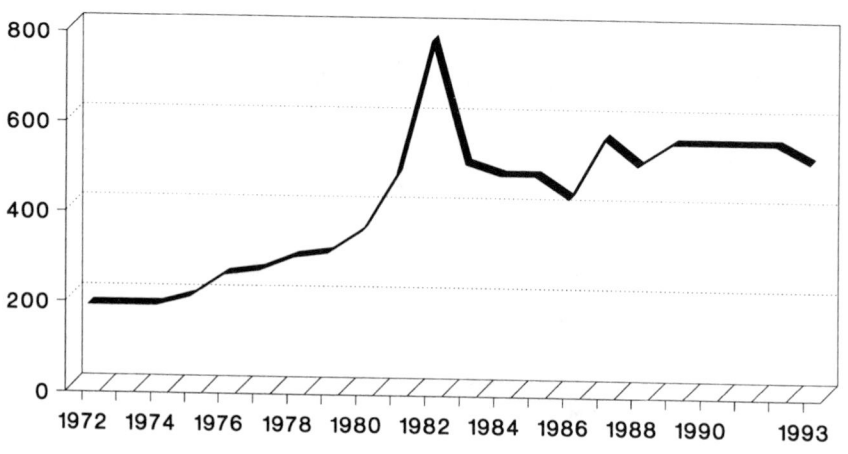

1896-S Quarter
Grade F-12

■ Retail Price

Source: COIN PRICES

1913-S Quarter
Grade XF-40

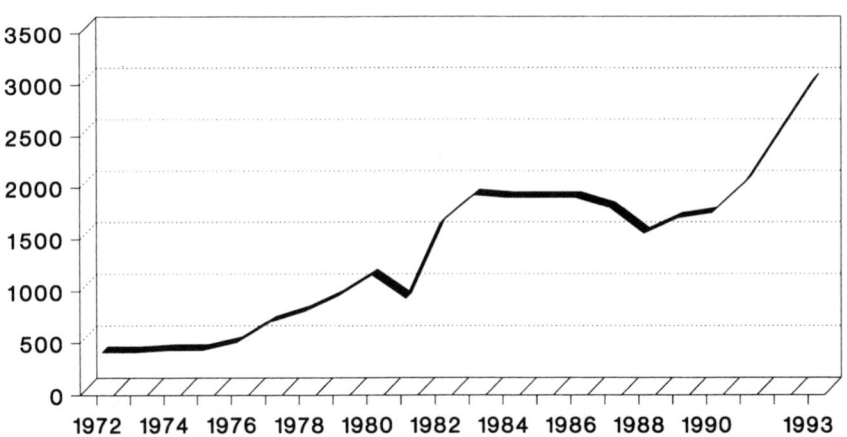

■ Retail Price

Source: COIN PRICES

Date	Mintage	G-4	VG-8	F-12	VF-20	XF-40	AU-50	MS-60	MS-65	Prf-65
1906O	2,056,000	2.75	4.50	20.00	31.00	68.00	180.	250.	2000.	—
1907	7,192,575	2.10	2.75	14.00	26.00	55.00	120.	205.	2000.	2350.
1907D	2,484,000	2.60	4.00	16.00	29.00	61.00	170.	275.	4100.	—
1907O	4,560,000	2.40	3.25	14.00	26.00	57.00	130.	225.	4000.	—
1907S	1,360,000	3.50	4.50	19.00	33.00	88.00	200.	340.	5600.	—
1908	4,232,545	2.20	3.00	14.00	26.00	56.00	125.	205.	2150.	4050.
1908D	5,788,000	2.50	3.25	14.00	26.00	56.00	125.	205.	2400.	—
1908O	6,244,000	2.50	3.25	14.00	26.00	56.00	125.	205.	2100.	—
1908S	784,000	7.00	11.50	38.00	88.00	215.	365.	625.	8000.	—
1909	9,268,650	2.00	2.75	13.00	25.00	55.00	120.	205.	1900.	2350.
1909D	5,114,000	2.50	3.00	13.50	26.00	60.00	155.	205.	2450.	—
1909O	712,000	7.00	13.00	38.00	88.00	180.	335.	625.	12,500.	—
1909S	1,348,000	2.60	4.25	15.00	28.00	60.00	170.	260.	2500.	—
1910	2,244,551	2.60	3.00	17.00	30.00	60.00	130.	190.	2050.	2350.
1910D	1,500,000	2.75	4.00	16.00	33.00	67.00	160.	265.	3000.	—
1911	3,720,543	2.10	3.00	14.00	26.00	55.00	120.	205.	1900.	2350.
1911D	933,600	3.00	4.00	65.00	160.	260.	425.	550.	7200.	—
1911S	988,000	2.75	3.75	16.50	30.00	88.00	195.	280.	1600.	—
1912	4,400,700	2.10	2.75	13.00	25.00	55.00	120.	205.	1900.	2350.
1912S	708,000	3.00	4.00	19.00	33.00	72.00	190.	325.	2450.	—
1913	484,613	6.50	10.00	45.00	110.	360.	550.	1000.	5500.	4300.
1913D	1,450,800	2.75	4.00	15.00	30.00	65.00	150.	260.	2300.	—
1913S	40,000	300.	475.	1400.	2100.	3000.	3500.	4300.	10,100.	—
1914	6,244,610	2.00	2.10	13.00	25.00	55.00	120.	205.	1900.	4050.
1914D	3,046,000	2.00	3.00	14.00	26.00	56.00	120.	205.	1900.	—
1914S	264,000	40.00	80.00	110.	160.	325.	535.	800.	4700.	—
1915	3,480,450	2.10	3.00	14.50	27.00	57.00	120.	205.	2000.	4300.
1915D	3,694,000	2.10	2.75	13.50	26.00	56.00	120.	205.	1900.	—
1915S	704,000	4.00	5.00	17.00	35.00	67.00	190.	285.	2300.	—
1916	1,788,000	2.10	3.00	14.50	27.00	57.00	125.	205.	1900.	—
1916D	6,540,800	2.00	2.60	13.00	25.00	55.00	120.	205.	1900.	—

Standing Liberty

Type I

Designer: Hermon A. MacNeil. **Size:** 24.3 millimeters. **Weight:** 6.25 grams. **Composition:** 90% silver (0.1809 ounces), 10% copper. **Notes:** ''MS-65FH'' values are for coins that have full detail on Liberty's head.

Date	Mintage	G-4	VG-8	F-12	VF-20	XF-40	AU-50	MS-60	MS-65	-65FH
1916	52,000	900.	1100.	1500.	2150.	2700.	3300.	4250.	13,500.	21,000.
1917	8,792,000	8.00	10.00	14.00	26.00	52.00	95.00	160.	1050.	1200.
1917D	1,509,200	12.00	14.00	22.00	48.00	85.00	120.	190.	1170.	1500.
1917S	1,952,000	12.00	14.50	20.00	56.00	115.	175.	200.	1465.	1975.

Type II

Notes: In 1917 the obverse design was modified to cover Liberty's bare right breast. On the reverse, three stars were added below the eagle.

Date	Mintage	G-4	VG-8	F-12	VF-20	XF-40	AU-50	MS-60	MS-65	-65FH
1917	13,880,000	11.00	13.00	16.00	22.00	35.00	60.00	125.	475.	1050.
1917D	6,224,400	16.00	21.00	42.00	53.00	82.00	110.	175.	1200.	3300.
1917S	5,522,000	15.00	20.00	28.00	47.50	70.00	100.	160.	1100.	2800.
1918	14,240,000	12.00	15.00	21.00	30.00	42.00	73.00	125.	500.	1200.
1918D	7,380,000	19.00	25.00	35.00	51.00	77.00	125.	180.	1550.	4800.
1918S	11,072,000	13.00	16.00	24.00	27.00	41.00	70.00	165.	1625.	15,000.
1918/17S	Inc.Ab.	950.	1200.	1625.	2200.	4000.	8100.	9400.	50,000.	70,000.
1919	11,324,000	22.00	29.00	40.00	46.00	60.00	82.00	135.	490.	1050.
1919D	1,944,000	40.00	63.00	100.	160.	250.	330.	425.	2600.	22,000.
1919S	1,836,000	38.00	58.00	95.00	195.	350.	475.	600.	3250.	21,000.
1920	27,860,000	13.00	15.00	19.00	24.00	35.00	60.00	125.	450.	1150.
1920D	3,586,400	20.00	30.00	47.50	70.00	100.	150.	200.	1975.	5250.
1920S	6,380,000	14.00	17.00	22.00	26.00	45.00	80.00	180.	2200.	20,000.
1921	1,916,000	60.00	80.00	110.	165.	230.	315.	400.	2300.	3000.
1923	9,716,000	12.00	14.00	22.00	26.00	33.00	60.00	125.	450.	1300.
1923S	1,360,000	85.00	140.	175.	260.	350.	430.	550.	1750.	3750.
1924	10,920,000	13.00	15.00	19.00	23.00	35.00	60.00	125.	450.	1100.
1924D	3,112,000	21.00	28.00	42.00	60.00	80.00	110.	140.	465.	5700.
1924S	2,860,000	15.00	18.00	21.00	27.00	77.00	165.	220.	2100.	4700.
1925	12,280,000	2.25	3.00	5.00	14.00	25.00	50.00	125.	495.	1050.
1926	11,316,000	2.25	3.00	5.00	14.00	25.00	52.00	125.	495.	1300.
1926D	1,716,000	5.50	7.00	11.00	18.50	40.00	72.00	125.	495.	13,000.
1926S	2,700,000	3.50	4.25	10.00	19.00	90.00	200.	300.	2500.	11,500.
1927	11,912,000	2.25	3.00	5.00	14.00	25.00	52.00	125.	500.	1100.
1927D	976,400	5.50	7.00	11.00	27.00	72.00	120.	135.	500.	3100.
1927S	396,000	7.00	10.00	45.00	150.	1050.	2400.	3450.	9500.	20,000.
1928	6,336,000	2.25	3.00	5.00	14.00	25.00	50.00	125.	500.	1150.
1928D	1,627,600	4.00	5.00	8.00	16.00	34.00	63.00	135.	475.	3800.
1928S	2,644,000	2.50	3.25	5.50	14.00	28.00	56.00	135.	450.	1050.
1929	11,140,000	2.25	3.00	4.50	13.00	25.00	50.00	125.	475.	1050.
1929D	1,358,000	4.00	5.00	6.50	15.50	30.00	58.00	135.	475.	3700.
1929S	1,764,000	2.40	2.75	5.25	13.50	25.00	52.00	130.	450.	1050.
1930	5,632,000	2.25	2.75	5.00	13.00	24.00	50.00	125.	475.	1050.
1930S	1,556,000	2.40	3.25	5.25	13.50	26.00	53.00	130.	475.	1100.

Washington

Reverse mintmark
(1932-1964)

Silver composition

Designer: John Flanagan. **Size:** 24.3 millimeters. **Weight:** 6.25 grams. **Composition:** 90% silver (0.1809 ounces), 10% copper.

Date	Mintage	G-4	VG-8	F-12	VF-20	XF-40	AU-50	MS-60	MS-65	Prf-65
1932	5,404,000	3.00	3.25	4.50	6.75	9.00	14.00	28.00	185.	—
1932D	436,800	34.00	38.00	45.00	65.00	150.	265.	400.	5000.	—
1932S	408,000	28.00	30.00	35.00	45.00	60.00	95.00	260.	3600.	—
1934	31,912,052	2.00	3.00	3.75	4.50	5.75	11.00	21.00	91.00	—
1934D	3,527,200	3.25	4.00	6.00	7.00	10.00	33.00	100.	960.	—
1935	32,484,000	2.00	3.00	3.75	4.50	5.75	11.00	20.00	84.00	—
1935D	5,780,000	2.40	4.00	6.00	7.00	10.00	39.00	112.	310.	—
1935S	5,660,000	2.40	3.00	4.50	5.00	7.50	18.00	53.00	190.	—
1936	41,303,837	2.00	3.00	4.00	4.50	6.00	11.00	17.00	74.00	950.
1936D	5,374,000	2.80	3.50	4.00	14.00	30.00	93.00	310.	910.	—
1936S	3,828,000	2.80	3.00	4.00	7.00	10.00	24.00	56.00	110.	—
1937	19,701,542	2.00	3.00	4.00	5.75	7.50	11.75	23.00	81.00	250.
1937D	7,189,600	2.75	3.00	4.00	7.00	9.00	14.00	38.00	105.	—
1937S	1,652,000	3.50	4.00	4.50	12.00	20.00	46.00	95.00	175.	—
1938	9,480,045	2.80	3.00	4.50	7.50	12.00	24.00	49.00	100.	150.
1938S	2,832,000	2.80	3.00	4.50	7.50	11.00	22.00	51.00	125.	—
1939	33,548,795	2.00	3.00	3.75	4.25	5.50	10.50	14.00	49.00.	150.
1939D	7,092,000	2.40	3.00	3.75	4.50	7.50	13.00	29.00	77.00	—

1932-D Quarter
Grade F-12

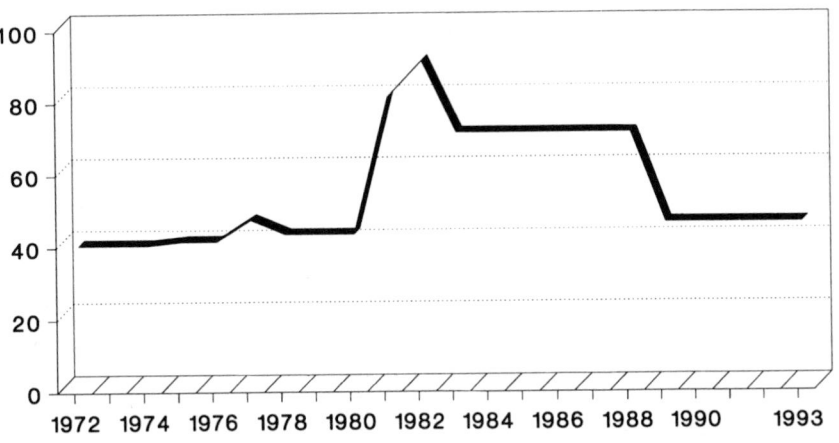

■ Retail Price

Source: COIN PRICES

PRICING SECTION

Date	Mintage	G-4	VG-8	F-12	VF-20	XF-40	AU-50	MS-60	MS-65	Prf-65
1939S	2,628,000	3.00	3.50	5.00	6.00	10.00	26.00	59.00	130.	—
1940	35,715,246	2.00	3.00	3.75	4.00	4.50	8.25	10.00	42.00	115.
1940D	2,797,600	3.25	3.50	7.00	10.00	15.50	28.00	62.00	110.	—
1940S	8,244,000	2.40	3.00	3.75	4.25	5.50	9.00	16.00	35.00	—
1941	79,047,287	—	—	1.50	2.00	3.25	4.50	7.50	23.00	115.
1941D	16,714,800	—	—	1.50	2.00	3.25	6.50	18.00	34.00	—
1941S	16,080,000	—	—	1.50	2.00	3.25	6.50	15.00	70.00	—
1942	102,117,123	—	—	1.50	2.00	3.25	4.00	6.50	23.00	110.
1942D	17,487,200	—	—	1.50	2.00	3.25	5.00	10.00	29.00	—
1942S	19,384,000	—	—	1.50	2.00	4.50	14.00	50.00	125.	—
1943	99,700,000	—	—	1.50	2.00	2.25	2.75	5.00	23.00	—
1943D	16,095,600	—	—	1.50	2.00	3.25	7.50	14.00	30.00	—
1943S	21,700,000	—	—	1.50	2.00	5.50	11.50	29.00	39.00	—
1944	104,956,000	—	—	1.50	2.00	3.25	3.75	4.50	16.00	—
1944D	14,600,800	—	—	1.50	2.00	3.25	5.00	9.00	21.00	—
1944S	12,560,000	—	—	1.50	2.00	3.25	5.50	9.00	26.00	—
1945	74,372,000	—	—	1.50	2.00	3.25	4.00	5.00	14.00	—
1945D	12,341,600	—	—	1.50	2.00	3.25	5.00	7.50	22.00	—
1945S	17,004,001	—	—	1.50	2.00	3.25	4.50	6.00	18.00	—
1946	53,436,000	—	—	1.50	2.00	2.25	2.50	4.75	15.00	—
1946D	9,072,800	—	—	1.50	2.00	2.25	2.75	4.00	12.00	—
1946S	4,204,000	—	—	1.50	2.00	2.25	2.50	4.00	19.00	—
1947	22,556,000	—	—	1.50	2.00	3.00	3.75	6.50	12.00	—
1947D	15,338,400	—	—	1.50	2.00	3.00	4.25	5.50	14.00	—
1947S	5,532,000	—	—	1.50	2.00	2.25	2.50	5.00	16.50	—
1948	35,196,000	—	—	1.50	2.00	2.25	2.50	4.00	10.00	—
1948D	16,766,800	—	—	1.50	2.00	2.25	2.50	5.00	12.00	—
1948S	15,960,000	—	—	1.50	2.00	3.25	3.60	5.00	12.50	—
1949	9,312,000	—	—	1.50	2.00	3.50	9.00	19.00	25.00	—
1949D	10,068,400	—	—	1.50	2.50	4.00	7.00	8.75	20.00	—
1950	24,971,512	—	—	1.50	2.50	3.00	3.75	5.00	8.00	50.00
1950D	21,075,600	—	—	1.50	2.50	2.75	3.00	4.50	8.00	—
1950D/S	Inc. Ab.	21.00	25.00	30.00	60.00	140.	215.	260.	515.	—
1950S	10,284,004	—	—	1.50	3.00	3.25	5.75	7.25	13.50	—
1950S/D	Inc. Ab.	21.00	25.00	30.00	60.00	170.	315.	460.	625.	—
1951	43,505,602	—	—	1.00	1.75	2.00	2.25	4.75	6.00	38.00
1951D	35,354,800	—	—	1.00	1.75	2.00	2.25	3.25	5.50	—
1951S	9,048,000	—	—	1.00	1.75	4.25	8.25	12.75	18.50	—
1952	38,862,073	—	—	1.00	1.75	2.00	2.25	3.00	5.50	30.00
1952D	49,795,200	—	—	1.00	1.75	2.00	1.95	3.25	6.00	—
1952S	13,707,800	—	—	1.00	2.00	2.50	5.25	8.50	11.50	—
1953	18,664,920	—	—	1.00	1.75	2.00	2.50	3.25	5.25	25.00
1953D	56,112,400	—	—	—	—	1.50	1.75	2.25	5.25	—
1953S	14,016,000	—	—	1.00	1.75	2.25	2.75	4.00	6.50	—
1954	54,645,503	—	—	—	—	—	1.50	2.00	4.75	12.00
1954D	42,305,500	—	—	—	1.25	1.50	1.75	2.00	4.50	—
1954S	11,834,722	—	—	—	1.25	1.50	1.75	2.00	5.25	—
1955	18,558,381	—	—	—	1.25	1.50	1.75	2.00	6.00	11.50
1955D	3,182,400	—	—	—	1.50	1.75	2.00	2.25	7.50	—
1956	44,813,384	—	—	—	1.00	1.50	1.75	2.00	4.00	6.00
1956D	32,334,500	—	—	—	1.00	1.75	2.25	2.75	4.00	—
1957	47,779,952	—	—	—	1.00	1.00	1.75	2.75	4.00	4.00
1957D	77,924,160	—	—	—	1.00	1.00	1.75	2.00	6.50	—
1958	7,235,652	—	—	—	1.00	1.00	2.00	2.50	6.50	6.00
1958D	78,124,900	—	—	—	1.00	1.00	1.75	2.00	4.50	—
1959	25,533,291	—	—	—	—	1.00	1.75	2.00	4.00	4.25
1959D	62,054,232	—	—	—	—	1.00	1.75	2.00	4.00	—
1960	30,855,602	—	—	—	—	1.00	1.75	2.75	5.00	3.75
1960D	63,000,324	—	—	—	—	1.00	1.75	2.00	4.00	—
1961	40,064,244	—	—	—	—	1.00	1.25	1.50	4.00	3.50
1961D	83,656,928	—	—	—	—	1.00	1.25	1.50	4.00	—
1962	39,374,019	—	—	—	—	1.00	1.25	1.50	4.00	3.50
1962D	127,554,756	—	—	—	—	1.00	1.25	1.50	4.00	—
1963	77,391,645	—	—	—	—	1.00	1.25	1.50	3.75	3.50
1963D	135,288,184	—	—	—	—	1.00	1.25	1.50	3.75	—
1964	564,341,347	—	—	—	—	1.00	1.25	1.50	3.75	—
1964D	704,135,528	—	—	—	—	1.00	1.25	1.50	3.75	—

Clad composition

Weight: 5.67 grams. **Composition:** clad layers of 75% copper and 25% nickel bonded to a pure-copper core.

Date	Mintage	MS-65	Prf-65	Date	Mintage	MS-65	Prf-65
1965	1,819,717,540	.80	—	1971	109,284,000	.50	—
1966	821,101,500	.80	—	1971D	258,634,428	.50	—
1967	1,524,031,848	1.00	—	1971S	Proof only	—	.95
1968	220,731,500	.80	—	1972	215,048,000	.40	—
1968D	101,534,000	1.00	—	1972D	311,067,732	.40	—
1968S	Proof only	—	1.50	1972S	Proof only	—	.95
1969	176,212,000	1.00	—	1973	346,924,000	.40	—
1969D	114,372,000	1.25	—	1973D	232,977,400	.40	—
1969S	Proof only	—	1.25	1973S	Proof only	—	.95
1970	136,420,000	.50	—	1974	801,456,000	.40	—
1970D	417,341,364	.50	—	1974D	353,160,300	.40	—
1970S	Proof only	—	.95	1974S	Proof only	—	1.50

  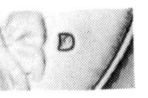

Obverse mintmark
(1968-present)

Bicentennial reverse, clad composition

Reverse designer: Jack L. Ahr.

Date	Mintage	G-4	VG-8	F-12	VF-20	XF-40	MS-60	MS-65	Prf-65
1976	809,784,016	—	—	—	—	—	—	.60	—
1976D	860,118,839	—	—	—	—	—	—	.60	—
1976S	—	—	—	—	—	—	—	—	.90

Bicentennial reverse, silver composition

Weight: 5.75 grams. Composition: clad layers of 80% silver and 20% copper bonded to a core of 20.9% silver and 79.1% copper (0.0739 total ounces of silver).

Date	Mintage	G-4	VG-8	F-12	VF-20	XF-40	MS-60	MS-65	Prf-65
1976S silver	11,000,000	—	—	—	—	—	—	1.10	1.95

Regular design resumed, clad composition

Notes: The 1979-S Type II proof has a clearer mintmark than the Type I.

Date	Mintage	MS-65	Prf-65	Date	Mintage	MS-65	Prf-65
1977	468,556,000	.40	—	1985D	519,962,888	3.25	—
1977D	258,898,212	.45	—	1985S	Proof only	—	1.75
1977S	Proof only	—	.95	1986P	551,199,333	3.00	—
1978	521,452,000	.40	—	1986D	504,298,660	3.50	—
1978D	287,373,152	.40	—	1986S	Proof only	—	2.50
1978S	Proof only	—	.95	1987P	582,499,481	.50	—
1979	515,708,000	.50	—	1987D	655,594,696	.50	—
1979D	489,789,780	.50	—	1987S	Proof only	—	1.25
1979S T-I	Proof only	—	.95	1988P	562,052,000	.55	—
1979S T-II	Proof only	—	1.45	1988D	596,810,688	.60	—
1980P	635,832,000	.50	—	1988S	Proof only	—	1.25
1980D	518,327,487	.50	—	1989P	512,868,000	.50	—
1980S	Proof only	—	.95	1989D	896,535,597	.50	—
1981P	601,716,000	.50	—	1989S	Proof only	—	1.35
1981D	575,722,833	.50	—	1990P	613,792,000	.50	—
1981S T-I	Proof only	—	.95	1990D	927,638,181	.50	—
1981S T-II	Proof only	—	3.00	1990S	Proof only	—	1.45
1982P	500,931,000	5.25	—	1991P	—	.50	—
1982D	480,042,788	2.25	—	1991D	—	.50	—
1982S	Proof only	—	2.25	1991S	Proof only	—	1.45
1983P	673,535,000	5.75	—	1992P	—	.50	—
1983D	617,806,446	8.25	—	1992D	—	.50	—
1983S	Proof only	—	1.85	1992S	Proof only	—	1.50
1984P	676,545,000	.85	—	1993P	—	.50	—
1984D	546,483,064	2.00	—	1993D	—	.50	—
1984S	Proof only	—	1.85	1993S	Proof only	—	1.50
1985P	775,818,962	2.00	—				

Half dollars

Flowing Hair

Designer: Robert Scot. **Size:** 32.5 millimeters. **Weight:** 13.48 grams. **Composition:** 89.24% silver (0.3869 ounces), 10.76% copper. **Notes:** The 1795 "recut date" variety had the date cut into the dies twice, so both sets of numbers are visible on the coin. The 1795 "3 leaves" variety has three leaves under each of the eagle's wings on the reverse.

Date	Mintage	G-4	VG-8	F-12	VF-20	XF-40	MS-60
1794	23,464	1150.	1950.	2950.	4000.	6950.	—
1795	299,680	440.	500.	825.	2000.	4000.	9500.
1795 recut date	Inc. Ab.	550.	625.	900.	2000.	3200.	9500.
1795 3 leaves	Inc. Ab.	1850.	2500.	3300.	5850.	11,000.	—

1797 Half Dollar
Grade F-12

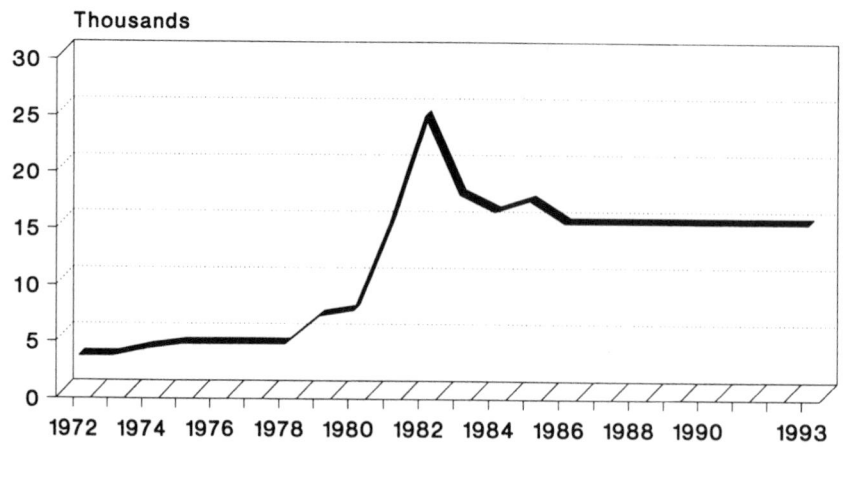

Source: COIN PRICES

Draped Bust

Small-eagle reverse

Designer: Robert Scot. **Size:** 32.5 millimeters. **Weight:** 13.48 grams. **Composition:** 89.24% silver (0.3869 ounces), 10.76% copper. **Notes:** The 1796 strikes have either 15 or 16 stars on the obverse.

Date	Mintage	G-4	VG-8	F-12	VF-20	XF-40	MS-60
1796 15 stars	3,918	10,000.	12,000.	15,000.	27,000.	39,000.	—
1796 16 stars	Inc. Ab.	10,000.	12,000.	15,000.	27,000.	39,000.	—
1797	Inc. Ab.	10,000.	12,000.	15,000.	27,000.	39,000.	—

Heraldic-eagle reverse

Notes: The two varieties of the 1803 strikes are distinguished by the size of the 3 in the date. The several varieties of the 1806 strikes are distinguished by the style of 6 in the date, size of the stars on the obverse, and whether the stem of the olive branch held by the reverse eagle extends through the claw.

Date	Mintage	G-4	VG-8	F-12	VF-20	XF-40	MS-60
1801	30,289	160.	325.	695.	1000.	1950.	9500.
1802	29,890	175.	375.	695.	1000.	1850.	9200.
1803 sm. 3	188,234	150.	250.	400.	695.	1000.	5400.
1803 lg. 3	Inc. Ab.	100.	150.	200.	400.	900.	5400.
1805	211,722	70.00	100.	140.	400.	800.	5200.
1805/4	Inc. Ab.	175.	250.	475.	650.	1375.	5200.
1806 round top 6, large stars	839,576	70.00	90.00	140.	325.	625.	5050.
1806 round top 6, small stars	Inc. Ab.	70.00	90.00	140.	325.	625.	5050.
1806 pointed top 6, stem not through claw	Inc. Ab.	70.00	90.00	140.	325.	625.	5050.
1806 pointed top 6, stem through claw	Inc. Ab.	70.00	90.00	140.	325.	625.	5050.
1806/5	Inc. Ab.	80.00	120.	200.	450.	775.	5050.
1806/inverted 6	Inc. Ab.	175.	225.	325.	675.	1175.	5050.
1807	301,076	90.00	125.	165.	315.	575.	5050.

Liberty Cap

Designer: John Reich. **Size:** 32.5 millimeters. **Weight:** 13.48 grams. **Composition:** 89.24% silver (0.3869 ounces), 10.76% copper. **Notes:** There are three varieties of the 1807 strikes. Two are distinguished by the size of the stars on the obverse. The third was struck from a reverse die that had a 5 cut over a 2 in the "50C." denomination. Two varieties of the 1811 are distinguished by the size of the 8 in the date. A third has a period between the 8 and second 1 in the date. One variety of the 1817 has a period between the 1 and 7 in the date. Two varieties of the 1819/18 overdate are distinguished by the size of the 9 in the date. Two varieties of the 1820 are distinguished by the size of the date. On the 1823 varieties, the "broken 3" appears to be almost separated in the middle of the 3 in the date; the "patched 3" has the error repaired; the "ugly 3" has portions of its detail missing. The 1827 "curled-2" and "square-2" varieties are distinguished by the numeral's base — either curled or square. Among the 1828 varieties, "knobbed 2" and "no knob" refers to whether the upper left serif of the digit is rounded. The 1830 varieties are distinguished by the size of the 0 in the date. The four 1834 varieties are distinguished by the sizes of the stars, date and letters in the inscriptions. The 1836 "50/00" variety was struck from a reverse die that had "50" recut over "00" in the denomination.

Date	Mintage	G-4	VG-8	F-12	VF-20	XF-40	AU-50	MS-60	MS-65
1807 sm. stars	750,500	75.00	100.	175.	300.	550.	950.	1250.	—
1807 lg. stars	Inc. Ab.	100.	120.	190.	310.	500.	1350.	2500.	—
1807 50/20 C.	Inc. Ab.	45.00	60.00	75.00	140.	350.	675.	1250.	—
1808	1,368,600	37.50	42.50	53.00	90.00	185.	450.	1875.	—
1808/7	Inc. Ab.	40.00	50.00	60.00	125.	200.	500.	2400.	—
1809	1,405,810	36.00	42.50	55.00	100.	440.	600.	2500.	—
1810	1,276,276	34.50	38.00	46.00	100.	225.	500.	1300.	—
1811 sm. 8	1,203,644	32.00	37.50	45.00	70.00	145.	450.	1975.	—
1811 lg. 8	Inc. Ab.	32.50	37.00	50.00	85.00	165.	450.	1975.	—
1811 dt. 18.11	Inc. Ab.	35.00	40.00	60.00	95.00	185.	495.	1800.	—
1812	1,628,059	32.50	37.50	45.00	100.	180.	350.	1200.	—
1812/11	Inc. Ab.	42.50	50.00	80.00	115.	225.	440.	850.	—
1813	1,241,903	32.50	37.50	45.00	95.00	225.	350.	1100.	—
1814	1,039,075	34.50	38.00	47.00	70.00	145.	500.	1800.	—
1814/13	Inc. Ab.	42.50	52.50	69.00	100.	200.	350.	900.	—
1815/12	47,150	750.	1000.	1350.	1875.	2800.	3600.	4500.	—
1817	1,215,567	31.50	33.00	40.00	65.00	135.	235.	700.	—
1817/13	Inc. Ab.	80.00	135.	185.	325.	500.	975.	1100.	—
1817/14					5 pieces known		—		—
1817 dt. 181.7	Inc. Ab.	37.00	47.00	70.00	115.	195.	395.	700.	—
1818	1,960,322	31.50	33.00	40.00	70.00	135.	235.	700.	—
1818/17	Inc. Ab.	31.50	33.00	40.00	70.00	135.	235.	700.	—
1819	2,208,000	31.50	33.00	40.00	70.00	135.	235.	700.	—
1819/18 sm. 9	Inc. Ab.	31.50	33.00	40.00	70.00	135.	235.	700.	—
1819/18 lg. 9	Inc. Ab.	31.50	33.00	40.00	70.00	135.	235.	700.	—
1820 sm. dt.	751,122	39.00	49.00	67.00	135.	210.	300.	700.	—
1820 lg. dt.	Inc. Ab.	39.00	50.00	67.00	135.	210.	300.	700.	—
1820/19	Inc. Ab.	37.00	49.00	75.00	130.	225.	275.	700.	—
1821	1,305,797	33.00	35.00	40.00	70.00	135.	245.	700.	—
1822	1,559,573	32.00	34.00	40.00	65.00	135.	245.	700.	—
1822/1	Inc. Ab.	50.00	69.00	110.	185.	300.	475.	1100.	—
1823	1,694,200	31.50	33.00	40.00	65.00	135.	235.	700.	—
1823 broken 3	Inc. Ab.	37.00	52.00	84.00	115.	220.	400.	700.	—
1823 patched 3	Inc. Ab.	37.00	50.00	75.00	95.00	195.	325.	700.	—
1823 ugly 3	Inc. Ab.	35.00	40.00	65.00	95.00	185.	265.	700.	—
1824	3,504,954	31.00	33.00	40.00	50.00	95.00	235.	700.	—
1824/21	Inc. Ab.	35.00	40.00	58.00	95.00	185.	250.	700.	—
1824/various dates									
	Inc. Ab.	31.50	33.00	40.00	65.00	145.	235.	700.	—
1825	2,943,166	31.50	33.00	40.00	50.00	95.00	235.	700.	—
1826	4,004,180	31.50	33.00	40.00	50.00	95.00	235.	700.	—
1827 curled 2	5,493,400	33.00	36.00	42.50	85.00	150.	245.	700.	—
1827 square 2	Inc. Ab.	31.50	33.00	40.00	50.00	95.00	235.	700.	—
1827/6	Inc. Ab.	35.00	40.00	60.00	90.00	145.	265.	1100.	—
1828 curled base 2, no knob									
	3,075,200	30.00	33.00	37.50	50.00	95.00	230.	700.	8500.
1828 curled base 2, knobbed 2									
	Inc. Ab.	35.00	45.00	60.00	85.00	150.	350.	750.	—
1828 small 8s, square base 2, large letters									
	Inc. Ab.	27.50	32.00	34.00	43.00	90.00	230.	700.	15,500.
1828 small 8s, square base 2, small letters									
	Inc. Ab.	27.50	32.00	65.00	125.	250.	350.	750.	—

Date	Mintage	G-4	VG-8	F-12	VF-20	XF-40	AU-50	MS-60	MS-65
1828 large 8s, square base 2									
	Inc. Ab.	27.50	32.00	34.00	43.00	90.00	230.	700.	—
1829	3,712,156	27.50	32.00	34.00	43.00	90.00	230.	700.	—
1829/27	Inc. Ab.	35.00	40.00	60.00	85.00	165.	250.	800.	—
1830 small 0 in date									
	4,764,800	27.50	32.00	34.00	43.00	89.00	230.	700.	8500.
1830 large 0 in date									
	Inc. Ab.	27.50	32.00	34.00	43.00	89.00	230.	700.	8500.
1831	5,873,660	27.50	32.00	34.00	43.00	89.00	230.	700.	8500.
1832 sm. lt.	4,797,000	27.50	32.00	34.00	43.00	89.00	230.	700.	8500.
1832 lg. let.	Inc. Ab.	30.00	38.00	45.00	65.00	195.	495.	1250.	8500.
1833	5,206,000	27.50	32.00	34.00	43.00	89.00	235.	700.	8500.
1834 small date, large stars, small letters									
	6,412,004	27.50	32.00	34.00	43.00	89.00	235.	700.	8500.
1834 small date, small stars, small letters									
	Inc. Ab.	27.50	32.00	34.00	43.00	89.00	235.	700.	8500.
1834 large date, small letters									
	Inc. Ab.	27.50	32.00	34.00	43.00	89.00	235.	700.	8500.
1834 large date, large letters									
	Inc. Ab.	27.50	32.00	34.00	43.00	89.00	235.	700.	8500.
1835	5,352,006	27.50	32.00	34.00	43.00	89.00	235.	700.	8500.
1836	6,545,000	27.50	32.00	34.00	43.00	89.00	235.	700.	8500.
1836 50/00	Inc. Ab.	50.00	60.00	80.00	160.	225.	475.	1100.	—

Reeded edge, "50 Cents" on reverse

Designer: Christian Gobrecht. **Size:** 30 millimeters. **Weight:** 13.36 grams. **Composition:** 90% silver (0.3867 ounces), 10% copper.

Date	Mintage	G-4	VG-8	F-12	VF-20	XF-40	AU-50	MS-60	MS-65
1836	1,200	600.	750.	950.	1450.	1900.	3500.	5000.	—
1837	3,629,820	32.00	38.00	41.00	60.00	125.	365.	750.	13,500.

"Half Dol." on reverse

Date	Mintage	G-4	VG-8	F-12	VF-20	XF-40	AU-50	MS-60	MS-65
1838	3,546,000	32.00	38.00	41.00	60.00	125.	475.	1200.	13,500.
1838O	Est. 20					Auction '82, MS-63, $47,000.			—
1839	3,334,560	32.00	38.00	41.00	60.00	125.	365.	750.	13,500.
1839O	178,976	85.00	125.	185.	375.	595.	—	3250.	—

Seated Liberty

Designer: Christian Gobrecht. **Size:** 30.6 millimeters. **Weight:** 13.36 grams. **Composition:** 90% silver (0.3867 ounces), 10% copper. **Notes:** Some 1839 strikes have drapery extending from Liberty's left elbow. One variety of the 1840 strikes has smaller lettering; another used the old reverse of 1838. Varieties of 1842 and 1846 are distinguished by the size of the numerals in the date.

Date	Mintage	G-4	VG-8	F-12	VF-20	XF-40	AU-50	MS-60	MS-65
1839 no drapery from elbow									
	Inc. Ab.	38.00	65.00	110.	250.	650.	1150.	2350.	107 K
1839 drapery	Inc. Ab.	20.00	25.00	40.00	70.00	115.	265.	450.	—

Date	Mintage	G-4	VG-8	F-12	VF-20	XF-40	MS-60	MS-65	Prf-65
1840 sm. let.	1,435,008	16.50	20.00	30.00	60.00	110.	350.	575.	15,000.
1840 rev. 1838	Inc. Ab.	85.00	120.	175.	250.	450.	700.	2000.	—
1840O	855,100	17.00	23.00	34.00	60.00	125.	300.	585.	—
1841	310,000	45.00	55.00	70.00	125.	265.	425.	1300.	—
1841O	401,000	24.00	35.00	45.00	90.00	150.	240.	875.	—
1842 sm. date	2,012,764	27.00	32.00	40.00	75.00	125.	325.	1300.	12,000.
1842 lg. date	Inc. Ab.	16.00	21.00	33.00	50.00	75.00	120.	1250.	12,000.
1842O sm. date	957,000	700.	1000.	1400.	2500.	5000.	—	—	—
1842O lg. date	Inc. Ab.	17.00	23.00	34.00	65.00	115.	245.	500.	—
1843	3,844,000	16.00	21.00	30.00	65.00	90.00	180.	410.	5500.
1843O	2,268,000	16.00	21.00	30.00	65.00	110.	250.	550.	—
1844	1,766,000	16.00	21.00	30.00	50.00	85.00	180.	410.	5500.
1844O	2,005,000	16.00	21.00	36.00	55.00	80.00	195.	525.	—
1845	589,000	30.00	40.00	50.00	90.00	170.	340.	900.	—
1845O	2,094,000	16.00	21.00	30.00	42.00	100.	240.	550.	—
1845O no drapery	Inc. Ab.	40.00	60.00	90.00	120.	195.	375.	750.	—
1846 med. dt.	2,210,000	16.00	20.00	28.00	40.00	70.00	175.	500.	9000.
1846 tall dt.	Inc. Ab.	22.00	30.00	60.00	80.00	125.	250.	650.	12,000.
1846/horizontal 6	Inc. Ab.	140.	185.	250.	375.	550.	1000.	2500.	—
1846O med.dt.	2,304,000	16.00	18.00	28.00	38.00	100.	225.	550.	12,000.
1846O tall dt.	Inc. Ab.	145.	225.	325.	550.	1000.	1800.	3600.	—
1847/1846	1,156,000	1500.	1900.	2500.	3250.	4500.	—	—	—
1847	Inc. Ab.	20.00	30.00	45.00	60.00	90.00	190.	480.	9000.
1847O	2,584,000	15.00	25.00	35.00	50.00	95.00	250.	640.	12,500.
1848	580,000	30.00	50.00	75.00	135.	240.	550.	1400.	9000.
1848O	3,180,000	18.00	25.00	40.00	50.00	95.00	285.	750.	9000.
1849	1,252,000	22.00	35.00	50.00	85.00	150.	365.	1250.	9000.
1849O	2,310,000	15.00	25.00	40.00	60.00	115.	250.	650.	9000.
1850	227,000	200.	250.	340.	400.	600.	875.	1500.	—

1855-S Half Dollar
Grade XF-40

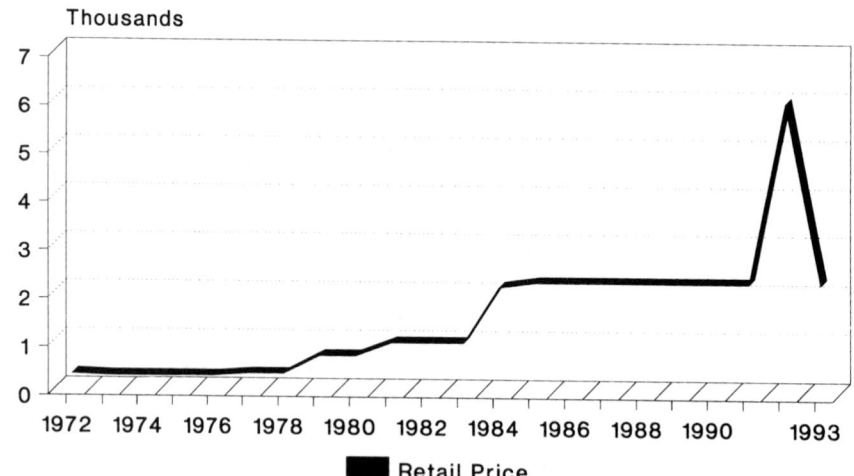

Source: COIN PRICES

Date	Mintage	G-4	VG-8	F-12	VF-20	XF-40	AU-50	MS-60	MS-65
1850O	2,456,000	15.00	25.00	40.00	55.00	115.	250.	650.	9000.
1851	200,750	225.	265.	325.	415.	450.	550.	1800.	—
1851O	402,000	37.00	45.00	57.00	90.00	175.	300.	610.	9000.
1852	77,130	300.	350.	425.	475.	650.	800.	1450.	—
1852O	144,000	65.00	80.00	125.	235.	350.	650.	1850.	—
1853O	Unrecorded			Garrett Sale, 1979, VF, $40,000.					

Arrows at date, reverse rays

Weight: 12.44 grams. **Composition:** 90% silver (0.36 ounces), 10% copper.

Date	Mintage	G-4	VG-8	F-12	VF-20	XF-40	AU-50	MS-60	MS-65	Prf-65
1853 rays on reverse	3,532,708	16.50	30.00	45.50	90.00	250.	505.	1700.	21,500.	—
1853O rays on reverse	1,328,000	19.00	30.00	45.50	100.	290.	700.	2100.	21,500.	—

Reverse rays removed

Date	Mintage	G-4	VG-8	F-12	VF-20	XF-40	AU-50	MS-60	MS-65	Prf-65
1854	2,982,000	15.00	20.00	29.00	50.00	100.	270.	675.	10,000.	—
1854O	5,240,000	15.00	20.00	29.00	50.00	100.	265.	500.	10,000.	—
1855	759,500	23.00	30.00	40.00	60.00	150.	325.	1200.	10,000.	22,500.
1855O	3,688,000	15.00	20.00	29.00	50.00	100.	270.	650.	10,000.	—
1855S	129,950	300.	380.	550.	1000.	2250.	6000.	—	—	—

Arrows at date removed

Date	Mintage	G-4	VG-8	F-12	VF-20	XF-40	AU-50	MS-60	MS-65	Prf-65
1856	938,000	18.00	25.00	32.00	47.50	90.00	150.	410.	12,500.	12,500.
1856O	2,658,000	15.00	21.00	28.00	45.00	82.00	150.	450.	12,500.	—
1856S	211,000	40.00	50.00	70.00	100.	225.	500.	1500.	19,000.	—
1857	1,988,000	15.00	18.00	28.00	45.00	82.00	150.	410.	12,500.	12,500.
1857O	818,000	18.00	21.00	25.00	55.00	100.	200.	850.	12,500.	—
1857S	158,000	45.00	65.00	110.	180.	290.	450.	1400.	19,000.	—
1858	4,226,000	15.00	18.00	35.00	60.00	80.00	150.	410.	5500.	12,500.
1858O	7,294,000	14.00	17.00	35.00	45.00	75.00	150.	450.	12,500.	—

Date	Mintage	G-4	VG-8	F-12	VF-20	XF-40	AU-50	MS-60	MS-65	Prf-65
1858S	476,000	20.00	30.00	48.00	75.00	175.	400.	950.	12,500.	—
1859	748,000	16.50	27.00	42.00	55.00	90.00	200.	650.	12,500.	7500.
1859O	2,834,000	15.00	25.00	40.00	50.00	85.00	150.	450.	12,500.	—
1859S	566,000	20.00	28.00	45.00	70.00	120.	200.	750.	12,500.	—
1860	303,700	18.00	21.00	27.00	70.00	145.	350.	1000.	12,500.	7500.
1860O	1,290,000	15.00	18.00	21.00	35.00	75.00	150.	450.	12,500.	—
1860S	472,000	18.00	30.00	50.00	70.00	130.	175.	850.	12,500.	—
1861	2,888,400	15.00	25.00	35.00	45.00	75.00	150.	410.	5500.	7500.
1861O	2,532,633	15.00	25.00	35.00	45.00	75.00	150.	450.	12,500.	—
1861S	939,500	17.00	20.00	24.00	45.00	75.00	150.	975.	19,000.	—
1862	253,550	24.00	32.00	45.00	80.00	150.	225.	750.	12,500.	7500.
1862S	1,352,000	16.00	27.00	35.00	60.00	90.00	175.	450.	5500.	—
1863	503,660	18.00	25.00	40.00	70.00	130.	250.	750.	12,500.	7500.
1863S	916,000	16.00	25.00	35.00	45.00	80.00	150.	410.	12,500.	—
1864	379,570	24.00	32.00	55.00	85.00	160.	200.	750.	12,500.	7500.
1864S	658,000	16.50	20.00	40.00	50.00	85.00	165.	450.	12,500.	—
1865	511,900	18.00	23.00	40.00	55.00	105.	165.	750.	12,500.	7500.
1865S	675,000	17.00	21.00	30.00	50.00	75.00	160.	450.	12,500.	—
1866	—	—	—	—	Proof, unique		—	—	—	—
1866S	60,000	60.00	80.00	150.	225.	335.	1000.	5000.	—	—

Motto above eagle

Notes: In 1866 the motto "In God We Trust" was added to the reverse. The "closed-3" and "open-3" varieties are distinguished by the amount of space between the upper left and lower left serifs of the 3.

Date	Mintage	G-4	VG-8	F-12	VF-20	XF-40	AU-50	MS-60	MS-65	Prf-65
1866	745,625	15.00	24.00	29.00	39.00	63.00	145.	800.	7000.	3750.
1866S	994,000	15.00	24.00	29.00	39.00	63.00	145.	800.	7000.	—
1867	449,925	16.00	27.00	35.00	55.00	100.	160.	1000.	7000.	3750.
1867S	1,196,000	15.00	24.00	29.00	39.00	63.00	145.	800.	7000.	—
1868	418,200	24.00	32.00	45.00	70.00	135.	170.	1000.	7100.	3750.
1868S	1,160,000	15.00	24.00	29.00	39.00	63.00	145.	800.	7000.	—
1869	795,900	15.00	24.00	29.00	39.00	63.00	145.	800.	7000.	3750.
1869S	656,000	15.00	27.00	35.00	47.00	80.00	145.	800.	7000.	—
1870	634,900	17.00	27.00	35.00	47.00	80.00	145.	800.	7000.	3750.
1870CC	54,617	600.	850.	1200.	2000.	3000.	—	—	—	—
1870S	1,004,000	15.00	24.00	29.00	42.00	75.00	145.	800.	7000.	—
1871	1,204,560	16.00	24.00	29.00	39.00	63.00	145.	800.	7000.	3750.
1871CC	153,950	120.	150.	200.	325.	600.	1250.	4000.	9150.	—
1871S	2,178,000	15.00	24.00	29.00	39.00	63.00	145.	800.	7000.	—
1872	881,550	15.00	24.00	29.00	39.00	63.00	145.	800.	7000.	3750.
1872CC	272,000	32.00	44.00	80.00	160.	350.	600.	2500.	8800.	—
1872S	580,000	23.00	28.00	40.00	80.00	145.	160.	900.	7000.	—
1873 closed 3	801,800	15.00	24.00	38.00	50.00	95.00	150.	760.	7000.	3750.
1873 open 3	Inc. Ab.	2500.	3000.	4000.	5000.	6500.	—	—	—	—
1873CC	122,500	110.	130.	200.	310.	475.	850.	3000.	8850.	3750.

1873S no arrows, 5,000 minted, no specimens known to survive.

Arrows at date

Weight: 12.5 grams. **Composition:** 90% silver (0.3618 ounces), 10% copper.

Date	Mintage	G-4	VG-8	F-12	VF-20	XF-40	AU-50	MS-60	MS-65	Prf-65
1873	1,815,700	16.50	25.00	36.00	80.00	225.	445.	950.	21,500.	14,000.
1873CC	214,560	60.00	75.00	95.00	225.	450.	900.	2500.	21,500.	—
1873S	233,000	45.00	60.00	90.00	165.	300.	575.	1850.	21,500.	—
1874	2,360,300	16.50	25.00	36.00	80.00	225.	445.	950.	21,500.	14,000.
1874CC	59,000	165.	210.	325.	500.	925.	1750.	4500.	21,500.	—
1874S	394,000	25.00	30.00	38.00	100.	275.	525.	2000.	21,500.	—

Arrows at date removed

Date	Mintage	G-4	VG-8	F-12	VF-20	XF-40	AU-50	MS-60	MS-65	Prf-65
1875	6,027,500	15.00	24.00	29.00	37.00	60.00	120.	800.	7000.	3750.
1875CC	1,008,000	17.00	33.00	35.00	45.00	100.	200.	850.	7000.	—
1875S	3,200,000	15.00	24.00	29.00	37.00	60.00	120.	350.	3500.	—
1876	8,419,150	15.00	24.00	32.00	40.00	60.00	135.	340.	3800.	3750.
1876CC	1,956,000	17.00	30.00	35.00	45.00	100.	200.	850.	7000.	—
1876S	4,528,000	15.00	24.00	32.00	40.00	60.00	120.	340.	3500.	—
1877	8,304,510	15.00	24.00	29.00	45.00	60.00	120.	340.	3500.	3750.
1877CC	1,420,000	17.00	33.00	35.00	45.00	95.00	160.	800.	7000.	—
1877S	5,356,000	15.00	24.00	29.00	37.00	65.00	120.	340.	3500.	—
1878	1,378,400	20.00	28.00	36.00	50.00	72.00	120.	340.	3500.	3750.
1878CC	62,000	250.	300.	400.	650.	1250.	1850.	3000.	9000.	—
1878S	12,000	6500.	7500.	8500.	12,500.	17,500.	20,000.	25,000.	—	—
1879	5,900	250.	275.	300.	375.	475.	700.	1600.	7000.	11,000.
1880	9,755	200.	220.	275.	310.	400.	600.	1500.	7000.	11,000.
1881	10,975	185.	210.	265.	300.	390.	575.	1400.	7000.	11,000.

1878-S Half Dollar
Grade F-12

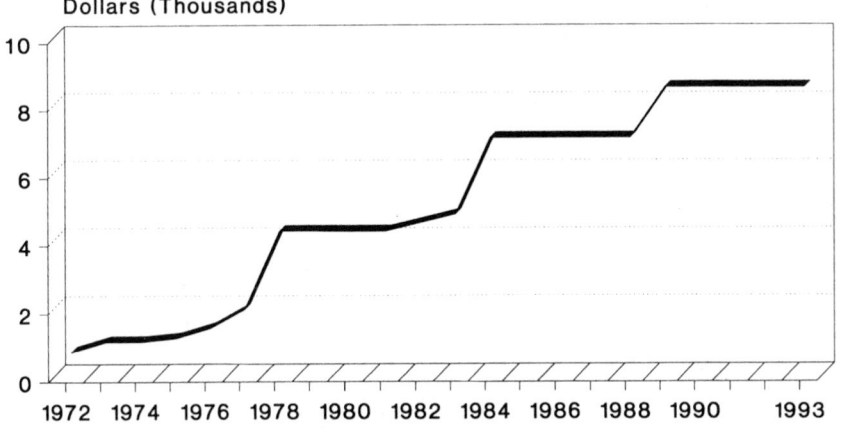

Dollars (Thousands)

Retail Price

Source: COIN PRICES

Date	Mintage	G-4	VG-8	F-12	VF-20	XF-40	AU-50	MS-60	MS-65	Prf-65
1882	5,500	250.	275.	300.	375.	475.	700.	1600.	7000.	11,000.
1883	9,039	200.	220.	275.	310.	400.	550.	1600.	7000.	11,000.
1884	5,275	280.	300.	370.	420.	525.	725.	1700.	7000.	11,000.
1885	6,130	275.	300.	350.	410.	525.	750.	1700.	7000.	11,000.
1886	5,886	285.	310.	350.	430.	550.	675.	1700.	7000.	11,000.
1887	5,710	325.	350.	400.	450.	575.	750.	1700.	7000.	11,000.
1888	12,833	175.	200.	235.	290.	375.	550.	1100.	7000.	11,000.
1889	12,711	185.	200.	235.	290.	395.	550.	1100.	7000.	11,000.
1890	12,590	185.	200.	235.	290.	375.	550.	1100.	7000.	11,000.
1891	200,600	30.00	35.00	55.00	80.00	115.	335.	1000.	7000.	11,000.

Barber

Designer: Charles E. Barber. **Size:** 30.6 millimeters. **Weight:** 12.5 grams. **Composition:** 90% silver (0.3618 ounces), 10% copper.

Date	Mintage	G-4	VG-8	F-12	VF-20	XF-40	AU-50	MS-60	MS-65	Prf-65
1892	935,245	17.00	23.00	37.00	70.00	170.	280.	420.	3300.	2800.
1892O	390,000	90.00	120.	160.	250.	400.	500.	925.	5900.	—
1892S	1,029,028	90.00	115.	160.	240.	380.	500.	775.	5900.	—
1893	1,826,792	11.00	16.50	38.00	65.00	150.	310.	460.	3500.	2800.
1893O	1,389,000	15.00	25.00	45.00	115.	260.	350.	550.	10,500.	—
1893S	740,000	50.00	60.00	140.	245.	345.	500.	1050.	10,500.	—
1894	1,148,972	13.00	20.00	48.00	73.00	170.	315.	500.	3500.	2850.
1894O	2,138,000	9.00	12.00	44.00	85.00	235.	340.	500.	7800.	—
1894S	4,048,690	7.50	10.75	40.00	60.00	190.	300.	460.	9600.	—
1895	1,835,218	7.50	10.00	36.00	75.00	165.	290.	495.	4450.	2900.
1895O	1,766,000	8.00	14.00	40.00	78.00	210.	340.	500.	8400.	—
1895S	1,108,086	14.00	23.00	43.00	90.00	250.	350.	475.	11,500.	—
1896	950,762	11.00	15.00	36.00	70.00	180.	290.	475.	8400.	2900.
1896O	924,000	16.00	20.00	72.00	140.	345.	580.	1100.	12,500.	—
1896S	1,140,948	52.00	60.00	100.	175.	350.	500.	1100.	11,500.	—
1897	2,480,731	6.50	7.50	23.00	58.00	130.	275.	425.	3300.	2800.
1897O	632,000	45.00	58.00	230.	400.	725.	1000.	1425.	7000.	—
1897S	933,900	70.00	85.00	240.	410.	625.	925.	1200.	9000.	—
1898	2,956,735	6.50	7.50	22.00	57.00	130.	275.	420.	3300.	2800.
1898O	874,000	13.00	25.00	58.00	135.	315.	425.	700.	7550.	—
1898S	2,358,550	7.75	14.00	32.00	73.00	200.	325.	575.	10,000.	—
1899	5,538,846	5.00	7.00	22.00	57.00	130.	275.	420.	3300.	2900.
1899O	1,724,000	7.25	10.50	38.00	80.00	210.	325.	550.	7200.	—
1899S	1,686,411	6.75	11.50	36.00	72.00	180.	315.	520.	6850.	—
1900	4,762,912	5.00	7.25	22.00	58.00	130.	275.	420.	3300.	2800.
1900O	2,744,000	7.00	10.00	37.00	82.00	240.	340.	685.	14,500.	—
1900S	2,560,322	7.00	10.00	31.00	86.00	180.	315.	500.	10,000.	—
1901	4,268,813	5.00	7.25	22.00	58.00	130.	275.	420.	4200.	2800.
1901O	1,124,000	7.00	11.50	43.00	105.	270.	420.	1250.	29,000.	—
1901S	847,044	11.00	15.00	78.00	215.	500.	825.	1400.	12,500.	—
1902	4,922,777	5.00	7.25	22.00	57.00	130.	275.	410.	3300.	2800.
1902O	2,526,000	6.00	10.00	35.00	72.00	170.	320.	650.	11,000.	—
1902S	1,460,670	6.50	10.50	38.00	77.00	200.	340.	520.	5150.	—
1903	2,278,755	8.00	12.00	30.00	66.00	145.	320.	460.	7500.	2800.
1903O	2,100,000	5.50	10.00	36.00	72.00	175.	315.	540.	9000.	—
1903S	1,920,772	6.00	10.50	37.00	73.00	210.	340.	510.	9000.	—
1904	2,992,670	5.00	7.50	23.00	58.00	135.	285.	420.	4550.	2900.
1904O	1,117,600	8.00	12.00	44.00	102.	275.	460.	1000.	11,000.	—
1904S	553,038	10.50	20.00	72.00	240.	495.	825.	1425.	13,750.	—
1905	662,727	8.50	10.50	43.00	72.00	215.	350.	500.	6000.	2850.
1905O	505,000	9.50	15.00	49.00	110.	225.	385.	660.	6600.	—
1905S	2,494,000	5.25	8.00	32.00	68.00	175.	320.	480.	10,350.	—
1906	2,638,675	5.00	7.00	22.00	57.00	125.	275.	410.	3300.	2800.
1906D	4,028,000	5.00	7.50	25.00	59.00	140.	275.	410.	3950.	—
1906O	2,446,000	5.25	8.00	30.00	66.00	160.	285.	500.	6850.	—
1906S	1,740,154	5.50	11.00	40.00	63.00	180.	325.	500.	6950.	—
1907	2,598,575	5.00	7.00	22.00	56.00	125.	275.	410.	3300.	2800.
1907D	3,856,000	5.00	7.00	25.00	58.00	140.	275.	410.	3300.	—
1907O	3,946,000	5.00	7.50	25.00	58.00	145.	280.	450.	3300.	—
1907S	1,250,000	6.50	11.00	37.00	72.00	250.	375.	775.	12,000.	—
1908	1,354,545	6.00	8.50	24.00	59.00	140.	295.	450.	3300.	2800.
1908D	3,280,000	5.00	7.50	25.00	60.00	145.	280.	460.	3300.	—
1908O	5,360,000	5.00	7.00	24.00	57.00	140.	275.	450.	3300.	—

Date	Mintage	G-4	VG-8	F-12	VF-20	XF-40	AU-50	MS-60	MS-65	Prf-65
1908S	1,644,828	5.50	10.50	36.00	72.00	180.	315.	660.	7550.	—
1909	2,368,650	4.75	7.00	22.00	56.00	120.	270.	405.	3300.	2800.
1909O	925,400	6.00	10.00	39.00	77.00	260.	450.	700.	6250.	—
1909S	1,764,000	5.25	7.50	24.00	71.00	165.	310.	500.	3850.	—
1910	418,551	8.00	12.00	51.00	105.	260.	400.	550.	3300.	3200.
1910S	1,948,000	5.00	7.50	25.00	66.00	165.	300.	550.	4200.	—
1911	1,406,543	5.25	8.00	25.00	60.00	140.	285.	425.	3300.	2800.
1911D	695,080	6.00	10.00	30.00	69.00	165.	310.	550.	3300.	—
1911S	1,272,000	5.25	8.00	28.00	66.00	155.	300.	525.	8400.	—
1912	1,550,700	5.00	7.00	23.00	58.00	150.	285.	420.	3600.	2800.
1912D	2,300,800	5.00	7.00	22.00	57.00	120.	275.	410.	3300.	—
1912S	1,370,000	5.25	7.00	25.00	60.00	155.	285.	465.	5000.	—
1913	188,627	15.00	21.00	80.00	175.	340.	650.	845.	3500.	5450.
1913D	534,000	6.00	9.00	31.00	66.00	175.	300.	470.	7100.	—
1913S	604,000	6.50	10.00	39.00	78.00	190.	350.	550.	3850.	—
1914	124,610	18.00	27.00	170.	325.	450.	750.	880.	11,000.	5600.
1914S	992,000	6.00	9.00	30.00	65.00	165.	325.	525.	3700.	—
1915	138,450	16.00	22.00	85.00	200.	350.	685.	975.	4800.	5600.
1915D	1,170,400	5.00	7.00	22.00	57.00	125.	275.	420.	3300.	—
1915S	1,604,000	5.00	7.00	24.00	58.00	130.	275.	475.	3300.	—

Walking Liberty

Obverse mintmark

Mintmark on obverse

Designer: Adolph A. Weinman. **Size:** 30.6 millimeters. **Weight:** 12.5 grams. **Composition:** 90% silver (0.3618 ounces), 10% copper.

Date	Mintage	G-4	VG-8	F-12	VF-20	XF-40	AU-50	MS-60	MS-65	Prf-65
1916	608,000	19.00	25.00	55.00	120.	160.	210.	275.	1575.	—
1916D	1,014,400	11.00	17.00	30.00	70.00	135.	175.	250.	1825.	—
1916S	508,000	40.00	48.00	115.	280.	510.	665.	800.	4550.	—
1917D	765,400	11.50	15.00	30.00	84.00	140.	210.	430.	5750.	—
1917S	952,000	12.50	20.00	38.00	210.	560.	975.	1600.	9700.	—

Reverse mintmark

Mintmark on reverse

Date	Mintage	G-4	VG-8	F-12	VF-20	XF-40	AU-50	MS-60	MS-65	Prf-65
1917	12,292,000	4.00	8.00	10.50	20.00	35.00	56.00	120.	885.	—
1917D	1,940,000	8.50	11.00	19.00	50.00	140.	310.	675.	14,250.	—
1917S	5,554,000	5.00	8.00	13.50	25.00	48.00	105.	280.	9100.	—
1918	6,634,000	4.00	9.00	17.00	45.00	130.	250.	410.	3775.	—
1918D	3,853,040	6.00	9.50	18.00	51.00	140.	315.	750.	17,000.	—
1918S	10,282,000	4.00	8.00	14.00	27.00	49.00	120.	330.	12,000.	—
1919	962,000	10.50	14.00	30.00	125.	375.	560.	915.	4700.	—
1919D	1,165,000	9.50	12.00	32.00	140.	450.	900.	2200.	39,000.	—
1919S	1,552,000	8.50	10.00	22.00	110.	600.	1100.	1700.	9100.	—
1920	6,372,000	4.00	8.00	13.00	23.00	53.00	91.00	220.	6100.	—
1920D	1,551,000	8.50	10.00	23.00	115.	300.	600.	1040.	8100.	—
1920S	4,624,000	6.00	8.00	14.00	42.00	135.	300.	590.	7300.	—
1921	246,000	50.00	68.00	160.	525.	1250.	1950.	2250.	10,750.	—
1921D	208,000	77.00	95.00	215.	595.	1750.	2500.	2650.	8850.	—
1921S	548,000	14.00	18.00	42.00	420.	2800.	6700.	7300.	32,500.	—
1923S	2,178,000	7.00	10.00	18.00	42.00	175.	490.	1100.	10,500.	—
1927S	2,392,000	4.00	7.00	11.00	25.00	84.00	245.	610.	8125.	—

1923-S Half Dollar
Grade XF-40

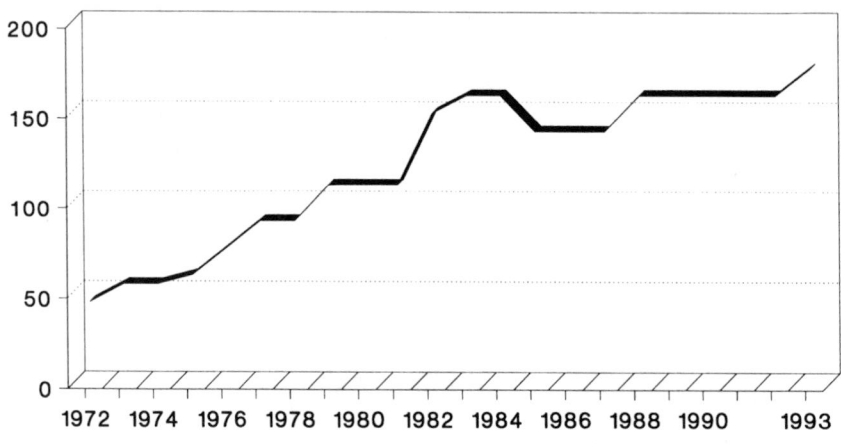

Retail Price

Source: COIN PRICES

Date	Mintage	G-4	VG-8	F-12	VF-20	XF-40	AU-50	MS-60	MS-65	Prf-65
1928S	1,940,000	4.00	7.00	12.50	30.00	105.	290.	620.	5850.	—
1929D	1,001,200	6.25	7.50	10.50	19.00	70.00	155.	245.	2050.	—
1929S	1,902,000	4.00	6.75	10.00	16.00	64.00	150.	300.	2250.	—
1933S	1,786,000	5.50	8.50	10.00	11.50	45.00	150.	450.	3050.	—
1934	6,964,000	2.50	2.75	3.50	4.50	11.00	26.50	40.00	350.	—
1934D	2,361,400	3.25	4.00	5.50	7.50	25.00	56.00	97.00	1300.	—
1934S	3,652,000	3.00	3.50	4.50	6.00	25.00	70.00	215.	2450.	—
1935	9,162,000	2.50	2.75	3.50	4.50	9.00	19.50	44.00	300.	—
1935D	3,003,800	3.25	4.00	5.50	7.50	25.00	56.00	105.	1100.	—
1935S	3,854,000	3.10	3.50	4.50	5.50	25.00	68.00	110.	1800.	—
1936	12,617,901	2.50	2.75	3.50	4.50	9.00	19.50	39.00	115.	2500.
1936D	4,252,400	2.95	3.50	4.50	5.50	17.00	47.00	85.00	340.	—
1936S	3,884,000	3.00	3.50	4.50	5.50	17.00	45.00	110.	565.	—
1937	9,527,728	2.50	2.75	3.50	4.50	9.00	19.50	36.00	170.	925.
1937D	1,676,000	6.00	7.00	8.75	10.50	28.00	125.	195.	610.	—
1937S	2,090,000	5.00	6.00	7.25	8.00	16.50	56.00	110.	495.	—
1938	4,118,152	3.00	3.50	4.50	6.50	11.00	33.00	60.00	215.	725.
1938D	491,600	18.00	20.00	28.00	42.00	100.	260.	395.	1080.	—
1939	6,820,808	2.50	2.75	3.50	4.50	10.00	22.00	40.00	115.	675.
1939D	4,267,800	3.00	3.50	4.50	5.50	10.50	24.00	39.00	115.	—
1939S	2,552,000	4.50	4.75	6.00	8.75	12.50	39.00	100.	220.	—
1940	9,167,279	2.45	3.50	4.00	5.50	9.00	14.00	24.00	110.	650.
1940S	4,550,000	2.45	3.50	4.00	5.50	10.00	21.00	28.00	385.	—
1941	24,207,412	2.45	2.65	3.50	4.50	8.00	9.00	24.00	100.	650.
1941D	11,248,400	2.45	2.65	3.50	4.50	6.00	16.00	32.00	110.	—
1941S	8,098,000	2.60	2.80	3.75	4.75	7.00	28.00	84.00	1250.	—
1942	47,839,120	2.45	2.65	3.50	4.50	5.50	9.00	25.00	115.	650.
1942D	10,973,800	2.45	2.65	3.50	4.50	6.00	16.00	28.00	220.	—
1942S	12,708,000	2.45	2.65	3.50	4.75	7.00	21.00	32.00	690.	—
1943	53,190,000	2.45	2.65	3.50	4.50	5.50	9.00	25.00	110.	—
1943D	11,346,000	2.45	2.65	3.50	4.50	6.00	20.00	43.00	130.	—
1943S	13,450,000	2.45	2.65	3.75	4.75	6.00	21.00	34.00	475.	—
1944	28,206,000	2.45	2.65	3.50	4.50	5.50	9.00	25.00	110.	—
1944D	9,769,000	2.45	2.65	3.50	4.50	6.00	18.00	34.00	110.	—
1944S	8,904,000	2.45	2.65	3.50	4.75	6.25	20.00	34.00	900.	—
1945	31,502,000	2.45	2.65	3.50	4.50	5.50	9.00	25.00	110.	—
1945D	9,966,800	2.45	2.65	3.50	4.50	6.00	15.00	30.00	115.	—
1945S	10,156,000	2.45	2.65	3.50	4.75	6.00	17.00	34.00	140.	—
1946	12,118,000	2.45	2.65	3.50	4.50	5.50	12.50	28.00	110.	—
1946D	2,151,000	4.50	4.75	6.00	8.75	9.50	17.00	26.00	110.	—
1946S	3,724,000	2.60	2.80	3.50	5.00	5.50	20.00	31.00	110.	—
1947	4,094,000	2.60	2.80	3.50	5.00	7.00	20.00	34.00	125.	—
1947D	3,900,600	2.60	2.80	3.50	5.00	7.00	20.00	36.00	110.	—

1953 Half Dollar
Grade MS-60

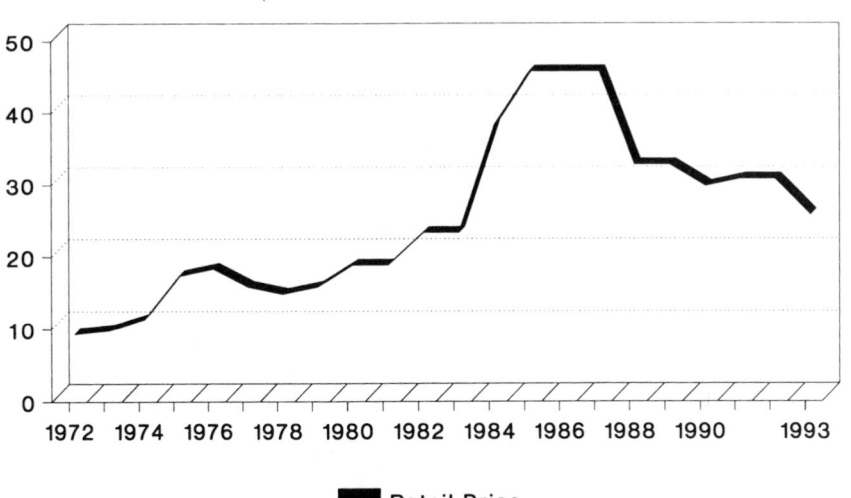

■ Retail Price

Source: COIN PRICES

Franklin

Designer: John R. Sinnock. **Size:** 30.6 millimeters. **Weight:** 12.5 grams. **Composition:** 90% silver (0.3618 ounces), 10% copper. **Notes:** "MS-65FBL" values are for coins with full lines across the bell on the reverse.

Date	Mintage	G-4	VG-8	F-12	VF-20	XF-40	AU-50	MS-60	MS-65	-65FBL	Prf-65
1948	3,006,814	—	3.50	4.00	4.50	9.00	10.00	17.50	82.00	—	—
1948D	4,028,600	—	3.50	4.00	4.50	8.00	9.00	10.00	150.	—	—
1949	5,614,000	—	3.50	4.00	6.00	11.00	15.00	37.50	90.00	250.	—
1949D	4,120,600	—	3.50	4.00	6.00	12.00	19.00	50.00	1375.	—	—
1949S	3,744,000	—	3.75	4.75	9.00	25.00	50.00	75.00	140.	450.	—
1950	7,793,509	—	—	4.00	4.50	9.00	12.00	37.50	95.00	—	440.
1950D	8,031,600	—	—	4.00	4.50	9.00	10.00	25.00	375.	—	—
1951	16,859,602	—	—	4.00	4.50	7.00	8.00	14.00	70.00	—	250.
1951D	9,475,200	—	—	3.50	4.25	5.00	12.50	40.00	195.	—	—
1951S	13,696,000	—	—	3.50	4.25	5.00	20.00	31.00	56.00	360.	—
1952	21,274,073	—	—	3.50	4.25	5.00	9.00	11.50	56.00	—	135.
1952D	25,395,600	—	—	3.00	3.50	4.50	9.00	10.00	170.	—	—
1952S	5,526,000	—	—	3.50	4.25	4.75	18.00	37.50	56.00	400.	—
1953	2,796,920	3.75	4.00	4.25	5.00	6.00	14.00	25.00	125.	—	95.00
1953D	20,900,400	—	—	3.00	3.50	4.00	8.00	8.75	165.	—	—
1953S	4,148,000	—	—	3.50	4.25	4.75	10.00	22.00	39.00	700.	—
1954	13,421,503	—	—	3.00	3.50	4.75	5.50	7.50	64.00	—	55.00
1954D	25,445,580	—	—	3.00	3.00	4.00	5.00	5.75	120.	—	—

Date	Mintage	G-4	VG-8	F-12	VF-20	XF-40	AU-50	MS-60	MS-65	-65FBL	Prf-65
1954S	4,993,400	—	—	3.50	4.25	4.75	6.50	7.50	34.00	165.	—
1955	2,876,381	4.50	5.00	6.50	7.00	7.50	8.00	8.50	44.00	—	50.00
1956	4,701,384	—	—	3.50	4.00	4.50	5.50	6.50	34.00	—	19.00
1957	6,361,952	—	—	3.50	4.00	4.50	7.00	8.50	34.00	—	16.50
1957D	19,966,850	—	—	3.00	3.50	4.50	5.00	5.75	34.00	—	—
1958	4,917,652	—	—	2.75	3.50	4.00	4.50	4.75	34.00	—	19.00
1958D	23,962,412	—	—	—	2.00	3.00	3.50	4.00	34.00	—	—
1959	7,349,291	—	—	—	2.00	3.00	4.50	5.65	125.	—	16.50
1959D	13,053,750	—	—	—	2.00	3.00	4.50	5.65	170.	—	—
1960	7,715,602	—	—	—	2.00	3.00	4.00	4.75	182.	—	15.00
1960D	18,215,812	—	—	—	2.00	3.00	3.50	4.50	750.	—	—
1961	11,318,244	—	—	—	2.00	3.00	3.50	4.50	315.	—	14.00
1961D	20,276,442	—	—	—	2.00	2.50	3.50	4.50	450.	—	—
1962	12,932,019	—	—	—	2.00	3.00	3.50	4.10	245.	—	14.00
1962D	35,473,281	—	—	—	2.00	2.50	3.00	4.10	500.	—	—
1963	25,239,645	—	—	—	2.00	2.50	2.65	2.75	82.00	—	14.00
1963D	67,069,292	—	—	—	2.00	2.10	2.25	2.50	75.00	—	—

Kennedy

Reverse mintmark (1964)

Obverse mintmark (1968-present)

90% silver composition

Designers: Gilroy Roberts and Frank Gasparro. **Size:** 30.6 millimeters. **Weight:** 12.5 grams. **Composition:** 90% silver (0.3618 ounces), 10% copper.

Date	Mintage	G-4	VG-8	F-12	VF-20	XF-40	MS-60	MS-65	Prf-65
1964	277,254,766	—	—	—	—	—	2.25	3.50	12.50
1964D	156,205,446	—	—	—	—	—	2.25	3.50	—

40% silver composition

Weight: 11.5 grams. **Composition:** clad layers of 80% silver and 20% copper bonded to a core of 20.9% silver and 79.1% copper (0.148 total ounces of silver).

Date	Mintage	G-4	VG-8	F-12	VF-20	XF-40	MS-60	MS-65	Prf-65
1965	65,879,366	—	—	—	—	—	1.25	2.50	—
1966	108,984,932	—	—	—	—	—	1.20	2.40	—
1967	295,046,978	—	—	—	—	—	1.00	2.25	—
1968D	246,951,930	—	—	—	—	—	1.00	2.25	—
1968S	3,041,506	—	—	—	—	—	Proof only	—	6.50
1969D	129,881,800	—	—	—	—	—	1.00	2.00	—
1969S	2,934,631	—	—	—	—	—	—	—	5.00
1970D	2,150,000	—	—	—	—	—	12.00	15.00	—
1970S	2,632,810	—	—	—	—	—	Proof only	—	7.50

Clad composition

Weight: 11.34 grams. **Composition:** clad layers of 75% copper and 25% nickel bonded to a pure-copper core.

Date	Mintage	G-4	VG-8	F-12	VF-20	XF-40	MS-60	MS-65	Prf-65
1971	155,640,000	—	—	—	—	—	1.50	2.50	—
1971D	302,097,424	—	—	—	—	—	1.00	1.50	—
1971S	3,244,183	—	—	—	—	Proof only		—	2.75
1972	153,180,000	—	—	—	—	—	2.00	2.50	—
1972D	141,890,000	—	—	—	—	—	2.00	2.50	—
1972S	3,267,667	—	—	—	—	—	—	—	2.50
1973	64,964,000	—	—	—	—	—	1.35	2.50	—
1973D	83,171,400	—	—	—	—	—	—	2.50	—
1973S	Proof only	—	—	—	—	—	—	—	2.50
1974	201,596,000	—	—	—	—	—	1.00	2.00	—
1974D	79,066,300	—	—	—	—	—	1.20	2.00	—
1974S	Proof only	—	—	—	—	—	—	—	3.50

Bicentennial design, clad composition

Reverse designer: Seth Huntington.

Date	Mintage	G-4	VG-8	F-12	VF-20	XF-40	MS-60	MS-65	Prf-65
1976	234,308,000	—	—	—	—	—	1.00	1.50	—
1976D	287,565,248	—	—	—	—	—	1.00	1.50	—
1976S	—	—	—	—	—	—	—	—	1.25

Bicentennial design, silver composition

Weight: 11.5 grams. **Composition:** 40% silver (0.148 ounces), 60% copper.

Date	Mintage	G-4	VG-8	F-12	VF-20	XF-40	MS-60	MS-65	Prf-65
1976S silver	11,000,000	—	—	—	—	—	—	6.00	5.75

Regular design resumed, clad composition

Notes: 1979-S Type II proof has a clearer mintmark than the Type I.

Date	Mintage	G-4	VG-8	F-12	VF-20	XF-40	MS-60	MS-65	Prf-65
1977	43,598,000	—	—	—	—	—	2.60	2.50	—
1977D	31,449,106	—	—	—	—	—	2.60	2.50	—
1977S	Proof only	—	—	—	—	—	—	—	1.75
1978	14,350,000	—	—	—	—	—	1.25	2.50	—
1978D	13,765,799	—	—	—	—	—	1.00	2.50	—
1978S	Proof only	—	—	—	—	—	—	—	1.75
1979	68,312,000	—	—	—	—	—	—	1.50	—
1979D	15,815,422	—	—	—	—	—	—	1.25	—
1979S T-I	Proof only	—	—	—	—	—	—	—	2.00
1979S T-II	Proof only	—	—	—	—	—	—	—	14.00
1980P	44,134,000	—	—	—	—	—	—	1.75	—
1980D	33,456,449	—	—	—	—	—	—	2.00	—
1980S	Proof only	—	—	—	—	—	—	—	1.65
1981P	29,544,000	—	—	—	—	—	—	2.00	—
1981D	27,839,533	—	—	—	—	—	—	2.00	—
1981S T-I	Proof only	—	—	—	—	—	—	—	1.65
1981S T-II	Proof only	—	—	—	—	—	—	—	13.50
1982P	10,819,000	—	—	—	—	—	—	1.50	—
1982D	13,140,102	—	—	—	—	—	—	1.50	—
1982S	Proof only	—	—	—	—	—	—	—	6.00
1983P	34,139,000	—	—	—	—	—	—	1.50	—
1983D	32,472,244	—	—	—	—	—	—	1.50	—
1983S	Proof only	—	—	—	—	—	—	—	5.50
1984P	26,029,000	—	—	—	—	—	—	1.50	—
1984D	26,262,158	—	—	—	—	—	—	1.50	—
1984S	Proof only	—	—	—	—	—	—	—	7.00
1985P	18,706,962	—	—	—	—	—	—	2.00	—
1985D	19,814,034	—	—	—	—	—	—	1.50	—
1985S	Proof only	—	—	—	—	—	—	—	5.00
1986P	13,107,633	—	—	—	—	—	—	2.00	—
1986D	15,336,145	—	—	—	—	—	—	1.50	—

Date	Mintage	G-4	VG-8	F-12	VF-20	XF-40	MS-60	MS-65	Prf-65
1986S	Proof only	—	—	—	—	—	—	—	14.00
1987P	2,890,758	—	—	—	—	—	—	3.00	—
1987D	2,890,758	—	—	—	—	—	—	2.25	—
1987S	Proof only	—	—	—	—	—	—	—	5.50
1988P	13,626,000	—	—	—	—	—	—	2.50	—
1988D	12,000,096	—	—	—	—	—	—	2.50	—
1988S	Proof only	—	—	—	—	—	—	—	7.25
1989P	24,542,000	—	—	—	—	—	—	2.50	—
1989D	23,000,216	—	—	—	—	—	—	2.50	—
1989S	Proof only	—	—	—	—	—	—	—	4.25
1990P	22,780,000	—	—	—	—	—	—	1.50	—
1990D	20,096,242	—	—	—	—	—	—	1.50	—
1990S	Proof only	—	—	—	—	—	—	—	4.75
1991P	—	—	—	—	—	—	—	1.50	—
1991D	—	—	—	—	—	—	—	1.50	—
1991S	Proof only	—	—	—	—	—	—	—	4.75
1992P	—	—	—	—	—	—	—	1.00	—
1992D	—	—	—	—	—	—	—	1.00	—
1992S	Proof only	—	—	—	—	—	—	—	4.75
1993P	—	—	—	—	—	—	—	1.00	—
1993D	—	—	—	—	—	—	—	1.00	—
1993S	Proof only	—	—	—	—	—	—	—	5.00

Silver dollars

Flowing Hair

Designer: Robert Scot. **Size:** 39-40 millimeters. **Weight:** 26.96 grams. **Composition:** 89.24% silver (0.7737 ounces), 10.76% copper. **Notes:** The two 1795 varieties have either two or three leaves under each of the eagle's wings on the reverse.

Date	Mintage	G-4	VG-8	F-12	VF-20	XF-40	MS-60
1794	1,758	10,000.	13,500.	18,500.	27,500.	42,500.	—
1795 2 leaves	203,033	750.	900.	1450.	2150.	3800.	40,000.
1795 3 leaves	Inc. Ab.	750.	900.	1450.	2150.	3800.	40,000.

Draped Bust

Small eagle

Designer: Robert Scot. **Size:** 39-40 millimeters. **Weight:** 26.96 grams. **Composition:** 89.24% silver (0.7737 ounces), 10.76% copper. **Notes:** The 1796 varieties are distinguished by the size of the numerals in the date and letters in "United States of America." The 1797 varieties are distinguished by the number of stars to the left and right of the word "Liberty" and by the size of the letters in "United States of America." The 1798 varieties have either 13 or 15 stars on the obverse.

Date	Mintage	G-4	VG-8	F-12	VF-20	XF-40	MS-60
1795	Inc. Ab.	600.	800.	1070.	1750.	3750.	17,000.
1796 small date, small letters							
	72,920	625.	800.	1150.	1950.	3650.	15,500.
1796 small date, large letters							
	Inc. Ab.	625.	750.	1050.	1800.	3400.	15,500.
1796 large date, small letters							
	Inc. Ab.	550.	700.	900.	1600.	3350.	15,500.
1797 9 stars left, 7 stars right, small letters							
	7,776	1500.	2000.	2750.	4500.	8450.	22,000.
1797 9 stars left, 7 stars right, large letters							
	Inc. Ab.	575.	750.	975.	1750.	3350.	15,500.
1797 10 stars left, 6 stars right							
	Inc. Ab.	575.	750.	975.	1750.	3350.	15,500.
1798 13 stars	327,536	900.	1150.	1450.	2400.	4500.	18,000.
1798 15 stars	Inc. Ab.	1100.	1600.	2100.	3150.	6900.	18,000.

Heraldic eagle

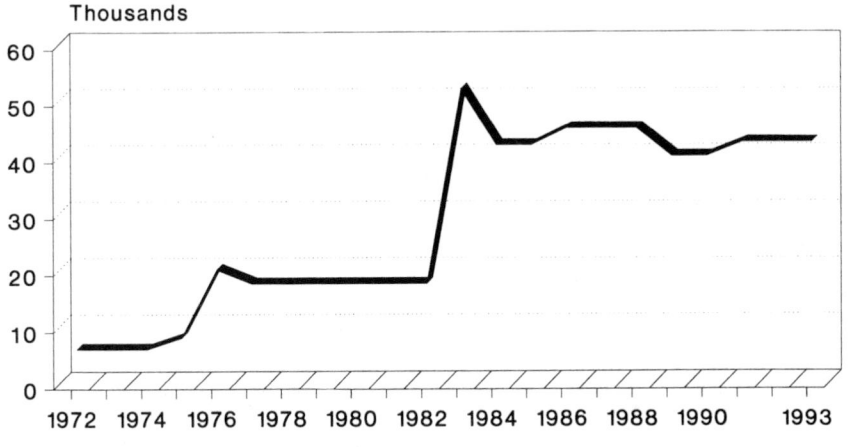

1794 Silver Dollar
Grade XF-40

Thousands

Retail Price

Source: COIN PRICES

Notes: The 1798 "knob 9" variety has a serif on the lower left of the 9 in the date. The 1798 varieties are distinguished by the number of arrows held by the eagle on the reverse and the number of berries on the olive branch. On the 1798 "high 8" variety, the 8 in the date is higher than the other numerals. The 1799 varieties are distinguished by the number and positioning of the stars on the obverse and by the size of the berries in the olive branch on the reverse. On the 1799 "irregular date" variety, the first 9 in the date is smaller than the other numerals. Some varieties of the 1800 strikes had letters in the legend cut twice into the dies; as the dies became worn, the letters were touched up. On the 1800 "very wide date, low 8" variety, the spacing between the numerals in the date is wider than other varieties, and the 8 is lower than the other numerals. The 1800 "small berries" variety refers to the size of the berries in the olive branch on the reverse. The 1800 "12 arrows" and "10 arrows" varieties refer to the number of arrows held by the eagle. The 1800 "Americai" variety appears to have the faint outline of an "I" after "America" in the reverse legend. The "close" and "wide" varieties of 1802 refer to the amount of space between the numerals in the date. For the 1802 "perfect date" varieties, all numerals in the date are of the same size. The 1803 large-3 and small-3 varieties are distinguished by the size of the 3 in the date.

Date	Mintage	G-4	VG-8	F-12	VF-20	XF-40	MS-60
1798 knob 9	Inc. Ab.	375.	450.	575.	850.	1675.	9000.
1798 10 arrows	Inc. Ab.	340.	390.	450.	700.	1300.	9000.
1798 4 berries	Inc. Ab.	340.	390.	450.	700.	1300.	9000.
1798 5 berries, 12 arrows							
	Inc. Ab.	340.	390.	450.	700.	1300.	9000.
1798 high 8	Inc. Ab.	340.	390.	450.	700.	1300.	9000.
1798 13 arrows	Inc. Ab.	340.	390.	450.	700.	1300.	9000.
1799/98 13 star reverse							
	423,515	340.	375.	460.	700.	1300.	15,000.
1799/98 15 star reverse							
	Inc. Ab.	400.	500.	850.	1150.	2000.	15,000.
1799 irregular date, 13 star reverse							
	Inc. Ab.	340.	375.	450.	675.	1250.	9000.
1799 irregular date, 15 star reverse							
	Inc. Ab.	340.	375.	450.	675.	1250.	9000.
1799 perfect date, 7 and 6 star obverse, no berries							
	Inc. Ab.	340.	375.	450.	675.	1250.	9000.
1799 perfect date, 7 and 6 star obverse, small berries							
	Inc. Ab.	340.	375.	450.	675.	1250.	9000.
1799 perfect date, 7 and 6 star obverse, medium large berries	Inc. Ab.	340.	375.	450.	675.	1250.	9000.
1799 perfect date, 7 and 6 star obverse, extra large berries	Inc. Ab.	340.	375.	450.	675.	1250.	9000.
1799 8 stars left, 5 stars right on obverse							
	Inc. Ab.	425.	500.	800.	1100.	2000.	9000.
1800 "R" in "Liberty" double cut							
	220,920	340.	375.	450.	675.	1300.	9000.
1800 first "T" in "States" double cut							
	Inc. Ab.	340.	375.	450.	675.	1300.	9000.
1800 both letters double cut							
	Inc. Ab.	340.	375.	450.	675.	1300.	9000.
1800 "T" in "United" double cut							
	Inc. Ab.	340.	375.	450.	675.	1300.	9000.
1800 very wide date, low 8							
	Inc. Ab.	340.	375.	450.	675.	1300.	9000.
1800 sm. berries	Inc. Ab.	340.	375.	450.	675.	1300.	9000.
1800 dot date	Inc. Ab.	340.	375.	450.	675.	1300.	9000.
1800 12 arrows	Inc. Ab.	340.	375.	450.	675.	1300.	9000.
1800 10 arrows	Inc. Ab.	340.	375.	450.	675.	1300.	9000.
1800 "Americai"	Inc. Ab.	360.	400.	500.	800.	1500.	9000.
1801	54,454	375.	450.	600.	850.	1900.	9000.
1801	Unrecorded		Proof restrike, rare				
1802/1 close	Inc. Ab.	360.	425.	550.	850.	1600.	9000.
1802/1 wide	Inc. Ab.	360.	425.	550.	850.	1600.	9000.
1802 close, perfect date							
	Inc. Ab.	375.	450.	600.	875.	1650.	9000.
1802 wide, perfect date							
	Inc. Ab.	375.	450.	600.	875.	1650.	9000.
1802	Unrecorded		Proof restrike, rare				
1803 lg. 3	85,634	360.	425.	600.	850.	1575.	9000.
1803 sm. 3	Inc. Ab.	375.	450.	650.	900.	1700.	9000.
1803	Unrecorded		Proof restrike, rare				
1804	15 known		3 varieties				—
			Auction '89, July 1989, MS-65, $990,000.				

Gobrecht

Designer: Christian Gobrecht. **Size:** 38.1 millimeters. **Weight:** 26.73 grams. **Composition:** 90% silver (0.7736 ounces), 10% copper. **Notes:** Several obverse and reverse combinations exist, as described. Restrikes were produced by the U.S. Mint between 1855 and 1860.

Date	Mintage	VF-20	XF-40	AU-50	Prf-60
1836 "C. Gobrecht F." below base. Rev: eagle flying left amid stars. Plain edge.	—	—	—	—	—
1836 Obv: same as above. Rev: eagle flying in plain field. Plain edge.	—	—	—	—	—

Date	Mintage	VF-20	XF-40	AU-50	Prf-60
1836 "C. Gobrecht F." on base. Rev: eagle flying left amid stars. Plain edge.	—	2500.	3750.	4750.	7500.
1836 Same as above, reeded edge.	—	—	—	—	—
1836 Obv: same as above. Rev: eagle flying in plain field. Plain edge.	—	—	—	—	10,000.

Obverse stars   Reverse stars

Date	Mintage	VF-20	XF-40	AU-50	Prf-60
1838 Similar obv., designer's name omitted, stars added around border. Rev: eagle flying left in plain field. Reeded edge.	—	3000.	4500.	—	7500.
1838 Same as above. Plain edge. Restrikes only.	3 known	—	—	—	—
1838 Obv: same as above. Rev: eagle flying left amid stars. Plain edge. Restrikes only.	2 known	—	—	—	—
1839 Obv: same as above. Rev: eagle in plain field. Reeded edge. Also known with plain edge and plain edge with eagle amid stars.	—	—	3750.	—	15,000.

Seated Liberty

No motto

Designer: Christian Gobrecht. **Size:** 38.1 millimeters. **Weight:** 26.73 grams. **Composition:** 90% silver (0.7736 ounces), 10% copper.

Date	Mintage	G-4	VG-8	F-12	VF-20	XF-40	AU-50	MS-60	MS-65	Prf-65
1840	61,005	130.	160.	225.	300.	475.	750.	1600.	—	—
1841	173,000	100.	130.	180.	220.	375.	575.	1300.	24,000.	—
1842	184,618	90.00	120.	160.	200.	300.	550.	1100.	24,000.	—
1843	165,100	90.00	120.	160.	200.	300.	550.	1400.	24,000.	—
1844	20,000	200.	250.	300.	425.	575.	800.	2000.	—	—
1845	24,500	150.	200.	250.	350.	500.	750.	3000.	—	—
1846	110,600	90.00	120.	160.	200.	275.	500.	1400.	24,000.	—
1846O	59,000	110.	140.	190.	325.	700.	2000.	4000.	—	—
1847	140,750	90.00	120.	160.	200.	300.	650.	850.	24,000.	—
1848	15,000	225.	250.	400.	550.	800.	1400.	2050.	—	—
1849	62,600	110.	140.	190.	240.	350.	700.	1600.	—	—
1850	7,500	400.	450.	600.	800.	1300.	2600.	3500.	—	—
1850O	40,000	200.	260.	350.	650.	1400.	3200.	5000.	—	—
1851	1,300	—	—	8000.	9500.	12,500.	15,000.	—	—	—
1852	1,100	—	—	6000.	7500.	10,500.	14,000.	—	—	—
1853	46,110	160.	190.	240.	375.	575.	800.	1300.	—	—

Date	Mintage	G-4	VG-8	F-12	VF-20	XF-40	AU-50	MS-60	MS-65	Prf-65
1854	33,140	900.	1200.	1500.	2000.	3000.	4200.	7000.	—	—
1855	26,000	750.	1000.	1300.	1900.	2650.	4500.	9000.	—	—
1856	63,500	250.	350.	450.	600.	800.	1300.	2000.	—	—
1857	94,000	250.	350.	450.	650.	900.	1400.	1800.	—	—
1858	Est. 200	—	—	—	—	Proof only	—	—	—	—
	Impaired Proof	—	—	—	4500.	5700.	6900.	—	—	—
1859	256,500	200.	250.	350.	450.	700.	1000.	2500.	24,000.	13,000.
1859O	360,000	85.00	100.	155.	195.	275.	500.	850.	24,000.	—
1859S	20,000	200.	275.	385.	600.	950.	3000.	—	—	—
1860	218,930	140.	180.	230.	300.	475.	700.	1300.	24,000.	13,000.
1860O	515,000	85.00	100.	155.	195.	275.	500.	850.	24,000.	—
1861	78,500	290.	400.	500.	800.	1000.	1400.	2000.	—	13,000.
1862	12,090	320.	425.	550.	850.	1050.	1450.	2200.	—	13,000.
1863	27,660	240.	290.	350.	500.	625.	1100.	1800.	—	13,000.
1864	31,170	175.	210.	260.	350.	550.	950.	2000.	—	13,000.
1865	47,000	175.	210.	250.	400.	625.	1100.	1800.	—	13,000.
1866	2 known without motto									

Motto added on reverse

Notes: In 1866 the motto "In God We Trust" was added to the reverse above the eagle.

Date	Mintage	G-4	VG-8	F-12	VF-20	XF-40	AU-50	MS-60	MS-65	Prf-65
1866	49,625	150.	200.	250.	350.	550.	900.	1600.	28,500.	12,000.
1867	47,525	170.	250.	300.	450.	675.	1000.	1800.	28,500.	12,000.
1868	162,700	140.	190.	225.	350.	525.	900.	2000.	28,500.	12,000.
1869	424,300	115.	150.	200.	325.	500.	800.	2000.	28,500.	12,000.
1870	416,000	100.	135.	175.	225.	325.	600.	1500.	28,500.	12,000.
1870CC	12,462	200.	275.	470.	700.	1100.	2250.	4250.	—	—
1870S	Unrecorded				Stacks, Nov. 1989, VF, $77,000.				—	—
1871	1,074,760	85.00	100.	160.	200.	315.	550.	1150.	28,500.	12,000.
1871CC	1,376	1650.	2350.	3200.	5000.	8500.	15,000.	—	—	—
1872	1,106,450	85.00	100.	160.	200.	295.	550.	1250.	28,500.	12,000.
1872CC	3,150	900.	1250.	1600.	2150.	3750.	6500.	15,000.	—	—
1872S	9,000	150.	225.	400.	575.	1100.	3000.	10,000.	—	—
1873	293,600	130.	150.	200.	250.	350.	600.	1350.	28,500.	12,000.
1873CC	2,300	2450.	3500.	5000.	8500.	14,000.	25,000.	40,000.	—	—
1873S	700			None known to exist				—	—	—

Trade

Designer: William Barber. **Size:** 38.1 millimeters. **Weight:** 27.22 grams. **Composition:** 90% silver (0.7878 ounces), 10% copper.

1875 Trade Dollar
Grade F-12

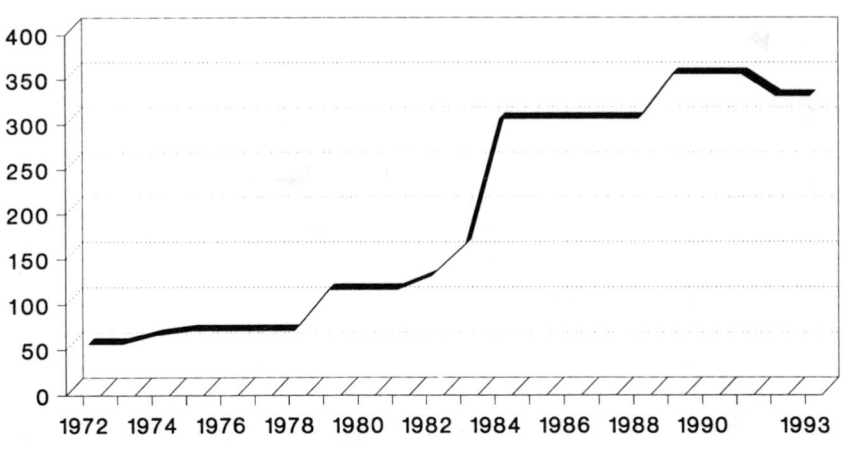

Retail Price

Source: COIN PRICES

Date	Mintage	G-4	VG-8	F-12	VF-20	XF-40	AU-50	MS-60	MS-65	Prf-65
1873	397,500	90.00	105.	115.	165.	250.	325.	1000.	19,000.	19,000.
1873CC	124,500	150.	175.	225.	275.	400.	675.	1500.	19,000.	—
1873S	703,000	130.	145.	160.	180.	260.	350.	1200.	12,000.	—
1874	987,800	80.00	90.00	100.	130.	190.	325.	700.	7500.	18,500.
1874CC	1,373,200	80.00	90.00	105.	125.	225.	350.	1000.	17,000.	—
1874S	2,549,000	70.00	80.00	95.00	115.	180.	285.	675.	7500.	—
1875	218,900	200.	225.	325.	450.	650.	800.	1850.	19,000.	6500.
1875CC	1,573,700	70.00	85.00	105.	130.	225.	375.	900.	18,500.	—
1875S	4,487,000	45.00	50.00	80.00	95.00	165.	275.	500.	7500.	—
1875S/CC	Inc.Ab.	225.	275.	375.	500.	800.	1000.	1500.	—	—
1876	456,150	70.00	75.00	100.	125.	165.	425.	675.	7500.	6500.
1876CC	509,000	85.00	95.00	115.	200.	300.	400.	900.	13,000.	—
1876S	5,227,000	50.00	60.00	80.00	95.00	165.	250.	480.	7500.	—
1877	3,039,710	45.00	55.00	80.00	100.	165.	250.	525.	7500.	19,000.
1877CC	534,000	120.	175.	200.	300.	400.	500.	1200.	13,000.	—
1877S	9,519,000	38.00	50.00	76.00	85.00	125.	275.	480.	7500.	—
1878	900			Proof only			—		—	22,000.
	Impaired Proof		—	—	1250.	1450.	1750.	—	—	—
1878CC	97,000	250.	550.	650.	950.	1600.	2450.	5500.	—	—
1878S	4,162,000	38.00	48.00	65.00	100.	125.	275.	480.	7500.	—
1879	1,541			Proof only			—		—	22,000.
	Impaired Proof		—	—	1000.	1200.	1400.	—	—	—
1880	1,987			Proof only			—		—	19,500.
	Impaired Proof		—	—	900.	1100.	1250.	—	—	—
1881	960			Proof only			—		—	20,000.
	Impaired Proof		—	—	1150.	1250.	1450.	—	—	—
1882	1,097			Proof only			—		—	20,000.
	Impaired Proof		—	—	1150.	1300.	1500.	—	—	—
1883	979			Proof only			—		—	20,000.
	Impaired Proof		—	—	1200.	1350.	1550.	—	—	—
1884	10				Superior, Aug. 1990, $75,000.					—
1885	5				Proof only, Stack's, Jan. 1989, $104,500.					—

1889-O Silver Dollar
Grade F-12

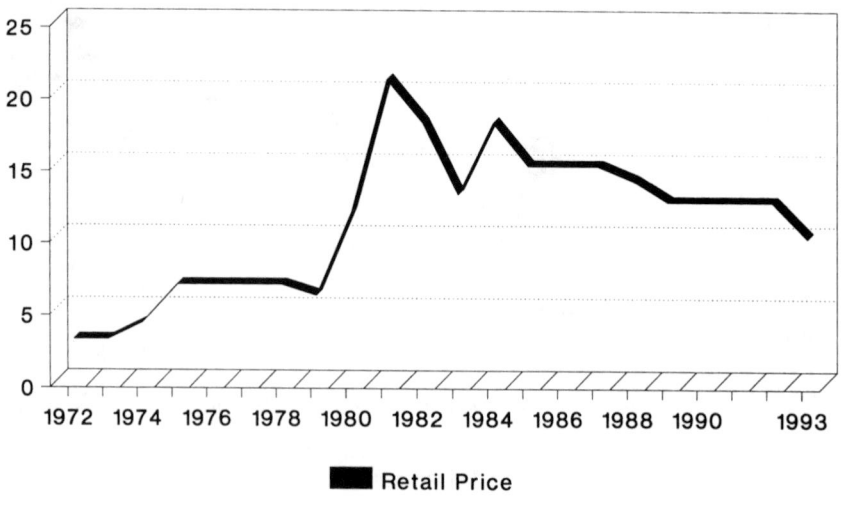

■ Retail Price

Source: COIN PRICES

Morgan

Reverse of 1879   7 over 8 tail feathers

Designer: George T. Morgan. **Size:** 38.1 millimeters. **Weight:** 26.73 grams. **Composition:** 90% silver (0.7736 ounces), 10% copper. **Notes:** "65DMPL" values are for coins grading MS-65 with deep-mirror prooflike surfaces. The 1878 "8 tail feathers" and "7 tail feathers" varieties are distinguished by the number of feathers in the eagle's tail. On the "reverse of 1878" varieties, the top of the top feather in the arrows held by the eagle is straight across and the eagle's breast is concave. On the "reverse of 1878 varieties," the top of the top feather in the arrows held by the eagle is slanted and the eagle's breast is convex. The 1890-CC "tail-bar variety" has a bar extending from the arrow feathers to the wreath on the reverse, the result of a die gouge.

Date	Mintage	G-4	VG-8	F-12	VF-20	XF-40	AU-50	MS-60	MS-63	MS-64	MS-65	Prf-65
1878 8 tail feathers												
	750,000	6.50	10.00	12.50	14.00	22.00	28.00	43.00	85.00	225.	1350.	6500.
1878 7 tail feathers, reverse of 1878												
	Inc. Ab.	6.50	9.00	10.00	11.50	12.50	19.00	25.00	65.00	225.	1200.	8450.
1878 7 tail feathers, reverse of 1879												
	Inc. Ab.	6.50	11.00	12.50	15.00	17.50	23.00	29.00	170.	415.	2750.	—
1878 7 over 8 tail feathers												
	9,759,550	6.50	12.50	15.00	19.00	28.00	42.00	63.00	125.	500.	2200.	—
1878CC	2,212,000	12.50	19.00	23.00	27.00	33.00	46.00	70.00	120.	250.	2200.	—
1878S	9,744,000	6.50	9.00	9.50	10.00	11.50	15.00	24.00	32.00	65.00	250.	—
1879	14,807,100	6.50	9.00	9.50	10.00	11.00	14.00	24.00	35.00	120.	1000.	4000.
1879CC	756,000	17.00	30.00	35.00	65.00	195.	500.	1300.	2350.	3550.	17,000.	—
1879O	2,887,000	6.50	9.00	9.50	10.00	11.50	22.00	34.00	215.	500.	6300.	—
1879S reverse of 1878												
	9,110,000	6.50	11.50	12.50	15.00	19.00	30.00	85.00	425.	1100.	5000.	—
1879S reverse of 1879												
	9,110,000	6.50	9.00	10.00	11.00	12.00	14.00	20.00	32.00	65.00	140.	—
1880	12,601,335	6.50	8.50	9.00	10.00	11.00	12.50	25.00	32.00	130.	1900.	4000.
1880CC reverse of 1878												
	591,000	25.00	31.00	41.00	60.00	91.00	125.	145.	240.	420.	1200.	—
1880CC reverse of 1879												
	591,000	25.00	31.00	41.00	60.00	88.00	115.	140.	175.	290.	600.	—
1880O	5,305,000	6.50	8.50	9.50	10.00	11.00	22.00	36.00	425.	1200.	19,000.	—
1880S	8,900,000	6.50	9.00	9.50	10.00	11.00	14.00	20.00	32.00	65.00	140.	—
1881	9,163,975	6.50	8.50	9.50	10.00	11.00	14.00	24.00	41.00	110.	1150.	4000.
1881CC	296,000	50.00	70.00	84.00	105.	120.	130.	145.	190.	270.	450.	—
1881O	5,708,000	6.50	8.50	9.00	10.00	11.00	12.50	20.00	36.00	180.	2100.	—
1881S	12,760,000	6.50	9.00	9.50	11.00	12.00	13.00	20.00	32.00	65.00	140.	—
1882	11,101,100	6.50	9.00	9.50	10.00	11.00	12.50	24.00	36.00	75.00	850.	4500.
1882CC	1,133,000	14.00	22.00	29.00	36.00	44.00	51.00	65.00	70.00	120.	300.	—
1882O	6,090,000	6.50	9.00	9.50	10.00	11.50	12.50	22.00	32.00	130.	1400.	—
1882S	9,250,000	6.50	9.00	10.00	11.00	12.00	15.00	21.00	32.00	65.00	140.	—
1883	12,291,039	6.50	9.00	9.50	10.00	11.00	12.50	22.00	32.00	65.00	150.	4000.
1883CC	1,204,000	14.00	22.00	29.00	36.00	44.00	50.00	65.00	65.00	90.00	250.	—
1883O	8,725,000	6.50	8.50	9.00	9.50	10.00	11.50	14.00	32.00	65.00	140.	—
1883S	6,250,000	6.50	10.00	11.50	14.00	19.00	95.00	315.	1250.	4300.	21,500.	—
1884	14,070,875	6.50	8.50	9.00	10.00	11.00	14.00	20.00	32.00	65.00	250.	4500.
1884CC	1,136,000	38.00	48.00	52.00	53.00	54.00	55.00	65.00	70.00	100.	250.	—
1884O	9,730,000	6.50	8.50	9.50	10.00	11.00	12.00	20.00	32.00	65.00	140.	—
1884S	3,200,000	7.50	10.00	11.50	14.00	28.00	190.	3800.	19,000.	47,000.	113,500.	—
1885	17,787,767	6.50	9.00	9.50	10.00	11.00	12.00	15.00	32.00	65.00	140.	4000.
1885CC	228,000	150.	160.	170.	180.	190.	200.	210.	230.	300.	550.	—
1885O	9,185,000	6.50	9.00	9.50	10.00	10.50	11.50	20.00	32.00	65.00	140.	—
1885S	1,497,000	7.50	10.00	14.00	16.50	20.00	44.00	80.00	210.	490.	2650.	—
1886	19,963,886	6.50	8.50	9.00	9.50	10.00	11.00	15.00	32.00	65.00	140.	4500.
1886O	10,710,000	6.50	9.50	11.50	14.00	17.50	45.00	205.	1500.	3150.	26,500.	—
1886S	750,000	11.00	12.50	15.00	20.00	31.00	50.00	100.	275.	600.	2400.	—
1887	20,290,710	6.50	9.00	9.50	10.00	10.50	11.50	15.00	32.00	65.00	140.	4000.
1887O	11,550,000	6.50	9.00	9.50	10.00	12.50	20.00	34.00	125.	550.	4650.	—
1887S	1,771,000	6.50	10.00	12.50	14.00	17.50	31.00	60.00	195.	550.	3800.	—
1888	19,183,833	6.50	9.00	9.50	10.00	11.00	12.00	17.00	32.00	65.00	190.	4800.
1888O	12,150,000	6.50	9.00	9.50	10.00	11.50	14.00	20.00	32.00	70.00	1250.	—
1888S	657,000	12.00	14.00	19.00	24.00	30.00	65.00	100.	295.	550.	2900.	—
1889	21,726,811	6.50	8.50	9.00	9.50	10.00	11.50	17.00	32.00	65.00	500.	4800.
1889CC	350,000	95.00	135.	165.	250.	630.	2500.	6600.	15,500.	26,500.	126,000.	—
1889O	11,875,000	6.50	9.00	10.00	11.00	15.00	30.00	70.00	215.	650.	4150.	—
1889S	700,000	11.00	12.50	17.50	22.00	25.00	45.00	75.00	225.	390.	1250.	—
1890	16,802,590	6.50	9.00	9.50	10.00	11.50	12.50	21.00	45.00	340.	3700.	4000.
1890CC	2,309,041	12.50	19.00	23.00	27.00	38.00	77.00	205.	415.	750.	6000.	—
1890CC tail bar												
	Inc. Ab.	12.50	19.00	23.00	27.00	38.00	77.00	205.	405.	750.	5500.	—
1890O	10,701,000	6.50	9.00	9.50	10.00	12.50	20.00	31.00	75.00	230.	5400.	—
1890S	8,230,373	6.50	9.00	9.50	11.00	13.00	22.00	38.00	70.00	190.	800.	—
1891	8,694,206	6.50	9.00	10.00	12.00	14.00	22.00	38.00	145.	600.	5500.	4000.
1891CC	1,618,000	14.00	20.00	25.00	29.00	38.00	75.00	110.	300.	650.	2650.	—
1891O	7,954,529	7.50	9.00	10.00	12.50	17.50	30.00	63.00	205.	900.	6500.	—
1891S	5,296,000	7.50	9.00	9.50	11.00	12.50	21.00	38.00	75.00	220.	1200.	—
1892	1,037,245	8.00	12.50	13.50	14.00	17.50	46.00	85.00	295.	800.	2850.	4000.
1892CC	1,352,000	18.00	26.00	32.00	44.00	82.00	175.	280.	700.	1100.	4050.	—
1892O	2,744,000	7.00	11.50	12.50	15.00	16.50	44.00	85.00	225.	450.	6000.	—
1892S	1,200,000	12.00	13.00	16.00	40.00	105.	1750.	10,000.	19,000.	28,500.	66,500.	—
1893	378,792	28.00	40.00	50.00	60.00	70.00	140.	225.	520.	1150.	5000.	4000.
1893CC	677,000	29.00	42.00	57.00	100.	380.	695.	1070.	2750.	5400.	33,000.	—
1893O	300,000	35.00	50.00	58.00	69.00	150.	345.	1200.	4600.	16,500.	82,000.	—
1893S	100,000	380.	580.	875.	1100.	2650.	12,000.	19,000.	44,000.	63,000.	138,500.	—
1894	110,972	120.	175.	210.	240.	290.	485.	800.	2400.	4650.	13,000.	4650.
1894O	1,723,000	8.00	11.50	19.00	22.00	27.00	115.	600.	2850.	4400.	30,000.	—
1894S	1,260,000	10.00	12.50	22.00	33.00	77.00	155.	300.	800.	1000.	4800.	—
1895	12,880	Proof only		3000.		5000.	9500.	10,500.	—	—	—	26,000.
1895O	450,000	30.00	50.00	63.00	82.00	165.	820.	6050.	14,500.	21,000.	33,000.	—
1895S	400,000	75.00	90.00	115.	160.	360.	585.	950.	2600.	4450.	17,500.	—
1896	9,967,762	6.50	8.50	9.00	9.50	10.00	11.50	20.00	38.00	65.00	200.	4000.
1896O	4,900,000	6.50	9.00	11.00	12.00	15.00	95.00	680.	5550.	19,500.	35,500.	—
1896S	5,000,000	8.00	10.00	15.00	35.00	100.	285.	640.	1000.	2250.	7500.	—
1897	2,822,731	6.50	8.50	9.00	9.50	10.00	11.50	14.00	32.00	65.00	350.	6000.

1897-O Silver Dollar
Grade MS-60

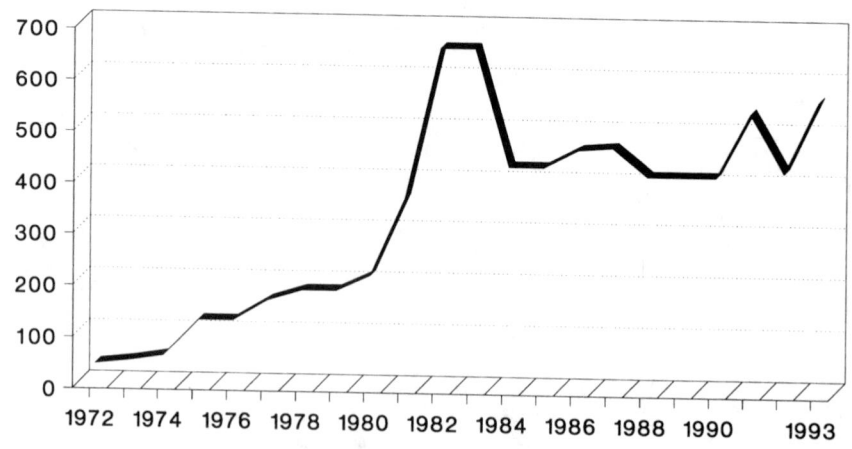

Retail Price

Source: COIN PRICES

Date	Mintage	G-4	VG-8	F-12	VF-20	XF-40	AU-50	MS-60	MS-63	MS-64	MS-65	Prf-65
1897O	4,004,000	6.50	9.00	10.00	11.50	15.00	63.00	565.	3550.	12,000.	23,500.	—
1897S	5,825,000	6.50	9.00	10.00	11.00	14.00	20.00	41.00	65.00	110.	400.	—
1898	5,884,735	6.50	9.00	9.50	10.00	11.00	12.00	15.00	32.00	65.00	200.	4500.
1898O	4,440,000	8.00	10.00	11.00	12.00	13.00	14.00	15.00	32.00	65.00	140.	—
1898S	4,102,000	6.50	11.50	12.50	16.50	24.00	50.00	110.	280.	500.	1950.	—
1899	330,846	13.00	19.00	26.00	30.00	40.00	56.00	75.00	105.	180.	950.	4800.
1899O	12,290,000	6.50	9.00	9.50	10.00	11.00	12.00	17.00	32.00	65.00	140.	—
1899S	2,562,000	6.50	11.50	12.50	17.50	25.00	56.00	105.	285.	450.	1200.	—
1900	8,880,938	6.50	8.50	9.00	9.50	10.00	11.50	20.00	32.00	65.00	200.	4500.
1900O	12,590,000	6.50	7.50	9.00	9.50	12.00	13.00	20.00	34.00	65.00	140.	—
1900O/CC	Inc. Ab.	11.00	16.50	19.00	22.00	27.00	75.00	170.	350.	590.	1750.	—
1900S	3,540,000	6.50	10.00	12.50	16.50	25.00	44.00	90.00	175.	330.	2350.	—
1901	6,962,813	8.00	14.00	16.50	25.00	38.00	155.	1150.	9500.	25,000.	85,000.	6250.
1901O	13,320,000	6.50	9.00	9.50	10.00	11.00	12.50	21.00	32.00	65.00	150.	—
1901S	2,284,000	7.50	12.50	15.00	21.00	38.00	88.00	215.	380.	650.	3400.	—
1902	7,994,777	7.00	9.50	10.00	11.00	12.00	22.00	36.00	63.00	150.	850.	6100.
1902O	8,636,000	6.50	9.00	9.50	10.00	10.50	11.50	15.00	32.00	65.00	160.	—
1902S	1,530,000	13.00	16.50	28.00	38.00	57.00	88.00	140.	290.	540.	3000.	—
1903	4,652,755	6.50	12.50	14.00	15.00	16.50	19.00	29.00	45.00	70.00	200.	4500.
1903O	4,450,000	100.	110.	120.	125.	130.	135.	140.	160.	190.	400.	—
1903S	1,241,000	9.00	13.00	19.00	56.00	160.	695.	1850.	3350.	3850.	5050.	—
1904	2,788,650	6.50	9.50	10.00	11.50	15.00	30.00	57.00	160.	500.	3150.	4500.
1904O	3,720,000	6.50	9.50	10.00	11.00	12.00	13.00	15.00	32.00	65.00	140.	—
1904S	2,304,000	9.00	12.50	16.50	32.00	110.	430.	800.	1500.	2300.	7500.	—
1921	44,690,000	5.50	6.50	7.00	7.50	8.00	9.00	11.00	25.00	30.00	150.	—
1921D	20,345,000	5.50	6.50	7.00	7.50	8.00	11.00	25.00	32.00	75.00	400.	—
1921S	21,695,000	5.50	6.50	7.00	7.50	8.00	11.00	25.00	36.00	180.	1450.	—

1903-O Silver Dollar
Grade MS-60

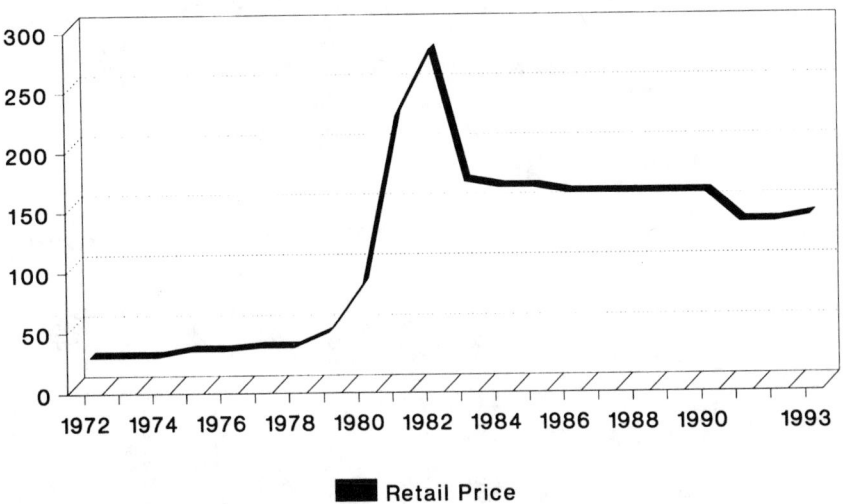

■ Retail Price

Source: COIN PRICES

1921 Morgan Dollar
Grade MS-60

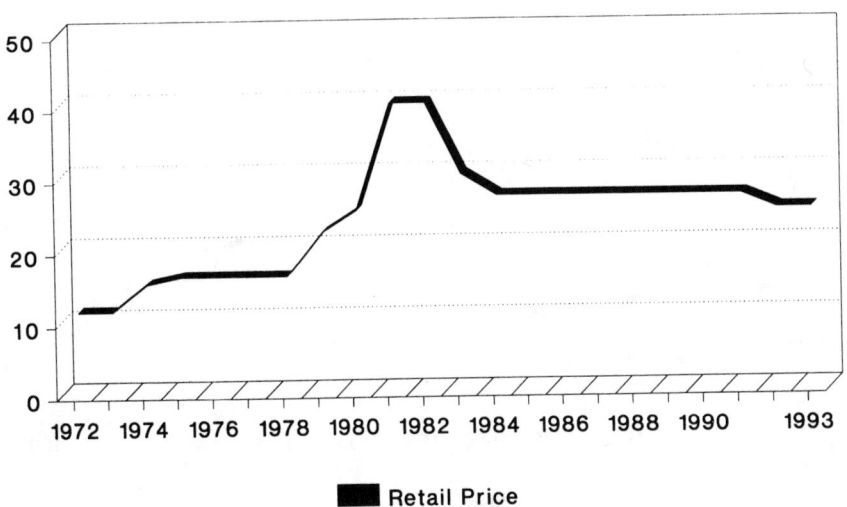

■ Retail Price

Source: COIN PRICES

Peace

Designer: Anthony de Francisci. **Size:** 38.1 millimeters. **Weight:** 26.73 grams. **Composition:** 90% silver (0.7736 ounces), 10% copper.

Date	Mintage	G-4	VG-8	F-12	VF-20	XF-40	AU-50	MS-60	MS-63	MS-64	MS-65
1921	1,006,473	15.00	19.00	25.00	34.00	41.00	75.00	120.	265.	500.	1550.
1922	51,737,000	6.00	6.50	6.50	7.00	7.25	7.50	10.00	18.00	50.00	200.
1922D	15,063,000	6.00	6.50	7.00	7.50	9.00	10.00	21.00	40.00	75.00	600.
1922S	17,475,000	6.00	6.50	7.00	7.50	9.00	10.00	21.00	55.00	380.	2500.
1923	30,800,000	6.00	6.50	6.50	7.00	7.25	7.50	10.00	18.00	55.00	200.
1923D	6,811,000	6.00	6.50	7.00	7.50	9.00	14.00	25.00	70.00	250.	2000.
1923S	19,020,000	6.00	6.50	7.00	7.50	9.00	10.00	21.00	65.00	500.	5500.
1924	11,811,000	6.00	6.50	7.00	7.50	8.00	9.00	11.00	22.00	55.00	300.
1924S	1,728,000	7.00	7.50	10.00	12.50	15.00	47.00	125.	390.	900.	8000.
1925	10,198,000	6.00	6.50	7.50	8.00	8.50	9.00	11.00	22.00	55.00	200.
1925S	1,610,000	7.00	7.50	9.00	11.00	14.00	26.00	50.00	140.	600.	6000.
1926	1,939,000	6.00	7.50	8.00	9.00	11.00	15.00	22.00	35.00	75.00	500.
1926D	2,348,700	6.50	7.50	8.00	9.00	12.50	27.00	45.00	110.	220.	750.
1926S	6,980,000	6.50	7.50	8.00	9.00	11.50	16.00	28.00	55.00	290.	2500.

1927-S Silver Dollar
Grade MS-60

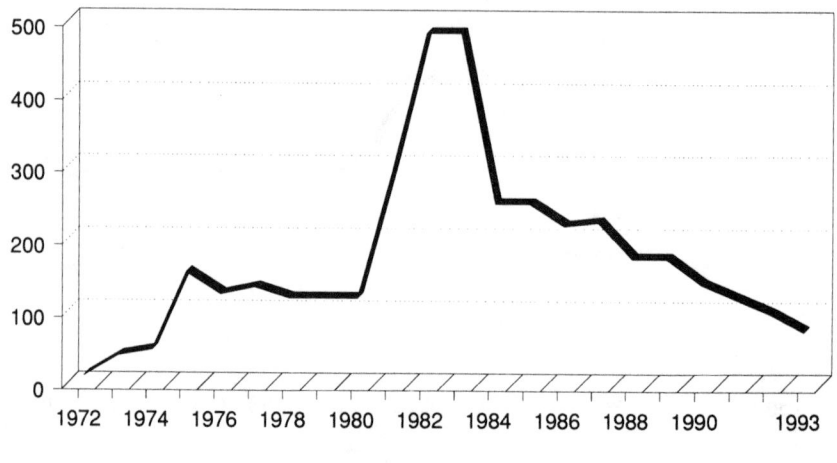

Retail Price

Source: COIN PRICES

Date	Mintage	G-4	VG-8	F-12	VF-20	XF-40	AU-50	MS-60	MS-63	MS-64	MS-65
1927	848,000	8.00	12.50	15.00	16.50	21.00	30.00	50.00	120.	350.	6300.
1927D	1,268,900	7.50	11.00	12.00	15.00	22.00	69.00	155.	300.	550.	4100.
1927S	866,000	9.00	12.00	13.00	14.00	19.00	55.00	75.00	190.	650.	6500.
1928	360,649	65.00	90.00	95.00	100.	110.	140.	175.	320.	600.	3150.
1928S	1,632,000	6.50	10.00	11.50	12.50	15.00	38.00	75.00	285.	1150.	17,500.
1934	954,057	8.00	12.50	14.00	15.00	20.00	32.00	70.00	155.	350.	1250.
1934D	1,569,500	6.50	11.50	12.50	14.00	17.50	32.00	100.	175.	500.	3300.
1934S	1,011,000	8.00	11.50	15.00	38.00	150.	440.	1100.	2600.	4300.	5500.
1935	1,576,000	6.50	10.00	11.50	12.50	16.50	22.00	41.00	75.00	295.	900.
1935S	1,964,000	6.50	8.50	10.00	12.50	16.50	60.00	100.	290.	500.	1300.

Clad dollars

Eisenhower

Designer: Frank Gasparro. **Size:** 38.1 millimeters. **Weight:** 24.59 grams (silver issues) and 22.68 grams (copper-nickel issues). **Clad composition:** 75% copper and 25% nickel bonded to a pure copper core. **Silver clad composition:** clad layers of 80% silver and 20% copper bonded to a core of 20.9% silver and 79.1% copper (0.3161 total ounces of silver).

Date	Mintage	(Proof)	MS-65	Prf-65
1971	47,799,000	—	2.80	—
1971D	68,587,424	—	1.60	—
1971S silver	6,868,530	(4,265,234)	3.80	4.10
1972	75,890,000	—	1.60	—
1972D	92,548,511	—	1.60	—
1972S silver	2,193,056	(1,811,631)	4.00	4.50
1973	2,000,056	—	3.80	—
1973D	2,000,000	—	3.80	—
1973S silver	1,833,140	(1,005,617)	4.30	31.00
1973S clad	—	2,769,624	—	5.30
1974	27,366,000	—	1.60	—
1974D	35,466,000	—	1.70	—
1974S silver	1,720,000	(1,306,579)	3.90	10.50
1974S clad	—	(2,617,350)	—	5.30

Type I Bicentennial reverse

Type II Bicentennial reverse

Bicentennial design

Reverse designer: Dennis R. Williams. **Notes:** In 1976 the lettering on the reverse was changed to thinner letters, resulting in Type I and Type II varieties for that year.

Date	Mintage	(Proof)	MS-65	Prf-65
1976 Type I	117,337,000	—	2.50	—
1976 Type II	Inc. Ab.	—	1.60	—
1976D Type I	103,228,274	—	1.80	—
1976D Type II	Inc. Ab.	—	1.60	—
1976S cld Type I	—	(2,909,369)	—	4.00
1976S cld Type II	—	(4,149,730)	—	4.75
1976S silver	11,000,000	(4,000,000)	6.50	7.90

Regular design resumed

Date	Mintage	(Proof)	MS-65	Prf-65
1977	12,596,000	—	1.60	—
1977D	32,983,006	—	1.70	—
1977S clad	—	(3,251,152)	—	5.00
1978	25,702,000	—	1.70	—
1978D	33,012,890	—	1.60	—
1978S clad	—	(3,127,788)	—	5.00

Anthony

Designer: Frank Gasparro. **Size:** 26.5 millimeters. **Weight:** 8.1 grams. **Composition:** clad layers of 75% copper and 25% nickel bonded to a pure copper core. **Notes:** The 1979-S and 1981-S Type II coins have a clearer mintmark than the Type I varieties for those years.

Date	Mintage	MS-65	Date	Mintage	MS-65
1979P	360,222,000	1.45	1980S	20,422,000	1.45
1979D	288,015,744	1.45	1980S Prf.	3,547,030	6.50
1979S	109,576,000	1.45	1981P	3,000,000	2.30
1979S Prf. Type I	3,677,175	5.75	1981D	3,250,000	2.50
1979S Prf. Type II	—	63.00	1981S	3,492,000	2.30
1980P	27,610,000	1.45	1981S Prf.Type I	4,063,083	6.70
1980D	41,628,708	1.45	1981S Prf. Type II	—	91.00

Type coins

Notes: Values listed are for the most common dates of each design type in grades MS-64 and proof-64. The -64 grade is relatively new. Except for Morgan dollars, Peace dollars and commemoratives, there is little history among other issues to support MS-64 and proof-64 values, other than as type coins. Among copper coins, the "red" and "brown" designations refer to coins that still retain their original color (red) and those that have toned over time (brown).

Description	MS-64	Proof-64
Draped Bust half cents (red & brown)	4150.	—
Classic Head half cents (red & brown)	650.	—
Braided Hair half cents (red & brown)	550.	—
Draped Bust large cents (red & brown)	9500.	—
Classic Head large cents (red & brown)	11,500.	—
Coronet large cents (red & brown)	850.	—
Braided Hair large cents (red & brown)	400.	—
Flying Eagle cents	800.	4150.
Indian Head cents, 1859 copper-nickel	650.	2000.
Indian Head cents, 1860-1864 copper-nickel	350.	900.
Indian Head cents, bronze (red & brown)	70.00	210.
Two-cent (red & brown)	220.	700.
Nickel three-cent	390.	450.
Silver three-cent, Type I	500.	—
Silver three-cent, Type II	1950.	4000.
Silver three-cent, Type III	550.	800.
Flowing Hair half dimes	16,000.	—
Draped Bust half dimes, small eagle	22,500.	—
Draped Bust half dimes, heraldic eagle	16,500.	—
Liberty Cap half dimes	1700.	—
Seated Liberty half dimes, no stars	2200.	—
Seated Liberty half dimes, no drapery	1700.	—
Seated Liberty half dimes, stars around rim	1150.	2450.
Seated Liberty half dimes, with arrows	1650.	11,500.
Seated Liberty half dimes, obverse legend	600.	900.
Shield nickels, with rays	800.	2650.
Shield nickels, no rays	400.	400.
Liberty nickels, no "Cents"	105.	450.
Liberty nickels, with "Cents"	210.	250.
Buffalo nickels, Type I	70.00	1150.
Buffalo nickels, Type II	—	900.
Jefferson nickels, wartime	—	100.
Draped Bust dimes, small eagle	16,500.	—
Draped Bust dimes, heraldic eagle	16,500.	—
Liberty Cap dimes, 1809-1827 (large size)	5000.	—
Liberty Cap dimes, 1828-1837 (reduced size)	2400.	—
Seated Liberty dimes, no stars	3900.	—
Seated Liberty dimes, no drapery	1750.	—
Seated Liberty dimes, stars around rim	1750.	3300.
Seated Liberty dimes, 1853-1855 with arrows	1700.	11,500.
Seated Liberty dimes, obverse legend	650.	950.
Seated Liberty dimes, 1873-1874 with arrows	2800.	2750.
Barber dimes	350.	950.
Mercury dimes	—	150.
Twenty-cent	2650.	3900.
Draped Bust quarters, heraldic eagle	25,000.	—
Liberty Cap quarters, 1815-1828 (large size)	9500.	—
Liberty Cap quarters, 1831-1838 (reduced size)	5050.	—
Seated Liberty quarters, no drapery	7000.	—
Seated Liberty quarters, no motto	2150.	2350.
Seated Liberty quarters, arrows and rays	7500.	—
Seated Liberty quarters, 1854-1855, with arrows	4050.	—
Seated Liberty quarters, with motto	1150.	1300.
Seated Liberty quarters, 1873-1874, with arrows	3550.	3350.
Barber quarters	700.	1150.
Standing Liberty quarters, Type I, full head	415.	—
Standing Liberty quarters, Type II	245.	—
Standing Liberty quarters, Type II, full head	400.	—
Flowing Hair half dollars	94,500.	—
Draped Bust half dollars, heraldic eagle	22,500.	—
Liberty Cap half dollars	3400.	—
Liberty Cap half dollars, reeded edge	5500.	—
Seated Liberty half dollars, no drapery	44,000.	—
Seated Liberty half dollars, no motto	3150.	3100.
Seated Liberty half dollars, arrows and rays	8000.	—
Seated Liberty half dollars, 1854-1855, with arrows	4150.	—
Seated Liberty half dollars, with motto	1750.	1750.
Seated Liberty half dollars, 1873-1874, with arrows	5000.	3550.
Barber half dollars	1300.	1900.
Walking Liberty half dollars	—	390.
Draped Bust dollars, small eagle	101,000.	—
Draped Bust dollars, heraldic eagle	36,500.	—
Seated Liberty dollars, no motto	7000.	6500.
Seated Liberty dollars, with motto	6500.	6000.
Morgan dollars	—	2850.
Trade dollars	3300.	3100.

Gold dollars
Liberty Head

Designer: James B. Longacre. **Size:** 13 millimeters. **Weight:** 1.672 grams. **Composition:** 90% gold (0.0484 ounces), 10% copper. **Notes:** On the "closed wreath" varieties of 1849, the wreath on the reverse extends closer to the numeral 1.

Date	Mintage	F-12	VF-20	XF-40	AU-50	MS-60
1849 open wreath	688,567	120.	145.	160.	200.	500.
1849 closed wreath	Inc. Ab.	120.	145.	160.	200.	500.
1849C closed wreath	11,634	285.	475.	875.	2200.	4200.
1849C open wreath	Inc. Ab.			Extremely Rare		—
1849Dopen wreath	21,588	285.	410.	750.	1250.	2900.
1849Oopen wreath	215,000	135.	165.	210.	440.	910.
1850	481,953	115.	150.	170.	190.	420.
1850C	6,966	390.	585.	975.	2200.	6200.
1850D	8,382	350.	550.	1150.	1950.	6000.
1850O	14,000	195.	260.	370.	775.	2700.
1851	3,317,671	115.	150.	170.	190.	420.
1851C	41,267	275.	450.	650.	1150.	2300.
1851D	9,882	275.	425.	775.	1500.	3800.
1851O	290,000	150.	175.	195.	250.	690.
1852	2,045,351	115.	150.	170.	190.	420.
1852C	9,434	275.	390.	775.	1300.	3200.
1852D	6,360	325.	700.	1375.	2000.	5700.
1852O	140,000	140.	165.	195.	300.	1050.
1853	4,076,051	115.	150.	170.	190.	420.
1853C	11,515	240.	490.	1000.	1650.	5200.
1853D	6,583	340.	700.	1075.	2300.	6500.
1853O	290,000	140.	160.	195.	220.	585.
1854	736,709	115.	150.	170.	190.	420.
1854D	2,935	550.	890.	1850.	6500.	14,500.
1854S	14,632	260.	315.	440.	725.	1800.

Small Indian Head

Designer: James B. Longacre. **Size:** 15 millimeters. **Weight:** 1.672 grams. **Composition:** 90% gold (0.0484 ounces), 10% copper.

Date	Mintage	F-12	VF-20	XF-40	AU-50	MS-60
1854	902,736	210.	290.	520.	750.	3000.
1855	758,269	210.	290.	520.	750.	3000.
1855C	9,803	675.	975.	2350.	5150.	10,000.
1855D	1,811	1400.	2300.	4700.	9500.	19,500.
1855O	55,000	370.	575.	800.	1500.	7700.
1856S	24,600	390.	650.	1250.	2500.	8000.

Large Indian Head

Designer: James B. Longacre. **Size:** 15 millimeters. **Weight:** 1.672 grams. **Composition:** 90% gold (0.0484 ounces), 10% copper. **Notes:** The 1856 varieties are distinguished by whether the 5 in the date is slanted or upright. The 1873 varieties are distinguished by the amount of space between the upper left and lower left serifs in the 3.

Date	Mintage	F-12	VF-20	XF-40	AU-50	MS-60	Prf-65
1856 upright 5	1,762,936	130.	160.	180.	325.	585.	—
1856 slanted 5	Inc. Ab.	120.	140.	170.	190.	370.	—
1856D	1,460	2600.	3900.	7000.	12,250.	22,500.	—
1857	774,789	120.	140.	170.	190.	375.	—
1857C	13,280	350.	575.	1150.	2850.	9750.	—
1857D	3,533	285.	850.	1800.	3800.	11,000.	—
1857S	10,000	285.	525.	750.	1950.	8550.	—
1858	117,995	120.	140.	170.	190.	375.	19,000.
1858D	3,477	390.	775.	1300.	2600.	7500.	—
1858S	10,000	300.	400.	625.	1800.	6500.	—
1859	168,244	120.	140.	160.	190.	425.	12,000.
1859C	5,235	300.	490.	1250.	2600.	10,500.	—
1859D	4,952	475.	875.	1400.	2700.	7500.	—
1859S	15,000	260.	310.	550.	1950.	7000.	—
1860	36,668	120.	140.	170.	190.	375.	12,000.
1860D	1,566	2300.	2750.	4700.	7700.	25,000.	—
1860S	13,000	200.	325.	400.	800.	2850.	—
1861	527,499	120.	140.	170.	190.	375.	18,000.
1861D	Unrecorded	4900.	6800.	13,500.	19,500.	39,500.	—
1862	1,361,390	120.	140.	170.	190.	375.	12,000.
1863	6,250	360.	450.	875.	1900.	4400.	12,000.
1864	5,950	285.	370.	475.	750.	1500.	12,000.
1865	3,725	285.	370.	585.	850.	1600.	12,000.
1866	7,130	290.	380.	450.	700.	1200.	12,000.
1867	5,250	345.	440.	550.	750.	1200.	12,000.
1868	10,525	260.	295.	400.	585.	1200.	12,000.
1869	5,925	325.	360.	520.	800.	1300.	12,000.
1870	6,335	260.	285.	425.	520.	1050.	12,000.
1870S	3,000	350.	475.	800.	1400.	3000.	—
1871	3,930	260.	285.	440.	525.	750.	18,000.
1872	3,530	285.	315.	480.	575.	900.	18,000.
1873 closed 3	125,125	325.	425.	850.	1200.	3250.	18,000.
1873 open 3	Inc. Ab.	120.	140.	170.	190.	425.	—
1874	198,820	120.	140.	170.	190.	425.	19,000.
1875	420	1800.	2500.	4200.	5900.	9100.	45,000.
1876	3,245	220.	250.	360.	475.	890.	12,000.
1877	3,920	150.	175.	350.	480.	760.	24,000.
1878	3,020	180.	215.	365.	470.	795.	12,000.
1879	3,030	165.	190.	300.	400.	550.	12,000.
1880	1,636	145.	160.	200.	235.	450.	12,000.
1881	7,707	145.	160.	200.	235.	450.	12,000.
1882	5,125	160.	175.	210.	235.	450.	12,000.
1883	11,007	145.	165.	200.	235.	450.	12,000.
1884	6,236	140.	160.	190.	230.	450.	12,000.
1885	12,261	145.	160.	200.	235.	450.	12,000.
1886	6,016	145.	165.	200.	235.	450.	12,000.
1887	8,543	145.	165.	200.	235.	450.	12,000.
1888	16,580	145.	165.	200.	235.	450.	12,000.
1889	30,729	145.	165.	200.	235.	365.	12,000.

Gold $2.50 (Quarter Eagle)

Liberty Cap

Designer: Robert Scot. **Size:** 20 millimeters. **Weight:** 4.37 grams. **Composition:** 91.67% gold (0.1289 ounces), 8.33% copper. **Notes:** The 1796 "no-stars" variety does not have stars on the obverse. The 1804 varieties are distinguished by the number of stars on the obverse.

Date	Mintage	F-12	VF-20	XF-40	MS-60
1796 no stars	963	9500.	21,000.	31,000.	—
1796 stars	432	7500.	9000.	14,000.	—
1797	427	7500.	9500.	14,500.	—
1798	1,094	2800.	4000.	6250.	40,000.
1802/1	3,035	2800.	3750.	5000.	28,000.
1804 13-star reverse	3,327	13,000.	18,500.	30,000.	14,500.
1804 14-star reverse	Inc. Ab.	2800.	3750.	5750.	16,000.
1805	1,781	2800.	3750.	5400.	18,500.
1806/4	1,616	2800.	3750.	5000.	14,500.
1806/5	Inc. Ab.	4750.	6500.	10,000.	—
1807	6,812	2800.	3500.	4500.	14,500.

Turban Head

Designer: John Reich. **Sizes:** 20 millimeters (1808), 18.5 millimeters (1821-1827), and 18.2 millimeters (1829-1834). **Weight:** 4.37 grams. **Composition:** 91.67% gold (0.1289 ounces), 8.33% copper.

Date	Mintage	F-12	VF-20	XF-40	MS-60
1808	2,710	9000.	12,500.	22,000.	45,000.
1821	6,448	3250.	4000.	5750.	14,000.
1824/21	2,600	3250.	4000.	5000.	10,500.
1825	4,434	3250.	4000.	5750.	10,500.
1826/25	760	3500.	5500.	7500.	19,000.
1827	2,800	3250.	4000.	6300.	14,000.
1829	3,403	3250.	3750.	4500.	8500.
1830	4,540	3250.	3750.	4500.	8500.
1831	4,520	3250.	3750.	4500.	8500.
1832	4,400	3250.	3750.	4500.	8500.
1833	4,160	3250.	3750.	4500.	8500.
1834	4,000	6750.	10,000.	16,500.	32,500.

Classic Head

Designer: William Kneass. **Size:** 18.2 millimeters. **Weight:** 4.18 grams. **Composition:** 89.92% gold (0.1209 ounces), 10.08% copper.

Date	Mintage	VF-20	XF-40	AU-50	MS-60	MS-65
1834	112,234	300.	550.	1100.	3000.	37,000.
1835	131,402	265.	500.	900.	2850.	37,000.
1836	547,986	255.	500.	900.	2850.	37,000.
1837	45,080	265.	500.	900.	2850.	37,000.
1838	47,030	265.	500.	900.	2850.	37,000.
1838C	7,880	1000.	2300.	5200.	19,500.	—
1839	27,021	265.	500.	1800.	6000.	37,000.
1839C	18,140	550.	1800.	3500.	13,600.	—
1839D	13,674	950.	2750.	5250.	18,000.	—
1839O	17,781	500.	1250.	2600.	6500.	55,000.

Coronet Head

Designer: Christian Gobrecht. **Size:** 18 millimeters. **Weight:** 4.18 grams. **Composition:** 90% gold (0.121 ounces), 10% copper. **Notes:** Varieties for 1843 are distinguished by the size of the numerals in the date. One 1848 variety has "Cal." inscribed on the reverse, indicating it was made from California gold. The 1873 "closed-3" and "open-3" varieties are distinguished by the amount of space between the upper left and lower left serifs in the 3 in the date.

Date	Mintage	F-12	VF-20	XF-40	AU-50	MS-60	Prf-65
1840	18,859	180.	245.	700.	1625.	3600.	—
1840C	12,822	325.	600.	1250.	4000.	12,000.	—
1840D	3,532	500.	2000.	4100.	9500.	—	—
1840O	33,580	225.	250.	900.	1800.	7500.	—
1841	—	—	—	30,000.	50,000.	—	—
1841C	10,281	275.	475.	1150.	3250.	16,000.	—
1841D	4,164	800.	1375.	2900.	7000.	15,500.	—
1842	2,823	350.	850.	3000.	6250.	14,500.	—
1842C	6,729	525.	1200.	2600.	5000.	14,500.	—
1842D	4,643	800.	1500.	2900.	9500.	16,000.	—
1842O	19,800	375.	375.	1125.	2900.	12,000.	—
1843	100,546	200.	225.	250.	375.	750.	—
1843C sm. dt.	26,064	750.	2500.	4900.	10,000.	24,000.	—
1843C lg. dt.	Inc. Ab.	300.	525.	900.	2850.	8000.	—
1843D	36,209	300.	650.	1100.	2500.	7500.	—
1843O sm. dt.	288,002	200.	225.	325.	450.	1150.	—
1843O lg. dt.	76,000	250.	350.	450.	1000.	2000.	—
1844	6,784	200.	400.	850.	2500.	7500.	—
1844C	11,622	325.	675.	1550.	3950.	16,000.	—
1844D	17,332	325.	625.	1200.	2700.	6500.	—
1845	91,051	200.	275.	325.	500.	1100.	—
1845D	19,460	325.	650.	1700.	2500.	8500.	—
1845O	4,000	750.	1500.	2400.	6000.	14,000.	—
1846	21,598	300.	400.	725.	2400.	7250.	—
1846C	4,808	275.	1000.	1750.	4400.	13,000.	—
1846D	19,303	350.	750.	1200.	2600.	7750.	—
1846O	66,000	200.	300.	525.	1600.	4250.	—
1847	29,814	200.	275.	400.	1100.	3800.	—
1847C	23,226	300.	600.	1150.	2300.	7450.	—
1847D	15,784	300.	600.	1250.	2750.	7500.	—
1847O	124,000	200.	275.	425.	1150.	3500.	—
1848	7,497	350.	625.	1000.	3500.	8200.	—

1848 "Cal."

Date	Mintage	F-12	VF-20	XF-40	AU-50	MS-60	Prf-65
1848 "Cal."	1,389	5000.	8000.	14,000.	17,000.	30,000.	—
1848C	16,788	300.	750.	1500.	3200.	9000.	—
1848D	13,771	350.	600.	1325.	2350.	8000.	—
1849	23,294	300.	500.	650.	1400.	3400.	—
1849C	10,220	325.	600.	1400.	4750.	19,000.	—
1849D	10,945	400.	700.	1550.	3150.	13,000.	—
1850	252,923	175.	200.	225.	300.	900.	—
1850C	9,148	275.	600.	1400.	3250.	14,000.	—
1850D	12,148	275.	700.	1200.	2850.	14,000.	—
1850O	84,000	200.	300.	575.	1400.	4400.	—
1851	1,372,748	135.	150.	185.	235.	300.	—
1851C	14,923	375.	675.	1400.	3650.	12,500.	—
1851D	11,264	275.	650.	1300.	3450.	12,000.	—
1851O	148,000	200.	250.	350.	1200.	4750.	—
1852	1,159,681	135.	150.	185.	235.	350.	—
1852C	9,772	350.	625.	1550.	4000.	17,000.	—
1852D	4,078	450.	850.	2400.	6500.	18,000.	—
1852O	140,000	200.	250.	300.	975.	1700.	—
1853	1,404,668	175.	185.	210.	250.	450.	—
1853D	3,178	500.	1350.	2650.	5000.	16,000.	—
1854	596,258	175.	185.	210.	250.	425.	—
1854C	7,295	250.	625.	1650.	4100.	14,000.	—
1854D	1,760	1400.	2700.	5000.	8000.	18,000.	—
1854O	153,000	200.	250.	300.	650.	1700.	—

PRICING SECTION

Date	Mintage	F-12	VF-20	XF-40	AU-50	MS-60	Prf-65
1854S	246	13,000.	20,000.	35,000.	—	—	—
1855	235,480	175.	185.	210.	275.	600.	—
1855C	3,677	500.	1300.	2850.	4800.	17,000.	—
1855D	1,123	2500.	3750.	7500.	14,000.	23,000.	—
1856	384,240	175.	185.	200.	225.	275.	32,000.
1856C	7,913	500.	850.	2000.	4500.	13,500.	—
1856D	874	4500.	7250.	13,000.	23,000.	42,000.	—
1856O	21,100	200.	250.	715.	2250.	7000.	—
1856S	71,120	200.	250.	435.	1050.	5100.	—
1857	214,130	175.	185.	210.	250.	390.	—
1857D	2,364	565.	1500.	3000.	4000.	10,000.	—
1857O	34,000	200.	250.	350.	1650.	6000.	—
1857S	69,200	200.	325.	500.	1600.	4000.	—
1858	47,377	200.	250.	300.	400.	1350.	20,000.
1858C	9,056	265.	600.	1300.	3000.	9000.	—
1859	39,444	200.	250.	300.	720.	1350.	20,000.
1859D	2,244	600.	1350.	2300.	6500.	23,000.	—
1859S	15,200	200.	300.	1200.	4000.	6250.	—
1860	22,675	200.	250.	300.	600.	1250.	20,000.
1860C	7,469	350.	750.	2250.	6000.	19,500.	—
1860S	35,600	200.	250.	700.	1450.	4200.	—
1861	1,283,878	150.	175.	200.	225.	350.	20,000.
1861S	24,000	200.	400.	1700.	3400.	5500.	—
1862	98,543	200.	250.	300.	550.	1450.	20,000.
1862/1	Inc. Ab.	—	850.	1900.	5750.	13,500.	—
1862S	8,000	650.	950.	2500.	5950.	15,500.	—
1863	30				RARCOA, Aug. 1990, proof only, $80,000.		
1863S	10,800	300.	465.	1700.	2700.	6600.	—
1864	2,874	2000.	5400.	11,500.	24,000.	42,000.	20,000.
1865	1,545	1550.	4325.	9600.	17,000.	32,000.	37,500.
1865S	23,376	200.	225.	630.	1250.	3700.	—
1866	3,110	550.	1200.	5000.	8000.	16,500.	20,000.
1866S	38,960	200.	300.	975.	2600.	8400.	—
1867	3,250	225.	360.	840.	1250.	5000.	20,000.
1867S	28,000	200.	250.	875.	2400.	5000.	—
1868	3,625	200.	300.	500.	840.	2600.	20,000.
1868S	34,000	200.	250.	500.	1250.	4400.	—
1869	4,345	200.	250.	500.	850.	4800.	20,000.
1869S	29,500	200.	250.	600.	1200.	4200.	—
1870	4,555	210.	275.	550.	1000.	3800.	20,000.
1870S	16,000	200.	285.	350.	1300.	4800.	—
1871	5,350	210.	275.	350.	900.	2400.	20,000.
1871S	22,000	225.	285.	350.	800.	2600.	—
1872	3,030	225.	360.	825.	2000.	5000.	20,000.
1872S	18,000	225.	285.	500.	1375.	4300.	—
1873 closed 3	178,025	200.	250.	300.	475.	1300.	20,000.
1873 open 3	Inc. Ab.	175.	200.	225.	250.	325.	—
1873S	27,000	200.	250.	575.	1100.	3700.	—
1874	3,940	200.	250.	500.	1000.	3700.	20,000.
1875	420	1500.	3600.	5250.	9000.	16,000.	32,000.
1875S	11,600	200.	250.	400.	800.	4500.	—
1876	4,221	210.	300.	750.	1450.	6000.	20,000.
1876S	5,000	210.	250.	800.	1275.	5100.	—
1877	1,652	325.	450.	800.	1700.	3500.	48,000.
1877S	35,400	125.	180.	210.	250.	850.	—
1878	286,260	125.	150.	160.	180.	245.	18,000.
1878S	178,000	125.	150.	160.	210.	425.	—
1879	88,990	125.	150.	160.	180.	270.	18,000.
1879S	43,500	125.	150.	160.	700.	1500.	—
1880	2,996	215.	250.	350.	600.	1500.	20,000.
1881	691	700.	1350.	3600.	7000.	14,500.	20,000.
1882	4,067	125.	225.	300.	350.	1200.	18,000.
1883	2,002	125.	225.	400.	700.	2200.	20,000.
1884	2,023	125.	225.	400.	500.	1500.	32,000.
1885	887	500.	800.	1700.	2750.	7000.	32,000.
1886	4,088	125.	210.	300.	550.	1400.	18,000.
1887	6,282	125.	190.	225.	500.	1300.	18,000.
1888	16,098	125.	190.	225.	300.	525.	18,000.
1889	17,648	125.	190.	250.	275.	450.	18,000.
1890	8,813	125.	190.	280.	295.	475.	18,000.
1891	11,040	125.	190.	250.	275.	450.	18,000.
1892	2,545	135.	195.	200.	325.	950.	18,000.
1893	30,106	125.	150.	200.	260.	300.	18,000.
1894	4,122	125.	150.	200.	325.	850.	18,000.
1895	6,199	125.	150.	200.	270.	425.	18,000.
1896	19,202	125.	150.	160.	180.	245.	18,000.
1897	29,904	125.	150.	160.	180.	245.	18,000.
1898	24,165	125.	150.	160.	180.	245.	18,000.
1899	27,350	125.	150.	160.	180.	245.	18,000.
1900	67,205	125.	150.	160.	180.	245.	18,000.
1901	91,322	125.	150.	160.	180.	245.	18,000.
1902	133,733	125.	150.	160.	180.	245.	18,000.
1903	201,257	125.	150.	160.	180.	245.	16,000.
1904	160,960	125.	150.	160.	180.	245.	16,000.
1905	217,944	125.	150.	160.	180.	245.	16,000.
1906	176,490	125.	150.	160.	180.	245.	16,000.
1907	336,448	125.	150.	160.	180.	245.	16,000.

1911-D Gold $2.50
Grade MS-60

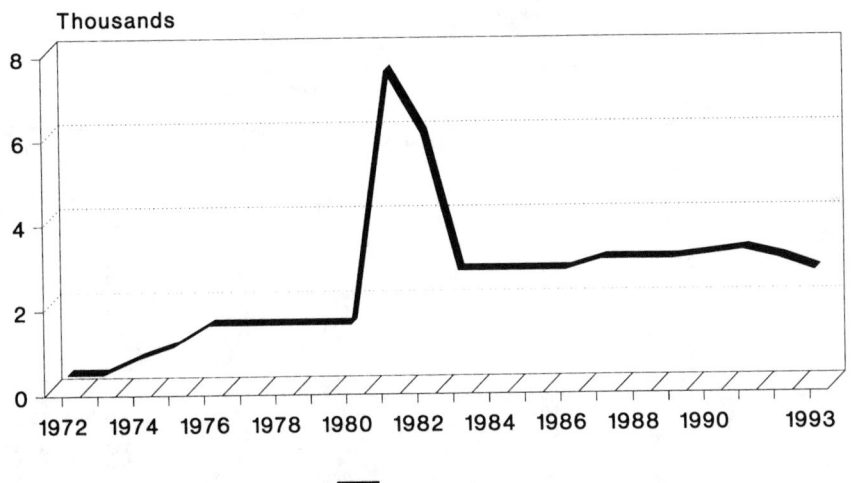

Retail Price

Source: COIN PRICES

Indian Head

Designer: Bela Lyon Pratt. **Size:** 18 millimeters. **Weight:** 4.18 grams. **Composition:** 90% gold (0.121 ounces), 10% copper.

Date	Mintage	VF-20	XF-40	AU-50	MS-60	MS-63	MS-65	Prf-65
1908	565,057	135.	155.	175.	260.	1050.	6000.	14,400.
1909	441,899	135.	155.	175.	310.	1150.	6600.	19,000.
1910	492,682	135.	155.	175.	295.	1250.	8400.	15,000.
1911	704,191	135.	155.	175.	290.	1150.	9100.	14,400.
1911D	55,680	700.	950.	1150.	2700.	6400.	30,000.	—
1912	616,197	135.	160.	180.	300.	1200.	12,250.	15,000.
1913	722,165	135.	155.	175.	265.	1200.	10,250.	14,400.
1914	240,117	140.	160.	190.	550.	2800.	19,000.	15,500.
1914D	448,000	135.	155.	175.	350.	1900.	19,000.	—
1915	606,100	135.	155.	175.	265.	1200.	6000.	15,000
1925D	578,000	135.	155.	175.	220.	1050.	6350.	—
1926	446,000	135.	155.	175.	220.	1050.	6000.	—
1927	388,000	135.	155.	175.	220.	1050.	6500.	—
1928	416,000	135.	155.	175.	220.	1050.	6700.	—
1929	532,000	135.	155.	175.	220.	1050.	8300.	—

Gold $3

Designer: James B. Longacre. **Size:** 20.5 millimeters. **Weight:** 5.015 grams. **Composition:** 90% gold (0.1452 ounces), 10% copper. **Notes:** The 1873 "closed-3" and "open-3" varieties are distinguished by the amount of space between the upper left and lower left serifs of the 3 in the date.

Date	Mintage	F-12	VF-20	XF-40	AU-50	MS-60	Prf-65
1854	138,618	365.	505.	650.	850.	2050.	35,000.
1854D	1,120	—	6500.	10,000.	23,500.	50,000.	—
1854O	24,000	365.	600.	950.	2150.	4100.	—
1855	50,555	365.	505.	650.	850.	2050.	—
1855S	6,600	550.	900.	2000.	5000.	12,750.	—
1856	26,010	365.	535.	690.	1200.	2150.	—
1856S	34,500	500.	760.	975.	1850.	7000.	—
1857	20,891	365.	535.	690.	1100.	2400.	—
1857S	14,000	510.	760.	925.	1750.	5200.	35,000.
1858	2,133	550.	800.	950.	1850.	4600.	—
1859	15,638	365.	505.	725.	1150.	2400.	35,000.
1860	7,155	550.	760.	850.	1200.	2400.	35,000.
1860S	7,000	525.	760.	1050.	4100.	11,000.	35,000.
1861	6,072	550.	760.	875.	1450.	3000.	—
1862	5,785	525.	760.	900.	1450.	3000.	35,000.
1863	5,039	600.	760.	925.	1650.	3000.	35,000.
1864	2,680	600.	760.	950.	1600.	3000.	35,000.
1865	1,165	700.	800.	1275.	3200.	10,000.	35,000.
1866	4,030	525.	760.	1275.	1600.	3000.	35,000.
1867	2,650	575.	800.	975.	1600.	3000.	35,000.
1868	4,875	525.	760.	900.	1600.	3000.	35,000.
1869	2,525	575.	760.	900.	1700.	3500.	35,000.
1870	3,535	525.	760.	900.	1600.	3500.	35,000.
1870S	Unique	Private Sale, 1992 XF-40 $1,500,000.					
1871	1,330	550.	880.	975.	1725.	3000.	35,000.
1872	2,030	525.	800.	950.	1600.	3000.	35,000.
1873 open 3	25			Proof only	—		—
1873 closed 3	Unknown	—	4000.	5000.	7000.	16,000.	—
1874	41,820	365.	525.	650.	1100.	3000.	35,000.
1875	20			Proof only RARCOA, Aug. 1990, proof, $159,000.			—
1876	45			Proof only			90,000.
1877	1,488	600.	900.	1450.	2750.	6000.	35,000.
1878	82,324	365.	500.	650.	850.	2050.	30,000.
1879	3,030	550.	800.	900.	1550.	3000.	30,000.
1880	1,036	550.	900.	925.	1800.	3000.	30,000.
1881	554	900.	1200.	1650.	3000.	4500.	32,000.
1882	1,576	550.	800.	1000.	1400.	3000.	30,000.
1883	989	550.	800.	925.	1700.	3300.	32,000.
1884	1,106	550.	800.	925.	2000.	3000.	30,000.
1885	910	550.	800.	1100.	1800.	3000.	32,000.
1886	1,142	550.	800.	925.	2000.	3500.	30,000.
1887	6,160	525.	625.	725.	1150.	2050.	30,000.
1888	5,291	525.	625.	725.	1150.	2050.	30,000.
1889	2,429	525.	625.	725.	1150.	2050.	30,000.

Gold $4 (Stella)

Flowing Hair   **Coiled Hair**

Designers: Charles E. Barber (Flowing Hair type) and George T. Morgan (Coiled Hair type). **Notes:** These are patterns, rather than coins struck for circulation. Examples in other metals also exist; values listed here are only for those struck in gold.

Date	Type	Mintage	VF-20	XF-40	AU-50	Prf-65
1879	Flowing Hair	415	—	—	—	90,000.
Impaired Proofs		—	10,000.	13,500.	26,000.	—
1879	Coiled Hair	10	—	—	—	500,000.
1880	Flowing Hair	15	—	—	—	225,000.
1880	Coiled Hair	10	—	—	—	500,000.

Gold $5 (Half Eagle)

Liberty Cap

Small eagle

Heraldic eagle

Designer: Robert Scot. **Size:** 25 millimeters. **Weight:** 8.75 grams. **Composition:** 91.67% gold (0.258 ounces), 8.33% copper. **Notes:** From 1795 through 1798, varieties exist with either a "small eagle" or a "large (heraldic) eagle" on the reverse. After 1798, only the heraldic eagle was used. Two 1797 varieties are distinguished by the number of stars on the obverse. 1798 varieties are distinguished by the size of the 8 in the date and the number of stars on the reverse. 1804 varieties are distinguished by the size of the 8 in the date. 1806 varieties are distinguished by whether the top of the 6 has a serif.

Date	Mintage	F-12	VF-20	XF-40	MS-60
1795 sm. eagle	8,707	5250.	7250.	9250.	31,500.
1795 lg. eagle	Inc. Ab.	6900.	10,000.	15,000.	48,000.
1796/95 small eagle	6,196	6000.	9100.	14,000.	—
1797/95 large eagle	3,609	5000.	7000.	9600.	30,000.
1797 15 stars, small eagle	Inc. Ab.	7500.	10,000.	18,500.	45,000.
1797 16 stars, small eagle	Inc. Ab.	7000.	9000.	17,500.	55,000. Extremely Rare
1798 sm.eagle	7 known				
1798 large eagle, small 8	24,867	1500.	1850.	3700.	10,500.
1798 large eagle, large 8, 13-star reverse	Inc. Ab.	1200.	1850.	3000.	7300.
1798 large eagle, large 8, 14-star reverse	Inc. Ab.	1600.	2300.	4300.	24,000.
1799	7,451	1300.	1600.	3000.	12,500.
1800	37,628	1150.	1550.	2150.	6000.
1802/1	53,176	1150.	1550.	2000.	6000.
1803/2	33,506	1150.	1550.	2000.	6000.
1804 sm. 8	30,475	1150.	1550.	2000.	6000.
1804 lg. 8	Inc. Ab.	1150.	1550.	2000.	6000.
1805	33,183	1150.	1550.	2200.	10,000.
1806 pointed 6	64,093	1150.	1550.	2000.	6000.
1806 round 6	Inc. Ab.	1150.	1550.	2000.	6000.
1807	32,488	1150.	1550.	2000.	6000.

Turban Head

Capped draped bust

Designer: John Reich. **Size:** 25 millimeters. **Weight:** 8.75 grams. **Composition:** 91.67% gold (0.258 ounces), 8.33% copper. **Notes:** The 1810 varieties are distinguished by the size of the numerals in the date and the size of the 5 in the "5D." on the reverse. The 1811 varieties are distinguished by the size of the 5 in the "5D." on the reverse.

Date	Mintage	F-12	VF-20	XF-40	MS-60
1807	51,605	1250.	1650.	2150.	6000.
1808	55,578	1250.	1650.	2150.	6000.
1808/7	Inc. Ab.	1400.	1550.	2400.	9500.
1809/8	33,875	1250.	1500.	2150.	6000.
1810 small date, small 5	100,287		Rare	—	—
1810 small date, large 5	Inc. Ab.				
1810 large date, small 5	Inc. Ab.	1300.	1650.	2400.	6000.
1810 large date, large 5	Inc. Ab.	3750.	4750.	7500.	24,000.
1811 small 5	Inc. Ab.	1250.	1400.	2000.	6000.
1811 large 5	99,581	1250.	1400.	2000.	5500.
1812	Inc. Ab.	1150.	1350.	2000.	6500.
	58,087	1000.	1350.	2000.	6250.

Capped head

Notes: 1820 varieties are distinguished by whether the 2 in the date has a curved base or square base, and by the size of the letters in the reverse inscriptions. 1832 varieties are distinguished by whether the 2 in the date has a curved base or square base and by the number of stars on the reverse. 1834 varieties are distinguished by whether the 4 has a serif at its far right.

Date	Mintage	F-12	VF-20	XF-40	MS-60
1813	95,428	1300.	1500.	2250.	6600.
1814/13	15,454	1600.	2000.	3100.	10,000.
1815	635		Norweb Sale, Oct.1987, AU-55, $82,500.		
1818	48,588	1500.	1900.	2850.	8500.
1819	51,723	—	Rare	—	—
1820 curved base 2, small letters	263,806	1500.	1900.	4500.	16,000.
1820 curved base 2, large letters	Inc. Ab.				
1820 sq. base 2	Inc. Ab.	1500.	1900.	4500.	16,000.
1821	Inc. Ab.	1500.	1900.	3100.	8500.
1822	34,641	2200.	3850.	7300.	23,000.
1823	(3 known) 17,796		Bowers & Ruddy, Oct. 1982, VF-30, $625,000.		
1824	14,485	1600.	2000.	3700.	14,500.
1825/21	17,340	2200.	3500.	8800.	—
1825/24	29,060	3250.	5000.	6500.	20,000.
1826	Inc. Ab.		Bowers & Merena, Mar. 1989, XF, $148,500.		
1827	18,069	2750.	6000.	7100.	25,000.
1828/7	24,913		Superior, June 1985, MS-65, $60,500.		
1828	28,029		Bowers & Merena, Jun. 1989, XF, $20,900.		
1829 lg. dt.	Inc. Ab.	—	—	—	—
1829 sm. dt.	57,442		Superior, July 1985, MS-65, $104,500.		
1830 sm. "5D."	Inc. Ab.		Private Sale, 1992 (XF-45), $89,000.		
1830 lg. "5D."	126,351	3500.	4700.	6000.	15,000.
1831	Inc. Ab.	3500.	5000.	6450.	16,500.
1832 curved base 2, 12-stars	140,594	3500.	4850.	6000.	16,500.
	157,487	—	Rare	—	—

Date	Mintage	F-12	VF-20	XF-40	MS-60
1832 square base 2, 13 stars	Inc. Ab.	4000.	6500.	8750.	21,000.
1833	193,630	3500.	4600.	5800.	15,500.
1834 plain 4	50,141	3500.	4600.	5800.	16,000.
1834 crosslet 4	Inc. Ab.	3500.	5000.	6500.	18,500.

Classic Head

Designer: William Kneass. **Size:** 22.5 millimeters. **Weight:** 8.36 grams. **Composition:** 89.92% gold (0.2418 ounces), 10.08% copper. **Notes:** 1834 varieties are distinguished by whether the 4 has a serif at its far right.

Date	Mintage	VF-20	XF-40	AU-50	MS-60	MS-65
1834 plain 4	658,028	300.	500.	850.	2950.	90,000.
1834 crosslet 4	Inc. Ab.	1150.	2375.	5250.	10,000.	—
1835	371,534	300.	500.	900.	2900.	62,000.
1836	553,147	300.	500.	850.	2900.	62,000.
1837	207,121	325.	525.	925.	3500.	62,000.
1838	286,588	300.	500.	900.	3250.	62,000.
1838C	17,179	1550.	4250.	9500.	20,000.	—
1838D	20,583	1450.	3500.	7000.	15,000.	—

Coronet Head

No motto

Designer: Christian Gobrecht. **Size:** 21.6 millimeters. **Weight:** 8.359 grams. **Composition:** 90% gold (0.242 ounces), 10% copper. **Notes:** Varieties for the 1842 Philadelphia strikes are distinguished by the size of the letters in the reverse inscriptions. Varieties for the 1842-C and -D strikes are distinguished by the size of the numerals in the date. Varieties for the 1843-O strikes are distinguished by the size of the letters in the reverse inscriptions.

Date	Mintage	F-12	VF-20	XF-40	MS-60	Prf-65
1839	118,143	200.	250.	435.	3500.	—
1839/8 curved date	Inc. Ab.	200.	300.	600.	1750.	—
1839C	17,205	450.	950.	1800.	16,500.	—
1839D	18,939	400.	800.	1700.	8500.	—
1840	137,382	190.	225.	350.	4100.	—
1840C	18,992	400.	700.	1650.	15,500.	—
1840D	22,896	400.	700.	1500.	11,000.	—
1840O	40,120	200.	325.	700.	7500.	—
1841	15,833	200.	375.	1200.	7500.	—
1841C	21,467	300.	675.	1450.	12,000.	—
1841D	30,495	325.	600.	1250.	12,000.	—
1841O	50		2 known	—		—
1842 sm. let.	27,578	150.	300.	1300.	10,000.	—
1842 lg. let.	Inc. Ab.	350.	700.	2000.	11,500.	—
1842C sm. dt.	28,184	1750.	3500.	11,750.	—	—
1842C lg. dt.	Inc. Ab.	350.	750.	1500.	13,750.	—
1842D sm. dt.	59,608	350.	650.	1250.	12,000.	—
1842D lg. dt.	Inc. Ab.	1250.	2250.	4500.	18,000.	—
1842O	16,400	350.	1000.	3500.	18,000.	—
1843	611,205	150.	180.	210.	1750.	—
1843C	44,201	350.	600.	1400.	9500.	—
1843D	98,452	350.	550.	1000.	8000.	—
1843O sm. let.	19,075	325.	550.	1400.	11,000.	—
1843O lg. let.	82,000	200.	250.	900.	15,000.	—
1844	340,330	150.	180.	250.	2100.	—

1852-C Gold $5
Grade MS-60

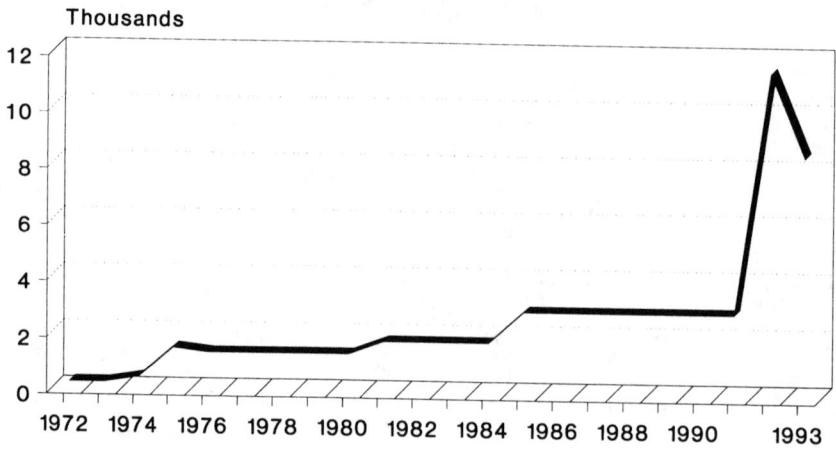

Thousands

■ Retail Price

Source: COIN PRICES

Date	Mintage	F-12	VF-20	XF-40	MS-60	Prf-65
1844C	23,631	300.	650.	1800.	13,500.	—
1844D	88,982	375.	550.	1050.	9250.	—
1844O	364,600	200.	225.	350.	5000.	—
1845	417,099	150.	180.	210.	2750.	—
1845D	90,629	360.	850.	1850.	10,000.	—
1845O	41,000	200.	350.	1100.	9500.	—
1846	395,942	150.	180.	210.	3000.	—
1846C	12,995	425.	900.	2500.	6750.	—
1846D	80,294	400.	550.	1350.	9250.	—
1846O	58,000	200.	350.	1200.	11,000.	—
1847	915,981	150.	180.	210.	1850.	—
1847C	84,151	375.	575.	1450.	13,000.	—
1847D	64,405	400.	500.	1100.	7250.	—
1847O	12,000	475.	1800.	4300.	19,000.	—
1848	260,775	150.	180.	250.	2500.	—
1848C	64,472	400.	650.	1400.	12,000.	—
1848D	47,465	400.	500.	1275.	10,000.	—
1849	133,070	150.	180.	300.	2700.	—
1849C	64,823	350.	500.	1100.	11,500.	—
1849D	39,036	350.	700.	1350.	11,500.	—
1850	64,491	200.	350.	875.	4350.	—
1850C	63,591	325.	550.	1100.	10,000.	—
1850D	43,984	350.	500.	1500.	18,000.	—
1851	377,505	150.	180.	265.	2800.	—
1851C	49,176	325.	600.	1100.	11,000.	—
1851D	62,710	350.	525.	1375.	11,500.	—
1851O	41,000	325.	650.	1500.	—	—
1852	573,901	150.	180.	210.	1850.	—
1852C	72,574	350.	550.	1100.	8500.	—
1852D	91,584	350.	500.	1000.	9000.	—
1853	305,770	150.	180.	210.	2250.	—
1853C	65,571	350.	525.	1000.	6600.	—
1853D	89,678	350.	500.	900.	6500.	—
1854	160,675	160.	200.	500.	3000.	—
1854C	39,283	400.	600.	1600.	8000.	—
1854D	56,413	350.	500.	1000.	6500.	—
1854O	46,000	250.	300.	500.	6300.	—
1854S	268	Bowers & Ruddy, Oct.1982, AU-55, $170,000.				—
1855	117,098	160.	200.	250.	2400.	—
1855C	39,788	350.	625.	1750.	9000.	—
1855D	22,432	400.	600.	1350.	10,000.	—

Date	Mintage	F-12	VF-20	XF-40	MS-60	Prf-65
1855O	11,100	350.	700.	2450.	16,500.	—
1855S	61,000	200.	425.	1100.	10,000.	—
1856	197,990	175.	310.	340.	3500.	—
1856C	28,457	350.	600.	1300.	12,000.	—
1856D	19,786	400.	600.	1300.	7800.	—
1856O	10,000	400.	800.	2300.	—	—
1856S	105,100	190.	300.	800.	—	—
1857	98,188	160.	200.	250.	3000.	—
1857C	31,360	300.	600.	1300.	8000.	—
1857D	17,046	300.	600.	1250.	8000.	—
1857O	13,000	300.	700.	2000.	—	—
1857S	87,000	200.	300.	700.	7000.	—
1858	15,136	200.	275.	800.	5250.	70,000.
1858C	38,856	375.	800.	1250.	11,000.	—
1858D	15,362	300.	600.	1000.	12,000.	—
1858S	18,600	350.	650.	2100.	—	—
1859	16,814	200.	275.	600.	6500.	—
1859C	31,847	300.	525.	1400.	13,000.	—
1859D	10,366	400.	725.	1500.	11,500.	—
1859S	13,220	450.	1250.	3500.	—	—
1860	19,825	200.	300.	600.	6500.	—
1860C	14,813	350.	800.	2000.	11,500.	—
1860D	14,635	300.	800.	1800.	13,500.	—
1860S	21,200	450.	1050.	2400.	18,500.	—
1861	688,150	150.	175.	210.	1900.	—
1861C	6,879	700.	1500.	3400.	25,000.	—
1861D	1,597	2500.	4000.	7000.	—	—
1861S	18,000	450.	1100.	4500.	—	—
1862	4,465	450.	750.	4500.	—	—
1862S	9,500	1400.	4500.	10,500.	—	—
1863	2,472	500.	1150.	3450.	—	—
1863S	17,000	425.	1200.	4750.	—	—
1864	4,220	400.	600.	2100.	11,500.	—
1864S	3,888	2200.	6750.	12,000.	—	—
1865	1,295	600.	1200.	3150.	—	—
1865S	27,612	425.	1200.	3600.	—	—
1866S	9,000	600.	1600.	4900.	—	—

With motto

Notes: In 1866 the motto "In God We Trust" was added above the eagle on the reverse. The 1873 "closed-3" and "open-3" varieties are distinguished by the amount of space between the upper left and lower left serifs of the 3 in the date.

Date	Mintage	VF-20	XF-40	AU-50	MS-60	MS-65	Prf-65
1866	6,730	725.	1800.	4400.	12,500.	—	35,000.
1866S	34,920	1150.	3500.	8500.	18,500.	—	—
1867	6,920	550.	1700.	3500.	8000.	—	35,000.
1867S	29,000	1350.	5000.	9000.	—	—	—
1868	5,725	650.	1400.	3700.	10,000.	—	35,000.
1868S	52,000	450.	550.	7200.	—	—	—
1869	1,785	875.	2300.	5000.	—	—	35,000.
1869S	31,000	375.	2100.	8000.	—	—	—
1870	4,035	700.	2800.	4500.	—	—	35,000.
1870CC	7,675	3000.	8000.	14,750.	—	—	—
1870S	17,000	1200.	3100.	9500.	—	—	—
1871	3,230	875.	2150.	6000.	—	—	35,000.
1871CC	20,770	975.	3000.	8700.	—	—	—
1871S	25,000	550.	1450.	6000.	17,500.	—	—
1872	1,690	750.	2000.	4700.	15,000.	—	35,000.
1872CC	16,980	850.	3000.	6750.	—	—	—
1872S	36,400	525.	1300.	7000.	—	—	—
1873 closed 3	49,305	225.	250.	625.	2800.	—	35,000.
1873 open 3	63,200	225.	250.	625.	2800.	—	—
1873CC	7,416	1800.	5000.	12,750.	—	—	—
1873S	31,000	875.	2700.	—	—	—	—
1874	3,508	625.	2200.	5000.	—	—	35,000.
1874CC	21,198	675.	1350.	4300.	12,000.	—	—
1874S	16,000	725.	2750.	7000.	—	—	—
1875	220	45,000.	55,000.	96,000.	—	—	110,000.
1875CC	11,828	1350.	4300.	13,000.	—	—	—

Date	Mintage	VF-20	XF-40	AU-50	MS-60	MS-65	Prf-65
1875S	9,000	950.	3300.	—	—	—	—
1876	1,477	1000.	2600.	5300.	15,500.	—	35,000.
1876CC	6,887	1150.	3900.	7700.	—	—	—
1876S	4,000	1500.	3900.	12,750.	—	—	—
1877	1,152	800.	2400.	4500.	12,000.	—	35,000.
1877CC	8,680	1000.	2900.	7000.	—	—	—
1877S	26,700	325.	900.	3600.	—	—	—
1878	131,740	135.	225.	250.	1000.	—	35,000.
1878CC	9,054	3500.	7500.	—	—	—	—
1878S	144,700	175.	275.	475.	1200.	—	—
1879	301,950	135.	175.	250.	525.	—	20,000.
1879CC	17,281	350.	1000.	2400.	—	—	—
1879S	426,200	200.	275.	325.	975.	—	—
1880	3,166,436	130.	150.	175.	200.	—	20,000.
1880CC	51,017	350.	650.	1750.	7500.	—	—
1880S	1,348,900	130.	150.	175.	200.	—	—
1881	5,708,802	130.	150.	175.	225.	5400.	20,000.
1881/80	Inc. Ab.	350.	700.	1800.	4050.	—	—
1881CC	13,886	500.	1500.	3800.	9000.	—	—
1881S	969,000	130.	140.	150.	175.	—	—
1882	2,514,568	130.	150.	175.	200.	5400.	20,000.
1882CC	82,817	375.	650.	1500.	5000.	—	—
1882S	969,000	130.	140.	150.	175.	—	—
1883	233,461	130.	150.	200.	550.	5400.	20,000.
1883CC	12,958	375.	650.	3100.	12,000.	—	—
1883S	83,200	195.	225.	330.	1150.	—	—
1884	191,078	150.	175.	260.	1250.	—	20,000.
1884CC	16,402	450.	825.	3700.	—	—	—
1884S	177,000	200.	275.	325.	775.	—	—
1885	601,506	130.	140.	150.	175.	—	20,000.
1885S	1,211,500	130.	150.	175.	225.	5400.	—
1886	388,432	150.	185.	225.	375.	—	20,000.
1886S	3,268,000	130.	150.	160.	225.	—	—
1887	87		Proof only	—	—	—	100,000.
1887S	1,912,000	130.	150.	185.	240.	—	—
1888	18,296	175.	250.	300.	1300.	—	20,000.
1888S	293,900	190.	275.	800.	2800.	—	—
1889	7,565	400.	700.	1500.	—	—	20,000.
1890	4,328	250.	400.	1500.	3500.	—	20,000.
1890CC	53,800	300.	400.	550.	1250.	—	—
1891	61,413	130.	235.	250.	775.	6500.	20,000.
1891CC	208,000	250.	375.	500.	850.	—	—
1892	753,572	130.	140.	150.	175.	—	20,000.
1892CC	82,968	300.	600.	700.	1400.	—	—
1892O	10,000	600.	1250.	2250.	4500.	—	—
1892S	298,400	175.	225.	325.	2500.	—	—
1893	1,528,197	130.	150.	185.	225.	5400.	20,000.
1893CC	60,000	300.	400.	625.	1750.	—	—
1893O	110,000	200.	300.	400.	1250.	—	—
1893S	224,000	175.	200.	325.	600.	6500.	—
1894	957,955	130.	150.	185.	300.	5400.	20,000.
1894O	16,600	195.	350.	475.	1350.	—	—
1894S	55,900	275.	350.	850.	3750.	6500.	—
1895	1,345,936	130.	140.	150.	175.	5400.	20,000.
1895S	112,000	250.	375.	1000.	3500.	26,000.	—
1896	59,063	140.	185.	225.	350.	5400.	20,000.
1896S	155,400	225.	275.	600.	2100.	—	—
1897	867,883	130.	140.	150.	175.	5400.	20,000.
1897S	354,000	165.	250.	525.	1800.	—	—
1898	633,495	130.	140.	150.	175.	5400.	20,000.
1898S	1,397,400	130.	165.	175.	300.	5400.	—
1899	1,710,729	130.	140.	150.	175.	5400.	20,000.
1899S	1,545,000	130.	140.	150.	175.	5400.	—
1900	1,405,730	130.	140.	150.	175.	5400.	20,000.
1900S	329,000	165.	200.	300.	700.	5400.	—
1901	616,040	130.	140.	150.	175.	5400.	12,500.
1901S	3,648,000	130.	140.	150.	175.	5400.	—
1902	172,562	130.	140.	150.	175.	5400.	12,500.
1902S	939,000	130.	140.	150.	175.	5400.	—
1903	227,024	130.	140.	150.	175.	5400.	15,000.
1903S	1,855,000	130.	140.	150.	175.	5400.	—
1904	392,136	130.	140.	150.	175.	5400.	12,500.
1904S	97,000	180.	225.	300.	800.	5400.	—
1905	302,308	130.	140.	150.	175.	5400.	12,500.
1905S	880,700	130.	175.	260.	900.	5400.	—
1906	348,820	130.	140.	150.	175.	5400.	12,500.
1906D	320,000	130.	140.	150.	175.	5400.	—
1906S	598,000	130.	140.	185.	275.	5400.	—
1907	626,192	130.	140.	150.	175.	5400.	20,000.
1907D	888,000	130.	140.	150.	175.	5250.	—
1908	421,874	130.	140.	150.	175.	5250.	—

Indian Head

Designer: Bela Lyon Pratt. **Size:** 21.6 millimeters. **Weight:** 8.359 grams. **Composition:** 90% gold (0.242 ounces), 10% copper.

Date	Mintage	VF-20	XF-40	AU-50	MS-60	MS-63	MS-65	Prf-65
1908	578,012	195.	215.	230.	425.	3400.	15,000.	22,000.
1908D	148,000	195.	215.	230.	425.	3400.	26,500.	—
1908S	82,000	225.	450.	540.	1850.	3700.	20,000.	—
1909	627,138	195.	215.	230.	445.	3400.	19,500.	26,500.
1909D	3,423,560	195.	215.	230.	425.	3400.	20,500.	—
1909O	34,200	600.	900.	1600.	6900.	30,000.	120,000.	—
1909S	297,200	215.	230.	240.	1175.	6600.	42,000.	—
1910	604,250	195.	215.	230.	430.	3700.	30.000.	24,000.
1910D	193,600	195.	215.	230.	510.	4800.	36,000.	—
1910S	770,200	195.	215.	230.	1800.	7200.	42,000.	—
1911	915,139	195.	215.	230.	425.	3400.	24,000.	25,000.
1911D	72,500	350.	500.	600.	5600.	19,000.	68,500.	—
1911S	1,416,000	195.	235.	250.	840.	6000.	42,000.	—
1912	790,144	195.	215.	230.	425.	3400.	21,500.	24,000.
1912S	392,000	215.	235.	250.	1550.	8500.	42,000.	—
1913	916,099	195.	215.	230.	425.	3400.	21,000.	25,000.
1913S	408,000	250.	300.	350.	2650.	15,000.	66,000.	—
1914	247,125	195.	215.	230.	425.	3400.	23,500.	25,000.
1914D	247,000	195.	215.	230.	435.	3700.	48,000.	—
1914S	263,000	215.	220.	255.	1050.	7550.	47,000.	—
1915	588,075	195.	215.	230.	425.	3400.	23,500.	33,000.
1915S	164,000	300.	325.	425.	2650.	8700.	66,000.	—
1916S	240,000	195.	215.	265.	660.	4700.	30,000.	—
1929	662,000	2000.	3500.	4850.	5400.	7700.	45,500.	—

Gold $10 (Eagle)

Liberty Cap

Small eagle

Designer: Robert Scot. **Size:** 33 millimeters. **Weight:** 17.5 grams. **Composition:** 91.67% gold (0.5159 ounces), 8.33% copper.

Date	Mintage	F-12	VF-20	XF-40	MS-60
1795	5,583	6000.	8500.	11,000.	39,500.
1796	4,146	6000.	8500.	11,000.	28,000.
1797 sm. eagle	3,615	6000.	9700.	23,500.	—

Heraldic eagle

Notes: The 1798/97 varieties are distinguished by the positioning of the stars on the obverse.

Date	Mintage	F-12	VF-20	XF-40	MS-60
1797 lg. eagle	10,940	2500.	3500.	5000.	14,000.
1798/97, 9 stars left, 4 right	900	4500.	7500.	17,000.	—
1798/97, 7 stars left, 6 right	842	10,000.	22,000.	—	—
1799	37,449	2400.	3000.	4500.	11,000.
1800	5,999	2400.	3250.	5000.	13,750.
1801	44,344	2400.	3000.	4000.	11,000.
1803	15,017	2600.	3250.	4000.	11,000.
1804	3,757	3750.	4200.	7000.	32,500.

Coronet Head

Old-style head, no motto

Designer: Christian Gobrecht. **Size:** 27 millimeters. **Weight:** 16.718 grams. **Composition:** 90% gold (0.4839 ounces), 10% copper.

Date	Mintage	F-12	VF-20	XF-40	MS-60	Prf-65
1838	7,200	550.	900.	2750.	—	—
1839 lg. lts.	38,248	450.	800.	1700.	16,000.	—

New-style head, no motto

Notes: The 1842 varieties are distinguished by the size of the numerals in the date.

Date	Mintage	F-12	VF-20	XF-40	MS-60	Prf-65
1839 sm. lts.	Inc. Ab.	700.	1600.	4000.	—	—
1840	47,338	350.	400.	750.	13,000.	—
1841	63,131	350.	375.	650.	14,000.	—
1841O	2,500	850.	2000.	5700.	—	—
1842 sm. dt.	81,507	350.	400.	700.	—	—
1842 lg. dt.	Inc. Ab.	350.	375.	750.	13,500.	—
1842O	27,400	225.	250.	700.	12,500.	—
1843	75,462	350.	375.	700.	7500.	—
1843O	175,162	350.	375.	600.	7750.	—
1844	6,361	475.	1100.	2950.	—	—
1844O	118,700	350.	375.	600.	11,000.	—
1845	26,153	350.	750.	2100.	—	—
1845O	47,500	350.	425.	700.	12,500.	—
1846	20,095	500.	900.	2850.	—	—
1846O	81,780	350.	450.	875.	—	—
1847	862,258	220.	250.	300.	5250.	—
1847O	571,500	220.	260.	400.	4500.	—
1848	145,484	300.	350.	400.	5500.	—
1848O	38,850	400.	600.	1400.	—	—
1849	653,618	220.	250.	275.	3850.	—
1849O	23,900	450.	700.	2400.	—	—
1850	291,451	220.	250.	275.	2500.	—
1850O	57,500	350.	400.	600.	—	—
1851	176,328	300.	325.	525.	9500.	—
1851O	263,000	250.	300.	550.	—	—
1852	263,106	300.	400.	525.	3850.	—
1852O	18,000	400.	550.	1875.	—	—
1853	201,253	220.	250.	275.	3850.	—
1853O	51,000	350.	400.	575.	—	—
1854	54,250	350.	400.	700.	—	—
1854O	52,500	350.	400.	575.	12,000.	—
1854S	123,826	250.	300.	575.	11,000.	—
1855	121,701	220.	250.	275.	2500.	—
1855O	18,000	350.	600.	2000.	—	—
1855S	9,000	850.	1700.	3800.	—	—
1856	60,490	275.	300.	360.	4800.	—
1856O	14,500	400.	600.	2100.	—	—
1856S	68,000	300.	350.	625.	10,000.	—
1857	16,606	300.	350.	1000.	—	—
1857O	5,500	700.	1000.	2300.	—	—
1857S	26,000	350.	525.	800.	—	—
1858	2,521	2500.	5000.	11,000.	—	—
1858O	20,000	300.	350.	850.	12,000.	—

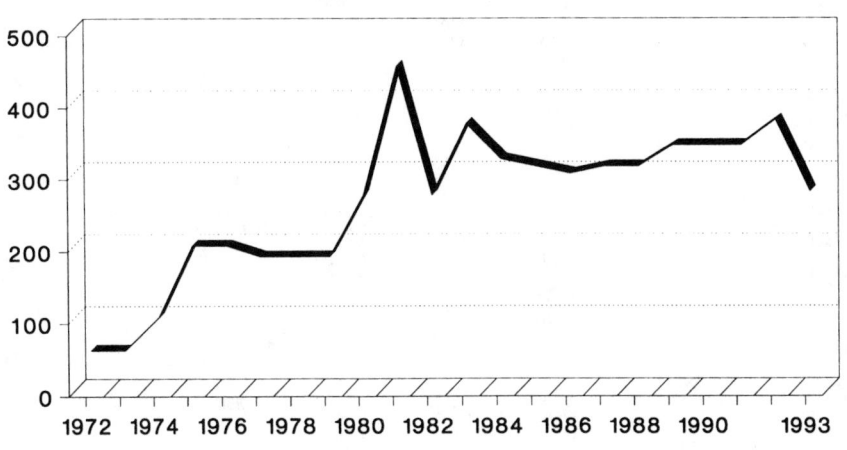

1853 Gold $10
Grade XF-40

■ Retail Price

Source: COIN PRICES

Date	Mintage	F-12	VF-20	XF-40	MS-60	Prf-65
1858S	11,800	750.	2150.	5100.	—	—
1859	16,093	300.	350.	1000.	—	—
1859O	2,300	1275.	3500.	9000.	—	—
1859S	7,000	900.	2500.	7400.	—	—
1860	15,105	300.	350.	1000.	12,500.	—
1860O	11,100	375.	575.	1200.	14,000.	—
1860S	5,000	750.	2700.	6900.	—	—
1861	113,233	250.	300.	340.	5000.	—
1861S	15,500	675.	1900.	4750.	—	—
1862	10,995	325.	475.	1350.	—	—
1862S	12,500	700.	1950.	4750.	—	—
1863	1,248	2000.	3650.	8750.	—	—
1863S	10,000	725.	1700.	4000.	—	—
1864	3,580	800.	1900.	4900.	—	—
1864S	2,500	2750.	5800.	11,500.	—	—
1865	4,005	750.	2150.	5250.	—	—
1865S	16,700	1450.	4500.	9250.	—	—
1865S/inverted 186	—	—	2500.	7500.	—	—
1866S	8,500	1300.	3000.	6500.	—	—

New-style head, with motto

Notes: In 1866 the motto "In God We Trust" was added above the eagle on the reverse. The 1873 "closed-3" and "open-3" varieties are distinguished by the amount of space between the upper left and lower left serifs of the 3 in the date.

Date	Mintage	VF-20	XF-40	AU-50	MS-60	MS-65	Prf-65
1866	3,780	750.	1600.	5500.	—	—	60,000.
1866S	11,500	1750.	3900.	9500.	—	—	—
1867	3,140	1750.	4500.	10,500.	—	—	60,000.
1867S	9,000	2400.	8000.	—	—	—	—
1868	10,655	600.	1375.	5750.	15,000.	—	60,000.
1868S	13,500	1600.	4250.	9500.	—	—	—
1869	1,855	1750.	4300.	11,500.	—	—	65,000.
1869S	6,430	1600.	4250.	11,500.	—	—	—
1870	4,025	750.	1450.	5000.	—	—	60,000.
1870CC	5,908	5750.	10,750.	25,000.	—	—	—
1870S	8,000	1600.	6000.	12,750.	—	—	—
1871	1,820	1600.	4000.	8750.	3500.	—	60,000.
1871CC	8,085	2000.	4750.	—	—	—	—
1871S	16,500	1750.	4700.	—	—	—	—
1872	1,650	3000.	8000.	—	—	—	60,000.
1872CC	4,600	1750.	7750.	—	—	—	—
1872S	17,300	900.	2000.	8500.	—	—	—
1873 closed 3	825	4200.	11,000.	24,000.	—	—	60,000.
1873CC	4,543	2250.	7500.	19,000.	—	—	—
1873S	12,000	1600.	3750.	9000.	—	—	—
1874	53,160	275.	325.	550.	2450.	—	60,000.
1874CC	16,767	875.	3200.	7500.	—	—	—
1874S	10,000	1700.	4200.	14,250.	—	—	—
1875	120			Akers, Aug. 1990, proof, $115,000.			—
1875CC	7,715	2500.	7500.	24,000.	—	—	—
1876	732	3000.	9000.	20,000.	—	—	50,000.
1876CC	4,696	2500.	6250.	19,000.	—	—	—
1876S	5,000	2100.	4000.	12,000.	—	—	—
1877	817	2500.	6500.	16,000.	—	—	40,000.
1877CC	3,332	2400.	5300.	11,500.	—	—	—
1877S	17,000	600.	2200.	7500.	—	—	—
1878	73,800	255.	325.	400.	2550.	—	50,000.
1878CC	3,244	3500.	8750.	19,500.	—	—	—
1878S	26,100	650.	1800.	8000.	—	—	—
1879	384,770	255.	265.	325.	850.	—	40,000.
1879CC	1,762	3700.	9000.	19,000.	—	—	—
1879O	1,500	2200.	7700.	17,000.	—	—	—
1879S	224,000	280.	325.	425.	1700.	—	—
1880	1,644,876	240.	245.	275.	400.	—	40,000.
1880CC	11,190	425.	675.	2200.	8500.	—	—
1880O	9,200	400.	950.	2300.	6000.	—	—
1880S	506,250	240.	250.	300.	600.	—	—
1881	3,877,260	240.	255.	280.	275.	—	40,000.
1881CC	24,015	400.	550.	1300.	4750.	—	—
1881O	8,350	400.	875.	2400.	7000.	—	—

PRICING SECTION

Date	Mintage	VF-20	XF-40	AU-50	MS-60	MS-65	Prf-65
1881S	970,000	240.	260.	300.	450.	6500.	—
1882	2,324,480	240.	260.	275.	290.	6500.	40,000.
1882CC	6,764	475.	1400.	2600.	7400.	—	—
1882O	10,820	400.	750.	1750.	3250.	—	—
1882S	132,000	240.	260.	275.	1100.	13,500.	—
1883	208,740	245.	260.	300.	450.	6500.	40,000.
1883CC	12,000	400.	850.	2200.	6000.	—	—
1883O	800	3200.	7500.	14,500.	30,000.	—	—
1883S	38,000	265.	350.	400.	1350.	13,500.	—
1884	76,905	245.	260.	375.	1850.	13,500.	86,000.
1884CC	9,925	525.	1100.	2900.	8000.	—	—
1884S	124,250	240.	245.	365.	1300.	6500.	—
1885	253,527	240.	245.	285.	775.	6500.	40,000.
1885S	228,000	240.	245.	325.	600.	6500.	—
1886	236,160	250.	275.	375.	1100.	6500.	40,000.
1886S	826,000	240.	245.	275.	340.	6500.	—
1887	53,680	275.	300.	475.	1800.	50,000.	40,000.
1887S	817,000	240.	245.	300.	425.	6500.	—
1888	132,996	275.	300.	365.	1500.	50,000.	40,000.
1888O	21,335	250.	260.	350.	750.	—	—
1888S	648,700	240.	245.	235.	500.	6500.	—
1889	4,485	400.	500.	1000.	2500.	—	40,000.
1889S	425,400	240.	245.	260.	375.	6500.	—
1890	58,043	275.	285.	425.	2000.	13,500.	40,000.
1890CC	17,500	300.	450.	600.	1400.	—	—
1891	91,868	245.	260.	275.	450.	13,500.	40,000.
1891CC	103,732	275.	350.	450.	750.	—	—
1892	797,552	240.	245.	260.	325.	6500.	40,000.
1892CC	40,000	375.	550.	600.	2100.	—	—
1892O	28,688	240.	275.	300.	600.	—	—
1892S	115,500	275.	285.	350.	750.	13,500.	—
1893	1,840,895	240.	245.	275.	325.	6500.	40,000.
1893CC	14,000	380.	600.	1075.	2700.	—	—
1893O	17,000	240.	250.	325.	675.	—	—
1893S	141,350	275.	285.	325.	800.	13,500.	—
1894	2,470,778	240.	245.	255.	335.	6500.	40,000.
1894O	107,500	240.	260.	350.	1300.	13,500.	—
1894S	25,000	300.	475.	1200.	3750.	13,500.	—
1895	567,826	240.	245.	255.	295.	6500.	40,000.
1895O	98,000	245.	285.	310.	650.	13,500.	—
1895S	49,000	250.	400.	1250.	4000.	40,000.	—
1896	76,348	250.	245.	275.	325.	6500.	40,000.
1896S	123,750	250.	350.	1000.	3750.	—	—
1897	1,000,159	240.	245.	255.	300.	6500.	40,000.
1897O	42,500	240.	275.	375.	850.	11,000.	—
1897S	234,750	240.	300.	500.	1850.	6500.	—
1898	812,197	240.	245.	255.	295.	6500.	40,000.
1898S	473,600	240.	245.	350.	525.	6500.	—
1899	1,262,305	240.	245.	255.	295.	6500.	40,000.
1899O	37,047	280.	290.	350.	950.	13,500.	—
1899S	841,000	240.	275.	300.	475.	6500.	—
1900	293,960	240.	245.	255.	295.	6500.	40,000.
1900S	81,000	280.	300.	400.	1300.	12,500.	—
1901	1,718,825	240.	245.	255.	295.	6500.	40,000.
1901O	72,041	275.	290.	320.	675.	13,500.	—
1901S	2,812,750	240.	245.	250.	295.	5500.	—
1902	82,513	240.	250.	275.	300.	12,500.	40,000.
1902S	469,500	240.	245.	255.	295.	6500.	—
1903	125,926	240.	245.	250.	300.	6500.	40,000.
1903O	112,771	240.	245.	300.	565.	6500.	—
1903S	538,000	240.	300.	340.	375.	6500.	—
1904	162,038	240.	245.	255.	295.	6500.	40,000.
1904O	108,950	240.	300.	350.	575.	6500.	—
1905	201,078	240.	245.	250.	295.	6500.	40,000.
1905S	369,250	240.	350.	425.	2500.	6500.	—
1906	165,497	240.	245.	250.	295.	6500.	40,000.
1906D	981,000	240.	245.	250.	310.	6500.	—
1906O	86,895	240.	290.	325.	650.	13,500.	—
1906S	457,000	250.	275.	300.	675.	6500.	—
1907	1,203,973	240.	245.	250.	295.	6500.	40,000.
1907D	1,030,000	240.	245.	250.	295.	6500.	—
1907S	210,500	250.	300.	400.	1000.	6500.	—

Indian Head

No motto

Designer: Augustus Saint-Gaudens. **Size:** 27 millimeters. **Weight:** 16.718 grams. **Composition:** 90% gold (0.4839 ounces), 10% copper. **Notes:** 1907 varieties are distinguished by whether the edge is rolled or wired, and whether the legend "E Pluribus Unum" has periods between each word.

Date	Mintage	VF-20	XF-40	AU-50	MS-60	MS-63	MS-65	Prf-65
1907 wire edge, periods before & after leg.								
	500	—	4500.	—	7800.	12,000.	39,000.	60,000.
1907 same, without stars on edge								
		—	Unique	—	—	—	—	—
1907 rolled edge, periods								
	42	—	—	—	21,500.	34,000.	60,000.	—
1907 without periods								
	239,406	425.	450.	500.	625.	2200.	9000.	—
1908 without motto								
	33,500	535.	585.	600.	900.	3350.	12,000.	—
1908D without motto								
	210,000	400.	425.	500.	720.	4100.	36,000.	—

1933 Gold $10
Grade MS-60

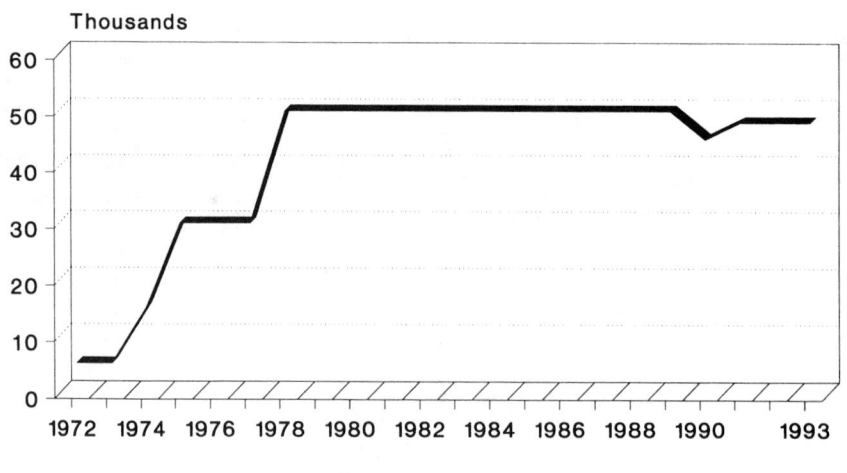

■ Retail Price

Source: COIN PRICES

With motto

Notes: In 1908 the motto "In God We Trust" was added on the reverse to the left of the eagle.

Date	Mintage	VF-20	XF-40	AU-50	MS-60	MS-63	MS-65	Prf-65
1908	341,486	375.	390.	400.	420.	1700.	7550.	35,000.
1908D	836,500	375.	400.	525.	710.	3500.	24,000.	—
1908S	59,850	400.	535.	700.	2500.	6600.	34,000.	—
1909	184,863	360.	390.	400.	480.	2450.	15,500.	39,000.
1909D	121,540	400.	440.	500.	975.	11,000.	42,000.	—
1909S	292,350	375.	425.	475.	840.	2650.	14,500.	—
1910	318,704	380.	390.	400.	430.	1600.	7550.	35,000.
1910D	2,356,640	360.	390.	400.	445.	1600.	7800.	—
1910S	811,000	475.	500.	550.	1050.	4100.	48,000.	—
1911	505,595	360.	375.	400.	430.	2300.	7200.	35,000.
1911D	30,100	400.	550.	750.	4800.	12,500.	90,000.	—
1911S	51,000	350.	450.	600.	1500.	3250.	9100.	—
1912	405,083	350.	390.	400.	435.	1600.	8400.	35,000.
1912S	300,000	350.	400.	510.	900.	2500.	46,000.	—
1913	442,071	350.	375.	400.	430.	1600.	8400.	35,000.
1913S	66,000	550.	650.	780.	5150.	25,000.	162,000.	—
1914	151,050	310.	325.	360.	370.	1800.	10,500.	35,000.
1914D	343,500	310.	325.	360.	370.	1700.	10,500.	—
1914S	208,000	350.	375.	500.	635.	3700.	39,500.	—
1915	351,075	310.	350.	380.	480.	1700.	7450.	42,000.
1915S	59,000	350.	500.	575.	2700.	8800.	73,000.	—
1916S	138,500	375.	475.	535.	725.	3500.	18,500.	—
1920S	126,500	6500.	7500.	8000.	15,000.	33,000.	120,000.	—
1926	1,014,000	380.	390.	400.	445.	1600.	6200.	—
1930S	96,000	3500.	5000.	7500.	8300.	12,500.	51,000.	—
1932	4,463,000	380.	390.	400.	445.	1600.	6000.	—
1933	312,500	—	—	—	48,000.	72,000.	340,000.	—

Gold $20
(Double Eagle)

Coronet Head

"Twenty D.," no motto

PRICING SECTION

Designer: James B. Longacre. **Size:** 34 millimeters. **Weight:** 33.436 grams. **Composition:** 90% gold (0.9677 ounces), 10% copper. **Notes:** In 1861 the reverse was redesigned by Anthony C. Paquet, but it was withdrawn soon after its release. The letters in the inscriptions on the Paquet-reverse variety are taller than those on the regular reverse.

Date	Mintage	VF-20	XF-40	AU-50	MS-60	MS-65	Prf-65
1849	1			Unique, in Smithsonion collection			
1850	1,170,261	530.	625.	1000.	4100.	—	—
18500	141,000	600.	1100.	3000.	7500.	—	—
1851	2,087,155	435.	500.	650.	2750.	—	—
18510	315,000	600.	750.	1700.	11,500.	—	—
1852	2,053,026	410.	500.	675.	2100.	—	—
18520	190,000	600.	750.	2400.	12,000.	—	—
1853	1,261,326	435.	600.	800.	5500.	—	—
18530	71,000	625.	1000.	3400.	7500.	—	—
1854	757,899	435.	625.	950.	6500.	—	—
18540	3,250	13,500.	30,000.	60,000.	—	—	—
1854S	141,468	550.	650.	1000.	4750.	28,000.	—
1855	364,666	425.	545.	1000.	9000.	28,000.	—
18550	8,000	3000.	6000.	14,750.	—	—	—
1855S	879,675	435.	575.	1200.	8750.	—	—
1856	329,878	450.	545.	1000.	8750.	—	—
18560	2,250	15,000.	30,000.	60,000.	—	—	—
1856S	1,189,750	450.	545.	850.	5800.	—	—
1857	439,375	450.	550.	825.	5000.	—	—
18570	30,000	800.	1600.	4500.	—	—	—
1857S	970,500	450.	545.	850.	6000.	—	—
1858	211,714	525.	700.	1850.	6500.	—	—
18580	35,250	1000.	1750.	6000.	8000.	—	—
1858S	846,710	450.	545.	925.	8500.	—	—
1859	43,597	900.	2250.	8000.	30,000.	—	—
18590	9,100	2750.	6750.	13,750.	—	—	—
1859S	636,445	450.	600.	1000.	6750.	—	—
1860	577,670	450.	600.	800.	6500.	—	—
18600	6,600	3000.	6250.	14,000.	—	—	—
1860S	544,950	450.	600.	1450.	7250.	—	—
1861	2,976,453	435.	450.	625.	2750.	—	—

Paquet reverse

1861 Paquet rev.	Inc. Ab.						
			Bowers & Merena, Nov. 1988, MS-67, $660,000.				—
18610	17,741	1750.	3750.	7000.	—	—	—
1861S	768,000	525.	600.	1500.	7500.	—	—
1861S Paquet rev.	Inc. Ab.	4500.	9750.	20,000.	—	—	—
1862	92,133	725.	1600.	3750.	14,750.	—	—
1862S	854,173	525.	775.	1700.	8000.	—	—
1863	142,790	500.	900.	1800.	12,500.	—	—
1863S	966,570	450.	545.	1400.	6750.	—	—
1864	204,285	500.	700.	2000.	10,500.	—	—
1864S	793,660	500.	825.	2800.	10,000.	—	—
1865	351,200	475.	550.	1050.	7000.	—	—
1865S	1,042,500	450.	545.	1400.	8000.	—	—
1866S	Inc. Below	1350.	3750.	7750.	—	—	—

"Twenty D.," with motto

Notes: In 1866 the motto "In God We Trust" was added to the reverse above the eagle. The 1873 "closed-3" and "open-3" varieties are distinguished by the amount of space between the upper left and lower left serif in the 3 in the date.

Date	Mintage	VF-20	XF-40	AU-50	MS-60	MS-65	Prf-65
1866	698,775	430.	625.	1500.	8000.	—	—
1866S	842,250	500.	800.	2600.	—	—	—
1867	251,065	430.	500.	750.	1500.	—	—
1867S	920,750	430.	625.	1675.	13,250.	—	—
1868	98,600	550.	900.	2450.	7500.	—	—
1868S	837,500	430.	725.	1900.	10,250.	—	—
1869	175,155	430.	750.	2200.	6000.	44,000.	—
1869S	686,750	430.	600.	1750.	6250.	—	—
1870	155,185	500.	1000.	2700.	—	—	—
1870CC	3,789	24,000.	40,000.	65,000.	125,000.	—	—
1870S	982,000	430.	550.	775.	6000.	—	—
1871	80,150	700.	1100.	2250.	6500.	—	—
1871CC	17,387	1850.	4500.	10,500.	35,000.	—	—
1871S	928,000	430.	550.	850.	5500.	—	—
1872	251,880	430.	475.	700.	4000.	—	—
1872CC	26,900	1100.	1650.	6100.	14,000.	—	—
1872S	780,000	430.	525.	675.	2500.	—	—
1873 closed 3	Est. 208,925	600.	825.	1700.	15,000.	—	—
1873 open 3	Est. 1,500,900	430.	440.	475.	650.	—	—
1873CC	22,410	950.	1600.	4500.	16,000.	—	—
1873S	1,040,600	430.	475.	520.	1950.	—	—
1874	366,800	475.	550.	825.	1900.	—	—
1874CC	115,085	550.	700.	2350.	11,500.	—	—
1874S	1,214,000	430.	500.	650.	2200.	—	—
1875	295,740	490.	525.	550.	975.	—	—
1875CC	111,151	525.	650.	750.	2400.	—	—
1875S	1,230,000	430.	475.	550.	1100.	—	—
1876	583,905	430.	475.	525.	950.	—	—
1876CC	138,441	525.	725.	1150.	7500.	—	—
1876S	1,597,000	430.	440.	455.	1100.	—	—

"Twenty Dollars"

Notes: In 1877 the denomination on the reverse was changed to read "Twenty Dollars" instead of "Twenty D."

Date	Mintage	VF-20	XF-40	AU-50	MS-60	MS-65	Prf-65
1877	397,670	430.	500.	550.	875.	—	—
1877CC	42,565	600.	850.	1600.	—	—	—
1877S	1,735,000	430.	445.	500.	1000.	—	—
1878	543,645	430.	500.	550.	750.	—	—
1878CC	13,180	750.	1850.	5250.	18,000.	—	—
1878S	1,739,000	430.	440.	475.	1500.	—	—
1879	207,630	450.	525.	575.	1650.	—	—
1879CC	10,708	850.	1500.	5250.	—	—	—
1879O	2,325	3250.	4250.	12,500.	45,000.	—	—
1879S	1,223,800	430.	500.	550.	1650.	—	—
1880	51,456	435.	475.	850.	—	—	—
1880S	836,000	450.	575.	750.	—	—	—
1881	2,260	3500.	7500.	16,500.	45,000.	—	—
1881S	727,000	430.	550.	700.	—	—	—
1882	630	8000.	15,000.	25,000.	50,000.	—	—
1882CC	39,140	675.	775.	1150.	4400.	—	—
1882S	1,125,000	430.	475.	510.	1000.	—	—
1883	92	—	—	—	—	—	—
1883CC	59,962	600.	625.	1000.	4700.	—	—
1883S	1,189,000	430.	425.	450.	725.	—	—
1884	71	Stacks, Nov. 1989, proof, $71,500.				—	—
1884CC	81,139	525.	800.	950.	2900.	—	—
1884S	916,000	430.	440.	450.	550.	—	—
1885	828	6500.	8750.	16,500.	30,000.	—	—
1885CC	9,450	1000.	1800.	4000.	12,000.	—	—
1885S	683,500	430.	475.	490.	575.	—	—
1886	1,106	8000.	12,500.	25,000.	32,000.	—	—
1887	121	—	—	—	—	—	65,000.
1887S	283,000	460.	490.	550.	1000.	—	—
1888	226,266	435.	475.	525.	1100.	—	—
1888S	859,600	430.	475.	500.	585.	—	—
1889	44,111	650.	700.	750.	1175.	—	—

1907-S Gold $20
Grade VF-20

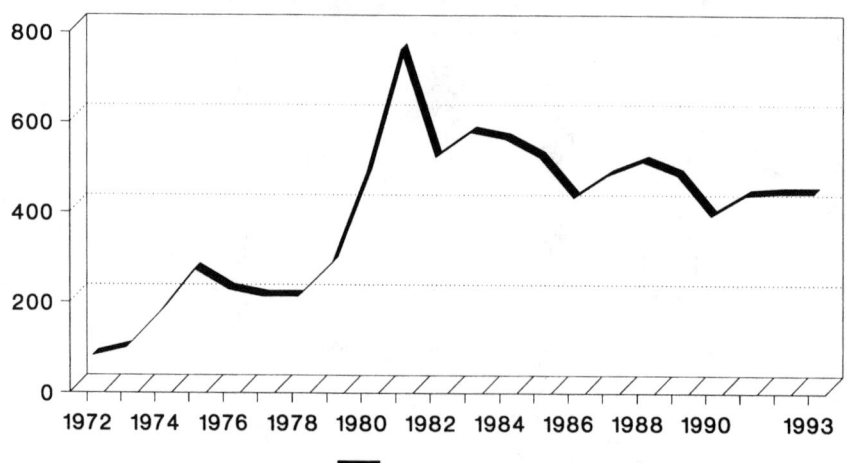

■ Retail Price

Source: COIN PRICES

Date	Mintage	VF-20	XF-40	AU-50	MS-60	MS-65	Prf-65
1889CC	30,945	650.	700.	1200.	3500.	—	—
1889S	774,700	430.	475.	500.	700.	—	—
1890	75,995	600.	675.	700.	1000.	—	—
1890CC	91,209	675.	725.	950.	4250.	—	—
1890S	802,750	435.	480.	500.	1400.	—	—
1891	1,442	3100.	4250.	8250.	27,000.	—	—
1891CC	5,000	1900.	2900.	5500.	13,750.	—	—
1891S	1,288,125	430.	440.	450.	525.	—	—
1892	4,523	1200.	1750.	2750.	7000.	—	—
1892CC	27,265	675.	850.	1550.	5750.	—	—
1892S	930,150	430.	440.	450.	520.	—	—
1893	344,339	430.	450.	475.	550.	—	—
1893CC	18,402	675.	925.	1300.	2800.	—	—
1893S	996,175	430.	450.	475.	500.	—	—
1894	1,368,990	430.	440.	450.	520.	—	—
1894S	1,048,550	430.	440.	475.	540.	—	—
1895	1,114,656	430.	440.	450.	520.	—	—
1895S	1,143,500	430.	440.	460.	550.	7200.	—
1896	792,663	430.	440.	450.	520.	—	—
1896S	1,403,925	430.	440.	450.	520.	—	—
1897	1,383,261	430.	440.	450.	520.	—	—
1897S	1,470,250	430.	440.	450.	520.	—	—
1898	170,470	450.	450.	475.	725.	—	—
1898S	2,575,175	430.	440.	450.	520.	7100.	—
1899	1,669,384	430.	440.	450.	520.	7100.	—
1899S	2,010,300	430.	440.	450.	520.	—	—
1900	1,874,584	430.	440.	450.	520.	7100.	—
1900S	2,459,500	430.	445.	470.	575.	7200.	—
1901	111,526	430.	440.	450.	575.	7000.	—
1901S	1,596,000	430.	440.	450.	550.	—	—
1902	31,254	550.	600.	700.	1025.	7200.	—
1902S	1,753,625	430.	440.	450.	500.	—	—
1903	287,428	430.	440.	450.	520.	7000.	—
1903S	954,000	430.	440.	450.	520.	7200.	—
1904	6,256,797	430.	440.	450.	520.	4500.	—
1904S	5,134,175	430.	440.	450.	520.	7000.	—
1905	59,011	525.	550.	575.	1475.	—	—
1905S	1,813,000	430.	405.	415.	500.	—	—
1906	69,690	600.	640.	800.	1000.	7000.	—
1906D	620,250	430.	440.	450.	525.	—	—
1906S	2,065,750	430.	440.	450.	520.	—	—
1907	1,451,864	430.	440.	450.	520.	7200.	—
1907D	842,250	430.	440.	450.	520.	7000.	—
1907S	2,165,800	430.	440.	450.	525.	—	—

1908-D Gold $20
Grade MS-60

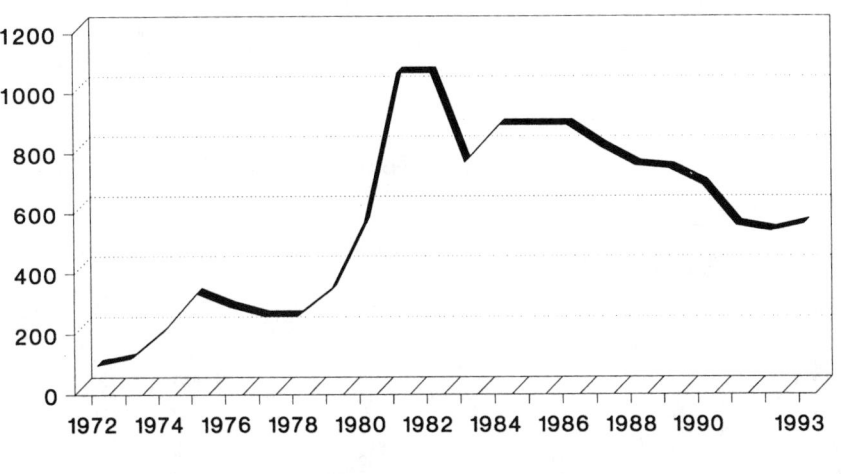

■ Retail Price

Source: COIN PRICES

Saint-Gaudens

No motto

Designer: Augustus Saint-Gaudens. **Size:** 34 millimeters. **Weight:** 33.436 grams. **Composition:** 90% gold (0.9677 ounces), 10% copper. **Notes:** The "Roman numerals" varieties for 1907 use Roman numerals for the date instead of Arabic numerals. The lettered-edge varieties have "E Pluribus Unum" on the edge, with stars between the words.

Date	Mintage	VF-20	XF-40	AU-50	MS-60	MS-63	MS-65	Prf-65
1907 extremely high relief, plain edge								
—			Unique	—		—	—	—
1907 extremely high relief, lettered edge								
Unrecorded			Prf-68 Private sale 1990 $1,500,000.			—	—	—
1907 high relief, Roman numerals, plain edge								
			Unique - AU-55 $150,000.			—	—	—
1907 high relief, Roman numerals, wire rim								
11,250	2500.	3600.	4000.	6400.	11,000.	30,000.	—
1907 high relief, Roman numerals, flat rim								
Inc. Ab.	3000.	4000.	4500.	6500.	12,500.	35,000.	—
1907 large letters on edge							Unique	—
1907 small letters on edge								
361,667	440.	465.	475.	545.	950.	4550.	—
1908	4,271,551	445.	450.	475.	490.	700.	1650.	—
1908D	663,750	440.	450.	470.	545.	1100.	10,750.	—

With motto

Notes: In 1908 the motto "In God We Trust" was added at the bottom of the reverse.

Date	Mintage	VF-20	XF-40	AU-50	MS-60	MS-63	MS-65	Prf-65
1908	156,359	440.	450.	465.	585.	1800.	13,250.	41,000.
1908D	349,500	440.	450.	465.	545.	1125.	3650.	—
1908S	22,000	800.	1150.	1350.	3000.	9600.	27,500.	—
1909/8	161,282	450.	500.	600.	1800.	6850.	48,000.	—
1909	Inc. Ab.	440.	450.	500.	875.	10,000.	38,500.	45,000.
1909D	52,500	575.	600.	650.	1325.	3250.	36,000.	—
1909S	2,774,925	440.	450.	460.	545.	775.	4800.	—
1910	482,167	440.	460.	470.	545.	880.	7900.	50,000.
1910D	429,000	440.	450.	460.	545.	870.	4550.	—
1910S	2,128,250	440.	450.	480.	545.	1100.	14,000.	—
1911	197,350	440.	450.	510.	545.	2300.	11,000.	41,000.
1911D	846,500	440.	450.	460.	550.	775.	2050.	—
1911S	775,750	440.	450.	460.	550.	875.	7200.	—
1912	149,824	450.	450.	510.	565.	2750.	13,250.	41,000.
1913	168,838	440.	460.	480.	565.	4150.	18,000.	41,000.
1913D	393,500	440.	450.	460.	545.	1000.	6000.	—
1913S	34,000	440.	465.	540.	1150.	5600.	27,500.	—
1914	95,320	450.	475.	535.	680.	2700.	11,000.	41,000.
1914D	453,000	440.	450.	460.	545.	800.	3750.	—
1914S	1,498,000	440.	450.	460.	545.	800.	3500.	—
1915	152,050	440.	475.	520.	630.	2700.	14,000.	56,000.
1915S	567,500	440.	450.	460.	545.	800.	2150.	—
1916S	796,000	440.	450.	465.	575.	800.	2050.	—
1920	228,250	440.	450.	460.	545.	1400.	15,500.	—
1920S	558,000	4500.	6000.	7200.	18,000.	39,500.	96,000.	—
1921	528,500	7200.	9550.	15,000.	30,000.	60,000.	144,000.	—
1922	1,375,500	440.	450.	460.	545.	800.	6000.	—
1922S	2,658,000	475.	525.	600.	740.	1825.	24,000.	—
1923	566,000	440.	450.	460.	545.	800.	7200.	—
1923D	1,702,250	440.	450.	460.	545.	800.	1700.	—
1924	4,323,500	440.	450.	460.	545.	775.	1550.	—
1924D	3,049,500	700.	1150.	1350.	2100.	5200.	48,000.	—
1924S	2,927,500	700.	800.	975.	1700.	4350.	42,000.	—
1925	2,831,750	440.	450.	460.	545.	775.	1400.	—
1925D	2,938,500	875.	1100.	1300.	2250.	6500.	45,000.	—
1925S	3,776,500	875.	950.	1200.	4700.	24,000.	60,000.	—
1926	816,750	440.	450.	460.	545.	775.	1750.	—
1926D	481,000	1000.	1350.	1600.	3500.	24,000.	60,000.	—
1926S	2,041,500	700.	950.	1100.	1900.	3500.	38,000.	—
1927	2,946,750	440.	450.	460.	545.	775.	1400.	—
1927D	180,000			Stack's, Mar.1991, MS-65, $522,500.			—	—
1927S	3,107,000	2000.	4500.	5500.	10,500.	26,000.	100,000.	—
1928	8,816,000	440.	450.	460.	545.	775.	1400.	—
1929	1,779,750	4000.	7000.	10,000.	15,000.	19,000.	57,000.	—
1930S	74,000	6000.	9000.	13,000.	22,500.	36,000.	72,000.	—
1931	2,938,250	4250.	8500.	10,000.	15,000.	24,000.	66,000.	—
1931D	106,500	5500.	7500.	9500.	15,000.	21,500.	60,000.	—
1932	1,101,750	7000.	9500.	12,000.	14,500.	20,000.	54,000.	—
1933	445,500			None placed in circulation			—	—

Proof sets

Notes: Proof sets have been sold off and on by the U.S. Mint since 1858. Listings here are for sets from what is commonly called the modern era, since 1936. Values for earlier individual proof coins are included in the regular date listings. Sets were not offered in years not listed. Since 1968, proof versions of circulating U.S. coins have been produced at the San Francisco Mint; before that they were produced at the Philadelphia Mint. In 1942 the five-cent coin was struck in two compositions. Some proof sets for that year contain only one type (five-coin set); others contain both types. Two types of packaging were used in 1955: a box and sealed Pliofilm packets. The 1960 large-date and small-date sets are distinguished by the size of the date on the cent. Some 1968 sets are missing the mintmark on the dime, the result of an error in the preparation of an obverse die. The 1970 large-date and small-date sets are distinguished by the size of the date on the cent. Some 1970 sets are missing the mintmark on the dime, the result of an error in the preparation of an obverse die. Some 1971 sets are missing the mintmark on the five-cent piece, the result of an error in the preparation of an obverse die. The 1976 three-piece set contains the quarter, half dollar and dollar with the Bicentennial designs. The 1979 and 1981 Type II sets have clearer mintmarks than the Type I sets for those years. Some 1983 sets are missing the mintmark on the dime, the result of an error in the preparation of an obverse die. Prestige sets contain the five regular-issue coins plus a commemorative silver dollar from that year: 1983, Olympics; 1984, Olympics; 1986, Statue of Liberty; 1987, Constitution Bicentennial; 1988, Olympics; 1989, Congress Bicentennial; 1990, Eisenhower; and 1991, Mount Rushmore. The 1992 prestige set contains the Olympic silver dollar and half dollar from that year.

Date	Sets Sold	Issue Price	Value
1936	3,837	1.89	3200.
1937	5,542	1.89	2100.
1938	8,045	1.89	1050.
1939	8,795	1.89	1030.
1940	11,246	1.89	760.
1941	15,287	1.89	680.
1942 6 coins	21,120	1.89	700.
1942 5 coins	Inc. Ab.	1.89	680.
1950	51,386	2.10	420.
1951	57,500	2.10	300.
1952	81,980	2.10	160.
1953	128,800	2.10	120.
1954	233,300	2.10	83.00
1955 box	378,200	2.10	63.00
1955 flat pack	Inc. Ab.	2.10	69.00
1956	669,384	2.10	38.00
1957	1,247,952	2.10	15.00
1958	875,652	2.10	22.00
1959	1,149,291	2.10	17.00
1960 large date	1,691,602	2.10	11.00
1960 small date	Inc. Ab.	2.10	24.00
1961	3,028,244	2.10	9.00
1962	3,218,019	2.10	9.00
1963	3,075,645	2.10	10.00
1964	3,950,762	2.10	9.00
1968S	3,041,509	5.00	5.00
1968 S no mint mark dime	—	5.00	7950.
1969S	2,934,631	5.00	5.00
1970S large date	2,632,810	5.00	7.50

Date	Sets Sold	Issue Price	Value
1970S small date	Inc. Ab.	5.00	98.00
1970S no mint mark dime			
	Est. 2,200	5.00	480.
1971S	3,224,138	5.00	5.40
1971S no mint mark nickel			
	Est. 1,655	5.00	720.
1972S	3,267,667	5.00	5.00
1973S	2,769,624	7.00	6.00
1974S	2,617,350	7.00	6.00
1975S	2,909,369	7.00	9.00
1976S 3 coins	3,998,621	12.00	10.00
1976S	4,149,730	7.00	7.50
1977S	3,251,152	9.00	6.80
1978S	3,127,788	9.00	7.50
1979S Type I	3,677,175	9.00	8.00
1979S Type II	Inc.Ab.	9.00	77.00
1980S	3,547,030	10.00	7.55
1981S Type I	4,063,083	11.00	7.55
1981S Type II	—	11.00	235.
1982S	3,857,479	11.00	5.50
1983S Prestige set	140,361	59.00	109.
1983S	3,138,765	11.00	7.00
1983S no mint mark dime	—	11.00	500.
1984S Prestige set	316,680	59.00	43.00
1984S	2,748,430	11.00	11.50
1985S	3,362,821	11.00	7.50
1986S Prestige set	599,317	48.50	35.00
1986S	2,411,180	11.00	27.50
1987S	3,972,233	11.00	5.50
1987S Prestige set	435,495	45.00	34.00
1988S	3,031,287	11.00	12.50
1988S Prestige set	231,661	45.00	46.00
1989S	3,009,107	11.00	10.00
1989S Prestige set	211,087	45.00	52.00
1990S	2,793,433	11.00	21.50
1990S no S 1¢	3,555	11.00	2350.
1990S Prestige set	506,126	45.00	35.00
1990S no S 1¢ Prestige set	—	45.00	2350.
1991S	—	11.00	24.00
1991S Prestige set	—	59.00	85.00
1992S	—	12.50	21.00
1992S Prestige set	—	59.00	69.00
1992S Silver	—	21.00	27.00
1992S Silver premier	—	37.00	39.00

1952 Proof Set
Issue Price: $2.10

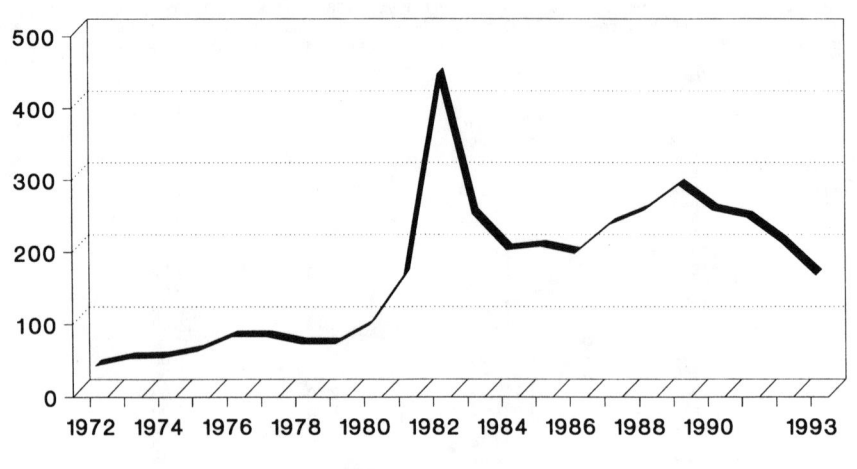

Retail Price

Source: COIN PRICES

Mint sets

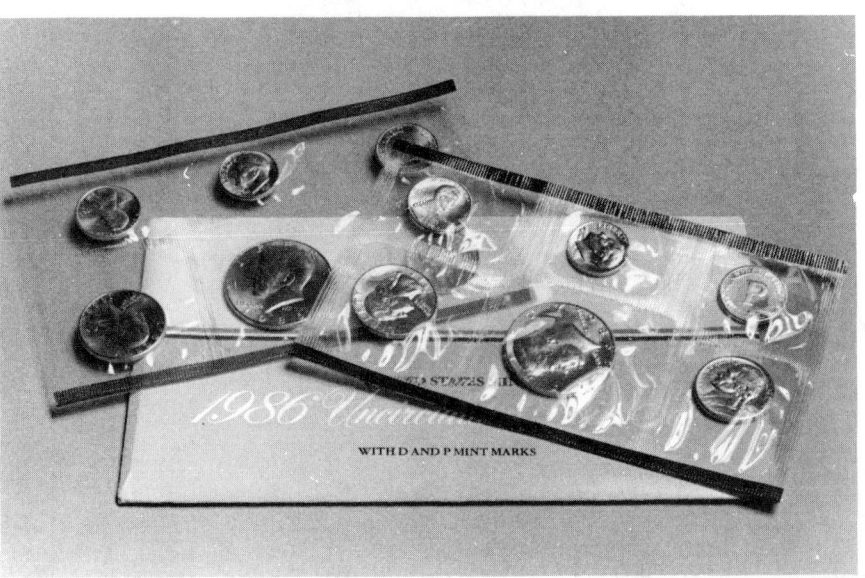

WITH D AND P MINT MARKS

Notes: Mint, or uncirculated, sets contain one uncirculated coin of each denomination from each mint produced for circulation that year. Values listed here are only for those sets packaged and marketed by the U.S. Mint. Sets were not offered in years not listed. In years when the Mint did not offer the sets, some private companies packaged and marketed uncirculated sets. Mint sets from 1947 through 1958 contain two examples of each coin mounted in cardboard holders, which caused the coins to tarnish. Beginning in 1959, the sets have been packaged in sealed Pliofilm packets and include only one specimen of each non-commemorative coin authorized for that year. Listings for 1965, 1966 and 1967 are for "special mint sets," which were of higher quality than regular mint sets and were prooflike. The 1965 sets were packaged in Pliofilm; the '66 and '67 sets in plastic cases. The 1970 large-date and small-date varieties are distinguished by the size of the date on the cent. The 1976 three-piece set contains the quarter, half dollar and dollar with the Bicentennial design. The 1971 and 1972 sets do not include a dollar coin; the 1979 set does not include an S-mintmarked dollar.

Date	Sets Sold	Issue Price	Value
1947	Est. 5,000	4.87	820.
1948	Est. 6,000	4.92	250.
1949	Est. 5,200	5.45	645.
1950	None issued	—	—
1951	8,654	6.75	415.
1952	11,499	6.14	280.
1953	15,538	6.14	265.
1954	25,599	6.19	115.
1955	49,656	3.57	76.00
1956	45,475	3.34	67.00
1957	32,324	4.40	101.
1958	50,314	4.43	99.00
1959	187,000	2.40	20.00
1960	260,485	2.40	14.00
1961	223,704	2.40	15.50
1962	385,285	2.40	14.50
1963	606,612	2.40	10.00
1964	1,008,108	2.40	8.50
1965 SMS*	2,360,000	4.00	3.90
1966 SMS*	2,261,583	4.00	5.60
1967 SMS*	1,863,344	4.00	7.00
1968	2,105,128	2.50	2.95
1969	1,817,392	2.50	3.20
1970 large date	2,038,134	2.50	12.50
1970 small date	Inc. Ab.	2.50	19.00
1971	2,193,396	3.50	3.20
1972	2,750,000	3.50	2.65
1973	1,767,691	6.00	8.50
1974	1,975,981	6.00	6.45
1975	1,921,488	6.00	7.30
1976 3 coins	4,908,319	9.00	10.50
1976	1,892,513	6.00	7.00

Date	Sets Sold	Issue Price	Value
1977	2,006,869	7.00	6.00
1978	2,162,609	7.00	6.15
1979	2,526,000	8.00	5.35
1980	2,815,066	9.00	6.75
1981	2,908,145	11.00	7.50
1982 & 1983	None issued	—	—
1984	1,832,857	7.00	5.00
1985	1,710,571	7.00	6.50
1986	1,153,536	7.00	22.50
1987	2,890,758	7.00	5.30
1988	1,646,204	7.00	3.90
1989	1,987,915	7.00	3.50
1990	1,809,184	7.00	6.30
1991	—	7.00	7.00
1992	—	7.00	9.10
1993	—	7.00	9.50

Uncirculated rolls

Notes: Listings are for rolls containing uncirculated coins. Large-date and small-date varieties for 1960 and 1970 apply to the one-cent coins.

Date	Cents	Nickels	Dimes	Quarters	Halves
1934	225.	1890.	1250.	1100.	1550.
1934D	900.	3800.	3400.	5550.	—
1934S	—	—	—	—	—
1935	95.00	1000.	900.	855.	1250.
1935D	195.	2400.	3300.	5650.	4050.
1935S	500.	1650.	1650.	4550.	6300.
1936	73.00	750.	750.	800.	1135.
1936D	145.	900.	2000.	—	2400.
1936S	110.	1000.	1150.	3650.	3300.
1937	57.00	500.	700.	750.	1200.
1937D	90.00	750.	1250.	1500.	4150.
1937S	100.	750.	1325.	5400.	3150.
1938	67.00	95.00	1010.	2140.	1900.
1938D	100.	135.	1050.	—	—
1938D Buffalo	—	450.	—	—	—
1938S	70.00	135.	1400.	2455.	—
1939	38.00	64.00	750.	595.	1250.
1939D	125.	1640.	650.	1100.	1300.
1939S	64.00	705.	1550.	2585.	2500.
1940	34.00	27.50	425.	490.	950.
1940D	29.00	82.00	750.	2250.	—
1940S	38.00	107.	700.	600.	1250.
1941	63.00	36.00	300.	250.	850.
1941D	140.	79.00	750.	900.	1250.
1941S	125.	165.	400.	950.	3500.
1942	24.00	164.	300.	230.	850.
1942P	—	315.	—	—	—
1942D	17.50	790.	700.	450.	1250.
1942S	180.	285.	800.	3200.	1650.
1943	24.00	125.	300.	160.	850.
1943D	39.00	110.	500.	600.	1650.
1943S	85.00	180.	750.	1150.	1400.
1944	17.50	125.	300.	125.	850.
1944D	19.00	415.	500.	315.	1100.
1944S	9.50	205.	440.	345.	1200.
1945	21.00	160.	285.	100.	850.
1945D	9.50	140.	300.	320.	1000.
1945S	7.00	140.	300.	215.	1150.
1946	10.50	26.50	32.00	180.	1000.
1946D	6.50	20.00	35.00	120.	850.
1946S	9.00	14.00	70.00	105.	1000.
1947	44.00	27.50	70.00	245.	1050.
1947D	5.70	26.50	100.	170.	950.
1947S	19.00	12.00	90.00	120.	—
1948	24.00	12.00	210.	135.	400.
1948D	11.50	43.00	160.	160.	285.
1948S	21.00	15.00	90.00	195.	—
1949	22.50	21.50	550.	800.	1000.
1949D	22.50	34.00	225.	300.	800.
1949S	48.00	48.00	910.	—	1200.
1950	19.50	21.00	90.00	100.	750.
1950D	20.00	225.	65.00	105.	565.
1950S	19.50	—	505.	250.	—
1951	26.50	44.00	65.00	135.	330.
1951D	11.50	33.00	80.00	120.	800.
1951S	28.00	95.00	265.	650.	600.
1952	17.50	35.50	75.00	90.00	215.
1952D	6.90	35.50	40.00	105.	175.
1952S	56.50	21.50	225.	380.	820.
1953	4.40	6.65	70.00	85.00	330.
1953D	3.90	6.30	22.00	50.00	160.
1953S	11.00	12.50	25.00	100.	285.

Date	Cents	Nickels	Dimes	Quarters	Halves
1954	7.50	5.00	22.00	50.00	160.
1954D	3.80	7.55	28.00	50.00	135.
1954S	3.15	7.50	25.00	55.00	140.
1955	4.15	11.50	30.00	55.00	150.
1955D	3.30	6.30	22.00	65.00	—
1955S	16.50	—	22.00	—	—
1956	2.50	3.80	30.00	55.00	160.
1956D	2.15	3.15	32.00	70.00	—
1957	1.90	4.25	25.00	50.00	145.
1957D	1.45	3.00	35.00	50.00	120.
1958	1.25	3.15	27.00	50.00	120.
1958D	1.45	3.00	25.00	45.00	105.
1959	.75	2.85	22.50	45.00	120.
1959D	.75	2.65	22.00	45.00	135.
1960 lg. dt.	.75	3.00	22.50	44.00	105.
1960 sm. dt.	73.00	—	—	—	—
1960D lg. dt.	.75	3.00	22.50	44.00	100.
1960D sm. dt.	1.10	—	—	—	—
1961	.85	3.15	22.50	45.00	100.
1961D	.75	3.00	22.50	44.00	110.
1962	.75	2.85	22.50	44.00	75.00
1962D	.85	3.45	22.50	45.00	75.00
1963	.85	3.00	22.50	44.00	55.00
1963D	.85	2.65	22.50	44.00	55.00
1964	.90	4.40	22.50	44.00	44.00
1964D	.90	4.40	22.50	44.00	44.00
1965	1.05	2.85	7.50	16.00	19.00
1966	.65	3.15	9.50	21.00	18.00
1967	1.10	4.55	9.50	32.00	17.50
1968	1.70	—	8.80	25.00	—
1968D	2.05	3.50	8.80	25.00	19.00
1968S	.70	3.80	—	—	—
1969	5.00	—	19.00	25.00	—
1969D	.85	5.00	11.50	25.00	19.00
1969S	1.25	5.00	—	—	—
1970	3.50	—	9.00	19.50	—
1970D	1.00	3.50	9.00	19.00	215.
1970S	1.10	3.50	—	—	—
1970S sm. dt.	1510.	—	—	—	—
1971	5.50	14.00	11.50	26.50	15.50
1971D	6.50	5.00	9.50	31.50	15.50
1971S	4.15	—	—	—	—
1972	1.00	4.15	10.00	14.00	19.00
1972D	1.05	5.00	9.00	19.50	19.00
1972S	1.05	—	—	—	—
1973	1.10	3.80	9.00	19.50	19.50
1973D	.75	3.50	9.00	22.50	17.50
1973S	1.00	—	—	—	—
1974	.70	3.00	9.00	19.00	15.50
1974D	.85	6.30	9.00	22.50	15.50
1974S	2.40	—	—	—	—
1975	1.00	10.10	12.00	—	—
1975D	1.45	6.30	10.00	—	—
1976	1.00	11.35	15.00	19.50	15.50
1976D	3.15	11.35	15.00	19.00	14.00
1977	1.25	3.80	7.55	15.50	25.00
1977D	.85	7.55	7.90	15.50	25.00
1978	1.05	3.45	8.50	19.50	25.00
1978D	1.05	3.80	9.00	15.50	24.00
1979	1.25	3.45	7.55	17.00	19.00
1979D	.85	4.75	7.55	17.00	17.50
1980	1.00	4.00	7.55	14.00	19.00
1980D	1.00	3.15	7.55	14.00	19.50
1981	1.00	3.45	7.55	15.50	21.00
1981D	.90	3.45	7.00	15.50	19.50
1982	.90	7.55	50.00	170.	17.50
1982D	.90	13.25	12.50	40.00	17.50
1983	1.25	15.00	31.50	210.	19.50
1983D	1.40	15.00	31.50	240.	19.00
1984	1.60	5.00	11.50	30.00	19.00
1984D	8.80	5.40	14.00	70.00	19.50
1985	2.40	6.30	13.00	65.00	20.00
1985D	1.55	6.50	10.00	110.	19.00
1986	5.00	5.80	14.00	95.00	21.00
1986D	1.75	7.90	14.00	110.	19.50
1987	3.15	3.80	7.90	19.00	40.00
1987D	1.75	3.80	7.90	15.50	35.00
1988	1.55	4.15	9.15	19.00	15.50
1988D	1.25	4.25	8.20	21.00	17.00
1989	.90	3.15	6.95	17.00	14.00
1990	.90	3.15	7.20	17.00	14.00
1990D	.95	3.50	7.20	14.00	15.50
1991	.95	3.50	7.90	14.00	15.50
1991D	.75	3.50	7.90	14.00	14.00
1992	.95	3.50	7.30	14.00	16.00
1992D	.75	3.50	7.30	14.00	14.00

Commemoratives, 1892-1954

Quarter

Designer: Charles E. Barber. **Size:** 24.3 millimeters. **Weight:** 6.25 grams. **Composition:** 90% silver (0.1809 ounces), 10% copper.

Date	Event	Mintage	AU-50	MS-60	MS-63	MS-64	MS-65
1893	Isabella (25¢)	24,214	215.	360.	700.	1200.	2800.

Half dollars

Designers: Alabama: Laura G. Fraser. Albany: Gertrude K. Lathrop. Arkansas: Edward E. Burr. Bay Bridge: Jacques Schnier. Boone: Augustus Lukeman. Bridgeport: Henry Kreis. California Jubilee: Jo Mora. Cincinnati: Constance Ort-mayer. Cleveland-Great Lakes: Brenda Putnam. Columbia: A. Wolfe Davidson. Columbian Expo: Olin L. Warner. Connecticut: Henry Kreis. Delaware: Carl L. Schmitz. Elgin: Trygve Rovelstad. Gettysburg: Frank Vittor. Grant: Laura G. Fraser. Hawaiian: Juliette M. Fraser. Hudson: Chester Beach. Huguenot-Walloon: George T. Morgan. Lincoln-Illinois: George T. Morgan. Iowa: Adam Pietz. Lexington-Concord: Chester Beach. Long Island: Howard K. Weinman. Lynchburg: Charles Keck. Maine: Anthony de Francisci. Maryland: Hans Schuler. Missouri: Robert Aitken. Monroe: Chester Beach. New Rochelle: Gertrude K. Lathrop. Norfolk: William M. and Marjorie E. Simpson. Oregon: James E. and Laura G. Fraser. Panama-Pacific: Charles E. Barber (obverse) and George T. Morgan (reverse). Pilgrim: Cyrus E. Dallin. Rhode Island: Arthur G. Carey and John H. Benson. Roanoke: William M. Simpson. Robinson-Arkansas: Henry Kreis (obverse) and Edward E. Burr. San Diego: Robert Aitken. Sesquicentennial: John F. Lewis. Spanish Trail: L.W. Hoffecker. Stone Mountain: Gutzon Borglum. Texas: Pompeo Coppini. Fort Vancouver: Laura G. Fraser. Vermont: Charles Keck. Booker T. Washington: Isaac S. Hathaway. Washington-Carver: Isaac S. Hathaway. Wisconsin: David Parsons. York County: Walter H. Rich. **Size:** 30.6 millimeters. **Weight:** 12.5 grams. **Composition:** 90% silver (0.3618 ounces), 10% copper. **Notes:** Values for ''PDS sets'' contain one example each from the Philadelphia, Denver and San Francisco mints. ''Type coin'' values are for the most inexpensive single coin available from the date and mintmark combinations listed. The Alabama half-dollar varieties are distinguished by whether ''2x2'' appears on the obverse behind the head. The Grant half-dollar varieties are distinguished by whether a star appears above the word ''Grant'' on the obverse. The Missouri half-dollar varieties are distinguished by whether ''2 ☆ 2'' appears on the obverse to the left of the head.

2x2

Date	Event	Mintage	AU-50	MS-60	MS-63	MS-64	MS-65
1921	Alabama 2X2	6,006	145.	275.	655.	1200.	4200.
1921	Alabama	59,038	95.00	195.	620.	950.	4150.

Date	Event	Mintage	AU-50	MS-60	MS-63	MS-64	MS-65
1936	Albany	17,671	195.	215.	245.	340.	825.

Date	Event	Mintage	AU-50	MS-60	MS-63	MS-64	MS-65
1937	Antietam	18,028	410.	450.	460.	485.	655.

Date	Event	Mintage	AU-50	MS-60	MS-63	MS-64	MS-65
1935	Arkansas PDS set	5,505	—	230.	255.	345.	1250.
1936	Arkansas PDS set	9,660	—	230.	255.	345.	1250.
1937	Arkansas PDS set	5,505	—	230.	255.	365.	1500.
1938	Arkansas PDS set	3,155	—	365.	580.	910.	2450.
1939	Arkansas PDS set	2,104	—	730.	950.	1600.	2600.
	Arkansas type coin	—	73.00	80.00	85.00	115.	410.

See also Robinson-Arkansas

Date	Event	Mintage	AU-50	MS-60	MS-63	MS-64	MS-65
1936	Bay Bridge	71,424	85.00	115.	135.	180.	560.

"1934" added to 1935-1938 issues

Date	Event	Mintage	AU-50	MS-60	MS-63	MS-64	MS-65
1934	Boone	10,007	92.00	97.00	110.	135.	195.
1935	Boone PDS set w/1934	5,005	—	545.	970.	1200.	1700.
1935	Boone PDS set	2,003	—	255.	275.	290.	545.
1936	Boone PDS set	5,005	—	255.	275.	290.	545.
1937	Boone PDS set	2,506	—	655.	710.	900.	1150.
1938	Boone PDS set	2,100	—	825.	910.	1400.	1750.
	Boone type coin	—	73.00	85.00	90.00	110.	180.

Date	Event	Mintage	AU-50	MS-60	MS-63	MS-64	MS-65
1936	Bridgeport	25,015	95.00	110.	120.	195.	475.

Date	Event	Mintage	AU-50	MS-60	MS-63	MS-64	MS-65
1925S	California Jubilee	86,594	85.00	110.	215.	365.	1100.

Date	Event	Mintage	AU-50	MS-60	MS-63	MS-64	MS-65
1936	Cincinnati PDS set	5,005	—	765.	835.	1100.	2400.
1936	Cincinnati type coin	—	215.	255.	275.	365.	800.

Date	Event	Mintage	AU-50	MS-60	MS-63	MS-64	MS-65
1936	Cleveland - Great Lakes	50,030	61.00	68.00	73.00	110.	340.

Date	Event	Mintage	AU-50	MS-60	MS-63	MS-64	MS-65
1936	Columbia PDS set	9,007	—	560.	610.	695.	945.
1936	Columbia type coin	—	175.	195.	215.	235.	325.

1892 Columbian Expo Half
Grade MS-60

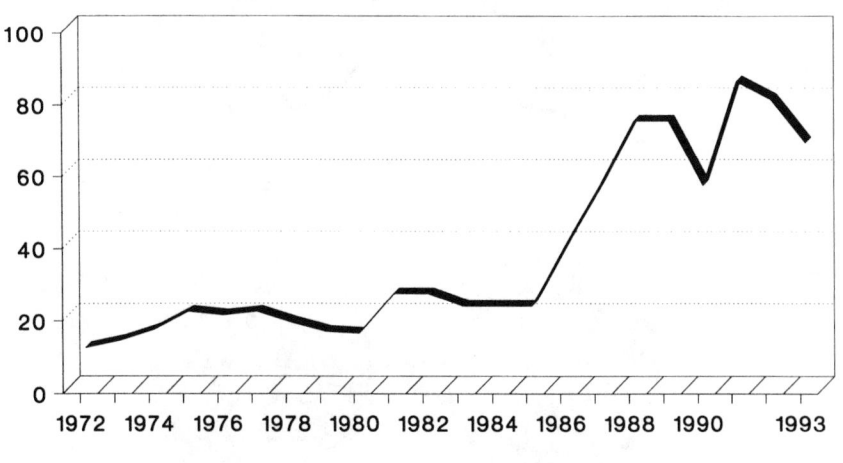

■ Retail Price

Source: COIN PRICES

Date	Event	Mintage	AU-50	MS-60	MS-63	MS-64	MS-65
1892	Columbian Expo	950,000	20.00	68.00	180.	420.	1400.
1893	Columbian Expo	1,550,405	17.00	61.00	165.	425.	1650.

Date	Event	Mintage	AU-50	MS-60	MS-63	MS-64	MS-65
1935	Connecticut	25,018	175.	210.	255.	400.	1050.

Date	Event	Mintage	AU-50	MS-60	MS-63	MS-64	MS-65
1936	Delaware	20,993	190.	215.	230.	275.	800.

Date	Event	Mintage	AU-50	MS-60	MS-63	MS-64	MS-65
1936	Elgin	20,015	180.	205.	230.	255.	425.

Date	Event	Mintage	AU-50	MS-60	MS-63	MS-64	MS-65
1936	Gettysburg	26,928	180.	225.	255.	350.	750.

Star added

Date	Event	Mintage	AU-50	MS-60	MS-63	MS-64	MS-65
1922	Grant with star	4,256	535.	885.	2450.	3550.	10,000.
1922	Grant	67,405	61.00	80.00	225.	400.	1200.

Date	Event	Mintage	AU-50	MS-60	MS-63	MS-64	MS-65
1928	Hawaiian	10,008	825.	1095.	1650.	2600.	4950.

Date	Event	Mintage	AU-50	MS-60	MS-63	MS-64	MS-65
1935	Hudson	10,008	410.	465.	600.	805.	2450.

Date	Event	Mintage	AU-50	MS-60	MS-63	MS-64	MS-65
1924	Huguenot-Walloon	142,080	63.00	85.00	115.	250.	950.

Date	Event	Mintage	AU-50	MS-60	MS-63	MS-64	MS-65
1918	Lincoln-Illinois	100,058	61.00	92.00	105.	210.	750.

Date	Event	Mintage	AU-50	MS-60	MS-63	MS-64	MS-65
1946	Iowa	100,057	61.00	73.00	80.00	85.00	115.

Date	Event	Mintage	AU-50	MS-60	MS-63	MS-64	MS-65
1925	Lexington-Concord	162,013	58.00	68.00	105.	215.	1200.

Date	Event	Mintage	AU-50	MS-60	MS-63	MS-64	MS-65
1936	Long Island	81,826	61.00	68.00	80.00	135.	560.

Date	Event	Mintage	AU-50	MS-60	MS-63	MS-64	MS-65
1936	Lynchburg	20,013	150.	160.	215.	290.	595.

Date	Event	Mintage	AU-50	MS-60	MS-63	MS-64	MS-65
1920	Maine	50,028	61.00	80.00	170.	300.	1000.

Date	Event	Mintage	AU-50	MS-60	MS-63	MS-64	MS-65
1934	Maryland	25,015	120.	140.	155.	205.	445.

2 ☆ 4

Date	Event	Mintage	AU-50	MS-60	MS-63	MS-64	MS-65
1921	Missouri 2 ☆ 4	5,000	245.	380.	850.	1700.	7400.
1921	Missouri	15,428	180.	310.	800.	1500.	7400.

Date	Event	Mintage	AU-50	MS-60	MS-63	MS-64	MS-65
1923S	Monroe	274,077	38.00	43.00	120.	535.	3850.

Date	Event	Mintage	AU-50	MS-60	MS-63	MS-64	MS-65
1938	New Rochelle	15,266	275.	295.	340.	365.	545.

Date	Event	Mintage	AU-50	MS-60	MS-63	MS-64	MS-65
1936	Norfolk	16,936	385.	400.	460.	475.	580.

1926 Oregon Trail Half Dollar
Grade MS-60

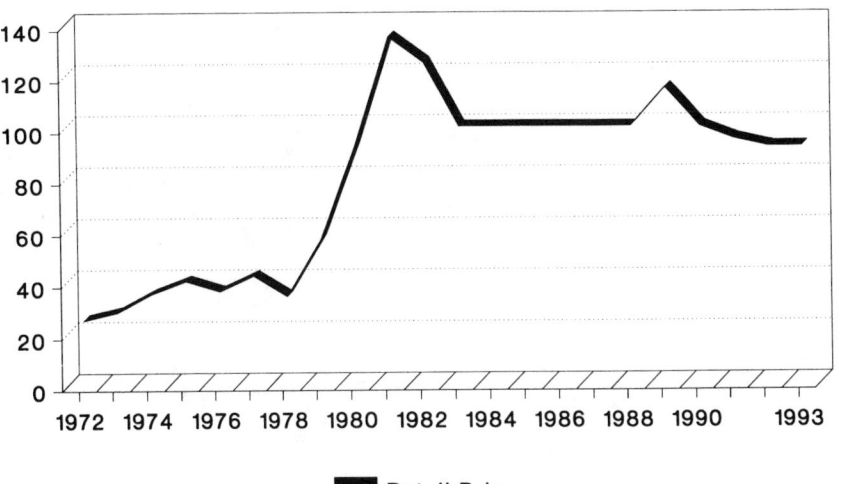

■ Retail Price

Source: COIN PRICES

Date	Event	Mintage	AU-50	MS-60	MS-63	MS-64	MS-65
1926	Oregon	47,955	85.00	92.00	135.	170.	290.
1926S	Oregon	83,055	85.00	92.00	135.	170.	290.
1928	Oregon	6,028	190.	210.	215.	290.	430.
1933D	Oregon	5,008	300.	315.	325.	350.	560.
1934D	Oregon	7,006	210.	215.	225.	245.	460.
1936	Oregon	10,006	120.	150.	160.	225.	305.
1936S	Oregon	5,006	135.	170.	180.	205.	330.
1937D	Oregon	12,008	110.	130.	155.	195.	305.
1938	Oregon PDS set	6,005	—	670.	680.	730.	1200.
1939	Oregon PDS set	3,004	—	970.	1300.	1650.	2050.
	Oregon type coin	—	92.00	97.00	135.	170.	290.

Date	Event	Mintage	AU-50	MS-60	MS-63	MS-64	MS-65
1915S	Panama - Pacific	27,134	195.	295.	730.	1550.	3050.

Date	Event	Mintage	AU-50	MS-60	MS-63	MS-64	MS-65
1920	Pilgrim	152,112	68.00	73.00	84.00	195.	900.
1921	Pilgrim	20,053	81.00	97.00	175.	340.	1000.

Date	Event	Mintage	AU-50	MS-60	MS-63	MS-64	MS-65
1936	Rhode Island PDS set	15,010	—	255.	275.	330.	1300.
1936	Rhode Island type coin	—	80.00	85.00	90.00	115.	440.

Date	Event	Mintage	AU-50	MS-60	MS-63	MS-64	MS-65
1937	Roanoke	29,030	180.	195.	215.	235.	300.

Date	Event	Mintage	AU-50	MS-60	MS-63	MS-64	MS-65
1936	Robinson-Arkansas	25,265	68.00	80.00	90.00	155.	535.
		(See also Arkansas)					

Date	Event	Mintage	AU-50	MS-60	MS-63	MS-64	MS-65
1935S	San Diego	70,132	61.00	73.00	80.00	95.00	115.
1936D	San Diego	30,092	61.00	73.00	80.00	90.00	140.

Date	Event	Mintage	AU-50	MS-60	MS-63	MS-64	MS-65
1926	Sesquicentennial	141,120	68.00	73.00	195.	775.	6000.

Date	Event	Mintage	AU-50	MS-60	MS-63	MS-64	MS-65
1935	Spanish Trail	10,008	670.	790.	830.	850.	1050.

Date	Event	Mintage	AU-50	MS-60	MS-63	MS-64	MS-65
1925	Stone Mountain	1,314,709	34.00	41.00	53.00	75.00	250.

Date	Event	Mintage	AU-50	MS-60	MS-63	MS-64	MS-65
1934	Texas	61,463	80.00	100.	110.	115.	175.
1935	Texas PDS set	9,994	—	290.	310.	345.	525.
1936	Texas PDS set	8,911	—	290.	310.	345.	525.
1937	Texas PDS set	6,571	—	330.	365.	425.	525.
1938	Texas PDS set	3,775	—	545.	850.	890.	1300.
	Texas type coins	—	80.00	95.00	100.	115.	175.

Date	Event	Mintage	AU-50	MS-60	MS-63	MS-64	MS-65
1925	Fort Vancouver	14,994	205.	275.	460.	600.	1700.

Date	Event	Mintage	AU-50	MS-60	MS-63	MS-64	MS-65
1927	Vermont	28,142	120.	155.	245.	365.	1400.

Date	Event	Mintage	AU-50	MS-60	MS-63	MS-64	MS-65
1946	B.T. Washington PDS set	200,113	—	36.00	49.00	61.00	150.
1947	B.T. Washington PDS set	100,017	—	45.00	49.00	61.00	270.
1948	B.T. Washington PDS set	8,005	—	92.00	105.	120.	180.
1949	B.T. Washington PDS set	6,004	—	205.	230.	255.	305.
1950	B.T. Washington PDS set	6,004	—	125.	135.	150.	210.
1951	B.T. Washington PDS set	7,004	—	125.	135.	150.	215.
	B.T. Washington type coin	—	10.00	12.00	19.00	23.00	50.00

Date	Event	Mintage	AU-50	MS-60	MS-63	MS-64	MS-65
1951	Washington-Carver PDS set	10,004	—	68.00	85.00	120.	610.
1952	Washington-Carver PDS set	8,006	—	80.00	85.00	155.	460.
1953	Washington-Carver PDS set	8,003	—	80.00	92.00	140.	485.
1954	Washington-Carver PDS set	12,006	—	68.00	85.00	97.00	580.
	Washington-Carver type coin	—	10.00	12.00	20.00	23.00	90.00

Date	Event	Mintage	AU-50	MS-60	MS-63	MS-64	MS-65
1936	Wisconsin	25,015	225.	230.	245.	255.	275.

Date	Event	Mintage	AU-50	MS-60	MS-63	MS-64	MS-65
1936	York County	25,015	205.	210.	215.	220.	305.

Silver dollar

Designer: Charles E. Barber. **Size:** 38.1 millimeters. **Weight:** 26.73 grams. **Composition:** 90% silver (0.7736 ounces), 10% copper.

Date	Event	Mintage	AU-50	MS-60	MS-63	MS-64	MS-65
1900	Lafayette ($1)	36,026	275.	640.	1750.	3800.	10,000.

Gold dollars

Designers: Louisiana: Charles E. Barber. Lewis and Clark Expo: Charles E. Barber. Panama-Pacific Expo: Charles Keck. McKinley Memorial: Charles E. Barber (obverse) and George T. Morgan (reverse). Grant: Laura G. Fraser. **Size:** 15 millimeters. **Weight:** 1.672 grams. **Composition:** 90% gold (0.0484 ounces), 10% copper. **Notes:** The Grant gold-dollar varieties are distinguished by whether a star appears on the obverse above the word "Grant."

Jefferson   McKinley

Date	Event	Mintage	AU-50	MS-60	MS-63	MS-64	MS-65
1903	Louisiana, Jefferson	17,500	340.	405.	1050.	1750.	2850.
1903	Louisiana, McKinley	17,500	330.	410.	1150.	1800.	2800.

Date	Event	Mintage	AU-50	MS-60	MS-63	MS-64	MS-65
1904	Lewis and Clark Expo	10,025	350.	800.	2350.	3650.	6500.
1905	Lewis and Clark Expo	10,041	495.	800.	3550.	5950.	16,000.

Date	Event	Mintage	AU-50	MS-60	MS-63	MS-64	MS-65
1915S	Panama-Pacific Expo	15,000	330.	435.	1050.	1400.	3250.

Date	Event	Mintage	AU-50	MS-60	MS-63	MS-64	MS-65
1916	McKinley Memorial	9,977	330.	425.	800.	1300.	3200.
1917	McKinley Memorial	10,000	325.	440.	1150.	2100.	4100.

With star

Date	Event	Mintage	AU-50	MS-60	MS-63	MS-64	MS-65
1922	Grant Memorial w/o star	5,016	950.	1400.	1950.	2700.	3100.
1922	Grant Memorial w/star	5,000	1100.	1550.	2400.	2550.	3250.

Gold $2.50

Designers: Panama-Pacific Expo: Charles E. Barber (obverse) and George T. Morgan (reverse). Sesquicentennial: John R. Sinnock. **Size:** 18 millimeters. **Weight:** 4.18 grams. **Composition:** 90% gold (0.121 ounces), 10% copper.

Date	Event	Mintage	AU-50	MS-60	MS-63	MS-64	MS-65
1915S	Panama-Pacific Expo	6,749	1025.	1350.	2500.	3200.	5550.

Date	Event	Mintage	AU-50	MS-60	MS-63	MS-64	MS-65
1926	Philadelphia Sesquicentennial	46,019	295.	350.	995.	1650.	9,500.

Gold $50

Designer: Robert Aitken. **Size:** 44 millimeters. **Weight:** 83.59 grams. **Composition:** 90% gold (2.42 ounces), 10% copper.

Date	Event	Mintage	AU-50	MS-60	MS-63	MS-64	MS-65
1915S	Panama-Pacific Expo, round	483	21,000.	23,500.	36,000.	50,500.	88,000.
1915S	Panama-Pacific Expo, octagon	645	18,500.	21,000.	28,500.	44,500.	76,000.

Commemoratives 1982-present

Silver half dollar

Designer: Elizabeth Jones. **Size:** 30.6 millimeters. **Weight:** 12.5 grams. **Composition:** 90% silver (0.3618 ounces), 10% copper.

Date	Mintage	(Proof)	MS-65	Prf-65
1982D Geo. Washington	2,210,458	—	5.00	—
1982S Geo. Washington	—	(4,894,044)	—	5.20

Clad half dollars

Designers: Statue of Liberty: Edgar Steever (obverse) and Sherl Joseph Winter (reverse). Congress: Patricia Lewis Verani (obverse) and William Woodward (reverse). Mount Rushmore: Marcel Jovine (obverse) and James Ferrell (reverse). 1992 Olympics: William C. Cousins (obverse) and Steven M. Bieda (reverse). **Size:** 30.6 millimeters. **Weight:** 11.34 grams. **Composition:** clad layers of 75% copper and 25% nickel bonded to a pure-copper core.

Date	Mintage	(Proof)	MS-65	Prf-65
1986D Statue of Liberty	928,008	—	4.50	—
1986S Statue of Liberty	—	(6,925,627)	—	4.10

Date	Mintage	(Proof)	MS-65	Prf-65
1989D Congress	163,753	—	13.00	—
1989S Congress	767,897	—	—	11.00

Date	Mintage	(Proof)	MS-65	Prf-65
1991D Mt. Rushmore	172,754	—	16.00	—
1991S Mt. Rushmore	753,257	—	—	20.00

Date	Mintage	(Proof)	MS-65	Prf-65
1992P Olympic	—	—	6.60	—
1992S Olympic	—	—	—	10.00

Date	Mintage	(Proof)	MS-65	Prf-65
1992D Columbus	—	—	10.50	—
1992S Columbus	—	—	—	12.00

Date	Mintage	(Proof)	MS-65	Prf-65
1993W Madison/Bill of Rights	—	—	16.50	—
1993S Madison/Bill of Rights	—	—	—	14.00

Silver dollars

Designers: 1983 Olympics: Elizabeth Jones. 1984 Olympics: Robert Graham. Statue of Liberty: John Mercanti. Constitution: Patricia Lewis Verani. 1988 Olympics: Patricia Lewis Verani (obverse) and Sherl Joseph Winter (reverse). Congress: William Woodward. Eisenhower: John Mercanti (obverse) and Marcel Jovine (reverse). Mount Rushmore: Marika Somogyi (obverse) and Frank Gasparro (reverse). Korean War: John Mercanti (obverse) and James Ferrell (reverse). United Service Organizations: Robert Lamb (obverse) and John Mercanti (reverse). 1992 Olympics: John R. Deecken (obverse) and Marcel Jovine (reverse). **Size:** 38.1 millimeters. **Weight:** 26.73 grams. **Composition:** 90% silver (0.76 ounces), 10% copper.

Date	Mintage	(Proof)	MS-65	Prf-65
1983P Olympic	294,543	—	16.00	—
1983D Olympic	174,014	—	26.00	—
1983S Olympic	174,014	(1,577,025)	19.00	11.00

Date	Mintage	(Proof)	MS-65	Prf-65
1984P Olympic	217,954	—	18.00	—
1984D Olympic	116,675	—	40.00	—
1984S Olympic	116,675	(1,801,210)	42.00	15.00

Date	Mintage	(Proof)	MS-65	Prf-65
1986P Statue of Liberty	723,635	—	16.00	—
1986S Statue of Liberty	—	(6,414,638)	—	12.00

Date	Mintage	(Proof)	MS-65	Prf-65
1987P Constitution	451,629	—	10.00	—
1987S Constitution	—	(2,747,116)	—	10.00

Date	Mintage	(Proof)	MS-65	Prf-65
1988D Olympic	191,368	—	28.00	—
1988S Olympic	—	(1,359,366)	—	12.00

Date	Mintage	(Proof)	MS-65	Prf-65
1989D Congress	135,203	—	35.00	—
1989S Congress	—	(762,198)	—	28.00

Date	Mintage	(Proof)	MS-65	Prf-65
1990W Eisenhower	241,669	—	28.00	—
1990P Eisenhower	—	(638,335)	—	19.00

Date	Mintage	(Proof)	MS-65	Prf-65
1991P Mt. Rushmore	133,139	—	44.00	—
1991S Mt. Rushmore	—	(738,419)	—	32.00

Date	Mintage	(Proof)	MS-65	Prf-65
1991D Korean War	213,049	—	23.00	—
1991P Korean War	—	(618,488)	—	25.00

Date	Mintage	(Proof)	MS-65	Prf-65
1991D USO	124,958	—	83.00	—
1991S USO	—	(321,275)	—	53.00

Date	Mintage	(Proof)	MS-65	Prf-65
1992D Columbus	—	—	30.00	—
1992P Columbus	—	—	—	31.00

Date	Mintage	(Proof)	MS-65	Prf-65
1992D Olympic	—	—	25.00	—
1992S Olympic	—	—	—	32.00

Date	Mintage	(Proof)	MS-65	Prf-65
1992D White House	—	—	88.00	—
1992W White House	—	—	—	89.00

Date	Mintage	(Proof)	MS-65	Prf-65
1993D Madison/Bill of Rights	—	—	26.00	—
1993S Madison/Bill of Rights	—	—	—	27.00

Gold $5

Designers: Statue of Liberty: Elizabeth Jones. Constitution: Marcel Jovine. 1988 Olympics: Elizabeth Jones (obverse) and Marcel Jovine (reverse). Congress: John Mercanti. Mount Rushmore: John Mercanti (obverse) and Robert Lamb (reverse). 1992 Olympics: James C. Sharpe (obverse) and James M. Peed (reverse). **Size:** 21.5 millimeters. **Weight:** 90% gold (0.24 ounces), 10% alloy.

Date	Mintage	(Proof)	MS-65	Prf-65
1986W Statue of Liberty	95,248	(404,013)	124.	124.

Date	Mintage	(Proof)	MS-65	Prf-65
1987W Constitution	214,225	(651,659)	117.	117.

Date	Mintage	(Proof)	MS-65	Prf-65
1988W Olympic	62,913	(281,456)	119.	119.

Date	Mintage	(Proof)	MS-65	Prf-65
1989W Congress	46,899	(164,690)	115.	115.

Date	Mintage	(Proof)	MS-65	Prf-65
1991W Mt. Rushmore	31,959	(111,991)	190.	190.

Date	Mintage	(Proof)	MS-65	Prf-65
1992W Olympic	—	—	220.	200.

Date	Mintage	(Proof)	MS-65	Prf-65
1992W Columbus	—	—	220.	220.

Date	Mintage	(Proof)	MS-65	Prf-65
1993W Madison/Bill of Rights	—	—	—	—

Gold $10

Designers: John Mercanti and James Peed (Mercanti designed the obverse from Peed's concept). **Size:** 27 millimeters. **Weight:** 26.73 grams. **Composition:** 90% gold (0.484 ounces), 10% copper.

Date	Mintage	(Proof)	MS-65	Prf-65
1984W Olympic	75,886	(381,085)	235.	235.
1984P Olympic	33,309	—	—	260.
1984D Olympic	34,533	—	—	235.
1984S Olympic	48,551	—	—	235.

Sets

1983-84 Olympics

Date	Price
1983 & 1984 proof dollars.	29.00
1983 & 1984 6 coin set. One 1983 and one 1984 uncirculated and proof dollar. One uncirculated and one proof gold $10.	420.
1983 collectors set- 1983 PDS uncirculated dollars.	48.00
1984 collectors set- 1984 PDS uncirculated dollars.	75.00
1983 silver proof dollar in case.	13.00
1984 silver proof dollar in case.	16.00
1983 & 1984 gold and silver uncirculated set. One 1983 and one 1984 uncirculated dollar and one 1984 uncirculated gold $10.	220.
1983 & 1984 gold and silver proof set. One 1983 and one 1984 proof dollar and one 1984 proof gold $10.	215.

1986 Statue of Liberty

Date	Price
1986 2 coin set: proof silver dollar and clad half dollar.	15.00
1986 3 coin set: proof silver dollar, clad half dollar and gold $5.	135.
1986 2 coin set: uncirculated silver dollar and clad half dollar.	21.00
1986 3 coin set: uncirculated silver dollar, clad half dollar and gold $5.	140.
1986 6 coin set: 1 each of the proof and uncirculated issues.	305.

1987 Constitution

Date	Price
1987 2 coin set: uncirculated silver dollar and gold $5.	110.
1987 2 coin set: proof silver dollar and gold $5.	110.
1987 4 coin set: 1 each of the proof and uncirculated issues.	230.

1988 Olympics

Date	Price
1988 2 coin set: uncirculated silver dollar and gold $5.	135.
1988 2 coin set: proof silver dollar and gold $5.	115.
1988 4 coin set: 1 each of proof and uncirculated issues.	255.

1989 Congress

Date	Price
1989 2 coin set: proof silver dollar and clad half dollar.	38.00
1989 3 coin set: proof silver dollar, clad half and gold $5.	145.
1989 2 coin set: uncirculated silver dollar and clad half dollar.	42.00
1989 3 coin set: uncirculated silver dollar, clad half and gold $5.	160.
1989 6 coin set: 1 each of the proof and uncirculated issues.	275.

1991 Mount Rushmore

Date	Price
1991 2 coin set: uncirculated half dollar and silver dollar.	35.00
1991 2 coin set: proof half dollar and silver dollar.	40.00
1991 3 coin set: uncirculated half dollar, silver dollar and gold $5.	235.
1991 3 coin set: proof half dollar, silver dollar and gold $5.	220.
1991 6 coin set: 1 each of proof and uncirculated issues.	450.

Columbus Quincentenary

Date	Price
1992 2 coin set: uncirculated half dollar and silver dollar.	42.00
1992 2 coin set: proof half dollar and silver dollar.	41.00
1992 3 coin set: uncirculated half dollar, silver dollar and gold $5.	220.
1992 3 coin set: proof half dollar, silver dollar and gold $5.	240.
1992 6 coin set: 1 each of proof and uncirculated issues.	450.

1992 Olympics

Date	Price
1992 2 coin set: uncirculated half dollar and silver dollar.	26.00
1992 2 coin set: proof half dollar and silver dollar.	38.00
1992 3 coin set: uncirculated half dollar, silver dollar and gold $5.	235.
1992 3 coin set: proof half dollar, silver dollar and gold $5.	220.
1992 6 coin set: 1 each of proof and uncirculated issues.	485.

Madison/Bill of Rights

Date	Price
1993 2 coin set: uncirculated half dollar and silver dollar.	31.50
1993 2 coin set: proof half dollar and silver dollar.	42.00
1993 3 coin set: uncirculated half dollar, silver dollar and gold $5.	—
1993 3 coin set: proof half dollar, silver dollar and gold $5.	265.
1993 6 coin set: 1 each of proof and uncirculated issues.	—

American Eagle bullion coins

Notes: American Eagle bullion coins are traded for their precious-metal content and compete with similar coins from other countries. Values for the non-proof issues will fluctuate with gold and silver prices.

Silver

One-ounce

Designers: Adolph A. Weinman (obverse) and John Mercanti (reverse). **Size:** 40.6 millimeters. **Weight:** 31.103 grams. **Composition:** 99.93% silver (0.999 ounces), 0.07% copper.

Prices based on $4.86 silver.

Date	Mintage	Unc	Prf.
1986	5,393,005	13.25	—
1986S	1,446,778	—	20.00
1987	11,442,335	7.00	—
1987S	904,732	—	18.00
1988	5,004,500	7.20	—
1988S	557,370	—	90.00
1989	5,203,327	7.25	—
1989S	617,694	—	20.00
1990	5,840,210	6.60	—
1990S	695,510	—	31.00
1991	7,191,066	6.85	—
1991S	—	—	29.00
1992	—	6.85	—
1992S	—	—	29.00
1993	—	6.85	—
1993S	—	—	—

Gold

Arabic numeral date   Roman numeral date

Tenth-ounce

Designers: Augustus Saint-Gaudens (obverse) and Miley Busiek (reverse). **Size:** 16.5 millimeters. **Weight:** 3.393 grams. **Composition:** 91.67% gold (0.1 ounces), 5.33% copper, 3% silver.

Prices based on $385.90 gold.

Date	Mintage	Unc	Prf.
1986	912,609	50.50	—
1987	580,266	50.50	—
1988	159,500	60.50	—
1988P	143,881	—	62.00
1989	264,790	53.00	—
1989P	82,924	—	64.00
1990	210,210	50.50	—
1990P	99,349	—	65.00
1991	165,200	50.50	—
1991P	—	—	66.00
1992	—	50.50	—
1992P	—	—	75.00
1993	—	50.50	—
1993P	—	—	—

Arabic numeral date   Roman numeral date

Quarter-ounce

Size: 22 millimeters. **Weight:** 8.483 grams. **Composition:** 91.67% gold (0.25 ounces), 5.33% copper, 3% silver.

Date	Mintage	Unc	Prf.
1986	726,031	105.	—
1987	269,255	105.	—
1988	49,000	105.	—
1988P	98,028	—	123.
1989	81,789	115.	—
1989P	53,593	—	129.
1990	41,000	105.	—
1990P	62,674	—	135.
1991	36,100	137.	—
1991P	—	—	135.
1992P	—	—	140.
1993	—	105.	—
1993P	—	—	—

Arabic numeral date   Roman numeral date

Half-ounce

Size: 27 millimeters. **Weight:** 16.966 grams. **Composition:** 91.67% gold (0.5 ounces), 5.33% copper, 3% silver.

Date	Mintage	Unc	Prf.
1986	599,566	212.	—
1987	131,255	212.	—
1987P	143,398	—	245.
1988	45,000	212.	—
1988P	76,528	—	245.
1989	44,829	212.	—
1989P	44,264	—	245.
1990	31,000	575.	—
1990P	51,636	—	337.
1991	24,100	450.	—
1991P	—	—	270.
1992	—	330.	—
1992P	—	—	260.
1993	—	212.	—
1993P	—	—	—

Arabic numeral date   **Roman numeral date**

One-ounce

Size: 32.7 millimeters. **Weight:** 33.931 grams. **Composition:** 91.67% gold (1 ounce), 5.33% copper, 3% silver.

Prices based on $385.90 gold.

Date	Mintage	Unc	Prf.
1986	1,362,650	398.	—
1986W	446,290	—	480.
1987	1,045,500	398.	—
1987W	147,498	—	484.
1988	465,000	398.	—
1988W	87,133	—	484.
1989	415,790	398.	—
1989W	53,960	—	470.
1990	373,210	398.	—
1990W	62,401	—	484.
1991	243,100	398.	—
1991W	—	—	550.
1992	—	398.	—
1992W	—	—	640.
1993	—	398.	—
1993W	—	—	—

U.S. minting varieties and errors

Introduction

The cataloging system used here for varieties and errors, compiled by Alan Herbert, began as the "PDS system," for "planchet," "die" and "striking," the three main divisions of the minting process. Two more divisions covering collectible modifications after the strike and alterations and damage have since been added.

The PDS system groups varieties of like cause. It can also be applied to foreign coins, with several classes added specifically to cover certain foreign minting processes.

Prices for U.S. coins listed here do not directly apply to foreign coins, but they can be used as a guide to the relative rarity of many foreign minting varieties. The prices quoted are the values for a common date and mint of the variety. In some instances, such as hubbing varieties, coins grading higher than MS-60 will bring a premium over the quoted prices.

The values quoted on the following pages are intended as a guide only; the ultimate price is determined by a willing buyer and seller. All prices are for grade uncirculated (MS-60), with a 20 percent to 50 percent or greater reduction for lesser grades.

Quick check index

If you have a coin and are not sure where to look for the possible variety:

If your coin shows doubling, check II-A, II-B, II-C, II-G, II-H, III-A, III-C-7, III-E, III-H-1, IV-D, or ejection doubling.

If part of the coin is missing, check I-B, I-C, or I-D.

If there is a raised line of coin metal, check II-D, II-G.

If there is a raised area of coin metal, check I-F, II-E, or II-F.

If the coin is out of round and too thin, check III-D.

If the coin appears to be the wrong metal, check I-A, I-E, I-G, and III-D.

If the die appears to have been damaged, check II-E, II-G, II-H. (Damage to the coin itself usually is not a minting variety.)

If the coin shows incomplete or missing design, check I-B-3, I-B-5, I-D, II-A, II-E, III-A, III-C, and III-D.

If only part of the planchet was struck, check II-E, II-G, III-A, III-B, III-C, III-E, III-F, III-G.

If something was struck into the coin, check III-B and III-C.

If something has happened to the coin's edge, check II-D-6, II-E-9 and 10, III-A-2, III-F, and III-H.

If your coin shows other than the normal design, check II-A or II-C.

If a layer of the coin metal is missing or a clad layer is missing, check I-D.

If you have an unstruck planchet, check I-H.

If your coin is a restrike, check IV-D.

If your coin has a counterstamp, additional engraving or apparent official modifications, check IV-A, IV-B, and IV-C.

Do not depend on the naked eye to examine your coins. Always use a magnifying lens. Circulation damage, wear, and alterations frequently can be mistaken for legitimate minting varieties.

Division I: Planchet varieties

These varieties and errors occur in the manufacture of the planchet on which the coin is struck and includes classes resulting from faulty metallurgy, mechanical damage, faulty processing or equipment, or human malfunction prior to the actual coin striking.

I-A: Improper alloy mix

Includes classes I-A-1, improper mix; and I-A-2, slag. Values for I-A-1 run from a few cents to a couple of dollars, depending on the denomination. Values for I-A-2 will run from several dollars on up, depending on the denomination and size of the slag area.

I-B: Damaged and defective planchets

This section involves planchets that are damaged, broken, or otherwise defective as a result of the production process. It does not include coins damaged after minting. Included are 23 classes, among them: I-B-1, defective planchets; I-B-2, mechanical damage; I-B-3, rolled thin; I-B-4, rolled thick; I-B-5, tapered; I-B-6, incomplete cladding; I-B-7, weld area planchet; I-B-8, unpunched center hole; I-B-9, uncentered center hole; I-B-10, clad stock missing clad layer; I-B-11, clad stock missing both clad layers; I-B-12, multiple punched center hole; I-B-13, incomplete punched center hole; I-B-14, wrong size or shape center hole; I-B-15, improperly prepared proof planchet; I-B-16, bubbled plating; I-B-17, broken planchet before strike; I-B-18, broken planchet after strike; I-B-19, improper annealing; I-B-20, unplated planchets; I-B-21, faulty upset planchet edge; I-B-22, rolled-in metal; I-B-23, included gas bubbles. (Values for I-B-20 cent planchets may range above $100.)

Defective planchet

Tapered planchet

	Defective I-B-1	Rolled Thin I-B-3	Rolled Thick I-B-4	Tapered I-B-5
Indian cent 1859-1909	10.	10.	50.	10.
Lincoln cent 1909-1942	5.	5.	15.	5.
Lincoln cent 1943	15.	25.	—	—
Lincoln cent 1944-1958	5.	5.	15.	5.
Lincoln cent 1959-1982	3.	10.	15.	3.
Lincoln cent 1976	5.	10.	20.	5.
Lincoln cent 1982-	5.	25.	35.	10.
Buffalo nickel 1913-1938	20.	—	—	—
Jefferson nickel 1938-	15.	—	20.	—
Jefferson nickel 1942-1945	10.	—	50.	—
Jefferson nickel 1976	25.	—	50.	—
Mercury dime 1916-1945	35.	—	75.	—
Roosevelt dime 1946-1964	25.	—	50.	—
Roosevelt dime 1965-	15.	—	25.	—
Roosevelt dime 1976	25.	—	50.	—
Washington quarter 1932-64	50.	Rare	100.	—
Washington quarter 1965-	20.	10.	Rare	—
Washington quarter 1976	50.	Rare	100.	—
Franklin half 1948-1963	50. up	—	Rare	—
Kennedy half 1964	50. up	—	Rare	—
Kennedy half 1965-1970	25. up	—	Rare	—
Kennedy half 1971-	20. up	—	Rare	—
Kennedy half 1976	100. up	—	Rare	—
Proof coins	25. up	Rare	Rare	Rare

I-C: Clipped planchets

Sixteen classes are listed in this section. Clips occur as the blanking-press punches overlap into areas of the coin-metal strip that have already been punched out, or where the end of the strip is broken or ragged, or over an incomplete punch.

The classes are I-C-1, curved clip to 5 percent; I-C-2, curved clip 6 percent to 10 percent or double clip; I-C-3, curved 11 percent to 25 percent; I-C-4, curved 26 percent to 60 percent; I-C-5, triple clip; I-C-6, multiple clip; I-C-7, incomplete punch; I-C-8, oval clip; I-C-9, crescent clip, 61 percent or larger; I-C-10, straight clip; I-C-11, ragged clip; I-C-12, outside corner clip; I-C-13, overlapping clips; I-C-14, inside corner clip; I-C-15, disc clip; and I-C-16, incomplete straight clip.

5 percent

50 percent

Ragged-edge clip

Multiple

Incomplete punch

	Curved to 5% I-C-1	Curved to 10% I-C-2	Curved to 25% I-C-3	Curved to 60% I-C-4	Triple Clip I-C-5	Multiple Clip I-C-6	Incomp Punch I-C-7	Oval Clip I-C-8	Crescent Clip 61%+ I-C-9	Straight Clip I-C-10	Ragged Clip I-C-11
Indian cent 1859-1909	10. up	15. up	25. up	50. up	35. up	50. up	—	—	—	—	50.
Lincoln cent 1909-1942	5.	10.	15.	25. up	15. up	25. up	20.	50.	50.	5.	10.
Lincoln cent 1943	5.	10.	35.	50. up	15.	50. up	100.	150.	—	25.	50.
Lincoln cent 1944-1958	3.	8.	12.	25. up	5.	15. up	15.	50.	40.	5.	10.
Lincoln cent 1959-1982	2.	5.	10.	25. up	5.	15. up	15.	45.	35.	5.	10.
Lincoln cent 1982-	1.	7.	15.	50. up	15.	50. up	35.	150.	—	25.	—
Buffalo nickel 1913-1938	5. up	15. up	25. up	100. up	50. up	100. up	35.	75.	—	25.	—
Jefferson nickel 1938-	2.	5.	10.	50. up	10. up	50. up	25.	50.	35.	5.	10.
Jefferson nickel 1942-1945	5.	10.	15.	150. up	25. up	100. up	35.	75.	50.	15.	20.
Mercury dime 1916-1945	10	25.	40.	75. up	30.	75. up	35.	—	75.	15.	25.
Roosevelt dime 1946-1964	2.	3.	5.	75. up	15.	50. up	30.	Rare	75.	10.	15.
Roosevelt dime 1965-	1.	2.	3.	50. up	10.	35. up	25.	100.	60.	5.	10.
Roosevelt dime 1976	2.	3.	5.	75. up	15.	50. up	30.	Rare	75.	10.	15.
Washington quarter 1932-64	5.	8.	10.	100. up	15.	75. up	35.	60.	—	10.	15.
Washington quarter 1965-	2.	3.	5.	50. up	10.	35. up	25.	50.	—	5.	10.
Washington quarter 1976	5.	8.	10. up	50. up	20.	75. up	50.	100.	—	15.	25.
Franklin half 1948-1963	10.	15.	40.	—	50.	—	—	—	—	50.	75.
Kennedy half 1964	10.	15.	25.	—	50.	—	—	—	—	50.	75.
Kennedy half 1965-1970	10.	15.	20.	—	25.	50.	50.	—	—	35.	50.
Kennedy half 1971-	5.	10.	15.	—	20.	40.	40.	—	—	30.	40.
Kennedy half 1976-	50.	20.	30.	—	100.	—	—	—	—	50.	75.
Morgan dollar 1878-1921	35.	75.	125.	—	—	—	—	—	—	—	—
Peace dollar 1921-1935	30.	65.	110.	—	—	—	—	—	—	—	—
Ike dollar (clad) 1971-78	15.	50.	100.	—	200.	500. up	—	—	1750.	50.	100.
Ike dollar (silver) 1971-1975	Rare to unknown in all classes										
Ike dollar (clad) 1976	Rare										
Ike dollar (silver) 1976	Rare to unknown in all classes										
Anthony dollar 1979-81	25.	50. up	175. up	250.	Rare	—	—	—	—	20.	35.
Commemoratives	Rare										
Proof coins	$25 to $200 cent to half dollar										

PRICING SECTION

I-D: Laminations and split planchets

There are 11 classes in this section, covering planchets that split, or crack parallel to the flat surfaces, or have chunks of metal rolled into the surface. I-D-10 (unstruck clad layer) ranges from $10 for a dime to $100 for a clad Eisenhower dollar. I-D-12 (broken planchet before strike) and I-D-13 (broken planchet after strike) are valued according to the size and coin.

The classes are I-D-1, lamination crack or up to 25 percent of surface missing; I-D-2, large lamination, over 25 percent missing; I-D-3, split unstruck planchet, rolled in metal; I-D-4, split before strike; I-D-5, split after strike; I-D-6, missing clad layer; I-D-7, both clad layers missing; I-D-8, struck clad layer, split off before strike; I-D-9, struck clad layer, split off after strike; I-D-10, unstruck clad layer; I-D-11, hinged split.

Split planchet	Layer peeled off	Metal split away	Lamination crack

	Lamination Crack or -25% of Surface Missing	Large Lamination +25% of Surface Missing	Rolled in Metal	Split Before Strike	Split After Strike	Missing Clad Layer	Missing Both Clad Layers	Struck & Split Before Strike	Struck & Split After Strike	Hinged Split Planchet
	I-D-1	I-D-2	I-D-3	I-D-4	I-D-5	I-D-6	I-D-7	I-D-8	I-D-9	I-D-11
Lincoln cent 1909-1942	1.	5.	2.	5.	3.	—	—	—	—	30.
Lincoln cent 1943	5.	15.	10.	50.	35.	—	—	—	—	100.
Lincoln cent 1944-1958	1.	5.	2.	5.	3.	—	—	—	—	25.
Lincoln cent 1959-1982	1.	3.	1.	3.	3.	—	—	—	—	20.
Lincoln cent 1982-	—	—	—	10.	15.	N/A	N/A	N/A	N/A	50.
Buffalo nickel 1913-1938	—	—	—	35.	35.	—	—	—	—	50.
Jefferson nickel 1938-	3.	10.	5.	15.	10.	—	—	—	—	35.
Jefferson nickel 1942-1945	Common	5.	5.	5.	5.	—	—	—	—	25.
Mercury dime 1916-1945	15.	50.	15.	—	—	—	—	—	—	—
Roosevelt dime 1946-1964	10.	35.	10.	—	—	—	—	—	—	50.
Roosevelt dime 1965-	3.	10.	5.	—	—	20.	35.	25.	35.	45.
Washington quarter 1932-64	15.	50.	10.	50.	50.	—	—	—	—	75.
Washington quarter 1965-	10.	25.	10.	—	—	25.	50.	50.	35.	60.
Washington quarter 1976	25.	50.	25.	—	—	50.	75.	75.	60.	100.
Walking Liberty 1916-47	—	—	—	150.	125.	—	—	—	—	—
Franklin half 1948-1963	20.	50. up	50. up	125.	100.	—	—	—	—	—
Kennedy half 1964	20.	50. up	50. up	100.	75.	—	—	—	—	150.
Kennedy half 1965-1970	15.	35. up	35. up	75.	50.	125.	200.	150.	100.	125.
Kennedy half 1971-	10.	25. up	25. up	50.	35.	100.	200.	125.	75.	100.
Kennedy half 1976	20.	50. up	50. up	100.	75.	150.	300.	200.	150.	200.
Morgan dollar 1878-1921	50. up	100. up	50. up	275.	175.	—	—	—	—	—
Peace dollar 1921-1935	50. up	100. up	50. up	275.	175.	—	—	—	—	—
Ike dollar (clad) 1971-78	35. up	75. up	35. up	250.	150.	500.	RARE	500.	400.	—
Ike dollar (silver) 1971-1975	Rare in all classes									
Ike Dollar (clad) 1976	Rare in all classes									
Ike Dollar (silver) 1976	Rare to unknown in all classes									
SBA dollar 1979-81	Rare in all classes									
Commemoratives	Rare to unknown in all classes									
Proof coins	Rare in all classes									
Gold coins	Rare in all classes									

I-E: Wrong-stock planchets

This section consists of planchets that were punched from strip intended for a different denomination, series, or for coins of another country. The classes are I-E-1, dime stock; I-E-2, quarter stock; I-E-3, half-dollar stock; I-E-4, dollar stock; I-E-5, foreign stock; and I-E-6, token or medal stock. I-E-7, punched from spoiled planchets (wrong thickness); I-E-8, punched from spoiled planchets (correct thickness); I-E-9, punched from tokens (wrong thickness); I-E-10, purchased planchets; I-E-11, half-cent stock; I-E-12, cent stock; I-E-13, experimental and pattern stock; I-E-14, proof stock; I-E-15, two-cent stock; I-E-16, silver three-cent stock; I-E-17, nickel three-cent stock; I-E-18, half-dime stock; I-E-19, 20-cent stock; I-E-20, clad stock; I-E-21, adjusted specifications; I-E-22, punched from trial strike; I-E-23, plated stock.

	Dime Stock	Quarter Stock	Half Dollar Stock
	I-E-1	I-E-2	I-E-3
Mercury dime 1916-1945	—	$200.	—
Roosevelt dime 1946-1964	—	100.	—
Roosevelt dime 1965-	—	75.	—
Washington quarter 1932-64	100.	—	—
Washington quarter 1965-	10.	—	125.

Quarter on dime stock

I-F: Extra metal

As planchets are punched from the strip, they can pick up extra metal that adheres to the punch press. This is found only in the rim area as a raised spur on the planchet or as an "island" on the rim on the struck coin. It cannot project above the normal surface of the coin, like a die break.

The classes are I-F-1, on Type I planchet; I-F-2, on Type II planchet; and I-F-3, on a struck coin.

	I-F-1	I-F-2	I-F-3
Cent 1909-1988	50.	25.	15.
Nickel 1938-1988	60.	50.	20.
Dime 1946-1988	75.	70.	35.

I-G: Sintered planchet

Color is not a minting variety. Many coins with a golden color are incorrectly described as the result of a "copper wash." The real cause is a thin coating of bronze or brass powder adhering to the planchets in the annealing drum. A thicker layer is classed as a sintered planchet. Although it is quite rare, it usually has a value of less than $50.

I-H: Unstruck planchets

Coin planchets may bypass parts of the processing and escape into circulation. The Type I-H-1 planchets are flat with sharp edges; the Type I-H-2 planchets have a slightly raised rim on both sides. Type I planchets are often difficult to authenticate. The classes are I-H-1, Type I planchet; I-H-2, Type II (upset edge) planchet.

	Type I I-H-1	Type II I-H-2		Type I I-H-1	Type II I-H-2
Half cent 1793-1857	50.	125.	Quarter 1796-1836	200.	200.
Large cent 1793-1857	15.	65.	Quarter 1837-1852	200.	200.
Small cent 1856-1864	250.	250.	Quarter 1853-1873	200.	200.
Indian cent 1854-1909	—	120.	Quarter 1873-1964	60.	50.
Lincoln cent 1909-1982	1.25	0.50	Quarter 1965-	2.	3.
Lincoln cent 1943	—	15.	Half dollar 1794-1836	250.	250.
Lincoln cent 1982-	5.	5.	Half dollar 1837-1852	250.	250.
Two-cent 1864-1873	150.	160.	Half dollar 1853-1873	250.	250.
Three-cent (nickel) 1865-89	200.	200.	Half dollar 1873-1964	240.	160.
Three-cent (silver) 1851-73	200.	200.	Half dollar 1965-1970	110.	330.
Nickel 1866-	3.	2.	Half dollar 1971-	2.	4.
Nickel 1942-1945 (silver)	235.	210.	Silver dollar 1794-1803	500.	500.
Half dime 1794-1873	150.	300.	Silver dollar 1840-1935	240.	160.
Dime 1798-1837	200.	200.	Trade dollar 1873-1885		Rare
Dime 1837-1853	150.	150.	Ike dollar (clad) 1971-78	35.	40.
Dime 1853-1873	200.	200.	Ike dollar (silver) 1971-1976	200.	250.
Dime 1873-1964	10.	10.	Anthony dollar 1979-81	125.	130.
Roosevelt dime 1965-	1.	2.			
Twenty cent 1875-1878		Rare			

Note: The market is flooded with many denominations of clad Type I and steel-cent Type I planchets.

I-I: Coin metal strip

The remains of the coin metal strip from which the planchets have been punched sometimes leave the mint as scrap and is acquired by collectors. A section of strip with punched holes (I-I-1) or a piece of chopped-up strip (I-I-2) are considered collectible. The sections are worth $5-$100. The chopped pieces are valued from a few cents to a few dollars, depending on the size of the piece and the metal.

	I-1
Cent planchet strip	15. up
Steel cent strip	10. up
Nickel strip	15. up
Clad dime strip	20. up
Clad quarter strip	35. up
Clad half-dollar strip	100. up

Division II: Die varieties

This division contains all the classes that deal with variations in the die itself, which result in a change in the intended design as a result of accident, intent, alteration, or other change in the die. Every class in this division repeats exactly on every coin struck by the given die.

II-A: Engraving varieties

With 37 classes, this is the largest section of the entire PDS system. II-A-1, overdates, are covered in the regular price charts, as are II-A-3, small dates. Other examples, however, are so scattered through the

coinage that it would be impossible to accurately price them except on a case-by-case basis.

The other classes are II-A-2, repunched dates; II-A-4, large date; II-A-5, small over large date; II-A-6, large over small; II-A-7, misspelled engraving; II-A-8, one letter over another; II-A-9, wrong number (other than date); II-A-10, one number over another (other than date); II-A-11, missing designer's initials; II-A-12, recutting; II-A-13, repunched numbers (other than date); II-A-14, repunched letter (other than mintmark); II-A-15, repunched design; II-A-16, modified design; II-A-17, normal design; II-A-18, design mistakes; II-A-19, broken punch; II-A-20, incomplete die; II-A-21, pattern; II-A-22, abnormal reeding; II-A-23, plugged die; II-A-24, wrong-size letters or numbers; II-A-25, letter over number; II-A-26, number over letter; II-A-27, trial design; II-A-28, numbered dies; II-A-29, expedient punch; II-A-30, misplaced device punch; II-A-31, layout marks; II-A-32, worn punch; II-A-33, misaligned punch; II-A-34, style overpunch; II-A-35, one design over another; II-A-36, wrong date; II-A-37, canceled die; and II-A-38, reducing-lathe doubling.

II-B: Hubbing varieties

This section includes seven classes of hub doubling, plus three more forms of hubbing varieties, all directly connected to the hub, which is the tool used to press the coin design into the face of the die. Each class of hub doubling is from a different cause, described by the title of the class. At the latest count, over 1,200 doubled dies have been reported among U.S. coinage, the most famous occurring on some cents of 1955 and 1972.

The classes are II-B-1, rotated hub doubling; II-B-2, distorted hub; II-B-3, design hub; II-B-4, offset hub; II-B-5, pivoted hub; II-B-6, distended hub; II-B-7, modified hub; II-B-8, hub cracks; II-B-9, hub breaks; II-B-10, worn or damaged hub; and II-B-11, tilted hub.

Rotated hub doubling

Hub break

	II-B-1	II-B-2	II-B-3	II-B-4	II-B-5	II-B-6	II-B-7	II-B-9
Flying Eagle cent 1856-58	750.	550.	600.	—	—	—	—	—
Indian cent 1873	—	—	500.	—	—	—	—	—
Lincoln cent 1909 "VDB"	—	—	125.	—	—	—	—	—
Lincoln cent 1917	—	—	—	—	175.	—	—	—
Lincoln cent 1936	—	—	8.	250.	100.	4.	—	—
Lincoln cent 1941	150.	—	—	150.	25.	4.	—	—
Lincoln cent 1955	775.	250.	—	—	—	3.	—	—

PRICING SECTION

	II-B-1	II-B-2	II-B-3	II-B-4	II-B-5	II-B-6	II-B-7	II-B-9
Lincoln cent 1960-P&D Lg/Sm, Sm/Lg	—	—	150.	—	—	4.	—	—
Lincoln cent 1964	—	4.	—	—	150.	—	—	—
Lincoln cent 1964 Pr	15.	—	—	—	35.	—	—	—
Lincoln cent 1969-S	5500.	—	—	—	—	—	—	—
Lincoln cent 1970-S	750.	—	5.	—	—	—	35.	—
Lincoln cent 1970-S Pr	250.	—	—	—	—	300.	—	—
Lincoln cent 1971	75.	75.	—	—	—	—	—	—
Lincoln cent 1971-S Pr	—	750.	—	—	—	—	—	—
Lincoln cent 1972	2.-225.	—	5.	—	—	—	—	—
Lincoln cent 1972-D	25.	—	—	—	—	—	—	—
Lincoln cent 1972-S Pr	300.	10.	—	—	—	—	—	—
Lincoln cent 1980	—	—	100.	—	—	—	—	—
Lincoln cent 1983	—	—	—	175.	—	—	—	—
Lincoln cent 1984	—	—	—	90.	—	—	—	—
Lincoln cent 1987-D	—	50.	—	—	—	—	—	—
Two-cent 1864-1873	—	275.	500.	350.	350.	—	—	—
Three-cent 1864-1871	—	—	325.	—	300.	—	—	—
Shield nickel 1866-1883	—	—	75.-425.	—	—	—	—	—
Buffalo nickel 1916/1916	—	—	—	—	9000.	—	—	—
Buffalo nickel 1918/1917-D	—	—	8500.	—	—	—	—	—
Jefferson nickel 1938 LD/SD	—	—	150.	—	—	—	—	—
Jefferson nickel 1939	—	200.	150.	—	—	40.	15.	—
Jefferson nickel 1943/1942	—	—	250.	—	—	—	—	—
Half dime 1861	—	—	—	—	550.	—	—	—
Mercury dime 1942/1941	—	—	1025.	—	—	—	—	—
Mercury dime 1942/2/1941-D	—	—	1175.	—	—	—	—	—
Roosevelt dime 1970	—	100.	—	—	—	—	—	—
Twenty-cent 1876-CC	—	—	69,300.	—	—	—	—	—
Standing Liberty quarter 1918/1917-S	—	—	8750.	—	—	—	—	—
Washington quarter 1934	15.-350.	—	—	—	—	—	—	—
Washington quarter 1936	625.	—	—	—	—	—	—	—
Washington quarter 1942-D	—	—	350.	—	—	—	—	—
Washington quarter 1943-S	—	—	250.	—	—	—	—	—
Washington quarter 1945	250.	—	—	—	—	—	—	—
Washington quarter 1968-S Pr	200.	—	—	—	—	—	—	—
Washington quarter 1976-D	450.	—	—	—	—	—	—	—
Walking Liberty half 1942	—	125.	—	—	—	—	—	—
Walking Liberty half 1946	—	150.	—	—	—	—	—	—
Kennedy half 1964-P&D	10.-25.	10.-75.	10.	—	—	—	—	—
Morgan dollar 1878 7/8 TF	—	—	63.	—	—	—	—	—
Morgan dollar 1878-CC	—	175.	—	—	—	—	—	—
Morgan dollar 1901	—	—	—	700.	—	—	—	—
Ike dollar 1976-PDS	—	—	20.	—	—	—	—	—
Anthony dollar 1979	—	25.	25.	—	—	—	—	—

Note: More than one die may exist for a given date. Prices for coins grading above MS-60 will be considerably higher.

II-C: Mintmark varieties

Mintmarks are punched into the die by hand. Variations resulting from mistakes in the punching are listed in this section. Unless exceptionally mispunched, values are usually estimated at 150 percent of numismatic value. Slightly tilted or displaced mintmarks have no value.

The classes are II-C-1, double punched; II-C-2, triple; II-C-3, quadruple; II-C-4, vertical/horizontal; II-C-5, vertical/upside down; II-C-6, overmintmark (such as D/S); II-C-7, small; II-C-8, large; II-C-9, large over small; II-C-10, missing; II-C-11, small over large; II-C-12, displaced; II-C-13, modified; II-C-14, tilted (45 degrees or more) mintmark; II-C-15, separated punches; II-C-16, normal mintmark; II-C-17, broken punch; II-C-18, mintmark touching design.

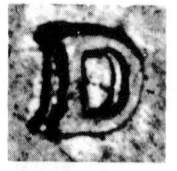

Double

Triple

	II-C-1	II-C-2	II-C-4	II-C-5	II-C-6	II-C-9	II-C-10	II-C-13	II-C-15
Indian cent 1908-S	225.	—	—	—	—	—	—	—	—
Lincoln cent 1909-S V/H	—	—	275.	—	—	—	—	—	—
Lincoln cent 1922	—	—	—	—	—	—	4000.	—	—
Lincoln cent 1944-D D/S	—	—	—	—	375.	—	—	—	—
Lincoln cent 1956-D	—	—	—	—	—	—	—	—	35.
Lincoln cent 1960-D V/H/H	—	3.	—	—	—	—	—	—	—
Lincoln cent 1961-D V/H	—	2.	—	—	—	—	—	—	—
Lincoln cent 1985-D	10.	—	—	—	—	—	—	—	—
Buffalo nickel 1935-D D/D/D	—	135.	—	—	—	—	—	—	—
Buffalo nickel 1937-D D/S	—	—	—	—	35.	—	—	—	—
Buffalo nickel 1938-D D/D/D/S	—	—	—	—	35.	—	—	—	—
Jefferson nickel 1942-D D/D/HD	—	—	30.	—	—	—	—	—	—
Jefferson nickel 1949-D D/S	—	—	—	—	330.	—	—	—	—
Jefferson nickel 1954-S S/D	—	—	—	—	31.	—	—	—	—
Jefferson nickel 1955-D D/S	—	—	—	—	15.-30. (10 dies)	—	—	—	—
Jefferson nickel 1971-(S) Pr	—	—	—	—	—	—	1055.	—	—
Seated Liberty dime 1890-S Lg/Sm	—	—	—	—	—	650.	—	—	—
Seated Liberty dime 1891-O V/H	—	—	600.	—	—	—	—	—	—
Roosevelt dime 1968-(S) Pr	—	—	—	—	—	—	8900.	—	—
Roosevelt dime 1970-(S) Pr	—	—	—	—	—	—	780.	—	—
Roosevelt dime 1975-(S) Pr	—	—	—	—	—	—	Two known	—	—
Roosevelt dime 1982-(P)	—	—	—	—	—	—	200.	—	—
Roosevelt dime 1983-(S) Pr	—	—	—	—	—	—	675.	—	—
Roosevelt dime 1985-P P&P	—	—	—	—	—	—	—	—	150.
Seated Liberty quarter 1856-S Lg/Sm	—	—	—	—	—	740.	—	—	—
Seated Liberty quarter 1877-S V/H	—	—	550.	—	—	—	—	—	—
Washington quarter 1950-D D/S	—	—	—	—	335.	—	—	—	—
Washington quarter 1950-S S/D	—	—	—	—	520.	—	—	—	—
Washington quarter 1956-D V/UD	—	—	—	30.	—	—	—	—	—
Seated Liberty half 1855-O V/H	—	—	1175.	—	—	—	—	—	—
Trade dollar 1875-S S/S/CC	—	—	—	—	1500.	—	—	—	—
Morgan dollar 1879-O V/H	—	—	1200.	—	—	—	—	—	—
Morgan dollar 1879-CC Lg/Sm	—	—	—	—	—	4850.	—	130.	—
Morgan dollar 1900-O O/CC	—	—	—	—	115. (8 dies)	—	—	230.	—
1979-S proof set (Variety II mintmark, all 6 coins) II-C-13								73.	
1981-S Proof Set (Variety II mintmark, all 6 coins) II-C-13								295.	

Note: More than 2,000 dies are known with mintmark varieties in most denominations and series. Those listed are some of the more valuable examples. Values are usually estimated at 150 percent of normal numismatic value for the grade, more for exceptional specimens. Prices for grades above MS-60 are substantially higher.

II-D: Die cracks

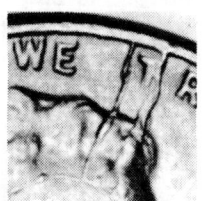

Cracks in the surface of the die allow coin metal to squeeze in, resulting in raised, irregular lines above the coin's normal surface. These are one of the commonest forms of die damage, making them easily collectible.

The classes are II-D-1, single die crack; II-D-2, multiple; II-D-3, head to rim (Lincoln cent); II-D-4, split die; II-D-5, rim to rim; and II-D-6, collar crack.

II-E: Die breaks

Breaks in the surface of the die allow coin metal to squeeze into the resulting holes, causing raised, irregular areas above the coin's normal surface. Die chips and small die breaks are nearly as common as die

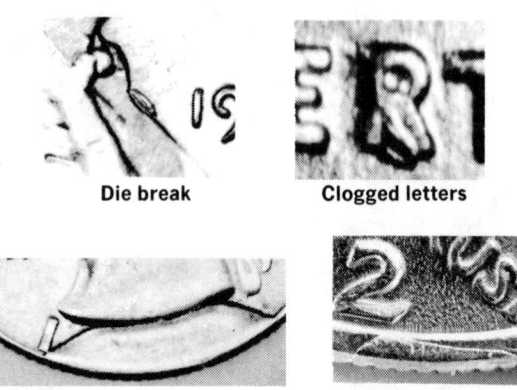

Die break   Clogged letters

Major die break ("cud")   Rim die break

cracks, but major die breaks ("cuds"), which extend in from the coin's edge, are quite rare on the larger coins. If the broken piece of the die is retained, the resulting design will be above or below the level of the rest of the surface.

The classes are II-E-1, die chip; II-E-2, small die break; II-E-3, large die break; II-E-4, rim die break; II-E-5, major die break; II-E-6, retained broken die; II-E-7, laminated die; II-E-8, split or chipped chrome plating; II-E-9, collar break; II-E-10, broken letter on edge die; II-E-11, missing letter on edge die; II-E-12, retained center broken die; and II-E-13, bar next to rim.

II-F: "BIE" varieties

A series of small die breaks or die chips in the letters of "Liberty," mostly on the wheat-reverse Lincoln cent, is actively collected. The name results from the resemblance to an "I" between the "B" and "E"

BIE error

on many of the dies, but they are found between all of the letters in different cases. Well over 1,500 dies are known and cataloged. Values range from 10 cents for common examples in circulated grades to $75 for the more scarce varieties in top grade.

II-G: Die dents, gouges, scratches, and polished dies

The die is subject to all sorts of damage, which will show on the struck coin. Any dent, gouge, pit, or scratch in the die will result in a matching raised area on the coin. This damage is repaired by polishing the die, resulting in removal or doubling of the design. All of these classes are quite common and have no value unless they are exceptional examples.

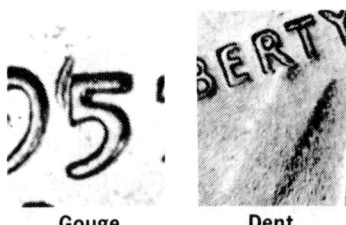

Scratches

Gouge   Dent

This section is divided into eight classes: II-G-1, dents; II-G-2, gouges or damaged die; II-G-3, scratches; II-G-4, polished die; II-G-5, polishing doubling (inside); II-G-6, polishing doubling (outside); II-G-7, worn or deformed die; II-G-8, pitted or rusted die.

II-H: Die clashes, collar clashes, and design transfer

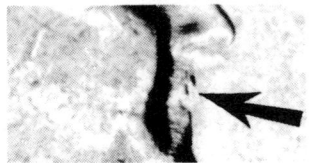

Die clashes occur when the dies hit each other, damaging the faces of the dies. The opposing design is thus transferred to the die and struck coin.

A collar clash results from the die hitting the collar, damaging the rim area of the die, which shows on the struck coin.

Design transfer ("ghost" images) result from deformation of the die from constant use. Only extreme examples have any value, as these are common forms of damage to the die. Heavy die and collar clashes will bring from a few cents to several dollars, depending on the coin's denomination.

II-I: Progressions

When additional changes occur in a die, the resulting variety is classed as a "progression." Up to a dozen or more stages of a given die pair may be traced by additional die breaks, die cracks, die substitutions, and so on. Values depend on the initial class of the variety, bringing a small premium for additional stages of the same die pair.

Division III: Striking varieties

Once the planchets have been prepared and the dies made, the planchets are struck by a pair of dies and become a coin. In this division are listed the misstrikes resulting from human or mechanical malfunction in the striking process. These are one-of-a-kind varieties, but there may be

many similar coins that fall in a given class. Multiples and combinations of classes must be considered on a case-by-case basis.

III-A: Die-adjustment strikes

As the dies are adjusted in the coin press, variations in the strike occur until the press is properly set up. These coins are normally scrapped, but on occasion reach circulation. The classes are III-A-1, die-adjustment strike; III-A-2, edge strike; III-A-3, weak strike; III-A-4, strong strike; III-A-5, jam strike; III-A-6, die trial; and III-A-7, edge die-adjustment strike.

	Die Adjustment Strike	Edge Strike	Weak Strike	Strong Strike	Jam Strike
	III-A-1	III-A-2	III-A-3	III-A-4	III-A-5
Indian cent 1859-1909	150.	—	—	—	—
Lincoln cent 1909-1942	50.	—	—	—	—
Lincoln cent 1943	150.	—	—	—	—
Lincoln cent 1944-1958	35.	—	—	—	—
Lincoln cent 1959-1982	25.	—	—	—	—
Lincoln cent 1976	35.	—	—	—	—
Lincoln cent 1982-	35.	—	—	—	—
Buffalo nickel 1913-1938	Unknown	—	—	—	—
Jefferson nickel 1938-	25.	—	—	—	—
Jefferson nickel 1942-1945	50.	—	—	—	—
Jefferson nickel 1976	35.	—	—	—	—
Mercury dime 1916-1945	100.	—	—	—	—
Roosevelt dime 1946-1964	50.	—	—	—	—
Roosevelt dime 1965-	35.	—	—	—	—
Roosevelt dime 1976	50.	—	—	—	—
Washington quarter 1932-64	125.	—	—	—	—
Washington quarter 1965-	75.	—	—	—	—
Washington quarter 1976	150.	—	—	—	—
Franklin half 1948-1963	275.	—	—	—	—
Kennedy half 1964	250.	—	—	—	—
Kennedy half 1965-1970	200.	—	—	—	—
Kennedy half 1971-	150.	—	—	—	—
Kennedy half 1976	350.	—	—	—	—
Morgan dollar 1878-1921	Rare	—	—	—	—
Peace dollar 1921-1935	Rare	—	—	—	—
Ike dollar 1971-78	300.	—	—	—	—
Ike dollar 1976	500.	—	—	—	—
Anthony dollar 1979-81	150.	—	—	—	—
Commemoratives	Rare	—	—	—	—

III-B: Indented, brockage, and counter-brockage strikes

Indented and uniface strikes involve an extra unstruck planchet between one of the dies and the planchet being struck. Brockage strikes involve a struck coin between one of the dies and the planchet, and a counter-brockage requires a brockage coin between one of the dies and the planchet.

A cap or capped-die strike results when a coin sticks to the die and is squeezed around it in the shape of a bottle cap. There are 18 classes in this section with variations on the planchet and coin relationship.

The classes are III-B-1, indented; III-B-2, uniface; III-B-3, indent of smaller planchet; III-B-4, partial brockage; III-B-5, full brockage; III-B-6, brockage of smaller coin; III-B-7, partial counter-brockage; III-B-8, full counter-brockage; III-B-9, brockage-counter-brockage; III-B-10, cap; III-B-11, indented second strike; III-B-12, brockage second strike; III-B-13,

counter-brockage second strike; III-B-14, multiple brockage; III-B-15, reverse (die) cap; and III-B-16, edge counter-brockage; III-B-17, indent of feed finger; III-B-18, brockage of struck fragment.

	III-B-1	III-B-8	III-B-10

	Indented Strike	Full Brockage	Full Counter Brockage	Cap (Capped Die)
	III-B-1	III-B-5	III-B-8	III-B-10
Indian cent 1859-1909	75.	150.	300.	1600.
Lincoln cent 1909-1942	15.	20.	125.	325.
Lincoln cent 1943	30.	75.	200.	Rare
Lincoln cent 1944-1958	10.	20.	100.	300.
Lincoln cent 1959-1982	5.	15.	75.	275.
Lincoln cent 1976	10.	20.	100.	300.
Lincoln cent 1982-	10.	20.	100.	Rare
Buffalo nickel 1913-1938	50.	75.	125.	Rare
Jefferson nickel 1938-	35.	50.	100.	300.
Jefferson nickel 1942-1945	50.	75.	150.	Rare
Jefferson nickel 1976	50.	75.	150.	Rare
Mercury dime 1916-1945	35.	50.	100.	300. up
Roosevelt dime 1946-1964	25.	35.	60.	250.
Roosevelt dime 1965-	20.	30.	50.	200.
Roosevelt dime 1976	25.	35.	60.	250.
Washington quarter 1932-64	40.	60.	125.	Rare
Washington quarter 1965-	25.	50.	100.	250.
Washington quarter 1976	50.	100.	200.	Rare
Franklin half 1948-1963	125.	500.	Rare	Rare
Kennedy half 1964	125.	450.	Rare	Rare
Kennedy half 1965-1970	100.	350.	Rare	Rare
Kennedy half 1971-	75.	250.	Rare	Rare
Kennedy half 1976	125.	500.	Rare	Rare
Morgan dollar 1878-1921			Rare in all classes	
Peace dollar 1921-1935			Rare in all classes	
Ike dollar 1971-78	200.	Rare	—	3500.
Ike dollar 1976			Rare in all classes	
Anthony dollar 1979-81	25.	100.	—	—
Proof coins			Rare in all classes	

III-C: Struck through abnormal objects

Just about anything can get between the die and planchet, and be struck into the coin's surface, leaving a distinctive indentation, such as the pattern of the weave of cloth. The object must be retained to identify certain classes, such as struck in wrong metal.

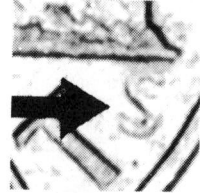

Cloth scrap	Filled die	Dropped letter

The classes are III-C-1, struck through cloth; III-C-2, wire; III-C-3, thread; III-C-4, filled die; III-C-5, dropped filling; III-C-6, wrong-metal fragments; III-C-7, struck coin fragments; III-C-8, rim burr; III-C-9, miscellaneous objects; and III-C-10, unstruck planchet fragments.

	Struck Through Cloth III-C-1	Wire III-C-2	Dropped Filling III-C-5	Struck Coin Fragment III-C-7
Indian cent 1859-1909	50.	50.	20.	75. up
Lincoln cent 1909-1942	35.	35.	15.	50. up
Lincoln cent 1943	—	75.	25.	100. up
Lincoln cent 1944-1958	25.	50.	10.	35. up
Lincoln cent 1959-1982	20.	50.	10.	25. up
Lincoln cent 1982-	25.	60.	15.	35. up
Buffalo nickel 1913-1938	60.	100.	10.	50. up
Jefferson nickel 1938-	50.	75.	10.	40. up
Jefferson nickel 1942-1945	60.	100.	15.	50. up
Mercury dime 1916-1945	60.	60.	15.	50. up
Roosevelt dime 1946-1964	50.	50.	15.	50. up
Roosevelt dime 1965-	35.	35.	10.	35. up
Roosevelt dime 1976	45.	45.	15.	45. up
Washington quarter 1932-64	75.	50.	15.	50. up
Washington quarter 1965-	45.	35.	10.	35. up
Washington quarter 1976	100.	75.	25.	100. up
Franklin half 1948-1963	75.	75.	25.	100. up
Kennedy half 1964	75.	75.	25.	100. up
Kennedy half 1965-1970	60.	60.	20.	100. up
Kennedy half 1971-	50.	50.	15.	75. up
Kennedy half 1976				Rare in all classes
Morgan dollar 1878-1921				Rare in all classes
Peace dollar 1921-1935				Rare in all classes
Ike dollar 1971-78				Rare in all classes
Ike dollar 1976				Rare in all classes
Anthony dollar 1979-81				Scarce to rare in all classes

Note: Some 1987, 1988 and 1989 quarters are found without mintmarks, classed as III-C-4, filled die. Values depend on market conditions. Filled dies have value only on current, uncirculated coins.

III-D: Struck on abnormal objects

This section contains coins struck on the wrong planchet, objects similar to a planchet, pieces of scrap and junk metal, two or more planchets stuck together, planchets that do not have the normal upset edge, and even on medal planchets. Anything the same size or smaller than a normal planchet can get into the dies and be struck.

Cent on dime planchet

Half dollar on dime planchet

Half dollar on quarter planchet

The classes are III-D-1, wrong metal on a cent planchet; III-D-2, on a nickel planchet; III-D-3, on a dime planchet; III-D-4, quarter planchet; III-D-5, half-dollar planchet; III-D-6, gold planchet; III-D-7, U.S. coin on foreign planchet; III-D-8, foreign coin on U.S. planchet; III-D-9, wrong-series planchet; III-D-10, scrap coin metal; III-D-11, junk non-coin metal; III-D-12, false planchet; III-D-13, bonded planchets; III-D-14, dollar planchet; III-D-15, medal planchet; III-D-16, Type I planchet; III-D-17, foreign coin on wrong foreign planchet; III-D-18, large planchet; III-D-19, hard planchet; III-D-20, small planchet; III-D-21, official samples; III-D-22, planchet fragment or lamination; and III-D-23, half-cent planchet.

	III-D-1	III-D-2	III-D-3	III-D-4	III-D-5	III-D-6	III-D-7	III-D-8
Flying Eagle cent 1856-58	—	—	2000.	—	—	—	—	—
Indian cent 1859-1909	—	—	1200.	—	—	—	—	—
Lincoln cent 1909-1942	—	—	375. up	—	—	—	100.	—
Lincoln cent 1943 (PD&S)	—	—	375. (On bronze $30,000)	—	—	—	2500.	—
Lincoln cent 1944-1958	—	—	150.-450.	—	—	—	100.	2000.
Lincoln cent 1959-1982	—	—	125.-450.	—	—	—	100.	100.
Lincoln cent 1976	—	—	150.	—	—	—	100.	100.
Lincoln cent 1982-	—	—	150.	—	—	—	100.	100.
Two-cent 1864-1873	800.	700.	1300.	—	—	—	—	—
Shield nickel 1866-1883	—	900.	Rare	—	—	—	—	—
Liberty nickel 1883-1912	650.	—	Rare	—	—	—	—	250.
Buffalo nickel 1913-1938	550.	—	Rare	—	—	—	—	—
Jefferson nickel 1938-	35.-500.	—	45.-550.	—	—	—	100.	—
Jefferson nickel 1942-1945	350.-850.	—	250.-400.	—	—	—	—	—
Jefferson nickel 1976	65.	—	100.	—	—	—	125.	—
Roosevelt dime 1965-	—	—	—	—	—	—	400.	—
Roosevelt dime 1976	—	—	—	—	—	—	1000.	—
Barber quarter 1892-1916	1200.	1200.	Rare	—	—	—	—	—
Standing Liberty 1916-30	800.	900.	Unknown	—	—	—	—	—
Washington quarter 1932-64	100.	55.-300.	100.-500.	—	—	—	300.	275.
Washington quarter 1965-	50.	35.-90.	50.-150.	—	—	—	200.	150.
Washington quarter 1976	—	250.	350.	—	—	—	—	—
Barber half 1891-1915						Rare in all classes		
Walking Liberty half 1916-47						Rare in all classes		
Franklin half 1948-1963	450.	500.	600.	300.	—	—	—	—
Kennedy half 1964	400.	450.	500.	250.	—	—	250.	—
Kennedy half 1965-1970	350.	400.	400.	200.	—	—	250.	—
Kennedy half 1971-	300.	350.	300.	100.	—	—	250.	400.
Kennedy half 1976	Rare	Rare	Rare	375.	—	—	—	—
Ike dollar 1971-78						Rare in all classes		
Ike dollar 1976						Rare in all classes		
Anthony dollar 1979-81	Rare	Rare	Rare	300.	—	—	—	—
Proof coins					Rare to unknown in all classes			

III-E: Double strikes

Only coins that receive two or more strikes fall in this section. Both sides of the coin are affected. Unless some object interferes, an equal area of both sides of the coin will be equally doubled. The exception is the second strike with a loose die, which will double only one side of a coin, but is a rare form occurring only on proofs.

A similar effect is flat-field doubling from die chatter, also only on proofs, which will add $1 to $10 to the coin's value and is relatively common.

The classes are III-E-1, close double strike (both centered); III-E-2, rotated second over centered first strike; III-E-3, off-center second over centered first; III-E-4, off-center second over off-centered first; III-E-5, saddle strike; III-E-6, multiple strike; III-E-7, obverse over reverse; III-E-8, struck over different denomination or series; III-E-9, U.S. over foreign; III-E-10, foreign over U.S.; III-E-11, foreign over foreign; III-E-12, chain

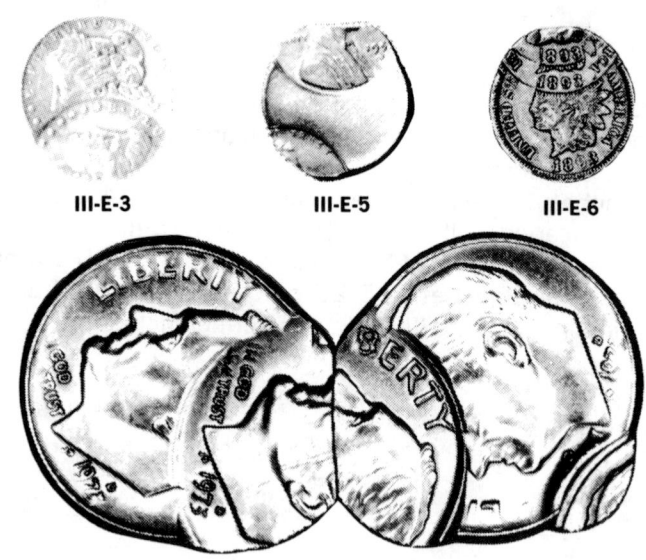

III-E-3   III-E-5   III-E-6

Chain strike (III-E-12)

strike; III-E-13, flat-field doubling (proof); III-E-14, second strike loose die (proof); III-E-15, second strike loose die (screw press); and III-E-16, first strike broadstrike, second strike off-center; III-E-17, second strike centered over off-center first strike (open collar); III-E-18, double strike on scrap or junk; III-E-19, struck on struck token or medal.

	III-E-1	III-E-2	III-E-3	III-E-4	III-E-5	III-E-6	III-E-7	III-E-8	III-E-9	III-E-10	III-E-11
Large cent 1793-1857	150.	200.	575.	—	—	—	350.	750.	—	—	—
Flying Eagle cent 1856-58	600.	175.	500.	—	—	300.	1500.	—	—	—	—
Indian cent 1859-1909	200.	150.	400.	—	—	—	250.	1000.	—	—	—
Lincoln cent 1909-1942	50.	60.	120.	—	—	—	200.	300.	—	—	—
Lincoln cent 1943	100.	150.	200.	—	—	—	400.	500.	—	—	—
Lincoln cent 1944-1958	50.	55.	60.	—	—	—	100.	250.	—	—	—
Lincoln cent 1959-1982	25.	45.	35.	—	—	—	150.	250.	—	—	—
Lincoln cent 1976	30.	50.	40.	—	—	—	150.	250.	—	—	—
Lincoln cent 1982-	30.	50.	50.	—	—	—	150.	250.	—	—	—
Liberty nickel 1883-1912	250.	350.	850.	—	—	—	350.	500.	—	—	—
Buffalo nickel 1913-1938	325.	125.	500.	—	—	—	225.	800.	—	—	—
Jefferson nickel 1938-	50.	75.	25.	—	—	—	150.	250.	—	—	—
Jefferson nickel 1942-1945	125.	150.	175.	—	—	—	200.	350.	—	—	—
Jefferson nickel 1976	60.	100.	35.	—	—	—	150.	250.	—	—	—
Half dime 1794-1873	500.	200.	650.	—	—	—	—	—	—	—	—
Dime 1798-1891	350.	200.	500.	—	—	—	—	1250.	—	—	—
Barber dime 1892-1916	300.	175.	400.	—	—	—	—	1200.	—	—	—
Mercury dime 1916-1945	200.	125.	350.	—	—	—	—	—	—	—	—
Roosevelt dime 1946-1964	50.	120.	100.	—	—	—	—	—	—	—	—
Roosevelt dime 1965-	45.	115.	55.	—	—	—	—	—	—	—	—
Roosevelt dime 1976	50.	125.	60.	—	—	—	—	—	—	—	—
Quarter 1796-1891	600.	—	750.	—	—	—	500.	—	—	—	—
Barber quarter 1892-1916	400.	200.	800.	—	—	—	500.	—	—	—	—
Standing Liberty quarter 1916-30								Rare in all classes			
Washington quarter 1932-64	120.	120.	140.	—	—	—	350.	500.	—	—	—
Washington quarter 1965-	75.	100.	50.	—	—	—	250.	400.	—	—	—
Washington quarter 1976	100.	150.	250.	—	—	—	Rare	Rare	—	—	—
Barber half 1891-1915	500.	600.	1000.	—	—	—	750.	—	—	—	—
Walking Liberty 1916-47	450.	500.	600.	—	—	—	700.	—	—	—	—
Franklin half 1948-1963	400.	450.	500.	—	—	—	500.	500.	—	—	—
Kennedy half 1964	400.	450.	500.	—	—	—	500.	500.	—	—	—
Kennedy half 1965-1970	275.	300.	400.	—	—	—	300.	450.	—	—	—
Kennedy half 1971-	200.	250.	300.	—	—	—	300.	400.	—	—	—
Kennedy half 1976								Rare in all classes			
Morgan dollar 1878-1921								Rare in all classes			
Peace dollar 1921-1935								Rare in all classes			
Ike dollar 1971-78								Rare in all classes			
Anthony dollar 1979-81								Rare in all classes			

III-F: Collar varieties

The collar is often referred to as the "third die" and is involved in a number of forms of misstrikes. The collar normally rises around the planchet, preventing it from squeezing sideways between the dies and at the same time forming the reeding on reeded-edge coins. If the collar is out of position or tilted, a form of partial collar results. If completely missing, it causes a broadstrike; if the planchet is not entirely between the dies, an off-center strike results.

The classes are III-F-1, flanged partial collar; III-F-2, tilted partial collar; III-F-3, centered broadstrike; III-F-4, uncentered broadstrike; III-F-5, off-center 10 percent to 30 percent; III-F-6, off-center 31 percent to 70 percent; III-F-7, off-center 71 percent and over; III-F-8, reversed partial collar; III-F-9, strike clip; III-F-10, reverse broadstrike; and III-F-11, rotated multisided planchet; III-F-12, collar too high; III-F-13, wire edge; III-F-14, split-off reeding; and III-F-15, reedless coin.

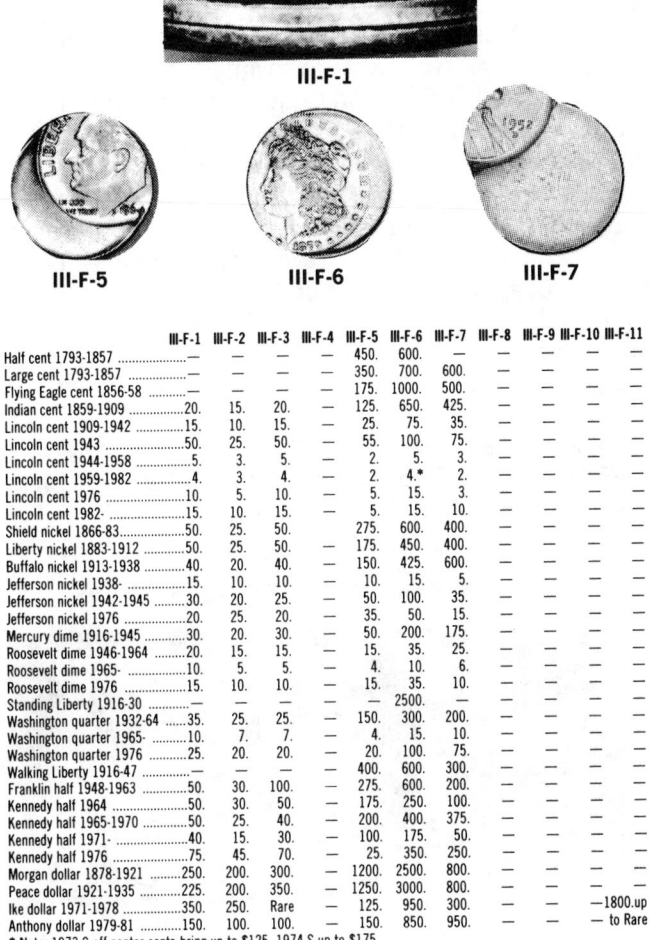

III-F-1

III-F-5   III-F-6   III-F-7

	III-F-1	III-F-2	III-F-3	III-F-4	III-F-5	III-F-6	III-F-7	III-F-8	III-F-9	III-F-10	III-F-11
Half cent 1793-1857	—	—	—	—	450.	600.	—	—	—	—	—
Large cent 1793-1857	—	—	—	—	350.	700.	600.	—	—	—	—
Flying Eagle cent 1856-58	—	—	—	—	175.	1000.	500.	—	—	—	—
Indian cent 1859-1909	20.	15.	20.	—	125.	650.	425.	—	—	—	—
Lincoln cent 1909-1942	15.	10.	15.	—	25.	75.	35.	—	—	—	—
Lincoln cent 1943	50.	25.	50.	—	55.	100.	75.	—	—	—	—
Lincoln cent 1944-1958	5.	3.	5.	—	2.	5.	3.	—	—	—	—
Lincoln cent 1959-1982	4.	3.	4.	—	2.	4.*	2.	—	—	—	—
Lincoln cent 1976	10.	5.	10.	—	5.	15.	3.	—	—	—	—
Lincoln cent 1982-	15.	10.	15.	—	5.	15.	10.	—	—	—	—
Shield nickel 1866-83	50.	25.	50.	—	275.	600.	400.	—	—	—	—
Liberty nickel 1883-1912	50.	25.	50.	—	175.	450.	400.	—	—	—	—
Buffalo nickel 1913-1938	40.	20.	40.	—	150.	425.	600.	—	—	—	—
Jefferson nickel 1938-	15.	10.	10.	—	10.	15.	5.	—	—	—	—
Jefferson nickel 1942-1945	30.	20.	25.	—	50.	100.	35.	—	—	—	—
Jefferson nickel 1976	20.	25.	20.	—	35.	50.	15.	—	—	—	—
Mercury dime 1916-1945	30.	20.	30.	—	50.	200.	175.	—	—	—	—
Roosevelt dime 1946-1964	20.	15.	15.	—	15.	35.	25.	—	—	—	—
Roosevelt dime 1965-	10.	5.	5.	—	4.	10.	6.	—	—	—	—
Roosevelt dime 1976	15.	10.	10.	—	15.	35.	10.	—	—	—	—
Standing Liberty 1916-30	—	—	—	—	—	2500.	—	—	—	—	—
Washington quarter 1932-64	35.	25.	25.	—	150.	300.	200.	—	—	—	—
Washington quarter 1965-	10.	7.	7.	—	4.	15.	10.	—	—	—	—
Washington quarter 1976	25.	20.	20.	—	20.	100.	75.	—	—	—	—
Walking Liberty 1916-47	—	—	—	—	400.	600.	300.	—	—	—	—
Franklin half 1948-1963	50.	30.	100.	—	275.	600.	200.	—	—	—	—
Kennedy half 1964	50.	30.	50.	—	175.	250.	100.	—	—	—	—
Kennedy half 1965-1970	50.	25.	40.	—	200.	400.	375.	—	—	—	—
Kennedy half 1971-	40.	15.	30.	—	100.	175.	50.	—	—	—	—
Kennedy half 1976	75.	45.	70.	—	25.	350.	250.	—	—	—	—
Morgan dollar 1878-1921	250.	200.	300.	—	1200.	2500.	800.	—	—	—	—
Peace dollar 1921-1935	225.	200.	350.	—	1250.	3000.	800.	—	—	—	—
Ike dollar 1971-1978	350.	250.	Rare	—	125.	950.	300.	—	—	—1800.up	
Anthony dollar 1979-81	150.	100.	100.	—	150.	850.	950.	—	—	— to Rare	

* Note: 1973-S off-center cents bring up to $125, 1974-S up to $175.

III-G: Misaligned and rotated (die) strikes

Misaligned die (III-G-1)

Normal   **90 degrees**   **135 degrees**

One (rarely both) of the dies may be offset misaligned — off to one side — or may be tilted (vertically misaligned) to one side. It may have been installed so that it is turned in relation to the other die, or may turn in the holder, or the shank may break, allowing the die face to rotate in relation to the opposing die. Values for offset misalignment range from $5 to $50, depending on the denomination. Vertical misaligned dies are rarely found and, like rotated dies, find only limited collector interest. Ninety- and 180-degree rotations are the most popular, bringing premiums of $5 to $400, again depending on the coin. Rotations of 14 degrees or less have no value.

The 1989-D Congress dollar is found with a nearly 180-degree rotated reverse and currently retails for around $2,000. A total of 30 have been reported.

The classes are III-G-1, offset misalignment; III-G-2, vertical misalignment; III-G-3, rotated 15 to 45 degrees; III-G-4, rotated 46 to 135 degrees; and III-G-5, rotated 136 to 180 degrees.

III-H: Lettered- and design-edge varieties

III-H-2

Some early U.S. coins and a number of foreign coins have lettered edges or designs on the edges. These are applied to the planchet before it is struck by the dies. Missing edge letters on early U.S. half dollars will add $10; overlapping edge letters will add $25 to the coin's value. Malfunctions of the application of the motto or design to the edge fall in this section.

The classes are III-H-1, overlapping edge letters or design; III-H-2, wrong edge motto or design; III-H-3, missing edge motto or design; III-H-4, jammed edge die; III-H-5, misplaced segment of edge die; and III-H-6, double-struck edge motto or design.

III-I: Defective strikes, mismatched dies, and die changes

The final section of the striking division covers coins not properly struck for reasons other than those in previous classes, coins struck with mismatched ("muled") dies, and those where it is possible to determine that a die was removed and a different die substituted. The mismatched-die varieties must be taken on a case-by-case basis, and the other two classes presently have little collector demand or premium. Some coins are struck with transposed dies (reverse die as hammer die), but this rarely affects value.

The classes are III-I-1, defective strikes; III-I-2, mismatched die; III-I-3, die substitutions; III-I-4, single strike proof; III-I-5, single die proof; and III-I-6, transposed dies.

Division IV: Official mint modifications

Several mint-produced varieties occur after the coin has been struck, resulting in the addition of a fourth division to the original PDS system. Since most of these coins are either unique or special varieties, each one must be taken on a case-by-case basis.

IV-A: Matte proofs

To provide a cataloging system, we have listed matte proofs (IV-A), including IV-A-1, matte proof; IV-A-II, matte proof on one side; and IV-A-3, sandblasted proofs.

IV-B: Additional engraving

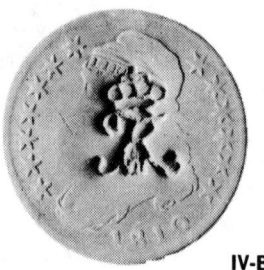

IV-B-1   IV-B-3

Classes consist of IV-B-1, punched or engraved lettering; IV-B-2, countermark; and IV-B-3, counterstamp.

IV-C: Restrikes

IV-C-7

Restrikes consist of IV-C-1, restrike on same denomination; IV-C-2, restrike on different denomination; IV-C-3, restrike on foreign coin; IV-C-4, restrike on token or medal; IV-C-5, restrike with original dies; IV-C-6, restrike with mismatched dies; IV-C-7, restrike with new dies; and IV-C-8, fantasy strike.

IV-D: Adjustment marks

Adjustment marks are one of the principal means of correcting a coin's weight. Such marks rarely add value to a coin but deserve mention.

IV-D: Machine doubling damage

The commonest form of doubling that occurs on coins is machine doubling damage, formerly called ejection doubling and by a variety of other names by other authors and writers, including "shift," shelf doubling, and micro doubling. It is important that the collector recognize it to avoid wasting time collecting it. Machine doubling has a number of causes, including loose or worn parts in the coin press, which allow the die to contact the coin after it is struck, damaging it in a manner that

causes parts of the design to appear doubled.

Machine doubling will usually be found on only one side of the design elements, appearing as a shelf above the field and never reaching the field. It never displays the notching that punching or hubbing varieties cause between the overlapping images and commonly will affect the date and mintmark, something that can't happen with a hubbing variety because the mintmark is added after the hubbing process. When you find doubling affecting only a small portion of the design on one side of a coin, always suspect machine doubling damage.

Since it is not a part of the strike and is, in fact, damage to the already struck coin, it has no collector value.

Canada

Large cents

1858-1910   1911-1920

BRONZE

KM#	Date	Mintage	VG-8	F-12	VF-20	XF-40	MS-60	MS-63
1	1858	421,000	30.00	35.00	50.00	70.00	165.00	400.00
	1859/8 wide 9	I.A.	20.00	25.00	35.00	50.00	125.00	250.00
	1859 narrow 9	9,579,000	1.00	2.00	3.00	5.00	20.00	120.00
	1859 double punched narrow 9 Type I							
		I.A.	160.00	220.00	300.00	475.00	875.00	1500.
	1859 double punched narrow 9 Type II							
		I.A.	25.00	32.50	45.00	65.00	135.00	275.00
7	1876H	4,000,000	1.00	2.00	3.00	5.00	35.00	160.00
	1881H	2,000,000	2.00	3.00	4.50	8.00	45.00	170.00
	1882H	4,000,000	1.00	1.75	2.25	5.00	25.00	90.00
	1884	2,500,000	1.50	2.50	3.50	6.00	35.00	140.00
	1886	1,500,000	2.75	3.50	5.00	9.25	50.00	180.00
	1887	1,500,000	2.00	2.75	4.25	6.50	35.00	140.00
	1888	4,000,000	1.00	1.50	2.00	3.50	24.00	90.00
	1890H	1,000,000	3.50	6.00	10.00	18.00	90.00	285.00
	1891 lg. date	1,452,000	3.00	5.00	8.00	15.00	60.00	225.00
	1891 S.D.L.L.	I.A.	35.00	55.00	65.00	90.00	250.00	650.00
	1891 S.D.S.L.	I.A.	25.00	35.00	50.00	70.00	165.00	425.00
	1892	1,200,000	2.25	4.00	6.00	8.50	30.00	110.00
	1893	2,000,000	1.25	2.00	3.50	5.75	25.00	85.00
	1894	1,000,000	4.25	6.50	9.00	14.00	75.00	200.00
	1895	1,200,000	2.50	4.25	5.75	8.00	45.00	150.00
	1896	2,000,000	1.25	1.75	2.25	4.00	25.00	90.00
	1897	1,500,000	1.25	2.00	2.50	4.50	25.00	95.00
	1898H	1,000,000	2.75	4.25	5.75	8.00	45.00	190.00
	1899	2,400,000	1.25	1.75	2.50	4.00	25.00	85.00
	1900	1,000,000	3.50	6.50	9.00	12.50	55.00	160.00
	1900H	2,600,000	1.00	1.75	2.25	3.75	20.00	70.00
	1901	4,100,000	1.00	1.50	2.00	3.25	20.00	60.00
8	1902	3,000,000	1.00	1.50	1.75	3.00	12.00	35.00
	1903	4,000,000	1.00	1.50	2.00	3.00	17.50	45.00
	1904	2,500,000	1.50	2.00	3.25	5.00	20.00	65.00
	1905	2,000,000	2.25	3.25	5.00	6.50	30.00	85.00
	1906	4,100,000	1.00	1.50	2.00	3.50	17.00	45.00
	1907	2,400,000	1.50	2.50	3.25	4.75	25.00	75.00
	1907H	800,000	6.00	8.00	12.00	20.00	70.00	220.00
	1908	2,401,506	1.50	2.75	3.75	5.00	22.00	65.00
	1909	3,973,339	1.00	1.25	2.00	3.00	17.50	45.00
	1910	5,146,487	.90	1.25	1.75	2.75	17.50	40.00
15	1911	4,663,486	.75	1.25	1.75	3.00	18.00	55.00
21	1912	5,107,642	.75	1.00	1.50	2.50	15.00	45.00
	1913	5,735,405	.75	1.00	1.50	2.50	12.00	45.00
	1914	3,405,958	1.00	1.25	2.00	3.50	25.00	85.00
	1915	4,932,134	.75	1.00	1.75	2.75	15.00	55.00
	1916	11,022,367	.45	.65	.90	2.00	12.00	45.00
	1917	11,899,254	.45	.65	.90	1.50	8.00	30.00
	1918	12,970,798	.45	.65	.90	1.50	8.00	30.00
	1919	11,279,634	.45	.65	.90	1.50	8.00	30.00
	1920	6,762,247	.45	.65	.90	1.50	10.00	35.00

Small cents

Dot

BRONZE

KM#	Date	Mintage	VG-8	F-12	VF-20	XF-40	MS-60	MS-63
28	1920	15,483,923	.15	.25	.90	1.50	8.50	30.00
	1921	7,601,627	.30	.50	1.75	4.00	12.00	50.00
	1922	1,243,635	8.00	10.00	13.00	20.00	95.00	225.00
	1923	1,019,002	12.50	15.00	22.00	32.00	150.00	425.00
	1924	1,593,195	3.50	5.00	6.50	10.00	70.00	160.00
	1925	1,000,622	11.00	13.00	19.00	27.00	125.00	325.00
	1926	2,143,372	1.50	2.00	3.00	7.00	50.00	140.00
	1927	3,553,928	.60	.85	2.00	4.00	22.50	85.00
	1928	9,144,860	.15	.20	.50	1.50	10.00	35.00
	1929	12,159,840	.15	.20	.50	1.50	10.00	35.00
	1930	2,538,613	1.50	1.75	2.50	5.00	25.00	75.00
	1931	3,842,776	.60	.85	1.75	3.50	19.00	60.00
	1932	21,316,190	.15	.20	.40	1.50	9.00	30.00
	1933	12,079,310	.15	.20	.40	1.50	9.00	30.00
	1934	7,042,358	.15	.20	.40	1.50	9.00	30.00
	1935	7,526,400	.15	.20	.40	1.50	9.00	30.00
	1936	8,768,769	.15	.20	.40	1.50	8.00	27.50
	1936 dot below dt	678,823	—	—	—	—	Unique	—
	1936 dot below dt	4 known	—	—	—	—	Specimen	—

Maple Leaf

KM#	Date	Mintage	VG-8	F-12	VF-20	XF-40	MS-60	MS-63
32	1937	10,040,231	.10	.20	.35	1.10	2.00	4.50
	1938	18,365,608	.10	.15	.25	.50	2.00	7.00
	1939	21,600,319	.10	.15	.25	.50	2.00	5.00
	1940	85,740,532	—	.10	.20	.40	1.50	4.00
	1941	56,336,011	—	.10	.25	.70	8.00	32.00
	1942	76,113,708	—	.10	.20	.70	7.00	25.00
	1943	89,111,969	—	.10	.20	.40	3.00	9.00
	1944	44,131,216	—	.10	.20	1.00	8.00	25.00
	1945	77,268,591	—	.10	.20	.35	1.25	4.00
	1946	56,662,071	—	.20	.30	.60	1.50	4.50
	1947	31,093,901	—	.10	.20	.35	1.50	5.00
	1947ML	47,855,448	—	.10	.20	.35	1.25	3.50

Modified Obverse Legend

KM#	Date	Mintage	VG-8	F-12	VF-20	XF-40	MS-60	MS-63
41	1948	25,767,779	.10	.20	.35	.60	2.00	7.00
	1949	33,128,933	—	.10	.15	.25	1.25	3.00
	1950	60,444,992	—	.10	.15	.25	1.25	3.00
	1951	80,430,379	—	.10	.15	.25	1.00	2.75
	1952	67,631,736	—	.10	.15	.25	1.00	2.75

Elizabeth II Effigy

KM#	Date	Mintage	VG-8	F-12	VF-20	XF-40	MS-60	MS-63
49	1953 w/o strap	67,806,016	—	.10	.15	.25	.60	1.75
	1953 w/strap	Inc. Ab.	.45	.90	1.25	2.75	11.00	25.00
	1954 w/strap	22,181,760	.10	.15	.30	.50	1.75	4.50
	1954 w/o strap	Inc. Ab.		Proof-Like Only		—	100.00	180.00
	1955 w/strap	56,403,193	—	.10	.15	.20	.50	1.00
	1955 w/o strap	Inc. Ab.	75.00	125.00	185.00	225.00	475.00	900.00
	1956	78,658,535	—	—	—	.10	.50	.80
	1957	100,601,792	—	—	—	.10	.30	.70
	1958	59,385,679	—	—	—	.10	.30	.70
	1959	83,615,343	—	—	—	.10	.25	.60
49	1960	75,772,775	—	—	—	.10	.25	.60
	1961	139,598,404	—	—	—	—	.15	.40
	1962	227,244,069	—	—	—	—	.10	.25
	1963	279,076,334	—	—	—	—	.10	.25
	1964	484,655,322	—	—	—	—	.10	.25

New Elizabeth II Effigy

KM#	Date	Mintage	VG-8	F-12	VF-20	XF-40	MS-60	MS-63
59.1	1965 sm. beads, pointed 5							
		304,441,082	—	—	—	.10	.45	1.00
	1965 sm. beads, blunt 5 I.A.		—	—	—	—	.10	.25
	1965 lg. beads, pointed 5 I.A.		—	—	1.50	4.00	13.00	25.00
	1965 lg. beads, blunt 5 I.A.		—	—	—	.10	.20	.35
	1966	184,151,087	—	—	—	—	.10	.20
	1968	329,695,772	—	—	—	—	.10	.20
	1969	335,240,929	—	—	—	—	.10	.20
	1970	311,145,010	—	—	—	—	.10	.20
	1971	298,228,936	—	—	—	—	.10	.20
	1972	451,304,591	—	—	—	—	.10	.20
	1973	457,059,852	—	—	—	—	.10	.20
	1974	692,058,489	—	—	—	—	.10	.20
	1975	642,318,000	—	—	—	—	.10	.20
	1976	701,122,890	—	—	—	—	.10	.20
	1977	453,762,670	—	—	—	—	.10	.20
	1978	911,170,647	—	—	—	—	.10	.20

Smaller Bust

KM#	Date	Mintage	VG-8	F-12	VF-20	XF-40	MS-60	MS-63
59.2	1979	754,394,064	—	—	—	—	.10	.20

Reduced Weight

KM#	Date	Mintage	VG-8	F-12	VF-20	XF-40	MS-60	MS-63
127	1980	912,052,318	—	—	—	—	.10	.15
	1981	1,209,468,500	—	—	—	—	.10	.15
	1981	199,000	—	—	—	—	Proof	1.00

New Elizabeth II Effigy

KM#	Date	Mintage	VG-8	F-12	VF-20	XF-40	MS-60	MS-63
132	1982	911,001,000	—	—	—	—	.10	.15
	1982	180,908	—	—	—	—	Proof	1.00
	1983	975,510,000	—	—	—	—	.10	.15
	1983	168,000	—	—	—	—	Proof	1.00
	1984	838,225,000	—	—	—	—	.10	.15
	1984	161,602	—	—	—	—	Proof	1.00
	1985	126,618,000	—	—	—	—	.10	.15
	1985	157,037	—	—	—	—	Proof	1.00
	1986	740,335,000	—	—	—	—	.10	.15
	1986	175,745	—	—	—	—	Proof	1.00
	1987	774,549,000	—	—	—	—	.10	.15
	1987	179,004	—	—	—	—	Proof	1.00
	1988	482,676,752	—	—	—	—	.10	.15
	1988	175,259	—	—	—	—	Proof	1.00
	1989	1,077,347,200	—	—	—	—	.10	.15
	1989	170,928	—	—	—	—	Proof	1.00

New Elizabeth II Effigy

KM#	Date	Mintage	VG-8	F-12	VF-20	XF-40	MS-60	MS-63
181	1990	218,035,000	—	—	—	—	.10	.15
	1990	140,649	—	—	—	—	Proof	1.00
	1991	696,629,000	—	—	—	—	.10	.15
	1991	—	—	—	—	—	Proof	1.00

Commemorative cents

KM#	Date	Mintage	VG-8	BRONZE F-12	VF-20	XF-40	MS-60	MS-63
65	1967 Confederation Centennial							
		345,140,645	—	—	—	—	.10	.20
204	1992 Confederation 125							
		—	—	—	—	—	.10	.15
		—	—	—	—	—	Proof	1.00

Five cents

Round 0's   Oval 0's

KM#	Date	Mintage	1.1620 g, .925 SILVER, .0346 oz ASW VG-8	F-12	VF-20	XF-40	MS-60	MS-63
2	1858 sm. date	1,500,000	7.25	11.00	15.00	25.00	225.00	400.00
	1858 lg. date over sm. date	Inc. Ab.	70.00	135.00	225.00	325.00	700.00	2000.
	1870 flat rim	2,800,000	6.50	10.00	20.00	40.00	175.00	420.00
	1870 wire rim	Inc. Ab.	6.50	10.00	20.00	45.00	200.00	430.00
	1871	1,400,000	6.50	10.00	18.00	35.00	165.00	420.00
	1872H	2,000,000	4.75	7.25	12.00	25.00	175.00	400.00
	1874H plain 4	800,000	12.00	20.00	35.00	65.00	350.00	700.
	1874H crosslet 4	Inc. Ab.	7.25	11.00	20.00	40.00	275.00	600.00
	1875H lg. date	1,000,000	75.00	140.00	250.00	425.00	1450.	3500.
	1875H sm. date	Inc. Ab.	60.00	100.00	200.00	325.00	1200.	2500.
	1880H	3,000,000	3.00	5.50	10.00	20.00	100.00	350.00
	1881H	1,500,000	3.50	6.00	11.00	24.00	130.00	400.00
	1882H	1,000,000	4.25	8.00	15.00	30.00	160.00	525.00
	1883H	600,000	9.00	18.00	35.00	60.00	350.00	850.00
	1884	200,000	55.00	90.00	140.00	300.00	1650.	4500.
	1885	1,000,000	4.75	10.00	20.00	40.00	300.00	900.00
	1886	1,700,000	3.50	6.50	12.00	24.00	175.00	375.00
	1887	500,000	10.00	15.00	30.00	50.00	250.00	600.00
	1888	1,000,000	3.00	5.00	10.00	20.00	125.00	300.00
	1889	1,200,000	14.00	25.00	40.00	80.00	375.00	1000.
	1890H	1,000,000	3.50	6.00	16.00	30.00	150.00	375.00
	1891	1,800,000	2.50	4.00	7.00	15.00	80.00	225.00
	1892	860,000	3.50	6.00	12.00	30.00	175.00	400.00
	1893	1,700,000	2.50	4.00	8.00	15.00	85.00	225.00
	1894	500,000	9.00	18.00	32.00	55.00	275.00	650.00
	1896	1,500,000	3.00	5.00	10.00	16.00	110.00	250.00
	1897	1,319,283	3.00	4.75	9.00	16.00	110.00	225.00
	1898	580,717	6.00	10.00	30.00	40.00	165.00	400.00
	1899	3,000,000	1.75	3.00	6.00	12.00	75.00	180.00
	1900 oval 0's	1,800,000	2.50	4.00	7.00	15.00	90.00	225.00
	1900 round 0's	Inc. Ab.	12.00	25.00	35.00	75.00	275.00	700.00
	1901	2,000,000	1.75	3.00	6.00	12.00	80.00	200.00
9	1902	2,120,000	1.50	2.00	3.00	6.50	35.00	60.00
	1902 lg. broad H	2,200,000	2.00	2.75	4.25	8.00	40.00	65.00
	1902 sm. narrow H	Inc. Ab.	6.00	10.00	20.00	40.00	120.00	190.00
13	1903	1,000,000	4.00	6.00	12.00	22.00	165.00	350.00
	1903H	2,640,000	1.75	3.00	5.00	10.00	75.00	190.00
	1904	2,400,000	1.75	3.00	6.00	12.00	90.00	300.00
	1905	2,600,000	1.75	3.00	5.00	10.00	75.00	180.00
	1906	3,100,000	1.50	2.00	3.00	7.00	65.00	140.00
	1907	5,200,000	1.50	2.00	3.00	7.00	60.00	120.00
	1908	1,220,524	4.00	6.50	11.00	20.00	90.00	200.00
	1909	1,983,725	1.75	2.25	6.00	12.00	125.00	325.00
	1910	3,850,325	1.25	1.75	3.00	6.00	45.00	85.00
16	1911	3,692,350	1.75	2.50	5.00	9.00	80.00	175.00
22	1912	5,863,170	1.25	2.00	3.00	5.00	45.00	100.00
	1913	5,488,048	1.25	2.00	3.00	5.00	30.00	60.00
	1914	4,202,179	1.25	2.00	3.25	6.00	50.00	115.00
	1915	1,172,258	6.00	10.00	18.00	40.00	200.00	425.00
	1916	2,481,675	2.75	4.00	6.50	15.00	95.00	225.00
	1917	5,521,373	1.25	1.75	2.50	4.00	40.00	75.00
	1918	6,052,298	1.25	1.75	2.50	4.00	30.00	65.00
	1919	7,835,400	1.25	1.75	2.50	4.00	30.00	65.00
22a	1920	10,649,851	1.1664 g, .800 SILVER, .0300 oz ASW 1.25	1.75	2.50	4.00	27.00	60.00
	1921	2,582,495	1150.	1050.	2550.	4000.	11,000.	20,000.

NOTE: Approximately 460 known, balance remelted.
NOTE: Stack's A.G. Carter Jr. Sale 12-89 Choice BU finest known realized $57,200.

	Near 6					Far 6	

NICKEL

KM#	Date	Mintage	VG-8	F-12	VF-20	XF-40	MS-60	MS-63
29	1922	4,794,119	.20	.75	2.00	6.00	35.00	75.00
	1923	2,502,279	.30	1.00	3.00	8.00	85.00	200.00
	1924	3,105,839	.20	.60	2.25	6.00	65.00	150.00
	1925	201,921	20.00	30.00	50.00	130.00	700.00	1500.
	1926 near 6	938,162	2.50	4.50	12.00	40.00	240.00	600.00
	1926 far 6	Inc. Ab.	50.00	90.00	150.00	300.00	1200.	2200.
	1927	5,285,627	.20	.60	2.00	5.00	45.00	120.00
	1928	4,577,712	.20	.60	2.00	5.00	40.00	80.00
	1929	5,611,911	.20	.60	2.00	5.00	45.00	120.00
	1930	3,704,673	.20	.60	2.00	5.00	70.00	150.00
	1931	5,100,830	.20	.60	2.00	5.00	70.00	150.00
	1932	3,198,566	.20	.60	2.25	6.00	75.00	150.00
	1933	2,597,867	.40	1.00	3.00	8.00	110.00	300.00
	1934	3,827,304	.20	.60	2.00	5.00	80.00	200.00
	1935	3,900,000	.20	.60	2.00	5.00	70.00	160.00
	1936	4,400,450	.20	.60	2.00	5.00	40.00	85.00

KM#	Date	Mintage	VG-8	F-12	VF-20	XF-40	MS-60	MS-63
33	1937 dot	4,593,263	.20	.35	1.75	3.00	10.00	25.00
	1938	3,898,974	.15	.75	1.75	7.00	65.00	150.00
	1939	5,661,123	.20	.50	1.75	4.50	40.00	70.00
	1940	13,920,197	.15	.30	1.00	2.00	14.00	40.00
	1941	8,681,785	.10	.25	1.00	2.50	17.00	42.00
	1942 round	6,847,544	.10	.30	1.00	2.50	14.00	40.00

Tombac (BRASS)

39	1942 - 12 sided	3,396,234	.30	.60	1.00	1.50	3.00	7.00

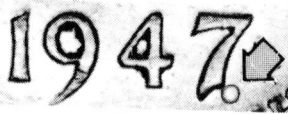 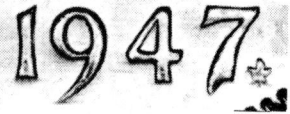

	Dot					Maple leaf	

NICKEL

KM#	Date	Mintage	VG-8	F-12	VF-20	XF-40	MS-60	MS-63
39a	1946	6,952,684	.15	.25	.50	2.00	10.00	22.50
	1947	7,603,724	.15	.25	.50	1.00	6.00	14.00
	1947 dot	Inc. Ab.	10.00	12.50	20.00	40.00	220.00	600.00
	1947 maple leaf	9,595,124	.15	.25	.50	1.00	6.00	12.00

Modified Obverse Legend

42	1948	1,810,789	.50	.80	1.00	2.00	15.00	25.00
	1949	13,037,090	.15	.15	.20	.60	4.00	7.00
	1950	11,970,521	.15	.15	.20	.60	4.00	7.00

CHROMIUM-PLATED STEEL

42a	1951 low relief*	4,313,410	.15	.20	.50	1.00	2.50	4.50
	1951 high relief* *	Inc. Ab.	200.00	325.00	500.00	750.00	1150.	2000.
	1952	10,891,148	.15	.20	.50	1.00	3.00	4.50

*NOTE: A in GRATIA points between denticles.
* *NOTE: A in GRATIA points to a denticle.

Elizabeth II Effigy - 12 Sided Coinage

KM#	Date	Mintage	VG-8	F-12	VF-20	XF-40	MS-60	MS-63
50	1953 w/o strap	16,635,552	.15	.25	.40	.75	3.00	4.50
	1953 w/strap	Inc.Ab.	.15	.25	.45	1.00	3.00	6.50
	1954	6,998,662	.15	.25	.50	1.00	4.50	7.50

NICKEL

KM#	Date	Mintage	VG-8	F-12	VF-20	XF-40	MS-60	MS-63
50a	1955	5,355,028	.15	.20	.25	.75	3.00	4.50
	1956	9,399,854	—	.20	.30	.45	1.75	3.00
	1957	7,387,703	—	—	.25	.30	1.25	2.75
	1958	7,607,521	—	—	.25	.30	1.25	2.75
	1959	11,552,523	—	—	—	.20	.65	1.25
	1960	37,157,433	—	—	—	.15	.25	.75
	1961	47,889,051	—	—	—	—	.20	.40
	1962	46,307,305	—	—	—	—	.20	.40

Round Coinage

KM#	Date	Mintage	VG-8	F-12	VF-20	XF-40	MS-60	MS-63
57	1963	43,970,320	—	—	—	—	.20	.40
	1964	78,075,068	—	—	—	—	.20	.40
	1964 XWL	—	6.00	8.00	10.00	12.50	20.00	30.00

New Elizabeth II Effigy

KM#	Date	Mintage	VG-8	F-12	VF-20	XF-40	MS-60	MS-63
60.1	1965	84,876,018	—	—	—	—	.20	.30
	1966	27,976,648	—	—	—	—	.20	.30
	1968	101,930,379	—	—	—	—	.20	.30
	1969	27,830,229	—	—	—	—	.20	.30
	1970	5,726,010	—	—	—	.25	.55	.75
	1971	27,312,609	—	—	—	—	.20	.30
	1972	62,417,387	—	—	—	—	.20	.30
	1973	53,507,435	—	—	—	—	.20	.30
	1974	94,704,645	—	—	—	—	.20	.30
	1975	138,882,000	—	—	—	—	.20	.30
	1976	55,140,213	—	—	—	—	.20	.30
	1977	89,120,791	—	—	—	—	.20	.30
	1978	137,079,273	—	—	—	—	.20	.30

Smaller bust

KM#	Date	Mintage	VG-8	F-12	VF-20	XF-40	MS-60	MS-63
60.2	1979	186,295,825	—	—	—	—	.20	.30
	1980	134,878,000	—	—	—	—	.20	.30
	1981	99,107,900	—	—	—	—	.20	.30
	1981	199,000	—	—	—	—	Proof	1.00

COPPER-NICKEL

KM#	Date	Mintage	VG-8	F-12	VF-20	XF-40	MS-60	MS-63
60.2a	1982	64,924,400	—	—	—	—	.20	.30
	1982	180,908	—	—	—	—	Proof	1.00
	1983	72,596,000	—	—	—	—	.20	.30
	1983	168,000	—	—	—	—	Proof	1.00
	1984	84,088,000	—	—	—	—	.20	.30
	1984	161,602	—	—	—	—	Proof	1.00
	1985	126,618,000	—	—	—	—	.20	.30
	1985	157,037	—	—	—	—	Proof	1.00
	1986	156,104,000	—	—	—	—	.20	.30
	1986	175,745	—	—	—	—	Proof	1.00
	1987	106,299,000	—	—	—	—	.10	.15
	1987	179,004	—	—	—	—	Proof	1.00
	1988	75,025,000	—	—	—	—	.10	.15
	1988	175,259	—	—	—	—	Proof	1.00
	1989	141,435,538	—	—	—	—	.10	.15
	1989	170,928	—	—	—	—	Proof	1.00

KM#	Date	Mintage	VG-8	F-12	VF-20	XF-40	MS-60	MS-63
182	1990	42,402,000	—	—	—	—	.10	.15
	1990	140,649	—	—	—	—	Proof	1.00
	1991	—	—	—	—	—	.10	.15
	1991	—	—	—	—	—	Proof	1.00

Commemorative five cents

KM#	Date	Mintage	VG-8	F-12	VF-20	XF-40	MS-60	MS-63
40	1943 Victory, Tombac (Brass)							
		24,760,256	.15	.25	.35	1.00	2.00	5.00
	CHROMIUM-PLATED STEEL							
40a	1944	11,532,784	.15	.25	.50	.90	2.00	4.00
	1945	18,893,216,	.15	.25	.50	.90	2.00	4.00

KM#	Date	Mintage	VG-8	F-12	VF-20	XF-40	MS-60	MS-63
48	1951 Nickel Bicentennial, Nickel							
		9,028,507	.15	.20	.25	.50	1.75	3.00

KM#	Date	Mintage	VG-8	F-12	VF-20	XF-40	MS-60	MS-63
66	1967 Confederation Centennial							
		36,876,574	—	—	—	—	.20	.30
205	1992 Confederation 125							
		—	—	—	—	—	.10	.15
		—	—	—	—	—	Proof	1.00

Ten cents

1858-1901

1902-1910

			2.3240 g, .925 SILVER, .0691 oz ASW					
KM#	Date	Mintage	VG-8	F-12	VF-20	XF-40	MS-60	MS-63
3	1858/5	Inc. Below	—	—	—		Rare	—
	1858	1,250,000	9.00	16.00	35.00	60.00	240.00	550.00
	1870 narrow 0	1,600,000	9.00	16.00	35.00	65.00	250.00	575.00
	1870 wide 0	Inc. Ab.	12.00	22.00	40.00	80.00	300.00	600.00
	1871	800,000	10.00	20.00	35.00	75.00	300.00	700.00
	1871H	1,870,000	13.00	22.00	55.00	100.00	375.00	800.00
	1872H	1,000,000	40.00	80.00	160.00	325.00	900.00	2250.
	1874H	600,000	6.00	12.00	25.00	55.00	240.00	620.00
	1875H	1,000,000	160.00	275.00	465.00	1000.	2750.	6750.
	1880H	1,500,000	4.75	9.00	18.00	40.00	225.00	600.00
	1881H	950,000	6.00	12.00	28.00	60.00	250.00	600.00
	1882H	1,000,000	5.50	14.00	25.00	55.00	290.00	600.00
	1883H	300,000	15.00	30.00	65.00	135.00	750.00	1500.
	1884	150,000	120.00	230.00	450.00	1100.	3250.	8000.
	1885	400,000	12.00	25.00	65.00	135.00	850.00	2250.
	1886 sm. 6	800,000	7.75	15.00	30.00	60.00	350.00	800.00
	1886 lg. 6	Inc. Ab.	10.00	20.00	50.00	110.00	450.00	925.00
	1887	350,000	15.00	30.00	75.00	185.00	1150.	2500.
	1888	500,000	4.00	8.00	20.00	40.00	225.00	500.00
	1889	600,000	350.00	550.00	1200.	2000.	5000.	10,000.
	1890H	450,000	7.75	14.00	30.00	70.00	325.00	700.00

KM#	Date	Mintage	VG-8	F-12	VF-20	XF-40	MS-60	MS-63
3	1891 21 leaves	800,000	8.00	15.00	32.50	80.00	350.00	800.00
	1891 22 leaves	Inc. Ab.	8.00	15.00	32.50	80.00	350.00	800.00
	1892/1	520,000	80.00	140.00	200.00	—	—	—
	1892	Inc. Ab.	6.00	12.00	25.00	60.00	400.00	800.00
	1893 flat top 3	500,000	12.00	22.50	55.00	100.00	400.00	1100.
	1893 rd. top 3	Inc. Ab.	300.00	650.00	1400.	2750.	5250.	11,500.
	1894	500,000	8.00	16.00	35.00	75.00	350.00	1000.
	1896	650,000	4.25	8.00	16.00	40.00	225.00	500.00
	1898	720,000	4.25	8.00	16.00	42.00	250.00	525.00
	1899 sm. 9's	1,200,000	3.50	6.00	15.00	35.00	200.00	550.00
	1899 lg. 9's	Inc. Ab.	6.00	12.00	25.00	65.00	300.00	850.00
	1900	1,100,000	2.25	5.00	14.00	30.00	140.00	360.00
	1901	1,200,000	2.25	5.00	14.00	30.00	140.00	360.00
10	1902	720,000	2.50	6.00	14.00	35.00	150.00	425.00
	1902H	1,100,000	2.00	4.25	10.00	25.00	100.00	225.00
	1903	500,000	7.00	14.00	35.00	95.00	750.00	1850.
	1903H	1,320,000	2.25	5.00	12.00	35.00	175.00	425.00
	1904	1,000,000	4.00	7.00	18.00	50.00	225.00	475.00
	1905	1,000,000	3.00	6.00	15.00	45.00	250.00	525.00
	1906	1,700,000	2.00	4.00	10.00	25.00	160.00	375.00
	1907	2,620,000	2.00	4.00	9.00	22.00	150.00	350.00
	1908	776,666	3.50	7.00	18.00	50.00	225.00	400.00
	1909 Victorian leaves, similar to 1902-1908 coinage							
		1,697,200	2.25	6.00	14.00	35.00	275.00	600.00
	1909 broad leaves similar to 1910-1912 coinage							
		Inc. Ab.	4.25	8.00	22.00	55.00	325.00	725.00
	1910	4,468,331	1.75	4.00	8.00	20.00	125.00	275.00
17	1911	2,737,584	4.00	9.00	15.00	44.00	140.00	325.00

Small leaves

Broad leaves

KM#	Date	Mintage	VG-8	F-12	VF-20	XF-40	MS-60	MS-63
23	1912	3,235,557	1.75	2.50	6.00	15.00	150.00	400.00
	1913 sm. leaves	3,613,937	1.00	2.25	5.00	14.00	145.00	400.00
	1913 lg. leaves	Inc. Ab.	90.00	160.00	285.00	600.00	3250.	6500.
	1914	2,549,811	1.25	2.50	5.00	12.00	150.00	425.00
	1915	688,057	4.00	9.00	22.00	75.00	375.00	725.00
	1916	4,218,114	1.00	1.50	4.00	8.00	90.00	225.00
	1917	5,011,988	.75	1.25	3.00	6.25	60.00	125.00
	1918	5,133,602	.75	1.25	3.00	6.25	50.00	90.00
	1919	7,877,722	.75	1.25	3.00	6.25	50.00	90.00
	2.3328 g, .800 SILVER, .0600 oz ASW							
23a	1920	6,305,345	.75	1.25	3.00	6.50	50.00	100.00
	1921	2,469,562	1.25	2.00	4.00	9.00	60.00	155.00
	1928	2,458,602	1.00	1.75	4.00	8.00	50.00	140.00
	1929	3,253,888	1.00	1.50	3.50	7.00	50.00	130.00
	1930	1,831,043	1.50	2.50	4.50	10.00	60.00	150.00
	1931	2,067,421	1.00	2.00	4.25	8.00	55.00	125.00
	1932	1,154,317	1.50	2.50	5.50	14.00	80.00	175.00
	1933	672,368	2.00	3.50	7.00	22.00	175.00	400.00
	1934	409,067	3.00	6.00	14.00	45.00	350.00	1500.
	1935	384,056	3.00	6.50	15.00	60.00	250.00	575.00
	1936	2,460,871	.60	1.25	3.00	6.50	45.00	75.00
	1936 dot on rev.	4 known	—	—	—		Specimen	—

Maple Leaf

KM#	Date	Mintage	VG-8	F-12	VF-20	XF-40	MS-60	MS-63
34	1937	2,500,095	.75	1.25	2.50	4.00	14.00	24.00
	1938	4,197,323	1.00	2.00	2.50	1.00	45.00	90.00
	1939	5,501,748	1.00	1.75	2.50	7.00	40.00	80.00
	1940	16,526,470	BV	1.00	1.75	4.00	15.00	30.00
	1941	8,716,386	BV	1.00	3.00	6.00	40.00	85.00
	1942	10,214,011	BV	1.00	2.00	3.00	30.00	45.00
	1943	21,143,229	BV	1.00	2.00	4.00	14.00	30.00
	1944	9,383,582	BV	1.00	2.00	5.00	25.00	45.00

KM#	Date	Mintage	VG-8	F-12	VF-20	XF-40	MS-60	MS-63
34	1945	10,979,570	BV	1.00	2.00	4.00	15.00	25.00
	1946	6,300,066	BV	1.00	2.25	4.50	25.00	45.00
	1947	4,431,926	BV	1.50	3.00	7.00	35.00	50.00
	1947 maple leaf	9,638,793	BV	1.00	2.00	3.50	10.00	18.00

Modified Obverse Legend

KM#	Date	Mintage	VG-8	F-12	VF-20	XF-40	MS-60	MS-63
43	1948	422,741	2.50	4.50	8.00	17.00	45.00	90.00
	1949	11,336,172	—	BV	1.25	2.00	8.00	14.00
	1950	17,823,075	—	BV	1.25	2.00	7.00	10.00
	1951	15,079,265	—	BV	1.00	2.00	6.00	9.00
	1952	10,474,455	—	BV	1.00	2.00	6.00	9.00

Elizabeth II Effigy

KM#	Date	Mintage	VG-8	F-12	VF-20	XF-40	MS-60	MS-63
51	1953 w/o straps	17,706,395	—	BV	1.00	1.50	3.50	6.00
	1953 w/straps	Inc. Ab.	—	BV	1.00	1.75	5.00	6.50
	1954	4,493,150	—	BV	1.00	1.75	7.00	12.00
	1955	12,237,294	—	BV	.75	1.00	3.50	5.00
	1956	16,732,844	—	BV	.75	1.00	2.75	4.00
	1956 dot below date	Inc. Ab.	1.50	2.75	4.00	4.75	12.00	16.00
	1957	16,110,229	—	—	BV	.60	1.50	2.00
	1958	10,621,236	—	—	BV	.60	1.50	2.00
	1959	19,691,433	—	—	BV	.50	1.25	2.00
	1960	45,446,835	—	—	—	BV	.75	1.00
	1961	26,850,859	—	—	—	BV	.75	1.00
	1962	41,864,335	—	—	—	BV	.75	1.00
	1963	41,916,208	—	—	—	BV	.75	1.00
	1964	49,518,549	—	—	—	BV	.75	1.00

New Elizabeth II Effigy

KM#	Date	Mintage	VG-8	F-12	VF-20	XF-40	MS-60	MS-63
61	1965	56,965,392	—	—	—	BV	.75	1.00
	1966	34,567,898	—	—	—	BV	.75	1.00

Reeding

		OTTAWA		Reeding		PHILADELPHIA		
KM#	Date	Mintage	VG-8	F-12	VF-20	XF-40	MS-60	MS-63
72	1968 Ottawa, .500 Silver	70,460,000	—	—	—	BV	.60	.75
72a	1968 Ottawa, Nickel	87,412,930	—	—	—	.15	.25	.40
73	1968 Philadelphia, Nickel	85,170,000	—	—	—	.15	.25	.40
	1969 lg.date, lg.ship	3 known	—	—	6500.	—	—	—

Redesigned Smaller Ship

KM#	Date	Mintage	VG-8	F-12	VF-20	XF-40	MS-60	MS-63
77.1	1969	55,833,929	—	—	—	.15	.25	.40
	1970	5,249,296	—	—	—	.25	.65	.95
	1971	41,016,968	—	—	—	.15	.25	.40
	1972	60,169,387	—	—	—	.15	.25	.40
	1973	167,715,435	—	—	—	.15	.25	.40
	1974	201,566,565	—	—	—	.15	.25	.40
	1975	207,680,000	—	—	—	.15	.25	.40
	1976	95,018,533	—	—	—	.15	.25	.40
	1977	128,452,206	—	—	—	.15	.25	.40
	1978	170,366,431	—	—	—	.15	.25	.40

Smaller bust

KM#	Date	Mintage	VG-8	F-12	VF-20	XF-40	MS-60	MS-63
77.2	1979	237,321,321	—	—	—	.15	.25	.40
	1980	170,111,533	—	—	—	.15	.25	.40
	1981	123,912,900	—	—	—	.15	.25	.40
	1981	199,000	—	—	—	—	Proof	1.50
	1982	93,475,000	—	—	—	.15	.25	.40
	1982	180,908	—	—	—	—	Proof	1.50
	1983	111,065,000	—	—	—	.15	.25	.40
	1983	168,000	—	—	—	—	Proof	1.50
	1984	121,690,000	—	—	—	.15	.25	.40
	1984	161,602	—	—	—	—	Proof	1.50
	1985	143,025,000	—	—	—	.15	.25	.40
	1985	157,037	—	—	—	—	Proof	1.50
	1986	168,620,000	—	—	—	.15	.25	.40
	1986	175,745	—	—	—	—	Proof	1.50
	1987	147,309,000	—	—	—	.15	.25	.40
	1987	179,004	—	—	—	—	Proof	1.50
	1988	162,998,558	—	—	—	.15	.25	.40
	1988	175,259	—	—	—	—	Proof	1.50
	1989	199,104,414	—	—	—	.15	.25	.40
	1989	170,528	—	—	—	—	Proof	1.50

New Elizabeth II Effigy

KM#	Date	Mintage	VG-8	F-12	VF-20	XF-40	MS-60	MS-63
183	1990	75,023,000	—	—	—	.15	.25	.40
	1990	140,649	—	—	—	—	Proof	1.50
	1991	46,693,000	—	—	—	.15	.25	.40
	1991	—	—	—	—	—	Proof	1.50

Commemorative ten cents

KM#	Date	Mintage	VG-8	F-12	VF-20	XF-40	MS-60	MS-63
67	1967 Confederation Centennial, .800 Silver							
		62,998,215	—	—	—	BV	.75	1.00
67a	1967 Confederation Centennial, .500 Silver							
		Inc. Ab.	—	—	—	BV	.75	1.00
206	1992 Confederation 125							
		—	—	—	—	.15	.25	.40
		—	—	—	—	—	Proof	1.50

Twenty cents

KM#	Date	Mintage	4.6480 g, .925 SILVER, .1382 oz ASW			XF-40	MS-60	MS-63
			VG-8	F-12	VF-20			
4	1858	750,000	50.00	70.00	100.00	200.00	950.00	1850.

Twenty-five cents

1870-1901

KM#	Date	Mintage	5.8100 g, .925 SILVER, .1728 oz ASW			XF-40	MS-60	MS-63
			VG-8	F-12	VF-20			
5	1870	900,000	7.50	14.00	35.00	85.00	500.00	1150.
	1871	400,000	10.00	18.00	45.00	140.00	550.00	1600.
	1871H	748,000	12.00	20.00	50.00	145.00	500.00	1300.
	1872H	2,240,000	5.00	7.00	18.00	60.00	300.00	800.00
	1874H	1,600,000	5.00	7.00	18.00	60.00	325.00	850.00
	1875H	1,000,000	175.00	350.00	900.00	1800.	4500.	9500.
	1880H narrow 0	400,000	22.00	50.00	125.00	275.00	800.00	2000.
	1880H wide 0	Inc. Ab.	70.00	125.00	275.00	550.00	1600.	3750.
	1880H wide/narrow 0	Inc. Ab.	90.00	150.00	300.00	600.00	—	—
	1881H	820,000	7.50	15.00	40.00	110.00	500.00	1250.

PRICING SECTION

KM#	Date	Mintage	VG-8	F-12	VF-20	XF-40	MS-60	MS-63
5	1882H	600,000	10.00	18.00	50.00	140.00	600.00	1400.
	1883H	960,000	7.00	12.00	30.00	100.00	600.00	1350.
	1885	192,000	60.00	120.00	300.00	600.00	2750.	5250.
	1886/3	540,000	8.00	18.00	50.00	150.00	800.00	2000.
	1886	Inc. Ab.	7.00	15.00	45.00	135.00	700.00	1700.
	1887	100,000	60.00	120.00	300.00	600.00	2750.	5250.
	1888	400,000	7.00	13.00	35.00	100.00	475.00	1100.
	1889	66,324	70.00	160.00	325.00	700.00	3000.	6000.
	1890H	200,000	12.00	20.00	50.00	150.00	850.00	2000.
	1891	120,000	35.00	60.00	165.00	350.00	1000.	2250.
	1892	510,000	7.00	12.00	30.00	100.00	475.00	1300.
	1893	100,000	50.00	100.00	230.00	450.00	1400.	2800.
	1894	220,000	10.00	20.00	50.00	140.00	675.00	1500.
	1899	415,580	4.00	7.00	18.00	60.00	375.00	850.00
	1900	1,320,000	3.00	6.00	15.00	55.00	300.00	700.00
	1901	640,000	3.00	6.00	15.00	55.00	300.00	700.00
11	1902	464,000	4.00	7.00	25.00	75.00	450.00	1200.
	1902H	800,000	3.00	5.00	18.00	45.00	175.00	400.00
	1903	846,150	4.00	7.00	25.00	75.00	375.00	850.00
	1904	400,000	7.00	18.00	60.00	150.00	825.00	2000.
	1905	800,000	5.00	10.00	30.00	90.00	750.00	1800.
	1906 lg. crown	1,237,843	4.00	6.00	18.00	65.00	275.00	850.00
	1906 sm. crown	Inc. Ab.	—	—	—	—	Rare	—
	1907	2,088,000	3.00	6.00	15.00	60.00	275.00	750.00
	1908	495,016	5.00	10.00	30.00	90.00	350.00	725.00
	1909	1,335,929	4.00	8.00	20.00	75.00	450.00	1150.
	1910	3,577,569	3.00	6.00	15.00	45.00	160.00	400.00
18	1911	1,721,341	6.00	14.00	27.50	70.00	350.00	700.00
24	1912	2,544,199	2.00	3.00	8.00	25.00	275.00	850.00
	1913	2,213,595	2.00	3.00	8.00	25.00	250.00	800.00
	1914	1,215,397	3.00	4.00	11.00	27.00	400.00	1100.
	1915	242,382	8.00	20.00	85.00	275.00	1700.	3500.
	1916	1,462,566	2.00	3.50	8.00	18.00	175.00	450.00
	1917	3,365,644	1.75	3.00	8.00	16.00	100.00	175.00
	1918	4,175,649	1.75	3.00	8.00	16.00	70.00	175.00
	1919	5,852,262	1.75	3.00	8.00	16.00	70.00	175.00

1902-1936
5.8319 g, .800 SILVER, .1500 oz ASW

KM#	Date	Mintage	VG-8	F-12	VF-20	XF-40	MS-60	MS-63
24a	1920	1,975,278	1.75	2.75	9.00	22.00	120.00	400.00
	1921	597,337	7.00	16.00	60.00	135.00	850.00	2000.
	1927	468,096	16.00	30.00	70.00	170.00	850.00	1700.
	1928	2,114,178	2.00	3.00	7.50	22.00	95.00	300.00
	1929	2,690,562	1.75	2.75	7.50	20.00	95.00	300.00
	1930	968,748	2.00	3.50	9.50	24.00	150.00	450.00
	1931	537,815	2.00	3.50	10.00	25.00	200.00	600.00
	1932	537,994	2.25	4.00	12.00	30.00	180.00	450.00
	1933	421,282	3.00	4.50	14.00	35.00	175.00	375.00
	1934	384,350	3.00	6.00	20.00	50.00	200.00	370.00
	1935	537,772	3.00	5.50	16.00	38.00	180.00	400.00
	1936	972,094	1.50	2.25	7.50	20.00	85.00	200.00

KM#	Date	Mintage	VG-8	F-12	VF-20	XF-40	MS-60	MS-63
24a	1936 dot	153,322	25.00	60.00	135.00	275.00	850.00	2000.

Maple Leaf Variety

KM#	Date	Mintage	VG-8	F-12	VF-20	XF-40	MS-60	MS-63
35	1937	2,690,176	BV	1.50	4.00	5.00	14.00	35.00
	1938	3,149,245	BV	1.50	4.25	7.00	70.00	170.00
	1939	3,532,495	BV	1.50	3.25	6.50	60.00	125.00
	1940	9,583,650	BV	1.50	2.75	3.75	13.00	30.00
	1941	6,654,672	BV	1.50	2.75	3.75	16.00	35.00
	1942	6,935,871	BV	1.50	2.75	3.75	16.00	35.00
	1943	13,559,575	BV	1.50	2.75	3.75	16.00	35.00
	1944	7,216,237	BV	1.50	2.75	4.00	30.00	70.00
	1945	5,296,495	BV	1.50	2.75	3.75	14.00	30.00
	1946	2,210,810	BV	1.50	3.25	6.50	40.00	70.00
	1947	1,524,554	BV	1.50	3.25	7.00	50.00	100.00
	1947 dot after 7	Inc. Ab.	20.00	40.00	60.00	115.00	275.00	600.00
	1947 maple leaf	4,393,938	BV	1.50	2.75	4.00	17.50	30.00
		Modified Obverse Legend						
44	1948	2,564,424	BV	1.75	3.25	6.00	50.00	120.00
	1949	7,988,830	—	BV	1.75	2.25	10.00	20.00
	1950	9,673,335	—	BV	1.75	2.25	9.00	17.50
	1951	8,290,719	—	BV	1.75	2.25	7.00	14.00
	1952	8,859,642	—	BV	1.75	2.25	7.00	14.00
		Elizabeth II Effigy						
52	1953 NSS	10,546,769	—	BV	1.75	2.25	5.00	7.00
	1953 SS	Inc. Ab.	—	BV	1.75	2.25	8.00	12.00
	1954	2,318,891	BV	1.75	2.75	7.00	25.00	35.00
	1955	9,552,505	—	—	BV	1.50	4.00	7.00
	1956	11,269,353	—	—	BV	1.25	3.50	5.00
	1957	12,770,190	—	—	BV	1.00	2.25	4.00
	1958	9,336,910	—	—	BV	1.00	2.25	4.00
	1959	13,503,461	—	—	—	BV	2.00	3.00
	1960	22,835,327	—	—	—	BV	2.00	3.00
	1961	18,164,368	—	—	—	BV	2.00	3.00
	1962	29,559,266	—	—	—	BV	2.00	2.25
	1963	21,180,652	—	—	—	BV	1.75	2.25
	1964	36,479,343	—	—	—	BV	1.75	2.25
		Machin Portrait						
62	1965	44,708,869	—	—	—	BV	1.75	2.25
	1966	25,626,315	—	—	—	BV	1.75	2.25
		5.8319 g, .500 SILVER, .0937 oz ASW						
62a	1968	71,464,000	—	—	—	BV	1.50	2.25
		NICKEL						
74.1	1968	88,686,931	—	—	—	.30	.50	.75
	1969	133,037,929	—	—	—	.30	.50	.75
	1970	10,302,010	—	—	—	.30	1.00	1.50
	1971	48,170,428	—	—	—	.30	.50	.75
	1972	43,743,387	—	—	—	.30	.50	.75
	1974	192,360,598	—	—	—	.30	.50	.75
	1975	141,148,000	—	—	—	.30	.50	.75
	1976	86,898,261	—	—	—	.30	.50	.75
	1977	99,634,555	—	—	—	.30	.50	.75
	1978	176,475,408	—	—	—	.30	.50	.75
		Smaller bust						
74.2	1979	131,042,905	—	—	—	.30	.50	.75
	1980	76,178,000	—	—	—	.30	.50	.75
	1981	131,580,272	—	—	—	.30	.50	.75
	1981	199,000	—	—	—	—	Proof	2.00
	1982	171,926,000	—	—	—	.30	.50	.75
	1982	180,908	—	—	—	—	Proof	2.00
	1983	13,162,000	—	—	—	.30	.50	.75
	1983	168,000	—	—	—	—	Proof	2.00
	1984	121,668,000	—	—	—	.30	.50	.75
	1984	161,602	—	—	—	—	Proof	2.00
	1985	158,734,000	—	—	—	.30	.50	.75
	1985	157,037	—	—	—	—	Proof	2.00
	1986	132,220,000	—	—	—	.30	.50	.75
	1986	175,745	—	—	—	—	Proof	2.00
	1987	53,408,000	—	—	—	.30	.50	.75
	1987	179,004	—	—	—	—	Proof	2.00
	1988	80,368,473	—	—	—	.30	.50	.75

KM#	Date	Mintage	VG-8	F-12	VF-20	XF-40	MS-60	MS-63
74.2	1988	175,259	—	—	—	—	Proof	2.00
	1989	119,796,307	—	—	—	.30	.50	.75
	1989	170,928	—	—	—	—	Proof	2.00

New Elizabeth II Effigy

KM#	Date	Mintage	VG-8	F-12	VF-20	XF-40	MS-60	MS-63
184	1990	31,258,000	—	—	—	.30	.50	.75
	1990	140,649	—	—	—	—	Proof	2.00
	1991	459,000	—	—	.30	.50	1.50	3.00
	1991	—	—	—	—	—	Proof	2.00

Commemorative twenty-five cents

KM#	Date	Mintage	VG-8	F-12	VF-20	XF-40	MS-60	MS-63
68	1967 Confederation Centennial, .800 Silver							
		48,855,500	—	—	—	BV	1.50	2.25
68a	1967 Confederation Centennial, .500 Silver							
		Inc. Ab.	—	—	—	BV	1.50	2.25

KM#	Date	Mintage	VG-8	F-12	VF-20	XF-40	MS-60	MS-63
81.1	1973 RCMP Centennial, 120 beads, Nickel							
		134,958,587	—	—	—	.30	.50	.75
81.2	1973 RCMP Centennial, 132 beads, Nickel							
		Inc. Ab.	15.00	25.00	35.00	55.00	85.00	120.
207	1992 Confederation 125, Nickel							
		—	—	—	—	—	—	1.00
		—	—	—	—	—	Proof	2.50

125th Anniversary of Confederation

KM#	Date	Mintage	VG-8	F-12	VF-20	XF-40	MS-60	MS-63
203	1992 New Brunswick, Nickel							
		10,000,000	—	—	—	—	—	.75
203a	1992 New Brunswick, .925 Silver							
		—	—	—	—	—	Proof	10.00

KM#	Date	Mintage	VG-8	F-12	VF-20	XF-40	MS-60	MS-63
212	1992 North West Territories, Nickel	10,000,000	—	—	—	—	—	.75
212a	1992 North West Territories, .925 Silver		—	—	—	—	Proof	10.00
213	1992 Newfoundland, Nickel	10,000,000	—	—	—	—	—	.75
213a	1992 Newfoundland, .925 Silver		—	—	—	—	Proof	10.00

KM#	Date	Mintage	VG-8	F-12	VF-20	XF-40	MS-60	MS-63
214	1992 Manitoba, Nickel	10,000,000	—	—	—	—	—	.75
214a	1992 Manitoba, .925 Silver		—	—	—	—	Proof	10.00
220	1992 Yukon, Nickel	10,000,000	—	—	—	—	—	.75
220a	1992 Yukon, .925 Silver		—	—	—	—	Proof	10.00

KM#	Date	Mintage	VG-8	F-12	VF-20	XF-40	MS-60	MS-63
221	1992 Alberta, Nickel	10,000,000	—	—	—	—	—	.75
221a	1992 Alberta, .925 Silver		—	—	—	—	Proof	10.00
222	1992 Prince Edward Island, Nickel	10,000,000	—	—	—	—	—	.75
222a	1992 Prince Edward Island, .925 Silver		—	—	—	—	Proof	10.00

KM#	Date	Mintage	VG-8	F-12	VF-20	XF-40	MS-60	MS-63
223	1992 Ontario, Nickel	10,000,000	—	—	—	—	—	.75
223a	1992 Ontario, .925 Silver		—	—	—	—	Proof	10.00
231	1992 Nova Scotia, Nickel		—	—	—	—	—	.75
231a	1992 Nova Scotia, .925 Silver		—	—	—	—	Proof	10.00

KM#	Date	Mintage	VG-8	F-12	VF-20	XF-40	MS-60	MS-63
232	1992 British Columbia, Nickel	—	—	—	—	—	—	.75
232a	1992 British Columbia, .925 Silver	—	—	—	—	—	Proof	10.00
233	1992 Saskatchewan, Nickel	—	—	—	—	—	—	.75
233a	1992 Saskatchewan, .925 Silver	—	—	—	—	—	Proof	10.00

KM#	Date	Mintage	VG-8	F-12	VF-20	XF-40	MS-60	MS-63
234	1992 Quebec, Nickel	—	—	—	—	—	—	.75
234a	1992 Quebec, .925 Silver	—	—	—	—	—	Proof	10.00

Fifty cents

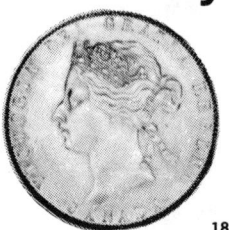 

1870-1901
11.6200 g, .925 SILVER, .3456 oz ASW

KM#	Date	Mintage	VG-8	F-12	VF-20	XF-40	MS-60	MS-63
6	1870	450,000	450.00	900.00	1800.	3200.	10,000.	16,500.
	1870 LCW	Inc. Ab.	25.00	45.00	90.00	225.00	3300.	6500.
	1871	200,000	40.00	90.00	200.00	450.00	4000.	7000.
	1871H	45,000	60.00	125.00	275.00	625.00	5000.	8750.
	1872H	80,000	20.00	50.00	130.00	275.00	3750.	7000.
	1872H inverted A for V in VICTORIA							
		Inc. Ab.	75.00	145.00	325.00	675.00	—	—
	1881H	150,000	35.00	75.00	125.00	275.00	3500.	7000.
	1888	60,000	80.00	160.00	350.00	750.00	5000.	9500.
	1890H	20,000	600.00	1100.	2000.	3500.	12,000.	22,000.
	1892	151,000	35.00	75.00	175.00	325.00	4000.	8500.
	1894	29,036	200.00	400.00	950.00	1750.	8000.	15,500.
	1898	100,000	30.00	75.00	160.00	300.00	4000.	8500.
	1899	50,000	65.00	160.00	325.00	800.00	5800.	12,000.
	1900	118,000	22.50	45.00	120.00	225.00	4000.	7250.
	1901	80,000	30.00	50.00	120.00	240.00	3500.	7000.

Victorian Leaves   Edwardian Leaves

KM#	Date	Mintage	VG-8	F-12	VF-20	XF-40	MS-60	MS-63
12	1902	120,000	8.00	18.00	70.00	150.00	1000.	3000.
	1903H	140,000	18.00	35.00	100.00	225.00	1400.	3900.
	1904	60,000	70.00	130.00	275.00	600.00	3100.	7000.
	1905	40,000	80.00	180.00	375.00	850.00	5000.	10,500.
	1906	350,000	8.00	22.00	60.00	150.00	1100.	3000.
	1907	300,000	8.00	18.00	50.00	125.00	1100.	3250.
	1908	128,119	20.00	45.00	120.00	285.00	1200.	2500.
	1909	302,118	12.50	35.00	90.00	225.00	1700.	3500.
	1910 Victorian lvs.	649,521	7.00	18.00	50.00	125.00	1000.	2650.
	1910 Edwardian lvs.	Inc. Ab.	7.00	18.00	50.00	125.00	1000.	2650.

Modified Obverse Legend

KM#	Date	Mintage	VG-8	F-12	VF-20	XF-40	MS-60	MS-63
19	1911	209,972	8.00	50.00	220.00	450.00	1250.	2800.

Modified Obverse Legend

KM#	Date	Mintage	VG-8	F-12	VF-20	XF-40	MS-60	MS-63
25	1912	285,867	4.50	16.00	65.00	150.00	1200.	2500.
	1913	265,889	4.50	16.00	65.00	155.00	1250.	3000.
	1914	160,128	12.00	40.00	130.00	375.00	1750.	3750.
	1916	459,070	3.00	14.00	50.00	110.00	700.00	1700.
	1917	752,213	3.00	14.00	35.00	85.00	475.00	1400.
	1918	754,989	3.00	8.00	22.00	70.00	400.00	1000.
	1919	1,113,429	3.00	8.00	22.00	65.00	375.00	950.00

1902-1936

KM#	Date	Mintage	11.6638 g, .800 SILVER, .3000 oz ASW			XF-40	MS-60	MS-63
			VG-8	F-12	VF-20			
25a	1920	584,691	3.00	10.00	35.00	120.00	600.00	1400.
	1921	75 to 100 pcs.known	10,000.	13,000.	18,000.	24,000.	37,500.	63,800.
NOTE: Bowers and Merena Victoria Sale 9-89 MS-65 realized $110,000.								
	1929	228,328	3.00	10.00	30.00	100.00	500.00	1400.
	1931	57,581	6.00	20.00	60.00	160.00	1200.	2400.
	1932	19,213	25.00	80.00	190.00	425.00	1800.	4000.
	1934	39,539	9.00	25.00	75.00	160.00	850.00	1800.
	1936	38,550	8.00	20.00	65.00	160.00	600.00	1200.
36	1937	192,016	2.50	4.00	7.00	10.00	30.00	70.00
	1938	192,018	3.00	7.00	14.00	30.00	130.00	300.00
	1939	287,976	3.00	5.00	8.00	18.00	100.00	250.00
	1940	1,996,566	BV	3.00	3.50	6.00	25.00	70.00
	1941	1,714,874	BV	2.25	3.50	6.00	25.00	70.00
	1942	1,974,164	BV	2.25	3.50	6.00	25.00	70.00
	1943	3,109,583	BV	2.25	3.50	6.00	25.00	70.00
	1944	2,460,205	BV	2.25	3.50	6.00	25.00	70.00
	1945	1,959,528	BV	2.25	3.50	6.00	25.00	70.00
	1946	950,235	BV	5.00	6.50	9.00	75.00	120.00
	1946 hoof in 6	Inc. Ab.	12.00	18.00	35.00	100.00	800.00	1700.
	1947 straight 7	424,885	3.00	4.00	6.00	14.00	80.00	175.00
	1947 curved 7	Inc. Ab.	2.00	3.50	7.00	14.00	80.00	190.00
	1947ML straight 7	38,433	10.00	16.00	30.00	50.00	150.00	300.00
	1947ML curved 7	Inc. Ab.	950.00	1250.	1700.	2000.	3200.	4750.

Modified Obverse Legend

KM#	Date	Mintage	VG-8	F-12	VF-20	XF-40	MS-60	MS-63
45	1948	37,784	32.50	42.50	55.00	85.00	175.00	275.00
	1949	858,991	2.25	3.00	6.50	9.00	40.00	100.00
	1949 hoof over 9	Inc. Ab.	5.00	10.00	25.00	65.00	350.00	700.00
	1950	2,384,179	3.00	5.00	9.00	20.00	175.00	300.00
	1950 lines in 0	Inc. Ab.	BV	2.50	3.00	4.00	12.00	20.00
	1951	2,421,730	BV	2.00	2.50	3.75	8.00	17.50
	1952	2,596,465	BV	2.50	3.00	3.75	8.00	18.00

Elizabeth II Effigy

KM#	Date	Mintage	VG-8	F-12	VF-20	XF-40	MS-60	MS-63
53	1953 sm. date	1,630,429	BV	2.50	3.00	3.50	8.00	12.00
	1953 lg.dt,straps	Inc. Ab.	BV	2.50	3.50	4.00	24.00	34.00
	1953 lg.dt,w/o straps	I.A.	3.00	5.00	6.00	12.00	85.00	140.00
	1954	506,305	2.25	3.25	4.75	7.00	23.00	30.00
	1955	753,511	BV	2.50	4.00	5.00	14.00	24.00
	1956	1,379,499	—	BV	2.00	3.50	6.00	9.00
	1957	2,171,689	—	—	BV	2.00	3.00	6.00
	1958	2,957,266	—	—	BV	2.00	2.75	6.00

KM#	Date	Mintage	VG-8	F-12	VF-20	XF-40	MS-60	MS-63
56	1959	3,095,535	—	—	BV	2.00	3.00	5.00
	1960	3,488,897	—	—	—	BV	2.25	3.25
	1961	3,584,417	—	—	—	BV	2.25	3.25
	1962	5,208,030	—	—	—	BV	2.25	3.25
	1963	8,348,871	—	—	—	BV	2.25	3.25
	1964	9,377,676	—	—	—	BV	2.25	3.25

New Elizabeth II Effigy

KM#	Date	Mintage	VG-8	F-12	VF-20	XF-40	MS-60	MS-63
63	1965	12,629,974	—	—	—	BV	2.25	3.25
	1966	7,920,496	—	—	—	BV	2.25	3.25

NICKEL

KM#	Date	Mintage	VG-8	F-12	VF-20	XF-40	MS-60	MS-63
75.1	1968	3,966,932	—	—	—	.50	.65	1.00
	1969	7,113,929	—	—	—	.50	.65	1.00
	1970	2,429,526	—	—	—	.50	.65	1.00
	1971	2,166,444	—	—	—	.50	.65	1.00
	1972	2,515,632	—	—	—	.50	.65	1.00
	1973	2,546,096	—	—	—	.50	.65	1.00
	1974	3,436,650	—	—	—	.50	.65	1.00
	1975	3,710,000	—	—	—	.50	.65	1.00
	1976	2,940,719	—	—	—	.50	.65	1.00

KM#	Date	Mintage	VG-8	Smaller bust F-12	VF-20	XF-40	MS-60	MS-63
75.2	1977	709,839	—	—	.50	.75	1.50	2.00

KM#	Date	Mintage	VG-8	F-12	VF-20	XF-40	MS-60	MS-63
75.3	1978 square jewels	3,341,892	—	—	—	.50	.75	1.00
	1978 round jewels	Inc. Ab.	—	—	.50	3.00	3.00	4.00
	1979	3,425,000	—	—	—	.50	.85	1.00
	1980	1,574,000	—	—	—	.50	.85	1.00
	1981	2,690,272	—	—	—	.50	.85	1.00
	1981	199,000	—	—	—	—	Proof	3.00
	1982 small beads	2,236,674	—	—	—	.50	.85	1.00
	1982 small beads	180,908	—	—	—	—	Proof	3.00
	1982 large beads	Inc. Ab.	—	—	—	.50	.85	1.00
	1983	1,177,000	—	—	—	.50	.85	1.00
	1983	168,000	—	—	—	—	Proof	3.00
	1984	1,502,989	—	—	—	.50	.85	1.00
	1984	161,602	—	—	—	—	Proof	3.00
	1985	2,188,374	—	—	—	.50	.85	1.00
	1985	157,037	—	—	—	—	Proof	3.00
	1986	781,400	—	—	—	.50	.85	1.00
	1986	175,745	—	—	—	—	Proof	3.00
	1987	373,000	—	—	—	.50	.85	1.00
	1987	179,004	—	—	—	—	Proof	3.00
	1988	220,000	—	—	—	.50	.85	1.00
	1988	175,259	—	—	—	—	Proof	3.00
	1989	266,419	—	—	—	.50	.85	1.00
	1989	170,928	—	—	—	—	Proof	3.00

KM#	Date	Mintage	VG-8	New Elizabeth II Effigy F-12	VF-20	XF-40	MS-60	MS-63
185	1990	207,000	—	—	—	.50	.85	1.00
	1990	140,649	—	—	—	—	Proof	3.00
	1991	490,000	—	—	—	.50	.85	1.00
	1991	—	—	—	—	—	Proof	3.00

Commemorative fifty cents

KM#	Date	Mintage	VG-8	F-12	VF-20	XF-40	MS-60	MS-63
69	1967 Confederation Centennial, Nickel							
		4,211,392	—	—	—	BV	3.00	4.00
208	1992 Confederation 125, Nickel							
		—	—	—	—	.50	.85	1.75
		—	—	—	—	—	Proof	3.00

Voyageur dollars

KM#	Date	Mintage	F-12	VF-20	XF-40	AU-50	MS-60	MS-63
		23.3276 g, .800 SILVER, .6000 oz ASW						
31	1936	339,600	8.00	12.00	15.00	22.00	45.00	80.00

Pointed 7	Blunt 7	Maple Leaf (blunt 7 only)

KM#	Date	Mintage	F-12	VF-20	XF-40	AU-50	MS-60	MS-63
37	1937	207,406	10.00	12.00	14.00	17.50	35.00	70.00
	1937	1,295	—	—	—	Proof	—	800.00
	1937	I.A.	—	—	—	Matte Proof	—	400.00
	1938	90,304	20.00	30.00	40.00	50.00	85.00	250.00
	1945	38,391	55.00	90.00	120.00	150.00	225.00	500.00
	1945	—	—	—	—		Specimen	2750.
	1946	93,055	12.50	20.00	28.00	35.00	80.00	250.00
	1947 pointed 7	Inc. Bl.	60.00	90.00	120.00	175.00	350.00	950.00
	1947 blunt 7	65,595	30.00	50.00	65.00	80.00	120.00	265.00
	1947 maple leaf	21,135	100.00	130.00	160.00	200.00	275.00	600.00
46	1948	18,780	425.00	525.00	675.00	750.00	900.	1250.
	1950 w/4 water lines	261,002	5.00	6.00	8.00	12.50	16.50	35.00
	1950 w/4 water lines, (1 known)					Matte Proof		—
	1950 Arnprior w/1-1/2 w.l.	I.A.	8.00	10.00	15.00	25.00	45.00	125.00
	1951 w/4 water lines	416,395	5.00	7.00	8.00	9.00	12.50	30.00
	1951 w/4 water lines	—	—	—	—	—	Proof	400.00
	1951 Arnprior w/1-1/2 w.l.	I.A.	22.00	30.00	40.00	70.00	120.00	350.00
	1952 w/4 water lines	406,148	5.00	6.00	7.00	8.00	12.00	30.00
	1952 Arnprior	I.A.	35.00	55.00	70.00	120.00	175.00	375.00
	1952 Arnprior	—	—	—	—	—	Proof	Rare
	1952 w/o water lines	I.A.	6.00	7.00	8.00	10.00	13.50	40.00

KM#	Date	Mintage	VF-20	XF-40	AU-50	MS-60	MS-63
54	1953 w/o strap, wire rim	1,074,578	4.00	5.00	6.00	7.00	18.00
	1953 w/strap, flat rim	Inc. Ab.	4.00	5.00	6.00	7.00	20.00
	1954	246,606	5.00	6.00	9.00	16.00	35.00
	1955 w/4 water lines	268,105	5.00	6.00	8.00	14.00	30.00
	1955 Arnprior w/1-1/2 w.l.*	I.A.	70.00	85.00	100.00	125.00	200.00
	1956	209,092	10.00	12.00	14.00	18.00	45.00
	1957 w/4 water lines	496,389	BV	4.00	5.00	6.00	15.00
	1957 w/1 water line	I.A.	5.00	6.00	8.00	12.00	30.00
	1959	1,443,502	—	BV	5.00	6.00	8.00
	1960	1,420,486	—	BV	6.00	7.00	8.00
	1961	1,262,231	—	BV	6.00	7.00	8.00
	1962	1,884,789	—	BV	6.00	7.00	8.00
	1963	4,179,981	—	BV	6.00	7.00	8.00

*NOTE: All genuine circulation strike 1955 Arnprior dollars have a die break running along the top of TI in the word GRATIA on the obverse.

Small Beads	Medium Beads	Large Beads

KM#	Date	Mintage	VF-20	XF-40	AU-50	MS-60	MS-63
		New Elizabeth II Effigy					
64.1	1965 sm. beads, pointed 5	10,768,569	—	BV	6.00	7.00	8.00
	1965 sm. beads, blunt 5	Inc. Ab.	—	BV	6.00	7.00	8.00
	1965 lg. beads, blunt 5	Inc. Ab.	—	BV	6.00	7.00	8.00

KM#	Date	Mintage	VF-20	XF-40	AU-50	MS-60	MS-63
64.1	1965 lg. beads, pointed 5	Inc. Ab.	BV	4.00	4.25	5.00	8.00
	1965 med. beads, pointed 5	Inc. Ab.	4.00	6.00	7.00	10.00	25.00
	1966 lg. beads	9,912,178	—	BV	6.00	7.00	8.00
	1966 sm. beads	*485 pcs.	—	600.	1000.	1200.	1500.

23.3276 g, .500 SILVER, .3750 oz ASW, 36mm

KM#	Date	Mintage	Smaller bust MS-63	Mintage	P/L	Spec.
64.2a	1972	—	—	341,598	—	16.00

NICKEL, 32mm

KM#	Date	Mintage	Large bust MS-63	Mintage	P/L	Spec.
76.1	1968	5,579,714	1.50	1,408,143	2.50	—
	1969	4,809,313	1.50	594,258	2.50	—
	1972	2,676,041	2.00	405,865	2.50	—

KM#	Date	Mintage	Smaller bust MS-63	Mintage	P/L	Spec.
76.2	1975	3,256,000	2.00	322,325	3.25	—
	1976	2,498,204	2.50	274,106	4.00	—

| 76.3 | 1975 mule w/1976 obv. | Inc. Ab. | — | | * | — |

*NOTE: Only known in proof-like sets w/1976 obv. slightly modified.

KM#	Date	Mintage	MS-63		P/L	Spec./Proof
117	1977	1,393,745	2.50	—	4.50	—
120	1978	2,948,488	2.00	—	3.50	—
	1979	2,954,842	2.00	—	5.50	—
	1980	3,291,221	2.00	—	9.00	—

KM#	Date	Mintage	MS-63	P/L	Proof
120	1981	2,778,900	2.00	5.00	6.50
	1982	1,098,500	2.00	5.50	10.00
	1983	2,267,525	2.00	6.00	15.00
	1984	1,223,486	2.00	6.00	—
	1984	161,602	—	—	15.00
	1985	3,104,092	2.00	7.00	—
	1985	157,037	—	—	35.00
	1986	3,089,225	2.00	12.00	—
	1986	175,259	—	—	30.00
	1987	287,330	2.00	8.00	—
	1987	179,004	—	—	30.00

Loon dollars

AUREATE NICKEL

KM#	Date	Mintage	MS-63	P/L	Proof
157	1987	205,405,000	3.00	—	—
	1987	178,120	—	—	20.00
	1988	138,893,539	2.00	7.50	—
	1988	175,259	—	—	25.00
	1989	184,773,902	2.00	7.50	—
	1989	170,928	—	—	25.00

New Elizabeth II Effigy

		Mintage	MS-63	P/L	Proof
186	1990	68,402,000	2.00	7.50	—
	1990	140,649	—	—	25.00
	1991	23,156,000	2.00	7.50	—
	1991	—	—	—	25.00

Commemorative dollars

KM#	Date	Mintage	23.3276 g, .800 SILVER, .6000 oz ASW F-12	VF-20	XF-40	AU-50	MS-60	MS-63
30	1935 Jubilee	428,707	15.00	25.00	35.00	45.00	70.00	175.00

KM#	Date	Mintage	F-12	VF-20	XF-40	AU-50	MS-60	MS-63
38	1939 Royal Visit	1,363,816	6.00	8.00	10.00	15.00	20.00	40.00
	1939 Royal Visit	—	—	—	—	—	Specimen	600.00
	1939 Royal Visit	—	—	—	—	—	Proof	2500.
47	1949 Newfoundland	672,218	9.00	15.00	22.50	27.50	40.00	65.00
	1949 Newfoundland	—	—	—	—	—	Specimen	425.00

KM#	Date	Mintage	F-12	VF-20	XF-40	AU-50	MS-60	MS-63
55	1958 Br. Columbia	3,039,630	BV	4.00	5.00	6.00	7.00	14.00

KM#	Date	Mintage	F-12	VF-20	XF-40	AU-50	MS-60	MS-63
58	1964 Charlottetown	7,296,832	—	BV	5.50	6.50	7.50	9.50

KM#	Date	Mintage	MS-63	P/L	Spec.
70	1967 Goose,Confederation Centennial	6,767,496	7.00	11.50	450.00

KM#	Date	Mintage	MS-63	P/L	Spec.
78	1970 Manitoba (Nickel, 32mm)	4,140,058	2.00	—	—
		645.869	—	3.25	—

KM#	Date	Mintage	MS-63	P/L	Spec.
79	1971 Br. Columbia (Nickel, 32mm)	4,260,781	2.00	3.00	—
		468,729	—	(c) 2.50	—

23.3276 g, .500 SILVER, .3750 oz ASW*

KM#	Date	Mintage	MS-63	P/L	Spec.
80	1971 Br. Columbia (.500 Silver, 36mm)	585,674	—	—	14.50

*NOTE: All silver dollars dated 1971 to date are minted to this standard.

KM#	Date	Mintage	MS-63	P/L	Spec.
82	1973 Pr. Edward Island (Nickel, 32mm)		2.50	—	—
		3,196,452			
		466,881	—	(c) 3.25	—

KM#	Date	Mintage	MS-63	P/L	Spec.
83	1973 Mountie (.500 Silver, 36mm)	1,031,271	—	—	15.00
83v	1973 Mountie, with metal crest on case	Inc. Ab.	—	—	17.00

KM#	Date	Mintage	MS-63	P/L	Spec.
88	1974 Winnipeg (Nickel, 32mm)	2,799,363	3.00	—	—
		363,786	—	(c) 5.00	—
88a	1974 Winnipeg (.500 Silver, 36mm)	728,947	—	—	14.50

KM#	Date	Mintage	MS-63	P/L	Spec.
97	1975 Calgary (.500 Silver, 36mm)	930,956	—	—	9.00

KM#	Date	Mintage	MS-63	P/L	Spec.
106	1976 Parliament Library (.500 Silver, 36mm)	578,708	—	—	22.50

KM#	Date	Mintage	MS-63	P/L	Spec.
118	1977 Silver Jubilee	744,848	—	—	15.50

KM#	Date	Mintage	MS-63	P/L	Spec.
121	1978 XI Games (.500 Silver, 36mm)	709,602	—	—	15.50

KM#	Date	Mintage	MS-63	P/L	Spec.
124	1979 Griffon (.500 Silver, 36mm)	826,695	—	—	26.00

KM#	Date	Mintage	MS-63	P/L	Spec.
128	1980 Arctic Territories (.500 Silver, 36mm)	539,617	—	—	65.00

KM#	Date	Mintage	MS-63	P/L	Proof
130	1981 Railroad (.500 Silver, 36mm)	699,494	50.00	—	35.00

KM#	Date	Mintage	MS-63	P/L	Proof
133	1982 Regina (.500 Silver, 36mm)	144,930	37.50	—	—
		758,958	—	—	10.00

KM#	Date	Mintage	MS-63	P/L	Proof
134	1982 Constitution (Nickel, 32mm)	9,709,422	2.00	—	—

KM#	Date	Mintage	MS-63	P/L	Proof
138	1983 Edmonton University Games	159,450	37.50	—	—
	(.500 Silver, 36mm)	506,847	—	—	16.50

KM#	Date	Mintage	MS-63	P/L	Proof
140	1984 Toronto Sesquicentennial	133,610	37.50	—	—
	(.500 Silver, 36mm)	732,542	—	—	11.50

KM#	Date	Mintage	MS-63	P/L	Proof
141	1984 Cartier (Nickel, 32mm)	7,009,323	2.25	—	—
		87,760	—	—	9.00

KM#	Date	Mintage	MS-63	P/L	Proof
143	1985 National Parks -Moose-	163,314	37.50	—	—
	(.500 Silver, 36mm)	733,354	—	—	11.50

KM#	Date	Mintage	MS-63	P/L	Proof
149	1986 Vancouver	125,949	37.50	—	—
	(.500 Silver, 36mm)	680,004	—	—	15.50

KM#	Date	Mintage	MS-63	P/L	Proof
154	1987 John Davis	118,722	37.50	—	—
	(.500 Silver, 36mm)	602,374	—	—	25.00

KM#	Date	Mintage	MS-63	P/L	Proof
161	1988 Ironworks	106,872	37.50	—	—
	(.500 Silver, 36mm)	255,013	—	—	45.00

KM#	Date	Mintage	MS-63	P/L	Proof
168	1989 MacKenzie River	99,774	25.00	—	—
	(.500 Silver, 36mm)	244,062	—	—	45.00

PRICING SECTION

KM#	Date	Mintage	MS-63	P/L	Proof
170	1990 Henry Kelsey	99,455	22.50	—	—
	(.500 Silver, 36mm)	254,959	—	—	23.50

KM#	Date	Mintage	MS-63	P/L	Proof
179	1991 S.S. Frontenac	73,843	14.50	—	—
	(.500 Silver, 36mm)	195,424	—	—	20.00

KM#	Date	Mintage	MS-63	P/L	Proof
210	1992 Stagecoach Service		15.00		21.50
	(.925 Silver, 36mm)	—		—	

125th Anniversary of the Confederation

KM#	Date	Mintage	MS-63	P/L	Proof
209	1992 Loon, Nickel	—	2.00	—	25.00
218	1992 Parliament, Nickel	—	2.00	—	22.50

NOTE: (c) Individually cased Proof-likes (P/L), Proofs or Specimens are from broken up Proof-like or specimen sets.

5 dollars

KM#	Date	Mintage	8.3592 g, .900 GOLD, .2419 oz AGW			AU-50	MS-60	MS-63
			F-12	VF-20	XF-40			
26	1912	165,680	120.00	140.00	165.00	220.00	325.00	600.00
	1913	98,832	120.00	140.00	165.00	220.00	325.00	600.00
	1914	31,122	200.00	300.00	375.00	500.00	750.00	1550.

Olympic Commemoratives

24.3000 g, .925 SILVER, .7227 oz ASW

Series I

KM#	Date	Mintage	MS-63	Proof
84	1973 Sailboats (Kingston)	—	5.50	—
		165.203	—	7.25

KM#	Date	Mintage	MS-63	Proof
85	1973 North America Map	—	5.50	—
		165,203	—	7.25

Series II

KM#	Date	Mintage	MS-63	Proof
89	1974 Olympic Rings	—	5.50	—
		97,431	—	7.25

KM#	Date	Mintage	MS-63	Proof
90	1974 Athlete with torch	—	5.50	—
		97,431	—	7.25

Series III

KM#	Date	Mintage	MS-63	Proof
91	1974 Rowing	—	5.50	—
		104,684	—	7.25

KM#	Date	Mintage	MS-63	Proof
92	1974 Canoeing	—	5.50	—
		104,684	—	7.25

Series IV

KM#	Date	Mintage	MS-63	Proof
98	1975 Marathon	—	5.50	—
		89,155	—	7.25

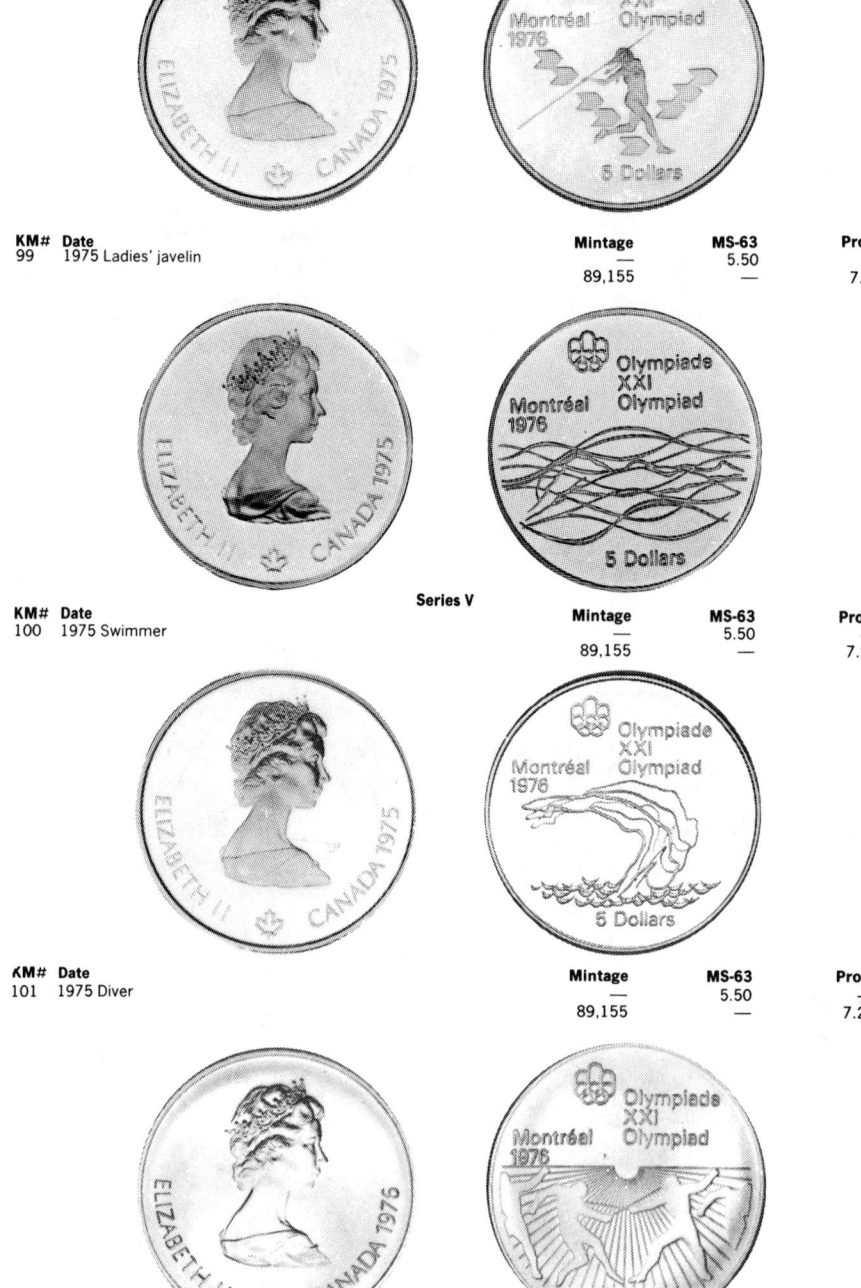

KM#	Date		Mintage	MS-63	Proof
99	1975 Ladies' javelin		—	5.50	—
			89,155	—	7.25

Series V

KM#	Date		Mintage	MS-63	Proof
100	1975 Swimmer		—	5.50	—
			89,155	—	7.25

KM#	Date		Mintage	MS-63	Proof
101	1975 Diver		—	5.50	—
			89,155	—	7.25

Series VI

KM#	Date		Mintage	MS-63	Proof
107	1976 Fencing		—	5.50	—
			82,302	—	10.00

KM#	Date	Mintage	MS-63	Proof
108	1976 Boxing		5.50	—
		82,302	—	10.00

Series VII

KM#	Date	Mintage	MS-63	Proof
109	1976 Olympic Village		5.50	—
		76,908	—	11.50

KM#	Date	Mintage	MS-63	Proof
110	1976 Olympic flame		5.50	—
		79,102	—	11.50

10 dollars

16.7185 g, .900 GOLD, .4838 oz AGW

KM#	Date	Mintage	F-12	VF-20	XF-40	AU-50	MS-60	MS-63
27	1912	74,759	200.00	300.00	380.00	500.00	750.00	1500.
	1913	149,232	200.00	300.00	380.00	500.00	775.00	1550.
	1914	140,068	210.00	320.00	425.00	625.00	975.00	1950.

Olympic Commemoratives

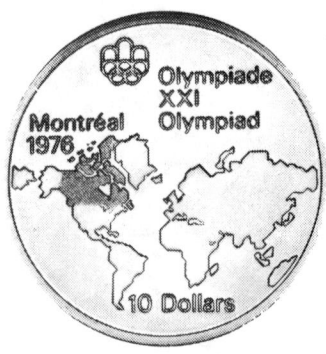

48.6000 g, .925 SILVER, 1.4454 oz ASW

Series I

KM#	Date	Mintage	MS-63	Proof
86.1	1973 World Map	103,426	11.50	—
		165,203	—	14.00
86.2	1974 World Map (Error-Mule)	320 pcs.	320.00	—

KM#	Date	Mintage	MS-63	Proof
87	1973 Montreal Skyline	—	11.00	—
		165,203	—	14.00

Series II

KM#	Date	Mintage	MS-63	Proof
93	1974 Head of Zeus	—	11.00	—
		104,684	—	14.00

KM#	Date	Mintage	MS-63	Proof
94	1974 Temple of Zeus	— 104,684	11.00 —	— 14.00

Series III

KM#	Date	Mintage	MS-63	Proof
95	1974 Cycling	— 97,431	11.00 —	— 14.00

KM#	Date	Mintage	MS-63	Proof
96	1974 Lacrosse	— 97,431	11.00 —	— 14.00

Series IV

KM#	Date	Mintage	MS-63	Proof
102	1975 Men's hurdles	—	11.00	—
		82,302	—	14.00

Series IV

KM#	Date	Mintage	MS-63	Proof
103	1975 Ladies' shot put	—	11.00	—
		82,302	—	14.00

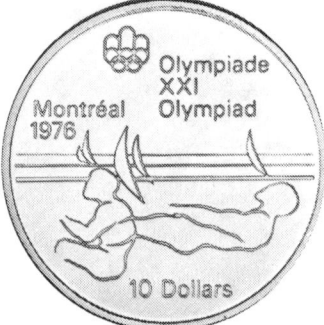

Series V

KM#	Date	Mintage	MS-63	Proof
104	1975 Sailing	—	11.00	—
		89,155	—	14.00

KM#	Date	Mintage	MS-63	Proof
105	1975 Paddler	—	11.00	—
		89,155	—	14.00

Series VI

KM#	Date	Mintage	MS-63	Proof
111	1976 Football	—	11.00	—
		76.908	—	17.50

KM#	Date	Mintage	MS-63	Proof
112	1976 Field Hockey	—	11.00	—
		76.908	—	17.50

Series VII

KM#	Date	Mintage	MS-63	Proof
113	1976 Olympic Stadium	—	11.00	—
		79,102	—	18.50

KM#	Date	Mintage	MS-63	Proof
114	1976 Olympic Velodrome	—	11.00	—
		79,102	—	18.50

15 dollars
Olympic Commemoratives

33.6300 g, .925 SILVER, 1.0000 oz ASW

KM#	Date	Mintage	MS-63	Proof
215	1992 Coaching Track	*275,000	—	45.00

KM#	Date	Mintage	MS-63	Proof
216	1992 High Jump, Rings, Speed Skating	*275,000	—	45.00

20 dollars

18.2733 g, .900 GOLD, .5288 oz AGW

KM#	Date	Mintage	MS-63	Proof
71	1967 Centennial	337,688	—	215.00

Olympic Commemoratives

33.6300 g, .925 SILVER, 1.0000 oz ASW

KM#	Date	Mintage	MS-63	Proof
145	1985 Winter Olympics, Downhill Skier, lettered edge			
	1985 Plain edge	406,360	—	32.00
		Inc. Ab.	—	425.00

KM#	Date	Mintage	MS-63	Proof
146	1985 Winter Olympics, Speed Skater, lettered edge	354,222	—	32.00
	1985 Plain edge	Inc. Ab.	—	340.00

KM#	Date	Mintage	MS-63	Proof
147	1986 Winter Olympics, Biathlon, lettered edge	308,086	—	32.00
	1986 Plain edge	Inc. Ab.	—	340.00

KM#	Date	Mintage	MS-63	Proof
148	1986 Winter Olympics, Hockey, lettered edge	396,602	—	32.00
	1986 Plain edge	Inc. Ab.	—	340.00

KM#	Date	Mintage	MS-63	Proof
150	1986 Winter Olympics, Cross Country Skier	303,199	—	32.00

KM#	Date	Mintage	MS-63	Proof
151	1986 Winter Olympics, Free Style Skier, lettered edge			
		294,322	—	32.00
	1986 Plain edge	Inc. Ab.	—	340.00

34.1070 g, .925 SILVER, 1.0000 oz ASW

KM#	Date	Mintage	MS-63	Proof
155	1987 Winter Olympics, Figure Skater	334,875	—	32.00

KM#	Date	Mintage	MS-63	Proof
156	1987 Winter Olympics, Curling	286,457	—	32.00

KM#	Date	Mintage	MS-63	Proof
159	1987 Winter Olympics, Ski Jumper	290,954	—	32.00

KM#	Date	Mintage	MS-63	Proof
160	1987 Winter Olympics, Bobsled	274,326	—	32.00

Aviation Commemoratives

31.1030 g, .925 SILVER w/1.0000 GOLD Cameo, 1.0000 oz ASW

KM#	Date	Mintage	MS-63	Proof
172	1990 Lancaster/Fauquier	43,596	—	60.00

KM#	Date	Mintage	MS-63	Proof
173	1990 Anson and Harvard	41,844	—	60.00

31.1030 g, .925 SILVER, .9743 oz ASW

KM#	Date	Mintage	MS-63	Proof
196	1991 Silver Dart	28,791	—	65.00

KM#	Date	Mintage	MS-63	Proof
197	1991 de Haviland "Beaver"	29,399	—	65.00

KM#	Date	Mintage	MS-63	Proof
224	1992 Curtiss JN-4 Canuck ("Jenny")	*50,000	—	50.00

KM#	Date	Mintage	MS-63	Proof
225	1992 de Haviland Gypsy Moth	*50,000	—	50.00

KM#	Date	Mintage	MS-63	Proof
236	1993 Fairchild 71C Float plane	*50,000	—	50.00

KM#	Date	Mintage	MS-63	Proof
237	1993 Lockheed 14	*50,000	—	50.00

100 dollars

13.3375 g, .583 GOLD, .2500 oz AGW   **16.9655 g, .917 GOLD, .5000 oz AGW**

KM#	Date	Mintage	MS-63	Proof
115	1976 Olympics, beaded borders, 27mm	650,000	105.00	—
116	1976 Olympics, reduced size, 25mm, plain borders	337,342	—	190.00

KM#	Date	Mintage	MS-63	Proof
119	1977 Queen's Silver Jubilee	180,396	—	220.00
122	1978 Canadian Unification	200,000	—	210.00

KM#	Date	Mintage	MS-63	Proof
126	1979 Year of the Child	250,000	—	200.00
129	1980 Arctic Territories	300,000	—	230.00

KM#	Date	Mintage	MS-63	Proof
131	1981 National Anthem	102,000	—	230.00
137	1982 New Constitution	121,708	—	225.00

KM#	Date	Mintage	MS-63	Proof
139	1983 St. John's, Newfoundland	83,128	—	230.00
142	1984 Jacques Cartier	67,662	—	230.00

KM#	Date	Mintage	MS-63	Proof
144	1985 National Parks - Big horn sheep	61,332	—	280.00
152	1986 Peace	76,409	—	230.00

13.3375 g, .583 GOLD, .2500 oz AGW

		Mintage	MS-63	Proof
158	1987 1988 Olympics - Torch and logo, lettered edge	142,750	—	160.00
	1987 Plain edge	Inc. Ab.	—	—
162	1988 Whales	52,594	—	300.00

KM#	Date	Mintage	MS-63	Proof
169	1989 Sainte-Marie	59,657	—	220.00
171	1990 Intl. Literacy Year	49,940	—	230.00

KM#	Date	Mintage	MS-63	Proof
180	1991 S.S. Empress of India	*33,966	—	215.00
211	1992 Montreal	—	—	210.00

175 dollars

16.9700 g, .917 GOLD, .5000 oz AGW

KM#	Date	Mintage	MS-63	Proof
217	1992 Olympics - Passing the Torch	*35,000	—	370.00

200 dollars

17.1060 g, .917 GOLD, .5042 oz AGW

KM#	Date	Mintage	MS-63	Proof
178	1990 Canada Flag Silver Jubilee	20,980	—	345.00
202	1991 Hockey	8,741	—	345.00
230	1992 Niagara Falls	*25,000	—	345.00

Sovereign

1908-1910   **7.9881 g, .917 GOLD, .2354 oz AGW**   **1911-1919**

C mint mark below horse's rear hooves

KM#	Date	Mintage	F-12	VF-20	XF-40	AU-50	MS-60	MS-63
14	1908C	636 pcs.	1000.	1700.	2300.	2800.	3300.	4100.
	1909C	16,273	175.00	250.00	325.00	550.00	875.00	1400.
	1910C	28,012	125.00	175.00	250.00	400.00	600.00	1200.
20	1911C	256,946	110.00	120.00	130.00	170.00	250.00	300.00
	1911C	—	—	—	—		Specimen	6500.
	1913C	3,715	400.00	550.00	750.00	1000.	1650.	2750.
	1914C	14,871	175.00	250.00	325.00	550.00	875.00	1400.
	1916C	Rare		*About 20 known		20,000.	25,000.	35,000.

NOTE: Stacks's A.G. Carter Jr. Sale 12-89 Gem BU realized $82,500.

	1917C	58,845	110.00	120.00	130.00	170.00	250.00	325.00
	1918C	106,516	110.00	120.00	130.00	170.00	250.00	325.00
	1919C	135,889	110.00	120.00	130.00	170.00	250.00	325.00

Silver bullion issues
5 dollars

31.1000 g, .9999 SILVER, 1.0000 oz ASW

KM#	Date	Mintage	MS-63	Proof
163	1988 Maple leaf	1,155,931	6.50	—
	1989 Maple leaf		6.50	—
	1989 Maple leaf	43,965	—	85.00

KM#	Date	Mintage	MS-63	Proof
		New Elizabeth II Effigy		
187	1990 Maple leaf	1,708,800	6.50	—
	1991 Maple leaf	644,300	7.50	—
	1992 Maple leaf		6.50	—
	1993 Maple leaf	—	6.50	—

Gold bullion issues
5 dollars

3.1200 g, .9999 GOLD, .1000 oz AGW

KM#	Date	Mintage	MS-63	Proof
135	1982 Maple leaf	246,000	BV + 15%	—
	1983 Maple leaf	304,000	BV + 15%	—
	1984 Maple leaf	262,000	BV + 15%	—
	1985 Maple leaf	398,000	BV + 15%	—
	1986 Maple leaf	529,516	BV + 15%	—
	1987 Maple leaf	459,000	BV + 15%	—
	1988 Maple leaf	506,500	BV + 15%	—
	1989 Maple leaf	—	BV + 15%	—
	1989 Maple leaf	16,992	—	100.00
	New Elizabeth II Effigy			
188	1990 Maple leaf	47,600	BV + 15%	—
	1991 Maple leaf	32,200	BV + 15%	—
	1992 Maple leaf	—	BV + 15%	—

10 dollars

7.7850 g, .9999 GOLD, .2500 oz AGW

KM#	Date	Mintage	MS-63	Proof
136	1982 Maple leaf	184,000	BV + 11 %	—
	1983 Maple leaf	308,800	BV + 11 %	—
	1984 Maple leaf	242,400	BV + 11 %	—
	1985 Maple leaf	620,000	BV + 11 %	—
	1986 Maple leaf	915,200	BV + 11 %	—
	1987 Maple leaf	376,000	BV + 11 %	—
	1988 Maple leaf	436,000	BV + 11%	—
	1989 Maple leaf	—	BV + 11%	—
	1989 Maple leaf	6,998	—	220.00
	New Elizabeth II Effigy			
189	1990 Maple leaf	63,400	BV + 11%	—
	1991 Maple leaf	41,600	BV + 11%	—
	1992 Maple leaf	—	BV + 11%	—

20 dollars

15.5515 g, .9999 GOLD, .5000 oz AGW

KM#	Date	Mintage	MS-63	Proof
153	1986 Maple leaf	529,200	BV + 7%	—
	1987 Maple leaf	332,800	BV + 7%	—
	1988 Maple leaf	538,400	BV + 7%	—
	1989 Maple leaf	—	BV + 7%	—
	1989 Maple leaf	6,998	—	365.00
	New Elizabeth II Effigy			
190	1990 Maple leaf	87,200	BV + 7%	—
	1991 Maple leaf	48,100	BV + 7%	—
	1992 Maple leaf	—	BV + 7%	—

50 dollars

31.1030 g, .999 GOLD, 1.0000 oz AGW
Rev: 999. Maple Leaf. 999.

KM#	Date	Mintage	MS-63	Proof
125.1	1979 Maple leaf	1,000,000	BV + 5%	—
	1980 Maple leaf	1,251,500	BV + 5%	—
	1981 Maple leaf	863,000	BV + 5%	—
	1982 Maple leaf	883,000	BV + 5%	—

31.1030 g, .9999 GOLD, 1.0000 oz AGW
Rev: 9999 Maple Leaf 9999

KM#	Date	Mintage	MS-63	Proof
125.2	1983 Maple leaf	843,000	BV + 5%	—
	1984 Maple leaf	1,067,500	BV + 5%	—
	1985 Maple leaf	1,908,000	BV + 5%	—
	1986 Maple leaf	779,115	BV + 5%	—
	1987 Maple leaf	978,000	BV + 5%	—
	1988 Maple leaf	826,500	BV + 5%	—
	1989 Maple leaf	—	BV + 5%	—
	1989 Maple leaf	17,781	—	700.00

New Elizabeth II Effigy

KM#	Date	Mintage	MS-63	Proof
191	1990 Maple leaf	815,000	BV + 5%	—
	1991 Maple leaf	290,000	BV + 5%	—
	1992 Maple leaf	—	BV + 5%	—

Platinum bullion issues
5 dollars

3.1203 g, .9995 PLATINUM, .1000 oz APW

KM#	Date	Mintage	MS-63	Proof
164	1988 Maple leaf	74,000	BV + 17%	—
	1989 Maple leaf	—	BV + 17%	—
	1989 Maple leaf	11,999	—	125.00

New Elizabeth II Effigy

KM#	Date	Mintage	MS-63	Proof
192	1990 Maple leaf	900 pcs.	BV + 17%	—
	1991 Maple leaf	1,300	BV + 17%	—
	1992 Maple leaf	—	BV + 17%	—

10 dollars

7.7857 g, .9995 PLATINUM, .2500 oz APW

KM#	Date	Mintage	MS-63	Proof
165	1988 Maple leaf	93,600	BV + 12%	—
	1989 Maple leaf	—	BV + 12%	—
	1989 Maple leaf	1,999	—	300.00

KM#	Date	Mintage	MS-63	Proof
	New Elizabeth II Effigy			
193	1990 Maple leaf	400 pcs.	BV + 12%	—
	1991 Maple leaf	1,800	BV + 12%	—
	1992 Maple leaf	—	BV + 12%	—

20 dollars

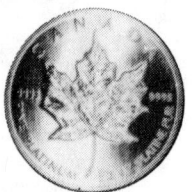

15.5519 g, .9995 PLATINUM, .5000 oz APW

KM#	Date	Mintage	MS-63	Proof
166	1988 Maple leaf	23,600	BV + 8%	—
	1989 Maple leaf	—	BV + 8%	—
	1989 Maple leaf	1,999	—	550.00
	New Elizabeth II Effigy			
194	1990 Maple leaf	1,300	BV + 8%	—
	1991 Maple leaf	2,800	BV + 8%	—
	1992 Maple leaf	—	BV + 8%	—

30 dollars

3.1100 g, .999 PLATINUM, .1000 oz APW

KM#	Date	Mintage	MS-63	Proof
174	1990 Polar bear swimming	1,928	Proof	80.00

KM#	Date	Mintage	MS-63	Proof
198	1991 Owls	*3,500	Proof	100.00
226	1992 Cougar head and shoulders	*3,500	Proof	100.00

50 dollars

31.1030 g, .9995 PLATINUM, 1.0000 oz APW

KM#	Date	Mintage	MS-63	Proof
167	1988 Maple leaf	37,500	BV + 6%	—
	1989 Maple leaf	1,500	BV + 6%	—
	1989 Maple leaf	5,965	—	1000.
	New Elizabeth II Effigy			
195	1990 Maple leaf	15,100	BV + 6%	—
	1991 Maple leaf	31,900	BV + 6%	—
	1992 Maple leaf	—	BV + 6%	—

75 dollars

7.7760 g, .999 PLATINUM, .2500 oz APW

KM#	Date	Mintage	MS-63	Proof
175	1990 Polar bear resting	1,928	Proof	220.00

KM#	Date	Mintage	MS-63	Proof
199	1991 Owls	*3,500	Proof	250.00
227	1992 Cougar prowling	*3,500	Proof	250.00

150 dollars

15.5520 g, .999 PLATINUM, .5000 oz APW

KM#	Date	Mintage	MS-63	Proof
176	1990 Polar bear walking	1,928	Proof	400.00

KM#	Date	Mintage	MS-63	Proof
200	1991 Owls	*3,500	Proof	450.00
228	1992 Cougar mother and cub	*3,500	Proof	450.00

300 dollars

31.1035 g, .999 PLATINUM, 1.0000 oz APW

KM#	Date	Mintage	MS-63	Proof
177	1990 Polar bear mother and cub	1,928	Proof	800.00

KM#	Date			Mintage	MS-63	Proof
201	1991 Owls			*3,500	Proof	875.00
229	1992 Cougar resting in tree			*3,500	Proof	875.00

Proof-like dollars

23.3276 g, .800 SILVER, .6000 oz ASW

KM#	Date	Mintage	Identification	Issue Price	Mkt Value
D3	1953	1,200	KM54, Canoe w/shoulder fold	—	500.00
D4	1954	5,300	KM54, Canoe	1.25	190.00
D5	1955	7,950	KM54, Canoe	1.25	165.00
D5a	1955	Inc. Ab.	KM54, Arnprior	1.25	320.00
D6	1956	10,212	KM54, Canoe	1.25	120.00
D7	1957	16,241	KM54, Canoe	1.25	50.00
D8	1958	33,237	KM55, British Columbia	1.25	35.00
D9	1959	45,160	KM54, Canoe	1.25	16.50
D10	1960	82,728	KM54, Canoe	1.25	15.00
D11	1961	120,928	KM54, Canoe	1.25	13.50
D12	1962	248,901	KM54, Canoe	1.25	12.00
D13	1963	963,525	KM54, Canoe	1.25	11.00
D14	1964	2,862,441	KM58, Charlottetown	1.25	11.00
D15	1965	2,904,352	KM64, Canoe	—	11.00
D16	1966	672,514	KM64, Canoe	—	12.00
D17	1967	1,036,176	KM70, Confederation	—	17.00

Mint sets

Olympic Commemoratives

KM#	Date	Mintage	Identification	Issue Price	Mkt Value
MS1	1973(4)	—	KM84-87, Series I	45.00	32.00
MS2	1974(4)	—	KM89-90,93-94, Series II	48.00	32.00
MS3	1974(4)	—	KM91-92,95-96, Series III	48.00	32.00
MS4	1975(4)	—	KM98-99,102-103, Series IV	48.00	32.00
MS5	1975(4)	—	KM100-101,104-105, Series V	60.00	32.00
MS6	1976(4)	—	KM107-108,111-112, Series VI	60.00	32.00
MS7	1976(4)	—	KM109-110,113-114, Series VII	60.00	35.00

Specimen sets

NOTE: Some authorities list these as proof sets. However, the Canadian Mint does not. The coins are double struck with higher than usual pressure, but are considered to have the same quality as proof issue from the Royal Mint, London.

KM#	Date	Mintage	Identification	Issue Price	Mkt Value
SS1	1858(4)	—	KM1-4 Reeded Edge	—	6000.
SS2	1858(4)	—	KM1-4 Plain Edge	—	6000.
SS3	1858(8)	—	KM1-4 Double Set	—	12,500.
SS4	1858(8)	—	KM1(overdate),2-4 Double Set	—	14,000.
SS5	1870(4)	100*	KM2,3,5,6 (reeded edges)	—	12,500.
SS6	1870(8)	—	KM2,3,5,6 Double Set (plain edges)	—	25,000.
SS7	1872H(4)	—	KM2,3,5,6	—	12,500.
SS8	1875H(3)	—	KM2(Large Date),3,5	—	20,000.
SS9	1880H(3)	—	KM2,3,5(Narrow 0)	—	7000.
SS10	1881H(5)	—	KM7,2,3,5,6	—	12,000.
SS11	1892(2)	—	KM3,5	—	10,000.
SS12	1902(5)	100*	KM8-12	—	10,000.
SS13	1902H(3)	—	KM9(Large H),10,11	—	6500.
SS14	1903H(3)	—	KM10,12,13	—	7000.

NOTE: A 1903H double set has been reported on display in Bombay, India.

KM#	Date	Mintage	Identification	Issue Price	Mkt Value
SS15	1908(5)	1,000*	KM8,10-13	—	2800.
SS16	1911(5)	1,000*	KM15-19	—	5500.
SS17	1911/12(8)	5	KM15-20,26-27	—	52,250.
SS18	1921(5)	—	KM22-25,28	—	80,000.
SS19	1922(2)	—	KM28,29	—	800.00
SS20	1923(2)	—	KM28,29	—	800.00
SS21	1924(2)	—	KM28,29	—	800.00
SS22	1925(2)	—	KM28,29	—	1800.
SS23	1926(2)	—	KM28,29 (Near 6)	—	1800.
SS24	1927(3)	—	KM24a,28,29	—	3200.
SS25	1928(4)	—	KM23a,24a,28,29	—	2800.
SS26	1929(5)	—	KM23a-25a,28,29	—	10,000.
SS27	1930(4)	—	KM23a,24a,28,29	—	6500.
SS28	1931(5)	—	KM23a-25a,28,29	—	8500.
SS29	1932(5)	—	KM23a-25a,28,29	—	10,000.
SS30	1934(5)	—	KM23-25,28,29	—	8500.
SS31	1936(5)	—	KM23-25,28,29	—	8500.
SS32	1936(6)	—	KM23a(dot),24a(dot),25a,28(dot),29,30	—	Rare
SS33	1937(6)	1025*	KM32-37 Matte Finish	—	850.00
SS34	1937(4)	—	KM32-35 Mirror Fields	—	500.00
SS35	1937(6)	75*	KM32-37 Mirror Fields	—	2000.
SS36	1938(6)	—	KM32-37	—	25,000.
SS-A36	1939(6)	—	KM32-35,38 Matte Finish	—	—
SS-B36	1939(6)	—	KM32-35,38 Mirror Fields	—	—
SS-C36	1942(2)	—	KM32,33	—	300.00
SS-D36	1943(2)	—	KM32,40	—	300.00
SS37	1944(5)	3	KM32,34-37,40a	—	20,000.
SS-A37	1944(2)	—	KM32,40a	—	300.00
SS38	1945(6)	6	KM32,34-37,40a	—	6500.
SS-A38	1945(2)	—	KM32,40a	—	300.00
SS39	1946(6)	15	KM32,34-37,39a	—	4000.
SS40	1947(6)	—	KM32,34-36(7 curved),37(pointed 7),39a	—	6000.
SS41	1947(6)	—	KM32,34-36(7 curved),37(blunt 7),39a	—	6000.
SS42	1947ML(6)	—	KM32,34-36(7 curved right),37,39a	—	6000.
SS43	1948(6)	30	KM41-46	—	5000.
SS44	1949(6)	20	KM41-45,47	—	2000.
SS44A	1949(2)	—	KM47	—	1000.
SS45	1950(6)	12	KM41-46	—	2100.
SS46	1950(6)	—	KM41-45,46(Arnprior)	—	2300.
SS47	1951(7)	12	KM41,48,42a,43-46 (w/water lines)	—	3750.
SS48	1952(6)	2,317	KM41,42a,43-46 (water lines)	—	4500
SS48A	1952(6)	—	KM41,42a,43-46 (w/o water lines)	—	4500.
SS49	1953(6)	28	KM49 w/o straps,50-54	—	1800.
SS50	1953(6)	—	KM49 w/straps,50-54	—	1800.
SS51	1964(6)	—	KM49,51,52,56-58	—	450.00
SS52	1965(6)	—	KM59.1-60.1,61-63,64.1	—	450.00

Double Dollar Prestige Sets

KM#	Date	Mintage	Identification	Issue Price	Mkt Value
SS56	1971(7)	66,860	KM59.1-60.1,74.1-75.1,77.1,79(2 pcs.)	12.00	15.00
SS57	1972(7)	36,349	KM59.1-60.1,74.1-75.1,76.1,(2 pcs.),77.1	12.00	50.00
				12.00	50.00
SS58	1973(7)	119,819	KM59.1-60.1,75.1,77.1,81.1,82,83	12.00	20.00
SS59	1973(7)	Inc. Ab.	KM59.1-60.1,75.1,77.1,81.2,82,83	—	150.00
SS60	1974(7)	85,230	KM59.1-60.1,74.1-75.1,77.1,88,88a	15.00	20.00
SS61	1975(7)	97,263	KM59.1-60.1,74.1-75.1,76.2,77.1,97	15.00	16.00
SS62	1976(7)	87,744	KM59.1-60.1,74.1-75.1,76.2,77.1,106	16.00	24.00
SS63	1977(7)	142,577	KM59.1-60.1,74.1,75.2,77.1,117.1,118	16.50	20.00
SS64	1978(7)	147,000	KM59.1-60.1,74.1,75.3,77.1,120,121	16.50	20.00
SS65	1979(7)	155,698	KM59.2-60.2,74.2,75.3,77.2,120,124	18.50	32.50
SS66	1980(7)	162,875	KM60.2,74.2,75.3,77.2,120,127,128	30.50	80.00

Regular Specimen Sets Resumed

KM#	Date	Mintage	Identification	Issue Price	Mkt Value
SS67	1981(6)	71,300	KM60.2,74.2,75.3,77.2,120,123	10.00	10.00
SS68	1982(6)	62,298	KM60.2a,74.2,75.3,77.2,120,123	11.50	10.00
SS69	1983(6)	60,329	KM60.2a,74.2,75.3,77.2,120,132	—	10.00
SS70	1984(6)	60,400	KM60.2a,74.2,75.3,77.2,120,132	10.00	10.00
SS71	1985(6)	61,553	KM60.2a,74.2,75.3,77.2,120,132	10.00	10.00
SS73	1986(6)	67,152	KM60.2a,74.2,75.3,77.2,120,132	10.00	18.00
SS72	1987(6)	75,194	KM60.2a,74.2,75.3,77.2,120,132	11.00	12.00
SS73	1988(6)	70,205	KM60.2a,74.2,75.3,77.2,132,157	12.30	16.00
SS74	1989(6)	75,306	KM60.2a,74.2,75.3,77.2,132,157	14.50	18.00
SS75	1990(6)	76,611	KM181-186	15.50	19.00
SS76	1991(6)	54,462	KM181-186	15.50	19.00
SS77	1992(6)	—	KM204-209	16.25	18.00

NOTE: *Estimated.

V.I.P. specimen sets

NOTE: A very limited number of cased Specimen sets were produced by the Mint beginning in 1969 for presentation to dignitaries visiting the Royal Canadian Mint or other parts of Canada. (A small quantity of 1970 cased Specimen sets were sold to the public for $13.00 each.) The coins, 1¢ to $1.00 were cased in long narrow leather cases (black and other colors).

KM#	Date	Mintage	Identification	Issue Price	Mkt Value
VS1	1969	2 known	—	—	1700.
VS2	1970	100	KM59.1-60.1,74.1-75.1,77.1,78	—	475.00
VS3	1971	69	KM59.1-60.1,74.1-75.1,77.1,79(2 pcs.)	—	375.00
VS4	1972	25	KM59.1-60.1,74.1-75.1,76.1,(2 pcs.),77.1	—	435.00
VS5	1973	26	KM59.1-60.1,75.1,77.1,81.1,82,83	—	435.00
VS6	1974	72	KM59.1-60.1,74.1-75.1,77.1,88,88a	—	375.00
VS7	1975	94	KM59.1-60.1,74.1-75.1,76.2,77.1,97	—	375.00
VS8	1976	—	KM59.1-60.1,74.1-75.1,76.2,77.1,106	—	375.00

Proof-like sets

NOTE: These sets do not have the quality of the Proof or Specimen Set, but are specially produced and packaged.

KM#	Date	Mintage	Identification	Issue Price	Mkt Value
PL1	1953(6)	1,200	KM49 w/o straps, 50-54	2.20	1250.
PL2	1953(6)	Inc. Ab.	KM49-54	2.20	750.00
PL3	1954(6)	3,000	KM49-54	2.50	320.00
PL4	1954(6)	Inc. Ab.	KM49 w/o straps, 50-54	2.50	500.00
PL5	1955(6)	6,300	KM49,50a,51-54	2.50	250.00
PL6	1955(6)	Inc. Ab.	KM49,50a,51-54,Arnprior	2.50	360.00
PL7	1956(6)	6,500	KM49,50a,51-54	2.50	145.00
PL8	1957(6)	11,862	KM49,50a,51-54	2.50	75.00
PL9	1958(6)	18,259	KM49,50a,51-53,55	2.50	60.00
PL10	1959(6)	31,577	KM49,50a,51,52,54,56	2.50	35.00
PL11	1960(6)	64,097	KM49,50a,51,52,54,56	3.00	20.00
PL12	1961(6)	98,373	KM49,50a,51,52,54,56	3.00	19.00
PL13	1962(6)	200,950	KM49,50a,51,52,54,56	3.00	17.00
PL14	1963(6)	673,006	KM49,51,52,54,56,57	3.00	12.00
PL15	1964(6)	1,653,162	KM49,51,52,56-58	3.00	12.00
PL16	1965(6)	2,904,352	KM59.1-60.1,61-63,64.1	4.00	12.00
PL17	1966(6)	672,514	KM59.1-60.1,61-63,64.1	4.00	12.00

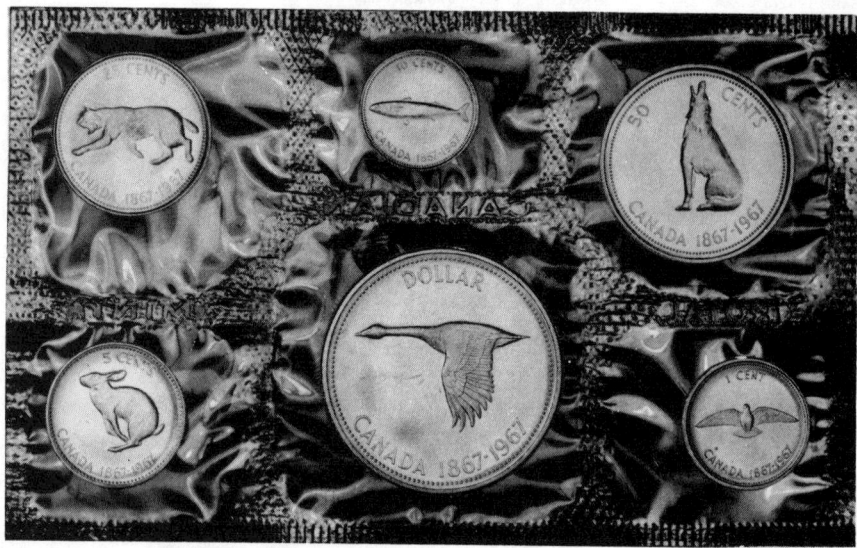

PL18	1967(6)	961,887	KM65-70 (pliofilm flat pack)	4.00	15.00
PL18A	1967(6)	70,583	KM65-70 and Silver Medal (red box)	12.00	18.00
PL18B	1967(7)	337,688	KM65-71 (black box)	40.00	275.00
PL19	1968(6)	521,641	KM59.1-60.1,72,74.1-76.1	4.00	3.00
PL20	1969(6)	326,203	KM59.1-60.1,74.1-77.1	4.00	3.25

KM#	Date	Mintage	Identification	Issue Price	Mkt Value
PL21	1970(6)	349,120	KM59.1-60.1,74.1-75.1,77.1,78	4.00	6.00
PL22	1971(6)	253,311	KM59.1-60.1,74.1-75.1,77.1,79	4.00	4.00
PL23	1972(6)	224,275	KM59.1-60.1,74.1-77.1	4.00	3.50
PL24	1973(6)	243,695	KM59.1-60.1,74.1-75.1 obv. 120 beads, 77.1,81.1,82	4.00	4.00
PL25	1973(6)	Inc. Ab.	KM59.1-60.1,74.1-75.1 obv. 132 beads, 77.1,81.2,82	4.00	150.00
PL26	1974(6)	213,589	KM59.1-60.1,74.1-75.1,77.1,88	5.00	4.00
PL27.1	1975(6)	197,372	KM59.1,60.1,74.1-77.1	5.00	4.00
PL27.2	1975(6)	Inc. Ab.	KM59.1,60.1,74.1-75.1,76.2,77.1	5.00	—
PL28	1976(6)	171,737	KM59.1,60.1,74.1-75.1,76.2,77.1	5.15	6.00
PL29	1977(6)	225,307	KM59.1,60.1,74.1,75.2,77.1,117.1	5.15	5.50
PL30	1978(6)	260,000	KM59.1-60.1,74.1,75.3,77.1,120	—	3.50
PL31	1979(6)	187,624	KM59.2-60.2,74.2,75.3,77.2,120	6.25	7.00
PL32	1980(6)	410,842	KM60.2,74.2,75.3,77.2,120,127	6.50	10.00
PL33	1981(6)	186,250	KM60.2,74.2,75.3,77.2,120,123	8.50	9.00
PL34	1982(6)	180,908	KM60.2,74.2,75.3,77.2,120,123	6.00	7.25
PL35	1982(6)	Inc. Ab.	KM60.2a,74.2,75.3,77.2,120,132	—	7.25
PL36	1983(6)	190,838	KM60.2a,74.2,75.3,77.2,120,132	—	11.50
PL37	1984(6)	181,249	KM60.2a,74.2,75.3,77.2,120,132	5.25	9.00
PL38	1985(6)	173,924	KM60.2a,74.2,75.3,77.2,120,132	5.25	10.00
PL40	1986(6)	167,338	KM60.2a,74.2,75.3,77.2,120,132	5.25	22.00
PL39	1987(6)	212,136	KM60.2a,74.2,75.3,77.2,120,132	5.25	10.00
PL41	1988(6)	182,048	KM60.2a,74.2,75.3,77.2,132,157	6.05	9.50
PL42	1989(6)	173,622	KM60.2a,74.2,75.3,77.2,132,157	6.60	13.00
PL43	1990(6)	170,791	KM181-186	7.40	10.00
PL44	1991(6)	130,867	KM181-186	7.40	9.00
PL45	1992(6)	—	KM204-209	8.25	9.50

Custom proof-like sets

KM#	Date	Mintage	Identification	Issue Price	Mkt Value
Each set contains two 1 cent pieces.					
CPL1	1971(7)	33,517	KM59.1(2 pcs.),60.1,74.1-75.1,77.1,79	6.50	6.00
CPL2	1972(7)	38,198	KM59.1(2 pcs.),60.1,74.1-77.1	6.50	6.00
CPL3	1973(7)	35,676	KM59.1(2 pcs.),60.1,75.1 obv. 120 beads, 77.1,81.1,82	6.50	5.75
CPL4	1973(7)	Inc. Ab.	KM59.1(2 pcs.),60.1,75.1 obv. 132 beads, 77.1,81.1,82	6.50	160.00
CPL5	1974(7)	44,296	KM59.1(2 pcs.),60.1,74.1-75.1,77.1,88	8.00	5.75
CPL6	1975(7)	36,851	KM59.1(2 pcs.),60.1,74.1-75.1,76.2,77.1	8.00	6.00
CPL7	1976(7)	28,162	KM59.1(2 pcs.),60.1,74.1-75.1,76.2,77.1	8.00	8.75
CPL8	1977(7)	44,198	KM59.1(2 pcs.),60.1,74.1,75.2,77.1,117	8.15	10.00
CPL9	1978(7)	41,000	KM59.1(2 pcs.),60.1,74.1,75.3,77.1,120	—	6.00
CPL10	1979(7)	31,174	KM59.2(2 pcs.),60.2,74.2,75.3,77.2,120	10.75	8.75
CPL11	1980(7)	41,447	KM60.2,74.2,75.3,77.2,120,127(2 pcs.)	10.75	11.50

Proof sets

KM#	Date	Mintage	Identification	Issue Price	Mkt Value
PS1	1981(7)	199,000	KM60.2,74.2,75.3,77.2,120,123,130	36.00	50.00
PS2	1982(7)	180,908	KM60.2a,74.2,75.3,77.2,120,123,133	36.00	25.00
PS3	1983(7)	166,779	KM60.2a,74.2,75.3,77.2,120,132,138	36.00	27.50
PS4	1984(7)	161,602	KM60.2a,74.2,75.3,77.2,120,132,140	30.00	32.50
PS5	1985(7)	157,037	KM60.2a,74.2,75.3,77.2,120,132,143	30.00	32.50
PS6	1986(7)	175,745	KM60.2a,74.2,75.3,77.2,120,132,149	30.00	32.50
PS7	1987(7)	179,004	KM60.2a,74.2,75.3,77.2,120,132,154	34.00	40.00
PS8	1988(7)	175,259	KM60.2a,74.2,75.3,77.2,132,157,161	37.50	50.00
PS9	1989(7)	170,928	KM60.2a,74.2,75.3,77.2,132,157,168	40.00	63.00
PS10	1989(4)	6,823	KM125.2,135-136,153	1190.	1250.
PS11	1989(4)	1,995	KM164-167	1700.	1975.
PS12	1989(3)	2,550	KM125.2,163,167	1530.	1625.
PS13	1989(3)	9,979	KM135,163-164	165.00	225.
PS14	1990(7)	158,068	KM170,181-186	41.00	50.00
PS15	1990(4)	2,629	KM174-177	1720.	1500.
PS16	1991(7)	14,629	KM179,181-186	—	45.00
PS17	1991(4)	873	KM198-201	1760.	1680.
PS18	1992(7)	—	KM204-210	42.75	45.00
PS19	1992 (4)	*3,500	KM226-229	1680.	1680.

Olympic Commemoratives (OCP)

KM#	Date	Mintage	Identification	Issue Price	Mkt Value
OCP1	1973(4)	—	KM84-87,Series I	78.50	42.50
OCP2	1974(4)	—	KM89,90,93,94,Series II	88.50	42.50
OCP3	1974(4)	—	KM91,92,95,96,Series III	88.50	42.50
OCP4	1975(4)	—	KM98,99,102,103,Series IV	88.50	42.50
OCP5	1975(4)	—	KM100,101,104,105,Series V	88.50	42.50
OCP6	1976(4)	—	KM107,108,111,112, Series VI	88.50	55.00
OCP7	1976(4)	—	KM109,110,113,114,Series VII	88.50	60.00

Newfoundland
Large cents

1865-1896   1904-1936

BRONZE

KM#	Date	Mintage	VG-8	F-12	VF-20	XF-40	MS-60	MS-63
1	1865	240,000	1.50	2.25	3.75	11.00	90.00	225.00
	1872H	200,000	1.50	2.25	3.75	11.00	65.00	160.00
	1872H	—	—	—	—	—	Proof	600.00
	1873	200,025	1.50	2.25	3.75	11.00	140.00	500.00
	1873	—	—	—	—	—	Proof	600.00
	1876H	200,000	1.50	2.25	3.75	11.00	125.00	400.00
	1876H	—	—	—	—	—	Proof	600.00
	1880 round O, even date							
		400,000	1.50	2.00	4.00	11.00	95.00	275.00
	1880 round O, low O	Inc. Ab.	1.50	2.25	4.50	11.00	100.00	325.00
	1880 oval O	Inc. Ab.	40.00	60.00	90.00	150.00	475.00	1100.
	1885	40,000	12.00	15.00	25.00	50.00	230.00	700.00
	1888	50,000	11.25	13.50	18.75	40.00	225.00	675.00
	1890	200,000	1.50	2.25	3.50	8.00	90.00	225.00
	1894	200,000	1.50	2.25	3.50	8.00	90.00	225.00
	1896	200,000	1.50	2.25	3.50	8.00	90.00	225.00
9	1904H	100,000	4.00	7.00	12.00	18.00	175.00	500.00
	1907	200,000	1.00	1.75	3.00	8.00	100.00	225.00
	1909	200,000	1.00	1.75	3.00	8.00	100.00	200.00
	1909	—	—	—	—	—	Proof	400.00
16	1913	400,000	.75	1.50	2.00	4.00	35.00	100.00
	1917C	702,350	.75	1.50	2.00	4.00	40.00	160.00
	1919C	300,000	.75	1.50	2.25	5.00	50.00	175.00
	1919C	—	—	—	—	—	Proof	150.00
	1920C	302,184	.75	1.50	2.25	5.00	50.00	175.00
	1929	300,000	.75	1.50	2.00	4.00	40.00	150.00
	1929	—	—	—	—	—	Proof	125.00
	1936	300,000	.75	1.25	1.75	3.00	25.00	70.00
	1936	—	—	—	—	—	Proof	250.00

Small cents

BRONZE

KM#	Date	Mintage	VG-8	F-12	VF-20	XF-40	MS-60	MS-63
18	1938	500,000	.25	.50	1.00	2.00	14.00	30.00
	1938	—	—	—	—	—	Proof	65.00
	1940	300,000	1.00	1.50	2.00	6.00	25.00	90.00
	1940 re-engraved date	—	12.00	24.00	28.00	35.00	150.00	350.00
	1941C	827,662	.25	.45	.60	1.25	12.50	30.00
	1941C re-engraved date	—	10.00	15.00	20.00	35.00	150.00	400.00
	1942	1,996,889	.25	.45	.60	1.25	12.50	25.00
	1943C	1,239,732	.25	.45	.60	1.25	12.50	25.00
	1944C	1,328,776	.50	1.00	1.50	3.50	25.00	70.00
	1947C	313,772	.50	.75	1.00	2.00	20.00	140.00

Five cents

KM#	Date	Mintage	1.1782 g, .925 SILVER, .0350 oz ASW					
			VG-8	F-12	VF-20	XF-40	MS-60	MS-63
2	1865	80,000	18.00	28.00	50.00	100.00	700.00	1500.
	1870	40,000	27.50	40.00	75.00	150.00	1000.	1750.
	1870	—	—	—	—	—	Proof	3900.
	1872H	40,000	18.00	25.00	45.00	100.00	600.00	1100.
	1873	44,260	30.00	40.00	80.00	175.00	1000.	1800.
	1873H	Inc. Ab.	675.00	1100.	1650.	2000.	3750.	—

KM#	Date	Mintage	VG-8	F-12	VF-20	XF-40	MS-60	MS-63
2	1876H	20,000	70.00	100.00	165.00	350.00	1700.	3000.
	1880	40,000	20.00	35.00	60.00	110.00	900.00	1600.
	1881	40,000	12.00	25.00	40.00	100.00	700.00	1500.
	1882H	60,000	10.00	18.00	35.00	85.00	600.00	1200.
	1882H	—	—	—	—	—	Proof	2800.
	1885	16,000	60.00	100.00	180.00	300.00	2000.	4250.
	1888	40,000	15.00	25.00	45.00	100.00	650.00	1000.
	1890	160,000	6.00	10.00	25.00	70.00	475.00	1100.
	1890	—	—	—	—	—	Proof	2100.
	1894	160,000	6.00	10.00	25.00	70.00	475.00	1100.
	1896	400,000	3.50	7.00	16.00	35.00	400.00	1000.
7	1903	100,000	2.00	4.00	16.00	40.00	400.00	1000.
	1904H	100,000	2.00	4.00	12.50	32.50	245.00	500.00
	1908	400,000	1.75	3.25	11.00	25.00	200.00	400.00
13	1912	300,000	1.00	1.75	4.00	16.00	175.00	300.00
	1917C	300,319	1.00	1.75	3.50	12.00	175.00	375.00
	1919C	100,844	1.50	3.00	8.00	22.00	350.00	500.00
	1929	300,000	1.00	1.75	3.25	12.00	150.00	275.00
	1929	—	—	—	—	—	Proof	750.00
19	1938	100,000	1.00	1.50	2.00	3.00	70.00	175.00
	1938	—	—	—	—	—	Proof	350.00
	1940C	200,000	1.00	1.50	2.00	3.00	40.00	140.00
	1941C	621,641	.75	1.00	1.50	2.25	18.00	25.00
	1942C	298,348	1.00	1.50	2.50	3.00	30.00	50.00
	1943C	351,666	.75	1.00	1.50	2.25	15.00	25.00
	1.1664 g, .800 SILVER, .0300 oz ASW							
19a	1944C	286,504	1.00	1.75	2.50	3.00	30.00	80.00
	1945C	203,828	.75	1.00	1.50	2.25	15.00	27.50
	1945C	—	—	—	—	—	Proof	250.00
	1946C	2,041	125.00	185.00	250.00	375.00	1400.	2000.
	1946C	—	—	—	—	—	Proof	4000.
	1947C	38,400	3.00	4.00	6.00	12.00	60.00	125.00
	1947C	—	—	—	—	—	Proof	400.00

Ten cents

1865-1896
2.3564 g, .925 SILVER, .0701 oz ASW

KM#	Date	Mintage	VG-8	F-12	VF-20	XF-40	MS-60	MS-63
3	1865	80,000	10.00	18.00	50.00	140.00	1200.	2500.
	1865 plain edge	—	—	—	—	—	Proof	5500.
	1870	30,000	100.00	150.00	300.00	600.00	3000.	6500.
	1872H	40,000	10.00	18.00	45.00	100.00	800.00	1850.
	1873 flat 3	23,614	12.00	24.00	60.00	175.00	1600.	3000.
	1873 round 3	Inc. Ab.	12.00	24.00	60.00	175.00	1600.	3000.
	1876H	10,000	20.00	35.00	75.00	225.00	1600.	3200.
	1880/70	10,000	20.00	35.00	75.00	225.00	1600.	3200.
	1882H	20,000	10.00	20.00	45.00	100.00	800.00	1750.
	1882H	—	—	—	—	—	Proof	3400.
	1885	8,000	35.00	80.00	190.00	450.00	2000.	4000.
	1888	30,000	10.00	16.00	50.00	130.00	1250.	2500.
	1890	100,000	4.00	10.00	20.00	70.00	700.00	1500.
	1890	—	—	—	—	—	Proof	3200.
	1894	100,000	4.00	10.00	20.00	70.00	650.00	1400.
	1894	—	—	—	—	—	Proof	1750.
	1896	230,000	3.00	7.00	18.00	65.00	550.00	1300.

1903-1947

KM#	Date	Mintage	VG-8	F-12	VF-20	XF-40	MS-60	MS-63
8	1903	100,000	3.00	7.00	22.00	60.00	600.00	1400.
	1904H	100,000	2.00	6.00	17.50	50.00	325.00	500.00

KM#	Date	Mintage	VG-8	F-12	VF-20	XF-40	MS-60	MS-63
14	1912	150,000	1.50	3.00	9.00	30.00	300.00	500.00
	1917C	250,805	1.25	2.00	6.00	20.00	360.00	650.00
	1919C	54,342	1.50	3.00	9.00	28.00	175.00	325.00
20	1938	100,000	1.00	1.50	2.50	6.00	100.00	250.00
	1938	—	—	—	—	—	Proof	500.00
	1940	100,000	.50	1.00	2.00	5.00	85.00	250.00
	1941C	483,630	.50	1.00	2.00	4.00	30.00	95.00
	1942C	293,736	.50	1.00	2.00	4.00	32.00	100.00
	1943C	104,706	.50	1.00	2.00	4.00	35.00	120.00
	2.3328 g, .800 SILVER, .0600 oz ASW							
20a	1944C	151,471	1.00	1.25	2.00	5.00	55.00	190.00
	1945C	175,833	.60	1.00	2.00	4.00	32.00	100.00
	1946C	38,400	2.00	4.00	8.00	16.00	65.00	300.00
	1947C	61,988	1.00	2.00	4.00	10.00	80.00	200.00

Twenty cents

KM#	Date	Mintage	4.7127 g, .925 SILVER, .1401 oz ASW VG-8	F-12	VF-20	XF-40	MS-60	MS-63
			1865-1900					
4	1865	100,000	8.00	14.00	35.00	100.00	900.00	2000.
	1865 plain edge	—	—	—	—	—	Proof	4500.
	1870	50,000	11.00	18.00	60.00	140.00	1250.	2600.
	1872H	90,000	7.00	12.00	30.00	90.00	750.00	1800.
	1873	45,797	9.00	15.00	40.00	120.00	1350.	2750.
	1876H	50,000	9.00	15.00	45.00	125.00	1350.	2500.
	1880/70	30,000	12.00	25.00	60.00	150.00	1350.	3000.
	1881	60,000	4.00	10.00	25.00	70.00	750.00	1750.
	1882H	100,000	1.00	8.00	25.00	70.00	750.00	1750.
	1882H	—	—	—	—	—	Proof	3700.
	1885	40,000	6.00	12.00	30.00	90.00	1300.	2500.
	1888	75,000	4.00	9.00	27.00	80.00	750.00	1750.
	1890	100,000	3.00	6.00	20.00	55.00	550.00	1500.
	1890	—	—	—	—	—	Proof	2750.
	1894	100,000	3.00	6.00	20.00	55.00	550.00	1500.
	1896 small 96	125,000	3.00	6.00	15.00	50.00	550.00	1500.
	1896 large 96	Inc. Ab.	3.50	9.00	20.00	65.00	600.00	1500.
	1899 small 99	125,000	6.00	12.00	30.00	75.00	700.00	1600.
	1899 large 99	Inc. Ab.	2.50	6.00	15.00	50.00	550.00	1500.
	1900	125,000	2.50	5.00	14.00	45.00	550.00	1500.

KM#	Date	Mintage	VG-8	F-12	VF-20	XF-40	MS-60	MS-63
			1904-1912					
10	1904H	75,000	6.00	12.00	45.00	100.00	925.00	2250.
	1904H	—	—	—	—	—	Proof	4150.
15	1912	350,000	2.00	3.00	10.00	35.00	350.00	900.00

Twenty-five cents

KM#	Date	Mintage	5.8319 g, .925 SILVER, .1734 oz ASW			XF-40	MS-60	MS-63
			VG-8	F-12	VF-20			
17	1917C	464,779	1.50	2.00	4.00	8.00	100.00	200.00
	1919C	163,939	1.50	2.25	4.25	12.00	130.00	350.00

Fifty cents

1870-1900

1904-1919

KM#	Date	Mintage	11.7818 g, .925 SILVER, .3504 oz ASW			XF-40	MS-60	MS-63
			VG-8	F-12	VF-20			
6	1870	50,000	8.00	12.00	35.00	135.00	1500.	2500.
	1870 plain edge	—	—	—	—	—	Proof	5500.
	1872H	48,000	8.00	12.00	35.00	135.00	1250.	2250.
	1873	37,675	15.00	25.00	60.00	250.00	2200.	5000.
	1874	80,000	8.00	12.00	40.00	160.00	2200.	5000.
	1876H	28,000	18.00	30.00	75.00	270.00	2200.	5200.
	1880	24,000	18.00	27.50	75.00	270.00	2200.	5200.
	1881	50,000	8.00	16.00	40.00	160.00	2200.	5400.
	1882H	100,000	6.00	12.00	30.00	130.00	1400.	3400.
	1882H	—	—	—	—	—	Proof	5500.
	1885	40,000	8.00	14.00	35.00	150.00	1800.	4750.
	1888	20,000	10.00	20.00	60.00	250.00	2000.	5200.
	1894	40,000	5.00	8.00	30.00	130.00	1500.	2600.
	1896	60,000	4.00	7.00	22.50	100.00	1200.	2400.
	1898	76,607	4.00	7.00	25.00	120.00	1200.	2250.
	1899 wide 9's	150,000	4.00	7.00	22.50	100.00	1200.	2250.
	1899 narrow 9's	Inc. Ab.	4.00	7.00	22.50	100.00	1200.	2250.
	1900	150,000	4.00	7.00	22.50	100.00	1200.	2250.
11	1904H	140,000	3.00	5.00	16.00	35.00	400.00	800.00
	1907	100,000	3.50	6.00	17.50	40.00	275.00	1000.
	1908	160,000	2.50	4.50	12.50	25.00	175.00	550.00
	1909	200,000	2.50	4.50	12.50	25.00	175.00	550.00
12	1911	200,000	2.00	3.00	8.00	20.00	225.00	550.00
	1917C	375,560	2.00	3.00	6.00	15.00	140.00	350.00
	1918C	294,824	2.00	3.00	6.00	15.00	140.00	350.00
	1919C	306,267	2.00	3.00	6.00	15.00	140.00	350.00

Two dollars

KM#	Date	Mintage	3.3284 g, .917 GOLD, .0981 oz AGW F-12	VF-20	XF-40	AU-50	MS-60	MS-63
5	1865	10,000	175.00	225.00	350.00	600.00	1250.	2800.
	1865 plain edge	about 10 known	—	—	—	—	Proof	10,000.
	1870	10,000	175.00	225.00	350.00	600.00	1250.	3000.
	1870 plain edge	—	—	—	—	—	Proof	10,000.
	1872	6,050	225.00	350.00	500.00	850.00	2500.	5250.
	1880	2,500	1000.	1500.	2000.	2800.	5500.	9000.
	1880	—	—	—	—	—	Proof	18,500.
	1881	10,000	120.00	190.00	235.00	350.00	750.00	1450.
	1882H	25,000	110.00	160.00	200.00	285.00	650.00	1200.
	1882H	—	—	—	—	—	Proof	6000.
	1885	10,000	120.00	190.00	235.00	350.00	750.00	1450.
	1888	25,000	110.00	160.00	200.00	285.00	650.00	1200.

New Brunswick
Half penny token

KM#	Date	Mintage	VG-8	COPPER F-12	VF-20	XF-40	MS-60	MS-63
1	1843	480,000	3.00	6.00	12.00	25.00	95.00	250.00
	1843	—	—	—	—	—	Proof	750.00

KM#	Date	Mintage	VG-8	F-12	VF-20	XF-40	MS-60	MS-63
3	1854	864,000	3.00	6.00	12.00	25.00	95.00	250.00

One penny token

KM#	Date	Mintage	VG-8	COPPER F-12	VF-20	XF-40	MS-60	MS-63
2	1843	480,000	3.00	6.00	12.00	30.00	150.00	300.00
	1843	—	—	—	—	—	Proof	800.00

KM#	Date	Mintage	VG-8	F-12	VF-20	XF-40	MS-60	MS-63
4	1854	432,000	3.00	6.00	12.00	35.00	160.00	320.00

Decimal coinage
Half cent

KM#	Date	Mintage	VG-8	BRONZE F-12	VF-20	XF-40	MS-60	MS-63
5	1861	222,800	40.00	60.00	80.00	110.00	320.00	850.00
	1861	—	—	—	—	—	Proof	2200.

One cent

KM#	Date	Mintage	VG-8	BRONZE F-12	VF-20	XF-40	MS-60	MS-63
6	1861	1,000,000	1.50	2.00	3.00	6.00	45.00	160.00
	1861	—	—	—	—	—	Proof	450.00
	1864 short 6	1,000,000	1.50	2.00	3.00	6.00	45.00	165.00
	1864 long 6	Inc. Ab.	1.50	2.00	3.00	6.00	45.00	150.00

Five cents

KM#	Date	Mintage	1.1620 g, .925 SILVER, .0346 oz ASW			XF-40	MS-60	MS-63
			VG-8	F-12	VF-20			
7	1862	100,000	20.00	35.00	80.00	160.00	800.00	1800.
	1862	—	—	—	—	—	Proof	2500.
	1864 small 6	100,000	20.00	35.00	80.00	160.00	850.00	1900.
	1864 large 6	Inc. Ab.	20.00	35.00	80.00	160.00	800.00	1800.

Ten cents

KM#	Date	Mintage	2.3240 g, .925 SILVER, .0691 oz ASW			XF-40	MS-60	MS-63
			VG-8	F-12	VF-20			
8	1862	150,000	15.00	35.00	80.00	160.00	725.00	1600.
	1862 recut 2	Inc. Ab.	15.00	35.00	80.00	160.00	725.00	1600.
	1862	—	—	—	—	—	Proof	2200.
	1864	100,000	15.00	35.00	80.00	160.00	725.00	1600.

Twenty cents

KM#	Date	Mintage	4.6480 g, .925 SILVER, .1382 oz ASW			XF-40	MS-60	MS-63
			VG-8	F-12	VF-20			
9	1862	150,000	10.00	14.00	30.00	100.00	725.00	1600.
	1862	—	—	—	—	—	Proof	2200.
	1864	150,000	10.00	14.00	30.00	100.00	725.00	1600.

Nova Scotia
Sterling coinage
Half penny token

COPPER

KM#	Date	Mintage	VG-8	F-12	VF-20	XF-40	MS-60	MS-63
1	1823	400,000	2.00	4.00	8.00	15.00	65.00	150.00
	1823 w/o hyphen	Inc. Ab.	5.00	10.00	20.00	35.00	170.00	350.00
	1824	118,636	2.50	5.00	12.50	22.50	100.00	225.00
	1832	800,000	1.50	3.00	7.50	12.50	55.00	150.00

KM#	Date	Mintage	VG-8	F-12	VF-20	XF-40	MS-60	MS-63
1a	1382(error)	—	150.00	300.00	550.00	—	—	—
	1832/1382	—	500.00	700.00	—	—	—	—
	1832 (imitation)	—	3.25	5.00	8.00	12.50	50.00	100.00

KM#	Date	Mintage	VG-8	F-12	VF-20	XF-40	MS-60	MS-63
3	1840 small 0	300,000	3.50	5.00	8.50	12.50	55.00	165.00
	1840 medium 0	Inc. Ab.	2.50	4.00	6.50	11.00	45.00	125.00
	1840 large 0	Inc. Ab.	4.00	6.00	10.00	16.00	60.00	185.00
	1843	300,000	3.00	5.00	8.00	12.00	50.00	160.00

KM#	Date	Mintage	VG-8	F-12	VF-20	XF-40	MS-60	MS-63
5	1856 w/o LCW	720,000	2.00	4.00	7.50	12.50	55.00	175.00
	1856 w/o LCW	—	—	—	—	—	Proof	600.00
	1856 w/o LCW, inverted A for V in PROVINCE				—	—	Proof	600.00

BRONZE

KM#	Date	Mintage	VG-8	F-12	VF-20	XF-40	MS-60	MS-63
5a	1856 w/LCW	—	—	—	—	—	Proof	600.00

One penny token

COPPER

KM#	Date	Mintage	VG-8	F-12	VF-20	XF-40	MS-60	MS-63
2	1824	217,776	3.00	6.00	10.00	22.50	100.00	250.00
	1832	200,000	2.00	4.00	7.50	18.00	80.00	230.00
2a	1832 (imitation)	—	5.50	16.00	24.00	40.00	—	—

KM#	Date	Mintage	VG-8	F-12	VF-20	XF-40	MS-60	MS-63
4	1840	150,000	2.00	4.00	7.00	15.00	60.00	175.00
	1843/0	150,000	9.00	12.50	18.00	30.00	85.00	—
	1843	Inc. Ab.	3.00	6.00	10.00	20.00	75.00	200.00

KM#	Date	Mintage	VG-8	F-12	VF-20	XF-40	MS-60	MS-63
6	1856 w/o LCW	360,000	2.50	4.50	8.50	12.00	55.00	135.00
	1856 w/LCW	Inc. Ab.	2.00	4.00	7.00	10.00	45.00	115.00

BRONZE

KM#	Date	Mintage	VG-8	F-12	VF-20	XF-40	MS-60	MS-63
6a	1856	—	—	—	—	—	Proof	400.00

Decimal coinage
Half cent

BRONZE

KM#	Date	Mintage	VG-8	F-12	VF-20	XF-40	MS-60	MS-63
7	1861	400,000	2.00	3.50	6.00	10.00	40.00	115.00
	1864	400,000	2.00	3.50	6.00	10.00	40.00	115.00
	1864	—	—	—	—	—	Proof	300.00

One cent

BRONZE

KM#	Date	Mintage	VG-8	F-12	VF-20	XF-40	MS-60	MS-63
8	1861	800,000	1.50	2.25	4.50	8.00	60.00	135.00
	1862	(Est.) 100,000	14.00	20.00	32.00	80.00	225.00	600.00
	1864	800,000	1.50	2.25	4.50	8.00	60.00	140.00

NOTE: The Royal Mint Report records mintage of 1,000,000 for 1862 which is considered incorrect.

Prince Edward Island
One cent

KM#	Date	Mintage	VG-8	BRONZE F-12	VF-20	XF-40	MS-60	MS-63
4	1871	2,000,000	1.25	2.00	3.50	8.00	70.00	175.00
	1871	—	—	—	—	—	Proof	2000.

Mexico

COLONIAL COB COINAGE

RULERS
Philip V, 1700-1724, 1724-1746
Luis I, 1724

MINT MARKS
Mo, MXo - Mexico City Mint

ASSAYERS INITIALS

Letter	Date	Name
L	1678-1703	Martin Lopez
J	1708-1723	Jose E. de Leon
D	1724-1727	?
R	1729-1730	Nicolas de Roxas
G	1730	—
F	1730-1733	Felipe Rivas de Angulo
F	1733-1784	Francisco de la Pena
M	1733-1763	Manuel de la Pena

1/2 REAL

.931 SILVER, 1.69 g
Philip V
Obv: Legend around crowned PHILIPVS monogram.
Rev: Legend around cross, lions and castles.

KM#	Date	Good	VG	Fine	VF
24	1701 L	30.00	40.00	55.00	90.00
	1702 L	25.00	35.00	50.00	65.00
	1703 L	25.00	35.00	50.00	65.00
	1704 L	30.00	42.50	65.00	85.00
	1705 L	30.00	42.50	65.00	85.00
	1706 L	30.00	42.50	65.00	85.00
	1707 L	30.00	42.50	65.00	85.00
	1708 J	35.00	50.00	70.00	110.00
	1709 J	30.00	42.50	65.00	85.00
	1710 J	30.00	42.50	65.00	85.00
	1711 J	30.00	42.50	65.00	85.00
	1712 J	30.00	42.50	65.00	85.00
	1714 J	30.00	42.50	65.00	85.00
	1715 J	30.00	42.50	65.00	85.00
	1716 J	30.00	42.50	65.00	85.00
	1717 J	30.00	42.50	65.00	85.00
	1718 J	30.00	42.50	65.00	85.00
	1719 J	30.00	42.50	65.00	85.00
	1720 J	30.00	42.50	65.00	85.00
	1721 J	30.00	42.50	65.00	85.00
	1722 J	42.50	55.00	80.00	125.00
	1723 J	42.50	55.00	80.00	125.00
	1724 J	50.00	65.00	85.00	140.00
	1724 D	50.00	65.00	85.00	140.00
	1725 D	50.00	65.00	85.00	140.00
	1726 D	35.00	50.00	70.00	110.00
	1727 D	35.00	50.00	70.00	110.00
	1728 D	35.00	50.00	70.00	110.00

.916 SILVER, 1.69 g

KM#	Date	Good	VG	Fine	VF
24a	1729 D	35.00	50.00	70.00	110.00
	1730 G	35.00	50.00	70.00	110.00
	1730 D	35.00	50.00	70.00	110.00
	1731 F	35.00	50.00	70.00	110.00
	1732 F	35.00	50.00	70.00	110.00
	1733 F	35.00	50.00	70.00	110.00
	Date off flan	15.00	20.00	25.00	30.00

.931 SILVER, 1.69 g
Luis I
Obv: Legend around crowned LVDOVICVS monogram.
Rev: Legend around cross, lions and castles.

KM#	Date	Good	VG	Fine	VF
25	1724 D	225.00	350.00	500.00	600.00
	1725 D	225.00	350.00	500.00	600.00
	1726 D	250.00	370.00	550.00	650.00
	Date off flan	100.00	200.00	250.00	300.00

REAL

ROYAL STRIKES

Philip V

Full struck sample specimens referred to as "Royal" strikes are seldom encountered and are considered rare.

CIRCULATION STRIKES

.931 SILVER, 3.38 g
Obv. leg: PHILIPVS V DEI G and date
around crowned arms.

	Date	Good	VG	Fine	VF
30	1701 L	45.00	60.00	70.00	115.00
	1702 L	45.00	60.00	70.00	115.00
	1703 L	45.00	60.00	70.00	115.00
	1703 L	45.00	60.00	70.00	115.00
	1704 L	45.00	60.00	70.00	115.00
	1705 L	45.00	60.00	70.00	115.00
	1706 L	45.00	60.00	70.00	115.00
	1707 L	45.00	60.00	70.00	115.00
	1708 J	45.00	60.00	70.00	115.00
	1709 J	45.00	60.00	70.00	115.00
	1710 J	45.00	60.00	70.00	115.00
	1711 J	45.00	60.00	70.00	115.00
	1712 J	45.00	60.00	70.00	115.00
	1713 J	35.00	45.00	57.50	85.00
	1714 J	35.00	45.00	57.50	85.00
	1715 J	45.00	60.00	70.00	100.00
	1716 J	45.00	60.00	70.00	100.00
	1717 J	45.00	60.00	70.00	100.00
	1718 J	45.00	60.00	70.00	100.00
	1719 J	45.00	60.00	70.00	100.00
	1720 J	45.00	60.00	70.00	100.00
	1721 J	45.00	60.00	70.00	100.00
	1722 J	45.00	60.00	70.00	100.00
	1723 J	45.00	60.00	70.00	100.00
	1724 J	45.00	60.00	70.00	100.00
	1726 D	45.00	60.00	70.00	100.00
	1727 D	45.00	60.00	70.00	100.00
	1728 D	45.00	60.00	70.00	100.00
	1729 F	45.00	60.00	70.00	100.00

.916 SILVER

	Date	Good	VG	Fine	VF
30a	1729 R	45.00	60.00	70.00	100.00
	1730 R	45.00	60.00	70.00	100.00
	1730 F	45.00	60.00	70.00	100.00
	1730 G	45.00	60.00	70.00	100.00
	1731 F	45.00	60.00	70.00	100.00
	Date off flan	10.00	15.00	20.00	30.00

2 REALES

ROYAL STRIKES

Philip V

Fully struck sample specimens referred to as "Royal" strikes are seldom encountered and are considered rare.

CIRCULATION STRIKES

.931 SILVER, 6.77 g
Obv. leg: PHILIPVS V DEI G and date
around crowned arms.

KM#	Date	Good	VG	Fine	VF
35	1701 L	25.00	40.00	50.00	75.00
	1702 L	25.00	40.00	50.00	75.00
	1703 L	25.00	40.00	50.00	75.00
	1704 L	35.00	75.00	150.00	250.00
	1705 L	25.00	40.00	50.00	75.00
	1706 L	25.00	40.00	50.00	75.00
	1707 L	35.00	75.00	150.00	250.00
	1708 J	25.00	40.00	50.00	75.00
	1710 J	25.00	40.00	50.00	75.00
	1711 J	25.00	40.00	50.00	75.00
	1712 J	25.00	40.00	50.00	75.00
	1713 J	25.00	40.00	50.00	75.00
	1714 J	25.00	40.00	50.00	80.00
	1715 J	25.00	40.00	50.00	80.00
	1716 J	25.00	40.00	50.00	75.00
	1717 J	25.00	40.00	50.00	75.00
	1718 J	25.00	40.00	50.00	75.00
	1719 J	25.00	40.00	50.00	75.00
	1720 J	25.00	40.00	50.00	75.00
	1721 J	25.00	40.00	60.00	100.00
	1722 J	25.00	40.00	50.00	75.00
	1723 J	25.00	40.00	50.00	75.00
	1724 J	36.00	50.00	60.00	100.00
	1725 D	36.00	57.50	75.00	125.00
	1725 R	36.00	40.00	50.00	100.00
	1726 D	36.00	57.50	75.00	125.00
	1727 D	36.00	57.50	75.00	125.00
	1728 D	28.00	37.50	75.00	125.00

.916 SILVER

KM#	Date	Good	VG	Fine	VF
35a	1729 R	28.00	37.50	75.00	125.00
	1730 R	28.00	37.50	75.00	125.00
	1731 MF	25.00	30.00	40.00	60.00
	1731/0 J	25.00	30.00	40.00	60.00
	1733 F	25.00	40.00	80.00	150.00
	Date off flan	10.00	20.00	30.00	40.00

4 REALES

ROYAL STRIKES

Philip V

Fully struck sample specimens referred to as "Royal" strikes are seldom encountered and are considered rare.

CIRCULATION STRIKES

.931 SILVER, 13.54 g
Obv. leg: PHILIPVS V DEI G and date
around crowned arms.

KM#	Date	Good	VG	Fine	VF
40	1701 L	80.00	125.00	225.00	375.00
	1702 L	80.00	125.00	225.00	375.00
	1703 L	45.00	90.00	150.00	250.00
	1704 L	80.00	125.00	225.00	375.00
	1705 L	65.00	100.00	200.00	300.00
	1706 L	65.00	100.00	200.00	300.00
	1707 L	65.00	100.00	200.00	300.00
	1708 J	30.00	70.00	120.00	200.00
	1709 J	65.00	100.00	200.00	300.00
	1710 J	50.00	90.00	175.00	250.00
	1711 J	50.00	90.00	175.00	250.00
	1712 J	80.00	125.00	225.00	375.00
	1713 J	80.00	125.00	225.00	375.00
	1714 J	65.00	100.00	200.00	300.00
	1715 J	80.00	125.00	225.00	375.00
	1716 J	65.00	100.00	200.00	300.00
	1717 J	80.00	125.00	225.00	375.00
	1718 J	80.00	125.00	225.00	375.00
	1719 J	65.00	100.00	200.00	300.00
	1720 J	65.00	100.00	200.00	300.00
	1721 J	65.00	100.00	200.00	300.00
	1722 J	90.00	150.00	300.00	500.00
	1723 J	90.00	150.00	300.00	500.00
	1725 D	90.00	150.00	300.00	500.00
	1726 D	90.00	150.00	300.00	500.00
	1727 D	90.00	150.00	300.00	500.00
	1728 D	80.00	125.00	225.00	375.00

.916 SILVER, 13.54 g

KM#	Date	Good	VG	Fine	VF
40a	1729 D	90.00	150.00	300.00	500.00
	1730 R	90.00	150.00	300.00	500.00
	1730 G	90.00	150.00	300.00	500.00
	1731 F	90.00	150.00	300.00	500.00
	1731 F	90.00	150.00	300.00	500.00
	1732/1 F	75.00	120.00	240.00	360.00
	1732 F	65.00	100.00	200.00	300.00
	1733 F	65.00	100.00	200.00	300.00
	1734 F	65.00	100.00	200.00	300.00
	Date off flan	40.00	50.00	70.00	100.00

Similar to KM#40a but 'klippe' planchet.

KM#	Date	Good	VG	Fine	VF
41	1733 MF	200.00	250.00	300.00	400.00
	1734 MF	250.00	300.00	400.00	500.00
	1734/3 MF	225.00	250.00	300.00	400.00
	1740/30 MF	250.00	275.00	350.00	450.00
	1742/32 MF	—	—	—	—
	1743/33 MF	—	—	—	—

.931 SILVER, 13.54 g
Luis I
Obv. leg: LVDOVICUS I DEI G
around crowned arms.

KM#	Date	Good	VG	Fine	VF
42	1724 D	650.00	1000.	1500.	2500.
	1725 D	750.00	1200.	2000.	3000.
	Date off flan	225.00	350.00	500.00	850.00

8 REALES
ROYAL STRIKES

Philip V

Fully struck sample specimens referred to as "Royal" strikes are seldom encountered and are considered rare.

CIRCULATION STRIKES

.931 SILVER, 27.07 g
Obv. leg: PHILIPVS V DEI G and date
around crowned arms.

KM#	Date	Good	VG	Fine	VF
47	1701 L	100.00	175.00	275.00	400.00
	1702 L	125.00	200.00	300.00	450.00
	1703 L	125.00	200.00	300.00	450.00
	1704 L	150.00	250.00	400.00	600.00
	1706 L	150.00	250.00	400.00	600.00
	1707 L	150.00	250.00	400.00	600.00
	1707 J	150.00	250.00	400.00	600.00
	1708 J	125.00	200.00	300.00	450.00
	1709 J	100.00	175.00	275.00	400.00
	1710 J	150.00	250.00	400.00	600.00
	1711 J	100.00	175.00	275.00	400.00
	1712 J	125.00	200.00	300.00	450.00
	1713 J	60.00	100.00	165.00	250.00

KM#	Date	Good	VG	Fine	VF
47	1714 J	60.00	100.00	165.00	250.00
	1715 J	100.00	175.00	275.00	400.00
	1716 J	100.00	175.00	275.00	400.00
	1717 J	100.00	175.00	275.00	400.00
	1718 J	100.00	175.00	275.00	400.00
	1719 J	100.00	175.00	275.00	400.00
	1720 J	100.00	175.00	275.00	400.00
	1721 J	125.00	200.00	300.00	450.00
	1722 J	100.00	175.00	275.00	400.00
	1723 J	125.00	200.00	300.00	450.00
	1724 D	125.00	200.00	300.00	450.00
	1725 D	180.00	350.00	500.00	900.00
	1726 D	180.00	350.00	500.00	900.00
	1727 D	180.00	350.00	500.00	900.00
	1728 D	200.00	400.00	600.00	1000.
	Date off flan	25.00	50.00	85.00	125.00

.916 SILVER

KM#	Date	Good	VG	Fine	VF
47a	1729 R	75.00	150.00	250.00	375.00
	1730 R	75.00	150.00	250.00	375.00
	1730 G	100.00	175.00	275.00	400.00
	1730 F	75.00	150.00	250.00	375.00
	1731/0 F	250.00	450.00	650.00	1200.
	1731 F	75.00	150.00	250.00	375.00
	1732 F	75.00	150.00	250.00	375.00
	1733 F	75.00	150.00	250.00	400.00
	Date off flan	25.00	50.00	85.00	125.00

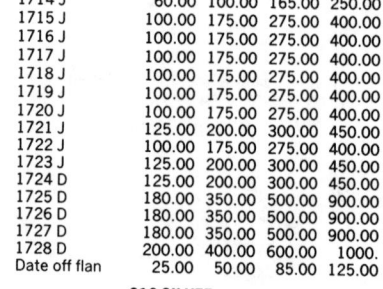

Similar to KM#47a but 'klippe' planchet.

KM#	Date	Good	VG	Fine	VF
48	1733 F	150.00	250.00	375.00	600.00
	1733 MF	100.00	150.00	250.00	375.00
	1734/3 MF	100.00	175.00	275.00	400.00
	1734 MF	100.00	175.00	275.00	400.00
	Date off flan	25.00	50.00	85.00	125.00

2 ESCUDOS

6.7700 g, .917 GOLD, .1996 oz AGW
Mint mark: MXo
Obv. leg: CAROLVS II DEI G and date
around crowned arms.
Rev: Legend around cross.

KM#	Date	Good	VG	Fine	VF
52	1701 L	600.00	750.00	900.00	1200.
	Date off flan	375.00	400.00	450.00	750.00

NOTE: Earlier dates (1690-1699) exist for this type.

ROYAL STRIKES

Philip V

Fully struck sample specimens referred to as "Royal" strikes are seldom encountered and are considered rare.

CIRCULATION STRIKES

.931 SILVER, 27.07 g
Luis I
Obv. leg: LVDOVICVS I DEI G.

KM#	Date	Good	VG	Fine	VF
49	1724 D	1500.	2000.	2500.	3000.
	1725 D	1500.	2000.	2500.	3000.
	Date off flan	400.00	600.00	1000.	1500.

ESCUDO

ROYAL STRIKES

Philip V

Fully struck sample specimens referred to as "Royal" strikes are seldom encountered and are considered rare.

CIRCULATION STRIKES

3.3800 g, .917 GOLD, .0997 oz AGW
Mint mark: MXo
Obv. leg: PHILIPVS V DEI G and date
around crowned arms.

KM#	Date	Good	VG	Fine	VF
51.1	1702 L	350.00	400.00	450.00	700.00
	1703 L	350.00	400.00	450.00	700.00
	1704 L	350.00	400.00	450.00	700.00
	1706 M	350.00	400.00	450.00	700.00
	1707 L	350.00	400.00	450.00	700.00
	1708 L	350.00	400.00	450.00	700.00
	1709 J	350.00	400.00	450.00	700.00
	1710 J	350.00	400.00	450.00	700.00
	1711 J	350.00	400.00	450.00	700.00
	1712 J	350.00	400.00	450.00	700.00
	Date off flan	250.00	300.00	350.00	450.00

Mint mark: Mo

KM#	Date	Good	VG	Fine	VF
51.2	1713 J	300.00	400.00	450.00	700.00
	1714 J	300.00	375.00	400.00	550.00
	Date off flan	250.00	300.00	350.00	450.00

6.7700 g, .917 GOLD, .1996 oz AGW
Mint mark: MXo
Obv. leg: PHILIPVS V DEI G and date
around crowned arms.

KM#	Date	Good	VG	Fine	VF
53.1	1704 L	400.00	500.00	650.00	850.00
	1705 L	400.00	500.00	650.00	850.00
	1707 L	400.00	500.00	650.00	850.00
	1708 J	400.00	500.00	650.00	850.00
	1709 J	400.00	500.00	650.00	850.00
	1710 J	400.00	500.00	650.00	850.00
	1711 J	400.00	500.00	600.00	850.00
	1712 J	400.00	500.00	600.00	850.00
	1713 J	400.00	500.00	600.00	850.00
	Date off flan	300.00	350.00	400.00	550.00

Mint mark: Mo

KM#	Date	Good	VG	Fine	VF
53.2	1714 J	350.00	400.00	600.00	750.00
	1717 J	350.00	400.00	600.00	750.00
	1722 J	350.00	400.00	600.00	800.00
	1723 J	350.00	400.00	600.00	800.00
	1729 R	350.00	400.00	600.00	800.00
	1731 F	350.00	400.00	600.00	700.00
	Date off flan	300.00	350.00	400.00	450.00

Luis I

KM#	Date	Good	VG	Fine	VF
A54	ND D	500.00	1000.	2000.	3000.

4 ESCUDOS
ROYAL STRIKES

Philip V
Fully struck sample specimens referred to as "Royal" strikes are seldom encountered and are considered rare.

CIRCULATION STRIKES

13.5400 g, .917 GOLD, .3992 oz AGW
Obv. leg: PHILIPVS V DEI G and date around crowned arms.
Rev: Legend around cross.

KM#	Date	Good	VG	Fine	VF
55.1	1701 L	700.00	800.00	1000.	1500.
	1702 L	700.00	800.00	1000.	1500.
	1703 L	700.00	800.00	1000.	1500.
	1704 L	700.00	800.00	1000.	1500.
	1705 L	700.00	800.00	1000.	1500.
	1706 L	700.00	800.00	1000.	1500.
	1707 L	700.00	800.00	1000.	1500.
	1708 J	700.00	800.00	1000.	1500.
	1709 J	700.00	800.00	1000.	1500.
	1710 J	700.00	800.00	1000.	1500.
	1711 J	700.00	800.00	1000.	1500.
	1712 J	700.00	800.00	1000.	1500.
	1713 J	700.00	800.00	1000.	1500.
	Date off flan	500.00	600.00	700.00	1000.

Mint mark: Mo

KM#	Date	Good	VG	Fine	VF
55.2	1714 J	700.00	800.00	1000.	1500.
	1720 J	700.00	800.00	1000.	1500.
	Date off flan	500.00	600.00	800.00	1100.

8 ESCUDOS
ROYAL STRIKES

Philip V
Fully struck sample specimens referred to as "Royal" strikes are seldom encountered and are considered rare.

CIRCULATION STRIKES

27.0700 g, .917 GOLD, .7980 oz AGW
Mint mark: MXo
Obv. leg: PHILIPVS V DEI G and date around crowned arms.
Rev: Legend around cross.

KM#	Date	Good	VG	Fine	VF
57.1	1701 L	1000.	1500.	2000.	2500.
	1702 L	1000.	1500.	2000.	2500.
	1703 L	1000.	1500.	2000.	2500.
	1704 L	1000.	1500.	2000.	2500.
	1705 L	1000.	1500.	2000.	2500.
	1706 L	1000.	1500.	2000.	2500.
	1707 L	1000.	1500.	2000.	2500.
	1708 J	1000.	1500.	2000.	2500.
	1709 J	1000.	1500.	2000.	2500.
	1710 J	1000.	1500.	2000.	2500.
	1711 J	1000.	1200.	1800.	2500.
	1712 J	1000.	1200.	1800.	2500.
	1713 J	600.00	900.00	1200.	1800.
	Date off flan	500.00	800.00	1000.	1500.

ROYAL STRIKES

Fully struck sample specimens referred to as "Royal" strikes are seldom encountered and are considered rare.

CIRCULATION STRIKES

Mint mark: Mo

KM#	Date	Good	VG	Fine	VF
57.2	1714 J	750.00	1000.	1600.	2250.
	1714 J date on rev.				
		750.00	1000.	1600.	2250.
	1715 J	750.00	1000.	1600.	2250.
	1717 J	800.00	1200.	2000.	3000.
	1718 J	800.00	1200.	2000.	3000.
	1720 J	800.00	1200.	2000.	3000.
	1723 J	800.00	1200.	2000.	3000.
	1728 D	800.00	1200.	2000.	3000.
	1729 R	800.00	1200.	2000.	3000.
	1730 R	800.00	1200.	2000.	3000.
	1730 F	800.00	1200.	2000.	3000.
	1731 F	800.00	1200.	2000.	3000.
	1732 F	800.00	1200.	2000.	3000.
	Date off flan	650.00	850.00	1100.	1500.

**Obv. leg: LVDOVICVS I DEI G and date
around crowned arms.
Rev: Legend around cross.**

58	1725 D	3000.	5000.	7500.	12,000.
	Date off flan	1500.	2500.	3500.	5000.

COLONIAL MILLED COINAGE
RULERS

Philip V, 1700-1746
Ferdinand VI, 1746-1759
Charles III, 1760-1788
Charles IV, 1788-1808
Ferdinand VII, 1808-1821

MINT MARKS
Mo - Mexico City Mint

ASSAYERS INITIALS

Letter	Date	Name
F	1733-1784	Francisco de la Pena
M	1733-1763	Manuel de la Pena
M	1754-1770	Manuel Assorin
F	1762-1770	Francisco de Rivera
M	1770-1777	Manuel de Rivera
F	1777-1803	Francisco Arance Cobos
M	1784-1801	Mariano Rodriguez
T	1801-1810	Tomas Butron Miranda
H	1803-1814	Henrique Buenaventura Azorin
J	1809-1833	Joaquin Davila Madrid
J	1812-1833	Jose Garcia Ansaldo

MONETARY SYSTEM

16 Pilones = 1 Real
8 Tlaco = 1 Real
16 Reales = 1 Escudo

1/8 (PILON)
(1/16 Real)

**COPPER
Obv: Crowned F VII monogram.
Rev: Castles and lions in wreath.**

KM#	Date	VG	Fine	VF	XF
59	1814	8.00	15.00	30.00	100.00
	1815	8.00	15.00	30.00	100.00

1/4 (TLACO)
(1/8 Real)

**COPPER
Obv. leg: FERDIN. VII. . around crowned F.VII.**

KM#	Date	VG	Fine	VF	XF
63	1814	10.00	20.00	40.00	125.00
	1815	10.00	20.00	40.00	125.00
	1816	10.00	20.00	40.00	125.00

2/4 (2 TLACO)
(1/4 Real)

**COPPER
Obv. leg: FERDIN. VII. . around crowned F.VII.**

64	1814	6.00	12.00	25.00	100.00
	1815/4	8.00	15.00	35.00	125.00
	1815	6.00	12.00	25.00	100.00
	1816	6.00	12.00	25.00	100.00
	1821	15.00	30.00	50.00	175.00

1/4 REAL

**.8450 g, .903 SILVER, .0245 oz ASW
Obv: Castle. Rev: Lion.**

62	1796	10.00	20.00	40.00	80.00
	1797	10.00	25.00	40.00	80.00
	1798	12.50	20.00	35.00	60.00
	1799/8	12.50	17.50	35.00	65.00
	1799	10.00	15.00	27.50	60.00
	1800	10.00	25.00	35.00	80.00
	1801	10.00	15.00	27.50	60.00
	1802	12.50	20.00	27.50	60.00
	1803	12.50	20.00	27.50	60.00
	1804	10.00	20.00	27.50	70.00
	1805/4	12.50	22.50	40.00	65.00
	1805	10.00	20.00	35.00	60.00
	1806	10.00	20.00	35.00	70.00
	1807/797	15.00	30.00	40.00	75.00
	1807	12.50	25.00	35.00	70.00
	1808	12.50	25.00	35.00	70.00
	1809/8	12.50	25.00	35.00	70.00
	1809	12.50	25.00	35.00	70.00
	1810	12.50	25.00	35.00	60.00
	1811	12.50	25.00	35.00	60.00
	1812	12.50	25.00	35.00	60.00
	1813	10.00	20.00	27.50	60.00
	1815	10.00	20.00	35.00	60.00
	1816	10.00	20.00	30.00	50.00

1/2 REAL

1.6900 g, .917 SILVER, .0498 oz ASW
Obv. leg: PHILIP.V.D.G. HISPAN.ET IND. REX.

KM#	Date	VG	Fine	VF	XF
65	1732	—	—	Rare	—
	1732 F	500.00	800.00	1200.	2000.
	1733 F(MX)	375.00	600.00	1000.	1500.
	1733 MF(MX)				
		400.00	600.00	1000.	1500.
	1733 F	200.00	325.00	550.00	800.00
	1733 MF	300.00	400.00	600.00	800.00
	1734/3 MF	10.00	25.00	35.00	60.00
	1734 MF	10.00	25.00	35.00	60.00
	1735/4 MF	7.50	20.00	35.00	60.00
	1735 MF	7.50	20.00	35.00	60.00
	1736/5 MF	7.50	20.00	35.00	60.00
	1736 MF	7.50	20.00	35.00	60.00
	1737/6 MF	7.50	20.00	35.00	60.00
	1737 MF	7.50	20.00	35.00	60.00
	1738/7 MF	7.50	20.00	35.00	60.00
	1738 MF	7.50	20.00	35.00	60.00
	1739 MF	7.50	20.00	35.00	60.00
	1740/30MF	5.00	10.00	20.00	45.00
	1740/39MF	5.00	10.00	20.00	45.00
	1740 MF	5.00	10.00	20.00	45.00
	1741/39MF	5.00	10.00	20.00	45.00
	1741/0MF	5.00	10.00	20.00	45.00
	1741 MF	5.00	10.00	20.00	45.00

Obv. leg:.PHS.V.D.G. HISP.ET IND.R.

KM#	Date	VG	Fine	VF	XF
66	1742 M	5.00	10.00	20.00	45.00
	1743 M	5.00	10.00	20.00	45.00
	1744/3 M	5.00	10.00	20.00	45.00
	1744 M	5.00	10.00	20.00	45.00
	1745 M	5.00	10.00	20.00	45.00
	1746 M	5.00	10.00	20.00	45.00
	1747 M	5.00	10.00	20.00	45.00

Obv. leg: FRD.VI.D.G.HISP.ET IND.R.

KM#	Date	VG	Fine	VF	XF
67	1747/6 M	—	—	—	—
	1747 M	6.00	12.00	25.00	50.00
	1748/7 M	6.00	12.00	25.00	50.00
	1748 M	6.00	12.00	25.00	50.00
	1749 M	6.00	12.00	25.00	50.00
	1750 M	6.00	12.00	25.00	50.00
	1751 M	6.00	12.00	30.00	60.00
	1752 M	6.00	12.00	25.00	50.00
	1753 M	6.00	12.00	25.00	50.00
	1754 M	7.50	15.00	40.00	100.00
	1755/6 M	6.00	12.00	25.00	50.00
	1755 M	6.00	12.00	25.00	50.00
	1756/5 M	6.00	12.00	25.00	50.00
	1756 M	6.00	12.00	25.00	50.00
	1757/6 M	6.00	12.00	25.00	50.00
	1757 M	6.00	12.00	25.00	50.00
	1758/7 M	6.00	12.00	25.00	50.00
	1758 M	6.00	12.00	25.00	50.00
	1759 M	6.00	12.00	25.00	50.00
	1760 M	7.50	15.00	30.00	60.00

Obv. leg: CAR.III.D.G.HISP.ET IND.R.

KM#	Date	VG	Fine	VF	XF
68	1760 M	5.00	7.50	12.50	50.00
	1761 M	5.00	7.50	12.50	50.00
	1762 M	4.00	6.00	10.00	50.00
	1763/2 M	5.00	7.50	12.50	55.00
	1763 M	4.00	6.00	10.00	50.00
	1764 M	5.00	7.50	12.50	50.00
	1765 M	5.00	7.50	12.50	50.00
	1766 M	5.00	7.50	12.50	50.00
	1767 M	7.50	13.50	27.50	65.00
	1768/6 M	6.00	10.00	18.00	60.00
	1768 M	4.00	6.00	12.50	50.00
	1769 M	6.00	10.00	20.00	50.00
	1770 M	6.00	10.00	20.00	50.00
	1770 F	10.00	15.00	30.00	75.00
	1771 F	6.00	10.00	20.00	50.00

1.6900 g, .903 SILVER, .0490 oz ASW
Obv. leg: CAROLUS.III.DEI.GRATIA.
Rev: Inverted FM and mint mark.

KM#	Date	VG	Fine	VF	XF
69.1	1772 FM	3.00	6.50	12.50	60.00
	1773 FM	3.00	5.00	10.00	50.00

Rev: Normal initials and mint mark.

KM#	Date	VG	Fine	VF	XF
69.2	1772 FF	6.00	10.00	20.00	75.00
	1773 FM	3.00	5.00	10.00	50.00
	1773 FM (error) CAROLS				
		300.00	—	—	—
	1774 FM	3.00	5.00	10.00	50.00
	1775 FM	3.00	5.00	10.00	50.00
	1776 FM	3.00	5.00	10.00	50.00
	1777 FM	6.00	10.00	20.00	60.00
	1778 FF	4.50	9.00	18.50	50.00
	1779 FF	3.00	5.00	10.00	50.00
	1780/g FF	3.00	5.00	10.00	50.00
	1780 FF	3.00	5.00	10.00	50.00
	1781 FF	2.50	4.00	8.50	50.00
	1782/1 FF	5.00	10.00	20.00	75.00
	1782 FF	3.00	5.00	10.00	50.00
	1783 FF	3.00	5.00	10.00	50.00
	1783 FM	125.00	300.00	450.00	—
	1784 FF	3.00	5.00	10.00	50.00
	1784 FM	6.00	10.00	20.00	75.00
	1785 FM	3.50	6.00	13.50	50.00
	1786 FM	3.00	5.00	10.00	50.00
	1787 FM	3.00	5.00	10.00	50.00
	1788 FM	3.00	5.00	10.00	50.00
	1789 FM	6.00	10.00	30.00	100.00

Obv: Armored bust of Charles III, leg: .CAROLUS.IV. .

KM#	Date	VG	Fine	VF	XF
70	1789 FM	6.00	10.00	20.00	90.00
	1790 FM	6.00	10.00	20.00	90.00

Obv: Armored bust of Charles III, leg: .CAROLUS.IIII. .

KM#	Date	VG	Fine	VF	XF
71	1790 FM	6.00	10.00	20.00	90.00

Obv: Armored bust of Charles IIII.
Rev: Pillars and arms.

KM#	Date	VG	Fine	VF	XF
72	1792 FM	6.00	10.00	20.00	45.00
	1793 FM	6.00	10.00	20.00	45.00
	1794/3 FM	7.50	12.50	25.00	75.00
	1794 FM	5.00	6.00	10.00	45.00
	1795 FM	4.00	6.00	10.00	45.00
	1796 FM	4.00	6.00	10.00	45.00
	1797 FM	4.00	6.00	10.00	45.00
	1798/7 FM	4.50	6.50	11.50	50.00
	1798 FM	4.00	6.00	10.00	45.00
	1799 FM	4.00	6.00	10.00	45.00
	1800/799 FM	4.50	7.50	10.00	50.00
	1800 FM	4.00	6.50	7.50	45.00
	1800 FT	—	—	—	—
	1801 FM	6.50	10.00	20.00	75.00
	1801 FT	4.00	6.00	10.00	45.00
	1802 FT	4.00	6.00	10.00	45.00
	1803 FT	5.00	9.00	15.00	45.00
	1804 TH	4.00	6.00	10.00	45.00
	1805 TH	4.00	6.00	10.00	45.00
	1806 TH	4.00	6.00	10.00	45.00
	1807/6 TH	4.50	6.50	11.50	50.00
	1807 TH	4.00	6.00	10.00	45.00
	1808/7 TH	4.50	6.50	11.50	50.00
	1808 TH	4.00	6.00	10.00	45.00

Obv: Armored bust of Ferdinand VII.

KM#	Date	VG	Fine	VF	XF
73	1808 TH	3.00	5.00	10.00	30.00
	1809 TH	3.00	5.00	10.00	30.00
	1810 TH	5.00	8.00	12.00	35.00
	1810 HJ	3.00	5.00	10.00	30.00
	1811 HJ	3.00	5.00	10.00	30.00
	1812 HJ	3.00	5.00	10.00	30.00
	1813 TH	3.50	6.00	10.00	30.00
	1813 JJ	10.00	20.00	40.00	100.00
	1813 HJ	7.50	15.00	30.00	90.00
	1814 JJ	5.00	8.00	12.00	35.00

Obv: Draped bust of Ferdinand VII.

KM#	Date	VG	Fine	VF	XF
74	1814 JJ	3.00	5.00	12.00	45.00
	1815 JJ	3.00	5.00	10.00	40.00
	1816 JJ	3.00	5.00	10.00	40.00
	1817/6 JJ	—	—	—	—
	1817 JJ	3.00	5.00	12.00	45.00
	1818/7 JJ	3.00	5.00	15.00	50.00
	1818 JJ	3.00	5.00	15.00	50.00
	1819 JJ	3.00	5.00	10.00	40.00
	1820 JJ	3.00	5.00	15.00	50.00
	1821 JJ	3.00	5.00	10.00	40.00

REAL

3.3800 g, .917 SILVER, .0996 oz ASW
Obv. leg: PHILIP.V.D.G.HISPAN.ET IND.REX.

KM#	Date	VG	Fine	VF	XF
75.1	1732	—	—	Rare	—
(75)	1732 F	125.00	225.00	350.00	500.00
	1733 F(MX)	150.00	300.00	425.00	600.00
	1733/2 MF(MX)				
		150.00	350.00	425.00	600.00
	1733 MF(MX)	150.00	350.00	425.00	600.00
	1733 F	—	—	Rare	—
	1733 MF	85.00	150.00	225.00	325.00
	1734/3 MF	15.00	30.00	60.00	125.00
	1734 MF	12.00	25.00	50.00	150.00
	1735 MF	12.00	25.00	50.00	150.00
	1736 MF	12.00	20.00	50.00	150.00
	1737 MF	12.00	20.00	50.00	150.00
	1738 MF	12.00	20.00	50.00	150.00
	1739 MF	12.00	20.00	50.00	150.00
	1740 MF	12.00	20.00	50.00	150.00
	1741 MF	12.00	20.00	50.00	150.00

Obv. leg: PHS.V.D.G.HISP.ET.IND.R.

KM#	Date	VG	Fine	VF	XF
75.2	1742 M	8.00	15.00	30.00	60.00
(75.1)	1743 M	8.00	15.00	30.00	90.00
	1744/3 M	8.00	15.00	30.00	90.00
	1744 M	8.00	15.00	30.00	90.00
	1745 M	8.00	15.00	30.00	60.00
	1746/5 M	10.00	20.00	60.00	200.00
	1746 M	10.00	20.00	60.00	200.00
	1747 M	8.00	15.00	35.00	90.00

Obv. leg: .FRD.VI.D.G.HISP.ET IND.R.

KM#	Date	VG	Fine	VF	XF
76	1747 M	8.00	15.00	30.00	60.00
	1748/7 M	8.00	15.00	30.00	60.00
	1748 M	8.00	15.00	30.00	60.00
	1749/8 M	8.00	15.00	30.00	60.00
	1749 M	8.00	15.00	30.00	60.00
	1750/49 M	8.00	15.00	30.00	60.00
	1750 M	8.00	15.00	30.00	60.00
	1751 M	10.00	20.00	40.00	80.00
	1752 M	8.00	15.00	30.00	60.00
	1753 M	8.00	15.00	30.00	60.00
	1754 M	10.00	20.00	40.00	80.00
	1755/4 M	8.00	15.00	30.00	60.00
	1755 M	8.00	15.00	30.00	60.00
	1756 M	10.00	20.00	40.00	80.00
	1757 M	10.00	20.00	40.00	80.00
	1758/5 M	8.00	15.00	30.00	60.00
	1758 M	8.00	15.00	30.00	60.00
	1759 M	10.00	20.00	40.00	80.00
	1760 M	10.00	20.00	40.00	80.00

Obv. leg: CAR.III.D.G.HISP.ET IND.R.

KM#	Date	VG	Fine	VF	XF
77	1760 M	8.00	12.00	20.00	60.00
	1761 M	6.00	9.00	17.50	50.00
	1762 M	6.00	9.00	17.50	50.00
	1763/2 M	7.00	10.00	17.50	50.00
	1763 M	6.00	9.00	17.50	50.00
	1764 M	10.00	15.00	50.00	100.00
	1765 M	10.00	15.00	50.00	100.00
	1766 M	6.00	9.00	17.50	50.00
	1767 M	10.00	15.00	50.00	100.00
	1768 M	6.00	9.00	17.50	50.00
	1769 M	6.00	9.00	17.50	50.00
	1770/69M	6.00	9.00	15.00	80.00
	1770 M	6.00	9.00	15.00	80.00
	1770 F	20.00	40.00	90.00	250.00
	1771 F	20.00	40.00	90.00	250.00

3.3800 g, .903 SILVER, .0981 oz ASW
Obv. leg: CAROLUS.III.DEI.GRATIA.
Rev: Inverted FM and mint mark.

KM#	Date	VG	Fine	VF	XF
78.1	1772 FM	3.00	7.50	12.50	60.00
	1773 FM	3.00	7.50	12.50	60.00

Rev: Normal initials and mint mark.

KM#	Date	VG	Fine	VF	XF
78.2	1773 FM	6.50	12.50	30.00	90.00
	1774 FM	3.00	7.50	12.50	60.00
	1775 FM	3.00	7.50	12.50	60.00
	1776 FM	3.00	7.50	12.50	60.00
	1777 FM	3.00	7.50	12.50	60.00
	1778 FM	3.00	7.50	12.50	60.00
	1779 FF	3.00	8.50	15.50	60.00
	1780 FF	3.00	7.50	12.50	60.00
	1781 FF	3.00	7.50	12.50	60.00
	1782 FF	3.00	7.50	12.50	60.00
	1783 FF	3.00	8.50	15.00	60.00
	1784 FF	3.00	8.50	15.00	60.00
	1785 FM	3.00	7.50	12.50	60.00
	1785 FF	3.00	8.50	13.50	60.00
	1786 FM	3.00	7.50	12.50	60.00
	1787 FM	12.00	25.00	50.00	125.00
	1787 FF	10.00	20.00	40.00	100.00
	1788 FM	3.00	9.00	15.00	60.00
	1788 FF	3.00	7.50	12.50	60.00
	1789 FM	5.00	10.00	15.00	75.00

Obv: Armored bust of Charles III, leg: CAROLUS.IV. .

KM#	Date	VG	Fine	VF	XF
79	1789 FM	8.00	15.00	25.00	100.00
	1790 FM	8.00	15.00	25.00	100.00

Obv: Armored bust of Charles III; leg: CAROLUS.IIII.

KM#	Date	VG	Fine	VF	XF
80	1790 FM	10.00	20.00	35.00	125.00

Obv: Armored bust of Charles IIII.

KM#	Date	VG	Fine	VF	XF
81	1792 FM	10.00	20.00	30.00	90.00
	1793 FM	15.00	30.00	50.00	150.00
	1794 FM	25.00	50.00	90.00	250.00
	1795 FM	15.00	30.00	50.00	150.00
	1796 FM	3.50	8.50	13.50	65.00
	1797/6 FM	5.00	10.00	20.00	80.00
	1797 FM	3.00	7.50	12.50	60.00
	1798/7 FM	3.50	8.50	13.50	65.00
	1798 FM	3.00	7.50	12.50	60.00
	1799 FM	3.00	7.50	13.50	60.00
	1800 FM	3.00	7.50	13.50	60.00
	1801 FM	8.00	15.00	25.00	80.00

KM#	Date	VG	Fine	VF	XF
81	1801 FT	3.00	8.50	16.50	60.00
	1802 FM	3.00	8.50	16.50	60.00
	1802 FT	3.00	7.50	12.50	60.00
	1803 FT	3.00	8.50	16.50	60.00
	1804 TH	3.00	7.50	12.50	60.00
	1805 TH	3.00	8.50	16.50	60.00
	1806 TH	3.00	7.50	12.50	60.00
	1807/6 TH	3.50	8.50	13.50	65.00
	1807 TH	3.00	7.50	12.50	60.00
	1808/7 TH	3.50	8.50	13.50	65.00
	1808 TH	3.00	7.50	12.50	60.00

Obv: Armored bust of Ferdinand VII.

KM#	Date	VG	Fine	VF	XF
82	1809 TH	4.00	7.50	15.00	100.00
	1810/09 TH	4.00	7.50	15.00	100.00
	1810 TH	4.00	7.50	15.00	100.00
	1810 HJ	6.00	10.00	20.00	125.00
	1811 HJ	4.00	7.50	15.00	100.00
	1811 TH	25.00	35.00	60.00	250.00
	1812 HJ	4.00	7.50	15.00	80.00
	1812 JJ	6.00	10.00	20.00	125.00
	1813 HJ	5.50	8.50	17.50	125.00
	1813 JJ	50.00	100.00	150.00	250.00
	1814 HJ	50.00	100.00	175.00	300.00
	1814 JJ	50.00	100.00	175.00	300.00

Obv: Draped bust of Ferdinand VII.

KM#	Date	VG	Fine	VF	XF
83	1814 JJ	25.00	50.00	100.00	350.00
	1815 JJ	5.50	8.50	17.50	125.00
	1815 HJ	15.00	30.00	60.00	150.00
	1816 JJ	4.00	7.50	12.50	75.00
	1817 JJ	4.00	7.50	12.50	75.00
	1818 JJ	30.00	60.00	125.00	500.00
	1819 JJ	5.50	8.50	17.50	75.00
	1820 JJ	5.00	8.50	17.50	75.00
	1821/0 JJ	7.50	12.50	27.50	110.00
	1821 JJ	5.00	8.50	12.50	50.00

2 REALES

6.7700 g, .917 SILVER, .1996 oz ASW
Obv. leg: PHILIP.V.D.G.HISPAN.ET IND. REX.

KM#	Date	VG	Fine	VF	XF
84	1732 F	800.00	1200.	1600.	2500.
	1733 F(MX)	500.00	750.00	1200.	2000.
	1733 F	500.00	675.00	1000.	1750.
	1733 MF(MX)				
		350.00	600.00	1000.	1500.
	1733 MF	500.00	750.00	1200.	2000.
	1734/3 MF	20.00	40.00	80.00	150.00
	1734 MF	20.00	40.00	80.00	150.00
	1735/3 MF	10.00	20.00	40.00	90.00
	1735/4 MF	10.00	20.00	40.00	90.00
	1735 MF	10.00	20.00	40.00	90.00
	1736/3 MF	15.00	30.00	60.00	125.00
	1736/4 MF	15.00	30.00	60.00	125.00

KM#	Date	VG	Fine	VF	XF
84	1736/5 MF	15.00	30.00	60.00	125.00
	1736 MF	15.00	30.00	60.00	125.00
	1737/3 MF	15.00	30.00	60.00	125.00
	1737 MF	15.00	30.00	60.00	125.00
	1738/7 MF	15.00	30.00	60.00	125.00
	1738 MF	15.00	30.00	60.00	125.00
	1739 MF	15.00	30.00	60.00	125.00
	1740/30 MF	15.00	30.00	60.00	125.00
	1740 MF	15.00	30.00	60.00	125.00
	1741 MF	15.00	30.00	60.00	125.00

KM#	Date	VG	Fine	VF	XF
87	1762 M	10.00	20.00	50.00	100.00
	1763/2 M	10.00	20.00	50.00	100.00
	1763 M	10.00	20.00	50.00	100.00
	1764 M	10.00	20.00	50.00	100.00
	1765 M	10.00	20.00	50.00	100.00
	1766 M	12.00	25.00	70.00	150.00
	1767 M	7.50	15.00	30.00	100.00
	1768/6 M	7.50	15.00	30.00	80.00
	1768 M	7.50	15.00	30.00	80.00
	1769 M	7.50	15.00	35.00	100.00
	1770 M	—	—	Rare	—
	1770 F	—	—	Rare	—
	1771 F	7.50	15.00	30.00	80.00

Obv. leg: PHS.V.D.G.HISP.ET IND.R.

	Date	VG	Fine	VF	XF
85	1742 M	10.00	20.00	50.00	100.00
	1743/2 M	10.00	20.00	50.00	100.00
	1743 M	10.00	20.00	50.00	100.00
	1744/2 M	10.00	20.00	50.00	100.00
	1744/3 M	10.00	20.00	50.00	100.00
	1744 M	10.00	20.00	50.00	100.00
	1745/4 M	10.00	20.00	50.00	100.00
	1745 M	10.00	20.00	50.00	100.00
	1746 M	10.00	20.00	50.00	100.00
	1747 M	10.00	20.00	50.00	100.00
	1749 M	150.00	225.00	300.00	600.00
	1750 M	150.00	225.00	300.00	600.00

6.7700 g, .903 SILVER, .1965 oz ASW
Obv. leg: CAROLUS.III.DEI.GRATIA.
Rev: Inverted FM and mint mark.

	Date	VG	Fine	VF	XF
88.1	1772 FM	5.00	10.00	15.00	100.00
	1773 FM	5.00	10.00	15.00	100.00

Rev: Normal initials and mint mark.

	Date	VG	Fine	VF	XF
88.2	1773 FM	5.00	10.00	15.00	100.00
	1774 FM	5.00	10.00	15.00	100.00
	1775 FM	5.00	10.00	15.00	100.00
	1776 FM	5.00	10.00	15.00	100.00
	1777 FM	5.00	10.00	15.00	100.00
	1778 FF	5.00	10.00	15.00	100.00
	1779 FF	5.00	10.00	15.00	100.00
	1780 FF	5.00	10.00	15.00	100.00
	1781 FF	5.00	10.00	15.00	100.00
	1782 FF	5.00	10.00	15.00	100.00
	1783 FF	5.00	10.00	15.00	100.00
	1784 FF	5.00	10.00	15.00	100.00
	1784 FF (error) DEI GRTIA	100.00	150.00	250.00	600.00
	1784 FM	100.00	150.00	250.00	600.00
	1785 FM	5.00	10.00	15.00	100.00
	1786 FM	5.00	10.00	15.00	100.00
	1786 FF	100.00	150.00	250.00	600.00
	1787 FM	5.00	10.00	15.00	100.00
	1788 FM	5.00	10.00	15.00	100.00
	1789 FM	11.50	25.00	40.00	150.00

Obv. leg: FRD.VI.D.G.HISP.ET IND.R.

	Date	VG	Fine	VF	XF
86	1747 M	12.00	25.00	45.00	125.00
	1748/7 M	12.00	25.00	45.00	125.00
	1748 M	10.00	20.00	30.00	100.00
	1749 M	10.00	20.00	30.00	100.00
	1750 M	10.00	20.00	30.00	100.00
	1751/41 M	12.00	25.00	45.00	125.00
	1751 M	10.00	20.00	30.00	100.00
	1752 M	10.00	20.00	30.00	100.00
	1753/2 M	12.00	25.00	60.00	150.00
	1753 M	12.00	25.00	60.00	150.00
	1754 M	12.00	25.00	60.00	150.00
	1755 M	12.00	25.00	60.00	150.00
	1756 M	12.00	25.00	60.00	150.00
	1757/6 M	10.00	20.00	30.00	100.00
	1757 M	10.00	20.00	30.00	100.00
	1758 M	10.00	20.00	30.00	100.00
	1759/8 M	10.00	20.00	30.00	100.00
	1759 M	10.00	20.00	30.00	100.00
	1760 M	15.00	25.00	45.00	100.00

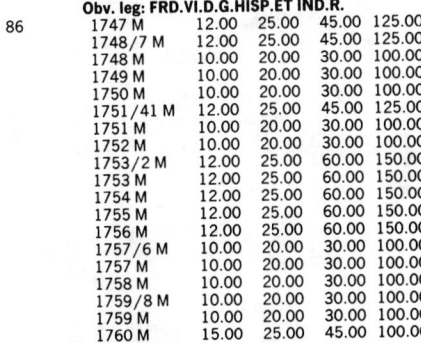

Obv: Armored bust of Charles III; leg: CAROLUS.IV. . .

	Date	VG	Fine	VF	XF
89	1789 FM	11.50	25.00	40.00	150.00
	1790 FM	11.50	25.00	40.00	150.00

Obv. leg: CAR.III.D.G.HISP.ET IND.R.

	Date	VG	Fine	VF	XF
87	1760 M	10.00	20.00	50.00	100.00
	1761 M	10.00	20.00	50.00	100.00

Obv: Armored bust of Charles III, leg: CAROLUS.IIII. . .

	Date	VG	Fine	VF	XF
90	1790 FM	12.50	27.50	60.00	200.00

Obv: Armored bust of Carolus IIII.

KM#	Date	VG	Fine	VF	XF
91	1792 FM	15.00	30.00	60.00	200.00
	1793 FM	15.00	30.00	60.00	200.00
	1794/3 FM	50.00	100.00	200.00	450.00
	1794 FM	40.00	75.00	150.00	400.00
	1795 FM	5.00	10.00	15.00	100.00
	1796 FM	5.00	10.00	15.00	100.00
	1797 FM	5.00	10.00	15.00	100.00
	1798 FM	5.00	10.00	15.00	100.00
	1799/8 FM	5.50	11.50	16.50	110.00
	1799 FM	5.00	10.00	15.00	100.00
	1800 FM	5.00	10.00	15.00	100.00
	1801 FT	5.00	10.00	15.00	100.00
	1801 FM	20.00	40.00	75.00	250.00
	1802 FT	5.00	10.00	15.00	100.00
	1803 FT	5.00	10.00	15.00	100.00
	1804 TH	5.00	10.00	15.00	100.00
	1805 TH	5.00	10.00	15.00	100.00
	1806/5 TH	5.50	11.50	16.50	110.00
	1806 TH	5.00	10.00	15.00	100.00
	1807/5 TH	5.50	11.50	16.50	110.00
	1807/6 TH	15.00	30.00	60.00	200.00
	1807 TH	5.00	10.00	15.00	100.00
	1808/7 TH	5.50	11.50	16.50	110.00
	1808 TH	5.00	10.00	15.00	100.00

Obv: Armored bust of Ferdinand VII.

KM#	Date	VG	Fine	VF	XF
92	1809 TH	6.50	12.50	45.00	150.00
	1810 TH	6.50	12.50	45.00	150.00
	1810 HJ	6.50	12.50	45.00	150.00
	1811 HJ	6.50	12.50	45.00	150.00
	1811 HJ/TH	40.00	80.00	150.00	300.00
	1811 TH	100.00	200.00	300.00	750.00

Obv: Draped bust of Ferdinand VII.

KM#	Date	VG	Fine	VF	XF
93	1812 HJ	15.00	30.00	100.00	300.00
	1812 TH	60.00	125.00	250.00	500.00
	1812 JJ	10.00	20.00	60.00	200.00
	1813 HJ	40.00	100.00	200.00	500.00
	1813 JJ	20.00	60.00	125.00	350.00
	1813 TH	15.00	30.00	100.00	400.00
	1814/13 JJ	15.00	30.00	100.00	400.00
	1814 JJ	15.00	30.00	100.00	400.00
	1815 JJ	5.00	10.00	30.00	100.00
	1816 JJ	5.00	10.00	30.00	100.00
	1817 JJ	5.00	10.00	30.00	100.00
	1818 JJ	5.00	10.00	30.00	100.00

KM#	Date	VG	Fine	VF	XF
93	1819 JJ	5.00	10.00	30.00	100.00
	1820 JJ	125.00	—	—	—
	1821/0 JJ	5.00	10.00	30.00	110.00
	1821 JJ	5.00	10.00	30.00	100.00

4 REALES

13.5400 g, .917 SILVER, .3992 oz ASW
Obv. leg: PHILLIP.V.D.G.HISPAN.ET IND.REX

KM#	Date	VG	Fine	VF	XF
94	1732	—	—	Rare Specimen	
	1732 F	2000.	3000.	5000.	10,000.
	1733 F	1500.	2000.	4000.	6000.
	1733 MF	1200.	1800.	2500.	4000.
	1733 MF(MX)	1500.	2200.	3250.	5000.
	1733 F(MX)	1500.	2500.	3500.	6000.
	1734/3 MF	150.00	300.00	600.00	1200.
	1734 MF	150.00	300.00	600.00	1200.
	1735 MF	100.00	200.00	300.00	500.00
	1736 MF	100.00	200.00	300.00	500.00
	1737 MF	100.00	200.00	300.00	500.00
	1738/7 MF	100.00	200.00	300.00	500.00
	1738 MF	100.00	200.00	300.00	500.00
	1739 MF	100.00	200.00	300.00	500.00
	1740/30 MF	100.00	200.00	300.00	600.00
	1740 MF	100.00	200.00	300.00	500.00
	1741 MF	100.00	200.00	300.00	500.00
	1742/1 MF	100.00	200.00	300.00	500.00
	1742 MF	100.00	200.00	300.00	500.00
	1743 MF	100.00	200.00	300.00	500.00
	1744/3 MF	100.00	200.00	300.00	600.00
	1744 MF	100.00	200.00	300.00	500.00
	1745 MF	100.00	200.00	300.00	500.00
	1746 MP	100.00	200.00	300.00	500.00
	1747 MF	150.00	275.00	400.00	650.00

Obv. leg: FERDND.VI.D.G.HISPAN.ET IND.REX

KM#	Date	VG	Fine	VF	XF
95	1747 MF	100.00	150.00	300.00	500.00
	1748/7 MF	100.00	150.00	300.00	500.00
	1748 MF	100.00	125.00	250.00	450.00
	1749 MF	150.00	225.00	350.00	650.00
	1750/40 MF	100.00	125.00	250.00	400.00
	1750 MF	100.00	125.00	250.00	450.00
	1751 MF	100.00	125.00	250.00	450.00
	1752 MF	100.00	125.00	250.00	450.00
	1753 MF	100.00	125.00	300.00	500.00
	1754 MM	250.00	375.00	500.00	850.00
	1754 MM	250.00	375.00	500.00	850.00
	1755 MM	100.00	125.00	225.00	400.00
	1756 MM	100.00	150.00	300.00	500.00
	1757 MM	100.00	150.00	250.00	450.00
	1758 MM	100.00	125.00	225.00	400.00
	1759 MM	100.00	125.00	225.00	400.00
	1760/59 MM	100.00	175.00	350.00	550.00
	1760 MM	100.00	175.00	350.00	550.00

Rev: Normal initials and mint mark.

KM#	Date	VG	Fine	VF	XF
97.2	1773 MF	200.00	300.00	400.00	800.00
	1774 FM	25.00	40.00	75.00	350.00
	1775 FM	25.00	40.00	75.00	350.00
	1776 FM	25.00	40.00	75.00	350.00
	1777 FM	25.00	40.00	75.00	350.00
	1778 FF	25.00	40.00	75.00	350.00
	1779 FF	25.00	40.00	75.00	350.00
	1780 FF	25.00	40.00	75.00	350.00
	1781 FF	250.00	350.00	500.00	1000.
	1782 FF	35.00	65.00	150.00	450.00
	1783 FF	25.00	40.00	75.00	350.00
	1784 FF	25.00	40.00	75.00	350.00
	1784 FM	100.00	200.00	350.00	600.00
	1785 FM	100.00	200.00	350.00	600.00
	1786 FM	25.00	40.00	75.00	350.00
	1787 FM	25.00	40.00	75.00	350.00
	1788 FM	25.00	40.00	75.00	350.00
	1789 FM	50.00	100.00	150.00	400.00

Obv. leg: CAROLVS.III.D.G.HISPAN.ET IND.REX

KM#	Date	VG	Fine	VF	XF
96	1760 MM	100.00	150.00	250.00	900.00
	1761 MM	100.00	150.00	250.00	900.00
	1761 MM cross between H and I				
		100.00	150.00	250.00	900.00
	1762 MM	75.00	100.00	150.00	450.00
	1762 MF	100.00	150.00	300.00	600.00
	1763/1 MM	100.00	150.00	300.00	600.00
	1763/2 MF	100.00	150.00	300.00	600.00
	1763 MM	100.00	150.00	300.00	600.00
	1763 MF	100.00	200.00	350.00	800.00
	1764 MM	400.00	600.00	1000.	2000.
	1764 MF	350.00	500.00	1000.	2000.
	1765 MF	350.00	500.00	1000.	2000.
	1766 MF	250.00	350.00	500.00	1250.
	1767 MF	100.00	150.00	300.00	600.00
	1768 MF	75.00	100.00	150.00	450.00
	1769 MF	75.00	100.00	150.00	450.00
	1770 MF	75.00	100.00	150.00	450.00
	1771 MF	125.00	200.00	300.00	700.00
	1771 FM	150.00	275.00	400.00	900.00

Obv: Armored bust of Charles III, leg: CAROLUS.IV. .

98	1789 FM	60.00	100.00	150.00	400.00
	1790 FM	25.00	50.00	100.00	350.00

13.5400 g, .903 SILVER, .3931 oz ASW
Obv. leg: CAROLUS.III.DEI.GRATIA.
Rev: Inverted FM and mint mark.

97.1	1772 FM	90.00	125.00	200.00	450.00
	1773 FM	100.00	175.00	300.00	650.00

Obv: Armored bust of Charles III, leg: CAROLUS.IIII. .

99	1790 FM	30.00	60.00	175.00	500.00

Obv: Armored bust of Charles IIII.

KM# 100	Date	VG	Fine	VF	XF
	1792 FM	25.00	40.00	75.00	350.00
	1793 FM	75.00	125.00	200.00	500.00
	1794/3 FM	25.00	40.00	80.00	375.00
	1794 FM	25.00	40.00	80.00	350.00
	1795 FM	25.00	40.00	80.00	350.00
	1796 FM	150.00	250.00	400.00	800.00
	1797 FM	40.00	75.00	150.00	500.00
	1798/7 FM	25.00	40.00	80.00	375.00
	1798 FM	25.00	40.00	80.00	350.00
	1799 FM	25.00	40.00	80.00	350.00
	1800 FM	25.00	40.00	80.00	350.00
	1801 FM	25.00	40.00	80.00	350.00
	1801 FT	60.00	100.00	150.00	500.00
	1802 FT	200.00	300.00	500.00	1000.
	1803 FT	60.00	125.00	200.00	550.00
	1803 FM	350.00	450.00	650.00	1250.
	1804 TH	25.00	50.00	150.00	450.00
	1805 TH	25.00	40.00	80.00	350.00
	1806 TH	25.00	40.00	80.00	350.00
	1807 TH	25.00	40.00	80.00	350.00
	1808/7 TH	25.00	50.00	150.00	450.00
	1808 TH	25.00	50.00	150.00	450.00

Obv: Armored bust of Ferdinand VII.

KM# 101	Date	VG	Fine	VF	XF
	1809 HJ	75.00	125.00	175.00	450.00
	1810 TH	75.00	125.00	175.00	450.00
	1810 HJ	75.00	125.00	175.00	450.00
	1811 HJ	75.00	125.00	175.00	450.00
	1812 HJ	500.00	750.00	1000.	2000.

Obv: Draped bust of Ferdinand VII.

KM# 102	Date	VG	Fine	VF	XF
	1816 JJ	150.00	200.00	350.00	600.00
	1817 JJ	250.00	400.00	500.00	1000.
	1818/7 JJ	250.00	400.00	500.00	1000.
	1818 JJ	250.00	400.00	500.00	1000.
	1819 JJ	175.00	250.00	350.00	700.00
	1820 JJ	175.00	250.00	350.00	700.00
	1821 JJ	75.00	125.00	200.00	425.00

8 REALES

27.0700 g, .917 SILVER, .7982 oz ASW
Obv. leg: PHILIP.V.D.G.HISPAN.ET IND.REX

103	Date	VG	Fine	VF	XF
	1732 F	—	—	Rare	—
	1733/2 F(MX)	—	—	Rare	—
	1733 F	—	—	Rare	—
	1733 F(MX)	—	—	Rare	—
	1733 MF(MX)	—	—	Rare	—
	1733 MF	700.00	1500.	2500.	4000.
	1734/3 MF	100.00	150.00	250.00	550.00
	1734 MF	100.00	150.00	250.00	500.00
	1735 MF	100.00	150.00	250.00	500.00
	1736 MF	100.00	150.00	250.00	500.00
	1737 MF	65.00	100.00	150.00	350.00
	1738/6 MF	65.00	100.00	150.00	350.00
	1738/7 MF	65.00	100.00	150.00	350.00
	1738 MF	65.00	100.00	150.00	350.00
	1739/6 MF	65.00	100.00	150.00	350.00
	1739/8 MF	65.00	100.00	150.00	350.00
	1739 MF	65.00	100.00	150.00	350.00
	1740/30 MF	65.00	100.00	150.00	350.00
	1740/39 MF	65.00	100.00	150.00	350.00
	1740 MF	65.00	100.00	150.00	350.00

KM#	Date	VG	Fine	VF	XF
103	1741/31 MF	65.00	100.00	150.00	350.00
	1741 MF	65.00	100.00	150.00	350.00
	1742/32 MF	75.00	125.00	200.00	450.00
	1742/1 MF	65.00	100.00	150.00	350.00
	1742 MF	65.00	100.00	150.00	350.00
	1743/2 MF	65.00	100.00	150.00	350.00
	1743 MF	65.00	100.00	150.00	350.00
	1744/34 MF	65.00	100.00	150.00	350.00
	1744/3 MF	65.00	100.00	150.00	350.00
	1744 MF	65.00	100.00	150.00	350.00
	1745 MF	65.00	100.00	150.00	350.00
	1746/5 MF	65.00	100.00	150.00	350.00
	1746 MF	65.00	100.00	150.00	350.00
	1747 MF	65.00	100.00	150.00	350.00

NOTE: Ponterio AMAT sale 3-91 AU 1732 F realized $28,000., XF 1733/2 F (MX) realized $27,000., XF 1733 F realized $11,500., XF 1733 MF (MX) realized $35,000.

Obv. leg: FERDND.VI.D.G.HISPAN.ET IND.REX
Rev: W/Royal crown on left pillar.

	Date	VG	Fine	VF	XF
104.1	1747 MF	50.00	100.00	175.00	300.00
	1748/7 MF	50.00	80.00	150.00	250.00
	1748 MF	50.00	75.00	100.00	200.00
	1749 MF	50.00	75.00	100.00	200.00
	1750 MF	50.00	75.00	100.00	200.00
	1751/0 MF	50.00	75.00	100.00	200.00
	1751 MF	50.00	75.00	100.00	200.00
	1752/1 MF	50.00	75.00	100.00	200.00
	1752 MF	50.00	75.00	100.00	200.00
	1753/2 MF	50.00	75.00	100.00	200.00
	1753 MF	50.00	75.00	100.00	200.00
	1754/3 MF	50.00	75.00	120.00	225.00
	1754 MF	50.00	75.00	100.00	200.00
	1754 MM/MF				
		250.00	600.00	1250.	2500.
	1754 MM	250.00	600.00	1250.	2500.
	1755/4 MM	50.00	80.00	150.00	250.00
	1755 MM	50.00	75.00	100.00	200.00
	1756/5 MM	50.00	75.00	100.00	200.00
	1756 MM	50.00	75.00	100.00	200.00
	1757/6 MM	50.00	75.00	100.00	200.00
	1757 MM	50.00	75.00	100.00	200.00
	1758 MM	50.00	75.00	100.00	200.00
	1759 MM	60.00	100.00	150.00	250.00
	1760/59 MM	60.00	100.00	150.00	250.00
	1760 MM	60.00	100.00	150.00	250.00

Rev: Imperial crown.

	Date	VG	Fine	VF	XF
104.2	1754 MM	75.00	125.00	200.00	400.00
	1754 MF	150.00	300.00	500.00	800.00

Obv. leg: CAROLUS.III.D.G.HISPAN.ET IND.REX

KM#	Date	VG	Fine	VF	XF
105	1760/59 MM CAROLUS.III/Ferdin.Vi				
		—	—	—	—
	1760 MM CAROLUS.III/FERDIN. VI. recut				
	die	60.00	100.00	150.00	325.00
	1760 MM	60.00	100.00	150.00	300.00
	1761/50 MM tip of cross between I and S in				
	leg.	65.00	110.00	165.00	325.00
	1761/51 MM tip of cross between I and S in				
	leg.	65.00	110.00	165.00	325.00
	1761/0 MM tip of cross between H and I in				
	leg.	65.00	110.00	165.00	300.00
	1761 MM tip of cross between H and I in leg.				
		60.00	100.00	150.00	275.00
	1761 MM tip of cross between I and S in leg.				
		60.00	100.00	150.00	300.00
	1762/1 MM tip of cross between H and I in				
	leg.	70.00	120.00	175.00	450.00
	1762/1 MM	70.00	120.00	175.00	450.00
	1762 MM tip of cross between H and I in leg.				
		50.00	75.00	100.00	200.00
	1762 MM tip of cross between I and S in leg.				
		50.00	75.00	100.00	200.00
	1762 MF	500.00	750.00	1000.	1500.
	1763/53 MF	50.00	75.00	100.00	250.00
	1763/1 MF	50.00	75.00	100.00	250.00
	1763/2 MM	300.00	450.00	750.00	1500.
	1763/2 MF	50.00	75.00	100.00	250.00
	1763/72 MF	50.00	75.00	100.00	250.00
	1763 MM	450.00	650.00	1150.	2500.
	1763 MF	50.00	75.00	100.00	250.00
	1764/54 MM	50.00	75.00	100.00	250.00
	1764/54 MF CAR/CRA				
		50.00	75.00	100.00	250.00
	1764/1 MF	50.00	75.00	100.00	250.00
	1764/3 MF	50.00	75.00	100.00	250.00
	1764 MF	50.00	75.00	100.00	250.00
	1765 MF	50.00	75.00	100.00	250.00
	1766/5 MF	50.00	75.00	100.00	250.00
	1766 MF	50.00	75.00	100.00	250.00
	1767/17 MF	50.00	75.00	100.00	250.00
	1767/6 MF	50.00	75.00	100.00	250.00
	1767 MF	50.00	75.00	100.00	250.00
	1768/6 MF	50.00	75.00	100.00	250.00
	1768/7 MF	50.00	75.00	100.00	250.00
	1768 MF	50.00	75.00	100.00	250.00
	1769 MF	50.00	75.00	100.00	250.00

KM#	Date	VG	Fine	VF	XF
105	1770/60 MF	50.00	75.00	100.00	250.00
	1770/60 FM	50.00	75.00	100.00	250.00
	1770/69 FM	50.00	75.00	100.00	250.00
	1770 MF	50.00	75.00	100.00	250.00
	1770 FM/F	50.00	75.00	100.00	250.00
	1770 FM	50.00	75.00	100.00	250.00
	1771/0 FM	50.00	75.00	100.00	250.00
	1771 FM	50.00	75.00	100.00	250.00
	1772 FM	—	—	Rare	—

27.0700 g, .903 SILVER, .7859 oz ASW

MF (error) inverted

FM (normal)

Obv. leg: CAROLUS.III.DEI.GRATIA.
Rev: Inverted FM or MF and mint mark

KM#	Date	VG	Fine	VF	XF
106.1	1772 FM	25.00	50.00	90.00	250.00
	1772 MF inverted MF (error)				
		150.00	350.00	750.00	1250.
	1773 FM	25.00	50.00	80.00	175.00

Rev: Normal initials and mint mark.

106.2	1773 FM	25.00	50.00	75.00	150.00
	1774 FM	25.00	45.00	60.00	135.00
	1775 FM	25.00	45.00	60.00	135.00
	1776 FM	25.00	45.00	60.00	135.00
	1777/6 FM	35.00	55.00	90.00	300.00
	1777 FM	25.00	45.00	60.00	135.00

KM#	Date	VG	Fine	VF	XF
106.2	1777 FF	35.00	50.00	80.00	250.00
	1778 FM	—	—	*Rare	—
	1778/7FF	25.00	45.00	60.00	135.00
	1778 FF	25.00	45.00	60.00	135.00
	1779 FF	25.00	45.00	60.00	135.00
	1780 FF	25.00	45.00	60.00	135.00
	1781 FF	25.00	45.00	60.00	135.00
	1782 FF	25.00	45.00	60.00	135.00
	1783 FF	25.00	45.00	60.00	135.00
	1783 FM	4000.	6000.	9000.	—
	1784 FF	150.00	300.00	500.00	1250.
	1784 FM	25.00	45.00	60.00	135.00
	1785 FM	25.00	45.00	60.00	135.00
	1786/5 FM	25.00	45.00	60.00	135.00
	1786 FM	25.00	45.00	60.00	135.00
	1787/6 FM	100.00	250.00	450.00	1200.
	1787 FM	25.00	45.00	60.00	135.00
	1788 FM	25.00	45.00	60.00	135.00
	1789 FM	50.00	100.00	150.00	225.00

*NOTE: Superior Casterline sale 5-89 VF realized $17,600.

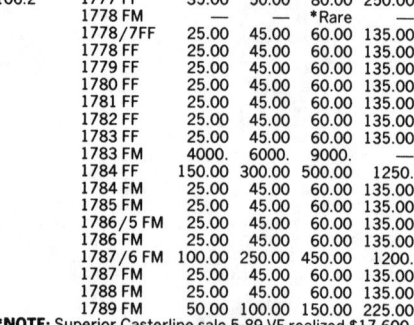

Obv: Armored bust of Charles III, leg: CAROLUS.IV. .

KM#	Date	VG	Fine	VF	XF
107	1789 FM	40.00	65.00	100.00	200.00
	1790 FM	30.00	50.00	80.00	190.00

Obv: Armored bust of Charles III, leg: CAROLUS.IIII. .

108	1790 FM	30.00	50.00	75.00	175.00

Obv: Armored bust of Ferdinand VII.

KM#	Date	VG	Fine	VF	XF
110	1808 TH	25.00	40.00	65.00	125.00
	1809/8 TH	25.00	40.00	65.00	125.00
	1809 HJ	25.00	40.00	65.00	125.00
	1809 HJ/TH	20.00	40.00	50.00	100.00
	1809 TH/JH	20.00	40.00	50.00	100.00
	1809 TH	20.00	40.00	50.00	100.00
	1810/09 HJ	25.00	40.00	65.00	125.00
	1810 HJ	25.00	40.00	65.00	125.00
	1810 HJ/TH	25.00	40.00	65.00	125.00
	1810 TH	75.00	150.00	300.00	600.00
	1811/0 HJ	20.00	40.00	50.00	100.00
	1811 HJ	20.00	40.00	50.00	100.00

27.0700 g, .903 SILVER, .7859 oz ASW
Obv: Armored bust of Charles IIII.

KM#	Date	VG	Fine	VF	XF
109	1791 FM	20.00	40.00	50.00	100.00
	1792 FM	20.00	40.00	50.00	100.00
	1793 FM	20.00	40.00	50.00	100.00
	1794 FM	20.00	40.00	50.00	100.00
	1795/4 FM	20.00	40.00	50.00	100.00
	1795 FM	20.00	40.00	50.00	100.00
	1796 FM	20.00	40.00	50.00	100.00
	1797 FM	20.00	40.00	50.00	100.00
	1798 FM	20.00	40.00	50.00	100.00
	1799 FM	20.00	40.00	50.00	100.00
	1800/700 FM	20.00	40.00	50.00	100.00
	1800 FM	20.00	40.00	50.00	100.00
	1801/791 FM	35.00	60.00	100.00	250.00
	1801/0 FM	35.00	60.00	100.00	250.00
	1801/0 FT/FM	20.00	40.00	50.00	100.00
	1801 FM	20.00	40.00	100.00	250.00
	1801 FT/M	35.00	60.00	100.00	250.00
	1801 FT	20.00	40.00	50.00	100.00
	1802/1 FT	35.00	60.00	100.00	250.00
	1802 FT	20.00	40.00	50.00	100.00
	1802 FT/FM	20.00	40.00	50.00	100.00
	1803 FT	20.00	40.00	50.00	110.00
	1803 FT/FM	20.00	40.00	50.00	100.00
	1803 TH	75.00	150.00	250.00	500.00
	1804/3 TH	35.00	60.00	100.00	250.00
	1804 TH	20.00	40.00	50.00	100.00
	1805/4 TH	40.00	80.00	125.00	275.00
	1805 TH	20.00	40.00	50.00	100.00
	1806 TH	20.00	40.00	50.00	100.00
	1807/6 TH	150.00	250.00	350.00	700.00
	1807 TH	20.00	40.00	50.00	100.00
	1870 TH(error 1807)	150.00	250.00	350.00	700.00
	1808/7 TH	20.00	40.00	50.00	100.00
	1808 TH	20.00	40.00	50.00	100.00

Obv: Draped bust of Ferdinand VII.

KM#	Date	VG	Fine	VF	XF
111	1811 HJ	20.00	40.00	60.00	125.00
	1812 HJ	50.00	75.00	125.00	250.00
	1812 JJ/HJ	20.00	40.00	50.00	90.00
	1812 JJ	20.00	40.00	50.00	90.00
	1813 HJ	50.00	75.00	125.00	250.00
	1813 JJ	20.00	40.00	50.00	90.00
	1814/3 HJ	1200.	2500.	5000.	—
	1814/3 JJ/HJ	20.00	40.00	50.00	90.00
	1814/3 JJ	20.00	40.00	50.00	90.00
	1814 JJ	20.00	40.00	50.00	90.00
	1814 HJ	500.00	800.00	1500.	3000.
	1815/4 JJ	20.00	40.00	50.00	90.00
	1815 JJ	20.00	40.00	50.00	90.00
	1816/5 JJ	20.00	40.00	50.00	85.00
	1816 JJ	20.00	40.00	50.00	85.00
	1817 JJ	20.00	40.00	50.00	85.00
	1818 JJ	20.00	40.00	50.00	85.00
	1819 JJ	20.00	40.00	50.00	85.00
	1820 JJ	20.00	40.00	50.00	85.00
	1821 JJ	20.00	40.00	50.00	85.00

1/2 ESCUDO

1.6900 g, .875 GOLD, .0475 oz AGW
Obv. leg: FERD.VII.D.G.HISP.ET IND.

KM#	Date	VG	Fine	VF	XF
112	1814 JJ	250.00	350.00	450.00	600.00
	1815/4 JJ	150.00	200.00	250.00	350.00
	1815 JJ	150.00	200.00	250.00	350.00
	1816 JJ	100.00	150.00	200.00	300.00
	1817 JJ	150.00	200.00	250.00	350.00
	1818 JJ	150.00	200.00	250.00	350.00
	1819 JJ	150.00	200.00	250.00	350.00
	1820 JJ	200.00	300.00	450.00	600.00

ESCUDO

3.3800 g, .917 GOLD, .0996 oz AGW
Obv. leg: PHILIP.V.D.G.HISPAN.ET IND.REX

113	1732 F	1000.	2000.	3000.	4000.
	1733/2 F	1000.	2000.	3000.	4000.
	1733 F	1000.	2000.	3000.	4000.
	1734/3 MF	150.00	250.00	400.00	950.00
	1734 MF	150.00	250.00	400.00	950.00
	1735/4 MF	150.00	250.00	400.00	950.00
	1735 MF	150.00	250.00	400.00	950.00
	1736/5 MF	150.00	250.00	400.00	950.00
	1736 MF	150.00	250.00	400.00	950.00
	1737 MF	200.00	300.00	600.00	1200.
	1738/7 MF	200.00	300.00	600.00	1200.
	1738 MF	200.00	300.00	600.00	1200.
	1739 MF	200.00	300.00	600.00	1200.
	1740 MF	200.00	300.00	600.00	1200.
	1741 MF	200.00	300.00	600.00	1200.
	1742 MF	200.00	300.00	600.00	1200.
	1743/2 MF	150.00	275.00	450.00	900.00
	1743 MF	150.00	250.00	400.00	800.00
	1744 MF	150.00	250.00	400.00	800.00
	1745 MF	150.00	250.00	400.00	800.00
	1746 MF	150.00	250.00	400.00	800.00
	1747 MF	—	—	Rare	—

Obv: Long bust; leg: FERD.VI.D.G.HISPAN.ET IND.REX.

114	1747 MF	600.00	900.00	1500.	2250.

Obv: Short bust

115.1	1748 MF	250.00	350.00	550.00	950.00
	1749 MF	300.00	450.00	700.00	1150.
	1750 MF	200.00	300.00	450.00	800.00
	1751 MF	200.00	300.00	450.00	800.00

KM#	Date	VG	Fine	VF	XF
115.2	1752 MF	150.00	250.00	400.00	750.00
	1753/2 MF	200.00	300.00	450.00	800.00
	1753 MF	200.00	300.00	450.00	800.00
	1754 MF	200.00	300.00	450.00	800.00
	1755 MM	200.00	300.00	450.00	800.00
	1756 MF	200.00	300.00	450.00	800.00
	1756 MM	200.00	300.00	450.00	800.00

Obv: Armored bust.

A116	1757 MM	200.00	300.00	450.00	800.00
	1758 MM	200.00	300.00	450.00	800.00
	1759 MM	200.00	300.00	450.00	800.00

Obv. leg: CAROLVS.III.D.G.HISPAN.ET IND.REX
Rev. leg: NOMINA MAGNA SEQUOR

116	1760 MM	500.00	1000.	1750.	2500.
	1761/0 MM	500.00	1000.	1750.	2500.
	1761 MM	500.00	1000.	1750.	2500.

Obv: Large bust, leg: CAR.III.D.G.HISP.ET IND.R.
Rev. leg: IN.UTROQ. FELIX.

117	1762 MF	250.00	375.00	600.00	1100.
	1762 MM	250.00	375.00	600.00	1100.
	1763 MF	250.00	375.00	600.00	1100.
	1763 MM	275.00	425.00	700.00	1200.
	1764 MM	250.00	375.00	600.00	1100.
	1765 MF	250.00	375.00	600.00	1100.
	1766 MF	250.00	375.00	600.00	1100.
	1767 MF	250.00	375.00	600.00	1100.
	1768 MF	250.00	375.00	600.00	1100.
	1769 MF	250.00	375.00	600.00	1100.
	1770 MF	250.00	375.00	600.00	1100.
	1771 MF	250.00	375.00	600.00	1100.

3.3800 g, .901 GOLD, .0979 oz AGW
Obv. leg: CAROL.III.D.G. HISPAN.ET IND.R.
Rev. leg: . . . . .FELIX.A.D.; FM and mint mark upright.

118.1	1772 FM	125.00	200.00	300.00	600.00
	1773 FM	125.00	200.00	300.00	600.00

Rev: Initial letters and mint mark inverted.

KM#	Date	VG	Fine	VF	XF
118.2	1772 FM	125.00	200.00	300.00	600.00
	1773 FM	125.00	200.00	300.00	600.00
	1774 FM	125.00	200.00	300.00	600.00
	1775 FM	125.00	200.00	300.00	600.00
	1776 FM	125.00	200.00	300.00	600.00

3.3800 g, .875 GOLD, .0950 oz AGW

118.2a	1777 FM	125.00	200.00	300.00	600.00
	1778 FF	125.00	200.00	300.00	600.00
	1779 FF	125.00	200.00	300.00	600.00
	1780 FF	125.00	200.00	300.00	600.00
	1781 FF	125.00	200.00	300.00	600.00
	1782 FF	125.00	200.00	300.00	600.00
	1783/2 FF	125.00	200.00	300.00	600.00
	1783 FF	125.00	200.00	300.00	600.00
	1784 FF	125.00	200.00	300.00	600.00
	1784 FM	125.00	200.00	300.00	600.00
	1785 FM	125.00	200.00	300.00	600.00
	1786 FM	125.00	200.00	300.00	600.00
	1787 FM	125.00	200.00	300.00	600.00
	1788 FM	125.00	200.00	300.00	600.00

Rev: Initial letters and mint mark upright.

118.1a	1787 FM	125.00	200.00	300.00	600.00
	1788 FM	125.00	200.00	300.00	600.00

Obv: Bust of Charles III, leg: CAROLUS.IV.D.G. .

119	1789 FM	125.00	200.00	300.00	600.00
	1790 FM	125.00	200.00	300.00	600.00

Obv: Armored bust of Charles IV.

120	1792 MF	125.00	200.00	250.00	375.00
	1793 FM	125.00	200.00	250.00	375.00
	1794 FM	125.00	200.00	250.00	375.00
	1795 FM	125.00	200.00	250.00	375.00
	1796 FM	125.00	200.00	250.00	375.00
	1797 FM	125.00	200.00	250.00	375.00
	1798 FM	125.00	200.00	250.00	375.00
	1799 FM	125.00	200.00	250.00	375.00
	1800 FM	125.00	200.00	250.00	350.00
	1801 FT	125.00	200.00	250.00	350.00
	1801 FM	125.00	200.00	250.00	350.00
	1802 FT	125.00	200.00	250.00	350.00
	1803 FT	125.00	200.00	250.00	350.00
	1804/3 TH	125.00	200.00	250.00	350.00
	1804 TH	125.00	200.00	250.00	350.00
	1805 TH	125.00	200.00	250.00	350.00
	1806 TH	125.00	200.00	250.00	350.00
	1807 TH	125.00	200.00	250.00	350.00
	1808 TH	125.00	200.00	250.00	350.00

Obv: Armored bust of Ferdinand VII.

121	1809 HJ	125.00	200.00	250.00	400.00
	1810 HJ	125.00	200.00	250.00	400.00
	1811 HJ	125.00	200.00	250.00	400.00
	1812 HJ	150.00	250.00	300.00	500.00

Obv: Undraped bust of Ferdinand VII.

KM#	Date	VG	Fine	VF	XF
122	1814 HJ	100.00	150.00	225.00	400.00
	1815 JJ	100.00	150.00	225.00	400.00
	1815 HJ	100.00	150.00	225.00	400.00
	1816 JJ	125.00	175.00	275.00	500.00
	1817 JJ	100.00	150.00	225.00	400.00
	1818 JJ	100.00	150.00	225.00	400.00
	1819 JJ	100.00	150.00	225.00	400.00
	1820 JJ	100.00	150.00	225.00	400.00

2 ESCUDOS

6.7700 g, .917 GOLD, .1996 oz AGW
Obv. leg: PHILIP.V.D.G.HISPAN.ET IND.REX
Rev. leg: INITIUM SAPIENTIAE TIMOR DOMINI

124	1732 F	1000.	1500.	2000.	3000.
	1733 F	750.00	1000.	1500.	2500.
	1734 MF	400.00	500.00	700.00	1300.
	1735 MF	400.00	500.00	700.00	1300.
	1736/5 MF	400.00	500.00	700.00	1300.
	1736 MF	400.00	500.00	700.00	1300.
	1737 MF	400.00	500.00	700.00	1300.
	1738/7 MF	400.00	500.00	700.00	1300.
	1738 MF	400.00	500.00	700.00	1300.
	1739 MF	400.00	500.00	700.00	1300.
	1740 MF	400.00	500.00	700.00	1300.
	1741 MF	400.00	500.00	700.00	1300.
	1742 MF	400.00	500.00	700.00	1300.
	1743 MF	400.00	500.00	700.00	1300.
	1744/3 MF	350.00	450.00	600.00	1200.
	1744 MF	400.00	500.00	700.00	1300.
	1745 MF	400.00	500.00	700.00	1300.
	1746 MF	400.00	500.00	700.00	1300.
	1747 MF	400.00	500.00	700.00	1300.

Obv: Large bust; leg: FERD.VI.D.G. .
Rev. leg: INITIUM. .

125	1747 MF	1500.	2000.	3000.	4500.

Obv: Small young bust; leg: FERD.VI.D.G. . . .
Rev. leg: NOMINA MAGNA SEQUOR

KM#	Date	VG	Fine	VF	XF
126.1	1748 MF	450.00	550.00	700.00	1250.
	1749/8 MF	450.00	550.00	700.00	1250.
	1749 MF	600.00	800.00	1000.	1800.
	1750 MF	400.00	500.00	600.00	1100.
	1751 MF	400.00	500.00	600.00	1100.
126.2	1752 MF	400.00	500.00	600.00	1100.
	1753 MF	400.00	500.00	600.00	1100.
	1754 MF	600.00	800.00	1000.	1800.
	1755 MM	400.00	500.00	600.00	1100.
	1756 MM	600.00	800.00	1000.	1800.
	1756 MF	450.00	550.00	700.00	1250.

Obv: Armored bust; leg: FERDND.VI.D.G. .

127	1757 MM	500.00	800.00	1300.	2200.
	1758 MM	500.00	800.00	1300.	2200.
	1759 MM	500.00	800.00	1300.	2200.

Obv: Young bust, leg: CAROLVS.III.D.G. .

128	1760 MM	550.00	900.00	1500.	2500.
	1761 MM	550.00	900.00	1500.	2500.

Obv: Large young bust, leg: CAROLUS.III.D.G. .
Rev. leg: IN.UTROQ.FELIX.AUSPICE.DEO

129	1762 MF	500.00	600.00	800.00	1500.
	1763 MF	500.00	600.00	800.00	1500.
	1764 MF	500.00	600.00	800.00	1500.
	1764 MM	500.00	600.00	800.00	1500.
	1765 MF	500.00	600.00	800.00	1500.
	1766 MF	500.00	600.00	800.00	1500.
	1767 MF	500.00	600.00	800.00	1500.
	1768 MF	500.00	600.00	800.00	1500.
	1769 MF	500.00	600.00	800.00	1500.
	1770 MF	500.00	600.00	1000.	1800.
	1771 MF	500.00	600.00	800.00	1500.

6.7700 g, .901 GOLD, .1961 oz AGW
Obv: Older bust, leg: CAROLUS.III.D.G. .
Rev: FM and mint mark upright.

130.1	1772 FM	300.00	450.00	600.00	1000.
	1773 FM	300.00	450.00	600.00	1000.

Rev: Initial letters and mint mark inverted.

130.2	1773 FM	300.00	450.00	600.00	1000.
	1774 FM	300.00	450.00	600.00	1000.
	1775 FM	300.00	450.00	600.00	1000.
	1776 FM	300.00	450.00	600.00	1000.

6.7700 g, .875 GOLD, .1904 oz AGW

KM#	Date	VG	Fine	VF	XF
130.2a	1777 FM	300.00	400.00	500.00	800.00
	1778 FF	300.00	400.00	500.00	800.00
	1779 FF	300.00	400.00	500.00	800.00
	1780 FF	300.00	400.00	500.00	800.00
	1781 FF/FM	300.00	400.00	500.00	800.00
	1781 FF	300.00	400.00	500.00	800.00
	1782 FF	300.00	400.00	500.00	800.00
	1783 FF	300.00	400.00	500.00	800.00
	1784 FF	300.00	400.00	500.00	800.00
	1784 FM	500.00	750.00	1000.	1500.
	1785 FM	300.00	400.00	500.00	800.00
	1786 FM	300.00	400.00	500.00	800.00
	1787 FM	300.00	400.00	500.00	800.00
	1788 FM	300.00	400.00	500.00	800.00

Rev: Initial letters and mint mark upright.

130.1a	1788 FM	300.00	400.00	500.00	800.00

Obv: Bust of Charles III, leg: CAROL.IV.D.G. .

131	1789 FM	300.00	400.00	650.00	1000.
	1790 FM	300.00	400.00	650.00	1000.

Obv: Armored bust of Charles IV.

132	1791 FM	300.00	400.00	650.00	1000.
	1792 FM	125.00	250.00	350.00	600.00
	1793 FM	125.00	250.00	350.00	600.00
	1794 FM	125.00	250.00	350.00	600.00
	1795 FM	125.00	250.00	350.00	600.00
	1796 FM	125.00	250.00	350.00	600.00
	1797 FM	125.00	250.00	400.00	750.00
	1798 FM	125.00	250.00	350.00	600.00
	1799 FM	125.00	250.00	350.00	600.00
	1800 FM	125.00	250.00	350.00	600.00
	1801 FM	125.00	250.00	350.00	600.00
	1802 FT	125.00	250.00	350.00	600.00
	1803 FT	125.00	250.00	350.00	600.00
	1804 TH	125.00	250.00	350.00	600.00
	1805 TH	125.00	250.00	350.00	600.00
	1806 TH	125.00	250.00	350.00	600.00
	1807 TH	125.00	250.00	350.00	600.00
	1808 TH	125.00	250.00	350.00	600.00

Obv: Undraped bust of Ferdinand VII.

134	1814 HJ	250.00	400.00	650.00	1200.
	1814 JJ	250.00	400.00	650.00	1200.
	1815 JJ	250.00	400.00	650.00	1200.
	1816 JJ	250.00	400.00	650.00	1200.
	1817 JJ	250.00	400.00	650.00	1200.
	1818 JJ	250.00	400.00	650.00	1200.
	1819 JJ	250.00	400.00	650.00	1200.
	1820 JJ	250.00	400.00	650.00	1200.

4 ESCUDOS

13.5400 g, .917 GOLD, .3992 oz AGW
Obv. leg: PHILIP.V.D.G.HISPAN.ET IND.REX
Rev. leg: INITIUM SAPIENTIAE TIMOR DOMINI

KM#	Date	VG	Fine	VF	XF
135	1732	—	—	Rare	—
	1732 F	—	—	Rare	—
	1733 F	—	—	Rare	—
	1734/3 F	1000.	1500.	2000.	3500.
	1734 MF	800.00	1200.	1750.	3000.
	1735 MF	800.00	1200.	1750.	3000.
	1736 MF	800.00	1200.	1750.	3000.
	1737 MF	600.00	1000.	1500.	2750.
	1738 MF	600.00	1000.	1500.	2750.
	1739 MF	600.00	1000.	1500.	2750.
	1740/30	600.00	1000.	1500.	2750.
	1740 MF	600.00	1000.	1500.	2750.
	1741 MF	600.00	1000.	1500.	2750.
	1742 MF	600.00	1000.	1500.	2750.
	1743 MF	600.00	1000.	1500.	2750.
	1744 MD	600.00	1000.	1500.	2750.
	1745 MF	600.00	1000.	1500.	2750.
	1746 MF	600.00	1000.	1500.	2750.
	1747 MF	600.00	1000.	1500.	2750.

Obv: Large bust; leg: FERDND.VI.D.G. .

KM#	Date	VG	Fine	VF	XF
136	1747 MF	—	—	Rare	—

Obv: Small bust; leg: FERDND.VI.D.G. .
Rev. leg: NOMINA MAGNA SEQUOR, 4S by arms.

KM#	Date	VG	Fine	VF	XF
137	1748 MF	1500.	3000.	5000.	7000.
	1749 MF	1500.	3000.	5000.	7000.
	1750 MF	1500.	3000.	5000.	7000.
	1751 MF	1500.	3000.	5000.	7000.

Rev: Without 4 S by arms.

KM#	Date	VG	Fine	VF	XF
138	1752 MF	800.00	1500.	2750.	4000.
	1753 MF	800.00	1500.	2750.	4000.
	1754 MF	800.00	1500.	2750.	4000.
	1755 MM	800.00	1500.	2750.	4000.
	1756 MM	800.00	1500.	2750.	4000.

Obv: Large full bust; leg: FERDND.VI.D.G. .

KM#	Date	VG	Fine	VF	XF
139	1757 MM	1250.	2500.	4500.	6500.
	1758 MM	1250.	2500.	4500.	6500.
	1759 MM	1250.	2500.	4500.	6500.

Obv: Young bust, leg: CAROLVS.III.D.G. .
Rev. leg: NOMINA MAGNA SEQUOR

KM#	Date	VG	Fine	VF	XF
140	1760 MM	2500.	5000.	7000.	10,000.
	1761 MM	2500.	5000.	7000.	10,000.

Obv: Large young bust, leg: CAROLUS.III.D.G. .
Rev. leg: IN.UTROQ.FELIX.AUSPICE.DEO.

KM#	Date	VG	Fine	VF	XF
141	1762 MF	800.00	1200.	1800.	3000.
	1763 MF	800.00	1200.	1800.	3000.
	1764 MF	—	—	Rare	—
	1765 MF	800.00	1200.	1800.	3000.
	1766 MF	800.00	1200.	1800.	3000.
	1767 MF	800.00	1200.	1800.	3000.
	1768 MF	800.00	1200.	1800.	3000.
	1769 MF	800.00	1200.	1800.	3000.
	1770 MF	800.00	1200.	1800.	3000.
	1771 MF	800.00	1200.	1800.	3000.

13.5400 g, .901 GOLD, .3922 oz AGW
Obv. leg: CAROL.III.D.G. .
Rev: FM and mint mark upright.

KM#	Date	VG	Fine	VF	XF
142.1	1772 FM	400.00	650.00	1000.	1850.
	1773 FM	400.00	650.00	1000.	1850.

Rev: Initial letters and mint mark inverted.

142.2	1773 FM	400.00	600.00	900.00	1600.
	1774 FM	400.00	600.00	900.00	1600.
	1775 FM	400.00	600.00	900.00	1600.
	1776 FM	400.00	600.00	900.00	1600.

13.5400 g, .875 GOLD, .3809 oz AGW

142.2a	1777 FM	400.00	600.00	900.00	1600.
	1778 FF	400.00	600.00	900.00	1600.
	1779 FF	400.00	600.00	900.00	1600.
	1780 FF	400.00	600.00	900.00	1600.
	1781 FF	400.00	600.00	900.00	1600.
	1782 FF	400.00	600.00	900.00	1600.
	1783 FF	400.00	600.00	900.00	1600.
	1784 FF	400.00	600.00	900.00	1600.
	1784 FM	400.00	600.00	900.00	1600.
	1785 FM	400.00	600.00	900.00	1600.
	1786 FM	400.00	600.00	900.00	1600.
	1787 FM	400.00	600.00	900.00	1600.
	1788 FM	400.00	600.00	900.00	1600.
	1789 FM	400.00	600.00	900.00	1600.

Rev: Initial letters and mint mark upright.

142.1a	1788 FM	400.00	650.00	1000.	1850.

Obv: Bust of Charles III, leg: CAROL.IV.D.G. .

143.1	1789 FM	500.00	700.00	1000.	1750.
	1790 FM	500.00	700.00	1000.	1750.

Obv: Bust of Charles III, leg: CAROL. IIII D.G. . . .

143.2	1790 FM	600.00	1000.	1800.	3000.

Obv: Armored bust of Charles IIII.

144	1792 FM	300.00	500.00	750.00	1400.
	1793 FM	300.00	500.00	750.00	1400.
	1794/3 FM	300.00	500.00	750.00	1400.
	1794 FM	300.00	500.00	750.00	1400.
	1795 FM	300.00	500.00	750.00	1400.
	1796 FM	300.00	500.00	750.00	1400.
	1797 FM	300.00	500.00	750.00	1400.
	1798/7 FM	300.00	500.00	750.00	1400.
	1798 FM	300.00	500.00	750.00	1400.
	1799 FM	300.00	500.00	750.00	1400.
	1800 FM	300.00	500.00	750.00	1400.
	1801 FM	300.00	500.00	750.00	1400.
	1801 FT	300.00	500.00	750.00	1400.
	1802 FT	300.00	500.00	750.00	1400.
	1803 FT	300.00	500.00	750.00	1400.
	1804/3 TH	300.00	500.00	750.00	1400.
	1804 TH	300.00	500.00	750.00	1400.
	1805 TH	300.00	500.00	750.00	1400.
	1806/5 TH	300.00	500.00	750.00	1400.
	1806 TH	300.00	500.00	750.00	1400.

KM#	Date	VG	Fine	VF	XF
144	1807 TH	300.00	500.00	750.00	1400.
	1808/0 TH	300.00	500.00	750.00	1400.
	1808 TH	300.00	500.00	750.00	1400.

Obv: Armored bust of Ferdinand VII.

145	1810 HJ	450.00	600.00	950.00	1600.
	1811 HJ	350.00	500.00	850.00	1400.
	1812 HJ	350.00	500.00	850.00	1400.

Obv: Undraped bust of Ferdinand VII.

146	1814 HJ	400.00	650.00	900.00	1600.
	1815 HJ	400.00	650.00	900.00	1600.
	1815 JJ	400.00	650.00	900.00	1600.
	1816 JJ	400.00	650.00	900.00	1600.
	1817 JJ	400.00	650.00	900.00	1600.
	1818 JJ	400.00	650.00	900.00	1600.
	1819 JJ	400.00	650.00	900.00	1600.
	1820 JJ	400.00	650.00	900.00	1600.

8 ESCUDOS

27.0700 g, .917 GOLD, .7981 oz AGW
Obv. leg: PHILIP.V.D.G.HISPAN.ET IND.REX
Rev. leg: INITIUM SAPIENTIAE TIMOR DOMINI

KM#	Date	VG	Fine	VF	XF
148	1732	—	—	Rare	—
	1732 F	—	—	Rare	—
	1733 F	—	—	Rare	—
	1734 MF	1000.	1600.	2600.	3750.
	1735 MF	1000.	1500.	2250.	3250.
	1736 MF	1000.	1500.	2250.	3250.
	1737 MF	1000.	1500.	2250.	3250.
	1738/7 MF	1000.	1500.	2250.	3250.
	1738 MF	1000.	1500.	2250.	3250.
	1739 MF	1000.	1500.	2250.	3250.
	1740 MF	1000.	1500.	2250.	3250.
	1741 MF	1000.	1500.	2250.	3250.
	1742 MF	1000.	1500.	2250.	3250.
	1743 MF	1000.	1500.	2250.	3250.
	1744 MF	1000.	1500.	2250.	3250.
	1745 MF	1000.	1500.	2250.	3250.
	1746 MF	1000.	1500.	2250.	3250.
	1747 MF	2000.	3000.	2250.	3250.

Obv: Large bust; leg: FERDND.VI.D.G. .

KM#	Date	VG	Fine	VF	XF
151	1752 MF	1000.	1500.	2500.	4000.
	1753 MF	1000.	1500.	2500.	4000.
	1754 MF	1000.	1500.	2500.	4000.
	1755 MM	1000.	1500.	2500.	4000.
	1756 MM	1000.	1500.	2500.	4000.

Obv: Young bust; leg: FERDND.VI.D.G. .

149	1747 MF	3000.	4000.	6500.	12,500.

Obv: Medium, full bust; leg: FERDND.VI.D.G. . . .

152	1757 MM	1200.	2000.	3000.	4000.
	1758 MM	1200.	2000.	3000.	4000.
	1759 MM	1200.	2000.	3000.	4000.

Obv: Young bust, leg: CAROLVS.III.D.G. .
w/Order of the Golden Fleece at date.

153	1760 MM	1500.	2500.	4250.	7000.
	1761 MM	1750.	3000.	5000.	8000.

Obv: Small bust; leg: FERDND.VI.D.G. .
Rev. leg: NOMINA MAGNA SEQUOR

150	1748 MF	1000.	1500.	2500.	4000.
	1749/8 MF	1000.	1500.	2500.	4000.
	1749 MF	1000.	1500.	2500.	4000.
	1750 MF	1000.	1500.	2500.	4000.
	1751 MF	1000.	1500.	2500.	4000.

Obv: Young bust, leg: CAROLVS.III.D.G. .
w/Order of the Golden Fleece on chest.

154	1761 MM	1500.	2750.	4500.	7500.

27.0700 g, .875 GOLD, .7616 oz AGW

KM# 156.2a	Date	VG	Fine	VF	XF
	1777/6 FM	500.00	700.00	1150.	1750.
	1777 FM	500.00	700.00	1150.	1750.
	1778 FF	500.00	700.00	1150.	1750.
	1779 FF	500.00	700.00	1150.	1750.
	1780 FF	500.00	700.00	1150.	1750.
	1781 FF	500.00	700.00	1150.	1750.
	1782 FF	500.00	700.00	1150.	1750.
	1783 FF	500.00	700.00	1150.	1750.
	1784 FF	500.00	700.00	1150.	1750.
	1784 FM	500.00	700.00	1150.	1750.
	1785 FM	500.00	700.00	1150.	1750.
	1786 FM	500.00	700.00	1150.	1750.
	1787 FM	500.00	700.00	1150.	1750.
	1788 FM	500.00	700.00	1150.	1750.

Rev: Initial letters and mint mark upright.

156.1a	1788 FM	600.00	900.00	1500.	2500.

Obv: Large bust, leg: CAROLUS.III.D.G. .
Rev. leg: IN.UTROQ.FELIX.AUSPICE

KM# 155	Date	VG	Fine	VF	XF
	1762 MF	1000.	1500.	2750.	5000.
	1762 MM	1000.	1500.	2750.	5000.
	1763 MF	1000.	1500.	2750.	5000.
	1763 MM	1000.	1500.	2750.	5000.
	1764 MF	1500.	3000.	4000.	6000.
	1764 MM	1500.	3000.	4000.	6000.
	1765/4 MF	1500.	3000.	4000.	6000.
	1765 MF	1500.	3000.	4000.	6000.
	1765 MM	1000.	1500.	2500.	4000.
	1766 MF	1000.	1500.	2500.	4000.
	1767 MF	1000.	1500.	2500.	4000.
	1768 MF	1000.	1500.	2500.	4000.
	1769 MF	1000.	1500.	2500.	4000.
	1770 MF	1000.	1500.	2500.	4000.
	1771 MF	1500.	3000.	4000.	6000.

Obv: Bust of Charles III, leg: CAROL.IV.D.G. .
Rev: IN UTROQ. . .A.D., arms, order chain.

157	1789 FM	500.00	750.00	1500.	3000.
	1790 FM	500.00	750.00	1500.	3000.

27.0700 g, .901 GOLD, .7841 oz AGW
Obv: Mature bust, leg: CAROL.III.D.G. .
Rev. leg: . . . .AUSPICE.DEO.; FM and mint mark upright.

156.1	1772 FM	500.00	750.00	1250.	2000.
	1773 FM	550.00	850.00	1350.	2250.

Rev: Initial letters and mint mark inverted.

156.2	1773 FM	500.00	700.00	1150.	1750.
	1774 FM	500.00	700.00	1150.	1750.
	1775 FM	500.00	700.00	1150.	1750.
	1776 FM	500.00	700.00	1150.	1750.

Obv: Bust of Charles III, leg: CAROL.IIII.D.G. .

158	1790 FM	500.00	750.00	1500.	3000.

Obv: Armored bust of Charles IIII.
Rev. leg: IN UTROQ. FELIX., arms, order chain.

159	1791 FM	375.00	475.00	650.00	900.00
	1792 FM	375.00	475.00	650.00	900.00
	1793 FM	375.00	475.00	650.00	900.00
	1794 FM	375.00	475.00	650.00	900.00
	1795 FM	375.00	475.00	650.00	900.00
	1796/5 FM	400.00	500.00	700.00	1000.
	1796 FM	375.00	475.00	650.00	900.00

KM#	Date	VG	Fine	VF	XF
159	1797 FM	375.00	475.00	650.00	900.00
	1798 FM	375.00	475.00	650.00	900.00
	1799 FM	375.00	475.00	650.00	900.00
	1800 FM	375.00	475.00	650.00	900.00
	1801/0 FT	400.00	500.00	700.00	1000.
	1801 FM	375.00	475.00	650.00	900.00
	1801 FT	375.00	475.00	650.00	900.00
	1802 FT	375.00	475.00	650.00	900.00
	1803 FT	375.00	475.00	650.00	900.00
	1804/3 TH	400.00	500.00	700.00	1000.
	1804 TH	375.00	475.00	650.00	900.00
	1805 TH	375.00	475.00	650.00	900.00
	1806 TH	375.00	475.00	650.00	900.00
	1807/6 TH	400.00	500.00	700.00	1000.
	1807 TH	450.00	550.00	750.00	1000.
	1808 TH	450.00	600.00	800.00	1100.

Obv: Armored bust of Ferdinand VII.

160	1808 TH	400.00	500.00	750.00	1000.
	1809 HJ	400.00	500.00	750.00	1000.
	1810 HJ	375.00	475.00	650.00	875.00
	1811/0 HJ	400.00	500.00	750.00	1000.
	1811 HJ	400.00	500.00	750.00	1000.
	1811 JJ	375.00	475.00	650.00	875.00
	1812 JJ	375.00	475.00	650.00	875.00

Obv: Undraped bust of Ferdinand VII.

161	1814 JJ	375.00	475.00	650.00	850.00
	1815/4 JJ	400.00	500.00	700.00	1000.
	1815/4 HJ	400.00	500.00	700.00	1000.
	1815 JJ	375.00	475.00	650.00	850.00
	1815 HJ	375.00	475.00	650.00	850.00
	1816/5 JJ	400.00	500.00	700.00	1000.
	1816 JJ	375.00	475.00	650.00	850.00
	1817 JJ	375.00	475.00	650.00	850.00
	1818/7 JJ	375.00	475.00	650.00	850.00
	1818 JJ	375.00	475.00	650.00	850.00
	1819 JJ	375.00	475.00	650.00	850.00
	1820 JJ	375.00	475.00	650.00	850.00
	1821 JJ	400.00	500.00	700.00	1000.

PROCLAMATION MEDALLIC ISSUES (Q)

The 'Q' used in the following listings refer to STANDARD CATALOG OF MEXICAN COINS, PAPER MONEY, STOCKS, BONDS and MEDALS, Krause Publications, Inc., copyright 1981.

Chiapa
REAL

SILVER
Obv: Crowned arms between pillars, IR below, leg: FERNANDO VII REY DE ESPANA Y DE SUS INDIAS. Rev: Legend in 5 lines within wreath, PROCLA/MADO/ENCIUD/R.DECHIAPPA/1808.

KM#	Date	Fine	VF	XF	Unc
Q8	1808	22.50	35.00	50.00	—

2 REALES

SILVER
Obv. leg: FERNANDO VII REY DE ESPANA Y DE SUS INDIAS.

Q10	1808	50.00	70.00	100.00	—

Mexico City
1/2 REAL

SILVER, 1.60 g
Obv. leg: A CARLOS IV REY DE ESPANA Y DE LAS YNDIAS. Rev. leg: PROCLAMADO EN MEXICO ANO DE 1789.

Q22	1789	20.00	28.50	40.00	—

BRONZE, 18mm

Q22a	1789	22.50	35.00	50.00	—

SILVER, 17mm
Obv: Crowned arms in double-lined circle.

Q23	1789	20.00	28.50	40.00	—

BRONZE

Q23a	1789	22.50	35.00	50.00	—

REAL

SILVER

Q24	1789	20.00	28.50	40.00	—

BRONZE, 21mm

Q24a	1789	22.50	35.00	50.00	—

SILVER
Obv: Crowned arms in double-lined circle.

Q-A24	1789	20.00	28.50	40.00	—

COPPER				
KM#	Date	Fine	VF	XF	Unc
Q-A24a	1789	22.50	35.00	50.00	—

2 REALES

SILVER, 6.70 g				
Q25	1789	35.00	50.00	75.00	—

BRONZE				
Q25a	1789	30.00	45.00	60.00	—

4 REALES

SILVER, 13.60 g				
Q27	1789	100.00	150.00	225.00	—

BRONZE				
Q27a	1789	70.00	100.00	150.00	—

8 REALES

SILVER, 27.00 g				
KM#	Date	Fine	VF	XF	Unc
Q28	1789	200.00	275.00	400.00	—

BRONZE				
Q28a	1789	70.00	100.00	150.00	—

Queretaro
2 REALES

SILVER
Obv. leg: FERNANDO VII REY DE ESPANA.

KM#	Date	Fine	VF	XF	Unc
Q64	1808	35.00	50.00	75.00	

4 REALES

SILVER				
Q-A66	1808	140.00	200.00	300.00	—

8 REALES

SILVER				
Q68	1808	300.00	425.00	600.00	—

WAR OF INDEPENDENCE
ROYALIST ISSUES
(1810-1821)

Provisional Mints
RULER
Ferdinand VII, 1808-1821

MINT MARKS

CA - Chihuahua
D - Durango
GA - Guadalajara
GO - Guanajuato
ZS - Zacatecas

MONETARY SYSTEM

16 Reales = 1 Escudo

CHIHUAHUA

The Chihuahua Mint was established by a decree of October 8, 1810 as a temporary mint. Their first coins were cast 8 reales using Mexico City coins as patterns and obliterating/changing the mint mark and moneyer initials. Two c/m were placed on the obverse - on the left, a T designating its having been received by the Royal Treasurer and on the right crowned pillars of Hercules with pomegranate beneath; the symbol of the comptroller.

In 1814 standard dies were available and from 1814 to 1822 standard 8 reales were struck. Only the one denomination was made at this mint.

MINT MARK: CA

8 REALES

CAST SILVER
Obv: Imaginary bust of Ferdinand VII; leg: FERDIN.VII.
DEI. GRATIA. c/m: 'T' at left and pomegranate
pillars at right.

KM#	Date	Good	VG	Fine	VF
123	1810 RP	—	—	Rare	—
	1811 RP	45.00	60.00	100.00	150.00
	1812 RP	30.00	40.00	60.00	90.00
	1813/2 RP	32.50	45.00	70.00	100.00
	1813 RP	30.00	40.00	60.00	90.00

27.0700 g, .903 SILVER, .7860 oz ASW
Obv: Draped bust of Ferdinand VII.
Rev: Similar to KM#123.

KM#	Date	VG	Fine	VF	XF
111.1	1813 RP	—	Reported, not confirmed		
	1814 RP	—	Reported, not confirmed		
	1815 RP	200.00	275.00	350.00	500.00
	1816 RP	80.00	125.00	150.00	275.00
	1817 RP	100.00	150.00	185.00	275.00
	1818 RP	100.00	150.00	185.00	275.00
	1819 RP	125.00	175.00	250.00	350.00
	1820 RP	200.00	275.00	350.00	500.00
	1821 RP	200.00	275.00	350.00	500.00
	1822 RP	400.00	600.00	800.00	1100.

NOTE: KM#111.1 is normally found counterstamped over earlier cast 8 Reales, KM#123.

DURANGO

The Durango mint was authorized as a temporary mint at the same time as the Chihuahua Mint, October 8, 1810. The mint opened sometime in 1811 and made coins of 6 denominations - 5 silver and 1 copper - during the period 1811 to 1822.

MINT MARK: D

1/8 REAL

COPPER
Obv: Crown above double F7 monogram.
Rev: EN DURANGO, value, date.

	Date				
60	1812	35.00	75.00	125.00	225.00
	1813	—	—	Rare	—
	1814	—	—	Rare	—

Rev: Spray added above date.

	Date				
61	1814	15.00	25.00	50.00	85.00
	1815	15.00	25.00	50.00	85.00
	1816	15.00	25.00	50.00	85.00
	1817	15.00	25.00	50.00	80.00
	1818	15.00	25.00	50.00	80.00
	1818 OCTAVO DD REAL (error)				
		45.00	75.00	—	—

1/2 REAL

1.6900 g, .903 SILVER, .0491 oz ASW
Obv: Draped bust of Ferdinand VII.

	Date				
74.1	1813 RM	250.00	350.00	600.00	1500.
	1814 MZ	250.00	350.00	600.00	1500.
	1816 MZ	250.00	350.00	600.00	1500.

REAL

3.3800 g, .903 SILVER, .0981 oz ASW
Obv: Draped bust of Ferdinand VII.

	Date				
83.1	1813 RM	250.00	350.00	500.00	1250.
	1814 MZ	250.00	350.00	500.00	1250.
	1815 MZ	250.00	300.00	500.00	1250.

2 REALES

6.7700 g, .903 SILVER, .1966 oz ASW
Obv: Armored bust of Ferdinand VII.

KM#	Date	VG	Fine	VF	XF
92.2	1811 RM	200.00	300.00	400.00	1500.
	1812 RM	—	—	Rare	—

Obv: Draped bust of Ferdinand VII.

93.1	1812 MZ	200.00	300.00	400.00	1500.
	1812 RM	—	—	Rare	—
	1813 MZ	300.00	500.00	800.00	2500.
	1813 RM	300.00	500.00	800.00	2500.
	1814 MZ	300.00	500.00	800.00	2500.
	1815 MZ	300.00	500.00	800.00	2500.
	1816 MZ	300.00	500.00	800.00	2500.
	1817 MZ	300.00	500.00	800.00	2500.

4 REALES

13.5400 g, .903 SILVER, .3931 oz ASW
Obv: Draped bust of Ferdinand VII.

102.1	1814 MZ	500.00	1000.	1500.	4000.
	1816 MZ	400.00	800.00	1200.	3000.
	1817 MZ	400.00	800.00	1200.	3000.

8 REALES

27.0700 g, .903 SILVER, .7860 oz ASW
Obv: Armored bust of Ferdinand VII.

110.1	1811 RM	500.00	800.00	1200.	4000.
	1812 RM	300.00	500.00	800.00	3000.
	1813 MZ	300.00	500.00	800.00	3000.
	1814 MZ	300.00	500.00	800.00	3000.

Obv: Draped bust of Ferdinand VII.

111.2	1812 MZ	300.00	400.00	600.00	1500.
	1812 RM	125.00	175.00	275.00	800.00
	1813 RM	150.00	200.00	325.00	850.00
	1813 MZ	125.00	175.00	275.00	750.00
	1814 MZ	150.00	225.00	275.00	750.00
	1815 MZ	75.00	125.00	225.00	600.00
	1816 MZ	50.00	75.00	125.00	325.00
	1817 MZ	30.00	50.00	90.00	250.00
	1818 MZ	50.00	75.00	125.00	350.00
	1818 RM	50.00	75.00	125.00	325.00
	1818 CG/RM	100.00	125.00	150.00	350.00
	1818 CG	50.00	75.00	125.00	325.00
	1819 CG/RM	50.00	100.00	150.00	300.00
	1819 CG	30.00	60.00	100.00	250.00
	1820 CG	30.00	60.00	100.00	250.00
	1821 CG	30.00	40.00	50.00	150.00
	1822 CG	30.00	50.00	75.00	160.00

NOTE: Occasionally these are found struck over Guadalajara 8 reales and are very rare in general, specimens dated prior to 1816 are rather weakly struck.

GUADALAJARA

The Guadalajara Mint made its first coins in 1812 and the mint operated until April 30, 1815. It was to reopen in 1818 and continue operations until 1822. It was the only Royalist mint to strike gold coins, both 4 and 8 escudos. In addition to these it struck the standard 5 denominations in silver.

MINT MARK: GA

1/2 REAL

1.6900 g, .903 SILVER, .0491 oz ASW
Obv: Draped bust of Ferdinand VII.

KM#	Date	VG	Fine	VF	XF
74.2	1812 MR	—	—	Rare	—
	1814 MR	40.00	100.00	200.00	300.00
	1815 MR	200.00	350.00	500.00	1000.

REAL

3.3800 g, .903 SILVER, .0981 oz ASW
Obv: Draped bust of Ferdinand VII.

83.2	1814 MR	125.00	175.00	275.00	600.00
	1815 MR	—	—	Rare	—

2 REALES

6.7700 g, .903 SILVER, .1966 oz ASW
Obv: Draped bust of Ferdinand VII.

93.2	1812 MR	300.00	500.00	800.00	2500.
	1814 MR	75.00	125.00	200.00	600.00
	1815/4 MR	425.00	725.00	1100.	3600.
	1815 MR	400.00	700.00	1000.	3500.
	1821 FS	200.00	250.00	350.00	900.00

4 REALES

13.5400 g, .903 SILVER, .3931 oz ASW
Obv: Draped bust of Ferdinand VII.

102.2	1814 MR	40.00	65.00	150.00	250.00
	1815 MR	80.00	150.00	300.00	500.00

4 ESCUDOS

13.5400 g, .875 GOLD, .3809 oz ASW
Obv: Uniformed bust of Ferdinand VII.

KM#	Date	VG	Fine	VF	XF
147	1812 MR	—	—	Rare	—

8 ESCUDOS

Obv: Large bust.

KM#	Date	VG	Fine	VF	XF
102.3	1814 MR	50.00	100.00	200.00	400.00

Obv: Large bust w/berries in laurel.

| 102.4 | 1814 MR | — | — | Rare | — |

8 REALES

27.0700 g, .875 GOLD, .7616 oz AGW
Obv: Large uniformed bust of Ferdinand VII.

KM#	Date	VG	Fine	VF	XF
162	1812 MR	—	Reported, not confirmed		
	1813 MR	4000.	7000.	10,000.	18,000.

Obv: Small uniformed bust of Ferdinand VII.

| 163 | 1813 MR | 7000. | 10,000. | 15,000. | 22,000. |

27.0700 g, .903 SILVER, .7860 oz ASW
Obv: Draped bust of Ferdinand VII.

111.3	1812 MR	1000.	1500.	3000.	4500.
	1813/2 MR	60.00	100.00	150.00	400.00
	1813 MR	60.00	100.00	150.00	400.00
	1814 MR	20.00	30.00	50.00	175.00
	1815 MR	150.00	200.00	250.00	750.00
	1818 FS	30.00	50.00	65.00	200.00
	1821/18 FS	30.00	50.00	75.00	200.00
	1821 FS	25.00	35.00	50.00	150.00
	1822/1 FS	30.00	50.00	75.00	200.00
	1822 FS	30.00	50.00	75.00	200.00

NOTE: Die varieties exist. Early dates are also encountered struck over other types.

Obv: Undraped bust of Ferdinand VII.

KM#	Date	VG	Fine	VF	XF
161.1	1821 FS	1500.	2500.	4500.	7500.

Obv: Draped bust of Ferdinand VII.

164	1821 FS	6000.	8500.	12,500.	20,000.

GUANAJUATO

Guanajuato Mint was authorized December 24, 1812 and started production shortly thereafter. For unknown reasons it closed on May 15, 1813. The mint was reopened in April of 1821 by the insurgent forces. They continued to make coins of the Spanish design to pay their army. After independence coins were made into the year 1822. Only the 2 and 8 reales coins were made.

MINT MARK: Go

2 REALES

6.7700 g, .903 SILVER, .1966 oz ASW
Obv: Draped bust of Ferdinand VII.

93.3	1821 JM	30.00	60.00	90.00	175.00
	1822 JM	25.00	45.00	65.00	125.00

8 REALES

27.0700 g, .903 SILVER, .7860 oz ASW
Obv: Draped bust of Ferdinand VII.

111.4	1812 JJ	750.00	1250.	1750.	2500.
	1813 JJ	125.00	175.00	275.00	600.00
	1821 JM	25.00	50.00	75.00	200.00
	1822/0 JM	40.00	100.00	150.00	300.00
	1822 JM	20.00	30.00	50.00	175.00

NUEVA VISCAYA

(Later became Durango State)

This 8 reales, intended for the province of Nueva Viscaya was minted in the newly opened Durango Mint during the months of February and March of 1811 before the regular coinage of Durango was started.

8 REALES

.903 SILVER
Obv. leg: MON.PROV. DE NUEV.VIZCAYA,
arms of Durango. Rev: Royal arms.

KM#	Date	Good	VG	Fine	VF
181	1811 RM	1250.	2000.	2750.	4500.

NOTE: Several varieties exist.

OAXACA

The city of Oaxaca was in the midst of a coin shortage when it became apparent the city would be taken by insurgent forces. The Royalist forces under Lt. Gen. Saravia had some coins made. They were cast in a blacksmith shop and were made in 3 denominations - 1/2, 1 and 8 reales. They were made only briefly in 1812 before the city fell to the opposing forces.

1/2 REAL

.903 SILVER
Obv: Cross separating castle, lion, F,7O.
Rev. leg: OAXACA around shield.

166	1812	1000.	1500.	2500.	3500.

REAL

.903 SILVER

167	1812	300.00	600.00	1000.	2000.

8 REALES

.903 SILVER

KM#	Date	Good	VG	Fine	VF
168	1812 c/m:A	1200.	1800.	3000.	4500.
	1812 c/m:B	1200.	1800.	3000.	4500.
	1812 c/m:C	1200.	1800.	3000.	4500.
	1812 c/m:D	1200.	1800.	3000.	4500.
	1812 c/m:K	1200.	1800.	3000.	4500.
	1812 c/m:L	1200.	1800.	3000.	4500.
	1812 c/m:Mo	1200.	1800.	3000.	4500.
	1812 c/m:N	1200.	1800.	3000.	4500.
	1812 c/m:O	1200.	1800.	3000.	4500.
	1812 c/m:R	1200.	1800.	3000.	4500.
	1812 c/m:V	1200.	1800.	3000.	4500.
	1812 c/m:Z	1200.	1800.	3000.	4500.

NOTE: The above issue usually has a second c/m: O between crowned pillars.

REAL DEL CATORCE
(City in San Luis Potosi)

Real del Catorce is an important mining center in the state of San Luis Potosi. In 1811 an 8 reales coin was issued under very tedious conditions while the city was still in Royalist hands. Few survive.

8 REALES

.903 SILVER
Obv. leg: EL R.D. CATORC. POR FERNA. VII.

Rev. leg: MONEDA. PROVISIONAL.VALE.8R.

KM#	Date	VG	Fine	VF	XF
169	1811	2000.	4000.	7500.	15,000.

SAN FERNANDO DE BEXAR

Struck by Jose Antonio de la Garza, the 'jolas' are the only known coins issued under Spanish rule in the continental United States of America.

1/8 REAL

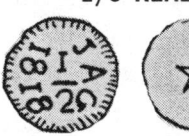 

COPPER

KM#	Date	Mintage	Good	VG	Fine	VF
170	1818	8,000	500.00	750.00	1200.	1600.

| 171 | 1818 | Inc. Ab. | 500.00 | 750.00 | 1200. | 1600. |

SAN LUIS POTOSI
Sierra De Pinos
Villa

1/4 REAL

COPPER

KM#	Date	Good	VG	Fine	VF
A172	1814	85.00	125.00	185.00	250.00

SILVER

| A172a | 1814 | — | — | Rare | — |

SOMBRERETE
(Under Royalist Vargas)

The Sombrerete Mint opened on October 8, 1810 in an area that boasted some of the richest mines in Mexico. The mint operated until July 16, 1811 when it closed only to reopen in 1812 and finally to close for good at the end of 1812. The man in charge of the mines, Fernando Vargas, was also in charge of the coinage. All of the coins bear his name.

1/2 REAL

.903 SILVER
Obv. leg: FERDIN.VII.SOMBRERETE..., around crowned globes. Rev. leg: VARGAS above lys in oval, sprays.

| 172 | 1811 | 35.00 | 60.00 | 100.00 | 175.00 |
| | 1812 | 50.00 | 90.00 | 150.00 | 225.00 |

REAL

.903 SILVER
Obv. leg: FERDIN.VII.SOMBRERETE. . ., around crowned globes. Rev. leg: VARGAS over lys in oval, sprays.

KM#	Date	Good	VG	Fine	VF
173	1811	40.00	60.00	100.00	160.00
	1812	30.00	40.00	80.00	125.00

2 REALES

.903 SILVER
Obv: R.CAXA.DE.SOMBRERETE, royal arms.
Rev. c/m: VARGAS, 1811, S between crowned pillars.

KM#	Date	Good	VG	Fine	VF
174	1811 SE	65.00	200.00	400.00	650.00

4 REALES

.903 SILVER
Obv. leg: R.CAXA.DE.SOMBRERETE, royal arms.
Rev. leg: Small VARGAS/1811.

KM#	Date	Good	VG	Fine	VF
175.1	1811	100.00	200.00	400.00	750.00

Rev: Large VARGAS/1812.

175.2	1812	50.00	150.00	250.00	400.00

8 REALES

.903 SILVER
Obv. leg: R.CAXA. DE SOMBRERETE.
Rev. c/m: VARGAS, date, S between crowned pillars.

KM#	Date	Good	VG	Fine	VF
176	1810	1000.	1500.	2500.	3500.
	1811	200.00	300.00	400.00	500.00

Obv. leg: R.CAXA. DE SOMBRETE, crowned arms.
Rev. leg: VARGAS/date/3

KM#	Date	Good	VG	Fine	VF
177	1811	100.00	150.00	200.00	300.00
	1812	100.00	150.00	200.00	300.00

VALLADOLID MICHOACAN
(Now Morelia)

Valladolid, capitol of Michoacan province, was a strategically important center for military thrusts into the adjoining provinces. The Royalists made every effort to retain the position. In 1813, with the advance of the insurgent forces, it became apparent that to maintain the position would be very difficult. During 1813 it was necessary to make coins in the city due to lack of traffic with other areas. These were made only briefly before the city fell and were also used by the insurgents with appropriate countermarks.

8 REALES

.903 SILVER
Obv: Royal arms in wreath, value at sides.
Rev: PROVISIONAL/DE VALLADOLID/1813.

KM#	Date	Good	VG	Fine	VF
178	1813	1000.	2000.	3000.	5000.

Obv: Bust, leg: FERDIN. VII.
Rev: Arms, pillars.

179	1813	1500.	2500.	3500.	5500.

ZACATECAS

The city of Zacatecas, in a rich mining area, has a long history of providing silver for the world. From the mid-1500's silver poured from its mines. On November 14, 1810 a mint began production for the Royalist cause. Zacatecas was the most prolific of the mints during the War of Independence. The 4 silver denominations were made here. The first type was a local type with the mountains of silver shown on the coins. These were made only in 1810 and 1811. Some of the 1811 were made by the insurgents after the town fell on April 15, 1811. The town was retaken by the Royalists on May 21, 1811. From then until 1822 the standard bust type of Ferdinand VII was made.

MINT MARKS: Z, ZS, Zs

1/2 REAL

.903 SILVER
Similar to KM#181 but w/local arms.
Flowers 1 and 4, castles 2 and 3.

KM#	Date	Good	VG	Fine	VF
180	1810	75.00	125.00	200.00	400.00
	1181 (error 1811)				
		30.00	50.00	75.00	150.00

Obv: Royal arms.
Rev. leg: MONEDA PROVISIONAL DE
ZACATECAS., mountain.

| 181 | 1811 | 30.00 | 50.00 | 75.00 | 100.00 |

Obv: Provincial bust FERDIN. VII.
Rev. leg: MONEDA PROVISIONAL DE ZACATECAS.

| 182 | 1811 | 30.00 | 40.00 | 60.00 | 80.00 |
| | 1812 | 25.00 | 35.00 | 50.00 | 70.00 |

1.6900 g, .903 SILVER, .0491 oz ASW
Obv: Armored bust of Ferdinand VII.

73.1	1813 FP	30.00	60.00	100.00	175.00
	1813 AG	20.00	40.00	60.00	100.00
	1814 AG	15.00	30.00	60.00	100.00
	1815 AG	12.50	25.00	40.00	60.00
	1816 AG	10.00	15.00	25.00	50.00
	1817 AG	10.00	15.00	25.00	50.00
	1818 AG	10.00	15.00	25.00	50.00
	1819 AG	10.00	15.00	25.00	50.00

Obv: Draped bust Ferdinand VII.

KM#	Date	VG	Fine	VF	XF
74.3	1819 AG	8.00	12.00	25.00	50.00
	1820 AG	8.00	12.00	25.00	50.00
	1820 RG	5.00	10.00	20.00	45.00
	1821 AG	50.00	100.00	150.00	250.00
	1821 RG	5.00	10.00	20.00	45.00

REAL

.903 SILVER
Obv: Local arms w/flowers and castles.

183	1810	100.00	150.00	300.00	500.00
	1181 (error 1811)				
		20.00	40.00	75.00	125.00

Obv: Royal arms.
Rev. leg: MONEDA PROVISIONAL DE
ZACATECAS., mountain.

KM#	Date	Good	VG	Fine	VF
184	1811	15.00	30.00	50.00	100.00

Obv: Provincial bust, leg: FERDIN. VII.
Rev. leg: MONEDA PROVISIONAL DE
ZACATECAS, arms, pillars.

| 185 | 1811 | 45.00 | 75.00 | 100.00 | 175.00 |
| | 1812 | 45.00 | 75.00 | 100.00 | 175.00 |

3.3800 g, .903 SILVER, .0981 oz ASW
Obv: Armored bust of Ferdinand VII.

82.1	1813 FP	50.00	100.00	150.00	250.00
	1814 FP	20.00	35.00	50.00	75.00
	1814 AG	20.00	35.00	50.00	75.00
	1815 AG	20.00	35.00	50.00	75.00
	1816 AG	10.00	20.00	30.00	60.00
	1817 AG	6.50	12.50	20.00	40.00
	1818 AG	6.50	12.50	20.00	40.00
	1819 AG	5.00	9.00	15.00	30.00
	1820 AG	4.00	7.50	12.50	25.00

Obv: Draped bust of Ferdinand VII.

KM#	Date	VG	Fine	VF	XF
83.3	1820 AG	5.00	10.00	17.50	40.00
	1820 RG	5.00	10.00	17.50	40.00
	1821 AG	15.00	30.00	45.00	75.00
	1821 AZ	10.00	20.00	30.00	60.00
	1821 RG	6.00	12.00	17.50	45.00
	1822 AZ	6.00	12.00	17.50	45.00
	1822 RG	15.00	30.00	45.00	75.00

2 REALES

.903 SILVER
Obv: Local arms w/flowers and castles.

KM#	Date	Good	VG	Fine	VF
186	1810	—	—	Rare	—
	1181 (error 1811)				
		25.00	40.00	60.00	100.00

Obv: Royal arms.
Rev. leg: MONEDA PROVISIONAL DE ZACATECAS.,
mountain above L.V.O.

KM#	Date	Good	VG	Fine	VF
187	1811	15.00	30.00	50.00	75.00

Obv: Armored bust, leg: FERDIN. VII.
Rev. leg: MONEDA PROVISIONAL DE
ZACATECAS, crowned arms, pillars.

	Date	Good	VG	Fine	VF
188	1811	40.00	75.00	150.00	225.00
	1812	30.00	60.00	125.00	200.00

6.7700 g, .903 SILVER, .1966 oz ASW
Obv: Large armored bust of Ferdinand VII.

	Date				
92.1	1813 FP	37.50	50.00	75.00	125.00
	1814 FP	37.50	50.00	75.00	125.00
	1814 AG	37.50	50.00	75.00	125.00
	1815 AG	6.50	12.50	25.00	50.00
	1816 AG	6.50	12.50	25.00	50.00
	1817 AG	6.50	12.50	25.00	50.00
	1818 AG	6.50	12.50	25.00	50.00

Obv: Small armored bust of Ferdinand VII.

A92	1819 AG	25.00	50.00	100.00	200.00

Obv: Draped bust of Ferdinand VII.

KM#	Date	VG	Fine	VF	XF
93.4	1818 AG	6.50	12.50	20.00	40.00
	1819 AG	10.00	20.00	40.00	75.00
	1820 AG	10.00	20.00	40.00	75.00
	1820 RG	10.00	20.00	40.00	75.00
	1821 AG	10.00	20.00	40.00	75.00
	1821 AZ/RG	10.00	20.00	40.00	75.00
	1821 AZ	10.00	20.00	40.00	75.00
	1821 RG	10.00	20.00	40.00	75.00
	1822 AG	10.00	20.00	40.00	75.00
	1822 AZ	15.00	30.00	60.00	120.00
	1822 RG	10.00	20.00	40.00	75.00

8 REALES

.903 SILVER
Obv: Local arm w/flowers and castles.
Rev: Similar to KM#190.

KM#	Date	Good	VG	Fine	VF
189	1810	300.00	450.00	600.00	800.00
	1181 (error 1811)	100.00	150.00	225.00	300.00

NOTE: Also exists with incomplete date.

Obv. leg: FERDIN.VII.DEI. ., royal arms.
Rev. leg: MONEDA PROVISIONAL DE
ZACATECAS, mountain above L.V.O.

190	1811	75.00	125.00	150.00	225.00

Rev: Crown with lower rear arc.

KM#	Date	Good	VG	Fine	VF
111.6	1821 RG	160.00	320.00	550.00	750.00

COUNTERMARKED COINAGE
Crown and Flag
(Refer to Multiple Countermarks)
LCM - La Comandancia Militar
NOTE: This countermark exists in 15 various sizes.

2 REALES

.903 SILVER
c/m: LCM on Mexico KM#92.

193.1	ND(1809) TH	100.00	150.00	200.00	275.00

c/m: LCM on Zacatecas KM#187.

193.2	ND(1811)	100.00	150.00	200.00	275.00

8 REALES

Obv: Armored bust of Ferdinand VII.
Rev. leg: MONEDA PROVISIONAL DE ZACATECAS, crowned arms, pillars.

KM#	Date	VG	Fine	VF	XF
191	1811	35.00	50.00	100.00	150.00
	1812	35.00	50.00	100.00	150.00

Obv: Draped bust of Ferdinand VII.
Rev. leg: MONEDA PROVISIONAL DE ZACATECAS crowned arms, pillars.

192	1812	50.00	75.00	125.00	200.00

27.0700 g, .903 SILVER, .7860 oz ASW
Obv: Draped bust of Ferdinand VII.

111.5	1813 AG	125.00	200.00	250.00	350.00
	1813 FP	75.00	125.00	175.00	275.00
	1814 AG	100.00	150.00	200.00	300.00
	1814 AG Dover horizontal D in IND				
		125.00	175.00	225.00	325.00
	1814 AG/FP	100.00	150.00	200.00	300.00
	1814 FP	150.00	250.00	350.00	450.00
	1815 AG	50.00	100.00	150.00	250.00
	1816 AG	35.00	50.00	65.00	125.00
	1817 AG	35.00	50.00	65.00	125.00
	1818 AG	30.00	40.00	50.00	100.00
	1819 AG	30.00	40.00	50.00	100.00
	1820 AG	30.00	40.00	50.00	100.00
	1820 RG	30.00	40.00	50.00	100.00
	1821/81 RG	75.00	150.00	225.00	300.00
	1821 RG	15.00	25.00	35.00	65.00
	1821 AZ	50.00	100.00	150.00	200.00
	1822 RG	40.00	60.00	100.00	175.00

CAST SILVER
c/m: LCM on Chihuahua KM#123.

KM#	Date	Good	VG	Fine	VF
194.1	ND(1811) RP	100.00	200.00	300.00	450.00
	ND(1812) RP	100.00	200.00	300.00	450.00

.903 SILVER
c/m: LCM on Chihuahua KM#111.1 struck over KM#123.

194.2	ND(1815) RP	200.00	275.00	400.00	550.00
	ND(1817) RP	125.00	175.00	225.00	300.00
	ND(1820) RP	125.00	175.00	225.00	300.00
	ND(1821) RP	125.00	175.00	225.00	300.00

c/m: LCM on Durango KM#111.2.

194.3	ND(1812) RM	70.00	125.00	190.00	250.00
	ND(1821) CG	70.00	125.00	190.00	250.00

c/m: LCM on Guadalajara KM#111.3.

194.4	ND(1813) MR	150.00	225.00	300.00	475.00
	ND(1820) FS	—	—	Rare	—

c/m: LCM on Guanajuato KM#111.4.

194.5	ND(1813) JM	225.00	350.00	475.00	650.00

c/m: LCM on Nueva Vizcaya KM#165.

194.6	ND(1811) RM	—	—	Rare	—

c/m: LCM on Mexico KM#111.

194.7	ND(1811) HJ	125.00	225.00	350.00	600.00
	ND(1812) JJ	110.00	135.00	190.00	325.00
	ND(1817) JJ	50.00	65.00	85.00	125.00
	ND(1818) JJ	50.00	65.00	85.00	125.00
	ND(1820) JJ	—	—	—	—

c/m: LCM on Sombrerete KM#176.

194.8	ND(1811)	—	—	Rare	—
	ND(1812)	—	—	Rare	—

c/m: LCM on Zacatecas KM#190.

KM#	Date	Good	VG	Fine	VF
194.9	ND(1811)	225.00	350.00	450.00	—

c/m: LCM on Zacatecas KM#111.5.

194.10	ND(1813) FP	—	—	—	—
	ND(1814) AG	—	—	—	—
	ND(1822) RG	—	—	—	—

LCV - Las Cajas de Veracruz
(The Royal Treasury
of the City of Veracruz)

L.C.V.

7 REALES

SILVER
c/m: LCV and 7 on underweight 8 Reales.

195	ND(-)	—	—	Rare	—

7-1/4 REALES

SILVER
c/m: LCV and 7-1/4 on underweight 8 Reales.

196	ND(-)	—	—	Rare	—

7-1/2 REALES

SILVER
c/m: LCV and 7-1/2 on underweight 8 Reales.

197	ND(-)	—	—	Rare	—

7-3/4 REALES

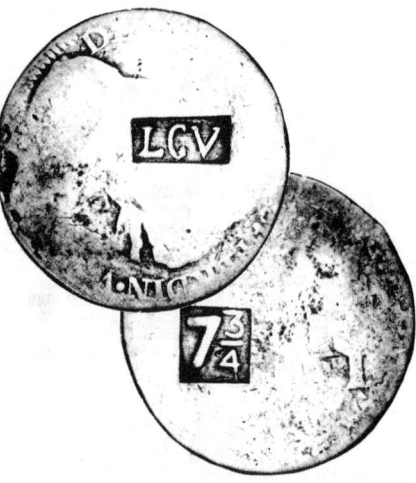

SILVER
c/m: LCV and 7-3/4 on underweight 8 Reales.

198	ND(-)	300.00	375.00	450.00	600.00

8 REALES

CAST SILVER
c/m: LCV on Chihuahua KM#123.

KM#	Date	Good	VG	Fine	VF
A198	ND(1811) RP	150.00	250.00	400.00	500.00

SILVER
c/m: LCV on Zacatecas KM#191.

KM#	Date	Good	VG	Fine	VF
199	ND(1811)	175.00	225.00	275.00	350.00
	ND(1812)	175.00	225.00	275.00	350.00

MS (Monogram) - Manuel Salcedo

8 REALES

SILVER
c/m: MS monogram on Mexico KM#110.

KM#	Date	Good	VG	Fine	VF
200	ND(1809) TH	150.00	250.00	400.00	500.00
	ND(1810) HJ	150.00	250.00	400.00	500.00
	ND(1811) HJ	150.00	250.00	400.00	500.00

MVA - Monclova

8 REALES

SILVER
c/m: MVA/1811 on Chihuahua KM#111.1; struck over cast Mexico KM#110.

KM#	Date	Good	VG	Fine	VF
201	ND(1809)	—	—	Rare	—
	ND(1816) RP	—	—	Rare	—
	ND(1821) RP	—	—	Rare	—

c/m: MVA/1812 on Chihuahua KM#111.1; struck over cast Mexico KM#109.

		Good	VG	Fine	VF
202.1	1812(1810)	125.00	175.00	250.00	350.00

c/m: MVA/1812 on cast Mexico KM#109.

		Good	VG	Fine	VF
202.2	1812(1798) FM	100.00	150.00	250.00	350.00
	1812(1802) FT	100.00	150.00	250.00	350.00

c/m: MVA/1812 on cast Mexico KM#110.

		Good	VG	Fine	VF
202.3	1812(1809) HJ	100.00	150.00	250.00	350.00
	1812(1809) TH	100.00	150.00	250.00	350.00
	1812(1810) HJ	100.00	150.00	250.00	350.00

c/m: MVA/1812 on Zacatecas KM#189.

		Good	VG	Fine	VF
202.5	1812(1813)	300.00	350.00	450.00	550.00

PDV - Provisional de Valladolid
VTIL - (Util = useful)
(Refer to Multiple countermarks)

INSURGENT COINAGE
Supreme National Congress
Of America
1/2 REAL

COPPER
Obv. leg: FERDIN. VII DEI GRATIA, eagle on bridge.
Rev. leg: S.P.CONG.NAT.IND.
GUV.T., value, bow, quiver, etc.

KM#	Date	Good	VG	Fine	VF
203	1811	30.00	45.00	60.00	100.00

REAL

SILVER
Similar to 1/2 Real, KM#203.

204	1811	50.00	75.00	125.00	200.00

2 REALES

SILVER

205	1812	250.00	350.00	500.00	700.00

8 REALES

CAST SILVER

206	1811	150.00	250.00	350.00	500.00
	1812	150.00	250.00	350.00	500.00

STRUCK SILVER

207	1811	—	Rare	—	—
	1812	300.00	600.00	1000.	1500.

COPPER
Obv. leg: FERDIN.VII. . . ., eagle on bridge.
Rev. leg: PROVICIONAL POR LA SUPREMA JUNTA
DE AMERICA, bow, sword and quiver.

KM#	Date	Good	VG	Fine	VF
208	1811	100.00	150.00	225.00	450.00
	1812	100.00	150.00	225.00	450.00

National Congress
1/2 REAL

COPPER
Obv. leg: VICE FERD. VII DEI GRATIA ET,
eagle on bridge.
Rev. leg: S. P. CONG. NAT. IND.
GUV. T., value, bow, quiver, etc.

209	1811	50.00	100.00	150.00	200.00
	1812	30.00	60.00	100.00	150.00
	1813	30.00	60.00	100.00	150.00
	1814	50.00	100.00	150.00	200.00

.903 SILVER

210	1812	30.00	60.00	100.00	150.00
	1813	50.00	100.00	175.00	275.00

NOTE: 1812 exists with the date reading inwards and outwards.

REAL

.903 SILVER

211	1812	25.00	45.00	65.00	100.00
	1813	25.00	45.00	65.00	100.00

NOTE: 1812 exists with the date reading either inward or outward.

2 REALES

COPPER

212	1812	100.00	150.00	200.00	250.00
	1813	25.00	50.00	75.00	100.00
	1814	35.00	75.00	110.00	150.00

.903 SILVER

KM#	Date	Good	VG	Fine	VF
213	1813	125.00	250.00	300.00	400.00

NOTE: These dies were believed to be intended for the striking of 2 Escudos.

4 REALES

.903 SILVER
Mint: Mexico City

KM#	Date				
214	1813	500.00	1000.	2000.	3000.

8 REALES

.903 SILVER
Mint: Mexico City
Obv: Small crowned eagle.

215.1	1812	500.00	1000.	2000.	3500.

Obv: Large crowned eagle.

215.2	1813	500.00	1000.	2000.	3500.

American Congress
REAL

.903 SILVER
Obv: Eagle on cactus,
leg: CONGRESO AMERICANO.
Rev: F.7 on spread mantle,
leg: DEPOSIT D.L.AUCTORI J.

KM#	Date	Good	VG	Fine	VF
216	ND (1813)	35.00	65.00	100.00	150.00

Obv: Eagle on cactus, leg: CONGR.AMER.
Rev: F.7 on spread mantle,
leg: DEPOS.D.L.AUT.D.

217	ND(1813)	35.00	65.00	100.00	150.00

NUEVA GALICIA
(Later became Jalisco State)

Nueva Galicia was a province in early colonial times that was similar to modern Zacatecas, etc. The name was adopted again during the War of Independence. The only issue was an 1812 2 reales of rather enigmatic origin.

2 REALES

.903 SILVER
Obv. leg: PROVYCIONAL....., N.G. in center, date.

KM#	Date	Good	VG	Fine	VF
218	1813	1000.	3000.	6000.	10,000.

OAXACA

Oaxaca was the hub of insurgent activity in the south. The issues of Oaxaca represent various episodic strikings of coins, usually under dire circumstances, by various individuals. The copper coins were made because of urgency and were to be redeemed at its face value in gold or silver. The silver coins were made after the copper coins when silver was available to the insurgent forces. Coinage started in July, 1811 and ran until October 1814.

SUD
(Under General Morelos)
1/2 REAL

COPPER
Obv: Bow, SUD.
Rev: Morelos monogram Mo, date.

KM#	Date	Good	VG	Fine	VF
219	1811	7.50	12.50	20.00	30.00
	1812	7.50	12.50	20.00	30.00
	1813	6.00	10.00	17.50	25.00
	1814	10.00	17.50	25.00	35.00

NOTE: Uniface strikes exist of #219.

STRUCK SILVER

KM#	Date	Good	VG	Fine	VF
220.1	1811	—	—	—	—
	1812	—	—	—	—
	1813	—	—	—	—

CAST SILVER

KM#	Date	Good	VG	Fine	VF
220.2	1811	—	—	—	—
	1812	—	—	—	—
	1813	25.00	50.00	100.00	150.00

NOTE: Most silver specimens available on today's market are considered spurious.

SILVER
Obv. leg: PROVICIONAL DE OAXACA, bow, arrow.
Rev. leg: AMERICA MORELOS, lion.

KM#	Date	Good	VG	Fine	VF
221	1812	35.00	60.00	100.00	150.00
	1813	35.00	60.00	100.00	150.00

COPPER

221a	1812	27.50	42.50	70.00	100.00
	1813	20.00	35.00	60.00	85.00

Obv: Similar to KM#220.
Rev: Similar to KM#221 but w/1/2 at left of lion.

A222	1813	27.50	42.50	70.00	100.00

REAL

COPPER

222	1811	5.00	10.00	20.00	40.00
	1812	4.00	8.00	15.00	30.00
	1813	4.00	8.00	15.00	30.00

STRUCK SILVER

222a	1812	—	—	—	—
	1813	—	—	—	—

CAST SILVER

223	1812	—	—	—	—
	1813	40.00	75.00	125.00	175.00

NOTE: Most silver specimens available on today's market are considered spurious.

COPPER
Obv: Bow, arrow/SUD.
Rev. leg: AMERICA MORELOS, lion.

KM#	Date	Good	VG	Fine	VF
224	1813	27.50	42.50	75.00	110.00

SILVER

225	1813	—	—	Rare	—

2 REALES

COPPER

226.1	1811	12.50	25.00	50.00	100.00
	1812	2.50	3.75	5.00	10.00
	1813	2.50	3.75	5.00	10.00

Obv: 3 large stars added.

226.2	1814	10.00	20.00	40.00	60.00

Obv. leg: SUD-OXA, bow, arrow.
Rev: Morelos monogram, value, date.

227	1813	60.00	100.00	200.00	300.00
	1814	60.00	100.00	200.00	300.00

Obv. leg: SUD. OAXACA

228	1814	60.00	100.00	200.00	325.00

CAST SILVER

229	1812	60.00	100.00	150.00	225.00
	1812 filled D in SUD				
		60.00	100.00	150.00	225.00

NOTE: Most silver specimens available on today's market are considered spurious.

4 REALES

NOTE: All known examples are modern fabrications.

Obv: Lines below bow slant right.

KM#	Date	Good	VG	Fine	VF
233.4	1813	10.00	17.50	30.00	50.00

CAST SILVER

KM#	Date	Good	VG	Fine	VF
230	1811	—	—	—	—
	1812	—	—	—	—

Obv. leg: SUD-OXA, bow, arrow.
Rev: Morelos monogram.

231	1813	125.00	250.00	400.00	800.00

COPPER
Obv. leg: SUD-OXA, bow, arrow.
Rev: Morelos monogram.

232	1814	100.00	150.00	200.00	400.00

8 REALES

Ornate flowery fields

234	1811	75.00	125.00	150.00	225.00
	1812	4.00	5.00	7.50	15.00
	1813	4.00	5.00	7.50	15.00
	1814	10.00	15.00	25.00	50.00

COPPER
Plain fields

KM#	Date	Good	VG	Fine	VF
233.1	1812	15.00	30.00	60.00	90.00

233.2	1812	6.00	8.00	12.00	15.00
	1813	6.00	8.00	12.00	15.00
	1814	10.00	12.00	15.00	20.00

Similar to KM#233.4 but lines below bow slant left.

233.3	1813	10.00	17.50	30.00	50.00

CAST SILVER

235	1811	—	—	—	—
	1812	100.00	200.00	300.00	400.00
	1813	75.00	150.00	250.00	350.00
	1814	—	—	—	—

NOTE: Most silver specimens available on today's market are considered spurious.

.903 SILVER, struck
Obv: PROV. D. OAXACA, M monogram.
Rev: Lion shield w/or w/o bow above.

KM#	Date	Good	VG	Fine	VF
236	1812	—	—	Rare	—

Obv: W/o leg.

237	1813	—	—	Rare	—

Obv: Bow/M/SUD..
Rev: PROV. DE, ..., arms.

238	1813	—	—	Rare	—

CAST SILVER
Similar to 4 Reales, KM#231.

239	1814	—	—	Rare	—

COPPER

240	1814	30.00	60.00	125.00	200.00

OAXACA spelled out

241	1814	—	—	Rare	—

Huautla
8 REALES

COPPER
Obv. leg: MONEDA PROVI.CIONAL PS.ES.
around bow, arrow/SUD.
Rev. leg: FABRICADO EN HUAUTLA

242	1812	500.00	800.00	1200.	1750.

Tierra Caliente
(Hot Country)
Under General Morelos
1/2 REAL

COPPER
Obv: Bow, T.C., SUD.
Rev: Morelos monogram, value, date.

KM#	Date	Good	VG	Fine	VF
243	1813	40.00	70.00	125.00	200.00

REAL

COPPER
Similar to 1/2 Real, KM#243.

244	1813	15.00	30.00	50.00	80.00

2 REALES

COPPER
Similar to 1/2 Real, KM#243.

245	1813	10.00	25.00	35.00	50.00

246	1814		25.00	50.00	100.00	175.00

CAST SILVER

247	1814	—	—	Rare	—

8 REALES

COPPER

248	1813	10.00	20.00	40.00	75.00

CAST SILVER

249	1813	—	—	—	—

NOTE: Most specimens available on todays market are considered spurious.

PUEBLA

The coins of Puebla emanated from Zacatlan, the headquarters of the hit-and-run insurgent leader Osorno. The mint opened in April of 1812 and operated until the end of 1813. The coins were 2 reales in silver and 1 and 1/2 reales in copper.

Zacatlan
(Struck by General Osorno)
1/2 REAL

COPPER
Obv: Osorno monogram, ZACATLAN, date.
Rev: Crossed arrows, wreath, value.

KM#	Date	Good	VG	Fine	VF
250	1813	—	—	Rare	—

REAL

COPPER

251	1813	100.00	150.00	250.00	450.00

2 REALES
COPPER

252	1813	125.00	200.00	325.00	550.00

VERACRUZ

Veracruz was the province that housed the town of Zongolica. In this town 2 priests and a lawyer decided to raise an army to fight for independence. Because of their isolation from other insurgent forces they decided to make coins for their area. Records show that they planned to or did mint coins of 1/2, 1, 2, 4, and 8 reales denominations. Extant specimens are known for only the three higher values.

Zongolica
2 REALES

.903 SILVER
Obv. leg: VIVA FERNANDO VII Y AMERICA,
bow and arrow.
Rev. leg: ZONGOLICA, value, crossed palm branch,
sword, date.

253	1812	100.00	200.00	300.00	600.00

4 REALES
.903 SILVER
Similar to 2 Reales, KM#253.

254	1812	600.00	800.00	1200.	2000.

8 REALES

.903 SILVER

KM#	Date	Good	VG	Fine	VF
255	1812	1200.	1600.	3000.	6000.

COUNTERMARKED COINAGE
Congress Of Chilpanzingo

Type A: Hand holding bow and arrow between quiver
w/arrows, sword and bow.

Type B: Crowned eagle on bridge.

1/2 REAL
SILVER
c/m: Type A on cast Mexico City KM#72.

256.1	ND(1812)	45.00	70.00	90.00	120.00

c/m: Type A on Zacatecas KM#181.

256.2	ND(1811)	55.00	75.00	100.00	125.00

REAL
SILVER
c/m: Type A on cast Mexico City KM#81.

A257	ND(1803)	20.00	30.00	50.00	80.00

2 REALES

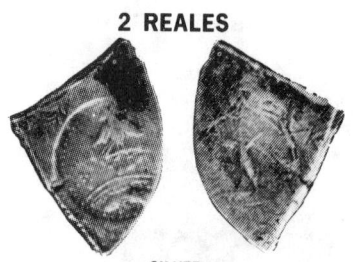

SILVER
c/m: Type B on 1/4 cut of 8 Reales.

KM#	Date	Good	VG	Fine	VF
257.1	ND	—	—	Unique	—

c/m: Type B on Zacatecas KM#186.

257.2	ND(1811)	—	—	Unique	—

8 REALES

SILVER
c/m: Type A on cast Mexico City KM#109.

258.1	ND(1805) TH	45.00	65.00	85.00	125.00

c/m: Type A on cast Mexico City KM#110.

258.2	ND(1810) HJ	50.00	75.00	100.00	150.00

c/m: Type A on cast Mexico City KM#111.

258.3	ND(1811) HJ	45.00	65.00	85.00	125.00
	ND(1812) HJ	100.00	125.00	175.00	275.00

c/m: Type B on Chihuahua KM#111.1.

259.1	ND(1816) RP	200.00	250.00	300.00	350.00

c/m: Type B on cast Mexico City KM#111.

259.2	ND(1811) HJ	130.00	140.00	150.00	175.00

c/m: Type B on Valladolid KM#178.

KM#	Date	Good	VG	Fine	VF
259.3	ND(1813)	1000.	2000.	3000.	5000.

c/m: Type B on Zacatecas KM#190.

259.4	ND(1810)	400.00	500.00	600.00	750.00

Ensaie
8 REALES

SILVER
c/m: Eagle over ENSAIE on Mexico City KM#110.

260.1	ND(1811) HJ	150.00	200.00	275.00	350.00

c/m: Eagle over ENSAIE crude sling below
on Zacatecas KM#189.

260.2	ND(1811)	200.00	400.00	600.00	800.00

c/m: Eagle over ENSAIE, crude sling below
on Zacatecas KM#190.

260.3	ND(1810)	—	—	—	—
	ND(1811)	100.00	150.00	200.00	300.00

c/m: Eagle over ENSAIE, crude sling below
on Zacatecas KM#191.

260.4	ND(1810)	500.00	700.00	900.00	1200.
	ND(1811)	275.00	325.00	400.00	500.00
	ND(1812)	225.00	275.00	300.00	400.00

Jose Maria Liceaga

J.M.L. with banner on cross, crossed olive branches.
(J.M.L./V., D.s, S.M.,S.Y.S.L., Ve, A.P.,
s.r.a., Sea, P.G.,S.,S.M.,E.)

1/2 REAL

SILVER
c/m: JML/SM on cast Mexico City 1/2 Real.

KM#	Date	Good	VG	Fine	VF
A260	ND	100.00	150.00	200.00	275.00

2 REALES

SILVER
c/m: J.M.L./Ve on 1/4 cut of 8 Reales.

| 261.1 | ND | 175.00 | 225.00 | 300.00 | — |

c/m: J.M.L./V. on Zacatecas KM#186-187.
| 261.2 | ND(1811) | 200.00 | 225.00 | 250.00 | 300.00 |

c/m: J.M.L./DS on Zacatecas KM#186-187.
| 261.3 | ND(1811) | 200.00 | 235.00 | 275.00 | 325.00 |

c/m: J.M.L./S.M. on Zacatecas KM#186-187.
| 261.4 | ND(1811) | 200.00 | 235.00 | 275.00 | 325.00 |

c/m: J.M.L./S.Y. on Zacatecas KM#186-187.
| 261.5 | ND(1811) | 200.00 | 235.00 | 275.00 | 325.00 |

8 REALES

SILVER
c/m: J.M.L./D.S. on Zacatecas KM#189-190.
| 262.1 | ND(1811) | 250.00 | 325.00 | 425.00 | 550.00 |

c/m: J.M.L./E on Zacatecas KM#189-190.
KM#	Date	Good	VG	Fine	VF
262.2	ND(1811)	225.00	300.00	400.00	550.00

c/m: J.M.L./P.G. on Durango KM#111.2.
| 262.3 | ND(1813) RM | 200.00 | 275.00 | 375.00 | 525.00 |

c/m: J.M.L./S.F. on Zacatecas KM#189-190.
| 262.4 | ND(1811) | 200.00 | 275.00 | 375.00 | 525.00 |

c/m: J.M.L./S.M. on Zacatecas KM#189-190.
| 262.5 | ND(1811) | 200.00 | 275.00 | 375.00 | 525.00 |

c/m: J.M.L./V.E. on Zacatecas KM#189-190.
| 262.6 | ND(1811) | 200.00 | 275.00 | 375.00 | 525.00 |

Don Jose Maria De Linares

8 REALES

SILVER
c/m: LINA/RES* on Mexico City KM#110.

KM#	Date	Good	VG	Fine	VF
263.1	ND(1808) TH	300.00	350.00	425.00	525.00

c/m: LINA/RES * on Zacatecas KM#189-190.

263.2	ND(1811)	350.00	425.00	500.00	600.00

c/m: LINA/RES* on Zacatecas, KM#191-192.

263.3	ND(1812)	300.00	350.00	425.00	525.00

L.V.S. - Labor Vincit Semper

NOTE: Some authorities believe L.V.S. is for 'La Villa de Sombrerete'.

8 REALES

CAST SILVER
c/m: L.V.S. on Chihuahua KM#123.

264.1	ND(1811) RP	275.00	350.00	450.00	550.00
	ND(1812) RP	200.00	250.00	300.00	375.00

c/m: L.V.S. on Chihuahua KM#111.1 overstruck on KM#123.

KM#	Date	Good	VG	Fine	VF
264.2	ND(1816) RP	250.00	300.00	325.00	375.00
	ND(1817) RP	250.00	300.00	325.00	375.00
	ND(1818) RP	250.00	300.00	325.00	375.00
	ND(1819) RP	400.00	450.00	500.00	600.00
	ND(1820) RP	450.00	500.00	550.00	650.00

c/m: L.V.S. on Guadalajara KM#111.3.

264.3	ND(1817)	185.00	220.00	250.00	310.00

c/m: L.V.S. on Nueva Vizcaya KM#165.

264.4	ND(1811) RM	1150.	3150.	5250.	8250.

c/m: L.V.S. on Sombrerete KM#177.

264.5	ND(1811)	300.00	350.00	450.00	550.00
	ND(1812)	300.00	350.00	450.00	550.00

c/m: L.V.S. on Zacatecas KM#189-190.

264.6	ND(1811)	350.00	400.00	450.00	550.00

c/m: L.V.S. on Zacatecas KM#192.

264.7	ND(1813)	350.00	400.00	450.00	550.00

Morelos
Morelos monogram

Type A: Stars above and below monogram in circle.

Type B: Dots above and below monogram in oval.

Type C: Monogram in rectangle.
NOTE: Many specimens of Type C available in today's market are considered spurious.

2 REALES

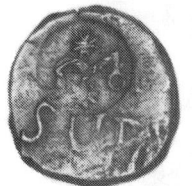

COPPER
c/m: Type A on Oaxaca Sud, KM#226.1.

KM#	Date	Good	VG	Fine	VF
A265	1812	—	—	—	—

8 REALES

SILVER
c/m: Type A on cast Mexico City KM#109.

265.1	ND(1797) FM	45.00	50.00	55.00	75.00
	ND(1798) FM	45.00	50.00	55.00	75.00
	ND(1800) FM	45.00	50.00	55.00	75.00
	ND(1807) TH	45.00	50.00	55.00	75.00

c/m: Type A on Mexico City KM#110.

265.2	ND(1809) TH	55.00	65.00	75.00	100.00
	ND(1811) HJ	55.00	65.00	75.00	100.00

c/m: Type A on Mexico City KM#111.

265.3	ND(1812) JJ	50.00	55.00	60.00	70.00

COPPER
c/m: Type A on Oaxaca Sud KM#233.

265.4	ND(1811)	12.50	17.50	25.00	35.00
	ND(1812)	12.50	17.50	25.00	35.00
	ND(1813)	12.50	17.50	25.00	35.00
	ND(1814)	12.50	17.50	25.00	35.00

CAST SILVER
c/m: Type A on Supreme National Congress KM#206.

KM#	Date	Good	VG	Fine	VF
265.5	ND(1811)	200.00	250.00	300.00	450.00

SILVER
c/m: Type A on Zacatecas KM#189-190.

265.6	ND(1811)	200.00	250.00	350.00	450.00

c/m: Type A on Zacatecas KM#191.

265.7	ND(1811)	200.00	250.00	350.00	450.00

c/m: Type B on Guatemala 8 Reales, C#67.

266.1	ND(1810) M	—	—	Rare	—

c/m: Type B on Mexico City KM#110.

266.2	ND(1809) TH	45.00	55.00	65.00	90.00

c/m: Type C on Zacatecas KM#189-190.

267	ND(1811)	300.00	350.00	400.00	500.00

Norte

Issued by the Supreme National Congress and the Army
of the North.

c/m: Eagle on cactus; star to left; NORTE below.

1/2 REAL

SILVER
c/m: On Zacatecas KM#180.

268	ND(1811)	250.00	300.00	375.00	450.00

2 REALES

SILVER
c/m: On Zacatecas KM#187.

KM#	Date	Good	VG	Fine	VF
269	ND(1811)	225.00	275.00	325.00	400.00

c/m: On Zacatecas KM#188.

A269	ND(1812)	—	—	—	—

4 REALES

SILVER
c/m: On Sombrerete KM#175.

B269	ND(1812)	100.00	150.00	200.00	275.00

8 REALES

SILVER
c/m: On Chihuahua KM#111.1.

270.1	ND(1813) RP	250.00	350.00	450.00	550.00

c/m: On Guanajuato KM#111.4.

270.2	ND(1813) JM	400.00	550.00	700.00	800.00

c/m: On Zacatecas KM#189-190.

270.3	ND(1811)	300.00	400.00	500.00	650.00

c/m: On Zacatecas KM#191.

KM#	Date	Good	VG	Fine	VF
270.4	ND(1811)	200.00	300.00	400.00	550.00
	ND(1812)	200.00	300.00	400.00	550.00

Osorno

c/m: Osorno monogram.
(Jose Francisco Osorno)

1/2 REAL

SILVER
c/m: On Mexico City KM#72.

KM#	Date	Good	VG	Fine	VF
271.1	ND(1798) FM	65.00	100.00	150.00	200.00
	ND(1802) FT	65.00	100.00	150.00	200.00
	ND(1806)	65.00	100.00	150.00	200.00

c/m: On Mexico City KM#73.

271.2	ND(1809)	65.00	100.00	150.00	200.00

REAL

SILVER
c/m: On Mexico City KM#81.

272.1	ND(1803) FT	65.00	100.00	150.00	200.00
	ND(1803) FT	65.00	100.00	150.00	200.00

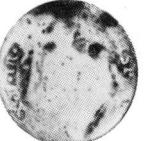

c/m: On Potosi Real.

272.2	ND	65.00	100.00	150.00	200.00

2 REALES

SILVER
c/m: On cast Mexico City KM#92.

A272.1	ND(1809) TH	75.00	125.00	175.00	250.00

c/m: On Zacatlan KM#252.

A272.2	ND(1813)	150.00	200.00	300.00	400.00

4 REALES

SILVER
c/m: On Mexico City KM#97.

KM#	Date	Good	VG	Fine	VF
273	ND(1782) FF	—	—	—	—

8 REALES

SILVER
c/m: On Lima 8 Reales, C#101.

274.1	ND(1811) JP	200.00	225.00	250.00	300.00

c/m: On Mexico City KM#110.

274.2	ND(1809) TH	125.00	150.00	225.00	300.00
	ND(1810) HJ	125.00	150.00	225.00	300.00
	ND(1811) HJ	125.00	150.00	225.00	300.00

S.J.N.G. - Suprema Junta National Gubernativa

(Refer to Multiple countermarks)

VILLA/GRAN

(Julian Villagran)

2 REALES

SILVER

c/m: On cast Mexico City KM#91.

KM#	Date	Good	VG	Fine	VF
298	ND(1799) FM	150.00	200.00	250.00	350.00
	ND(1802) FT	150.00	200.00	250.00	350.00

8 REALES

SILVER
c/m: VILLA/GRAN on cast Mexico City KM#109.

275	ND(1796) FM	200.00	250.00	300.00	350.00
	ND(1806) TH	200.00	250.00	300.00	350.00

UNCLASSIFIED COUNTERMARKS

General Vicente Guerrero

The countermark of an eagle facing left within a pearled oval has been attributed by some authors as that of General Vicente Guerrero, a leader of the insurgents in the south, 1816-1821.

1/2 REAL

SILVER
c/m: Eagle on Mexico City 1/2 Real.

276	ND	40.00	60.00	80.00	175.00

REAL

SILVER
c/m: Eagle on Mexico City KM#78.

277	ND(1772) FM	35.00	50.00	75.00	150.00

2 REALES

SILVER
c/m: Eagle on Mexico City KM#88.

278.1	ND(1784) FM	50.00	75.00	125.00	250.00

c/m: Eagle on Mexico City KM#91.

278.2	ND(1807) PJ	35.00	65.00	85.00	200.00

8 REALES

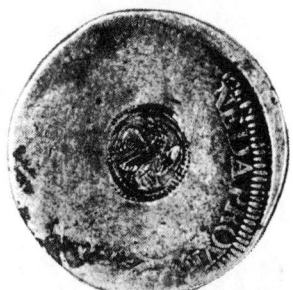

SILVER
c/m: Eagle on Zacatecas KM#191.

KM#	Date	Good	VG	Fine	VF
279	ND(1811)	100.00	150.00	200.00	350.00

ZMY
8 REALES

SILVER
c/m: ZMY on Zacatecas KM#191.

286	ND(1812)	100.00	150.00	210.00	275.00

MULTIPLE COUNTERMARKS

Many combinations of Royalist and Insurgent counter-marks are found usually on the cast copies produced by the Chihuahua and Mexico City Mints and also the crude provisional mint issues of this period. Struck Mexico Mint coins were used for molds to cast necessity coinage and were countermarked to show issuing authority. Some were marked again by opposing forces or by friendly forces to allow circulation in their area of occupation. Some countermarks are only obtainable with companion markings.

Chilpanzingo
Crown and Flag
8 REALES

SILVER
c/m: Chilpanzingo Type B and
crown and flag on Zacatecas KM#189-190.

280	ND(1811)	—	—	—	—

Chilpanzingo/LVA
8 REALES

SILVER
c/m: Chilpanzingo Type A and LVA on Mexico City
KM#109.

KM#	Date	Good	VG	Fine	VF
297	ND(1805) TH	—	—	—	—

Chilpanzingo/LVS
8 REALES

SILVER
c/m: Chilpanzingo Type A and
script LVS on cast Mexico City KM#110.

281	ND(1809) HJ	50.00	75.00	150.00	250.00

Chilpanzingo/Morelos
8 REALES

SILVER
c/m: Chilpanzingo Type A and Morelos
monogram Type A on cast Mexico City KM#109.

KM#	Date	Good	VG	Fine	VF
284	ND(1806) TH	35.00	45.00	55.00	150.00
	ND(1807) TH	—	—	—	—

c/m: Chilpanzingo Type A and Morelos monogram
Type A on struck Mexico City KM#110.

285.1	ND(1809) TH	35.00	50.00	100.00	250.00

c/m: Chilpanzingo Type A and Morelos monogram
Type A on cast Mexico City KM#110.

285.2	ND(1810) HJ	35.00	45.00	55.00	150.00
	ND(1811) HJ	—	—	—	—

c/m: Chilpanzingo Type A and Morelos monogram
Type A on cast Mexico City KM#111.

285.3	ND(1811) HJ	—	—	—	—

Chilpanzingo/Morelos/LVS
8 REALES

SILVER
c/m: Chilpanzingo Type A, Morelos Type A and
LVS monogram on cast Mexico City KM#110.

286	ND(1809) HJ	35.00	50.00	75.00	200.00

Chilpanzingo/P.D.V.
8 REALES

SILVER
c/m: Chilpanzingo Type B and P.D.V. (Provisional
De Valladolid) on Valladolid KM#178.

KM#	Date	Good	VG	Fine	VF
287	ND(1813)	—	—	—	—

Chilpanzingo/S.J.N.G.
8 REALES

SILVER
c/m: Chilpanzingo Type B and S.J.N.G. (Suprema
Junta Nacional Gubernativa) on Zacatecas KM#189-190.

288	ND(1811)	—	—	—	—

C.M.S./S.C.M.
2 REALES

SILVER
c/m: C.M.S. (Comandancia Militar Suriana) and eagle
w/S.C.M. (Soberano Congreso Mexicano) on
Mexico City 2 Reales.

289	ND	—	—	—	—

ENSAIE/J.M.L.
8 REALES

SILVER
c/m: ENSAIE and J.M.L. on Zacatecas, KM#190.

KM#	Date	Good	VG	Fine	VF
A290	ND(1811)	—		—	—

8 REALES

SILVER
c/m: J.M.L./D.S. and VTIL on Mexico City KM#110.

KM#	Date	Good	VG	Fine	VF
291	ND(1810) HJ	—	—	—	—

ENSAIE/VTIL
8 REALES

SILVER
c/m: ENSAIE and VTIL on Zacatecas KM#189-190.

290	ND(1811)	—	—	—	—

L.C.M./Morelos
8 REALES

SILVER
c/m: LCM and Morelos monogram
Type A on cast Mexico City KM#109.

282	ND(1792) FM	—	—	—	—

J.M.L./VTIL
2 REALES

SILVER
c/m: J.M.L./D.S. and VTIL on Zacatecas, KM#186.

A286	ND(1811)	75.00	125.00	175.00	250.00

c/m: J.M.L./V.E. and VTIL on Zacatecas KM#186.

B286	ND(1810)	75.00	125.00	175.00	250.00
	ND(1811)	75.00	125.00	175.00	250.00

Morelos/Morelos
8 REALES

SILVER
c/m: Morelos Type A and C on cast Mexico City KM#109.

283	ND(1806) TH	—	—	—	—

LCM/MVA-1812
8 REALES

SILVER
c/m: LCM and MVA/1812 on Chihuahua KM#123.

KM#	Date	Good	VG	Fine	VF
292	1812(1810) RP	—	—	—	—

c/m: LCM and MVA 1812 on Chihuahua KM#110.
A293   1812(1810) HJ   —   —   —   —

c/m: LCM and MVA/1812 on Chihuahua KM#111.1.
293   1812(1818)   200.00 300.00 450.00 700.00

L.V.A./Morelos
8 REALES

SILVER
c/m: Script LVA and Morelos monogram Type A
on cast Mexico City KM#110.

294   ND(-) HJ   —   —   —   —

M.d.S./S.C.M.
2 REALES

SILVER
c/m: M.d.S. (Militar del Sur) and eagle w/S.C.M.
(Soberano Congreso Mexicano) on Mexico City 2 Reales.

KM#	Date	Good	VG	Fine	VF
295	ND	—	—	—	—

OSORNO/VILLAGRAN
8 REALES

SILVER
c/m: Osorno monogram and VILLA/GRAN on cast
Mexico City KM#110.

296   ND(1809) TH   —   —   —   —

S.J.N.G./VTIL
8 REALES

SILVER
c/m: S.J.N.G. and VTIL on Zacatecas KM#191.

297   ND   35.00   50.00   75.00   200.00

EMPIRE OF ITURBIDE
RULERS
Augustin I Iturbide, 1822-1823

MINT MARKS
Mo - Mexico City Mint

ASSAYERS INITIALS
JA - Jose Garcia Ansaldo, 1812-1833
JM - Joaquin Davila Madrid,
   1809-1833

1/8 REAL

COPPER
Mint: Nueva Viscaya

KM#	Date	Mintage	Good	VG	Fine	VF
299	1821	—	25.00	50.00	85.00	150.00
	1822	—	7.50	12.50	25.00	45.00
	1823	—	7.50	12.50	25.00	45.00

1/4 REAL

COPPER
Mint: Nueva Viscaya

300	1822	—	175.00	275.00	425.00	500.00

1/2 REAL

.903 SILVER
Mint mark: Mo

KM#	Date	Mintage	Fine	VF	XF	Unc
301	1822 JM	—	17.50	30.00	60.00	310.00
	1823 JM	—	12.50	25.00	50.00	285.00

REAL

.903 SILVER
Mint mark: Mo

302	1822 JM	—	50.00	110.00	225.00	750.00

2 REALES

.903 SILVER
Mint mark: Mo

303	1822 JM	—	25.00	55.00	225.00	800.00
	1823 JM	—	20.00	45.00	175.00	750.00

8 REALES

.903 SILVER
Mint mark: Mo

KM#	Date	Mintage	Fine	VF	XF	Unc
304	1822 JM	—	45.00	95.00	225.00	825.00

Obv: Bust similar to 8 Escudos, KM#313.
Rev: Similar to KM#304.

305	1822 JM	—	—	—	Rare	—

Type I. Obv: Leg. divided. Rev: 8 R.J.M. at upper left of eagle.

306.1	1822 JM	—	60.00	145.00	325.00	1150.

Rev: Cross on crown.

306.2	1822 JM	—	—	—	Rare	—

Type II. Obv: Similar to KM#306.
Rev: Similar to KM#310.

307	1822 JM	—	135.00	325.00	550.00	2150.

Type III. Obv: Continuous leg. w/long smooth truncation. Rev: Similar to KM#306.

308	1822 JM	—	175.00	500.00	950.00	1400.

NOTE: Variety with long, straight truncation is valued at $5,000. in uncirculated condition.

8 SCUDOS

Type IV. Obv: Similar to KM#308.
Rev: Similar to KM#310.

KM#	Date	Mintage	Fine	VF	XF	Unc
309	1822 JM	—	50.00	125.00	225.00	800.00

.875 GOLD
Mint mark: Mo
Obv. leg: AUGUSTINUS.

KM#	Date	Mintage	Fine	VF	XF	Unc
313.1	1822 JM	—	1200.	2000.	3500.	—

NOTE: Superior Casterline sale 5-89 choice AU realized $11,000.

Obv. leg: AUGSTINUS (error).

313.2	1822 JM	—	1250.	2250.	4000.	—

Type V. Obv: continuous leg. w/short
irregular truncation. Rev: 8 R.J.M. below eagle.

310	1822 JM	—	50.00	125.00	200.00	725.00
	1823 JM	—	50.00	125.00	200.00	725.00

Type VI. Obv: Bust w/long truncation.
Rev: Similar to KM#310.

311	1822 JM	—	—	—	Rare	

4 SCUDOS

.875 GOLD
Mint mark: Mo

312	1823 JM	—	1000.	1750.	2500.	4500.
314	1823 JM	—	1000.	1800.	3000.	5000.

REPUBLIC

MINT MARKS

A, AS - Alamos
CE - Real de Catorce
CA,CH - Chihuahua
C, Cn, Gn(error) - Culiacan
D, Do - Durango
EoMo - Estado de Mexico
Ga - Guadalajara
GC - Guadalupe y Calvo
G, Go - Guanajuato
H, Ho - Hermosillo
M, Mo - Mexico City
O, OA - Oaxaca
SLP, PI, P, I/P - San Luis Potosi
Z, Zs - Zacatecas

ASSAYERS INITIALS

ALAMOS MINT

Initials	Years	Mintmaster
PG	1862-1868	Pascual Gaxiola
DL, L	1866-1879	Domingo Larraguibel
AM	1872-1874	Antonio Moreno
ML, L	1878-1895	Manuel Larraguibel

REAL DE CATORCE MINT

Initials	Years	Mintmaster
ML	1863	Mariano Leon

CHIHUAHUA MINT

MR	1831-1834	Mariano Cristobal Ramirez
AM	1833-1839	Jose Antonio Mucharraz
MJ	1832	Jose Mariano Jimenez
RG	1839-1856	Rodrigo Garcia
JC	1856-1865	Joaquin Campa
BA	1858	Bruno Arriada
FP	1866	Francisco Potts
JG	1866-1868	Jose Maria Gomez del Campo
MM, M	1868-1895	Manuel Merino
AV	1873-1880	Antonio Valero
EA	1877	Eduardo Avila
JM	1877	Jacobo Mucharraz
GR	1877	Guadalupe Rocha
MG	1880-1882	Manuel Gameros

CULIACAN MINT

CE	1846-1870	Clemente Espinosa de los Monteros
C	1870	???
PV	1860-1861	Pablo Viruega
MP, P	1871-1876	Manuel Onofre Parodi
GP	1876	Celso Gaxiola & Manuel Onofre Parodi
CG, G	1876-1878	Celso Gaxiola
JD, D	1878-1882	Juan Dominguez
AM, M	1882-1899	Antonio Moreno
F	1870	Fernando Ferrari
JQ, Q	1899-1903	Jesus S. Quiroz
FV, V	1903	Francisco Valdez
MH, H	1904	Merced Hernandez
RP, P	1904-1905	Ramon Ponce de Leon

DURANGO MINT

RL	1825-1832	???
RM	1830-1848	Ramon Mascarenas
OMC	1840	Octavio Martinez de Castro
CM	1848-1876	Clemente Moron
JMR	1849-1852	Jose Maria Ramirez
CP, P	1853-1864 1867-1873	Carlos Leon de la Pena
LT	1864-1865	???
JMP, P	1877	Carlos Miguel de la Palma
PE, E	1878	Pedro Espejo
TB, B	1878-1880	Trinidad Barrera
JP	1880-1894	J. Miguel Palma
MC, C	1882-1890	Manuel M. Canseco or Melchor Calderon

Initials	Years	Mintmaster
JB	1885	Jacobo Blanco
ND, D	1892-1895	Norberto Dominguez

ESTADO DE MEXICO MINT

L	1828-1830	Luis Valazquez de la Cadena
F	1828-1830	Francisco Parodi

GUADALAJARA MINT

FS	1818-1835	Francisco Suarez
JM	1830-1832	???
JG	1836-1839 1842-1867	Juan de Dios Guzman
MC	1839-1846	Manuel Cueras
JM	1867-1869	Jesus P. Manzano
IC, C	1869-1877	Ignacio Canizo y Soto
MC	1874-1875	Manuel Contreras
JA, A	1877-1881	Julio Arancivia
FS, S	1880-1882	Fernando Sayago
TB, B	1883-1884	Trinidad Barrera
AH, H	1884-1885	Antonio Hernandez y Prado
JS, S	1885-1895	Jose S. Schiafino

GUADALUPE Y CALVO MINT

MP	1844-1852	Manuel Onofre Parodi

GUANAJUATO MINT

JJ	1825-1826	Jose Mariano Jimenez
MJ, MR, JM, PG, PJ, PF	???	
PM	1841-1848, 1853-1861	Patrick Murphy
YF	1862-1868	Yldefonso Flores
YE	1862-1863	Ynocencio Espinoza
FR	1870-1878	Faustino Ramirez
SB, RR	???	
RS	1891-1900	Rosendo Sandoval

HERMOSILLO MINT

PP	1835-1836	Pedro Peimbert
FM	1871-1876	Florencio Monteverde
MP	1866	Manuel Onofre Parodi
PR	1866-1875	Pablo Rubio
R	1874-1875	Pablo Rubio
GR	1877	Guadalupe Rocha
AF, F	1876-1877	Alejandro Fourcade
JA, A	1877-1883	Jesus Acosta
FM, M	1883-1886	Fernando Mendez
FG, G	1886-1895	Fausto Gaxiola

MEXICO CITY MINT

Because of the great number of assayers for this mint (Mexico City is a much larger mint than any of the others) there is much confusion as to which initial stands for which assayer at any one time. Therefore we feel that it would be of no value to list the assayers.

OAXACA MINT

AE	1859-1891	Agustin Endner
E	1889-1890	Agustin Endner
FR	1861-1864	Francisco de la Rosa
EN	1890	Eduardo Navarro Luna
N	1890	Eduardo Navarro Luna

POTOSI MINT

JS	1827-1842	Juan Sanabria
AM	1838 1843-1849	Jose Antonio Mucharraz
PS	1842-1843 1848-1849,1857-1861,1867-1870	Pomposo Sanabria
S	1869-1870	Pomposo Sanabria
MC	1849-1859	Mariano Catano
RO	1859-1865	Romualdo Obregon
MH, H	1870-1885	Manuel Herrera Razo
O	1870-1873	Juan R. Ochoa
CA, G	1867-1870	Carlos Aguirre Gomez
BE, E	1879-1881	Blas Escontria
LC, C	1885-1886	Luis Cuevas
MR, R	1886-1893	Mariano Reyes

ZACATECAS MINT

A	1825-1829	Adalco
Z	1825-1828	Mariano Zaldivar
V	1824-1831	Jose Mariano Vela
O	1829-1867	Manuel Ochoa
M	1831-1867	Manuel Miner

Initials	Years	Mintmaster
VL	1860-1866	Vicente Larranaga
JS	1867-1868	J.S. de Santa Ana
	1876-1886	
YH	1868-1874	Ygnacio Hierro
JA	1874-1876	Juan H. Acuna
FZ	1886-1905	Francisco de P. Zarate
FM	1904-1905	Francisco Mateos

State and Federal Issues
1/16 REAL
(Medio Octavo)

COPPER
Mint: Jalisco
Obv. leg: DEPARTAMENTO DE JALISCO

KM#	Date	Mintage	Good	VG	Fine	VF
316	1860	—	3.00	5.00	10.00	50.00

Obv. leg: ESTADO LIBRE DE JALISCO

317	1861	—	3.00	5.00	10.00	50.00

Mint: Mexico City
Obv. leg: REPUBLICA MEXICANA

KM#	Date	Mintage	VG	Fine	VF	XF
315	1831	—	10.00	15.00	35.00	100.00
	1832/1	—	12.00	17.50	35.00	125.00
	1832	—	10.00	15.00	35.00	100.00
	1833	—	10.00	15.00	35.00	100.00

BRASS

315a	1832	—	15.00	22.50	60.00	150.00
	1833	—	12.00	17.50	50.00	100.00
	1835	— 400.00	800.00	1250.	2300.	

1/8 REAL
(Octavo Real)

COPPER
Mint: Chihuahua
Obv. leg: ESTADO SOBERANO DE CHIHUAHUA

KM#	Date	Mintage	Good	VG	Fine	VF
318	1833	—	—	—	Rare	—
	1834	—	—	—	Rare	—
	1835/3	—	—	—	Rare	—

Obv. leg: ESTADO DE CHIHUAHUA

319	1855	—	3.50	5.00	18.00	60.00

Mint: Durango
Rev. leg: LIBERTAD

320	1824	—	5.00	10.00	35.00	100.00
	1828	— 150.00	250.00	400.00	900.00	

NOTE: These pieces were frequently struck over 1/8

Real, dated 1821-23 of Nueva Vizcaya. All known examples are collectable contemporary counterfeits.

Rev. leg: OCTo.DE.R.DE DO., date.

KM#	Date	Mintage	Good	VG	Fine	VF
321	1828	—	6.00	15.00	35.00	100.00

Obv. leg: ESTADO DE DURANGO

322	1833	—	—	—	Rare	—

Obv. leg: REPUBLICA MEXICANA

323	1842/33	—	15.00	20.00	40.00	125.00
	1842	—	10.00	15.00	30.00	100.00

Obv. leg: REPUBLICA MEXICANA
Rev. leg: DEPARTAMENTO DE DURANGO

324	1845	—	25.00	50.00	100.00	250.00
	1846	—	—	—	Rare	—
	1847	—	3.00	5.00	8.00	35.00

Obv. leg: REPUBLICA MEXICANA
Rev. leg: ESTADO DE DURANGO

325	1851	—	3.00	5.00	8.00	30.00
	1852/1	—	3.00	5.00	8.00	30.00
	1852	—	3.00	5.00	8.00	30.00
	1854	—	6.00	10.00	17.50	65.00

Mint: Guanajuato
Obv. leg: ESTADO LIBRE DE GUANAJUATO

326	1829	—	3.00	5.00	10.00	30.00
	1829 error w/GUANJUATO					
		—	3.00	5.00	10.00	30.00
	1830	—	8.00	12.00	20.00	75.00

BRASS

KM#	Date	Mintage	Good	VG	Fine	VF
327	1856	—	8.00	12.00	20.00	75.00

25mm

328	1856	—	4.00	6.00	10.00	30.00
	1857	—	4.00	6.00	10.00	30.00

COPPER

328a	1857	—	10.00	20.00	35.00	60.00

Mint: Jalisco
Obv. leg: ESTADO LIBRE DE JALISCO

329	1828	—	3.00	5.00	8.00	25.00
	1831	— 100.00	200.00	300.00	400.00	
	1832/28	—	3.00	5.00	8.00	25.00
	1832	—	3.00	5.00	8.00	25.00
	1833	—	3.00	5.00	8.00	25.00
	1834	— 50.00	100.00	175.00	300.00	

330	1856	—	4.00	7.00	10.00	25.00
	1857	—	4.00	7.00	10.00	25.00
	1858	—	4.00	7.00	10.00	25.00
	1861	— 100.00	200.00	300.00	400.00	
	1862/1	—	4.00	7.00	10.00	25.00
	1862	—	4.00	7.00	10.00	25.00

Obv. leg: DEPARTAMENTO DE JALISCO

KM#	Date	Mintage	Good	VG	Fine	VF
331	1858	—	3.00	5.00	8.00	20.00
	1859	—	3.00	5.00	8.00	20.00
	1860/59	—	3.00	5.00	8.00	20.00
	1860	—	3.00	5.00	8.00	20.00
	1862	—	6.00	10.00	20.00	60.00

Mint: Mexico City
27mm
Obv. leg: REPUBLICA MEXICANA

KM#	Date	Mintage	VG	Fine	VF	XF
332	1829	— 450.00	900.00	1500.	2500.	

21mm
Obv. leg: REPUBLICA MEXICANA

KM#	Date	Mintage	Good	VG	Fine	VF
333	1829	—	10.00	15.00	30.00	60.00
	1830	—	2.00	3.00	5.00	15.00
	1831	—	2.00	4.00	6.00	20.00
	1832	—	2.00	4.00	6.00	20.00
	1833/2	—	2.00	4.00	6.00	20.00
	1833	—	2.00	3.00	5.00	15.00
	1834	—	2.00	3.00	5.00	15.00
	1835/4	—	2.25	4.00	6.00	20.00
	1835	—	2.00	3.00	5.00	15.00

Obv. leg: LIBERTAD

334	1841	—	7.00	15.00	30.00	75.00
	1842	—	3.00	5.00	10.00	30.00
	1850	—	15.00	20.00	30.00	80.00
	1861	—	8.00	12.00	25.00	70.00

Mint: Occidente
Obv. leg: ESTADO DE OCCIDENTE

335	1828 reverse S					
		—	15.00	30.00	45.00	100.00
	1829	—	15.00	30.00	45.00	100.00

Mint: Potosi
Obv. leg: ESTADO LIBRE DE SAN LUIS POTOSI

336	1829	—	6.00	9.00	15.00	50.00
	1830	—	8.00	12.00	20.00	60.00
	1831	—	5.00	8.00	12.00	40.00
	1859	—	5.00	8.00	12.00	40.00

Mint: Sonora
Obv. leg: ESTO LIBE Y SOBO DE SONORA, 28mm.

KM#	Date	Mintage	Good	VG	Fine	VF
337	1859	—	—	Rare	—	—

Obv. leg: ESTADO LIBRE DE CHIHUAHUA

KM#	Date	Mintage	Good	VG	Fine	VF
341	1846	—	4.00	6.00	12.00	50.00

NOTE: Varieties with or without fraction bar.

Mint: Zacatecas
Obv. leg: ESTo LIBe FEDo DE ZACATECAS

KM#	Date	Mintage	Good	VG	Fine	VF
338	1825	—	3.00	5.00	10.00	25.00
	1827	—	3.00	5.00	10.00	25.00
	1827 inverted A for V in OCTAVO					
		—	12.00	20.00	40.00	100.00
	1829	—	—	—	Rare	—
	1830	—	3.00	5.00	8.00	20.00
	1831	—	4.00	6.00	10.00	25.00
	1832	—	3.00	5.00	8.00	20.00
	1833	—	3.00	5.00	8.00	20.00
	1835	—	4.00	6.00	10.00	25.00
	1846	—	4.00	6.00	10.00	25.00
	1851	—	125.00	175.00	250.00	350.00
	1852	—	4.00	6.00	10.00	25.00
	1858	—	3.00	5.00	8.00	20.00
	1859	—	3.00	5.00	8.00	20.00
	1862	—	3.00	5.00	8.00	20.00
	1863 reversed 6 in date					
		—	3.00	5.00	8.00	20.00

Obv. leg: ESTADO DE CHIHUAHUA

KM#	Date	Mintage	Good	VG	Fine	VF
342	1855	—	3.00	5.00	10.00	50.00
	1856	—	3.00	5.00	10.00	50.00

Obv. leg: DEPARTAMENTO DE CHIHUAHUA

KM#	Date	Mintage	Good	VG	Fine	VF
343	1855	—	3.00	5.00	10.00	50.00
	1855 DE/reversed D and E					
		—	3.00	5.00	10.00	50.00

Obv. leg: DEPARTAMENTO DE ZACATECAS

KM#	Date	Mintage	Good	VG	Fine	VF
339	1836	—	4.00	8.00	15.00	40.00
	1845	—	6.00	10.00	20.00	50.00
	1846	—	4.00	8.00	15.00	40.00

1/4 REAL
(Un Quarto/Una Quartilla)
(Copper/Brass Series)

Obv. leg: E. CHIHA LIBERTAD

KM#	Date	Mintage	Good	VG	Fine	VF
344	1860	—	2.00	4.00	8.00	25.00
	1861	—	2.00	4.00	8.00	25.00
	1865/1	—	2.50	5.50	10.00	30.00
	1865	—	10.00	20.00	35.00	95.00
	1866/5	—	10.00	20.00	35.00	95.00
	1866	—	2.00	4.00	8.00	25.00

COPPER
Mint: Chihuahua
Obv. leg: ESTADO SOBERANO DE CHIHUAHUA

KM#	Date	Mintage	Good	VG	Fine	VF
340	1833	—	8.00	12.00	35.00	75.00
	1834	—	5.00	8.00	12.00	50.00
	1835	—	5.00	8.00	12.00	50.00

Mint: Durango
Obv. leg: REPUBLICA MEXICANA

KM#	Date	Mintage	Good	VG	Fine	VF
345	1845	—	—	—	Rare	—

Obv. leg: REPUBLICA MEXICANA
Rev: DURANGO, date, value.

KM#	Date	Mintage	Good	VG	Fine	VF
346	1858	—	—	—	Rare	—

Obv. leg: ESTADO DE DURANGO
Rev. leg: CONSTITUCION

KM#	Date	Mintage	Good	VG	Fine	VF
347	1858	—	3.00	6.00	12.00	50.00

NOTE: Variety exists in brass.

Obv. leg: DEPARTAMENTO DE DURANGO
Rev. leg: LIBERTAD EN EL ORDEN.

348	1860	—	2.00	5.00	15.00	45.00
	1866	—	2.00	5.00	15.00	45.00

Obv. leg: ESTADO DE DURANGO
Rev. leg: INDEPENDENCIA Y LIBERTAD

349	1866	—	3.00	5.00	12.00	45.00

Rev. leg: SUFRAGIO LIBRE

350	1872	—	2.00	4.00	10.00	20.00

NOTE: Variety exists in brass.

 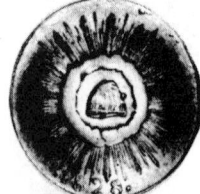

Mint: Guanajuato
Obv. leg: ESTADO LIBRE DE GUANAJUATO

351	1828	—	4.00	7.00	10.00	45.00
	1828 error w/GUANJUATO					
		—	4.00	7.00	10.00	45.00
	1829	—	4.00	7.00	10.00	45.00

Obv. leg: EST. LIB. DE GUANAXUATO
Rev. leg: OMNIA VINCIT LABOR

KM#	Date	Mintage	Good	VG	Fine	VF
352	1856	—	12.00	25.00	50.00	100.00
	1857	—	6.00	9.00	15.00	45.00
		BRASS				
352a	1856	—	4.00	7.00	10.00	30.00
	1857	—	4.00	7.00	10.00	30.00

COPPER
Mint: Jalisco
Obv. leg: ESTADO LIBRE DE JALISCO

353	1828	—	4.00	6.00	12.00	35.00
	1829/8	—	3.00	5.00	8.00	35.00
	1829	—	3.00	5.00	8.00	35.00
	1830/20	—	3.00	5.00	8.00	30.00
	1830/29	—	3.00	5.00	8.00	30.00
	1830	—	3.00	5.00	8.00	30.00
	1831	—	—	—	Rare	—
	1832/20	—	3.00	5.00	8.00	30.00
	1832/28	—	3.00	5.00	8.00	30.00
	1832	—	3.00	5.00	8.00	30.00
	1833/2	—	3.00	5.00	8.00	30.00
	1834	—	3.00	5.00	8.00	30.00
	1835/3	—	3.00	5.00	8.00	30.00
	1835	—	3.00	5.00	8.00	30.00
	1836	—	—	—	Rare	—

Obv. leg: DEPARTAMENTO DE JALISCO

354	1836	—	—	—	Rare	—

Obv. leg: ESTADO LIBRE DE JALISCO

KM#	Date	Mintage	Good	VG	Fine	VF
355	1858	—	3.00	5.00	8.00	20.00
	1861	—	3.00	5.00	10.00	25.00
	1862	—	3.00	5.00	8.00	20.00

Obv. leg: DEPARTAMENTO DE JALISCO

KM#	Date	Mintage	Good	VG	Fine	VF
356	1858	—	3.00	5.00	8.00	20.00
	1859/8	—	3.00	5.00	8.00	20.00
	1859	—	3.00	5.00	8.00	20.00
	1860	—	3.00	5.00	8.00	20.00

Mint: Mexico City
Obv. leg: REPUBLICA MEXICANA.

KM#	Date	Mintage	VG	Fine	VF	XF
357	1829	—	8.00	20.00	60.00	150.00

Reduced size.

KM#	Date	Mintage	VG	Fine	VF	XF
358	1829	—	12.00	25.00	50.00	150.00
	1830	—	2.00	3.00	4.00	10.00
	1831	—	2.00	3.00	4.00	10.00
	1832	—	5.50	10.00	20.00	35.00
	1833	—	2.00	3.00	4.00	10.00
	1834/3	—	2.00	3.00	4.00	10.00
	1834	—	2.00	3.00	4.00	10.00
	1835	—	2.00	3.00	4.00	10.00
	1836	—	2.00	3.00	4.00	10.00
	1837	—	5.00	10.00	20.00	40.00

BRASS
c/m: JM

358a.1	1831	—	8.00	15.00	35.00	75.00

W/o countermark

358a.2	1831	—	—	—	—	—

COPPER
Mint: Potosi
Obv. leg: ESTADO LIBRE DE SAN LUIS POTOSI
Rev. leg: MEXICO LIBRE

KM#	Date	Mintage	Good	VG	Fine	VF
359	1828	—	3.00	4.00	6.00	15.00
	1829	—	3.00	4.00	6.00	15.00
	1830	—	3.00	4.00	6.00	15.00
	1832	—	3.00	4.00	6.00	15.00
	1859 large LIBRE	—	3.00	4.00	6.00	15.00
	1859 small LIBRE	—	3.00	4.00	6.00	15.00
	1860	—	3.00	4.00	6.00	15.00

Rev. leg: REPUBLICA MEXICANA

KM#	Date	Mintage	Good	VG	Fine	VF
360	1862	1,367	3.00	4.00	6.00	10.00
	1862 LIBR Inc. Ab.		3.00	4.00	6.00	10.00

Milled edge
Obv. leg: ESTADO LIBRE Y SOBERANO DE S.L. POTOSI
Rev. leg: LIBERTAD Y REFORMA

361	1867	3.177	3.00	4.00	7.00	20.00
	1867 AFG I.A.		3.00	4.00	7.00	20.00

Plain edge

362	1867 Inc. Ab.		3.00	4.00	7.00	20.00
	1867 AFG I.A.		3.00	4.00	7.00	20.00

Mint: Sinaloa
Obv. leg: ESTADO LIBRE Y SOBERANO DE SINALOA

363	1847	—	3.00	5.00	8.00	20.00
	1848	—	3.00	5.00	8.00	20.00
	1859	—	2.00	3.00	4.00	9.00
	1861	—	2.00	3.00	4.00	9.00
	1862	—	2.00	3.00	4.00	9.00
	1863	—	2.50	3.50	5.00	10.00
	1864/3	—	2.50	3.50	5.00	10.00
	1864	—	2.00	3.00	4.00	9.00
	1865	—	2.00	3.00	4.00	9.00
	1866/5	7.401	2.50	3.50	5.00	10.00
	1866 Inc. Ab.		2.00	3.00	4.00	9.00

BRASS

363a	1847	—	5.00	10.00	20.00	50.00

COPPER
Mint: Sonora
Obv. leg: EST.D.SONORA UNA CUART

364	1831	—	—	—	Rare	—
	1832	—	3.00	5.00	9.00	50.00
	1833/2	—	2.50	4.00	7.00	40.00

KM#	Date	Mintage	Good	VG	Fine	VF
364	1833	—	2.50	4.00	7.00	40.00
	1834	—	2.50	4.00	7.00	40.00
	1835/3	—	2.50	4.00	7.00	40.00
	1835	—	2.50	4.00	7.00	40.00
	1836	—	2.50	4.00	7.00	40.00

Obv. leg: ESTO.LIBE.Y SOBO.DE SONORA

KM#	Date	Mintage	Good	VG	Fine	VF
365	1859	—	3.00	5.00	8.00	20.00
	1861/59	—	4.00	6.50	11.00	25.00
	1861	—	3.00	5.00	8.00	20.00
	1862	—	3.00	5.00	8.00	20.00
	1863/2	—	7.00	15.00	30.00	50.00

BRASS
Mint: Zacatecas
Obv. leg: ESTO LIBE FEDO DE ZACATECAS

KM#	Date	Mintage	Good	VG	Fine	VF
366	1824	—	—	—	Rare	—
	1825	—	3.00	5.00	8.00	20.00
	1826	—	100.00	150.00	200.00	300.00
	1827/17	—	3.00	5.00	8.00	20.00
	1829	—	3.00	5.00	8.00	20.00
	1830	—	3.00	5.00	8.00	20.00
	1831	—	50.00	100.00	125.00	250.00
	1832	—	3.00	5.00	8.00	20.00
	1833	—	3.00	5.00	8.00	20.00
	1834	—	—	—	Rare	—
	1835	—	3.00	5.00	8.00	20.00
	1846	—	3.00	5.00	8.00	20.00
	1847	—	3.00	5.00	8.00	20.00
	1852	—	3.00	5.00	8.00	20.00
	1853	—	3.00	5.00	8.00	20.00
	1855	—	5.00	10.00	20.00	65.00
	1858	—	3.00	5.00	8.00	20.00
	1859	—	3.00	5.00	8.00	20.00
	1860	—	100.00	150.00	200.00	300.00
	1862/57	—	3.50	5.00	8.00	20.00
	1862/59/7	—	10.00	20.00	40.00	80.00
	1862	—	3.00	5.00	8.00	20.00
	1863/2	—	3.00	5.00	8.00	20.00
	1863	—	3.00	5.00	8.00	20.00
	1864/58	—	5.00	10.00	25.00	60.00

COPPER
Obv. leg: DEPARTAMENTO DE ZACATECAS

KM#	Date	Mintage	Good	VG	Fine	VF
367	1836	—	5.00	8.00	12.00	25.00
	1845	—	—	—	Rare	—
	1846	—	3.00	5.00	8.00	20.00

SILVER SERIES

0.8450 g, .903 SILVER, .0245 oz ASW
Mint mark: CA

KM#	Date	Mintage	VG	Fine	VF	XF
368	1843 RG	—	75.00	125.00	300.00	500.00
	Mint mark: C					
368.1	1855 LR	—	50.00	100.00	200.00	400.00
	Mint mark: Do					
368.2	1842 LR	—	12.00	20.00	40.00	125.00
	1843 LR	—	20.00	25.00	60.00	150.00
	Mint mark: Ga					
368.3	1842 JG	—	2.50	5.50	8.00	20.00
	1843/2 JG	—	—	—	—	—
	1843 JG	—	6.00	9.00	12.50	30.00
	1843 MC	—	4.00	6.50	9.00	25.00
	1844 MC	—	4.00	6.50	9.00	25.00
	1844 LR	—	2.50	5.00	7.50	15.00
	1845 LR	—	2.50	4.50	7.50	15.00
	1846 LR	—	5.00	8.00	10.00	25.00
	1847 LR	—	4.00	6.50	9.00	25.00
	1848 LR	—	—	—	Rare	—
	1850 LR	—	—	—	Rare	—
	1851 LR	—	6.00	10.00	20.00	50.00
	1852 LR	—	50.00	100.00	135.00	200.00
	1854/3 LR	—	50.00	100.00	135.00	200.00
	1854 LR	—	5.00	10.00	12.50	30.00
	1855 LR	—	5.00	8.00	10.00	30.00
	1857 LR	—	6.50	10.00	15.00	27.50
	1862 LR	—	5.50	10.00	15.00	30.00
	Mint mark: GC					
368.4	1844 LR	—	50.00	75.00	125.00	200.00
	Mint mark: Go					
368.5	1842 PM	—	4.00	6.00	10.00	20.00
	1842 LR	—	2.00	4.00	8.00	15.00
	1843/2 LR	—	4.00	6.00	10.00	20.00
	1843 LR	—	2.00	4.00	8.00	15.00
	1844/3 LR	—	—	—	—	—
	1844 LR	—	2.00	4.00	8.00	15.00
	1845 LR	—	8.00	15.00	30.00	60.00
	1846/5 LR	—	—	—	—	—
	1846 LR	—	4.00	6.00	10.00	20.00
	1847 LR	—	2.00	4.00	8.00	15.00
	1848/7 LR	—	2.00	4.00	8.00	15.00
	1848 LR	—	2.00	4.00	8.00	15.00
	1849/7 LR	—	8.00	15.00	30.00	60.00
	1849 LR	—	2.00	4.00	8.00	15.00
	1850 LR	—	2.00	4.00	8.00	15.00
	1851 LR	—	2.00	4.00	8.00	15.00
	1852 LR	—	2.00	4.00	8.00	15.00
	1853 LR	—	2.00	4.00	8.00	15.00
	1855 LR	—	4.00	8.00	15.00	30.00
	1856/4 LR	—	—	—	—	—
	1856 LR	—	5.00	10.00	20.00	35.00
	1862/1 LR	—	3.00	5.00	10.00	20.00
	1862 LR	—	2.00	4.00	8.00	15.00
	1863 LR	—	2.00	4.00	8.00	15.00
	Mint mark: Mo					
368.6	1842 LR	—	2.00	4.00	8.00	15.00
	1843 LR	—	2.00	4.00	8.00	15.00
	1844/3 LR	—	8.00	12.00	20.00	40.00
	1844 LR	—	4.00	6.00	10.00	20.00
	1845 LR	—	4.00	6.00	10.00	20.00
	1846 LR	—	2.00	4.00	8.00	15.00
	1850 LR	—	5.00	10.00	20.00	35.00
	1858 LR	—	4.00	8.00	15.00	30.00
	1859 LR	—	4.00	6.00	10.00	20.00
	1860 LR	—	4.00	6.00	10.00	20.00
	1861 LR	—	4.00	6.00	10.00	20.00
	1862 LR	—	4.00	6.00	10.00	20.00
	1863/53 LR	—	—	—	—	—
	1863 LR	—	4.00	6.00	10.00	20.00
	Mint mark: S.L.PI					
368.7	1842	—	2.00	4.00	8.00	15.00
	1843/2	—	4.00	6.00	10.00	20.00
	1843	—	2.00	4.00	8.00	15.00

KM#	Date	Mintage	VG	Fine	VF	XF
368.7	1844	—	2.00	4.00	8.00	15.00
	1845/3	—	4.00	6.00	10.00	25.00
	1845/4	—	4.00	6.00	10.00	25.00
	1845	—	2.00	4.00	8.00	15.00
	1847/5	—	4.00	6.00	10.00	20.00
	1847	—	2.00	4.00	8.00	15.00
	1851/47	—	4.00	8.00	15.00	30.00
	1854	—	125.00	200.00	275.00	400.00
	1856	—	4.00	8.00	15.00	30.00
	1857	—	5.00	10.00	20.00	35.00
	1862/57	—	10.00	20.00	40.00	85.00

Mint mark: Zs

KM#	Date	Mintage	VG	Fine	VF	XF
368.8	1842/1 LR	—	4.00	8.00	15.00	30.00
	1842 LR	—	4.00	6.00	10.00	20.00

1/2 REAL

1.6900 g, .903 SILVER, .0490 oz ASW
Mint mark: Mo
Obv: Hooked neck eagle

KM#	Date	Mintage	Fine	VF	XF	Unc
369	1824 JM	—	40.00	60.00	125.00	500.00

Mint mark: A

KM#	Date	Mintage				Unc
370	1862 PG	—	—	—	—	Rare	—

Mint mark: Ca
Obv: Facing eagle

KM#	Date	Mintage	Fine	VF	XF	Unc
370.1	1844 RG	—	75.00	125.00	175.00	275.00
	1845 RG	—	75.00	125.00	150.00	250.00

Mint mark: C, Co

KM#	Date	Mintage	Fine	VF	XF	Unc
370.2	1846 CE	—	30.00	50.00	75.00	150.00
	1848/7 CE	—	15.00	25.00	45.00	90.00
	1849/8 CE	—	15.00	25.00	45.00	90.00
	1849 CE	—	—			
	1852 CE	—	12.50	20.00	40.00	80.00
	1853/1 CE	—	12.50	20.00	40.00	80.00
	1854 CE	—	20.00	35.00	50.00	100.00
	1856 CE	—	12.50	20.00	40.00	80.00
	1857/6 CE	—	20.00	35.00	50.00	100.00
	1857 CE	—	15.00	25.00	45.00	90.00
	1858 CE (error 1 for 1/2)	—	12.50	20.00	40.00	80.00
	1860/59 PV	—	20.00	35.00	50.00	100.00
	1860 PV	—	12.50	20.00	40.00	80.00
	1861 PV	—	12.50	20.00	40.00	80.00
	1863 CE (error 1 for 1/2)	—	15.00	25.00	45.00	90.00
	1867 CE	—	12.50	20.00	40.00	80.00
	1869 CE (error 1 for 1/2)	—	12.50	20.00	40.00	80.00

Mint mark: D, Do

KM#	Date	Mintage	Fine	VF	XF	Unc
370.3	1832 RM	—	125.00	225.00	350.00	600.00
	1832 RM/L	—	—	—	—	—
	1833/2 RM/L	—	75.00	100.00	150.00	225.00
	1833/1 RM/L	—	12.50	20.00	40.00	80.00
	1833 RM	—	25.00	40.00	75.00	150.00
	1834/1 RM	—	25.00	40.00	75.00	150.00
	1834 RM	—	12.50	20.00	40.00	80.00
	1837/1 RM	—	12.50	20.00	40.00	80.00
	1837/4 RM	—	12.50	20.00	40.00	80.00
	1837/6 RM	—	12.50	20.00	40.00	80.00
	1841/33 RM	—	15.00	25.00	50.00	100.00
	1842/32 RM	—	12.50	20.00	40.00	80.00

KM#	Date	Mintage	Fine	VF	XF	Unc
370.3	1842 RM	—	12.50	20.00	40.00	80.00
	1842 RM 8R (error)	—	12.50	20.00	40.00	80.00
	1842 RM 1/2/8R	—	12.50	20.00	40.00	80.00
	1843/33 RM	—	15.00	25.00	50.00	100.00
	1843 RM	—	—	—	—	—
	1845/31 RM	—	12.50	20.00	40.00	80.00
	1845/34 RM	—	12.50	20.00	40.00	80.00
	1845/35 RM	—	12.50	20.00	40.00	80.00
	1845 RM	—	15.00	25.00	50.00	100.00
	1846 RM	—	30.00	50.00	80.00	150.00
	1848/5 RM	—	35.00	55.00	110.00	200.00
	1848/36 RM	—	25.00	40.00	75.00	150.00
	1849 JMR	—	25.00	40.00	75.00	150.00
	1850 RM	—	—	—	Rare	—
	1850 JMR	—	25.00	40.00	75.00	150.00
	1851 JMR	—	20.00	35.00	50.00	100.00
	1852/1 JMR	—	65.00	125.00	225.00	500.00
	1852 JMR	—	30.00	50.00	80.00	150.00
	1853 CP	—	12.50	20.00	40.00	80.00
	1854 CP	—	25.00	40.00	75.00	150.00
	1855 CP	—	25.00	40.00	60.00	125.00
	1856/5 CP	—	20.00	35.00	50.00	100.00
	1857 CP	—	20.00	35.00	50.00	100.00
	1858/7 CP	—	20.00	35.00	50.00	100.00
	1859 CP	—	20.00	35.00	50.00	100.00
	1860/59 CP	—	40.00	60.00	125.00	225.00
	1861 CP	—	125.00	200.00	300.00	500.00
	1862 CP	—	25.00	40.00	60.00	125.00
	1864 LT	—	50.00	100.00	200.00	350.00
	1869 CP	—	40.00	75.00	125.00	225.00

Mint mark: EoMo

KM#	Date	Mintage	Fine	VF	XF	Unc
370.4	1829 LF	—	175.00	300.00	450.00	1250.

Mint mark: Ga

KM#	Date	Mintage	Fine	VF	XF	Unc
370.5	1825 FS	—	25.00	40.00	75.00	150.00
	1826 FS	—	10.00	15.00	35.00	70.00
	1828/7 FS	—	12.50	20.00	40.00	80.00
	1829 FS	—	7.50	15.00	30.00	60.00
	1830/29 FS	—	40.00	60.00	100.00	200.00
	1831 LP	—	—	—	Rare	—
	1832 FS	—	10.00	20.00	35.00	70.00
	1834/3 FS	—	65.00	100.00	175.00	250.00
	1834 FS	—	10.00	20.00	35.00	70.00
	1835/4/3 FS/LP	—	15.00	25.00	40.00	80.00
	1837/6 JG	—	50.00	100.00	150.00	250.00
	1838/7 JG	—	15.00	25.00	40.00	80.00
	1839/8 JG/FS	—	35.00	75.00	150.00	250.00
	1839 MC	—	10.00	20.00	35.00	70.00
	1840/39 MC/JG	—	—	—	—	—
	1840 MC	—	15.00	25.00	40.00	80.00
	1841 MC	—	20.00	35.00	50.00	100.00
	1842/1 JG	—	15.00	25.00	40.00	80.00
	1842 JG	—	10.00	20.00	35.00	70.00
	1843/2 JG	—	15.00	30.00	50.00	100.00
	1843 JG	—	10.00	20.00	35.00	70.00
	1843 MC/JG	—	10.00	20.00	35.00	70.00
	1843 MC	—	10.00	20.00	35.00	70.00
	1844 MC	—	10.00	20.00	35.00	70.00
	1845 MC	—	10.00	20.00	35.00	70.00
	1845 JG	—	10.00	20.00	35.00	70.00
	1846 MC	—	10.00	20.00	35.00	70.00
	1846 JG	—	10.00	20.00	35.00	70.00
	1847 JG	—	10.00	20.00	35.00	70.00
	1848/7 JG	—	10.00	20.00	35.00	70.00
	1849 JG	—	10.00	20.00	35.00	70.00
	1850/49 JG	—	—	—	—	—
	1850 JG	—	10.00	20.00	35.00	70.00
	1851/0 JG	—	10.00	20.00	35.00	70.00
	1852 JG	—	10.00	20.00	35.00	70.00
	1853 JG	—	10.00	20.00	35.00	70.00
	1854 JG	—	10.00	20.00	35.00	70.00
	1855/4 JG	—	10.00	20.00	35.00	70.00
	1855 JG	—	10.00	20.00	35.00	70.00
	1856 JG	—	10.00	20.00	35.00	70.00
	1857 JG	—	10.00	20.00	35.00	70.00
	1858/7 JG	—	10.00	20.00	35.00	70.00
	1858 JG	—	10.00	20.00	35.00	70.00
	1859/7 JG	—	10.00	20.00	35.00	70.00
	1860/59 JG	—	10.00	20.00	35.00	70.00

KM#	Date	Mintage	Fine	VF	XF	Unc
370.5	1861 JG	—	5.00	12.50	25.00	50.00
	1862/1 JG	—	15.00	25.00	40.00	80.00
Mint mark: GC						
370.6	1844 MP	—	50.00	100.00	150.00	350.00
	1845 MP	—	25.00	50.00	100.00	200.00
	1846 MP	—	25.00	50.00	100.00	200.00
	1847 MP	—	25.00	50.00	100.00	300.00
	1848 MP	—	20.00	40.00	75.00	150.00
	1849 MP	—	25.00	50.00	100.00	200.00
	1850 MP	—	30.00	60.00	125.00	250.00
	1851 MP	—	25.00	50.00	100.00	200.00
Mint mark: Go						
370.7	1826 MJ	—	125.00	250.00	400.00	1000.
	1827/6 MJ	—	7.50	15.00	30.00	75.00
	1828/7 MJ	—	7.50	15.00	30.00	75.00
	1828 MJ denomination 2/1					
	1828 JG	—	—	—	—	—
	1828 MR	—	50.00	100.00	150.00	250.00
	1829/8 MJ	—	5.00	10.00	25.00	50.00
	1829 MJ	—	5.00	10.00	25.00	50.00
	1829 MJ reversed N in MEXICANA					
		—	5.00	10.00	25.00	50.00
	1830 MJ	—	5.00	10.00	25.00	50.00
	1831/29 MJ	—	15.00	30.00	60.00	150.00
	1831 MJ	—	10.00	20.00	40.00	80.00
	1832/1 MJ	—	7.50	15.00	30.00	75.00
	1832 MJ	—	7.50	15.00	30.00	75.00
	1833 MJ round top 3					
		—	10.00	20.00	40.00	80.00
	1833 MJ flat top 3					
		—	10.00	20.00	40.00	80.00
	1834 PJ	—	5.00	10.00	25.00	50.00
	1835 PJ	—	5.00	10.00	25.00	50.00
	1836/5 PJ	—	7.50	15.00	30.00	75.00
	1836 PJ	—	5.00	10.00	25.00	50.00
	1837 PJ	—	5.00	10.00	25.00	50.00
	1838/7 PJ	—	5.00	10.00	25.00	50.00
	1839 PJ	—	5.00	10.00	25.00	50.00
	1839 PJ (error: REPUBLIGA)					
		—	5.00	10.00	25.00	50.00
	1840/39 PJ	—	7.50	10.00	25.00	75.00
	1840 PJ straight J					
		—	5.00	10.00	25.00	50.00
	1840 PJ curved J					
		—	5.00	10.00	25.00	50.00
	1841/31 PJ	—	5.00	10.00	25.00	50.00
	1841 PJ	—	5.00	10.00	25.00	50.00
	1842/1 PJ	—	5.00	10.00	25.00	50.00
	1842/1 PM	—	5.00	10.00	25.00	50.00
	1842 PM/J	—	5.00	10.00	25.00	50.00
	1842 PJ	—	5.00	10.00	25.00	50.00
	1842 PM	—	5.00	10.00	25.00	50.00
	1843/33 PM 1/2 over 8					
		—	5.00	10.00	25.00	50.00
	1843 PM convex wings					
		—	5.00	10.00	25.00	50.00
	1843 PM concave wings					
		—	5.00	10.00	25.00	50.00
	1844/3 PM	—	5.00	10.00	25.00	50.00
	1844 PM	—	10.00	20.00	40.00	90.00
	1845/4 PM	—	5.00	10.00	25.00	50.00
	1845 PM	—	5.00	10.00	25.00	50.00
	1846/4 PM	—	5.00	10.00	25.00	50.00
	1846/5 PM	—	5.00	10.00	25.00	50.00
	1846 PM	—	5.00	10.00	25.00	50.00
	1847/6 PM	—	7.50	15.00	30.00	60.00
	1847 PM	—	7.50	15.00	30.00	60.00
	1848/35 PM	—	5.00	10.00	25.00	50.00
	1848 PM	—	5.00	10.00	25.00	50.00
	1848 PF/M	—	5.00	10.00	25.00	50.00
	1849/39 PF	—	5.00	10.00	25.00	50.00
	1849 PF	—	5.00	10.00	25.00	50.00
	1849 PF (error: MEXCANA)					
		—	5.00	10.00	25.00	50.00
	1850 PF	—	5.00	10.00	25.00	50.00
	1851 PF	—	5.00	10.00	25.00	50.00
	1852/1 PF	—	5.00	10.00	25.00	50.00
	1852 PF	—	2.50	7.50	17.50	40.00
	1853 PF/R	—	5.00	10.00	25.00	50.00
	1853 PF	—	5.00	10.00	25.00	50.00
	1854 PF	—	5.00	10.00	25.00	50.00

KM#	Date	Mintage	Fine	VF	XF	Unc
370.7	1855 PF	—	5.00	10.00	25.00	50.00
	1856/4 PF	—	5.00	10.00	25.00	50.00
	1856/5 PF	—	5.00	10.00	25.00	50.00
	1856 PF	—	5.00	10.00	25.00	50.00
	1857/6 PF	—	5.00	10.00	25.00	50.00
	1857 PF	—	5.00	10.00	25.00	50.00
	1858/7 PF	—	7.50	15.00	30.00	60.00
	1858 PF	—	5.00	10.00	25.00	50.00
	1859 PF	—	5.00	10.00	25.00	50.00
	1860 PF small 1/2					
		—	5.00	10.00	25.00	50.00
	1860 PF large 1/2					
		—	5.00	10.00	25.00	50.00
	1860/59 PF	—	5.00	10.00	25.00	50.00
	1861 PF small 1/2					
		—	5.00	10.00	25.00	50.00
	1861 PF large 1/2					
		—	5.00	10.00	25.00	50.00
	1862/1 YE	—	5.00	10.00	25.00	50.00
	1862 YE	—	2.50	7.50	17.50	40.00
	1862 YF	—	5.00	10.00	25.00	50.00
	1867 YF	—	2.50	7.50	17.50	40.00
	1868 YF	—	2.50	7.50	17.50	40.00
NOTE: Varieties exist.						
Mint mark: Ho						
370.8	1839 PP	—	—	—	Unique	—
	1862 FM	—	65.00	125.00	200.00	400.00
	1867 PR/FM 6/inverted 6, & 7/1					
		—	100.00	175.00	250.00	450.00
Mint mark: Mo						
370.9	1825 JM	—	10.00	20.00	40.00	80.00
	1826/5 JM	—	10.00	20.00	40.00	80.00
	1826 JM	—	5.00	10.00	20.00	60.00
	1827/6 JM	—	5.00	10.00	20.00	60.00
	1827 JM	—	5.00	10.00	20.00	60.00
	1828/7 JM	—	7.50	15.00	25.00	75.00
	1828 JM	—	10.00	20.00	40.00	80.00
	1829 JM	—	7.50	15.00	25.00	75.00
	1830 JM	—	5.00	10.00	20.00	60.00
	1831 JM	—	5.00	10.00	20.00	60.00
	1832 JM	—	7.50	12.50	27.50	60.00
	1833 JM	—	7.50	12.50	27.50	60.00
	1834 ML	—	5.00	10.00	20.00	60.00
	1835 ML	—	5.00	10.00	20.00	60.00
	1836/5 ML/MF					
		—	7.50	15.00	25.00	65.00
	1836 ML	—	7.50	15.00	25.00	65.00
	1838 ML	—	5.00	10.00	20.00	60.00
	1839/8 ML	—	5.00	10.00	25.00	65.00
	1839 ML	—	5.00	10.00	20.00	50.00
	1840 ML	—	5.00	10.00	20.00	50.00
	1841 ML	—	5.00	10.00	20.00	50.00
	1842 ML	—	5.00	10.00	20.00	50.00
	1842 MM	—	5.00	10.00	20.00	50.00
	1843 MM	—	10.00	20.00	40.00	80.00
	1844 MF	—	5.00	10.00	20.00	50.00
	1845/4 MF	—	5.00	10.00	25.00	60.00
	1845 MF	—	5.00	10.00	20.00	50.00
	1846 MF	—	5.00	10.00	20.00	50.00
	1847 RC	—	10.00	20.00	40.00	80.00
	1848/7 GC/RC					
		—	5.00	10.00	20.00	50.00
	1849 GC	—	5.00	10.00	20.00	50.00
	1850 GC	—	5.00	10.00	20.00	50.00
	1851 GC	—	5.00	10.00	20.00	50.00
	1852 GC	—	5.00	10.00	20.00	50.00
	1853 GC	—	5.00	10.00	20.00	50.00
	1854 GC	—	5.00	10.00	20.00	50.00
	1855 GC	—	5.00	10.00	20.00	50.00
	1855 GF/GC	—	7.50	12.50	25.00	65.00
	1856/5 GF	—	7.50	12.50	25.00	65.00
	1857 GF	—	5.00	10.00	20.00	50.00
	1858 FH	—	3.00	5.00	12.50	40.00
	1858/9 FH	—	5.00	10.00	20.00	50.00
	1859 FH	—	3.00	6.00	15.00	50.00
	1860 FH/GC					
		—	5.00	10.00	20.00	50.00
	1860/59 FH	—	7.50	12.50	25.00	65.00
	1860 FH	—	3.00	6.00	15.00	50.00
	1860 TH	—	5.00	10.00	20.00	50.00
	1861 CH	—	3.00	6.00	15.00	45.00
	1862/52 CH	—	5.00	10.00	20.00	50.00

KM#	Date	Mintage	Fine	VF	XF	Unc
370.9	1862 CH	—	3.00	6.00	15.00	45.00
	1863/55 TH/GC					
		—	5.00	10.00	20.00	50.00
	1863 CH/GC	—	5.00	10.00	20.00	50.00
	1863 CH	—	3.00	6.00	15.00	45.00

Mint mark: Pi

KM#	Date	Mintage	Fine	VF	XF	Unc
370.10	1831 JS	—	7.50	12.50	25.00	65.00
	1841/36 JS	—	20.00	40.00	75.00	125.00
	1842/1 PS	—	20.00	40.00	75.00	125.00
	1842/1 PS P/J					
		—	60.00	80.00	150.00	300.00
	1842 PS/JS	—	50.00	75.00	125.00	250.00
	1842 JS	—	20.00	40.00	75.00	125.00
	1843/2 PS	—	17.50	25.00	40.00	80.00
	1843 PS	—	15.00	25.00	35.00	70.00
	1843 AM	—	10.00	15.00	25.00	60.00
	1844 AM	—	10.00	15.00	30.00	65.00
	1845 AM	—	250.00	375.00	500.00	1500.
	1846/5 AM	—	40.00	75.00	125.00	200.00
	1847/6 AM	—	15.00	25.00	40.00	80.00
	1848 AM	—	15.00	25.00	40.00	80.00
	1849 MC/AM	—	15.00	25.00	40.00	80.00
	1849 MC	—	12.50	20.00	35.00	70.00
	1850/49 MC	—				
	1850Pi MC	—	10.00	15.00	25.00	60.00
	1850P MC	—	—	—	—	—
	1851 MC	—	10.00	15.00	25.00	60.00
	1852 MC	—	10.00	20.00	30.00	65.00
	1853 MC	—	7.50	12.50	20.00	60.00
	1854 MC	—	7.50	12.50	20.00	60.00
	1855 MC	—	15.00	20.00	35.00	70.00
	1856 MC	—	15.00	25.00	50.00	100.00
	1857 MC	—	7.50	12.50	20.00	60.00
	1857 PS	—	10.00	15.00	30.00	65.00
	1858 MC	—	12.50	20.00	35.00	70.00
	1858 PS	—	12.50	20.00	35.00	70.00
	1859 MC	—	—	—	Rare	—
	1860/59 PS	—	12.50	20.00	35.00	70.00
	1861 RO	—	10.00	15.00	30.00	60.00
	1862/1 RO	—	15.00	25.00	50.00	125.00
	1862 RO	—	15.00	25.00	50.00	125.00
	1863/2 RO	—	15.00	25.00	45.00	100.00

Mint mark: Z, Zs

KM#	Date	Mintage	Fine	VF	XF	Unc
370.11	1826 AZ	—	5.00	10.00	20.00	60.00
	1826 AO	—	5.00	10.00	20.00	60.00
	1827 AO	—	5.00	10.00	20.00	60.00
	1828/7 AO	—	5.00	10.00	20.00	60.00
	1829 AO	—	5.00	10.00	20.00	60.00
	1830 OV	—	5.00	10.00	20.00	60.00
	1831 OV	—	25.00	50.00	75.00	150.00
	1831 OM	—	5.00	10.00	20.00	60.00
	1832 OM	—	5.00	10.00	20.00	60.00
	1833 OM	—	5.00	10.00	20.00	60.00
	1834 OM	—	5.00	10.00	20.00	60.00
	1835/4 OM	—	5.00	10.00	20.00	60.00
	1835 OM	—	5.00	10.00	20.00	60.00
	1836 OM	—	5.00	10.00	20.00	60.00
	1837 OM	—	10.00	20.00	40.00	80.00
	1838 OM	—	5.00	10.00	20.00	60.00
	1839 OM	—	7.50	15.00	30.00	65.00
	1840 OM	—	10.00	25.00	45.00	90.00
	1841 OM	—	10.00	25.00	45.00	90.00
	1842/1 OM	—	5.00	10.00	20.00	60.00
	1842 OM	—	5.00	10.00	20.00	60.00
	1843 OM	—	40.00	75.00	115.00	250.00
	1844 OM	—	5.00	10.00	20.00	60.00
	1845 OM	—	5.00	10.00	20.00	60.00
	1846 OM	—	7.50	15.00	30.00	65.00
	1847 OM	—	5.00	10.00	20.00	50.00
	1848 OM	—	5.00	10.00	20.00	50.00
	1849 OM	—	5.00	10.00	20.00	50.00
	1850 OM	—	5.00	10.00	20.00	50.00
	1851 OM	—	5.00	10.00	20.00	50.00
	1852 OM	—	5.00	10.00	20.00	50.00
	1853 OM	—	5.00	10.00	20.00	50.00
	1854/3 OM	—	5.00	10.00	20.00	50.00
	1854 OM	—	5.00	10.00	20.00	50.00
	1855/3 OM	—	7.50	15.00	30.00	65.00
	1855 OM	—	5.00	10.00	20.00	50.00
	1856 OM	—	5.00	10.00	20.00	50.00
	1857 MO	—	5.00	10.00	20.00	50.00
	1858 MO	—	5.00	10.00	20.00	50.00
	1859 MO	—	6.00	8.50	17.50	35.00
	1859 VL	—	6.00	8.50	17.50	40.00

KM#	Date	Mintage	Fine	VF	XF	Unc
370.11	1860/50 VL inverted A for V					
		—	5.00	10.00	20.00	50.00
	1860/59 VL inverted A for V					
			5.00	10.00	20.00	50.00
	1860 MO	—	5.00	10.00	20.00	50.00
	1860 VL	—	5.00	10.00	20.00	50.00
	1861/0 VL inverted A for V					
		—	7.50	15.00	30.00	65.00
	1861 VL inverted A for V					
		—	5.00	10.00	20.00	50.00
	1862 VL inverted A for V					
		—	5.00	10.00	20.00	50.00
	1863/1 VL inverted A for V					
		—	7.50	15.00	30.00	65.00
	1863 VL inverted A for V					
		—	5.00	10.00	20.00	50.00
	1869 YH	—	5.00	10.00	20.00	50.00

REAL

3.3800 g, .903 SILVER, .0981 oz ASW
Mint mark: Do

KM#	Date	Mintage	Fine	VF	XF	Unc
371	1824 RL	—	2750.	3250.	4000.	5500.

Mint mark: Ca

KM#	Date	Mintage	Fine	VF	XF	Unc
372	1844 RG	—	500.00	1000.	1500.	2500.
	1845 RG	—	500.00	1000.	1500.	2500.
	1855 RG	—	100.00	150.00	225.00	400.00

Mint mark: C

KM#	Date	Mintage	Fine	VF	XF	Unc
372.1	1846 CE	—	12.50	25.00	40.00	110.00
	1848 CE	—	12.50	25.00	40.00	110.00
	1850 CE	—	12.50	25.00	40.00	110.00
	1851/0 CE	—	12.50	25.00	40.00	110.00
	1852/1 CE	—	7.50	15.00	30.00	100.00
	1853/2 CE	—	7.50	15.00	30.00	100.00
	1854 CE	—	7.50	15.00	30.00	100.00
	1856 CE	—	40.00	65.00	100.00	225.00
	1857/4 CE	—	10.00	20.00	35.00	100.00
	1857/6 CE	—	10.00	20.00	35.00	100.00
	1858 CE	—	5.00	7.50	15.00	100.00
	1859 CE	—	—	—	—	—
	1860 PV	—	5.00	7.50	15.00	100.00
	1861 PV	—	5.00	7.50	15.00	100.00
	1863 CE					
		3 known	—	—	1650.	2250.
	1869 CE	—	5.00	7.50	15.00	100.00

Mint mark: Do

KM#	Date	Mintage	Fine	VF	XF	Unc
372.2	1832/1 RM	—	5.00	10.00	20.00	90.00
	1832 RM/RL	—	10.00	15.00	30.00	100.00
	1832 RM	—	5.00	10.00	20.00	100.00
	1834/24 RM/RL					
		—	15.00	25.00	50.00	150.00
	1834/3 RM/RL					
		—	15.00	25.00	50.00	150.00
	1834 RM	—	10.00	20.00	40.00	110.00
	1836/4 RM	—	5.00	7.50	15.00	100.00
	1836 RM	—	5.00	7.50	15.00	100.00
	1837 RM	—	12.50	20.00	40.00	110.00
	1841 RM	—	7.50	15.00	30.00	100.00
	1842/32 RM	—	10.00	20.00	40.00	110.00
	1842 RM	—	7.50	15.00	30.00	100.00
	1843 RM	—	5.00	7.50	15.00	100.00
	1844/34 RM	—	15.00	25.00	45.00	125.00
	1845 RM	—	5.00	7.50	15.00	100.00
	1846 RM	—	7.50	15.00	30.00	100.00
	1847 RM	—	10.00	15.00	35.00	100.00

KM#	Date	Mintage	Fine	VF	XF	Unc
372.2	1848/31 RM	—	10.00	15.00	35.00	100.00
	1848/33 RM	—	10.00	15.00	35.00	100.00
	1848/5 RM	—	10.00	15.00	35.00	100.00
	1848 RM	—	7.50	12.50	20.00	100.00
	1849/8 CM	—	10.00	15.00	30.00	100.00
	1850 JMR	—	15.00	25.00	45.00	125.00
	1851 JMR	—	15.00	25.00	45.00	120.00
	1852 JMR	—	15.00	25.00	45.00	120.00
	1853 CP	—	12.50	20.00	35.00	100.00
	1854/1 CP	—	10.00	15.00	25.00	100.00
	1854 CP	—	7.50	12.50	20.00	100.00
	1855 CP	—	10.00	15.00	35.00	100.00
	1856 CP	—	12.50	20.00	35.00	100.00
	1857 CP	—	12.50	20.00	35.00	100.00
	1858 CP	—	12.50	20.00	35.00	100.00
	1859 CP	—	7.50	12.50	20.00	100.00
	1860/59 CP	—	10.00	15.00	25.00	100.00
	1861 CP	—	15.00	25.00	40.00	110.00
	1862/1 CP	—	225.00	300.00	450.00	1250.
	1864 LT	—	15.00	25.00	40.00	110.00

Mint mark: EoMo

KM#	Date	Mintage	Fine	VF	XF	Unc
372.3	1828 LF	—	200.00	300.00	450.00	1500.

Mint mark: Ga

KM#	Date	Mintage	Fine	VF	XF	Unc
372.4	1826 FS	—	15.00	30.00	50.00	125.00
	1828/7 FS	—	15.00	30.00	50.00	125.00
	1829/8/7 FS	—	—	—	—	—
	1829 FS	—	15.00	30.00	50.00	125.00
	1830 FS	—	250.00	350.00	500.00	—
	1831 LP	—	15.00	30.00	50.00	125.00
	1831 LP/FS	—	300.00	450.00	600.00	—
	1832 FS	—	250.00	350.00	500.00	—
	1833/2 G FS	—	100.00	150.00	275.00	550.00
	1833 FS	—	75.00	125.00	225.00	500.00
	1834/3 FS	—	75.00	125.00	225.00	500.00
	1835 FS	—	—	—	—	—
	1837/6 JG/FS					
		—	12.50	20.00	35.00	100.00
	1838/7 JG/FS					
		—	12.50	20.00	35.00	100.00
	1839 JG	—	250.00	350.00	500.00	—
	1840 JG	—	12.50	20.00	35.00	100.00
	1840 MC	—	7.50	12.50	25.00	70.00
	1841 MC	—	50.00	75.00	125.00	250.00
	1842/0 JG/MC					
		—	10.00	15.00	30.00	100.00
	1842 JG	—	7.50	12.50	20.00	100.00
	1843 JG	—	150.00	200.00	300.00	750.00
	1843 MC	—	5.00	7.50	15.00	100.00
	1844 MC	—	7.50	12.50	20.00	100.00
	1845 MC	—	10.00	15.00	25.00	100.00
	1845 JG	—	5.00	7.50	20.00	100.00
	1846 JG	—	12.50	20.00	35.00	100.00
	1847/6 JG	—	10.00	15.00	25.00	100.00
	1847 JG	—	10.00	15.00	25.00	100.00
	1848 JG	—	400.00	550.00	700.00	—
	1849 JG	—	7.50	12.50	20.00	100.00
	1850 JG	—	175.00	275.00	400.00	—
	1851 JG	—	10.00	15.00	25.00	100.00
	1852 JG	—	10.00	15.00	25.00	100.00
	1853/2 JG	—	10.00	15.00	25.00	100.00
	1854 JG	—	10.00	15.00	25.00	100.00
	1855 JG	—	15.00	25.00	40.00	100.00
	1856 JG	—	7.50	12.50	20.00	100.00
	1857/6 JG	—	12.50	20.00	35.00	100.00
	1858/7 JG	—	15.00	25.00	40.00	110.00
	1859/8 JG	—	25.00	50.00	75.00	150.00
	1860/59 JG	—	30.00	60.00	90.00	225.00
	1861/0 JG	—	20.00	30.00	50.00	125.00
	1861 JG	—	25.00	50.00	100.00	250.00
	1862 JG	—	7.50	12.50	20.00	100.00

Mint mark: GC

KM#	Date	Mintage	Fine	VF	XF	Unc
372.5	1844 MP	—	40.00	60.00	100.00	250.00
	1845 MP	—	40.00	60.00	100.00	250.00
	1846 MP	—	40.00	60.00	100.00	250.00
	1847 MP	—	40.00	60.00	100.00	250.00
	1848 MP	—	40.00	60.00	100.00	250.00
	1849/7 MP	—	40.00	60.00	100.00	250.00
	1849/8 MP	—	40.00	60.00	100.00	250.00
	1849 MP	—	40.00	60.00	100.00	250.00
	1850 MP	—	40.00	60.00	100.00	250.00
	1851 MP	—	40.00	60.00	100.00	250.00

Mint mark: Go

KM#	Date	Mintage	Fine	VF	XF	Unc
372.6	1826/5 JJ	—	5.00	7.50	15.00	85.00
	1826 MJ	—	4.00	6.00	15.00	85.00
	1827 MJ	—	4.00	6.00	15.00	65.00
	1827 JM	—	10.00	15.00	25.00	75.00
	1828/7 MR	—	4.00	6.00	15.00	85.00
	1828 MJ, straight J, small 8					
		—	6.00	15.00	85.00	
	1828Go MJ, full J, large 8					
		—	4.00	6.00	15.00	85.00
	1828G MJ, full J, large 8					
		—	4.00	6.00	15.00	85.00
	1828 MR	—	4.00	6.00	15.00	85.00
	1829/8 MG small eagle					
		—	4.00	6.00	15.00	85.00
	1829 MJ small eagle					
		—	4.00	6.00	15.00	85.00
	1829 MJ large eagle					
		—	4.00	6.00	15.00	85.00
	1830 MJ small initials					
		—	4.00	6.00	15.00	85.00
	1830 MJ medium initials					
		—	4.00	6.00	15.00	85.00
	1830 MJ large initials					
		—	4.00	6.00	15.00	85.00
	1830 MJ reversed N in MEXICANA					
		—	4.00	6.00	15.00	85.00
	1831/0 MJ reversed N in MEXICANA					
		—	4.00	6.00	15.00	85.00
	1831 MJ	—	4.00	6.00	15.00	85.00
	1832/1 MJ	—	15.00	30.00	50.00	125.00
	1832 MJ	—	15.00	30.00	50.00	125.00
	1833 MJ top of 3 round					
		—	4.00	6.00	15.00	85.00
	1833 MJ top of 3 flat					
		—	4.00	6.00	15.00	85.00
	1834 PJ	—	4.00	6.00	15.00	85.00
	1835 PJ	—	7.50	12.50	20.00	85.00
	1836 PJ	—	4.00	6.00	15.00	85.00
	1837 PJ	—	15.00	30.00	50.00	125.00
	1838/7 PJ	—	10.00	20.00	35.00	85.00
	1839 PJ	—	4.00	6.00	15.00	85.00
	1840/39 PJ	—	4.00	6.00	15.00	85.00
	1840 PJ	—	4.00	6.00	15.00	85.00
	1841/31 PJ	—	10.00	20.00	35.00	85.00
	1841 PJ	—	4.00	6.00	15.00	85.00
	1842 PJ	—	4.00	6.00	15.00	85.00
	1842 PM	—	4.00	6.00	15.00	85.00
	1843 PM convex wings					
		—	4.00	6.00	15.00	85.00
	1843 PM concave wings					
		—	4.00	6.00	15.00	85.00
	1844 PM	—	4.00	6.00	15.00	85.00
	1845/4 PM	—	4.00	6.00	15.00	85.00
	1845 PM	—	4.00	6.00	15.00	85.00
	1846/5 PM	—	7.50	12.50	20.00	85.00
	1846 PM	—	4.00	6.00	15.00	85.00
	1847/6 PM	—	4.00	6.00	15.00	85.00
	1847 PM	—	4.00	6.00	15.00	85.00
	1848 PM	—	4.00	6.00	15.00	85.00
	1849 PF	—	10.00	20.00	35.00	85.00
	1850 PF	—	4.00	6.00	15.00	85.00
	1851 PF	—	10.00	20.00	35.00	100.00
	1853/2 PF	—	7.50	12.50	20.00	75.00
	1853 PF	—	4.00	6.00	15.00	75.00
	1854/3 PF	—	4.00	6.00	15.00	75.00
	1854 PF large eagle					
		—	4.00	6.00	15.00	75.00
	1854 PF small eagle					
		—	4.00	6.00	15.00	75.00
	1855/3 PF	—	4.00	6.00	15.00	75.00
	1855/4 PF	—	4.00	6.00	15.00	75.00
	1855 PF	—	4.00	6.00	15.00	75.00
	1856/5 PF	—	4.00	6.00	15.00	75.00
	1856 PF	—	4.00	6.00	15.00	75.00
	1857/6 PF	—	4.00	6.00	15.00	75.00
	1857 PF	—	4.00	6.00	15.00	75.00
	1858 PF	—	4.00	6.00	15.00	75.00
	1859 PF	—	4.00	6.00	15.00	75.00
	1860/50 PF	—	4.00	6.00	15.00	75.00
	1860 PF	—	4.00	6.00	15.00	75.00
	1861 PF	—	4.00	6.00	15.00	75.00
	1862 YE	—	4.00	6.00	15.00	75.00

KM#	Date	Mintage	Fine	VF	XF	Unc
372.6	1862/1 YF	—	7.50	12.50	20.00	75.00
	1862 YF	—	4.00	6.00	15.00	75.00
	1867 YF	—	4.00	6.00	15.00	75.00
	1868/7 YF	—	4.00	6.00	15.00	75.00

Mint mark: Ho

KM#	Date	Mintage	Fine	VF	XF	Unc
372.7	1867 small 7/1 PR					
		—	50.00	65.00	100.00	250.00
	1867 large 7/small 7 PR					
		—	50.00	65.00	100.00	250.00
	1868 PR	—	50.00	65.00	100.00	250.00

Mint mark: Mo

KM#	Date	Mintage	Fine	VF	XF	Unc
372.8	1825 JM	—	10.00	20.00	40.00	110.00
	1826 JM	—	7.50	15.00	30.00	100.00
	1827/6 JM	—	7.50	15.00	30.00	75.00
	1827 JM	—	5.00	10.00	20.00	70.00
	1828 JM	—	7.50	15.00	30.00	100.00
	1830/29 JM	—	5.00	10.00	20.00	100.00
	1830 JM	—	5.00	12.50	25.00	100.00
	1831 JM	—	100.00	200.00	300.00	750.00
	1832 JM	—	5.00	10.00	20.00	100.00
	1833/2 MJ	—	5.00	10.00	20.00	100.00
	1850 GC	—	5.00	10.00	20.00	100.00
	1852 GC	—	275.00	425.00	575.00	—
	1854 GC	—	10.00	20.00	40.00	100.00
	1855 GF	—	5.00	10.00	20.00	80.00
	1856 GF	—	5.00	10.00	20.00	80.00
	1857 GF	—	5.00	10.00	20.00	80.00
	1858 FH	—	5.00	10.00	20.00	80.00
	1859 FH	—	5.00	10.00	20.00	80.00
	1861 CH	—	5.00	10.00	20.00	80.00
	1862 CH	—	5.00	10.00	20.00	80.00
	1863/2 CH	—	7.50	12.50	25.00	80.00

Mint mark: Pi

KM#	Date	Mintage	Fine	VF	XF	Unc
372.9	1831 JS	—	5.00	10.00	20.00	125.00
	1837 JS	—	750.00	850.00	1000.	—
	1838/7 JS	—	250.00	300.00	375.00	—
	1838 JS	—	20.00	35.00	60.00	125.00
	1840/39 JS	—	7.50	15.00	30.00	125.00
	1840 JS	—	7.50	15.00	30.00	125.00
	1841 JS	—	7.50	15.00	30.00	125.00
	1842 JS	—	15.00	30.00	55.00	150.00
	1842 PS	—	5.00	10.00	20.00	125.00
	1843 PS	—	12.50	20.00	35.00	125.00
	1843 AM	—	40.00	60.00	80.00	150.00
	1844 AM	—	40.00	60.00	80.00	150.00
	1845 AM	—	7.50	15.00	30.00	125.00
	1846/5 AM	—	7.50	15.00	30.00	125.00
	1847/6 AM	—	7.50	15.00	30.00	125.00
	1847 AM	—	7.50	15.00	30.00	125.00
	1848/7 AM	—	7.50	15.00	30.00	125.00
	1849 PS	—	7.50	15.00	30.00	125.00
	1849/8 SP	—	60.00	100.00	150.00	—
	1849 SP	—	15.00	25.00	40.00	125.00
	1850 MC	—	5.00	10.00	20.00	125.00
	1851/0 MC	—	7.50	15.00	30.00	125.00
	1851 MC	—	7.50	15.00	30.00	125.00
	1852/1/0 MC					
		—	10.00	20.00	35.00	125.00
	1852 MC	—	7.50	15.00	30.00	125.00
	1853/1 MC	—	12.50	20.00	35.00	125.00
	1853 MC	—	10.00	20.00	35.00	125.00
	1854/3 MC	—	20.00	40.00	60.00	150.00
	1855/4 MC	—	20.00	40.00	60.00	150.00
	1855 MC	—	15.00	25.00	45.00	125.00
	1856 MC	—	15.00	25.00	45.00	125.00
	1857 PS	—	20.00	35.00	55.00	135.00
	1857 MC	—	20.00	40.00	60.00	150.00
	1858 MC	—	12.50	20.00	35.00	125.00
	1859 PS	—	10.00	15.00	30.00	125.00
	1860/59 PS	—	10.00	15.00	30.00	125.00
	1861 PS	—	7.50	12.50	20.00	125.00
	1861 RO	—	12.50	20.00	35.00	125.00
	1862/1 RO	—	12.50	20.00	35.00	90.00
	1862 RO	—	7.50	12.50	20.00	125.00

Mint mark: Zs

KM#	Date	Mintage	Fine	VF	XF	Unc
372.10	1826 AZ	—	5.00	12.50	35.00	120.00
	1826 AO	—	5.00	12.50	35.00	120.00
	1827 AO	—	5.00	12.50	35.00	120.00
	1828/7 AO	—	5.00	12.50	35.00	120.00
	1828 AO	—	5.00	12.50	35.00	120.00
	1828 AO inverted V for A					
		—	5.00	12.50	35.00	120.00

KM#	Date	Mintage	Fine	VF	XF	Unc
372.10	1829 AO	—	5.00	12.50	35.00	120.00
	1830 ZsOV	—	5.00	12.50	35.00	120.00
	1830 ZOV	—	5.00	12.50	35.00	120.00
	1831 OV	—	5.00	12.50	35.00	120.00
	1831 OM	—	5.00	12.50	30.00	120.00
	1832 OM	—	5.00	12.50	30.00	120.00
	1833/2 OM	—	5.00	12.50	30.00	120.00
	1833 OM	—	5.00	12.50	30.00	120.00
	1834/3 OM	—	5.00	12.50	30.00	120.00
	1834 OM	—	5.00	12.50	30.00	120.00
	1835/4 OM	—	20.00	35.00	60.00	150.00
	1835 OM	—	4.00	8.00	20.00	65.00
	1836/5 OM	—	4.00	8.00	20.00	85.00
	1836 OM	—	4.00	8.00	20.00	85.00
	1837 OM	—	4.00	8.00	20.00	85.00
	1838 OM	—	4.00	8.00	20.00	85.00
	1839 OM	—	4.00	8.00	20.00	85.00
	1840 OM	—	4.00	8.00	20.00	85.00
	1841 OM	—	20.00	40.00	60.00	150.00
	1842/1 OM	—	4.00	8.00	20.00	85.00
	1842 OM	—	4.00	8.00	20.00	85.00
	1843 OM	—	4.00	8.00	20.00	85.00
	1844 OM	—	4.00	8.00	20.00	85.00
	1845/4 OM	—	5.00	12.50	30.00	100.00
	1845 OM	—	4.00	8.00	20.00	85.00
	1846 OM old font and obv.					
		—	4.00	8.00	20.00	85.00
	1846 OM new font and obv.					
		—	4.00	8.00	20.00	85.00
	1847 OM	—	4.00	8.00	20.00	85.00
	1848 OM	—	4.00	8.00	20.00	85.00
	1849 OM	—	10.00	25.00	50.00	125.00
	1850 OM	—	4.00	6.00	15.00	85.00
	1851 OM	—	4.00	6.00	15.00	85.00
	1852 OM	—	4.00	6.00	15.00	85.00
	1853 OM	—	4.00	6.00	15.00	85.00
	1854/2 OM	—	4.00	6.00	15.00	85.00
	1854/3 OM	—	4.00	6.00	15.00	85.00
	1854 OM	—	4.00	6.00	15.00	85.00
	1855/4 OM	—	4.00	6.00	15.00	85.00
	1855 OM	—	4.00	6.00	15.00	85.00
	1855 MO	—	4.00	6.00	15.00	85.00
	1856 MO	—	4.00	6.00	15.00	85.00
	1856 MO/OM	—	4.00	6.00	15.00	85.00
	1857 MO	—	4.00	6.00	15.00	85.00
	1858 MO	—	4.00	6.00	15.00	85.00
	1859 MO	—	4.00	6.00	15.00	75.00
	1860 VL	—	4.00	6.00	15.00	75.00
	1861 VL	—	4.00	6.00	15.00	75.00
	1862 VL	—	5.00	12.50	30.00	100.00
	1868 JS	—	25.00	45.00	90.00	175.00
	1869 YH	—	4.00	8.00	20.00	75.00

2 REALES

6.7600 g, .903 SILVER, .1962 oz ASW
Mint mark: D, Do
Obv: Hooked-neck eagle.

KM#	Date	Mintage	Fine	VF	XF	Unc
373	1824 Do RL	—	50.00	125.00	300.00	750.00
	1824 D RL	—	100.00	200.00	500.00	1500.

Mint mark: Mo

KM#	Date	Mintage	Fine	VF	XF	Unc
373.1	1824 JM	—	20.00	50.00	100.00	300.00

PRICING SECTION

Mint mark: A
Obv: Facing eagle, reeded edge.

KM#	Date	Mintage	Fine	VF	XF	Unc
374	1872 AM	.015	40.00	60.00	100.00	350.00

Mint mark: Ce

KM#	Date	Mintage	Fine	VF	XF	Unc
374.1	1863 ML	—	125.00	200.00	325.00	675.00

Mint mark: Ca

KM#	Date	Mintage	Fine	VF	XF	Unc
374.2	1832 MR	—	30.00	60.00	100.00	200.00
	1833 MR	—	30.00	60.00	125.00	500.00
	1834 MR	—	35.00	75.00	125.00	500.00
	1834 AM	—	35.00	75.00	125.00	500.00
	1835 AM	—	35.00	75.00	125.00	500.00
	1836 AM	—	20.00	40.00	80.00	200.00
	1844 RG	—	—	—	Unique	—
	1845 RG	—	20.00	40.00	80.00	200.00
	1855 RG	—	20.00	40.00	80.00	200.00

Mint mark: C

KM#	Date	Mintage	Fine	VF	XF	Unc
374.3	1846/1146 CE	—	25.00	50.00	100.00	225.00
	1847 CE	—	12.50	20.00	40.00	200.00
	1848 CE	—	12.50	20.00	40.00	200.00
	1850 CE	—	25.00	50.00	75.00	200.00
	1851 CE	—	12.50	20.00	40.00	200.00
	1852/1 CE	—	12.50	20.00	40.00	200.00
	1853/2 CE	—	12.50	20.00	40.00	200.00
	1854 CE	—	15.00	30.00	50.00	200.00
	1856 CE	—	20.00	35.00	70.00	200.00
	1857 CE	—	12.50	20.00	40.00	200.00
	1860 PV	—	12.50	20.00	40.00	200.00
	1861 PV	—	12.50	20.00	40.00	200.00
	1869 CE	—	12.50	20.00	40.00	200.00

Mint mark: Do

KM#	Date	Mintage	Fine	VF	XF	Unc
374.4	1826 RL	—	20.00	40.00	60.00	200.00
	1832 RM style of pre-1832	—	20.00	40.00	60.00	200.00
	1832 RM style of post-1832	—	20.00	40.00	60.00	200.00
	1834/2 RM	—	20.00	40.00	60.00	200.00
	1834/3 RM	—	20.00	40.00	60.00	200.00
	1835/4 RM/RL	—	200.00	300.00	500.00	—
	1841/31 RM	—	50.00	75.00	125.00	250.00
	1841 RM	—	50.00	75.00	125.00	250.00
	1842/32 RM	—	12.50	20.00	40.00	200.00
	1843 RM/RL	—	12.50	20.00	40.00	200.00
	1844 RM	—	35.00	50.00	80.00	200.00
	1845/34 RM/RL	—	12.50	20.00	40.00	200.00
	1846/36 RM	—	100.00	150.00	200.00	350.00
	1848/36 RM	—	12.50	20.00	40.00	200.00
	1848/37 RM	—	12.50	20.00	40.00	200.00
	1848/7 RM	—	12.50	20.00	40.00	200.00
	1848 RM	—	12.50	20.00	40.00	200.00
	1849 CM/RM	—	12.50	20.00	40.00	200.00
	1849 CM	—	12.50	20.00	40.00	200.00
	1851 JMR/RL	—	12.50	20.00	40.00	200.00
	1852 JMR	—	12.50	20.00	40.00	200.00
	1854 CP/CR	—	30.00	50.00	80.00	200.00
	1855 CP	—	250.00	350.00	500.00	—
	1856 CP	—	100.00	150.00	250.00	500.00
	1858 CP	—	12.50	20.00	40.00	200.00
	1859/8 CP	—	12.50	20.00	40.00	200.00
	1861 CP	—	12.50	20.00	40.00	200.00

Mint mark: EoMo

KM#	Date	Mintage	Fine	VF	XF	Unc
374.5	1828 LF	—	325.00	525.00	900.00	2500.

Mint mark: Ga

KM#	Date	Mintage	Fine	VF	XF	Unc
374.6	1825 FS	—	20.00	40.00	80.00	200.00
	1826 FS	—	20.00	40.00	80.00	200.00
	1828/7 FS	—	100.00	150.00	225.00	400.00
	1829 FS	—	—	—	Rare	—
	1832/0 FS/LP	—	100.00	150.00	225.00	350.00
	1832 FS	—	12.50	20.00	40.00	200.00
	1833/2 FS/LP	—	12.50	20.00	40.00	200.00
	1834/27 FS	—	—	—	Rare	—
	1834 FS	—	12.50	20.00	40.00	200.00
	1835 FS	—	2100.	—	—	—
	1837 JG	—	12.50	20.00	40.00	200.00
	1838 JG	—	12.50	20.00	40.00	200.00
	1840/30 MC	—	12.50	20.00	40.00	200.00

KM#	Date	Mintage	Fine	VF	XF	Unc
374.6	1841 MC	—	12.50	20.00	40.00	200.00
	1842/32 JG/MC	—	35.00	50.00	100.00	200.00
	1842 JG	—	20.00	40.00	80.00	200.00
	1843 JG	—	12.50	20.00	40.00	200.00
	1843 MC/JG	—	12.50	20.00	40.00	200.00
	1844 MC	—	12.50	20.00	40.00	200.00
	1845/3 MC/JG	—	12.50	20.00	40.00	200.00
	1845/4 MC/JG	—	12.50	20.00	40.00	200.00
	1845 JG	—	12.50	20.00	40.00	200.00
	1846 JG	—	12.50	20.00	40.00	200.00
	1847/6 JG	—	25.00	40.00	80.00	200.00
	1848/7 JG	—	12.50	20.00	40.00	200.00
	1849 JG	—	12.50	20.00	40.00	200.00
	1850/40 JG	—	12.50	20.00	40.00	200.00
	1851 JG	—	250.00	350.00	500.00	—
	1852 JG	—	12.50	20.00	40.00	200.00
	1853/1 JG	—	12.50	20.00	40.00	200.00
	1854/3 JG	—	250.00	350.00	500.00	—
	1855 JG	—	35.00	50.00	80.00	200.00
	1856 JG	—	12.50	20.00	40.00	200.00
	1857 JG	—	250.00	350.00	500.00	—
	1859/8 JG	—	12.50	20.00	40.00	—
	1859 JG	—	12.50	20.00	40.00	200.00
	1862/1 JG	—	12.50	20.00	40.00	200.00

Mint mark: GC

KM#	Date	Mintage	Fine	VF	XF	Unc
374.7	1844 MP	—	40.00	60.00	125.00	275.00
	1845 MP	—	40.00	60.00	125.00	275.00
	1846 MP	—	50.00	100.00	150.00	300.00
	1847 MP	—	35.00	50.00	100.00	250.00
	1848 MP	—	50.00	100.00	150.00	300.00
	1849 MP	—	50.00	100.00	150.00	300.00
	1850 MP	—	50.00	100.00	150.00	300.00
	1851/0 MP	—	50.00	100.00	150.00	300.00
	1851 MP	—	50.00	100.00	150.00	300.00

Mint mark: Go

KM#	Date	Mintage	Fine	VF	XF	Unc
374.8	1825 JJ	—	7.50	15.00	30.00	150.00
	1826/5 JJ	—	7.50	15.00	30.00	150.00
	1826 JJ	—	7.50	10.00	25.00	150.00
	1826 MJ	—	7.50	10.00	25.00	150.00
	1827/6 MJ	—	7.50	10.00	25.00	150.00
	1827 MJ	—	7.50	10.00	25.00	150.00
	1828/7 MR	—	7.50	15.00	30.00	150.00
	1828 MJ	—	7.50	10.00	20.00	150.00
	1828 JM	—	7.50	10.00	20.00	150.00
	1829 MJ	—	7.50	10.00	20.00	150.00
	1831 MJ	—	7.50	10.00	20.00	150.00
	1832 MJ	—	7.50	10.00	20.00	150.00
	1833 MJ	—	7.50	10.00	20.00	150.00
	1834 PJ	—	7.50	10.00	20.00	150.00
	1835/4 PJ	—	7.50	15.00	30.00	150.00
	1835 PJ	—	7.50	10.00	20.00	150.00
	1836 PJ	—	7.50	10.00	20.00	150.00
	1837/6 PJ	—	7.50	10.00	20.00	150.00
	1837 PJ	—	7.50	10.00	20.00	150.00
	1838/7 PJ	—	7.50	10.00	20.00	150.00
	1838 PJ	—	7.50	10.00	20.00	150.00
	1839/8 PJ	—	7.50	15.00	30.00	150.00
	1839 PJ	—	7.50	10.00	20.00	150.00
	1840 PJ	—	7.50	10.00	20.00	150.00
	1841 PJ	—	7.50	10.00	20.00	150.00
	1842 PJ	—	7.50	10.00	20.00	150.00
	1842 PM/PJ	—	7.50	10.00	20.00	150.00
	1842 PM	—	7.50	10.00	20.00	150.00
	1843/2 PM concave wings, thin rays, sm. letters	—	7.50	10.00	20.00	150.00
	1843 PM convex wings, thick rays, lg. letters	—	7.50	10.00	20.00	150.00
	1844 PM	—	7.50	10.00	20.00	150.00
	1845/4 PM	—	7.50	10.00	20.00	150.00
	1845 PM	—	7.50	10.00	20.00	150.00
	1846/5 PM	—	10.00	15.00	35.00	150.00
	1846 PM	—	7.50	10.00	20.00	150.00
	1847 PM	—	7.50	10.00	20.00	150.00
	1848/7 PM	—	7.50	15.00	30.00	150.00
	1848 PM	—	7.50	15.00	30.00	150.00
	1848 PF	—	100.00	150.00	250.00	500.00
	1849/8 PF/PM	—	7.50	10.00	20.00	150.00
	1849 PF	—	7.50	10.00	20.00	150.00

KM#	Date Mintage	Fine	VF	XF	Unc
374.8	1850/40 PF —	7.50	10.00	20.00	150.00
	1850 PF —	7.50	10.00	20.00	150.00
	1851 PF —	7.50	10.00	20.00	150.00
	1852/1 PF —	7.50	10.00	20.00	150.00
	1852 PF —	7.50	10.00	20.00	150.00
	1853 PF —	7.50	10.00	20.00	150.00
	1854/3 PF —	7.50	10.00	20.00	150.00
	1854 PF old font and obv.				
	—	7.50	10.00	20.00	150.00
	1854 PF new font and obv.				
	—	7.50	10.00	20.00	150.00
	1855 PF —	7.50	10.00	20.00	150.00
	1855 PF star in G of mint mark				
	—	7.50	10.00	20.00	150.00
	1856/5 PF —	10.00	15.00	35.00	150.00
	1856 PF —	10.00	15.00	25.00	150.00
	1857/6 PF —	7.50	10.00	20.00	150.00
	1857 PF —	7.50	10.00	20.00	150.00
	1858/7 PF —	7.50	10.00	20.00	150.00
	1858 PF —	7.50	10.00	20.00	150.00
	1859/7 PF —	7.50	10.00	20.00	150.00
	1859 PF —	7.50	10.00	20.00	150.00
	1860/50 PF —	7.50	10.00	20.00	150.00
	1860/59 PF —	7.50	10.00	20.00	150.00
	1860 PF —	7.50	10.00	20.00	150.00
	1861/51 PF —	7.50	10.00	20.00	150.00
	1861/57 PF —	7.50	10.00	20.00	150.00
	1861/0 PF —	7.50	10.00	20.00	150.00
	1861 PF —	7.50	10.00	20.00	150.00
	1862/1 YE —	7.50	10.00	20.00	125.00
	1862 YE —	7.50	10.00	20.00	125.00
	1862/57 YE —	7.50	10.00	20.00	125.00
	1862 YE/PF —	7.50	10.00	20.00	125.00
	1862 YF —	7.50	10.00	20.00	125.00
	1863/52 YF —	7.50	10.00	20.00	125.00
	1863 YF —	7.50	10.00	20.00	125.00
	1867/57 YF —	7.50	10.00	20.00	125.00
	1868/57 YF —	10.00	15.00	25.00	125.00

NOTE: Varieties exist.

KM#	Date Mintage	Fine	VF	XF	Unc
	Mint mark: Ho				
374.9	1861 FM —	200.00	300.00	400.00	650.00
	1862/52 Ho FM/C. CE				
	—	250.00	350.00	500.00	—
	1867/1 PR/FM				
	—	75.00	150.00	250.00	500.00

KM#	Date Mintage	Fine	VF	XF	Unc
	Mint mark: Mo				
374.10	1825 JM —	10.00	15.00	30.00	175.00
	1826 JM —	10.00	15.00	30.00	175.00
	1827 JM —	10.00	15.00	30.00	175.00
	1828 JM —	10.00	15.00	30.00	175.00
	1829/8 JM —	10.00	15.00	30.00	175.00
	1829 JM —	10.00	15.00	30.00	175.00
	1830 JM —	40.00	60.00	125.00	250.00
	1831 JM —	10.00	15.00	30.00	175.00
	1832 JM —	100.00	200.00	400.00	—
	1833/2 MJ/JM				
	—	10.00	15.00	30.00	175.00
	1834 ML —	50.00	100.00	200.00	400.00
	1836 ML	—	Reported, not confirmed		
	1836 MF —	10.00	15.00	30.00	175.00
	1837 ML —	10.00	15.00	30.00	175.00
	1840 ML —	150.00	225.00	350.00	—
	1841 ML —	10.00	15.00	30.00	175.00
	1842 ML	—	—	Rare	—
	1847 RC —	10.00	15.00	30.00	175.00
	1848 GC —	10.00	15.00	30.00	175.00
	1849 GC —	10.00	15.00	30.00	175.00
	1850 GC —	10.00	15.00	30.00	175.00
	1851 GC —	40.00	60.00	125.00	250.00
	1852 GC —	10.00	15.00	30.00	175.00
	1853 GC —	10.00	15.00	30.00	175.00
	1854/44 GC —	10.00	15.00	30.00	175.00
	1855 GC —	10.00	15.00	30.00	175.00
	1855 GF/GC —	10.00	15.00	30.00	175.00
	1855 GF —	10.00	15.00	30.00	175.00
	1856/5 GF/GC				
	—	10.00	15.00	30.00	175.00
	1857 GF —	10.00	15.00	30.00	175.00
	1858 FH —	7.50	12.50	25.00	150.00
	1858 FH/GF —	7.50	12.50	25.00	150.00
	1859 FH —	7.50	12.50	25.00	150.00

KM#	Date Mintage	Fine	VF	XF	Unc
374.10	1860 FH —	7.50	12.50	25.00	150.00
	1860 TH —	7.50	12.50	25.00	150.00
	1861 TH	—	Reported, not confirmed		
	1861 CH —	7.50	12.50	25.00	150.00
	1862 CH —	7.50	12.50	25.00	150.00
	1863 CH —	7.50	12.50	25.00	150.00
	1863 TH —	7.50	12.50	25.00	150.00
	1867 CH —	7.50	12.50	25.00	150.00
	1868 CH —	10.00	15.00	30.00	150.00
	1868 PH —	7.50	12.50	25.00	150.00

NOTE: Varieties exist.

KM#	Date Mintage	Fine	VF	XF	Unc
	Mint mark: Pi				
374.11	1829 JS —	10.00	15.00	30.00	200.00
	1830/20 JS —	20.00	30.00	60.00	200.00
	1837 JS —	10.00	15.00	30.00	200.00
	1841 JS —	10.00	15.00	30.00	200.00
	1842/1 JS —	10.00	15.00	30.00	200.00
	1842 JS —	10.00	15.00	30.00	200.00
	1842 PS —	20.00	35.00	60.00	200.00
	1843 PS —	12.50	20.00	40.00	200.00
	1843 AM —	10.00	15.00	30.00	200.00
	1844 AM —	10.00	15.00	30.00	200.00
	1845 AM —	10.00	15.00	30.00	200.00
	1846 AM —	10.00	15.00	30.00	200.00
	1849 MC —	10.00	15.00	30.00	200.00
	1850 MC —	10.00	15.00	30.00	200.00
	1856 MC —	40.00	60.00	125.00	250.00
	1857 MC	—	—	—	—
	1858 MC —	12.50	20.00	40.00	200.00
	1859 MC —	50.00	70.00	100.00	200.00
	1861 PS —	10.00	15.00	30.00	200.00
	1862 RO —	12.50	20.00	40.00	200.00
	1863 RO —	100.00	250.00	350.00	500.00
	1868 PS —	10.00	15.00	30.00	200.00
	1869/8 PS —	10.00	15.00	30.00	200.00
	1869 PS —	10.00	15.00	30.00	200.00

KM#	Date Mintage	Fine	VF	XF	Unc
	Mint mark: Zs				
374.12	1825 AZ —	10.00	15.00	30.00	150.00
	1826 AV (A is inverted V)				
	—	7.50	10.00	25.00	150.00
	1826 AZ (A is inverted V)				
	—	7.50	10.00	25.00	150.00
	1826 AO —	10.00	15.00	30.00	150.00
	1827 AO (A is inverted V)				
	—	6.00	8.00	12.00	150.00
	1828/7 AO —	15.00	30.00	60.00	175.00
	1828 AO —	7.50	10.00	25.00	100.00
	1828 AO (A is inverted V)				
	—	7.50	10.00	25.00	150.00
	1829 AO —	7.50	10.00	25.00	150.00
	1829 OV —	7.50	10.00	25.00	150.00
	1830 OV —	7.50	10.00	25.00	150.00
	1831 OV —	7.50	10.00	25.00	150.00
	1831 OM/OV —	7.50	10.00	25.00	150.00
	1831 OM —	7.50	10.00	25.00	150.00
	1832/1 OM —	15.00	30.00	60.00	150.00
	1832 OM —	7.50	10.00	25.00	150.00
	1833/27 OM —	7.50	10.00	25.00	150.00
	1833/2 OM —	7.50	10.00	25.00	150.00
	1833 OM —	7.50	10.00	25.00	150.00
	1834 OM —	40.00	60.00	125.00	200.00
	1835 OM —	7.50	10.00	25.00	150.00
	1836 OM —	7.50	10.00	25.00	150.00
	1837 OM —	7.50	10.00	25.00	150.00
	1838 OM —	15.00	30.00	60.00	150.00
	1839 OM —	7.50	10.00	20.00	150.00
	1840 OM —	7.50	10.00	20.00	150.00
	1841/0 OM —	7.50	10.00	20.00	150.00
	1841 OM —	7.50	10.00	20.00	150.00
	1842 OM —	7.50	10.00	20.00	150.00
	1843 OM —	7.50	10.00	20.00	150.00
	1844 OM —	7.50	10.00	20.00	150.00
	1845 OM small letters and leaves				
	—	7.50	10.00	20.00	150.00
	1845 OM large letters and leaves				
	—	7.50	10.00	20.00	150.00
	1846 OM —	7.50	10.00	20.00	150.00
	1847 OM —	7.50	10.00	20.00	150.00
	1848 OM —	7.50	10.00	20.00	150.00
	1849 OM —	7.50	10.00	20.00	150.00
	1850 OM —	7.50	10.00	20.00	150.00
	1851 OM —	7.50	10.00	20.00	150.00
	1852 OM —	7.50	10.00	20.00	150.00
	1853 OM —	7.50	10.00	20.00	150.00

KM#	Date	Mintage	Fine	VF	XF	Unc
374.12	1854/3 OM	—	7.50	10.00	20.00	150.00
	1854 OM	—	7.50	10.00	20.00	150.00
	1855/4 OM	—	7.50	10.00	20.00	150.00
	1855 OM	—	7.50	10.00	20.00	150.00
	1855 MO	—	7.50	10.00	20.00	150.00
	1856/5 MO	—	7.50	10.00	20.00	150.00
	1856 MO	—	7.50	10.00	20.00	150.00
	1857 MO	—	7.50	10.00	20.00	150.00
	1858 MO	—	7.50	10.00	20.00	150.00
	1859 MO	—	7.50	10.00	20.00	150.00
	1860/59 MO	—	7.50	10.00	20.00	150.00
	1860 MO	—	7.50	10.00	20.00	100.00
	1860 VL	—	7.50	10.00	20.00	150.00
	1861 VL	—	7.50	10.00	20.00	150.00
	1862 VL	—	7.50	10.00	20.00	100.00
	1863 MO	—	12.50	20.00	40.00	150.00
	1863 VL	—	7.50	10.00	20.00	150.00
	1864 MO	—	7.50	10.00	20.00	150.00
	1864 VL	—	7.50	10.00	20.00	150.00
	1865 MO	—	7.50	10.00	20.00	150.00
	1867 JS	—	7.50	10.00	20.00	150.00
	1868 JS	—	10.00	15.00	35.00	150.00
	1868 YH	—	7.50	10.00	20.00	150.00
	1869 YH	—	7.50	10.00	20.00	150.00
	1870 YH	—	7.50	10.00	20.00	150.00

NOTE: Varieties exist.

4 REALES

13.5400 g, .903 SILVER, .3925 oz ASW
Mint mark: Ce.
Obv: Facing eagle.

KM#	Date	Mintage	Fine	VF	XF	Unc
375	1863 ML large C					
		—	200.00	500.00	850.00	4000.
	1863 ML small C					
		—	350.00	650.00	1000.	4500.

Mint mark: C

KM#	Date	Mintage	Fine	VF	XF	Unc
375.1	1846 CE	—	400.00	550.00	900.00	—
	1850 CE	—	75.00	125.00	250.00	600.00
	1852 CE	—	200.00	300.00	500.00	1250.
	1857 CE	—	—	—	Rare	—
	1858 CE	—	100.00	200.00	350.00	1000.
	1860 PV	—	25.00	50.00	125.00	600.00

Mint mark: Ga

KM#	Date	Mintage	Fine	VF	XF	Unc
375.2	1842/1 JG	—	—	Reported, not confirmed		
	1842 JG	—	—	Reported, not confirmed		
	1843 MC	—	20.00	40.00	80.00	400.00
	1844/3 MC	—	30.00	60.00	125.00	400.00
	1844 MC	—	20.00	40.00	80.00	400.00
	1845 MC	—	20.00	40.00	80.00	400.00
	1845 JG	—	20.00	40.00	80.00	400.00
	1846 JG	—	20.00	40.00	80.00	400.00
	1847 JG	—	40.00	80.00	150.00	400.00
	1848/7 JG	—	40.00	80.00	150.00	400.00
	1849 JG	—	40.00	80.00	150.00	400.00
	1850 JG	—	65.00	125.00	250.00	550.00
	1852 JG	—	—	—	Rare	—
	1854 JG	—	—	—	Rare	—
	1855 JG	—	100.00	200.00	400.00	1250.
	1856 JG	—	—	—	Rare	—
	1857/6 JG	—	65.00	125.00	250.00	550.00
	1858 JG	—	125.00	250.00	450.00	1250.
	1859/8 JG	—	125.00	250.00	450.00	1250.
	1860 JG	—	—	—	Rare	—
	1863/2 JG	—	150.00	300.00	1250.	6000.
	1863 JG	—	150.00	300.00	1250.	6000.

Mint mark: GC

KM#	Date	Mintage	Fine	VF	XF	Unc
375.3	1844 MP	—	1000.	2000.	3000.	—
	1845 MP	—	3000.	4000.	5000.	9000.
	1846 MP	—	1700.	2800.	—	—
	1847 MP	—	1500.	2500.	—	—
	1849 MP	—	2000.	3000.	—	—
	1850 MP	— 500.00	1000.			

Mint mark: Go

KM#	Date	Mintage	Fine	VF	XF	Unc
375.4	1835 PJ	—	12.50	25.00	60.00	350.00
	1836/5 PJ	—	15.00	30.00	75.00	350.00
	1836 PJ	—	15.00	30.00	75.00	350.00
	1837 PJ	—	12.50	25.00	60.00	350.00
	1838/7 PJ	—	15.00	30.00	75.00	350.00
	1838 PJ	—	12.50	30.00	75.00	350.00
	1839 PJ	—	12.50	25.00	60.00	350.00
	1840/30 PJ	—	20.00	50.00	100.00	350.00
	1841/31 PJ	—	150.00	250.00	450.00	1250.
	1842 PJ	—	—	—	Rare	—
	1842 PM	—	15.00	30.00	75.00	350.00
	1843/2 PM eagle w/convex wings, thick rays					
		—	12.50	25.00	60.00	350.00
	1843 PM eagle w/concave wings, thin rays					
		—	12.50	25.00	60.00	350.00
	1844/3 PM	—	15.00	30.00	75.00	350.00
	1844 PM	—	20.00	50.00	100.00	350.00
	1845/4 PM	—	20.00	50.00	100.00	350.00
	1845 PM	—	20.00	50.00	100.00	350.00
	1846/5 PM	—	15.00	30.00	75.00	350.00
	1846 PM	—	15.00	30.00	75.00	350.00
	1847/6 PM	—	15.00	30.00	75.00	350.00
	1847 PM	—	15.00	30.00	75.00	350.00
	1848/7 PM	—	20.00	50.00	100.00	350.00
	1848 PM	—	20.00	50.00	100.00	350.00
	1849 PF	—	20.00	50.00	100.00	350.00
	1850 PF	—	12.50	25.00	60.00	350.00
	1851 PF	—	12.50	25.00	60.00	350.00
	1852 PF	—	15.00	30.00	75.00	350.00
	1853 PF	—	15.00	30.00	75.00	350.00
	1854 PF large eagle					
		—	15.00	30.00	75.00	350.00
	1854 PF small eagle					
		—	15.00	30.00	75.00	350.00
	1855/4 PF	—	15.00	30.00	75.00	350.00
	1855 PF	—	12.50	25.00	60.00	350.00
	1856 PF	—	12.50	25.00	60.00	350.00
	1857 PF	—	20.00	50.00	100.00	350.00
	1858 PF	—	20.00	50.00	100.00	350.00
	1859 PF	—	20.00	50.00	100.00	350.00
	1860/59 PF	—	15.00	30.00	75.00	350.00
	1860 PF	—	15.00	30.00	75.00	350.00
	1861/51 PF	—	15.00	30.00	75.00	350.00
	1861 PF	—	20.00	50.00	100.00	350.00
	1862/1 YE	—	15.00	30.00	75.00	350.00
	1862/1 YF	—	15.00	30.00	75.00	350.00
	1862 YE/PF	—	15.00	30.00	75.00	350.00
	1862 YE	—	15.00	30.00	75.00	350.00
	1862 YF	—	15.00	30.00	75.00	350.00
	1863/53 YF	—	15.00	30.00	75.00	350.00
	1863 YF/PF	—	15.00	30.00	75.00	350.00
	1863 YF	—	15.00	30.00	75.00	350.00
	1867/57 YF/PF					
		—	15.00	30.00	75.00	350.00
	1868/58 YF/PF					
		—	15.00	30.00	75.00	350.00
	1870 FR	—	15.00	30.00	75.00	350.00

NOTE: Varieties exist. Some 1862 dates appear to be 1869 because of weak dies.

Mint mark: Ho

KM#	Date	Mintage	Fine	VF	XF	Unc
375.5	1861 FM	—	200.00	350.00	500.00	1850.
	1867/1 PR/FM					
		—	150.00	275.00	400.00	1750.

Mint mark: Mo

KM#	Date	Mintage	Fine	VF	XF	Unc
375.6	1827/6 JM	—	200.00	400.00	—	—
	1850 GC	—	—	—	Rare	—
	1852 GC	—	—	—	Rare	—
	1854 GC	—	—	—	Rare	—
	1855 GF/GC	—	50.00	100.00	200.00	500.00
	1855 GF	—	100.00	200.00	350.00	800.00
	1856 GF/GC	—	20.00	50.00	100.00	350.00
	1856 GF	—	—	—	Rare	—
	1859 FH	—	20.00	50.00	100.00	350.00

KM#	Date	Mintage	Fine	VF	XF	Unc
375.6	1861 CH	—	15.00	30.00	75.00	300.00
	1862 CH	—	20.00	50.00	100.00	350.00
	1863/2 CH	—	20.00	50.00	100.00	350.00
	1863 CH	—	75.00	150.00	300.00	650.00
	1867 CH	—	20.00	50.00	100.00	350.00
	1868 CH/PH	—	30.00	75.00	150.00	400.00
	1868 CH	—	20.00	50.00	100.00	350.00
	1868 PH	—	30.00	75.00	150.00	400.00

Mint mark: O

KM#	Date	Mintage	Fine	VF	XF	Unc
375.7	1861 FR ornamental edge					
		—	225.00	450.00	700.00	2500.
	1861 FR herringbone edge					
		—	275.00	550.00	800.00	2500.
	1861 FR obliquely reeded edge					
		—	200.00	400.00	650.00	—

Mint mark: Pi

KM#	Date	Mintage	Fine	VF	XF	Unc
375.8	1837 JS	—	—	—	Rare	—
	1838 JS	—	150.00	250.00	400.00	800.00
	1842 PS	—	50.00	100.00	200.00	450.00
	1843/2 PS	—	50.00	100.00	200.00	450.00
	1843/2 PS 3 cut from 8 punch					
		—	50.00	100.00	200.00	450.00
	1843 AM	—	30.00	75.00	150.00	450.00
	1843 PS	—	50.00	100.00	200.00	450.00
	1844 AM	—	30.00	75.00	150.00	450.00
	1845/4 AM	—	20.00	50.00	100.00	450.00
	1845 AM	—	20.00	50.00	100.00	450.00
	1846 AM	—	20.00	50.00	100.00	450.00
	1847 AM	—	75.00	150.00	250.00	550.00
	1848 AM	—	—	—	Rare	—
	1849 MC/AM	—	20.00	50.00	100.00	450.00
	1849 MC	—	20.00	50.00	100.00	450.00
	1849 PS	—	20.00	50.00	100.00	450.00
	1850 MC	—	20.00	50.00	100.00	450.00
	1851 MC	—	20.00	50.00	100.00	450.00
	1852 MC	—	20.00	50.00	100.00	450.00
	1853 MC	—	20.00	50.00	100.00	450.00
	1854 MC	—	100.00	200.00	400.00	1100.
	1855 MC	—	200.00	350.00	500.00	1500.
	1856 MC	—	300.00	450.00	700.00	—
	1857 MC	—	—	—	Rare	—
	1857 PS	—	—	—	Rare	—
	1858 MC	—	100.00	200.00	400.00	1000.
	1859 MC	—	2000.	3000.	—	—
	1860 PS	—	300.00	450.00	700.00	—
	1861 PS	—	30.00	75.00	150.00	450.00
	1861 RO/PS	—	30.00	75.00	150.00	450.00
	1861 RO	—	50.00	100.00	200.00	450.00
	1862 RO	—	30.00	75.00	150.00	450.00
	1863 RO	—	30.00	75.00	150.00	450.00
	1864 RO	—	1600.	2600.	—	—
	1868 PS	—	30.00	75.00	150.00	450.00
	1869/8 PS	—	30.00	75.00	150.00	450.00
	1869 PS	—	30.00	75.00	150.00	450.00

Mint mark: Zs

KM#	Date	Mintage	Fine	VF	XF	Unc
375.9	1830 OM	—	20.00	50.00	100.00	350.00
	1831 OM	—	15.00	30.00	75.00	350.00
	1832/1 OM	—	20.00	50.00	100.00	350.00
	1832 OM	—	20.00	50.00	100.00	350.00
	1833/2 OM	—	20.00	50.00	100.00	350.00
	1833/27 OM	—	15.00	30.00	75.00	350.00
	1833 OM	—	15.00	30.00	75.00	350.00
	1834/3 OM	—	20.00	50.00	100.00	350.00
	1834 OM	—	15.00	30.00	75.00	350.00
	1835 OM	—	15.00	30.00	75.00	350.00
	1836 OM	—	15.00	30.00	75.00	350.00
	1837/5 OM	—	20.00	50.00	100.00	350.00
	1837/6 OM	—	20.00	50.00	100.00	350.00
	1837 OM	—	20.00	50.00	100.00	350.00
	1838/7 OM	—	15.00	30.00	75.00	350.00
	1839 OM	—	250.00	375.00	500.00	—
	1840 OM	—	—	—	Rare	—
	1841 OM	—	15.00	30.00	75.00	350.00
	1842 OM small letters					
		—	75.00	150.00	300.00	800.00
	1842 OM large letters					
		—	15.00	30.00	75.00	350.00
	1843 OM	—	15.00	30.00	75.00	350.00
	1844 OM	—	20.00	50.00	100.00	350.00
	1845 OM	—	20.00	50.00	100.00	350.00
	1846/5 OM	—	25.00	60.00	125.00	350.00
	1846 OM	—	20.00	50.00	100.00	350.00
	1847 OM	—	15.00	30.00	75.00	350.00

KM#	Date	Mintage	Fine	VF	XF	Unc
375.9	1848/6 OM	—	50.00	75.00	125.00	350.00
	1848 OM	—	20.00	50.00	100.00	350.00
	1849 OM	—	20.00	50.00	100.00	350.00
	1850 OM	—	20.00	50.00	100.00	350.00
	1851 OM	—	15.00	30.00	75.00	350.00
	1852 OM	—	15.00	30.00	75.00	350.00
	1853 OM	—	20.00	50.00	100.00	350.00
	1854/3 OM	—	30.00	75.00	150.00	350.00
	1855/4 OM	—	20.00	50.00	100.00	350.00
	1855 OM	—	15.00	30.00	75.00	350.00
	1856 OM	—	15.00	30.00	75.00	350.00
	1856 MO	—	20.00	50.00	100.00	350.00
	1857/5 MO	—	20.00	50.00	100.00	350.00
	1857 O/M	—	20.00	50.00	100.00	350.00
	1857 MO	—	15.00	30.00	75.00	350.00
	1858 MO	—	20.00	50.00	100.00	350.00
	1859 MO	—	15.00	30.00	75.00	350.00
	1860/59 MO	—	20.00	50.00	100.00	350.00
	1860 MO	—	15.00	30.00	75.00	350.00
	1860 VL	—	20.00	50.00	100.00	350.00
	1861/0 VL	—	20.00	50.00	100.00	350.00
	1861 VL	—	15.00	30.00	75.00	350.00
	1862/1 VL	—	20.00	50.00	100.00	350.00
	1862 VL	—	20.00	50.00	100.00	350.00
	1863 VL	—	20.00	50.00	100.00	350.00
	1863 MO	—	20.00	50.00	100.00	350.00
	1864 VL	—	15.00	30.00	75.00	350.00
	1868 JS	—	20.00	50.00	100.00	350.00
	1868 YH	—	15.00	30.00	75.00	350.00
	1869 YH	—	15.00	30.00	75.00	350.00
	1870 YH	—	15.00	30.00	75.00	350.00

8 REALES

27.0700 g, .903 SILVER, .7859 oz ASW
Mint mark: Do
Obv: Hooked-neck eagle.

KM#	Date	Mintage	Fine	VF	XF	Unc
376	1824 RL	—	200.00	350.00	1250.	2750.

NOTE: Varieties exist.

Mint mark: Go

KM#	Date	Mintage	Fine	VF	XF	Unc
376.1	1824 JM	—	200.00	325.00	1000.	3500.
	1825/4 JJ	—	550.00	800.00	1500.	6000.
	1825 JJ	—	500.00	750.00	1400.	5500.

Mint mark: Mo

KM#	Date	Mintage	Fine	VF	XF	Unc
376.2	1823 JM edge: circle and rectangle pattern					
		—	—	—	Rare	—
	1823 JM edge: laurel leaves					
		—	150.00	300.00	650.00	2500.
	1824 JM	—	125.00	250.00	450.00	2000.
	1824 JM (error) REPULICA					
		—	—	—	Rare	—

NOTE: These are rarely found with detail on the eagles breast and bring a premium if even slight feather detail is present there.

Mint mark: A, As

KM#	Date	Mintage	Fine	VF	XF	Unc
377	1864 PG	—	650.00	900.00	1200.	—
	1865/4 PG	—	—	—	Rare	—
	1865 PG	—	500.00	750.00	1000.	—
	1866/5 PG	—	—	—	Rare	—
	1866 PG	—	—	—	Rare	—
	1866 DL	—	—	—	Rare	—
	1867 DL	—	—	—	Rare	—
	1868 DL	—	50.00	100.00	150.00	300.00
	1869/8 DL	—	50.00	100.00	150.00	—
	1869 DL	—	60.00	85.00	150.00	300.00
	1870 DL	—	30.00	60.00	150.00	300.00
	1871 DL	—	20.00	35.00	75.00	200.00
	1872 AM/DL	—	25.00	50.00	100.00	300.00
	1872 AM	—	25.00	50.00	100.00	250.00
	1873 AM	.509	15.00	30.00	60.00	175.00
	1874 DL	—	15.00	30.00	60.00	175.00
	1875A DL 7/7—	40.00	80.00	150.00	300.00
	1875A DL	—	15.00	25.00	50.00	150.00
	1875AsDL	—	30.00	60.00	125.00	250.00
	1876 DL	—	15.00	25.00	50.00	150.00
	1877 DL	.515	15.00	25.00	50.00	150.00
	1878 DL	.513	15.00	25.00	50.00	150.00
	1879 DL	—	20.00	35.00	75.00	175.00
	1879 ML	—	30.00	60.00	125.00	300.00
	1880 ML	—	12.00	15.00	25.00	125.00
	1881 ML	.966	12.00	15.00	25.00	125.00
	1882 ML	.480	12.00	15.00	25.00	125.00
	1883 ML	.464	12.00	15.00	25.00	125.00
	1884 ML	—	12.00	15.00	25.00	125.00
	1885 ML	.280	12.00	15.00	25.00	125.00
	1886 ML	.857	12.00	15.00	20.00	100.00
	1886/0 As/Cn ML/JD					
	Inc. Ab.	15.00	20.00	30.00	125.00
	1887 ML	.650	12.00	15.00	20.00	100.00
	1888/7 ML	.508	30.00	60.00	100.00	400.00
	1888 ML Inc. Ab.	12.00	15.00	20.00	100.00
	1889 ML	.427	12.00	15.00	20.00	100.00
	1890 ML	.450	12.00	15.00	20.00	100.00
	1891 ML	.533	12.00	15.00	20.00	100.00
	1892 ML	.465	12.00	15.00	20.00	100.00
	1893 ML	.734	10.00	12.00	18.00	75.00
	1894 ML	.725	10.00	12.00	18.00	75.00
	1895 ML	.477	10.00	12.00	18.00	75.00

NOTE: Varieties exist.

Mint mark: Ce

KM#	Date	Mintage	Fine	VF	XF	Unc
377.1	1863 ML	—	375.00	625.00	1000.	2250.
	1863 CeML/PiMC					
		—	375.00	650.00	1100.	2750.

Mint mark: Ca

KM#	Date	Mintage	Fine	VF	XF	Unc
377.2	1831 MR	—	1000.	1750.	2250.	3250.
	1832 MR	—	125.00	200.00	300.00	600.00
	1833 MR	—	500.00	750.00	1250.	—
	1834 MR	—	—	—	Rare	—
	1834 AM	—	—	—	Rare	—
	1835 AM	—	150.00	250.00	400.00	800.00
	1836 AM	—	100.00	150.00	225.00	450.00
	1837 AM	—	—	—	Rare	—
	1838 AM	—	100.00	200.00	300.00	600.00
	1839 RG	—	1250.	2500.	—	—
	1840 RG 1 dot after date					
		—	400.00	600.00	800.00	1500.
	1840 RG 3 dots after date					
		—	400.00	600.00	800.00	1500.
	1841 RG	—	50.00	100.00	150.00	300.00
	1842 RG	—	25.00	40.00	65.00	125.00
	1843 RG	—	40.00	80.00	125.00	250.00
	1844/1 RG	—	35.00	70.00	100.00	200.00
	1844 RG	—	25.00	40.00	65.00	125.00
	1845 RG	—	25.00	40.00	65.00	125.00
	1846 RG	—	30.00	60.00	100.00	250.00
	1847 RG	—	40.00	80.00	125.00	250.00
	1848 RG	—	30.00	60.00	100.00	200.00
	1849 RG	—	30.00	60.00	100.00	200.00
	1850/40 RG	—	40.00	80.00	125.00	250.00
	1850 RG	—	30.00	60.00	100.00	200.00
	1851/41 RG	—	100.00	200.00	300.00	500.00
	1851 RG	—	150.00	250.00	400.00	750.00
	1852/42 RG	—	150.00	250.00	400.00	750.00
	1852 RG	—	150.00	250.00	400.00	750.00
	1853/43 RG	—	150.00	250.00	400.00	750.00
	1853 RG	—	150.00	250.00	400.00	750.00
	1854/44 RG	—	100.00	200.00	300.00	500.00
	1854 RG	—	50.00	100.00	150.00	300.00
	1855/45 RG	—	100.00	200.00	350.00	650.00
	1855 RG	—	75.00	125.00	200.00	400.00
	1856/45 RG	—	200.00	400.00	600.00	1000.
	1856/5 JC	—	600.00	1000.	1250.	1750.
	1857 JC/RG	—	40.00	80.00	125.00	250.00
	1857 JC	—	50.00	100.00	150.00	250.00
	1858 JC	—	20.00	30.00	50.00	120.00
	1858 BA	—	—	—	Rare	—
	1859 JC	—	40.00	80.00	125.00	250.00
	1860 JC	—	20.00	40.00	90.00	175.00
	1861 JC	—	15.00	25.00	50.00	120.00
	1862 JC	—	15.00	25.00	50.00	120.00
	1863 JC	—	20.00	35.00	75.00	150.00
	1864 JC	—	20.00	35.00	75.00	150.00
	1865 JC	—	100.00	200.00	350.00	600.00
	1865 FP	—	—	—	Rare	—
	1866 JC	—	—	—	Rare	—
	1866 FP	—	—	—	Rare	—
	1866 JG	—	—	—	Rare	—
	1867 JG	—	100.00	200.00	350.00	600.00
	1868 JG	—	75.00	150.00	200.00	350.00
	1868 MM	—	50.00	100.00	150.00	300.00
	1869 MM	—	20.00	35.00	65.00	125.00
	1870 MM	—	20.00	35.00	65.00	125.00
	1871/0 MM	—	15.00	25.00	50.00	100.00

KM#	Date	Mintage	Fine	VF	XF	Unc
377.2	1871 MM	—	15.00	25.00	50.00	100.00
	1871 MM first M/inverted M					
		—	20.00	35.00	65.00	125.00
	1873 MM	—	20.00	35.00	65.00	125.00
	1873 MM/T					
		—	15.00	25.00	50.00	100.00
	1874 MM	—	12.00	15.00	30.00	100.00
	1875 MM	—	12.00	15.00	30.00	100.00
	1876 MM	—	12.00	15.00	30.00	100.00
	1877 EA	.472	12.00	15.00	30.00	100.00
	1877 GR	I.A.	25.00	45.00	65.00	150.00
	1877 JM	I.A.	12.00	15.00	30.00	100.00
	1877 AV	I.A.	100.00	200.00	350.00	750.00
	1878 AV	.439	12.00	15.00	25.00	75.00
	1879 AV	—	12.00	15.00	25.00	75.00
	1880 AV	—	250.00	400.00	600.00	1200.
	1880 PM	—	500.00	750.00	1000.	1500.
	1880 MG normal initials					
		—	12.00	15.00	25.00	100.00
	1880 MG tall initials					
		—	12.00	15.00	25.00	100.00
	1880 MM	—	12.00	15.00	25.00	100.00
	1881 MG	1.085	10.00	12.00	20.00	60.00
	1882 MG	.779	10.00	12.00	20.00	60.00
	1882 MM	I.A.	10.00	12.00	20.00	60.00
	1882 MM M sideways					
		Inc. Ab.	20.00	40.00	90.00	150.00
	1883 sideways M MM					
		.818	—	—	—	—
	1883 MM	I.A.	10.00	12.00	20.00	60.00
	1884/3 MM	—	12.00	15.00	30.00	75.00
	1884 MM	—	10.00	12.00	20.00	60.00
	1885/4 MM					
		1.345	15.00	25.00	50.00	100.00
	1885/6 MM	I.A.	15.00	25.00	50.00	100.00
	1885 MM	I.A.	10.00	12.00	20.00	60.00
	1886 MM	2.483	10.00	12.00	20.00	60.00
	1887 MM	2.625	10.00	12.00	20.00	60.00
	1888/7 MM					
		2.434	15.00	25.00	50.00	100.00
	1888 MM	I.A.	10.00	12.00	20.00	60.00
	1889 MM	2.681	10.00	12.00	20.00	60.00
	1890 MM	2.137	10.00	12.00	20.00	60.00
	1891/0 MM					
		2.268	15.00	25.00	50.00	100.00
	1891 MM	I.A.	10.00	12.00	20.00	80.00
	1892 MM	2.527	10.00	12.00	20.00	60.00
	1893 MM	2.632	10.00	12.00	20.00	60.00
	1894 MM	2.642	10.00	12.00	20.00	60.00
	1895 MM	1.112	10.00	12.00	20.00	60.00

NOTE: Varieties exist.

Mint mark: C, Cn

KM#	Date	Mintage	Fine	VF	XF	Unc
377.3	1846 CE	—	150.00	300.00	800.00	1500.
	1847 CE	—	600.00	1000.	1500.	—
	1848 CE	—	150.00	300.00	600.00	1000.
	1849 CE	—	75.00	125.00	200.00	400.00
	1850 CE	—	75.00	125.00	200.00	400.00
	1851 CE	—	125.00	250.00	450.00	1000.
	1852/1 CE	—	100.00	150.00	250.00	500.00
	1852 CE	—	100.00	200.00	350.00	650.00
	1853/0 CE	—	200.00	350.00	700.00	1300.
	1853/2/0	—	200.00	400.00	750.00	1400.
	1853 CE thick rays					
		—	100.00	175.00	300.00	600.00
	1853 CE (error:) MEXIGANA					
		—	200.00	350.00	650.00	—
	1854 CE	—	—	—	Rare	—
	1854 CE large eagle & hat					
		—	150.00	300.00	600.00	1000.
	1855/6 CE	—	40.00	60.00	100.00	200.00
	1855 CE	—	25.00	40.00	60.00	125.00
	1856 CE	—	50.00	100.00	175.00	350.00
	1857 CE	—	20.00	30.00	45.00	100.00
	1858 CE	—	30.00	40.00	60.00	125.00
	1859 CE	—	20.00	30.00	45.00	100.00
	1860/9 PV/CV					
		—	50.00	70.00	100.00	200.00
	1860/9 PV/E	—	50.00	70.00	100.00	200.00
	1860 CE	—	25.00	40.00	55.00	100.00
	1860 PV	—	40.00	60.00	80.00	150.00
	1861/0 CE	—	40.00	60.00	100.00	250.00

KM#	Date	Mintage	Fine	VF	XF	Unc
377.3	1861 PV/CE	—	75.00	125.00	200.00	350.00
	1861 CE	—	20.00	35.00	50.00	150.00
	1862 CE	—	20.00	35.00	50.00	150.00
	1863/2 CE	—	30.00	50.00	75.00	200.00
	1863 CE	—	20.00	30.00	50.00	150.00
	1864 CE	—	30.00	60.00	100.00	300.00
	1865 CE	—	125.00	200.00	325.00	650.00
	1866 CE	—	—	Rare	—	
	1867 CE	—	125.00	200.00	375.00	750.00
	1868/7 CE	—	30.00	40.00	75.00	150.00
	1868/8	—	50.00	100.00	150.00	300.00
	1868 CE	—	30.00	40.00	75.00	150.00
	1869 CE	—	30.00	40.00	75.00	175.00
	1870 CE	—	35.00	50.00	90.00	200.00
	1873 MP	—	50.00	100.00	150.00	300.00
	1874C MP	—	20.00	30.00	45.00	100.00
	1874CN MP	—	125.00	200.00	300.00	600.00
	1875 MP	—	12.00	15.00	20.00	75.00
	1876 GP	—	12.00	15.00	30.00	90.00
	1876 CG	—	12.00	15.00	20.00	75.00
	1877 CG	.339	12.00	15.00	20.00	75.00
	1877 GnCG (error)					
		—	65.00	125.00	200.00	400.00
	1877 JA	Inc. Ab.	35.00	75.00	125.00	250.00
	1878/7 CG	.483	35.00	75.00	125.00	250.00
	1878 CG	Inc. Ab.	15.00	25.00	35.00	125.00
	1878 JD	Inc. Ab.	15.00	20.00	30.00	125.00
	1878 JD D/retrograde D					
		Inc. Ab.	20.00	30.00	40.00	150.00
	1879 JD	—	12.00	15.00	30.00	90.00
	1880/70 JD	—	15.00	20.00	30.00	90.00
	1880 JD	—	12.00	15.00	20.00	75.00
	1881/0 JD					
		1.032	15.00	20.00	30.00	90.00
	1881C JD					
		Inc. Ab.	12.00	15.00	20.00	75.00
	1881CnJD	I.A.	40.00	60.00	90.00	150.00
	1882 JD	.397	12.00	15.00	20.00	75.00
	1883 AM	I.A.	12.00	15.00	20.00	125.00
	1884 AM	—	12.00	15.00	20.00	75.00
	1885/6 AM	.227	20.00	30.00	45.00	100.00
	1885C AM	I.A.	75.00	125.00	250.00	500.00
	1885CnAM	I.A.	12.00	15.00	20.00	75.00
	1885GnAM (error)					
		Inc. Ab.	60.00	100.00	150.00	300.00
	1886 AM	.571	12.00	15.00	20.00	75.00
	1887 AM	.732	12.00	15.00	20.00	75.00
	1888 AM	.768	12.00	15.00	20.00	75.00
	1889 AM	1.075	12.00	15.00	20.00	75.00
	1890 AM	.874	10.00	12.00	18.00	60.00
	1891 AM	.777	10.00	12.00	18.00	60.00
	1892 AM	.681	10.00	12.00	18.00	60.00
	1893 AM	1.144	10.00	12.00	18.00	60.00
	1894 AM	2.118	10.00	12.00	18.00	60.00
	1895 AM	1.834	10.00	12.00	18.00	60.00
	1896 AM	2.134	10.00	12.00	18.00	60.00
	1897 AM	1.580	10.00	12.00	18.00	60.00

NOTE: Varieties exist.

Mint mark: Do

KM#	Date	Mintage	Fine	VF	XF	Unc
377.4	1825 RL	—	30.00	55.00	85.00	175.00
	1826 RL	—	40.00	100.00	250.00	500.00
	1827/6 RL	—	35.00	60.00	80.00	175.00

KM#	Date	Mintage	Fine	VF	XF	Unc
377.4	1827 RL	—	30.00	50.00	75.00	150.00
	1828/7 RL	—	35.00	60.00	80.00	175.00
	1828 RL	—	25.00	50.00	75.00	150.00
	1829 RL	—	25.00	50.00	75.00	150.00
	1830 RM B on eagles claw					
		—	25.00	50.00	75.00	150.00
	1831 RM B on eagles claw					
		—	20.00	30.00	50.00	125.00
	1832 RM Mexican dies, B on eagles claw					
		—	25.00	50.00	100.00	200.00
	1832/1 RM/RL French dies					
		—	25.00	35.00	75.00	150.00
	1833/2 RM/RL					
		—	20.00	35.00	75.00	150.00
	1833 RM	—	15.00	30.00	50.00	125.00
	1834/3/2 RM/RL					
		—	20.00	35.00	75.00	150.00
	1834 RM	—	15.00	25.00	45.00	100.00
	1835/4 RM/RL					
		—	25.00	40.00	80.00	150.00
	1835 RM	—	20.00	35.00	55.00	125.00
	1836/1 RM	—	20.00	30.00	50.00	125.00
	1836/4 RM	—	20.00	30.00	50.00	125.00
	1836/5/4 RM/RL					
		—	75.00	150.00	250.00	500.00
	1836 RM	—	20.00	30.00	50.00	125.00
	1836 RM M on snake					
		—	20.00	30.00	50.00	125.00
	1837/1 RM	—	20.00	30.00	50.00	125.00
	1837 RM	—	20.00	30.00	50.00	125.00
	1838/1 RM	—	20.00	30.00	50.00	125.00
	1838/7 RM	—	20.00	30.00	50.00	125.00
	1838 RM	—	20.00	30.00	50.00	125.00
	1839/1 RM/RL					
		—	20.00	30.00	50.00	125.00
	1839/1 RM	—	20.00	30.00	50.00	125.00
	1839 RM	—	20.00	30.00	50.00	125.00
	1840/38/31 RM					
		—	20.00	30.00	50.00	125.00
	1840/39 RM	—	20.00	30.00	50.00	125.00
	1840 RM	—	20.00	30.00	50.00	125.00
	1841/31 RM	—	25.00	50.00	75.00	175.00
	1842/31 RM B below cactus					
		—	125.00	250.00	400.00	750.00
	1842/31 RM	—	40.00	80.00	125.00	250.00
	1842/32 RM	—	40.00	80.00	125.00	250.00
	1842 RM eagle of 1832-41					
		—	20.00	30.00	50.00	125.00
	1842 RM pre 1832 eagle resumed					
		—	20.00	30.00	50.00	125.00
	1842 RM	—	40.00	80.00	125.00	250.00
	1843/33 RM	—	50.00	90.00	150.00	250.00
	1844/34 RM	—	100.00	200.00	300.00	500.00
	1844/35 RM	—	100.00	200.00	300.00	500.00
	1845/31 RM	—	35.00	75.00	125.00	250.00
	1845/34 RM	—	35.00	75.00	125.00	250.00
	1845/35 RM	—	35.00	75.00	125.00	250.00
	1845 RM	—	20.00	30.00	50.00	125.00
	1846/31 RM	—	20.00	30.00	50.00	125.00
	1846/36 RM	—	20.00	30.00	50.00	125.00
	1846 RM	—	20.00	30.00	50.00	125.00
	1847 RM	—	25.00	50.00	75.00	150.00
	1848/7 RM	—	125.00	250.00	400.00	750.00
	1848/7 CM/RM					
		—	100.00	200.00	350.00	700.00
	1848 CM/RM	—	100.00	200.00	350.00	700.00
	1848 RM	—	100.00	200.00	300.00	600.00
	1848 CM	—	50.00	100.00	200.00	400.00
	1849/39 CM	—	100.00	200.00	350.00	700.00
	1849 CM	—	100.00	200.00	350.00	700.00
	1849 JMR/CM oval O					
		—	200.00	325.00	450.00	800.00
	1849 DoJMR oval O					
		—	200.00	400.00	600.00	1000.
	1849 DoJMR round O					
		—	200.00	400.00	600.00	1000.
	1850 JMR	—	100.00	150.00	250.00	500.00
	1851/0 JMR	—	100.00	150.00	250.00	500.00
	1851 JMR	—	100.00	150.00	250.00	500.00
	1852 CP/JMR					
		—	—	—	Rare	—
	1852 CP	—	—	—	Rare	—
	1852 JMR	—	175.00	250.00	375.00	550.00
	1853 CP/JMR					
		—	175.00	275.00	400.00	700.00

KM#	Date	Mintage	Fine	VF	XF	Unc
377.4	1853 CP	—	200.00	350.00	600.00	1200.
	1854 CP	—	25.00	35.00	65.00	300.00
	1855 CP eagle type of 1854					
		—	50.00	100.00	175.00	350.00
	1855 CP eagle type of 1856					
		—	50.00	100.00	175.00	350.00
	1856 CP	—	50.00	100.00	175.00	350.00
	1857 CP	—	35.00	75.00	175.00	350.00
	1858/7 CP	—	25.00	35.00	70.00	150.00
	1858 CP	—	20.00	30.00	60.00	150.00
	1859 CP	—	20.00	30.00	60.00	150.00
	1860/59 CP	—	30.00	50.00	100.00	200.00
	1860 CP	—	20.00	30.00	60.00	150.00
	1861/0 CP	—	30.00	50.00	100.00	200.00
	1861 CP	—	20.00	30.00	50.00	125.00
	1862/1 CP	—	25.00	35.00	60.00	125.00
	1862 CP	—	20.00	30.00	55.00	100.00
	1863/2 CP	—	25.00	50.00	75.00	175.00
	1863/53 CP	—	30.00	60.00	90.00	200.00
	1863 CP	—	25.00	50.00	75.00	175.00
	1864 CP	—	100.00	150.00	250.00	500.00
	1864 LT	—	25.00	40.00	80.00	175.00
	1865 LT	—	—	—	Rare	—
	1866 CM	—	—	—	Rare	—
	1867 CM	—	—	—	Rare	—
	1867/6 CP	—	200.00	400.00	600.00	1200.
	1867 CP	—	175.00	300.00	500.00	1000.
	1867 CP/CM	—	175.00	300.00	500.00	1000.
	1867 CP/LT	—	175.00	300.00	500.00	1000.
	1868 CP	—	25.00	40.00	80.00	175.00
	1869 CP	—	20.00	30.00	50.00	125.00
	1870/69 CP	—	20.00	30.00	50.00	125.00
	1870/9 CP	—	20.00	30.00	50.00	125.00
	1870 CP	—	20.00	30.00	50.00	125.00
	1873 CP	—	125.00	225.00	325.00	600.00
	1873 CM	—	30.00	50.00	100.00	200.00
	1874/3 CM	—	12.00	15.00	20.00	100.00
	1874 CM	—	10.00	15.00	20.00	60.00
	1874 JH	—	—	—	Rare	—
	1875 CM	—	10.00	15.00	20.00	75.00
	1875 JH	—	100.00	175.00	275.00	500.00
	1876 CM	—	10.00	15.00	20.00	75.00
	1877 CM	.431	—	—	Rare	—
	1877 CP	Inc. Ab.	10.00	15.00	20.00	75.00
	1877 JMP	I.A.	—	—	Rare	—
	1878 PE	.409	15.00	25.00	40.00	90.00
	1878 TB	Inc. Ab.	10.00	15.00	20.00	75.00
	1879 TB	—	10.00	15.00	20.00	75.00
	1880/70 TB	—	150.00	250.00	375.00	650.00
	1880/70 TB/JP					
		—	150.00	250.00	375.00	650.00
	1880/70 JP	—	15.00	25.00	40.00	90.00
	1880 TB	—	150.00	250.00	375.00	650.00
	1880 JP	—	10.00	15.00	20.00	75.00
	1881 JP	.928	10.00	15.00	20.00	75.00
	1882 JP	.414	10.00	15.00	20.00	75.00
	1882 MC/JP					
		Inc. Ab.	30.00	60.00	100.00	200.00
	1882 MC	I.A.	25.00	50.00	75.00	150.00
	1883/73 MC					
		.452	15.00	25.00	40.00	90.00
	1883 MC	I.A.	10.00	15.00	20.00	75.00
	1884/3 MC	—	20.00	30.00	60.00	110.00
	1884 MC	—	10.00	15.00	20.00	75.00
	1885 MC	.547	10.00	12.00	18.00	65.00
	1885 JB	Inc. Ab.	25.00	35.00	50.00	125.00
	1886/3 MC	.955	15.00	25.00	40.00	90.00
	1886 MC	I.A.	10.00	12.00	18.00	65.00
	1887 MC	1.004	10.00	12.00	18.00	65.00
	1888 MC	.996	10.00	12.00	18.00	65.00
	1889 MC	.874	10.00	12.00	18.00	65.00
	1890 MC	1.119	10.00	12.00	18.00	65.00
	1890 JP	Inc. Ab.	10.00	12.00	18.00	65.00
	1891 JP	1.487	10.00	12.00	18.00	65.00
	1892 JP	1.597	10.00	12.00	18.00	65.00
	1892 ND	Inc. Ab.	25.00	50.00	100.00	200.00
	1893 ND	1.617	10.00	12.00	18.00	65.00
	1894 ND	1.537	10.00	12.00	18.00	65.00

KM#	Date	Mintage	Fine	VF	XF	Unc
377.4	1895/3 ND	.761	15.00	25.00	40.00	90.00
	1895 ND	I.A.	10.00	12.00	18.00	65.00

NOTE: Varieties exist.

Mint mark: EoMo

KM#	Date	Mintage	Fine	VF	XF	Unc
377.5	1828 LF/LP	—	500.00	1000.	2500.	—
	1828 LF	—	500.00	1000.	2500.	—
	1829 LF	—	400.00	800.00	1500.	—
	1830/20 LF	—	—	—	Rare	—
	1830 LF	—	1000.	2000.	3000.	—

Mint mark: Ga

KM#	Date	Mintage	Fine	VF	XF	Unc
377.6	1825 FS	—	150.00	275.00	425.00	850.00
	1826/5 FS	—	125.00	250.00	400.00	800.00
	1827/87 FS	—	125.00	250.00	400.00	800.00
	1827 FS	—	225.00	350.00	500.00	1000.
	1287 FS (error)	8500.	—	—	—	—
	1828 FS	—	200.00	375.00	550.00	1100.
	1829/8 FS	—	200.00	375.00	550.00	1100.
	1829 FS	—	175.00	325.00	475.00	950.00
	1830/29 FS	—	175.00	300.00	450.00	900.00
	1830 FS	—	100.00	175.00	350.00	600.00
	1830 LP/FS	—	—	—	Rare	—
	1831 LP	—	200.00	400.00	600.00	1200.
	1831 FS/LP	—	300.00	500.00	750.00	1500.
	1831 FS	—	—	—	—	—
	1832/1 FS	—	50.00	100.00	175.00	300.00
	1832/1 FS/LP					
		—	60.00	125.00	200.00	350.00
	1832 FS	—	25.00	50.00	100.00	200.00
	1833/2/1 FS/LP					
		—	45.00	75.00	125.00	250.00
	1833/2 FS	—	25.00	50.00	100.00	200.00
	1834/2 FS	—	60.00	125.00	200.00	350.00
	1834/3 FS	—	60.00	125.00	200.00	350.00
	1834/0 FS	—	60.00	125.00	200.00	350.00
	1834 FS	—	50.00	100.00	150.00	300.00
	1835 FS	—	25.00	50.00	100.00	200.00
	1836/1 JG/FS					
		—	40.00	80.00	125.00	250.00
	1836 FS	—	—	—	Rare	—
	1836 JG/FS	—	25.00	50.00	100.00	200.00
	1836 JG	—	25.00	50.00	100.00	200.00
	1837/6 JG/FS					
		—	50.00	100.00	175.00	300.00
	1837 JG	—	40.00	80.00	125.00	250.00

KM#	Date	Mintage	Fine	VF	XF	Unc
377.6	1838/7 JG	—	100.00	175.00	300.00	550.00
	1838 JG	—	100.00	150.00	275.00	500.00
	1839 MC	—	100.00	200.00	300.00	550.00
	1839 MC/JG	—	100.00	200.00	300.00	550.00
	1839 JG	—	60.00	125.00	200.00	350.00
	1840/30 MC	—	50.00	75.00	150.00	275.00
	1840 MC	—	30.00	60.00	125.00	250.00
	1841 MC	—	30.00	60.00	125.00	250.00
	1842/1 JG/MG					
		—	100.00	150.00	250.00	450.00
	1842/1 JG/MC					
		—	100.00	150.00	250.00	450.00
	1842 JG	—	25.00	50.00	100.00	200.00
	1842 JG/MG	—	25.00	50.00	100.00	200.00
	1843/2 MC/JG					
		—	25.00	50.00	100.00	200.00
	1843 MC/JG	—	25.00	50.00	100.00	200.00
	1843 JG	—	400.00	600.00	800.00	1500.
	1843 MC	—	50.00	100.00	150.00	300.00
	1844 MC	—	50.00	100.00	150.00	300.00
	1845 MC	—	75.00	150.00	250.00	450.00
	1845 JG	—	600.00	1000.	1500.	—
	1846 JG	—	40.00	80.00	150.00	300.00
	1847 JG	—	100.00	150.00	225.00	400.00
	1848/7 JG	—	55.00	85.00	125.00	250.00
	1848 JG	—	50.00	75.00	100.00	200.00
	1849 JG	—	90.00	125.00	175.00	300.00
	1850 JG	—	50.00	100.00	150.00	300.00
	1851 JG	—	125.00	200.00	350.00	650.00
	1852 JG	—	100.00	150.00	250.00	450.00
	1853/2 JG	—	125.00	175.00	250.00	475.00
	1853 JG	—	90.00	125.00	175.00	300.00
	1854/3 JG	—	65.00	90.00	125.00	250.00
	1854 JG	—	50.00	75.00	125.00	250.00
	1855/4 JG	—	50.00	100.00	150.00	275.00
	1855 JG	—	25.00	50.00	100.00	200.00
	1856/4 JG	—	60.00	125.00	175.00	300.00
	1856/5 56	—	60.00	125.00	175.00	300.00
	1856 JG	—	50.00	100.00	150.00	275.00
	1857 JG	—	50.00	100.00	225.00	400.00
	1858 JG	—	100.00	150.00	300.00	500.00
	1859/7 JG	—	25.00	50.00	100.00	175.00
	1859/8 JG	—	25.00	50.00	100.00	175.00
	1859 JG	—	20.00	40.00	80.00	125.00
	1860 JG w/o dot					
		—	400.00	800.00	1200.	2000.
	1860 JG dot in loop of eagles tail					
	(base alloy)	—	—	—	Rare	—
	1861 JG	—	—	—	Rare	—
	1862 JG	—	—	—	Rare	—
	1863/52 JG	—	—	—	—	—
	1863/59 JG	—	45.00	50.00	85.00	135.00
	1863/2 JG	—	30.00	50.00	90.00	175.00
	1863/4 JG	—	40.00	60.00	125.00	200.00
	1863 JG	—	25.00	45.00	75.00	150.00
	1863 FV	—	—	—	Rare	—
	1867 JM	—	—	—	Rare	—
	1868/7 JM	—	50.00	75.00	125.00	200.00
	1868 JM	—	50.00	75.00	125.00	200.00
	1869 JM	—	50.00	75.00	125.00	200.00
	1869 IC	—	75.00	125.00	200.00	375.00
	1870/60 IC	—	60.00	90.00	150.00	275.00
	1870 IC	—	60.00	90.00	150.00	275.00
	1873 IC	—	15.00	25.00	50.00	125.00
	1874 IC	—	10.00	15.00	20.00	85.00
	1874 MC	—	25.00	50.00	100.00	200.00
	1875 IC	—	15.00	30.00	60.00	125.00
	1875 MC	—	10.00	15.00	20.00	85.00
	1876 IC	.559	15.00	30.00	50.00	100.00
	1876 MC	Inc. Ab.	125.00	175.00	250.00	375.00
	1877 IC	.928	10.00	15.00	20.00	85.00
	1877 JA	Inc. Ab.	10.00	15.00	20.00	85.00
	1878 JA	.764	10.00	15.00	20.00	85.00
	1879 JA	—	10.00	15.00	20.00	85.00
	1880/70 FS	—	15.00	25.00	50.00	125.00
	1880 JA	—	10.00	15.00	20.00	85.00
	1880 FS	—	10.00	15.00	20.00	85.00
	1881 FS	1.300	10.00	15.00	20.00	85.00
	1882/1 FS	.537	15.00	25.00	50.00	125.00
	1882 FS	I.A.	10.00	15.00	20.00	85.00
	1882 TB/FS	I.A.	75.00	150.00	250.00	450.00
	1882 TB	I.A.	50.00	100.00	175.00	300.00
	1883 TB	.561	15.00	25.00	40.00	125.00
	1884 TB	—	10.00	12.00	18.00	85.00
	1884 AH	—	10.00	12.00	18.00	85.00

PRICING SECTION

KM#	Date	Mintage	Fine	VF	XF	Unc
377.6	1885 AH	.443	10.00	12.00	18.00	85.00
	1885 JS	Inc. Ab.	30.00	60.00	100.00	200.00
	1886 JS	1.039	10.00	12.00	18.00	85.00
	1887 JS	.878	10.00	12.00	18.00	85.00
	1888 JS	1.159	10.00	12.00	18.00	85.00
	1889 JS	1.583	10.00	12.00	18.00	85.00
	1890 JS	1.658	10.00	12.00	18.00	85.00
	1891 JS	1.507	10.00	12.00	18.00	85.00
	1892/1 JS	1.627	15.00	25.00	50.00	125.00
	1892 JS	I.A.	10.00	12.00	18.00	75.00
	1893 JS	1.952	10.00	12.00	18.00	75.00
	1894 JS	2.046	10.00	12.00	18.00	75.00
	1895 JS	1.146	10.00	12.00	18.00	60.00

NOTE: Varieties exist. The 1830 LP/FS is currently only known with a Philippine countermark.

Mint mark: GC

KM#	Date	Mintage	Fine	VF	XF	Unc
377.7	1844 MP	—	350.00	500.00	1000.	2000.
	1844 MP (error) reversed S in Ds, Gs					
		—	400.00	600.00	1200.	2250.
	1845 MP eagle's tail square					
		—	125.00	225.00	300.00	600.00
	1845 MP eagle's tail round					
		—	225.00	450.00	650.00	1200.
	1846 MP eagle's tail square					
		—	100.00	150.00	350.00	750.00
	1846 MP eagle's tail round					
		—	100.00	150.00	350.00	750.00
	1847 MP	—	150.00	250.00	400.00	800.00
	1848 MP	—	175.00	300.00	500.00	900.00
	1849 MP	—	175.00	300.00	525.00	1000.
	1850 MP	—	175.00	300.00	575.00	1100.
	1851 MP	—	400.00	600.00	900.00	1600.
	1852 MP	—	500.00	800.00	1250.	2250.

Mint mark: Go

KM#	Date	Mintage	Fine	VF	XF	Unc
377.8	1825 JJ	—	40.00	70.00	150.00	300.00
	1826 JJ straight J's					
		—	40.00	80.00	175.00	350.00
	1826 JJ full J's					
		—	30.00	60.00	125.00	250.00
	1826 MJ	—	—	—	Rare	—
	1827 MJ	—	40.00	75.00	125.00	250.00
	1827 MJ/JJ	—	40.00	75.00	125.00	250.00
	1827 MR	—	100.00	200.00	350.00	600.00
	1828 MJ	—	30.00	60.00	125.00	250.00
	1828/7 MR	—	200.00	400.00	600.00	1200.
	1828 MR	—	200.00	400.00	600.00	1200.
	1829 MJ	—	20.00	35.00	55.00	150.00

KM#	Date	Mintage	Fine	VF	XF	Unc
377.8	1830 MJ oblong beading and narrow J					
		—	20.00	30.00	55.00	150.00
	1830 MJ regular beading and wide J					
		—	20.00	30.00	55.00	150.00
	1831 MJ colon after date					
		—	12.00	20.00	30.00	100.00
	1831 MJ 2 stars after date					
		—	12.00	20.00	30.00	100.00
	1832 MJ	—	12.00	20.00	30.00	100.00
	1832 MJ 1 of date over inverted 1					
		—	20.00	35.00	65.00	125.00
	1833 MJ	—	12.00	20.00	30.00	100.00
	1833 JM	—	1000.	1500.	2000.	2500.
	1834 PJ	—	12.00	20.00	30.00	100.00
	1835 PJ star on cap					
		—	12.00	20.00	30.00	100.00
	1835 PJ dot on cap					
		—	12.00	20.00	30.00	100.00
	1836 PJ	—	12.00	20.00	30.00	100.00
	1837 PJ	—	12.00	20.00	30.00	100.00
	1838 PJ	—	12.00	20.00	30.00	100.00
	1839 PJ/JJ	—	12.00	20.00	30.00	100.00
	1839 PJ	—	12.00	20.00	30.00	100.00
	1840/30 PJ	—	20.00	30.00	50.00	150.00
	1840 PJ	—	12.00	20.00	30.00	125.00
	1841/31 PJ	—	12.00	20.00	30.00	100.00
	1841 PJ	—	12.00	20.00	30.00	100.00
	1842/31 PM/PJ					
		—	25.00	35.00	60.00	150.00
	1842 PJ	—	20.00	30.00	50.00	125.00
	1842 PM/PJ	—	12.00	20.00	30.00	100.00
	1842 PM	—	12.00	20.00	30.00	100.00
	1843 PM dot after date					
		—	12.00	20.00	30.00	100.00
	1843 PM triangle of dots after date					
		—	12.00	20.00	30.00	100.00
	1844 PM	—	12.00	20.00	30.00	100.00
	1845 PM	—	12.00	20.00	30.00	100.00
	1846/5 PM eagle type of 1845					
		—	20.00	30.00	50.00	150.00
	1846 PM early type of 1847					
		—	15.00	25.00	35.00	125.00
	1847 PM	—	12.00	20.00	30.00	75.00
	1848/7 PM	—	20.00	35.00	65.00	150.00
	1848 PM	—	20.00	35.00	65.00	150.00
	1848 PF	—	12.00	20.00	30.00	75.00
	1849 PF	—	12.00	20.00	30.00	75.00
	1850 PF	—	12.00	20.00	30.00	75.00
	1851/0 PF	—	20.00	30.00	50.00	100.00
	1851 PF	—	12.00	20.00	30.00	75.00
	1852/1 PF	—	20.00	30.00	50.00	100.00
	1852 PF	—	12.00	20.00	30.00	75.00
	1853/2 PF	—	20.00	30.00	50.00	100.00
	1853 PF	—	12.00	20.00	30.00	75.00
	1854 PF	—	12.00	20.00	30.00	75.00
	1855 PF large letters					
		—	12.00	20.00	30.00	75.00
	1855 PF small letters					
		—	12.00	20.00	30.00	75.00
	1856/5 PF	—	20.00	30.00	50.00	100.00
	1856 PF	—	12.00	20.00	30.00	75.00
	1857/5 PF	—	20.00	30.00	50.00	100.00
	1857/6 PF	—	20.00	30.00	50.00	100.00
	1857 PF	—	12.00	20.00	30.00	75.00
	1858 PF	—	12.00	20.00	30.00	75.00
	1859/7 PF	—	20.00	30.00	50.00	100.00
	1859/8 PF	—	12.00	20.00	30.00	100.00
	1859 PF	—	12.00	20.00	30.00	75.00
	1860/50 PF	—	20.00	30.00	50.00	100.00
	1860/59 PF	—	12.00	18.00	25.00	85.00
	1860 PF	—	12.00	15.00	20.00	75.00
	1861/51 PF	—	15.00	20.00	30.00	100.00
	1861/0 PF	—	12.00	15.00	20.00	75.00
	1861 PF	—	12.00	15.00	20.00	75.00
	1862 YE/PF	—	12.00	15.00	20.00	75.00
	1862 YE	—	12.00	15.00	20.00	75.00
	1862 YF	—	12.00	15.00	20.00	75.00
	1862 YF/PF	—	12.00	15.00	20.00	75.00
	1863/53 YF	—	12.00	18.00	25.00	75.00
	1863/54 YF	—	15.00	20.00	30.00	100.00
	1863 YE	—	—	—	Rare	—
	1863 YF	—	12.00	15.00	20.00	75.00
	1867/57 YF	—	15.00	20.00	30.00	100.00
	1867 YF	—	12.00	15.00	20.00	75.00

KM#	Date	Mintage	VG	Fine	VF	XF
377.8	1868/58 YF	—	15.00	20.00	30.00	100.00
	1868 YF	—	12.00	15.00	20.00	75.00
	1870/60 FR	—	20.00	30.00	50.00	150.00
	1870 YF	—	—	—	Rare	—
	1870 FR/YF	—	12.00	18.00	25.00	85.00
	1870 FR	—	12.00	15.00	20.00	75.00
	1873 FR	—	12.00	15.00	20.00	75.00
	1874/3 FR	—	15.00	20.00	30.00	85.00
	1874 FR	—	15.00	25.00	35.00	100.00
	1875/6 FR	—	15.00	20.00	30.00	85.00
	1875 FR small circle w/dot on eagle					
		—	12.00	15.00	20.00	75.00
	1876/5 FR	—	15.00	20.00	30.00	85.00
	1876 FR	—	12.00	15.00	20.00	60.00
	1877 FR	2.477	12.00	15.00	20.00	60.00
	1878/7 FR					
		2.273	15.00	20.00	30.00	75.00
	1878/7 SM	—	15.00	20.00	30.00	75.00
	1878 FR	I.A.	12.00	15.00	20.00	65.00
	1878 SM,S/F	—	15.00	20.00	25.00	70.00
	1878 SM	—	12.00	15.00	20.00	65.00
	1879/7 SM	—	15.00	20.00	30.00	75.00
	1879/8 SM	—	15.00	20.00	30.00	75.00
	1879/8 SM/FR					
		—	15.00	20.00	30.00	75.00
	1879 SM	—	12.00	15.00	20.00	65.00
	1879 SM/FR	—	15.00	20.00	30.00	75.00
	1880/70 SB	—	15.00	20.00	30.00	75.00
	1880 SB/SM	—	12.00	15.00	20.00	65.00
	1881/71 SB	—				
		3.974	15.00	20.00	30.00	75.00
	1881/0 SB	I.A.	15.00	20.00	30.00	75.00
	1881 SB	I.A.	12.00	15.00	20.00	65.00
	1882 SB	2.015	12.00	15.00	20.00	75.00
	1883 SB	2.100	35.00	75.00	125.00	250.00
	1883 BR	I.A.	12.00	15.00	20.00	65.00
	1883 BR/SR	—	12.00	15.00	20.00	65.00
	1883 BR/SB					
		Inc. Ab.	12.00	15.00	20.00	65.00
	1884/73 BR	—	20.00	30.00	40.00	100.00
	1884/74 BR	—	20.00	30.00	40.00	100.00
	1884/3 BR	—	20.00	30.00	40.00	100.00
	1884 BR	—	12.00	15.00	20.00	65.00
	1884/74 RR	—	50.00	100.00	175.00	350.00
	1884 RR	—	50.00	100.00	175.00	350.00
	1885/75 RR					
		2.363	15.00	20.00	30.00	75.00
	1885 RR	I.A.	12.00	15.00	20.00	65.00
	1886/75 RR					
		4.127	15.00	20.00	25.00	70.00
	1886/76 RR					
		Inc. Ab.	12.00	15.00	20.00	65.00
	1886/5 RR/BR					
		Inc. Ab.	12.00	15.00	20.00	65.00
	1886 RR	I.A.	12.00	15.00	20.00	65.00
	1887 RR	4.205	10.00	15.00	20.00	65.00
	1888 RR	3.985	10.00	15.00	20.00	65.00
	1889 RR	3.646	10.00	15.00	20.00	65.00
	1890 RR	3.615	10.00	15.00	20.00	65.00
	1891 RS	3.197	10.00	15.00	20.00	65.00
	1891 RR	—	Contemporary counterfeit			
	1892 RS	3.672	10.00	15.00	20.00	65.00
	1893 RS	3.854	10.00	15.00	20.00	65.00
	1894 RS	4.127	10.00	15.00	20.00	65.00
	1895/1 RS					
		3.768	15.00	20.00	25.00	75.00
	1895/3 RS	I.A.	15.00	20.00	25.00	75.00
	1895 RS	I.A.	10.00	15.00	20.00	65.00
	1896/1 Go/As RS/ML					
		5.229	15.00	20.00	25.00	75.00
	1896/1 RS	I.A.	12.00	15.00	20.00	65.00
	1896 Go/Ga RS					
		Inc. Ab.	—	—	—	—
	1896 RS	I.A.	10.00	12.00	18.00	60.00
	1897 RS	4.344	10.00	12.00	18.00	60.00

NOTE: Varieties exist.

Mint mark: Ho

KM#	Date	Mintage	Fine	VF	XF	Unc
377.9	1835 PP	—	—	—	—	—
	1836 PP	—	—	—	Unique	—
	1839 PR	—	—	—	Unique	—
	1861 FM	—	—	—	Rare	—
	1862 FM	—	—	—	Rare	—
	1862 FM reeded edge					
		—	—	—	Rare	—
	1863 FM	—	150.00	300.00	800.00	—
	1864 FM	—	—	—	Rare	—
	1864 PR	—	—	—	Rare	—
	1865 FM	—	250.00	500.00	950.00	—
	1866 FM	—	—	—	Rare	—
	1866 MP	—	—	—	Rare	—
	1867 PR	—	100.00	175.00	275.00	500.00
	1868 PR	—	20.00	35.00	65.00	175.00
	1869 PR	—	40.00	60.00	125.00	250.00
	1870 PR	—	50.00	80.00	150.00	300.00
	1871/0 PR	—	50.00	75.00	125.00	250.00
	1871 PR	—	30.00	50.00	90.00	200.00
	1872/1 PR	—	35.00	60.00	90.00	200.00
	1872 PR	—	30.00	50.00	75.00	175.00
	1873 PR	.351	30.00	50.00	85.00	150.00
	1874 PR	—	15.00	20.00	40.00	125.00
	1875 PR	—	15.00	20.00	40.00	125.00
	1876 AF	—	15.00	20.00	40.00	125.00
	1877 AF	.410	20.00	30.00	50.00	150.00
	1877 GR	I.A.	100.00	150.00	225.00	400.00
	1877 JA	I.A.	25.00	50.00	85.00	175.00
	1878 JA	.451	15.00	20.00	40.00	100.00
	1879 JA	—	15.00	20.00	40.00	100.00
	1880 JA	—	15.00	20.00	40.00	100.00
	1881 JA	.586	15.00	20.00	40.00	100.00
	1882 HoJA O above H					
		.240	25.00	40.00	65.00	125.00
	1882 HoJA O after H					
		Inc. Ab.	25.00	40.00	65.00	125.00
	1883/2 JA	.204	225.00	375.00	550.00	1000.
	1883/2 FM/JA					
		Inc. Ab.	25.00	40.00	75.00	150.00
	1883 FM	Inc. Ab.	20.00	30.00	60.00	125.00
	1883 JA	Inc. Ab.	200.00	350.00	500.00	1000.
	1884/3 FM	—	20.00	25.00	50.00	125.00
	1884 FM	—	15.00	20.00	40.00	100.00
	1885 FM	.132	15.00	20.00	40.00	100.00
	1886 FM	.225	20.00	30.00	45.00	125.00
	1886 FG	Inc. Ab.	20.00	30.00	45.00	125.00
	1887 FG	.150	20.00	35.00	65.00	150.00
	1888 FG	.364	12.00	18.00	25.00	100.00
	1889 FG	.490	12.00	18.00	25.00	100.00
	1890 FG	.565	12.00	18.00	25.00	100.00
	1891 FG	.738	12.00	18.00	25.00	100.00
	1892 FG	.643	12.00	18.00	25.00	100.00
	1893 FG	.518	12.00	18.00	25.00	100.00
	1894 FG	.504	12.00	18.00	25.00	100.00
	1895 FG	.320	12.00	18.00	25.00	100.00

NOTE: Varieties exist.

Mint mark: Mo

KM#	Date	Mintage	Fine	VF	XF	Unc
377.10	1824 JM round tail					
		—	75.00	125.00	250.00	500.00
	1824 JM square tail					
		—	75.00	125.00	250.00	500.00
	1825 JM	—	25.00	35.00	50.00	150.00
	1826/5 JM	—	25.00	40.00	75.00	150.00
	1826 JM	—	20.00	30.00	50.00	125.00
	1827 JM medal alignment					
		—	25.00	35.00	50.00	125.00
	1827 JM coin alignment					
		—	25.00	35.00	50.00	125.00
	1828 JM	—	30.00	60.00	100.00	200.00
	1829 JM	—	20.00	30.00	50.00	125.00
	1830/20 JM	—	35.00	55.00	100.00	200.00
	1830 JM	—	30.00	50.00	90.00	175.00
	1831 JM	—	30.00	50.00	100.00	200.00
	1832/1 JM	—	25.00	40.00	60.00	125.00
	1832 JM	—	20.00	30.00	40.00	100.00
	1833 MJ	—	25.00	40.00	80.00	175.00
	1833 ML	—	500.00	750.00	950.00	2000.
	1834/3 ML	—	25.00	35.00	50.00	125.00
	1834 ML	—	20.00	30.00	40.00	100.00
	1835 ML	—	20.00	30.00	40.00	125.00
	1836 ML	—	50.00	100.00	150.00	300.00
	1836 ML/MF	—	50.00	100.00	150.00	300.00
	1836 MF	—	30.00	50.00	80.00	175.00
	1836 MF/ML	—	35.00	60.00	90.00	200.00
	1837/6 ML	—	30.00	50.00	75.00	150.00
	1837/6 MM	—	30.00	50.00	75.00	150.00
	1837/6 MM/ML					
		—	30.00	50.00	75.00	150.00
	1837/6 MM/MF					
		—	30.00	50.00	75.00	150.00
	1837 ML	—	30.00	50.00	75.00	150.00
	1837 MM	—	75.00	125.00	175.00	325.00
	1838 MM	—	30.00	50.00	75.00	150.00
	1838 ML	—	20.00	35.00	60.00	125.00
	1838 ML/MM	—	20.00	35.00	60.00	125.00
	1839 ML	—	15.00	25.00	35.00	100.00
	1840 ML	—	15.00	25.00	35.00	100.00
	1841 ML	—	15.00	25.00	35.00	75.00
	1842 ML	—	15.00	25.00	35.00	75.00
	1842 MM	—	15.00	25.00	35.00	75.00
	1843 MM	—	15.00	25.00	35.00	75.00
	1844 MF/MM	—	—	—	—	—
	1844 MF	—	15.00	25.00	35.00	75.00
	1845/4 MF	—	15.00	25.00	35.00	75.00
	1845 MF	—	15.00	25.00	35.00	75.00
	1846/5 MF	—	15.00	25.00	35.00	100.00
	1846 MF	—	15.00	25.00	35.00	100.00
	1847/6 MF	—	—	—	Rare	—
	1847 MF	—	—	—	Rare	—
	1847 RC	—	20.00	30.00	40.00	100.00
	1847 RC/MF	—	15.00	25.00	35.00	75.00
	1848 GC	—	15.00	25.00	35.00	75.00
	1849/8 GC	—	20.00	35.00	50.00	100.00
	1849 GC	—	15.00	25.00	35.00	75.00
	1850/40 GC	—	25.00	50.00	100.00	200.00
	1850/49 GC	—	25.00	50.00	100.00	200.00
	1850 GC	—	20.00	40.00	75.00	150.00
	1851 GC	—	20.00	40.00	60.00	125.00
	1852 GC	—	15.00	30.00	45.00	100.00
	1853 GC	—	15.00	25.00	40.00	100.00
	1854 GC	—	15.00	25.00	40.00	100.00
	1855 GC	—	20.00	35.00	65.00	125.00
	1855 GF	—	12.00	15.00	20.00	75.00

KM#	Date	Mintage	Fine	VF	XF	Unc
377.10	1855 GF/GC	—	12.00	15.00	20.00	75.00
	1856/4 GF	—	15.00	25.00	40.00	100.00
	1856/5 GF	—	15.00	25.00	40.00	100.00
	1856 GF	—	12.00	15.00	20.00	75.00
	1857 GF	—	10.00	15.00	20.00	75.00
	1858/7 FH/GF					
		—	10.00	15.00	20.00	75.00
	1858 FH	—	10.00	15.00	20.00	75.00
	1859 FH	—	10.00	15.00	20.00	75.00
	1860/59 FH	—	15.00	20.00	25.00	75.00
	1860 FH	—	10.00	15.00	20.00	65.00
	1860 TH	—	12.00	18.00	30.00	100.00
	1861 TH	—	10.00	15.00	20.00	75.00
	1861 CH	—	10.00	15.00	20.00	75.00
	1862 CH	—	10.00	15.00	20.00	75.00
	1863 CH	—	10.00	15.00	20.00	75.00
	1863 CH/TH	—	10.00	15.00	20.00	75.00
	1863 TH	—	10.00	15.00	20.00	75.00
	1867 CH	—	10.00	15.00	20.00	65.00
	1868 CH	—	10.00	15.00	20.00	65.00
	1868 CH/PH	—	10.00	15.00	20.00	65.00
	1868 PH	—	10.00	15.00	20.00	65.00
	1869 CH	—	10.00	15.00	20.00	65.00
	1873 MH	—	10.00	15.00	20.00	65.00
	1873 MH/HH	—	12.00	18.00	25.00	75.00
	1874/69 MH	—	15.00	25.00	45.00	100.00
	1874 MH	—	12.00	18.00	25.00	75.00
	1874 BH/MH	—	12.00	15.00	20.00	65.00
	1874 BH	—	10.00	15.00	20.00	65.00
	1875 BH	—	10.00	15.00	20.00	65.00
	1876/4 BH	—	12.00	18.00	25.00	75.00
	1876/5 BH	—	12.00	18.00	25.00	75.00
	1876 BH	—	10.00	15.00	20.00	65.00
	1877 MH	.898	10.00	15.00	20.00	65.00
	1877 MH/BH					
		Inc. Ab.	12.00	18.00	25.00	75.00
	1878 MH	2.154	10.00	15.00	20.00	65.00
	1879/8 MH	—	10.00	15.00	20.00	75.00
	1879 MH	—	10.00	15.00	20.00	65.00
	1880/79 MH	—	15.00	20.00	30.00	75.00
	1880 MH	—	10.00	15.00	20.00	75.00
	1881 MH	5.712	10.00	15.00	20.00	65.00
	1882/1 MH					
		2.746	12.00	15.00	20.00	75.00
	1882 MH	I.A.	10.00	15.00	20.00	65.00
	1883/2 MH					
		2.726	12.00	18.00	25.00	85.00
	1883 MH	I.A.	10.00	15.00	20.00	65.00
	1884/3 MH	—	15.00	20.00	30.00	75.00
	1884 MH	—	10.00	15.00	20.00	65.00
	1885 MH	3.649	10.00	15.00	20.00	65.00
	1886 MH	7.558	10.00	12.00	18.00	60.00
	1887 MH	7.681	10.00	12.00	18.00	60.00
	1888 MH	7.179	10.00	12.00	18.00	60.00
	1889 MH	7.332	10.00	15.00	20.00	65.00
	1890 MH	7.412	10.00	12.00	18.00	60.00
	1890 AM	I.A.	10.00	12.00	18.00	60.00
	1891 AM	8.076	10.00	12.00	18.00	60.00
	1892 AM	9.392	10.00	12.00	18.00	60.00
	1893 AM	10.773	10.00	12.00	18.00	55.00
	1894 AM	12.394	10.00	12.00	18.00	45.00
	1895 AM	10.474	10.00	12.00	18.00	45.00
	1895 AB	I.A.	10.00	12.00	18.00	60.00
	1896 AB	9.327	10.00	12.00	18.00	60.00
	1896 AM	I.A.	10.00	12.00	18.00	60.00
	1897 AM	8.621	10.00	12.00	18.00	60.00

NOTE: Varieties exist. 1874 CP is a die struck counterfeit.

Mint mark: O, Oa

KM#	Date	Mintage	Fine	VF	XF	Unc
377.11	1858O AE	—	—	—	Rare	—
	1858OaAE	—	—	—	Rare	—
	1859 AE A in O of mm					
		—	250.00	550.00	1000.	—
	1860 AE A in O of mm					
		—	200.00	400.00	600.00	—
	1861 O FR	—	125.00	250.00	500.00	1000.
	1861OaFR	—	200.00	400.00	600.00	—
	1862O FR	—	50.00	100.00	200.00	375.00
	1862OaFR	—	75.00	150.00	250.00	450.00
	1863O FR	—	30.00	60.00	100.00	250.00
	1863O AE	—	30.00	60.00	100.00	250.00
	1863OaAE A in O of mm					
		—	100.00	150.00	250.00	450.00
	1863OaAE A above O in mm					
		—	—	—	Rare	—
	1864 FR	—	25.00	50.00	75.00	200.00
	1867 AE	—	40.00	80.00	150.00	400.00
	1868 AE	—	25.00	50.00	100.00	250.00
	1869 AE	—	30.00	60.00	100.00	250.00
	1873 AE	—	200.00	300.00	600.00	1250.
	1874 AE	.142	15.00	30.00	50.00	200.00
	1875/4 AE	.131	25.00	50.00	75.00	200.00
	1875 AE	I.A.	15.00	30.00	40.00	125.00
	1876 AE	.140	20.00	35.00	55.00	200.00
	1877 AE	.139	20.00	30.00	50.00	200.00
	1878 AE	.125	15.00	25.00	50.00	200.00
	1879 AE	.153	15.00	30.00	45.00	150.00
	1880 AE	.143	15.00	30.00	45.00	150.00
	1881 AE	.134	20.00	35.00	60.00	150.00
	1882 AE	.100	20.00	35.00	60.00	150.00
	1883 AE	.122	15.00	30.00	45.00	150.00
	1884 AE	.142	15.00	30.00	50.00	150.00
	1885 AE	.158	15.00	25.00	40.00	125.00
	1886 AE	.120	15.00	30.00	45.00	150.00
	1887/6 AE	.115	25.00	50.00	80.00	200.00
	1887 AE	I.A.	15.00	25.00	40.00	125.00
	1888 AE	.145	15.00	25.00	40.00	125.00
	1889 AE	.150	20.00	30.00	60.00	175.00
	1890 AE	.181	20.00	30.00	60.00	175.00
	1891 EN	.160	15.00	25.00	40.00	125.00
	1892 EN	.120	15.00	25.00	40.00	125.00
	1893 EN	.066	45.00	75.00	115.00	225.00

NOTE: Varieties exist.

Mint mark: Pi

KM#	Date	Mintage	Fine	VF	XF	Unc
377.12	1827 JS	—	—	—	Rare	—
	1828/7 JS	—	250.00	400.00	600.00	1200.
	1828 JS	—	200.00	350.00	500.00	1000.
	1829 JS	—	35.00	65.00	125.00	250.00
	1830 JS	—	30.00	50.00	100.00	200.00
	1831/0 JS	—	30.00	60.00	125.00	250.00
	1831 JS	—	25.00	35.00	65.00	200.00
	1832/22 JS	—	25.00	35.00	55.00	150.00
	1832 JS	—	25.00	35.00	55.00	150.00
	1833/2 JS	—	30.00	40.00	50.00	150.00
	1833 JS	—	20.00	30.00	40.00	125.00
	1834/3 JS	—	25.00	35.00	50.00	125.00
	1834 JS	—	15.00	25.00	40.00	125.00
	1835 JS denomination 8R					
		—	20.00	30.00	60.00	150.00
	1835 JS denomination 8Rs					
		—	15.00	25.00	40.00	125.00
	1836 JS	—	20.00	30.00	45.00	125.00
	1837 JS	—	30.00	50.00	80.00	175.00

KM#	Date	Mintage	Fine	VF	XF	Unc
377.12	1838 JS	—	20.00	30.00	45.00	125.00
	1839 JS	—	20.00	40.00	60.00	125.00
	1840 JS	—	20.00	30.00	50.00	125.00
	1841PiJS	—	25.00	40.00	80.00	175.00
	1841iPJS (error)					
		—	50.00	100.00	200.00	400.00
	1842/1 JS	—	40.00	60.00	90.00	175.00
	1842/1 PS/JS					
		—	35.00	55.00	85.00	175.00
	1842 JS eagle type of 1843					
		—	30.00	50.00	75.00	150.00
	1842 PS	—	30.00	50.00	75.00	150.00
	1842 PS/JS eagle type of 1841					
		—	30.00	50.00	75.00	150.00
	1843/2 PS round top 3					
		—	50.00	75.00	150.00	250.00
	1843 PS flat top 3					
		—	30.00	60.00	125.00	225.00
	1843 AM round top 3					
		—	20.00	30.00	50.00	125.00
	1843 AM flat top 3					
		—	20.00	30.00	50.00	125.00
	1844 AM	—	20.00	30.00	50.00	125.00
	1845/4 AM	—	25.00	50.00	100.00	225.00
	1845 AM	—	25.00	50.00	100.00	225.00
	1846/5 AM	—	25.00	35.00	50.00	125.00
	1846 AM	—	15.00	25.00	40.00	125.00
	1847 AM	—	30.00	50.00	80.00	150.00
	1848/7 AM	—	30.00	60.00	90.00	175.00
	1848 AM	—	30.00	50.00	80.00	150.00
	1849/8 PS/AM					
		—	—	—	Rare	—
	1849 PS/AM	—	—	—	Rare	—
	1849 MC/PS	—	60.00	125.00	250.00	500.00
	1849 AM	—	—	—	Rare	—
	1849 MC	—	60.00	125.00	250.00	500.00
	1850 MC	—	40.00	80.00	150.00	300.00
	1851 MC	—	125.00	200.00	300.00	600.00
	1852 MC	—	75.00	125.00	200.00	400.00
	1853 MC	—	125.00	175.00	300.00	600.00
	1854 MC	—	100.00	150.00	250.00	500.00
	1855 MC	—	100.00	150.00	250.00	500.00
	1856 MC	—	65.00	100.00	200.00	400.00
	1857 MC	—	—	—	Rare	—
	1857 PS/MC	—	150.00	225.00	375.00	700.00
	1857 PS	—	125.00	200.00	350.00	650.00
	1858 MC/PS	—	250.00	400.00	650.00	1200.
	1858 MC	—	250.00	400.00	650.00	1200.
	1858 PS	—	—	—	Rare	—
	1859/8 MC/PS					
		—	—	—	Rare	—
	1859 MC/PS	—	—	—	Rare	—
	1859 PS/PC	—	—	—	Rare	—
	1859 PS	—	—	—	Rare	—
	1860 FC	—	2000.	4000.	6500.	—
	1860 FE	—	—	—	Rare	—
	1860 MC	—	2000.	4000.	6500.	—
	1860 PS	—	400.00	600.00	900.00	1750.
	1861 PS	—	30.00	60.00	90.00	175.00
	1861 RO	—	25.00	35.00	55.00	125.00
	1862/1 RO	—	20.00	25.00	50.00	125.00
	1862 RO	—	15.00	20.00	40.00	100.00
	1862 RO oval O in RO					
		—	15.00	20.00	40.00	100.00
	1862 RO round O in RO, 6 is inverted 9					
		—	20.00	30.00	50.00	125.00
	1863/2 RO	—	25.00	35.00	65.00	150.00
	1863 RO	—	15.00	20.00	40.00	125.00
	1863 6/inverted 6					
		—	25.00	35.00	55.00	125.00
	1863 FC	—	—	—	Rare	—
	1864 RO	—	—	—	Rare	—
	1867 CA	—	—	—	Rare	—
	1867 LR	—	—	—	Rare	—
	1867 PS	—	30.00	60.00	125.00	275.00
	1868/7 PS	—	30.00	60.00	125.00	250.00
	1868 PS	—	20.00	30.00	50.00	125.00
	1869/8 PS	—	20.00	25.00	45.00	125.00
	1869 PS	—	15.00	20.00	40.00	125.00
	1870/69 PS	—	—	—	Rare	—
	1870 PS	—	—	—	Rare	—
	1873 MH	—	15.00	20.00	40.00	135.00
	1874/3 MH	—	15.00	20.00	30.00	125.00
	1874 MH	—	10.00	12.00	18.00	100.00
	1875 MH	—	10.00	12.00	18.00	100.00

PRICING SECTION

KM#	Date	Mintage	Fine	VF	XF	Unc
377.12	1876/5 MH	—	15.00	20.00	30.00	125.00
	1876 MH	—	10.00	12.00	18.00	100.00
	1877 MH	1.018	10.00	12.00	18.00	100.00
	1878 MH	1.046	12.00	15.00	25.00	125.00
	1879/8 MH	—	15.00	20.00	30.00	125.00
	1879 MH	—	10.00	12.00	18.00	100.00
	1879 BE	—	25.00	50.00	75.00	150.00
	1879 MR	—	30.00	50.00	100.00	200.00
	1880 MR	—	250.00	400.00	800.00	—
	1880 MH	—	10.00	12.00	18.00	100.00
	1881 MH	2.100	10.00	12.00	18.00	100.00
	1882/1 MH	1.602	15.00	20.00	30.00	125.00
	1882 MH	I.A.	10.00	12.00	18.00	100.00
	1883 MH	1.545	10.00	12.00	18.00	100.00
	1884/3 MH	—	15.00	20.00	30.00	125.00
	1884 MH/MM		12.00	15.00	20.00	85.00
	1884 MH	—	10.00	12.00	18.00	75.00
	1885/4 MH	1.736	15.00	20.00	30.00	125.00
	1885/8 MH	I.A.	15.00	20.00	30.00	125.00
	1885 MH	I.A.	10.00	12.00	18.00	75.00
	1885 LC	I.A.	12.00	18.00	25.00	100.00
	1886 LC	3.347	10.00	12.00	18.00	75.00
	1886 MR	I.A.	10.00	12.00	18.00	75.00
	1887 MR	2.922	10.00	12.00	18.00	75.00
	1888 MR	2.438	10.00	12.00	18.00	75.00
	1889 MR	2.103	10.00	12.00	18.00	75.00
	1890 MR	1.562	10.00	12.00	18.00	65.00
	1891 MR	1.184	10.00	12.00	18.00	65.00
	1892 MR	1.336	10.00	12.00	18.00	65.00
	1893 MR	.530	10.00	12.00	18.00	75.00

NOTE: Varieties exist.

Mint mark: Zs

KM#	Date	Mintage	Fine	VF	XF	Unc
377.13	1825 AZ	—	25.00	35.00	60.00	150.00
	1826/5 AZ	—	25.00	45.00	75.00	175.00
	1826 AZ	—	20.00	35.00	60.00	150.00
	1826 AV	—	225.00	450.00	700.00	1500.
	1826 AO	—	350.00	650.00	1000.	2000.
	1827 AO/AZ	—	35.00	50.00	125.00	250.00
	1827 AO	—	25.00	45.00	85.00	175.00
	1828 AO	—	15.00	20.00	40.00	125.00
	1829 AO	—	15.00	20.00	40.00	125.00
	1829 OV	—	50.00	90.00	150.00	300.00
	1830 OV	—	15.00	20.00	40.00	125.00
	1831 OV	—	25.00	50.00	90.00	175.00
	1831 OM	—	15.00	25.00	50.00	125.00
	1832/1 OM	—	20.00	25.00	40.00	125.00
	1832 OM	—	15.00	20.00	35.00	100.00
	1833/2 OM	—	20.00	30.00	40.00	125.00
	1833 OM/MM	—	15.00	25.00	35.00	100.00
	1833 OM	—	15.00	20.00	30.00	100.00
	1834 OM	—	15.00	20.00	30.00	100.00
	1835 OM	—	15.00	20.00	35.00	100.00
	1836/4 OM	—	20.00	30.00	45.00	125.00
	1836/5 OM	—	20.00	30.00	45.00	125.00
	1836 OM	—	15.00	20.00	30.00	100.00
	1837 OM	—	15.00	20.00	30.00	100.00
	1838/7 OM	—	20.00	30.00	40.00	125.00
	1838 OM	—	15.00	20.00	30.00	100.00
	1839 OM	—	15.00	20.00	30.00	100.00
	1840 OM	—	15.00	20.00	30.00	100.00
	1841 OM	—	15.00	20.00	30.00	100.00

KM#	Date	Mintage	Fine	VF	XF	Unc
377.13	1842 OM eagle type of 1841	—	15.00	20.00	30.00	100.00
	1842 OM eagle type of 1843	—	15.00	20.00	30.00	100.00
	1843 OM	—	15.00	20.00	30.00	100.00
	1844 OM	—	15.00	20.00	30.00	100.00
	1845 OM	—	15.00	20.00	30.00	100.00
	1846 OM	—	15.00	20.00	30.00	100.00
	1847 OM	—	15.00	20.00	30.00	100.00
	1848/7 OM	—	20.00	30.00	40.00	125.00
	1848 OM	—	15.00	20.00	30.00	100.00
	1849 OM	—	15.00	20.00	30.00	100.00
	1850 OM	—	15.00	20.00	30.00	100.00
	1851 OM	—	15.00	20.00	30.00	100.00
	1852 OM	—	15.00	20.00	30.00	100.00
	1853 OM	—	30.00	45.00	65.00	200.00
	1854/3 OM	—	20.00	30.00	50.00	150.00
	1854 OM	—	15.00	25.00	40.00	125.00
	1855 OM	—	20.00	30.00	60.00	125.00
	1855 MO	—	30.00	60.00	90.00	175.00
	1856/5 MO	—		30.00	40.00	125.00
	1856 MO	—	15.00	20.00	30.00	100.00
	1857/5 MO	—		30.00	40.00	125.00
	1857 MO	—	15.00	20.00	30.00	100.00
	1858/7 MO	—	15.00	20.00	30.00	100.00
	1858 MO	—	15.00	20.00	30.00	100.00
	1859/8 MO	—	15.00	20.00	30.00	100.00
	1859 MO	—	15.00	20.00	30.00	100.00
	1859 VL/MO	—	25.00	50.00	75.00	150.00
	1859 VL	—	20.00	40.00	60.00	125.00
	1860/50 MO	—	10.00	12.00	18.00	75.00
	1860/59 MO	—	10.00	12.00	18.00	75.00
	1860 MO	—	10.00	12.00	18.00	75.00
	1860 VL/MO	—	10.00	12.00	18.00	75.00
	1860 VL	—	10.00	12.00	18.00	75.00
	1861/0 VL/MO	—	10.00	12.00	18.00	75.00
	1861/0 VL	—	10.00	12.00	18.00	75.00
	1861 VL	—	10.00	12.00	18.00	75.00
	1862/1 VL	—	15.00	20.00	30.00	100.00
	1862 VL	—	10.00	12.00	18.00	75.00
	1863 VL	—	10.00	12.00	18.00	75.00
	1863 MO	—	10.00	12.00	18.00	75.00
	1864/3 VL	—	15.00	20.00	30.00	100.00
	1864 VL	—	10.00	12.00	18.00	75.00
	1864 MO	—	15.00	20.00	30.00	100.00
	1865/4 MO	—	200.00	450.00	700.00	1500.
	1865 MO	—	175.00	400.00	600.00	1250.
	1866 VL	—	Contemporary counterfeit			
	1867 JS	—	—	—	Rare	—
	1868 JS	—	10.00	12.00	18.00	75.00
	1868 YH	—	10.00	12.00	18.00	75.00
	1869 YH	—	10.00	12.00	18.00	75.00
	1870 YH	—	—	—	Rare	—
	1873 YH	—	10.00	12.00	18.00	75.00
	1874 YH	—	10.00	12.00	18.00	75.00
	1874 JA/YA	—	10.00	12.00	18.00	75.00
	1874 JA	—	10.00	12.00	18.00	75.00
	1875 JA	—	10.00	12.00	18.00	75.00
	1876 JA	—	10.00	12.00	18.00	75.00
	1876 JS	—	10.00	12.00	18.00	75.00
	1877 JS	2.700	10.00	12.00	18.00	75.00
	1878 JS	2.310	10.00	12.00	18.00	75.00
	1879/8 JS	—	15.00	20.00	30.00	100.00
	1879 JS	—	10.00	12.00	18.00	75.00
	1880 JS	—	10.00	12.00	18.00	75.00
	1881 JS	5.592	10.00	12.00	18.00	75.00
	1882/1 JS	2.485	15.00	20.00	30.00	100.00
	1882 JS straight J	Inc. Ab.	10.00	12.00	18.00	60.00
	1882 JS full J	Inc. Ab.	10.00	12.00	18.00	60.00
	1883/2 JS	2.563	15.00	20.00	30.00	100.00
	1883 JS	I.A.	10.00	12.00	18.00	75.00
	1884 JS	—	10.00	12.00	18.00	75.00
	1885 JS	2.252	10.00	12.00	18.00	60.00
	1886/5 JS	5.303	15.00	20.00	30.00	100.00
	1886/8 JS	I.A.	15.00	20.00	30.00	100.00
	1886 JS	I.A.	10.00	12.00	18.00	60.00
	1886 FZ	I.A.	10.00	12.00	18.00	60.00
	1887ZsFZ	4.733	10.00	12.00	18.00	60.00
	1887Z FZ	I.A.	20.00	30.00	50.00	100.00

KM#	Date	Mintage	Fine	VF	XF	Unc
377.13	1888/7 FZ					
		5.132	12.00	15.00	25.00	75.00
	1888 FZ	I.A.	10.00	12.00	18.00	60.00
	1889 FZ	4.344	10.00	12.00	18.00	60.00
	1890 FZ	3.887	10.00	12.00	18.00	60.00
	1891 FZ	4.114	10.00	12.00	18.00	60.00
	1892/1 FZ					
		4.238	12.00	15.00	25.00	75.00
	1892 FZ	I.A.	10.00	12.00	18.00	60.00
	1893 FZ	3.872	10.00	12.00	18.00	60.00
	1894 FZ	3.081	10.00	12.00	18.00	60.00
	1895 FZ	4.718	10.00	12.00	18.00	60.00
	1896 FZ	4.226	10.00	12.00	18.00	50.00
	1897 FZ	4.877	10.00	12.00	18.00	50.00

NOTE: Varieties exist.

1/2 ESCUDO

1.6900 g, .875 GOLD, .0475 oz AGW
Mint mark: C
Obv: Facing eagle.

KM#	Date	Mintage	VG	Fine	VF	XF
378	1848 CE	—	35.00	50.00	75.00	150.00
	1853 CE	—	35.00	50.00	75.00	150.00
	1854 CE	—	35.00	50.00	75.00	150.00
	1856 CE	—	50.00	100.00	150.00	250.00
	1857 CE	—	35.00	50.00	75.00	150.00
	1859 CE	—	35.00	50.00	75.00	150.00
	1860 CE	—	35.00	50.00	75.00	150.00
	1862 CE	—	35.00	50.00	75.00	125.00
	1863 CE	—	35.00	50.00	75.00	125.00
	1866 CE	—	35.00	50.00	75.00	125.00
	1867 CE	—	35.00	50.00	75.00	125.00
	1870 CE	—	—	—	—	—

Mint mark: Do

KM#	Date	Mintage	VG	Fine	VF	XF
378.1	1833 RM/RL	—	35.00	50.00	75.00	150.00
	1834/3 RM	—	35.00	50.00	75.00	150.00
	1835/3 RM	—	35.00	50.00	75.00	150.00
	1836/4 RM	—	35.00	50.00	75.00	150.00
	1837 RM	—	35.00	50.00	75.00	150.00
	1838 RM	—	40.00	60.00	100.00	175.00
	1843 RM	—	40.00	60.00	100.00	175.00
	1844/33 RM	—	40.00	60.00	100.00	175.00
	1844/33 RM/RL					
		—	40.00	60.00	100.00	175.00
	1846 RM	—	40.00	60.00	100.00	175.00
	1848 RM	—	40.00	60.00	100.00	175.00
	1850/33 JMR	—	40.00	60.00	100.00	175.00
	1851 JMR	—	40.00	60.00	100.00	200.00
	1852 JMR	—	40.00	60.00	100.00	175.00
	1853/33 CP	—	75.00	150.00	300.00	500.00
	1853 CP	—	35.00	50.00	75.00	150.00
	1854 CP	—	35.00	50.00	75.00	150.00
	1855 CP	—	35.00	50.00	75.00	150.00
	1859 CP	—	35.00	50.00	75.00	150.00
	1861 CP	—	35.00	50.00	75.00	150.00
	1864 LT	—	75.00	125.00	250.00	400.00

Mint mark: Ga

KM#	Date	Mintage	VG	Fine	VF	XF
378.2	1825 FS	—	40.00	60.00	100.00	175.00
	1829 FS	—	40.00	60.00	100.00	175.00
	1831 FS	—	40.00	60.00	100.00	175.00
	1834 FS	—	40.00	60.00	100.00	175.00
	1835 FS	—	40.00	60.00	100.00	175.00
	1837 JG	—	40.00	60.00	100.00	175.00
	1838 JG	—	40.00	60.00	100.00	175.00
	1839 JG	—	40.00	60.00	100.00	175.00
	1842 JG	—	40.00	60.00	100.00	175.00
	1847 JG	—	40.00	60.00	100.00	175.00
	1850 JG	—	35.00	50.00	75.00	150.00
	1852 JG	—	35.00	50.00	75.00	150.00
	1859 JG	—	40.00	60.00	100.00	175.00
	1861 JG	—	35.00	50.00	75.00	150.00

Mint mark: GC

KM#	Date	Mintage	Fine	VF	XF	Unc
378.3	1846 MP	—	50.00	75.00	100.00	175.00
	1847 MP	—	50.00	75.00	100.00	175.00
	1848/7 MP	—	50.00	75.00	100.00	200.00
	1851 MP	—	50.00	75.00	100.00	175.00

Mint mark: Go

KM#	Date	Mintage	Fine	VF	XF	Unc
378.4	1845 PM	—	30.00	40.00	65.00	125.00
	1849 PF	—	30.00	40.00	65.00	125.00
	1851/41 PF	—	30.00	40.00	65.00	125.00
	1851 PF	—	30.00	40.00	65.00	125.00
	1852 PF	—	30.00	40.00	65.00	125.00
	1853 PF	—	30.00	40.00	65.00	125.00
	1855 PF	—	30.00	50.00	80.00	150.00
	1857 PF	—	30.00	40.00	65.00	125.00
	1858/7 PF	—	30.00	40.00	65.00	125.00
	1859 PF	—	30.00	40.00	65.00	125.00
	1860 PF	—	30.00	40.00	65.00	125.00
	1861 PF	—	30.00	40.00	65.00	125.00
	1862/1 YE	—	30.00	40.00	65.00	125.00
	1863 YF	—	30.00	40.00	65.00	125.00

Mint mark: Mo

KM#	Date	Mintage	Fine	VF	XF	Unc
378.5	1825/1 JM	—	50.00	75.00	125.00	200.00
	1825/4 JM	—	50.00	75.00	125.00	200.00
	1825 JM	—	30.00	40.00	80.00	150.00
	1827/6 JM	—	30.00	40.00	80.00	150.00
	1827 JM	—	30.00	40.00	80.00	150.00
	1829 JM	—	30.00	40.00	80.00	150.00
	1831/0 JM	—	30.00	40.00	80.00	150.00
	1831 JM	—	30.00	40.00	60.00	125.00
	1832 JM	—	30.00	40.00	60.00	125.00
	1833 MJ olive & oak branches reversed					
		—	30.00	50.00	90.00	175.00
	1834 ML	—	30.00	40.00	60.00	125.00
	1835 ML	—	30.00	40.00	60.00	150.00
	1838 ML	—	30.00	50.00	90.00	175.00
	1839 ML	—	30.00	50.00	90.00	175.00
	1840 ML	—	30.00	40.00	60.00	125.00
	1841 ML	—	30.00	40.00	60.00	125.00
	1842 ML	—	30.00	40.00	80.00	150.00
	1842 MM	—	30.00	40.00	80.00	150.00
	1843 MM	—	30.00	40.00	60.00	125.00
	1844 MF	—	30.00	40.00	60.00	125.00
	1845 MF	—	30.00	40.00	60.00	125.00
	1846/5 MF	—	30.00	40.00	60.00	125.00
	1846 MF	—	30.00	40.00	60.00	125.00
	1848 GC	—	30.00	40.00	60.00	125.00
	1850 GC	—	30.00	40.00	60.00	125.00
	1851 GC	—	30.00	40.00	60.00	125.00
	1852 GC	—	30.00	40.00	60.00	125.00
	1853 GC	—	30.00	40.00	60.00	125.00
	1854 GC	—	30.00	40.00	60.00	125.00
	1855 GF	—	30.00	40.00	60.00	125.00
	1856/4 GF	—	30.00	40.00	60.00	125.00
	1857 GF	—	30.00	40.00	60.00	125.00
	1858/7 FH/GF					
		—	35.00	50.00	75.00	150.00
	1858 FH	—	30.00	40.00	60.00	125.00
	1859 FH	—	30.00	40.00	60.00	125.00
	1860/59 FH	—	30.00	40.00	60.00	125.00
	1861 CH/FH	—	30.00	40.00	80.00	150.00
	1862 CH	—	30.00	40.00	60.00	125.00
	1863/57 CH/GF					
		—	30.00	40.00	60.00	125.00
	1868/58 PH	—	30.00	40.00	80.00	150.00
	1869/59 CH	—	30.00	40.00	80.00	150.00

Mint mark: Zs

KM#	Date	Mintage	VG	Fine	VF	XF
378.6	1860 VL	—	35.00	50.00	75.00	150.00
	1862/1 VL	—	35.00	50.00	75.00	150.00
	1862 VL	—	30.00	40.00	65.00	125.00

ESCUDO

3.3800 g, .875 GOLD, .0950 oz AGW
Mint mark: C
Obv: Facing eagle.

KM#	Date	Mintage	VG	Fine	VF	XF
379	1846 CE	—	75.00	100.00	200.00	350.00
	1847 CE	—	50.00	75.00	125.00	175.00
	1848 CE	—	50.00	75.00	125.00	175.00
	1849/8 CE	—	60.00	100.00	150.00	225.00
	1850 CE	—	50.00	75.00	125.00	175.00
	1851 CE	—	60.00	100.00	150.00	225.00
	1853/1 CE	—	60.00	100.00	150.00	225.00
	1854 CE	—	50.00	75.00	125.00	175.00
	1856/5/4 CE—		60.00	100.00	150.00	225.00
	1856 CE	—	50.00	75.00	125.00	175.00
	1857/1 CE	—	60.00	100.00	150.00	225.00
	1857 CE	—	50.00	75.00	125.00	175.00
	1861 PV	—	50.00	75.00	125.00	175.00
	1862 CE	—	50.00	75.00	125.00	175.00
	1863 CE	—	50.00	75.00	125.00	175.00
	1866 CE	—	50.00	75.00	125.00	175.00
	1870 CE	—	50.00	75.00	125.00	175.00

Mint mark: Do

KM#	Date	Mintage	VG	Fine	VF	XF
379.1	1833/2 RM/RL					
		—	75.00	125.00	200.00	300.00
	1834 RM	—	60.00	100.00	150.00	200.00
	1835 RM	—	—	—	—	—
	1836 RM/RL	—	60.00	100.00	150.00	200.00
	1838 RM	—	60.00	100.00	150.00	200.00
	1846/38 RM	—	75.00	125.00	200.00	300.00
	1850 JMR	—	75.00	125.00	175.00	225.00
	1851/31 JMR					
		—	75.00	125.00	200.00	300.00
	1851 JMR	—	75.00	125.00	175.00	225.00
	1853 CP	—	75.00	125.00	175.00	225.00
	1854/34 CP	—	75.00	125.00	175.00	225.00
	1854/44 CP/RP					
		—	75.00	125.00	175.00	225.00
	1855 CP	—	75.00	125.00	175.00	225.00
	1859 CP	—	75.00	125.00	175.00	225.00
	1861 CP	—	75.00	125.00	175.00	225.00
	1864 LT/CP	—	75.00	125.00	175.00	225.00

Mint mark: Ga

KM#	Date	Mintage	VG	Fine	VF	XF
379.2	1825 FS	—	60.00	90.00	125.00	200.00
	1826 FS	—	60.00	90.00	125.00	200.00
	1829 FS	—	—	—	—	—
	1831 FS	—	60.00	90.00	125.00	200.00
	1834 FS	—	60.00	90.00	125.00	200.00
	1835 JG	—	60.00	90.00	125.00	200.00
	1842 JG/MC	—	60.00	90.00	125.00	200.00
	1843 MC	—	60.00	90.00	125.00	200.00
	1847 JG	—	60.00	90.00	125.00	200.00
	1848/7 JG	—	60.00	90.00	125.00	200.00
	1849 JG	—	60.00	90.00	125.00	200.00
	1850/40 JG	—	60.00	125.00	225.00	325.00
	1850 JG	—	60.00	90.00	125.00	200.00
	1852/1 JG	—	60.00	90.00	125.00	200.00
	1856 JG	—	60.00	90.00	125.00	200.00
	1857 JG	—	60.00	90.00	125.00	200.00
	1859/7 JG	—	60.00	90.00	125.00	200.00
	1860/59 JG	—	60.00	90.00	125.00	200.00
	1860 JG	—	60.00	90.00	125.00	200.00

Mint mark: GC

KM#	Date	Mintage	VG	Fine	VF	XF
379.3	1844 MP	—	75.00	100.00	175.00	250.00
	1845 MP	—	75.00	100.00	175.00	250.00
	1846 MP	—	75.00	100.00	175.00	250.00
	1847 MP	—	75.00	100.00	175.00	250.00
	1848 MP	—	75.00	100.00	175.00	250.00
	1849 MP	—	75.00	100.00	175.00	250.00
	1850 MP	—	75.00	100.00	175.00	250.00
	1851 MP	—	75.00	100.00	175.00	250.00

Mint mark: Go

KM#	Date	Mintage	VG	Fine	VF	XF
379.4	1845 PM	—	60.00	75.00	125.00	200.00
	1849 PF	—	60.00	75.00	125.00	200.00
	1851 PF	—	60.00	75.00	125.00	200.00
	1853 PF	—	60.00	75.00	125.00	200.00
	1860 PF	—	75.00	125.00	200.00	300.00
	1862 YE	—	60.00	75.00	125.00	200.00

Mint mark: Mo

KM#	Date	Mintage	VG	Fine	VF	XF
379.5	1825 JM	—	50.00	70.00	100.00	150.00
	1827/6 JM	—	50.00	70.00	100.00	150.00
	1827 JM	—	50.00	70.00	100.00	150.00
	1830/29 JM	—	50.00	70.00	100.00	150.00
	1831 JM	—	50.00	70.00	100.00	150.00
	1832 JM	—	50.00	70.00	100.00	175.00
	1833 MJ	—	50.00	70.00	100.00	150.00
	1834 ML	—	50.00	70.00	125.00	175.00

KM#	Date	Mintage	VG	Fine	VF	XF
379.5	1841 ML	—	50.00	70.00	125.00	175.00
	1843 MM	—	50.00	70.00	100.00	150.00
	1845 MF	—	50.00	70.00	100.00	150.00
	1846/5 MF	—	50.00	70.00	100.00	150.00
	1848 GC	—	50.00	70.00	100.00	150.00
	1850 GC	—	50.00	70.00	125.00	175.00
	1856/4 GF	—	50.00	70.00	100.00	150.00
	1856/5 GF	—	50.00	70.00	100.00	150.00
	1856 GF	—	50.00	70.00	100.00	150.00
	1858 FH	—	50.00	70.00	125.00	175.00
	1859 FH	—	50.00	70.00	100.00	150.00
	1860 TH	—	50.00	70.00	125.00	175.00
	1861 CH	—	50.00	70.00	100.00	150.00
	1862 CH	—	50.00	70.00	125.00	175.00
	1863 TH	—	50.00	70.00	100.00	150.00
	1869 CH	—	50.00	70.00	100.00	150.00

Mint mark: Zs

KM#	Date	Mintage	VG	Fine	VF	XF
379.6	1853 OM	—	100.00	125.00	200.00	300.00
	1860/59 VL V is inverted A					
		—	75.00	100.00	200.00	350.00
	1860 VL	—	75.00	100.00	150.00	200.00
	1862 VL	—	75.00	100.00	150.00	200.00

2 ESCUDOS

6.7700 g, .875 GOLD, .1904 oz AGW
Mint mark: C
Obv: Facing eagle.

KM#	Date	Mintage	VG	Fine	VF	XF
380	1846 CE	—	100.00	150.00	225.00	325.00
	1847 CE	—	100.00	150.00	225.00	325.00
	1848 CE	—	100.00	150.00	225.00	325.00
	1852 CE	—	100.00	150.00	225.00	325.00
	1854 CE	—	100.00	175.00	250.00	375.00
	1856/4 CE	—	100.00	175.00	250.00	375.00
	1857 CE	—	100.00	150.00	225.00	325.00

Mint mark: Do

KM#	Date	Mintage	VG	Fine	VF	XF
380.1	1833 RM	—	300.00	450.00	700.00	1200.
	1837/4 RM	—	—	—	—	—
	1837 RM	—	—	—	—	—
	1844 RM	—	275.00	400.00	600.00	1000.

Mint mark: EoMo

KM#	Date	Mintage	VG	Fine	VF	XF
380.2	1828 LF	—	700.00	1000.	1750.	2500.

Mint mark: Ga

KM#	Date	Mintage	VG	Fine	VF	XF
380.3	1835 FS	—	100.00	150.00	225.00	325.00
	1836/5 JG	—	100.00	150.00	225.00	300.00
	1839/5 JG	—	—	—	—	—
	1839 JG	—	100.00	150.00	200.00	275.00
	1840 MC	—	100.00	150.00	200.00	275.00
	1841 MC	—	100.00	150.00	250.00	400.00
	1847/6 JG	—	100.00	150.00	225.00	300.00
	1848/7 JG	—	100.00	150.00	225.00	300.00
	1850/40 JG	—	100.00	150.00	200.00	250.00
	1851 JG	—	100.00	150.00	200.00	275.00
	1852 JG	—	100.00	150.00	225.00	325.00
	1853 JG	—	100.00	150.00	200.00	275.00
	1854/2 JG	—	—	—	—	—
	1858 JG	—	100.00	150.00	200.00	275.00
	1859/8 JG	—	100.00	150.00	225.00	300.00
	1859 JG	—	100.00	150.00	200.00	275.00
	1860/50 JG	—	100.00	150.00	225.00	300.00
	1860 JG	—	100.00	150.00	225.00	300.00
	1861/59 JG	—	100.00	150.00	200.00	275.00
	1861/0 JG	—	100.00	150.00	200.00	275.00
	1863/1 JG	—	100.00	150.00	200.00	275.00
	1870 IC	—	100.00	150.00	200.00	275.00

Mint mark: GC

KM#	Date	Mintage	VG	Fine	VF	XF
380.4	1844 MP	—	150.00	200.00	275.00	400.00
	1845 MP	—	750.00	1250.	2000.	3000.
	1846 MP	—	750.00	1250.	2000.	3000.
	1847 MP	—	125.00	175.00	350.00	500.00

PRICING SECTION

KM#	Date	Mintage	VG	Fine	VF	XF
380.4	1848 MP	—	150.00	200.00	350.00	450.00
	1849 MP	—	150.00	200.00	300.00	400.00
	1850 MP	—	150.00	200.00	300.00	400.00
	Mint mark: Go					
380.5	1845 PM	—	100.00	150.00	250.00	400.00
	1849 PF	—	100.00	150.00	250.00	400.00
	1853 PF	—	100.00	150.00	250.00	400.00
	1856 PF	—	100.00	150.00	250.00	400.00
	1859 PF	—	100.00	150.00	250.00	400.00
	1860/59 PF	—	100.00	150.00	250.00	400.00
	1860 PF	—	100.00	150.00	250.00	400.00
	1862 YE	—	100.00	150.00	250.00	400.00
	Mint mark: Ho					
380.6	1861 FM	—	500.00	1000.	1500.	2000.
	Mint mark: Mo					
380.7	1825 JM	—	100.00	150.00	200.00	275.00
	1827/6 JM	—	100.00	150.00	200.00	275.00
	1827 JM	—	100.00	150.00	200.00	275.00
	1830/29 JM	—	100.00	150.00	200.00	275.00
	1831 JM	—	100.00	150.00	200.00	275.00
	1833 ML	—	100.00	150.00	200.00	275.00
	1841 ML	—	100.00	150.00	200.00	275.00
	1844 MF	—	100.00	150.00	200.00	275.00
	1845 MF	—	100.00	150.00	200.00	275.00
	1846 MF	—	125.00	200.00	400.00	600.00
	1848 GC	—	100.00	150.00	200.00	275.00
	1850 GC	—	100.00	150.00	200.00	275.00
	1856/5 GF	—	100.00	150.00	200.00	275.00
	1856 GF	—	100.00	150.00	200.00	275.00
	1858 FH	—	100.00	150.00	200.00	275.00
	1859 FH	—	100.00	150.00	200.00	275.00
	1861 TH	—	100.00	150.00	200.00	275.00
	1861 CH	—	100.00	150.00	200.00	300.00
	1862 CH	—	100.00	150.00	200.00	300.00
	1863 TH	—	100.00	150.00	200.00	300.00
	1868 PH	—	100.00	150.00	200.00	300.00
	1869 CH	—	100.00	150.00	200.00	300.00
	Mint mark: Zs					
380.8	1860 VL	—	150.00	300.00	600.00	1200.
	1862 VL	—	250.00	500.00	800.00	1200.
	1864 MO	—	150.00	300.00	600.00	1200.

4 ESCUDOS

13.5400 g, .875 GOLD, .3809 oz AGW
Mint mark: C
Facing eagle

381	1846 CE	—	1200.	1700.	—	—
	1847 CE	—	400.00	650.00	850.00	1250.
	1848 CE	—	600.00	900.00	1250.	1750.
	Mint mark: Do					
381.1	1832 RM/LR	—	—	—	Rare	—
	1832 RM	—	600.00	900.00	1250.	1750.
	1833 RM/RL	—	—	—	Rare	—
	1852 JMR	—	—	—	Rare	—
	Mint mark: Ga					
381.2	1844 MC	—	500.00	750.00	1000.	1500.
	1844 JG	—	400.00	650.00	850.00	1250.
	Mint mark: GC					
381.3	1844 MP	—	400.00	650.00	850.00	1250.
	1845 MP	—	350.00	500.00	700.00	1000.
	1846 MP	—	400.00	650.00	850.00	1250.
	1848 MP	—	400.00	650.00	850.00	1250.
	1850 MP	—	500.00	750.00	1000.	1500.

		Mint mark: Go				
KM#	Date	Mintage	VG	Fine	VF	XF
381.4	1829/8 MJ	—	250.00	400.00	550.00	750.00
	1829 JM	—	250.00	400.00	550.00	750.00
	1829 MJ	—	250.00	400.00	550.00	750.00
	1831 MJ	—	250.00	400.00	550.00	750.00
	1832 MJ	—	250.00	400.00	550.00	750.00
	1833 MJ	—	250.00	400.00	600.00	850.00
	1834 PJ	—	300.00	500.00	700.00	1000.
	1835 PJ	—	300.00	500.00	700.00	1000.
	1836 PJ	—	250.00	400.00	600.00	850.00
	1837 PJ	—	250.00	400.00	600.00	850.00
	1838 PJ	—	250.00	400.00	600.00	850.00
	1839 PJ	—	300.00	500.00	700.00	1000.
	1840 PJ	—	250.00	400.00	600.00	850.00
	1841 PJ	—	300.00	500.00	700.00	1000.
	1845 PM	—	250.00	400.00	600.00	850.00
	1847/5 YE	—	300.00	500.00	700.00	1000.
	1847 PM	—	300.00	500.00	700.00	1000.
	1849 PF	—	300.00	500.00	700.00	1000.
	1851 PF	—	300.00	500.00	700.00	1000.
	1852 PF	—	250.00	400.00	600.00	850.00
	1855 PF	—	250.00	400.00	600.00	850.00
	1857/5 PF	—	250.00	400.00	600.00	850.00
	1858/7 PF	—	250.00	400.00	600.00	850.00
	1858 PF	—	250.00	400.00	600.00	850.00
	1859/7 PF	—	300.00	500.00	700.00	1000.
	1860 PF	—	300.00	500.00	800.00	1200.
	1862 YE	—	250.00	400.00	600.00	850.00
	1863 YF	—	250.00	400.00	600.00	850.00
	Mint mark: Ho					
381.5	1861 FM	—	1000.	1500.	2500.	3500.
	Mint mark: Mo					
381.6	1825 JM	—	250.00	400.00	600.00	900.00
	1827/6 JM	—	250.00	400.00	550.00	850.00
	1829 JM	—	250.00	450.00	700.00	1000.
	1831 JM	—	250.00	450.00	700.00	1000.
	1832 JM	—	300.00	500.00	800.00	1200.
	1844 MF	—	250.00	450.00	700.00	1000.
	1850 GC	—	250.00	450.00	700.00	1000.
	1856 GF	—	250.00	400.00	550.00	850.00
	1857/6 GF	—	250.00	400.00	550.00	850.00
	1857 GF	—	250.00	400.00	550.00	850.00
	1858 FH	—	250.00	450.00	700.00	1000.
	1859/8 FH	—	250.00	450.00	700.00	1000.
	1861 CH	—	400.00	800.00	1200.	1600.
	1863 CH	—	250.00	450.00	700.00	1000.
	1868 PH	—	250.00	400.00	550.00	850.00
	1869 CH	—	250.00	400.00	500.00	800.00
	Mint mark: O, Oa					
381.7	1861 FR	—	1500.	2500.	4000.	6500.
	Mint mark: Zs					
381.8	1862 VL	—	750.00	1250.	2250.	3500.

8 ESCUDOS

Tail Curved   **Tail Looped**

27.0700 g, .875 GOLD, .7616 oz AGW
Mint mark: Mo
Obv: Hooked-neck eagle.

KM#	Date	Mintage	Fine	VF	XF	Unc
382.1	1823 JM snake's tail curved					
		—	3500.	6500.	10,000.	—

NOTE: Superior Casterline sale 5-89 choice AU realized $18,700.

KM#	Date	Mintage	Fine	VF	XF	Unc
382.2	1823 JM snake's tail looped					
		—	3500.	6500.	10,000.	—

Mint mark: A
Obv: Facing eagle.

KM#	Date	Mintage	Fine	VF	XF	Unc
383	1864 PG	—	650.00	1250.	2250.	—
	1866 DL	—	—	—	7500.	—
	1868/7 DL	—	1500.	2250.	3250.	—
	1869 DL	—	650.00	1250.	2250.	—
	1870 DL	—	1500.	2250.	3250.	—
	1872 AM	—	—	—	Rare	—

Mint mark: Ca

KM#	Date	Mintage	Fine	VF	XF	Unc
383.1	1841 RG	—	400.00	750.00	1250.	1750.
	1842 RG	—	375.00	500.00	1000.	1500.
	1843 RG	—	375.00	500.00	1000.	1500.
	1844 RG	—	350.00	500.00	1000.	1500.
	1845 RG	—	350.00	500.00	1000.	1500.
	1846 RG	—	500.00	1250.	1500.	2000.
	1847 RG	—	1000.	2500.	—	—
	1848 RG	—	350.00	500.00	1000.	1500.
	1849 RG	—	350.00	500.00	1000.	1500.
	1850/40 RG	—	350.00	500.00	1000.	1500.
	1851/41 RG	—	350.00	500.00	1000.	1500.
	1852/42 RG	—	350.00	500.00	1000.	1500.
	1853/43 RG	—	350.00	500.00	1000.	1500.
	1854/44 RG	—	350.00	500.00	1000.	1500.
	1855/43 RG	—	400.00	650.00	1250.	1750.
	1856/46 RG	—	350.00	500.00	750.00	1250.
	1857 JC/RG	—	350.00	500.00	750.00	1250.
	1858 JC	—	350.00	500.00	750.00	1250.
	1858 BA/RG	—	350.00	500.00	750.00	1250.
	1859 JC/RG	—	350.00	500.00	750.00	1250.
	1860 JC/RG	—	350.00	500.00	1000.	1500.
	1861 JC	—	375.00	500.00	750.00	1250.
	1862 JC	—	375.00	500.00	750.00	1250.
	1863 JC	—	500.00	1000.	1750.	2250.
	1864 JC	—	400.00	750.00	1250.	1750.
	1865 JC	—	750.00	1500.	2500.	3500.
	1866 JC	—	375.00	500.00	1000.	1500.
	1866 FP	—	600.00	1250.	2000.	2500.
	1866 JG	—	350.00	500.00	1000.	1500.
	1867 JG	—	375.00	500.00	750.00	1250.
	1868 JG concave wings					
		—	375.00	500.00	750.00	1250.

KM#	Date	Mintage	Fine	VF	XF	Unc
383.1	1869 MM regular eagle					
		—	375.00	500.00	750.00	1250.
	1870/60 MM	—	375.00	500.00	750.00	1250.
	1871/61 MM	—	375.00	500.00	1000.	1500.

Mint mark: C

KM#	Date	Mintage	Fine	VF	XF	Unc
383.2	1846 CE	—	375.00	500.00	1000.	1750.
	1847 CE	—	375.00	500.00	800.00	1250.
	1848 CE	—	375.00	500.00	1000.	1750.
	1849 CE	—	375.00	450.00	700.00	1250.
	1850 CE	—	375.00	450.00	700.00	1250.
	1851 CE	—	375.00	500.00	800.00	1250.
	1852 CE	—	375.00	500.00	800.00	1250.
	1853/1 CE	—	375.00	450.00	700.00	1250.
	1854 CE	—	375.00	450.00	700.00	1250.
	1855/4 CE	—	375.00	500.00	1000.	1750.
	1855 CE	—	375.00	500.00	800.00	1250.
	1856 CE	—	375.00	450.00	700.00	1250.
	1857 CE	—	375.00	450.00	700.00	1250.
	1857 CE w/o periods after C's					
		—	—	—	—	—
	1858 CE	—	375.00	450.00	700.00	1250.
	1859 CE	—	375.00	450.00	700.00	1250.
	1860/58 CE	—	375.00	500.00	800.00	1250.
	1860 CE	—	375.00	500.00	800.00	1250.
	1860 PV	—	375.00	450.00	700.00	1250.
	1861 PV	—	375.00	500.00	800.00	1250.
	1861 CE	—	375.00	500.00	800.00	1250.
	1862 CE	—	375.00	500.00	800.00	1250.
	1863 CE	—	375.00	500.00	800.00	1250.
	1864 CE	—	375.00	450.00	700.00	1250.
	1865 CE	—	375.00	500.00	800.00	1250.
	1866/5 CE	—	375.00	450.00	700.00	1250.
	1866 CE	—	375.00	450.00	700.00	1250.
	1867 CB (error)					
		—	375.00	450.00	700.00	1250.
	1867 CE/CB	—	375.00	450.00	700.00	1250.
	1868 CB (error)					
		—	375.00	500.00	800.00	1250.
	1869 CE	—	375.00	500.00	800.00	1250.
	1870 CE	—	375.00	500.00	800.00	1250.

Mint mark: Do

KM#	Date	Mintage	Fine	VF	XF	Unc
383.3	1832 RM	—	850.00	1750.	2000.	3000.
	1833 RM/RL	—	375.00	500.00	800.00	1250.
	1834 RM	—	375.00	500.00	800.00	1250.
	1835 RM	—	375.00	500.00	800.00	1250.
	1836 RM/RL	—	375.00	500.00	800.00	1250.
	1836 RM M on snake					
		—	375.00	500.00	800.00	1250.
	1837 RM	—	375.00	500.00	800.00	1250.

KM#	Date	Mintage	Fine	VF	XF	Unc
383.3	1838/6 RM	—	375.00	500.00	800.00	1250.
	1838 RM	—	375.00	500.00	800.00	1250.
	1839 RM	—	375.00	450.00	700.00	1250.
	1840/30 RM/RL					
		—	400.00	600.00	1000.	1750.
	1841/30 RM	—	550.00	750.00	1250.	2000.
	1841/31 RM	—	375.00	500.00	800.00	1250.
	1841/34 RM	—	375.00	500.00	800.00	1250.
	1841 RM/RL	—	375.00	500.00	800.00	1250.
	1842/32 RM	—	375.00	500.00	800.00	1250.
	1843/33 RM	—	550.00	750.00	1250.	2000.
	1843/1 RM	—	375.00	500.00	800.00	1250.
	1843 RM	—	375.00	500.00	800.00	1250.
	1844/34 RM/RL					
		—	500.00	1000.	1500.	2500.
	1844 RM	—	450.00	800.00	1250.	2000.
	1845/36 RM	—	400.00	600.00	1000.	1750.
	1845 RM	—	400.00	600.00	1000.	1750.
	1846 RM	—	375.00	500.00	800.00	1250.
	1847/37 RM	—	375.00	500.00	800.00	1250.
	1848/37 RM	—	—	—	—	—
	1848/38 CM	—	375.00	500.00	800.00	1250.
	1849/39 CM	—	375.00	500.00	800.00	1250.
	1849 JMR	—	400.00	750.00	1250.	2000.
	1850 JMR	—	400.00	750.00	1250.	2000.
	1851 JMR	—	400.00	750.00	1250.	2000.
	1852/1 JMR	—	450.00	800.00	1250.	2000.
	1852 CP	—	450.00	800.00	1250.	2000.
	1853 CP	—	450.00	800.00	1250.	2000.
	1854 CP	—	400.00	600.00	1000.	1750.
	1855/4 CP	—	375.00	500.00	800.00	1250.
	1855 CP	—	375.00	500.00	800.00	1250.
	1856 CP	—	400.00	600.00	1000.	1750.
	1857 CP French style eagle, 1832-57					
		—	375.00	500.00	800.00	1250.
	1857 CP Mexican style eagle					
		—	375.00	500.00	800.00	1250.
	1858 CP	—	375.00	500.00	800.00	1250.
	1859 CP	—	375.00	500.00	800.00	1250.
	1860/59 CP	—	450.00	700.00	1250.	2200.
	1861/0 CP	—	400.00	600.00	1000.	1750.
	1862/52 CP	—	375.00	500.00	800.00	1250.
	1862/1 CP	—	375.00	500.00	800.00	1250.
	1862 CP	—	375.00	500.00	800.00	1250.
	1863/53 CP	—	375.00	500.00	800.00	1250.
	1864 LT	—	375.00	500.00	800.00	1250.
	1865/4 LT	—	500.00	1000.	1650.	2750.
	1866/4 CM	-	1250.	2000.	2500.	—
	1866 CM	—	400.00	600.00	1000.	1750.
	1867/56 CP	—	400.00	600.00	1000.	1750.
	1867/4 CP	—	375.00	500.00	800.00	1250.
	1868/4 CP/LT					
		—	—	—	—	—
	1869 CP	—	500.00	1250.	1750.	2750.
	1870 CP	—	400.00	600.00	1000.	1750.

Mint mark: EoMo

KM#	Date	Mintage	Fine	VF	XF	Unc
383.4	1828 LF	—	2500.	4500.	7500.	—
	1829 LF	—	2500.	4500.	7500.	—

Mint mark: Ga

KM#	Date	Mintage	Fine	VF	XF	Unc
383.5	1825 FS	—	500.00	1000.	1250.	1750.
	1826 FS	—	500.00	1000.	1250.	1750.
	1830 FS	—	500.00	1000.	1250.	1750.
	1836 FS	—	750.00	1500.	2000.	3000.
	1836 JG	—	1000.	2500.	3500.	—
	1837 JG	—	1000.	2500.	3500.	—
	1840 MC	—	750.00	1500.	2000.	3000.
	1841/31 MC	—	1000.	2500.	—	—
	1841 MC	—	850.00	1650.	2250.	—
	1842 JG	—	—	—	—	—
	1843 MC	—	—	—	—	—
	1845 MC	—	400.00	750.00	1000.	1500.
	1847 JG	—	2250.	—	—	—
	1849 JG	—	500.00	1000.	1250.	1750.
	1850 JG	—	400.00	750.00	1000.	1500.
	1851 JG	—	400.00	750.00	1000.	1500.
	1852/1 JG	—	500.00	1000.	1250.	1750.
	1855 JG	—	1000.	2500.	3500.	—
	1856 JG	—	400.00	750.00	1000.	1500.
	1857 JG	—	400.00	750.00	1000.	1500.
	1861/0 JG	—	500.00	1000.	1250.	1750.
	1861 JG	—	400.00	600.00	1000.	1750.
	1863/1 JG	—	500.00	1000.	1250.	1750.
	1866 JG	—	400.00	750.00	1000.	1500.

Mint mark: GC

KM#	Date	Mintage	Fine	VF	XF	Unc
383.6	1844 MP	—	550.00	750.00	1250.	2000.
	1845 MP eagle's tail square					
		—	550.00	750.00	1250.	2000.
	1845 MP eagle's tail round					
		—	550.00	750.00	1250.	2000.
	1846 MP eagle's tail square					
		—	450.00	650.00	1000.	1750.
	1846 MP eagle's tail round					
		—	450.00	650.00	1000.	1750.
	1847 MP	—	450.00	650.00	1000.	1750.
	1848 MP	—	550.00	750.00	1250.	2000.
	1849 MP	—	550.00	750.00	1250.	2000.
	1850 MP	—	450.00	650.00	1000.	1750.
	1851 MP	—	450.00	650.00	1000.	1750.
	1852 MP	—	550.00	750.00	1250.	2000.

Mint mark: Go

KM#	Date	Mintage	Fine	VF	XF	Unc
383.7	1828 MJ	—	700.00	1750.	2250.	3000.
	1829 MJ	—	600.00	1500.	2000.	2750.
	1830 MJ	—	375.00	500.00	750.00	1000.
	1831 MJ	—	600.00	1500.	2000.	2750.
	1832 MJ	—	500.00	1250.	1750.	2500.
	1833 MJ	—	375.00	500.00	750.00	1000.
	1834 PJ	—	375.00	500.00	750.00	1000.
	1835 PJ	—	375.00	500.00	750.00	1000.
	1836 PJ	—	400.00	650.00	900.00	1250.
	1837 PJ	—	400.00	650.00	900.00	1250.
	1838/7 PJ	—	375.00	500.00	750.00	1000.
	1838 PJ	—	375.00	500.00	800.00	1200.
	1839/8 PJ	—	375.00	500.00	750.00	1000.
	1839 PJ regular eagle					
		—	375.00	500.00	800.00	1200.
	1840 PJ concave wings					
		—	375.00	500.00	750.00	1000.
	1841 PJ	—	375.00	500.00	750.00	1000.
	1842 PJ	—	375.00	475.00	650.00	1000.
	1842 PM	—	375.00	500.00	750.00	1000.
	1843 PM small eagle					
		—	375.00	500.00	750.00	1000.
	1844/3 PM	—	400.00	650.00	900.00	1250.
	1844 PM	—	375.00	500.00	750.00	1000.
	1845 PM	—	375.00	500.00	750.00	1000.
	1846/5 PM	—	375.00	500.00	800.00	1200.
	1846 PM	—	375.00	500.00	750.00	1000.
	1847 PM	—	400.00	650.00	900.00	1250.
	1848/7 PM	—	375.00	500.00	750.00	1000.
	1848 PM	—	375.00	500.00	750.00	1000.

KM#	Date	Mintage	Fine	VF	XF	Unc
383.7	1848 PF	—	375.00	500.00	750.00	1000.
	1849 PF	—	375.00	425.00	650.00	900.00
	1850 PF	—	375.00	425.00	650.00	900.00
	1851 PF	—	375.00	500.00	750.00	1000.
	1852 PF	—	375.00	500.00	750.00	1000.
	1853 PF	—	375.00	425.00	650.00	900.00
	1854 PF eagle of 1853					
		—	375.00	500.00	750.00	1000.
	1854 PF eagle of 1855					
		—	375.00	500.00	750.00	1000.
	1855/4 PF	—	400.00	650.00	900.00	1250.
	1855 PF	—	375.00	500.00	750.00	1000.
	1856 PF	—	375.00	500.00	750.00	1000.
	1857 PF	—	375.00	500.00	750.00	1000.
	1858 PF	—	375.00	500.00	750.00	1000.
	1859 PF	—	375.00	400.00	550.00	750.00
	1860/50 PF	—	375.00	425.00	650.00	900.00
	1860/59 PF	—	400.00	650.00	900.00	1250.
	1860 PF	—	375.00	500.00	750.00	1100.
	1861/0 PF	—	375.00	400.00	500.00	750.00
	1861 PF	—	375.00	400.00	500.00	750.00
	1862/1 YE	—	375.00	500.00	750.00	1000.
	1862 YE	—	375.00	500.00	750.00	1000.
	1862 YF	—	—	—	—	—
	1863/53 YF	—	375.00	500.00	750.00	1000.
	1863 PF	—	375.00	500.00	750.00	1000.
	1867/57 YF/PF					
		—	375.00	500.00	750.00	1000.
	1867 YF	—	375.00	500.00	750.00	1000.
	1868/58 YF	—	375.00	500.00	750.00	1000.
	1870 FR	—	375.00	425.00	650.00	900.00

Mint mark: Ho

KM#	Date	Mintage	Fine	VF	XF	Unc
383.8	1863 FM	—	400.00	650.00	1000.	2000.
	1864 FM	—	600.00	1250.	1750.	2750.
	1864 PR/FM	—	400.00	650.00	1000.	2000.
	1865 FM/PR	—	500.00	800.00	1250.	2500.
	1867/57 PR	—	400.00	650.00	1000.	2000.
	1868 PR	—	500.00	800.00	1250.	2500.
	1868 PR/FM	—	500.00	800.00	1250.	2500.
	1869 PR/FM	—	400.00	650.00	1000.	2000.
	1869 PR	—	400.00	650.00	1000.	2000.
	1870 PR	—	400.00	650.00	1000.	2000.
	1871/0 PR	—	500.00	800.00	1250.	2500.
	1871 PR	—	500.00	800.00	1250.	2500.
	1872/1 PR	—	600.00	1250.	1750.	2750.
	1873 PR	—	400.00	650.00	1000.	2000.

Mint mark: Mo

KM#	Date	Mintage	Fine	VF	XF	Unc
383.9	1824 JM lg. book reverse					
		—	500.00	1000.	1250.	2000.
	1825 JM sm. book reverse					
		—	375.00	450.00	600.00	1000.
	1826/5 JM	—	700.00	1750.	2250.	3000.
	1827 JM	—	375.00	600.00	725.00	1000.
	1828 JM	—	375.00	600.00	725.00	1000.
	1829 JM	—	375.00	600.00	725.00	1000.
	1830 JM	—	375.00	600.00	725.00	1000.
	1831 JM	—	375.00	600.00	725.00	1000.
	1832/1 JM	—	375.00	600.00	725.00	1000.
	1832 JM	—	375.00	600.00	725.00	1000.
	1833 MJ	—	400.00	750.00	1000.	1500.
	1833 ML	—	375.00	450.00	600.00	900.00
	1834 ML	—	375.00	450.00	600.00	900.00
	1835/4 ML	—	500.00	1000.	1250.	2000.
	1836 ML	—	375.00	450.00	600.00	900.00
	1836 MF	—	500.00	700.00	1200.	2000.
	1837/6 ML	—	375.00	450.00	600.00	900.00
	1838 ML	—	375.00	450.00	600.00	900.00
	1839 ML	—	375.00	450.00	600.00	900.00
	1840 ML	—	375.00	450.00	600.00	900.00
	1841 ML	—	375.00	450.00	600.00	900.00
	1842/1 ML	—	—	—	—	—
	1842 ML	—	375.00	450.00	600.00	900.00
	1842 MM	—	—	—	—	—
	1843 MM	—	375.00	450.00	600.00	900.00
	1844 MF	—	375.00	450.00	600.00	900.00
	1845 MF	—	375.00	450.00	600.00	900.00
	1846 MF	—	500.00	1000.	1250.	2000.
	1847 MF	—	950.00	2250.	—	—
	1847 RC	—	375.00	500.00	800.00	1250.
	1848 GC	—	375.00	450.00	600.00	900.00
	1849 GC	—	375.00	450.00	600.00	900.00
	1850 GC	—	375.00	450.00	600.00	900.00
	1851 GC	—	375.00	450.00	600.00	900.00
	1852 GC	—	375.00	450.00	600.00	900.00
	1853 GC	—	375.00	450.00	600.00	900.00
	1854/44 GC	—	375.00	450.00	600.00	900.00
	1854/3 GC	—	375.00	450.00	600.00	900.00
	1855 GF	—	375.00	450.00	600.00	900.00
	1856/5 GF	—	375.00	450.00	600.00	900.00
	1856 GF	—	375.00	450.00	600.00	900.00
	1857 GF	—	375.00	450.00	600.00	900.00
	1858 FH	—	375.00	450.00	600.00	900.00
	1859 FH	—	400.00	750.00	1000.	1500.
	1860 FH	—	375.00	450.00	600.00	900.00
	1860 TH	—	375.00	450.00	600.00	900.00
	1861/51 CH	—	375.00	450.00	600.00	900.00
	1862 CH	—	375.00	450.00	600.00	900.00
	1863/53 CH	—	375.00	450.00	600.00	900.00
	1863/53 TH	—	375.00	450.00	600.00	900.00
	1867 CH	—	375.00	450.00	600.00	900.00
	1868 CH	—	375.00	450.00	600.00	900.00
	1868 PH	—	375.00	450.00	600.00	900.00
	1869 CH	—	375.00	450.00	600.00	900.00

NOTE: Formerly reported 1825/3 JM is merely a reworked 5.

Large book.

Small book.

Mint mark: O

KM#	Date	Mintage	Fine	VF	XF	Unc
383.10	1858 AE	—	2000.	3000.	4000.	6000.
	1859 AE	—	1000.	2500.	3750.	5500.
	1860 AE	—	1000.	2500.	3750.	5500.
	1861 FR	—	450.00	900.00	1500.	2750.
	1862 FR	—	450.00	900.00	1500.	2750.
	1863 FR	—	450.00	900.00	1500.	2750.
	1864 FR	—	500.00	900.00	1500.	2750.
	1867 AE	—	450.00	900.00	1500.	2750.

KM#	Date	Mintage	Fine	VF	XF	Unc
383.10	1868 AE	—	450.00	900.00	1500.	2750.
	1869 AE	—	450.00	900.00	1500.	2750.

Mint mark: Zs

KM#	Date	Mintage	Fine	VF	XF	Unc
383.11	1858 MO	—	400.00	750.00	1000.	2000.
	1859 MO	—	375.00	450.00	650.00	900.00
	1860/59 VL/MO					
		—	2000.	3000.	4000.	—
	1860/9 MO	—	400.00	750.00	1000.	2000.
	1860 MO	—	375.00	500.00	700.00	1000.
	1861/0 VL	—	375.00	500.00	700.00	1000.
	1861 VL	—	375.00	500.00	700.00	1000.
	1862 VL	—	375.00	500.00	700.00	1100.
	1863 VL	—	375.00	500.00	700.00	1000.
	1863 MO	—	375.00	500.00	700.00	1000.
	1864 MO	—	750.00	1000.	1500.	3000.
	1865 MO	—	375.00	500.00	700.00	1000.
	1865 MP	—	Contemporary counterfeit			
	1868 JS	—	400.00	600.00	800.00	1250.
	1868 YH	—	400.00	600.00	800.00	1250.
	1869 YH	—	400.00	600.00	800.00	1250.
	1870 YH	—	400.00	600.00	800.00	1250.
	1871 YH	—	400.00	600.00	800.00	1250.

EMPIRE OF MAXIMILIAN
RULER
Maximilian, Emperor, 1864-1867
MINT MARKS
Refer To Republic Coinage
MONETARY SYSTEM
100 Centavos = 1 Peso (8 Reales)
CENTAVO

COPPER
Mint mark: M

384	1864	—	35.00	60.00	150.00	900.00

5 CENTAVOS

1.3537 g, .903 SILVER, .0393 oz ASW
Mint mark: G

385	1864	.090	17.50	35.00	65.00	225.00
	1865	—	20.00	30.00	50.00	200.00
	1866	—	65.00	140.00	300.00	1800.

Mint mark: M

385.1	1864	—	12.50	20.00	40.00	200.00
	1866/4	—	25.00	40.00	75.00	365.00
	1866	—	20.00	35.00	65.00	350.00

Mint mark: P

385.2	1864	—	100.00	215.00	950.00	2000.

Mint mark: Z

385.3	1865	—	20.00	30.00	100.00	300.00

10 CENTAVOS

2.7073 g, .903 SILVER, .0786 oz ASW

Mint mark: G

KM#	Date	Mintage	Fine	VF	XF	Unc
386	1864	.045	17.50	35.00	65.00	225.00
	1865	—	25.00	40.00	80.00	275.00

Mint mark: M

386.1	1864	—	12.50	20.00	40.00	200.00
	1866/4	—	20.00	30.00	55.00	275.00
	1866/5	—	20.00	30.00	65.00	300.00
	1866	—	20.00	30.00	65.00	300.00

Mint mark: P

386.2	1864	—	60.00	110.00	200.00	550.00

Mint mark: Z

386.3	1865	—	25.00	50.00	120.00	450.00

50 CENTAVOS

13.5365 g, .903 SILVER, .3929 oz ASW
Mint mark: Mo

387	1866	.031	30.00	50.00	100.00	550.00

PESO

27.0700 g, .903 SILVER, .7857 oz ASW
Mint mark: Go

388	1866	—	300.00	425.00	650.00	2250.

Mint mark: Mo

388.1	1866	2.148	25.00	40.00	80.00	325.00
	1867	1.238	35.00	60.00	120.00	400.00

Mint mark: Pi

388.2	1866	—	40.00	80.00	150.00	600.00

20 PESOS

33.8400 g, .875 GOLD, .9520 oz AGW
Mint mark: Mo

KM#	Date	Mintage	Fine	VF	XF	Unc
389	1866	8,274	500.00	850.00	1150.	2250.

GOLD PESO FANTASIES

Modern gold 'Peso' fantasies of Maximilian exist. Five varieties exist, some dated 1865. One has an eagle in a plain field above a wreath on the reverse. On the second type a numeral '1' appears to either side of the eagle, and the metallic content is designated below: LEY-ORO-K22.

TRIAL STRIKES (TS)

KM#	Date	Mintage	Identification	Mkt.Val.
TS1	1866 Mo	—	20 Pesos, Copper	—

REPUBLIC DECIMAL COINAGE

100 Centavos = 1 Peso

UN (1) CENTAVO

COPPER
Mint mark: Mo
Obv: Seated Liberty.

KM#	Date	Mintage	Fine	VF	XF	Unc
390	1863 round top 3, reeded edge					
		—	10.00	15.00	30.00	150.00
	1863 round top 3, plain edge					
		—	10.00	15.00	30.00	150.00
	1863 flat top 3					
		—	8.00	12.50	25.00	150.00

Mint mark: SLP

KM#	Date	Mintage	Fine	VF	XF	Unc
390.1	1863	1.025	10.00	25.00	50.00	300.00

Mint mark: As
Obv: Standing eagle.

KM#	Date	Mintage	Fine	VF	XF	Unc
391	1875	—	—	—	Rare	—
	1876	.050	75.00	100.00	175.00	650.00
	1880	—	25.00	50.00	100.00	400.00
	1881	—	30.00	60.00	125.00	250.00
	Mint mark: Cn					
391.1	1874	.266	12.50	17.50	35.00	150.00
	1875/4	.153	15.00	20.00	45.00	150.00
	1875	Inc. Ab.	10.00	15.00	25.00	150.00
	1876	.154	5.00	8.00	15.00	150.00
	1877/6	.993	7.50	11.50	17.50	175.00
	1877	Inc. Ab.	6.00	9.00	15.00	150.00
	1880	.142	7.50	10.00	12.50	150.00
	1881	.167	7.50	10.00	25.00	175.00
	1897 large N in mm.					
		.300	2.50	5.00	12.00	50.00
	1897 small N in mm.					
		Inc. Ab.	2.50	5.00	9.00	45.00
	Mint mark: Do					
391.2	1879	.110	10.00	17.50	35.00	150.00
	1880	.069	40.00	90.00	175.00	500.00
	1891	—	8.00	11.00	30.00	150.00
	1891 Do/Mo	—	8.00	11.00	30.00	150.00
	Mint mark: Ga					
391.3	1872	.263	15.00	30.00	60.00	200.00
	1873	.333	6.00	9.00	25.00	150.00
	1874	.076	15.00	25.00	50.00	175.00
	1875	—	10.00	15.00	30.00	150.00
	1876	.303	3.00	6.00	17.50	150.00
	1877	.108	4.00	6.00	20.00	150.00
	1878	.543	4.00	6.00	15.00	150.00
	1881/71	.975	7.00	9.00	20.00	175.00
	1881	Inc. Ab.	7.00	9.00	20.00	175.00
	1889 Ga/Mo	—	3.50	5.00	25.00	125.00
	1890	—	4.00	7.50	20.00	100.00
	Mint mark: Go					
391.4	1874	—	20.00	40.00	80.00	250.00
	1875	.190	11.50	20.00	60.00	200.00
	1876	—	125.00	200.00	350.00	750.00
	1877	—	—	—	Rare	—
	1878	.576	8.00	11.00	30.00	175.00
	1880	.890	6.00	10.00	25.00	175.00
	Mint mark: Ho					
391.5	1875	3,500	450.00	—	—	—
	1876	8,508	50.00	100.00	225.00	500.00
	1880 short H, round O					
		.102	7.50	15.00	35.00	150.00
	1880 tall H, oval O					
		Inc. Ab.	7.50	15.00	35.00	150.00
	1881	.459	5.00	10.00	25.00	150.00
	Mint mark: Mo					
391.6	1869	1.874	7.50	25.00	60.00	200.00
	1870/69	1.200	10.00	25.00	60.00	225.00
	1870	Inc. Ab.	8.00	20.00	50.00	200.00
	1871	.918	8.00	15.00	40.00	200.00
	1872/1	1.625	6.50	10.00	30.00	200.00
	1872	Inc. Ab.	6.00	9.00	25.00	200.00
	1873	1.605	4.00	7.50	20.00	200.00
	1874/3	1.700	5.00	7.00	15.00	100.00
	1874	Inc. Ab.	3.00	5.50	15.00	100.00
	1874.	Inc. Ab.	5.00	10.00	25.00	200.00
	1875	1.495	6.00	8.00	30.00	100.00
	1876	1.600	3.00	5.50	12.50	100.00
	1877	1.270	3.00	5.50	13.50	100.00
	1878/5	1.900	7.50	11.00	22.50	125.00
	1878/6	Inc. Ab.	7.50	11.00	22.50	125.00
	1878/7	Inc. Ab.	7.50	11.00	20.00	125.00
	1878	Inc. Ab.	6.00	9.00	13.50	100.00
	1879/8	1.505	4.50	6.50	13.50	100.00
	1879	Inc. Ab.	3.00	5.50	11.50	75.00
	1880/70	1.130	5.50	7.50	15.00	100.00
	1880/72	I.A.	20.00	50.00	100.00	250.00
	1880/79	I.A.	15.00	35.00	75.00	175.00
	1880	Inc. Ab.	4.25	6.00	12.50	75.00
	1881	1.060	4.50	7.00	15.00	75.00
	1886	12.687	1.50	2.00	8.50	40.00
	1887	7.292	1.50	2.00	5.00	35.00
	1888/78	9.984	2.50	3.00	10.00	30.00
	1888/7	Inc. Ab.	2.50	3.00	10.00	30.00
	1888	Inc. Ab.	1.50	2.00	8.50	30.00
	1889	19.970	2.00	3.00	8.00	30.00

KM#	Date	Mintage	Fine	VF	XF	Unc
391.6	1890/89					
		18.726	2.50	3.00	10.00	40.00
	1890/990	I.A.	2.50	3.00	10.00	40.00
	1890	Inc. Ab.	1.50	2.00	8.50	30.00
	1891	14.544	1.50	2.00	8.50	30.00
	1892	12.908	1.50	2.00	8.50	30.00
	1893/2	5.078	2.50	3.00	10.00	35.00
	1893	Inc. Ab.	1.50	2.00	8.50	30.00
	1894/3	1.896	3.00	6.00	15.00	50.00
	1894	Inc. Ab.	2.00	3.00	10.00	35.00
	1895/3	3.453	3.00	4.50	12.50	35.00
	1895/85	I.A.	3.00	6.00	15.00	50.00
	1895	Inc. Ab.	2.00	3.00	8.50	25.00
	1896	3.075	2.00	3.00	8.50	25.00
	1897	4.150	1.50	2.00	8.50	25.00

NOTE: Varieties exist.

Mint mark: Oa

KM#	Date	Mintage	Fine	VF	XF	Unc
391.7	1872	.016	300.00	500.00	1200.	—
	1873	.011	350.00	600.00	—	—
	1874	4,835	450.00	—	—	—
	1875	2,860	500.00	—	—	—

Mint mark: Pi

KM#	Date	Mintage	Fine	VF	XF	Unc
391.8	1871	—	—	—	Rare	—
	1877	.249	—	—	Rare	—
	1878	.751	12.50	25.00	50.00	200.00
	1891 Pi/Mo	—	10.00	17.50	35.00	150.00
	1891	—	8.00	15.00	30.00	150.00

Mint mark: Zs

KM#	Date	Mintage	Fine	VF	XF	Unc
391.9	1872	.055	22.50	30.00	100.00	300.00
	1873	1.460	4.00	8.00	25.00	150.00
	1874/3	.685	5.50	11.00	30.00	250.00
	1874	Inc. Ab.	4.00	8.00	25.00	200.00
	1875/4	.200	8.50	17.00	45.00	250.00
	1875	Inc. Ab.	7.00	14.00	35.00	200.00
	1876	—	5.00	10.00	25.00	200.00
	1877	—	50.00	125.00	300.00	750.00
	1878	—	4.50	9.00	25.00	200.00
	1880	.100	5.00	10.00	30.00	200.00
	1881	1.200	4.25	8.00	25.00	150.00

COPPER-NICKEL
Mint: Mexico City

KM#	Date	Mintage	Fine	VF	XF	Unc
392	1882	99.955	7.50	12.50	17.50	35.00
	1883	Inc. Ab.	.50	.75	1.00	1.50

Obv: Restyled eagle.

KM#	Date	Mintage	Fine	VF	XF	Unc
393	1898	1.529	4.00	6.00	15.00	40.00

NOTE: Varieties exist.

Mint mark: C
Reduced size

KM#	Date	Mintage	Fine	VF	XF	Unc
394	1901	.220	15.00	22.50	35.00	75.00
	1902	.320	15.00	22.50	55.00	100.00
	1903	.536	7.50	12.50	20.00	45.00

KM#	Date	Mintage	Fine	VF	XF	Unc
394	1904/3	.148	35.00	50.00	75.00	125.00
	1905	.110	100.00	150.00	300.00	550.00

NOTE: Varieties exist.

Mint mark: M,Mo

KM#	Date	Mintage	Fine	VF	XF	Unc
394.1	1899	.051	150.00	175.00	300.00	800.00
	1900 wide date					
		4.010	2.50	4.00	7.50	25.00
	1900 narrow date					
		Inc. Ab.	2.50	4.00	7.50	25.00
	1901	1.494	3.00	8.00	17.50	50.00
	1902/899					
		2.090	30.00	60.00	100.00	175.00
	1902	Inc. Ab.	2.25	4.00	10.00	35.00
	1903	8.400	1.50	2.25	4.00	20.00
	1904	10.250	1.50	2.00	4.00	20.00
	1905	3.643	2.25	4.00	10.00	40.00

NOTE: Varieties exist.

2 CENTAVOS

COPPER-NICKEL
Mint: Mexico City

KM#	Date	Mintage	Fine	VF	XF	Unc
395	1882	50.023	2.00	3.00	7.50	15.00
	1883/2	Inc. Ab.	2.00	3.00	7.50	15.00
	1883	Inc. Ab.	.50	.75	1.00	2.50

5 CENTAVOS

1.3530 g, .903 SILVER, .0392 oz ASW
Mint mark: Ca
Obv: Facing eagle. Rev: Denomination in wreath.

KM#	Date	Mintage	Fine	VF	XF	Unc
396	1868	—	40.00	65.00	125.00	400.00
	1869	*.030	25.00	40.00	100.00	350.00
	1870	.035	30.00	50.00	100.00	350.00

Mint mark: SLP

KM#	Date	Mintage	Fine	VF	XF	Unc
396.1	1863	—	75.00	125.00	350.00	1200.

Mint mark: Mo
Rev: Cap and rays.

KM#	Date	Mintage	Fine	VF	XF	Unc
397	1867/3	—	25.00	50.00	125.00	275.00
	1867	—	20.00	40.00	100.00	250.00
	1868/7	—	25.00	50.00	150.00	325.00
	1868	—	20.00	40.00	100.00	250.00

NOTE: Varieties exist.

Mint mark: P

KM#	Date	Mintage	Fine	VF	XF	Unc
397.1	1868/7	.034	25.00	50.00	125.00	300.00
	1868	Inc. Ab.	20.00	45.00	100.00	250.00
	1869	.014	200.00	300.00	600.00	—

Mint mark: As
Obv: Standing eagle.

KM#	Date	Mintage	Fine	VF	XF	Unc
398	1874 DL	—	7.50	15.00	30.00	100.00
	1875 DL	—	7.50	15.00	30.00	100.00
	1876 L	—	20.00	40.00	60.00	150.00

PRICING SECTION

KM#	Date	Mintage	Fine	VF	XF	Unc
398	1878 L mule, gold peso obverse	—	250.00	350.00	650.00	—
	1879 L mule, gold peso obverse	—	30.00	60.00	100.00	250.00
	1880 L mule, gold peso obverse	.012	50.00	75.00	125.00	300.00
	1886 L	.043	10.00	20.00	40.00	150.00
	1886 L mule, gold peso obverse	Inc. Ab.	50.00	75.00	125.00	200.00
	1887 L	.020	25.00	50.00	75.00	150.00
	1888 L	.032	10.00	20.00	40.00	100.00
	1889 L	.016	25.00	50.00	100.00	200.00
	1890 L	.030	25.00	50.00	75.00	150.00
	1891 L	8,000	50.00	75.00	125.00	350.00
	1892 L	.013	20.00	40.00	60.00	125.00
	1893 L	.024	10.00	20.00	40.00	80.00
	1895 L	.020	10.00	20.00	40.00	80.00

Mint mark: CH, Ca

KM#	Date	Mintage	Fine	VF	XF	Unc
398.1	1871 M	.014	20.00	40.00	100.00	250.00
	1873 M crude date	—	100.00	150.00	250.00	500.00
	1874 M crude date	—	25.00	50.00	75.00	150.00
	1886 M	.025	7.50	15.00	30.00	100.00
	1887 M	.037	7.50	15.00	30.00	100.00
	1887 Ca/MoM	Inc. Ab.	10.00	20.00	40.00	125.00
	1888 M	.145	1.50	3.00	6.00	25.00
	1889 M	.044	5.00	10.00	20.00	50.00
	1890 M	.102	1.50	3.00	6.00	25.00
	1891 M	.164	1.50	3.00	6.00	25.00
	1892 M	.085	1.50	3.00	6.00	25.00
	1892 M 9/inverted 9	Inc. Ab.	2.00	4.00	7.50	30.00
	1893 M	.133	1.50	3.00	6.00	25.00
	1894 M	.108	1.50	3.00	6.00	25.00
	1895 M	.074	2.00	4.00	7.50	30.00

Mint mark: Cn

KM#	Date	Mintage	Fine	VF	XF	Unc
398.2	1871 P	—	125.00	200.00	350.00	—
	1873 P	4,992	50.00	100.00	200.00	400.00
	1874 P	—	25.00	50.00	100.00	200.00
	1875 P	—	—	—	Rare	—
398.2	1876 P	—	25.00	50.00	100.00	200.00
	1886 M	.010	25.00	50.00	100.00	200.00
	1887 M	.010	25.00	50.00	100.00	200.00
	1888 M	.119	1.50	3.00	6.00	30.00
	1889 M	.066	4.00	7.50	15.00	50.00
	1890 M	.180	1.50	3.00	6.00	25.00
	1890 D (error)	Inc. Ab.	125.00	175.00	250.00	—
	1891 M	.087	2.00	4.00	7.50	25.00
	1894 M	.024	4.00	7.50	15.00	40.00
	1896 M	.016	7.50	12.50	25.00	75.00
	1897 M	.223	1.50	2.50	5.00	20.00

Mint mark: Do

KM#	Date	Mintage	Fine	VF	XF	Unc
398.3	1874 M	—	100.00	150.00	225.00	500.00
	1877 P	4,795	75.00	125.00	225.00	450.00
	1878/7 E/P	4,300	200.00	300.00	450.00	—
	1879 B	—	125.00	200.00	350.00	—
	1880 B	—	—	—	Rare	—
	1881 P	3,020	300.00	500.00	800.00	—
	1887 C	.042	5.00	8.00	17.50	60.00
	1888/9 C	.091	6.00	10.00	20.00	70.00
	1888 C	Inc. Ab.	4.00	7.50	15.00	55.00
	1889 C	.049	3.50	6.00	12.50	50.00
	1890 C	.136	4.00	7.50	15.00	55.00
	1890 P	Inc. Ab.	5.00	8.00	17.50	60.00
	1891/0 P	.048	3.50	6.00	12.50	50.00
	1891 P	Inc. Ab.	3.00	5.00	10.00	45.00
	1894 D	.038	3.50	6.00	12.50	50.00

Mint mark: Ga

KM#	Date	Mintage	Fine	VF	XF	Unc
398.4	1877 A	—	15.00	30.00	60.00	150.00
	1881 S	.156	4.00	7.50	15.00	60.00
	1886 S	.087	2.00	4.00	7.50	25.00
	1888 S lg.G	.262	2.00	4.00	10.00	30.00
	1888 S sm.g I.A.		2.00	4.00	10.00	30.00
	1889 S	.178	1.50	3.00	7.50	25.00
	1890 S	.068	4.00	7.50	12.50	35.00
	1891 S	.050	4.00	6.50	10.00	35.00
	1892 S	.078	2.00	4.00	7.50	25.00
	1893 S	.044	4.00	7.50	15.00	45.00

Mint mark: Go

KM#	Date	Mintage	Fine	VF	XF	Unc
398.5	1869 S	.080	15.00	30.00	75.00	175.00
	1871 S	.100	5.00	10.00	25.00	75.00
	1872 S	.030	30.00	60.00	125.00	250.00
	1873 S	.040	30.00	60.00	125.00	250.00
	1874 S	—	7.00	12.00	25.00	75.00
	1875 S	—	8.00	15.00	30.00	75.0C
	1876 S	—	8.00	15.00	30.00	75.00
	1877 S	—	7.00	12.00	20.00	75.00
	1878/7 S	.020	8.00	15.00	25.00	75.00
	1879 S	—	8.00	15.00	25.00	75.00
	1880 S	.055	15.00	30.00	60.00	200.00
	1881/0 S	.160	5.00	8.00	17.50	60.00
	1881 S	Inc. Ab.	4.00	6.00	12.00	45.00
	1886 R	.230	1.50	3.00	6.00	30.00
	1887 R	.230	1.50	2.50	5.00	30.00
	1888 R	.320	1.50	2.50	5.00	20.00
	1889 R	.060	4.00	6.00	12.00	45.00
	1890 R	.250	1.50	2.50	5.00	20.00
	1891/0 R	.168	1.80	3.00	6.00	30.00
	1891 R	Inc. Ab.	1.50	2.50	5.00	20.00
	1892 R	.138	1.50	3.00	6.00	25.00
	1893 R	.200	1.25	2.50	5.00	20.00
	1894 R	.200	1.25	2.50	5.00	20.00
	1896 R	.525	1.25	2.00	4.00	15.00
	1897 R	.596	1.50	2.00	4.00	15.00

Mint mark: Ho

KM#	Date	Mintage	Fine	VF	XF	Unc
398.6	1874/69 R	—	125.00	225.00	350.00	—
	1874 R	—	100.00	200.00	325.00	—
	1878/7 A	.022	—	—	Rare	—
	1878 A	Inc. Ab.	20.00	40.00	80.00	175.00
	1878 A mule, gold peso obverse	Inc. Ab.	40.00	80.00	150.00	300.00
	1880 A	.043	7.50	15.00	30.00	75.00
	1886 G	.044	5.00	10.00	20.00	75.00
	1887 G	.020	5.00	10.00	20.00	75.00
	1888 G	.012	7.50	15.00	30.00	85.00
	1889 G	.067	3.00	6.00	12.50	40.00
	1890 G	.050	3.00	6.00	12.50	40.00
	1891 G	.046	3.00	6.00	12.50	40.00
	1893 G	.084	2.50	5.00	10.00	30.00
	1894 G	.068	2.00	4.00	10.00	30.00

Mint mark: Mo

KM#	Date	Mintage	Fine	VF	XF	Unc
398.7	1869/8 C	.040	8.00	15.00	40.00	120.00
	1870 C	.140	4.00	7.00	20.00	60.00
	1871 C	.103	9.00	20.00	40.00	100.00
	1871 M	Inc. Ab.	7.50	12.50	25.00	60.00
	1872 M	.266	5.00	8.00	20.00	55.00
	1873 M	.020	40.00	60.00	100.00	225.00
	1874/69 M	—	7.50	15.00	30.00	75.00
	1874 M	—	4.00	7.00	17.50	50.00
	1874/3 B	—	5.00	8.00	22.50	55.00
	1874 B	—	5.00	8.00	22.50	55.00
	1875 B	—	4.00	7.00	15.00	50.00
	1875 B/M	—	6.00	9.00	17.50	50.00
	1876/5 B	—	4.00	7.00	15.00	50.00
	1876 B	—	4.00	7.00	12.50	50.00
	1877/6 M	.080	4.00	7.00	15.00	60.00
	1877 M	Inc. Ab.	4.00	7.00	12.50	60.00
	1878/7 M	.100	4.00	7.00	15.00	55.00
	1878 M	Inc. Ab.	2.50	5.00	12.50	45.00
	1879/8 M	—	8.00	12.50	22.50	55.00
	1879 M	—	4.50	7.00	15.00	50.00
	1879 M 9/inverted 9	—	10.00	15.00	25.00	75.00
	1880/76 M/B	—	5.00	7.50	15.00	50.00
	1880/76 M	—	5.00	7.50	15.00	50.00
	1880 M	—	4.00	6.00	12.00	40.00
	1881/0 M	.180	4.00	6.00	10.00	35.00
	1881 M	Inc. Ab.	3.00	4.50	9.00	35.00
	1886/0 M	.398	2.00	2.75	7.50	25.00
	1886/1 M	I.A.	2.00	2.75	7.50	25.00
	1886 M	Inc. Ab.	1.75	2.25	6.00	20.00
	1887 m	.720	1.75	2.00	5.00	20.00
	1887 M/m	I.A.	2.00		6.00	20.00
	1888/7 M	1.360	2.25	2.50	5.00	20.00
	1888 M	Inc. Ab.	1.75	2.00	5.00	20.00
	1889/8 M	1.242	2.25	2.50	6.00	20.00
	1889 M	Inc. Ab.	1.75	2.00	5.00	20.00
	1890/00 M	1.694	1.75	2.75	6.00	20.00

KM#	Date	Mintage	Fine	VF	XF	Unc
398.7	1890 M	Inc. Ab.	1.50	2.00	5.00	20.00
	1891 M	1.030	1.75	2.00	5.00	20.00
	1892 M	1.400	1.75	2.00	5.00	20.00
	1892 M 9/inverted 9					
		Inc. Ab.	2.00	2.75	7.50	20.00
	1893 M	.220	1.75	2.00	5.00	15.00
	1894 M	.320	1.75	2.00	5.00	15.00
	1895 M	.078	3.00	5.00	8.00	25.00
	1896 B	.080	1.75	2.00	5.00	20.00
	1897 M	.160	1.75	2.00	5.00	15.00

NOTE: Varieties exist.

Mint mark: Oa

KM#	Date	Mintage	Fine	VF	XF	Unc
398.8	1890 E	.048	—	—	Rare	—
	1890 N	Inc. Ab.	65.00	125.00	200.00	350.00

Mint mark: Pi

KM#	Date	Mintage	Fine	VF	XF	Unc
398.9	1869 S	—	300.00	400.00	500.00	—
	1870 G/MoC					
		.020	—	—	Rare	—
	1870 O	Inc. Ab.	200.00	300.00	400.00	—
	1871 O	5,400	—	—	Rare	—
	1872 O	—	75.00	100.00	175.00	400.00
	1873	5,000	—	—	Rare	—
	1874 H	—	30.00	50.00	100.00	225.00
	1875 H	—	7.50	12.50	30.00	75.00
	1876 H	—	10.00	20.00	45.00	100.00
	1877 H	—	7.50	12.50	20.00	60.00
	1878/7 H	—	—	—	Rare	—
	1878 H	—	60.00	90.00	150.00	300.00
	1880 H	6,200	—	—	Rare	—
	1881 H	4,500	—	—	Rare	—
	1886 R	.033	12.50	25.00	50.00	125.00
	1887/0 R	.169	4.00	7.50	15.00	45.00
	1887 R	Inc. Ab.	3.00	5.00	10.00	35.00
	1888 R	.210	2.00	4.00	9.00	30.00
	1889/7 R	.197	2.50	5.00	10.00	35.00
	1889 R	Inc. Ab.	2.00	4.00	9.00	30.00
	1890 R	.221	2.00	3.00	6.00	25.00
	1891/89 R/B					
		.176	2.00	4.00	8.00	25.00
	1891 R	Inc. Ab.	2.00	3.00	6.00	20.00
	1892/89 R	.182	2.00	4.00	8.00	25.00
	1892/0 R	I.A.	2.00	4.00	8.00	25.00
	1892 R	Inc. Ab.	2.00	3.00	6.00	20.00
	1893 R	.041	5.00	10.00	20.00	60.00

NOTE: Varieties exist.

Mint mark: Zs

KM#	Date	Mintage	Fine	VF	XF	Unc
398.10	1870 H	.040	12.50	25.00	50.00	125.00
	1871 H	.040	12.50	25.00	50.00	125.00
	1872 H	.040	12.50	25.00	50.00	125.00
	1873/2 H	.020	35.00	65.00	125.00	275.00
	1873 H	Inc. Ab.	25.00	50.00	100.00	250.00
	1874 H	—	7.50	12.50	25.00	75.00
	1874 A	—	40.00	75.00	150.00	300.00
	1875 A	—	7.50	12.50	25.00	75.00
	1876 A	—	50.00	75.00	100.00	200.00
	1876 S	—	12.50	25.00	50.00	125.00
	1877 S	—	3.00	6.00	12.00	40.00
	1878 S	.060	3.00	6.00	12.00	40.00
	1879/8 S	—	3.00	6.00	15.00	50.00
	1879 S	—	3.00	6.00	12.00	40.00
	1880/79 S	.130	6.00	10.00	20.00	60.00
	1880 S	Inc. Ab.	5.00	8.00	16.00	45.00
	1881 S	.210	2.50	5.00	10.00	35.00
	1886/4 S	.360	6.00	10.00	20.00	60.00
	1886 S	Inc. Ab.	2.00	3.00	6.00	20.00
	1886 Z	Inc. Ab.	5.00	10.00	25.00	65.00
	1887 Z	.400	2.00	3.00	6.00	25.00
	1888/7 Z	.500	2.00	3.00	6.00	25.00
	1888 Z	Inc. Ab.	2.00	3.00	6.00	25.00
	1889 Z	.520	2.00	3.00	6.00	25.00
	1889 Z 9/inverted 9					
		Inc. Ab.	2.00	3.00	6.00	25.00
	1889 ZsZ/MoM					
		Inc. Ab.	2.00	3.00	6.00	25.00
	1890 Z	.580	1.75	2.50	5.00	20.00
	1890 ZsZ/MoM					
		Inc. Ab.	2.00	3.00	6.00	25.00
	1891 Z	.420	1.75	2.50	5.00	20.00

KM#	Date	Mintage	Fine	VF	XF	Unc
398.10	1892 Z	.346	1.75	2.50	5.00	20.00
	1893 Z	.258	1.75	2.50	5.00	20.00
	1894 Z	.228	1.75	2.50	5.00	20.00
	1894 ZoZ (error)					
		Inc. Ab.	2.00	4.00	8.00	30.00
	1895 Z	.260	1.75	2.50	5.00	20.00
	1896 Z	.200	1.75	2.50	5.00	20.00
	1896 6/inverted 6					
		Inc. Ab.	2.00	3.00	6.00	25.00
	1897/6 Z	.200	2.00	3.00	6.00	25.00
	1897 Z	Inc. Ab.	1.75	2.50	5.00	20.00

COPPER-NICKEL
Mint: Mexico City

KM#	Date	Mintage	Fine	VF	XF	Unc
399	1882	Inc. Ab.	.50	1.00	2.50	7.50
	1883	Inc. Ab.	25.00	50.00	80.00	250.00

.903 SILVER
Mint mark: Cn
Obv: Restyled eagle.

KM#	Date	Mintage	Fine	VF	XF	Unc
400	1898 M	.044	1.75	4.00	8.00	20.00
	1899 M	.111	5.50	8.50	20.00	50.00
	1899 Q	Inc. Ab.	1.75	2.25	4.50	12.50
	1900/800 Q					
		.239	3.50	5.00	12.50	30.00
	1900 Q round Q, single tail					
		Inc. Ab.	1.75	2.50	6.00	15.00
	1900 Q narrow C, oval Q					
		Inc. Ab.	1.75	2.50	6.00	15.00
	1900 Q wide C, oval Q					
		Inc. Ab.	1.75	2.50	6.00	15.00
	1901 Q	.148	1.75	2.25	4.50	12.50
	1902 Q narrow C, heavy serifs					
		.262	1.75	2.50	6.00	15.00
	1902 Q wide C, light serifs					
		Inc. Ab.	1.75	2.50	6.00	15.00
	1903/1 Q	.331	2.00	2.50	6.00	15.00
	1903 Q	Inc. Ab.	1.75	2.25	4.50	12.50
	1903/1898 V					
		Inc. Ab.	3.50	4.50	9.00	22.50
	1903 V	Inc. Ab.	1.75	2.25	4.50	12.50
	1904 H	.352	1.75	2.25	5.00	15.00

NOTE: Varieties exist.

Mint mark: Go

KM#	Date	Mintage	Fine	VF	XF	Unc
400.1	1898 R mule, gold peso obverse					
		.180	7.50	15.00	30.00	75.00
	1899 R	.260	1.75	2.25	4.50	12.50
	1900 R	.200	1.75	2.25	4.50	12.50

NOTE: Varieties exist.

Mint mark: Mo

KM#	Date	Mintage	Fine	VF	XF	Unc
400.2	1898 M	.080	2.00	4.00	7.00	25.00
	1899 M	.168	1.75	2.25	4.50	12.50
	1900/800 M					
		.300	4.50	6.50	10.00	30.00
	1900 M	Inc. Ab.	1.75	2.25	4.50	12.50
	1901 M	.100	1.75	2.25	4.50	12.50
	1902 M	.144	1.25	2.00	3.75	10.00
	1903 M	.500	1.25	2.00	3.75	10.00
	1904/804 M					
		1.090	1.75	2.50	6.00	15.00
	1904/94 M	I.A.	1.75	2.50	6.00	15.00
	1904 M	Inc. Ab.	1.25	2.00	6.00	12.50
	1905 M	.344	1.75	3.75	7.50	17.50

Mint mark: Zs

KM#	Date	Mintage	Fine	VF	XF	Unc
400.3	1898 Z	.100	1.75	2.25	4.50	12.50
	1899 Z	.050	2.00	3.00	7.00	20.00
	1900 Z	.055	1.75	2.50	5.00	15.00
	1901 Z	.040	1.75	2.50	5.00	15.00
	1902/1 Z	.034	2.00	4.50	9.00	22.50
	1902 Z	Inc. Ab.	1.75	3.75	7.50	17.50
	1903 Z	.217	1.25	2.00	5.00	12.50
	1904 Z	.191	1.75	2.50	5.00	12.50
	1904 M	Inc. Ab.	1.75	2.50	6.00	15.00
	1905 M	.046	2.00	4.50	9.00	22.50

10 CENTAVOS

2.7070 g, .903 SILVER, .0785 oz ASW
Mint mark: Ca
Obv: Eagle. Rev: Value within wreath.

KM#	Date	Mintage	Fine	VF	XF	Unc
401	1868/7	—	30.00	60.00	150.00	550.00
	1868	—	30.00	60.00	150.00	550.00
	1869	.015	25.00	50.00	125.00	600.00
	1870	.017	22.50	45.00	100.00	550.00

Mint mark: SLP

401.2	1863	—	75.00	150.00	275.00	900.00

Mint mark: Mo

402	1867/3	—	50.00	100.00	150.00	450.00
	1867	—	20.00	40.00	60.00	250.00
	1868/7	—	20.00	40.00	80.00	275.00
	1868	—	20.00	45.00	75.00	250.00

Mint mark: P

402.1	1868/7	.038	45.00	90.00	175.00	650.00
	1868	Inc. Ab.	20.00	40.00	100.00	550.00
	1869/7	4,900	55.00	125.00	250.00	800.00

Mint mark: As

403	1874 DL	—	20.00	40.00	80.00	175.00
	1875 L	—	5.00	10.00	25.00	75.00
	1876 L	—	7.50	12.50	35.00	100.00
	1878/7 L	—	7.50	12.50	35.00	110.00
	1878 L	—	5.00	10.00	30.00	100.00
	1879 L	—	7.50	12.50	35.00	100.00
	1880 L	.013	7.50	12.50	35.00	100.00
	1882 L	.022	7.50	12.50	35.00	100.00
	1883 L	8,520	25.00	50.00	100.00	225.00
	1884 L	—	5.00	10.00	30.00	100.00
	1885 L	.015	5.00	10.00	25.00	100.00
	1886 L	.045	5.00	10.00	25.00	100.00
	1887 L	.015	5.00	10.00	25.00	100.00
	1888 L	.038	5.00	10.00	25.00	100.00
	1889 L	.020	5.00	10.00	25.00	100.00
	1890 L	.040	5.00	10.00	25.00	100.00
	1891 L	.038	5.00	10.00	25.00	100.00
	1892 L	.057	3.00	6.00	20.00	100.00
	1893 L	.070	7.50	12.50	35.00	100.00

NOTE: Varieties exist.

Mint mark: CH,Ca

403.1	1871 M	8,150	15.00	30.00	60.00	150.00
	1873 M crude date					
		—	35.00	75.00	125.00	175.00
	1874 M	—	10.00	17.50	35.00	100.00
	1880/70 G					
		7,620	20.00	40.00	80.00	175.00
	1880 G/g	I.A.	15.00	25.00	50.00	125.00
	1881	340 pcs.	—	—	Rare	—
	1883 M	9,000	10.00	20.00	40.00	125.00
	1884 M	—	10.00	20.00	40.00	125.00
	1886 M	.045	7.50	12.50	30.00	100.00
	1887/3 M/G					
		.096	5.00	10.00	20.00	75.00
	1887 M	Inc. Ab.	2.00	4.00	8.00	75.00

KM#	Date	Mintage	Fine	VF	XF	Unc
403.1	1888 M	.299	1.50	2.50	5.00	75.00
	1888 Ca/Mo					
		Inc. Ab.	1.50	2.50	5.00	75.00
	1889/8 M	.115	2.00	4.00	8.00	75.00
	1889 M small 89 (5 Centavo font)					
		Inc. Ab.	2.00	4.00	8.00	75.00
	1890/80 M	.140	2.00	4.00	8.00	75.00
	1890/89 M	I.A.	2.00	4.00	8.00	75.00
	1890 M	Inc. Ab.	1.50	3.00	7.00	75.00
	1891 M	.163	1.50	3.00	7.00	75.00
	1892 M	.169	1.50	3.00	7.00	75.00
	1892 M 9/inverted 9					
		Inc. Ab.	2.00	4.00	8.00	75.00
	1893 M	.246	1.50	3.00	7.00	75.00
	1894 M	.163	1.50	3.00	7.00	75.00
	1895 M	.127	1.50	3.00	7.00	75.00

NOTE: Varieties exist.

Mint mark: Cn

403.2	1871 P	—	—	—	Rare	—
	1873 P	8,732	20.00	50.00	100.00	225.00
	1881 D	9,440	75.00	175.00	325.00	500.00
	1882 D	.012	75.00	125.00	200.00	400.00
	1885 M mule gold 2-1/2 Peso obv.					
		.018	25.00	50.00	100.00	200.00
	1886 M mule, gold 2-1/2 Peso obv.					
		.013	50.00	100.00	150.00	300.00
	1887 M	.011	20.00	40.00	75.00	175.00
	1888 M	.056	5.00	10.00	25.00	125.00
	1889 M	.042	5.00	10.00	20.00	75.00
	1890 M	.132	2.00	4.00	7.50	75.00
	1891 M	.084	5.00	10.00	20.00	75.00
	1892/1 M	.037	4.00	8.00	15.00	75.00
	1892 M	Inc. Ab.	2.50	5.00	10.00	75.00
	1894 M	.043	2.50	5.00	10.00	75.00
	1895 M	.023	2.50	5.00	10.00	60.00
	1896 M	.121	1.50	2.50	5.00	50.00

Mint mark: Do

403.3	1878 E	2,500	100.00	175.00	300.00	600.00
	1879 B	—	—	—	Rare	—
	1880/70 B	—	—	—	Rare	—
	1880/79 B	—	—	—	Rare	—
	1884 C	—	30.00	60.00	100.00	225.00
	1886 C	.013	75.00	150.00	300.00	500.00
	1887 C	.081	4.00	8.00	15.00	100.00
	1888 C	.031	6.00	12.00	30.00	100.00
	1889 C	.055	4.00	8.00	15.00	100.00
	1890 C	.050	4.00	8.00	15.00	100.00
	1891 P	.139	2.00	4.00	8.00	80.00
	1892 P	.212	2.00	4.00	8.00	80.00
	1892 D	Inc. Ab.	2.00	4.00	8.00	80.00
	1893 D	.258	2.00	4.00	8.00	80.00
	1893 D/C	I.A.	2.50	5.00	10.00	80.00
	1894 D	.184	1.50	3.00	6.00	80.00
	1894 D/C	I.A.	2.00	4.00	8.00	80.00
	1895 D	.142	1.50	3.00	6.00	80.00

Mint mark: Ga

403.4	1871 C	4,734	75.00	125.00	200.00	500.00
	1873/1 C	.025	10.00	15.00	35.00	150.00
	1873 C	Inc.Ab.	10.00	15.00	35.00	150.00
	1874 C	—	10.00	15.00	35.00	150.00
	1877 A	—	10.00	15.00	30.00	150.00
	1881 S	.115	5.00	10.00	25.00	150.00
	1883 B	.090	4.00	8.00	15.00	90.00
	1884 B	—	5.00	10.00	20.00	90.00
	1884 B/S	—	6.00	12.50	25.00	90.00
	1884 H	—	3.00	5.00	10.00	90.00
	1885 H	.093	3.00	5.00	10.00	90.00
	1886 S	.151	2.50	4.00	9.00	90.00
	1887 S	.162	1.50	3.00	6.00	90.00
	1888 S	.225	1.50	3.00	6.00	90.00
	1888 GaS/HoG					
		Inc. Ab.	1.50	3.00	6.00	90.00
	1889 S	.310	1.50	3.00	6.00	40.00
	1890 S	.303	1.50	3.00	6.00	40.00
	1891 S	.199	5.00	10.00	20.00	45.00
	1892 S	.329	1.50	3.00	6.00	40.00
	1893 S	.225	1.50	3.00	6.00	40.00
	1894 S	.243	1.50	3.00	6.00	40.00
	1895 S	.080	1.50	3.00	6.00	40.00

NOTE: Varieties exist.

Mint mark: Go

KM#	Date	Mintage	Fine	VF	XF	Unc
403.5	1869 S	7,000	20.00	40.00	80.00	200.00
	1871/0 S	.060	15.00	25.00	50.00	125.00
	1872 S	.060	15.00	25.00	50.00	125.00
	1873 S	.050	15.00	25.00	50.00	125.00
	1874 S	—	15.00	25.00	50.00	125.00
	1875 S	—	250.00	350.00	500.00	800.00
	1876 S	—	10.00	20.00	40.00	100.00
	1877 S	—	80.00	120.00	200.00	400.00
	1878/7 S	.010	10.00	20.00	45.00	110.00
	1878 S	Inc. Ab.	7.50	12.00	20.00	75.00
	1879 S	—	7.50	12.00	20.00	75.00
	1880 S	—	100.00	200.00	300.00	450.00
	1881/71 S	.100	3.00	5.00	10.00	75.00
	1881/0 S	I.A.	3.50	5.00	10.00	75.00
	1881 S	Inc. Ab.	3.00	5.00	10.00	75.00
	1882/1 S	.040	3.00	6.00	12.00	75.00
	1883 B	—	3.00	5.00	10.00	75.00
	1884 B	—	1.50	3.00	6.00	75.00
	1884 S	—	6.00	12.50	25.00	90.00
	1885 R	.100	1.50	3.00	6.00	75.00
	1886 R	.095	3.00	5.00	10.00	75.00
	1887 R	.330	2.50	5.00	10.00	75.00
	1888 R	.270	1.50	3.00	6.00	75.00
	1889 R	.205	2.00	4.00	8.00	75.00
	1889 GoR/HoG					
		Inc. Ab.	3.00	5.00	10.00	75.00
	1890 R	.270	1.50	3.00	6.00	35.00
	1890 GoR/Cn M					
		Inc. Ab.	1.50	3.00	6.00	35.00
	1891 R	.523	1.50	3.00	6.00	35.00
	1891 GoR/HoG					
		Inc. Ab.	1.50	3.00	6.00	35.00
	1892 R	.440	1.50	3.00	6.00	35.00
	1893/1 R	.389	3.00	5.00	10.00	35.00
	1893 R	Inc. Ab.	1.50	3.00	6.00	35.00
	1894 R	.400	1.50	2.50	5.00	35.00
	1895 R	.355	1.50	2.50	5.00	35.00
	1896 R	.190	1.50	2.50	5.00	35.00
	1897 R	.205	1.50	2.50	5.00	35.00

NOTE: Varieties exist.

Mint mark: Ho

KM#	Date	Mintage	Fine	VF	XF	Unc
403.6	1874 R	—	30.00	60.00	100.00	200.00
	1876 F	3,140	200.00	300.00	450.00	750.00
	1878 A	—	5.00	10.00	15.00	85.00
	1879 A	—	25.00	50.00	90.00	175.00
	1880 A	—	3.00	6.00	12.50	85.00
	1881 A	.028	4.00	7.00	15.00	85.00
	1882/1 A	.025	5.00	10.00	20.00	85.00
	1882/1 a	I.A.	6.00	12.50	25.00	85.00
	1882 A	Inc. Ab.	4.00	7.00	15.00	85.00
	1883	7,000	65.00	100.00	200.00	400.00
	1884 A	—	35.00	75.00	150.00	300.00
	1884 M	—	7.50	15.00	30.00	85.00
	1885 M	.021	12.50	25.00	50.00	100.00
	1886 M	.010	—	—	Rare	—
	1886 M	Inc. Ab.	7.50	12.50	25.00	85.00
	1887 G	—	25.00	50.00	75.00	150.00
	1888 G	.025	6.00	12.50	25.00	85.00
	1889 G	.042	3.00	6.00	10.00	85.00
	1890 G	.048	3.00	6.00	10.00	85.00
	1891/80 G	.136	3.00	6.00	10.00	85.00
	1891/0 G	I.A.	3.00	6.00	10.00	85.00
	1891 G	Inc. Ab.	3.00	6.00	10.00	85.00
	1892 G	.067	3.00	6.00	10.00	85.00
	1893 G	.067	3.00	6.00	10.00	85.00

Mint mark: Mo

KM#	Date	Mintage	Fine	VF	XF	Unc
403.7	1869/8 C	.030	10.00	20.00	40.00	100.00
	1869 C	Inc. Ab.	8.00	17.50	35.00	90.00
	1870 C	.110	3.00	7.50	15.00	50.00
	1871 C	.084	50.00	75.00	125.00	250.00
	1871 M	Inc. Ab.	12.00	17.50	45.00	125.00
	1872/69 M	.198	10.00	20.00	35.00	100.00
	1872 M	Inc. Ab.	3.00	7.50	15.00	65.00
	1873 M	.040	10.00	15.00	30.00	75.00
	1874 M	—	5.00	10.00	20.00	65.00
	1874/64 B	—	5.00	10.00	20.00	65.00
	1874 B/M	—	20.00	40.00	60.00	125.00
	1874 B	—	5.00	10.00	15.00	65.00
	1875 B	—	20.00	40.00	60.00	125.00
	1876/5 B	—	3.00	5.00	9.00	65.00
	1876/5 B/M	—	3.00	5.00	9.00	65.00
	1877/6 M	—	3.00	5.00	9.00	65.00

Mint mark: Mo (continued)

KM#	Date	Mintage	Fine	VF	XF	Unc
403.7	1877/6 M/B	—	3.00	5.00	9.00	65.00
	1877 M	—	3.00	5.00	9.00	65.00
	1878/7 M	.100	3.00	5.00	9.00	65.00
	1878 M	Inc. Ab.	3.00	5.00	9.00	65.00
	1879/69 M	—	3.00	5.00	9.00	65.00
	1879 M/C	—	3.00	5.00	9.00	65.00
	1880/79 M	—	3.00	5.00	9.00	65.00
	1881/0 M	.510	3.00	5.00	9.00	35.00
	1881 M	Inc. Ab.	3.00	5.00	9.00	35.00
	1882/1 M	.550	3.00	5.00	9.00	35.00
	1882 M	Inc. Ab.	3.00	5.00	9.00	35.00
	1883/2 M	.250	3.00	5.00	9.00	35.00
	1884 M	—	3.00	5.00	9.00	35.00
	1885 M	.470	3.00	5.00	9.00	35.00
	1886 M	.603	3.00	5.00	9.00	35.00
	1887 M	.580	3.00	5.00	9.00	35.00
	1888/7 MoM					
		.710	3.00	5.00	9.00	35.00
	1888 MoM	I.A.	3.00	5.00	9.00	35.00
	1888 MOM	I.A.	3.00	5.00	9.00	35.00
	1889/8 M	.622	3.00	5.00	9.00	35.00
	1889 M	Inc. Ab.	3.00	5.00	9.00	35.00
	1890/89 M	.815	3.00	5.00	9.00	35.00
	1890 M	Inc. Ab.	3.00	5.00	9.00	35.00
	1891 M	.859	1.50	2.50	7.00	25.00
	1892 M	1.030	1.50	2.50	7.00	25.00
	1893 M	.310	1.50	2.50	7.00	25.00
	1893 M/C	I.A.	1.50	2.50	7.00	25.00
	1894 M	.350	5.00	10.00	20.00	60.00
	1895 M	.320	1.50	2.50	7.00	25.00
	1896 B/G	.340	1.50	2.50	7.00	25.00
	1896 M	Inc. Ab.	35.00	70.00	100.00	150.00
	1897 M	.170	1.50	2.50	5.00	20.00

NOTE: Varieties exist.

Mint mark: Oa

KM#	Date	Mintage	Fine	VF	XF	Unc
403.8	1889 E	.021	200.00	400.00	600.00	
	1890 E	.031	100.00	150.00	250.00	500.00
	1890 N	Inc. Ab.	—	—	Rare	

Mint mark: Pi

KM#	Date	Mintage	Fine	VF	XF	Unc
403.9	1869/8 S	4,000	—	—	Rare	—
	1870/69 O	.018	—	—	Rare	—
	1870 O	Inc. Ab.	125.00	200.00	325.00	600.00
	1871 O	.021	50.00	100.00	150.00	300.00
	1872 O	.016	150.00	225.00	350.00	650.00
	1873 O	4,750	—	—	Rare	—
	1874 H	—	25.00	50.00	100.00	200.00
	1875 H	—	75.00	125.00	200.00	400.00
	1876 H	—	75.00	125.00	200.00	400.00
	1877 H	—	75.00	125.00	200.00	400.00
	1878 H	—	250.00	500.00	750.00	—
	1879 H	—	—	—	—	—
	1880 H	—	150.00	250.00	350.00	—
	1881 H	7,600	250.00	350.00	500.00	—
	1882 H	4,000	—	—	Rare	—
	1883 H	—	125.00	200.00	300.00	500.00
	1884 H	—	25.00	50.00	100.00	200.00
	1885 H	.051	25.00	50.00	100.00	200.00
	1885 C	Inc. Ab.	—	—	Rare	—
	1886 C	.052	15.00	30.00	60.00	150.00
	1886 R	Inc. Ab.	5.00	10.00	20.00	65.00
	1887 R	.118	2.50	5.00	10.00	50.00
	1888 R	.136	2.50	5.00	10.00	50.00
	1889/7 R	.131	7.50	12.50	20.00	60.00
	1890 R	.204	1.50	3.00	7.50	40.00
	1891/89 R	.163	2.50	5.00	10.00	40.00
	1891 R	Inc. Ab.	1.50	3.50	6.00	30.00
	1892/0 R	.200	2.00	4.00	8.00	40.00
	1892 R	Inc. Ab.	1.50	2.50	5.00	40.00
	1893 R	.048	7.50	10.00	17.50	60.00

NOTE: Varieties exist.

Mint mark: Zs

KM#	Date	Mintage	Fine	VF	XF	Unc
403.10	1870 H	.020	100.00	150.00	200.00	400.00
	1871/0 H	.010	—	—	—	—
	1871 H	Inc. Ab.	—	—	—	—
	1872 H	.010	150.00	200.00	275.00	500.00
	1873 H	.010	250.00	350.00	600.00	—
	1874/3 H	—	50.00	75.00	150.00	300.00
	1874 A	—	200.00	300.00	500.00	—
	1875 A	—	5.00	10.00	25.00	100.00
	1876 A	—	5.00	10.00	25.00	100.00
	1876 S	—	100.00	200.00	300.00	500.00

KM#	Date	Mintage	Fine	VF	XF	Unc
403.10	1877 S small S					
		—	7.50	12.50	25.00	100.00
	1877 S regular S					
		—	7.50	12.50	25.00	100.00
	1878/7 S	.030	5.00	10.00	20.00	80.00
	1878 S	Inc. Ab.	5.00	10.00	20.00	80.00
	1879 S	—	5.00	10.00	20.00	80.00
	1880 S	—	5.00	10.00	20.00	80.00
	1881/0 S	.120	3.00	6.00	12.50	50.00
	1881 S	Inc. Ab.	3.00	6.00	12.50	50.00
	1882/1 S	.064	12.50	25.00	50.00	125.00
	1882 S	Inc. Ab.	12.50	25.00	50.00	125.00
	1883/73 S	.102	2.00	4.00	8.00	50.00
	1883 S	Inc. Ab.	2.00	4.00	8.00	50.00
	1884/3 S	—	2.00	4.00	8.00	50.00
	1884 S	—	2.00	4.00	8.00	50.00
	1885 S	.297	1.50	2.50	5.00	50.00
	1885 S small S in mint mark					
		Inc. Ab.	2.50	4.00	8.00	50.00
	1885 Z w/o assayers initial (error)					
		Inc. Ab.	3.50	7.50	15.00	65.00
	1886 S	.274	1.50	2.50	5.00	30.00
	1886 Z	I.A.	12.50	25.00	50.00	125.00
	1887 ZsZ	.233	1.50	2.50	5.00	30.00
	1887 Z Z (error)					
		Inc. Ab.	3.50	7.50	15.00	50.00
	1888 ZsZ	.270	1.50	2.50	5.00	30.00
	1888 Z Z (error)					
		Inc. Ab.	3.50	7.50	15.00	40.00
	1889/7 Z/S					
		.240	4.00	8.00	12.50	40.00
	1889 Z/S	I.A.	1.50	4.00	8.00	30.00
	1889 Z	Inc. Ab.	1.50	2.50	5.00	30.00
	1890 ZsZ	.410	1.50	2.50	5.00	30.00
	1890 Z Z (error)					
		Inc. Ab.	3.75	7.50	15.00	40.00
	1891 Z	1.105	1.50	2.50	5.00	30.00
	1891 ZsZ double s					
		Inc. Ab.	2.00	4.00	7.00	30.00
	1892 Z	1.102	1.50	2.50	5.00	30.00
	1893 Z	1.011	1.50	2.50	5.00	25.00
	1894 Z	.892	1.50	2.50	5.00	30.00
	1895 Z	.920	1.50	2.50	5.00	30.00
	1896/5 ZsZ	.700	1.50	2.50	5.00	30.00
	1896 ZsZ	I.A.	1.50	2.50	5.00	30.00
	1896 Z Z (error)					
		Inc. Ab.	3.75	7.50	15.00	40.00
	1897/6 ZsZ	.900	2.00	5.00	10.00	30.00
	1897/6 Z Z (error)					
		Inc. Ab.	3.75	7.50	15.00	40.00
	1897 Z	Inc. Ab.	1.50	2.50	5.00	30.00

NOTE: Varieties exist.

Mint mark: Cn
Obv: Restyled eagle.

KM#	Date	Mintage	Fine	VF	XF	Unc
404	1898 M	9,870	50.00	100.00	150.00	300.00
	1899 Q round Q, single tail					
		.080	5.00	7.50	15.00	40.00
	1899 Q oval Q, double tail					
		Inc. Ab.	5.00	7.50	15.00	40.00
	1900 Q	.160	1.50	2.50	5.00	20.00
	1901 Q	.235	1.50	2.50	5.00	20.00
	1902 Q	.186	1.50	2.50	5.00	20.00
	1903 Q	.256	1.50	2.50	6.00	20.00
	1903 V	Inc. Ab.	1.50	2.50	5.00	15.00
	1904 H	.307	1.50	2.50	5.00	15.00

NOTE: Varieties exist.

Mint mark: Go

KM#	Date	Mintage	Fine	VF	XF	Unc
404.1	1898 R	.435	1.50	2.50	5.00	20.00
	1899 R	.270	1.50	2.50	5.00	25.00
	1900 R	.130	7.50	12.50	25.00	60.00

Mint mark: Mo

KM#	Date	Mintage	Fine	VF	XF	Unc
404.2	1898 M	.130	1.50	2.50	5.00	17.50
	1899 M	.190	1.50	2.50	5.00	17.50
	1900 M	.311	1.50	2.50	5.00	17.50
	1901 M	.080	2.50	3.50	7.00	20.00
	1902 M	.181	1.50	2.50	5.00	17.50
	1903 M	.581	1.50	2.50	5.00	17.50
	1904 M	1.266	1.25	2.00	4.50	15.00
	1904 MM (error)					
		Inc. Ab.	2.50	5.00	10.00	25.00
	1905 M	.266	2.00	3.75	7.50	20.00

Mint mark: Zs

KM#	Date	Mintage	Fine	VF	XF	Unc
404.3	1898 Z	.240	1.50	2.50	7.50	20.00
	1899 Z	.105	1.50	3.00	10.00	22.00
	1900 Z	.219	7.50	10.00	20.00	45.00
	1901 Z	.070	2.50	5.00	10.00	25.00
	1902 Z	.120	2.50	5.00	10.00	25.00
	1903 Z	.228	1.50	3.00	10.00	20.00
	1904 Z	.368	1.50	3.00	10.00	20.00
	1904 M	Inc. Ab.	1.50	3.00	10.00	25.00
	1905 M	.066	7.50	15.00	30.00	60.00

20 CENTAVOS

5.4150 g, .903 SILVER, .1572 oz ASW
Mint mark: Cn
Obv: Restyled eagle.

KM#	Date	Mintage	Fine	VF	XF	Unc
405	1898 M	.114	5.00	12.50	35.00	140.00
	1899 M	.044	12.00	20.00	45.00	225.00
	1899 Q	Inc. Ab.	20.00	35.00	100.00	250.00
	1900 Q	.068	6.50	12.50	35.00	140.00
	1901 Q	.185	5.00	10.00	30.00	120.00
	1902/802 Q					
		.098	6.00	10.00	30.00	120.00
	1902 Q	Inc. Ab.	4.00	9.00	30.00	120.00
	1903 Q	.093	4.00	9.00	30.00	120.00
	1904/3 H	.258	—	—	—	—
	1904 H	Inc. Ab.	5.00	10.00	30.00	120.00

Mint mark: Go

KM#	Date	Mintage	Fine	VF	XF	Unc
405.1	1898 R	.135	4.00	8.00	20.00	100.00
	1899 R	.215	4.00	8.00	20.00	100.00
	1900/800 R					
		.038	10.00	20.00	50.00	150.00

Mint mark: Mo

KM#	Date	Mintage	Fine	VF	XF	Unc
405.2	1898 M	.150	4.00	8.00	20.00	85.00
	1899 M	.425	4.00	8.00	20.00	85.00
	1900/800 M					
		.295	4.00	8.00	20.00	85.00
	1901 M	.110	4.00	8.00	20.00	85.00
	1902 M	.120	4.00	8.00	20.00	85.00
	1903 M	.213	4.00	8.00	20.00	85.00
	1904 M	.276	4.00	8.00	20.00	85.00
	1905 M	.117	6.50	20.00	50.00	150.00

NOTE: Varieties exist.

Mint mark: Zs

KM#	Date	Mintage	Fine	VF	XF	Unc
405.3	1898 Z	.195	5.00	10.00	20.00	100.00
	1899 Z	.210	5.00	10.00	20.00	100.00
	1900/800 Z					
		.097	5.00	10.00	20.00	100.00
	1901/0 Z	.130	25.00	50.00	100.00	250.00
	1901 Z	Inc. Ab.	5.00	10.00	20.00	100.00
	1902 Z	.105	5.00	10.00	20.00	100.00
	1903 Z	.143	5.00	10.00	20.00	100.00
	1904 Z	.246	5.00	10.00	20.00	100.00
	1904 M	Inc. Ab.	5.00	10.00	20.00	100.00
	1905 M	.059	10.00	20.00	50.00	150.00

25 CENTAVOS

6.7680 g, .903 SILVER, .1965 oz ASW
Mint mark: A,As

KM#	Date	Mintage	Fine	VF	XF	Unc
406	1874 L	—	20.00	40.00	80.00	200.00
	1875 L	—	15.00	30.00	60.00	200.00
	1876 L	—	30.00	50.00	90.00	200.00
	1877 L	.011	50.00	100.00	200.00	400.00
	1877.	Inc. Ab.	10.00	25.00	50.00	200.00
	1878 L	.025	10.00	25.00	50.00	200.00
	1879 L	—	10.00	25.00	50.00	200.00
	1880 L	—	10.00	25.00	50.00	200.00
	1880.L	—	10.00	25.00	50.00	200.00
	1881 L	8,800	—	—	Rare	—
	1882 L	7,777	15.00	35.00	75.00	200.00
	1883 L	.028	10.00	25.00	50.00	200.00
	1884 L	—	10.00	25.00	50.00	200.00
	1885 L	—	20.00	40.00	80.00	200.00
	1886 L	.046	10.00	25.00	60.00	200.00
	1887 L	.012	10.00	25.00	50.00	200.00
	1888 L	.020	10.00	25.00	50.00	200.00
	1889 L	.014	10.00	25.00	50.00	200.00
	1890 L	.023	10.00	25.00	50.00	200.00

Mint mark: CA,CH,Ca

KM#	Date	Mintage	Fine	VF	XF	Unc
406.1	1871 M	.018	25.00	50.00	100.00	200.00
	1872 M very crude date					
		.024	50.00	100.00	150.00	300.00
	1883 M	.012	10.00	25.00	50.00	175.00
	1885/3 M	.035	10.00	25.00	50.00	175.00
	1885 M	Inc.Ab.	10.00	25.00	50.00	175.00
	1886 M	.022	10.00	25.00	50.00	175.00
	1887/6 M	.026	10.00	15.00	30.00	175.00
	1887 M	Inc. Ab.	10.00	15.00	30.00	175.00
	1888 M	.014	10.00	25.00	50.00	175.00
	1889 M	.050	10.00	15.00	30.00	175.00

Mint mark: Cn

KM#	Date	Mintage	Fine	VF	XF	Unc
406.2	1871 P	—	250.00	500.00	750.00	—
	1872 P	2,780	300.00	550.00	800.00	—
	1873 P	.020	100.00	150.00	250.00	500.00
	1874 P	—	20.00	50.00	125.00	250.00
	1875 P	—	250.00	500.00	750.00	—
	1876 P	—	—	—	Rare	—
	1878/7 D/S	—	100.00	150.00	250.00	500.00
	1878 D	—	100.00	150.00	250.00	500.00
	1879 D	—	15.00	35.00	70.00	175.00
	1880 D	—	250.00	500.00	750.00	—
	1881/0 D	.018	15.00	30.00	60.00	175.00
	1882 D	—	200.00	350.00	600.00	—
	1882 M	—	—	—	Rare	—
	1883 M	.015	50.00	100.00	150.00	300.00
	1884 M	—	20.00	40.00	80.00	175.00
	1885/4 M	.019	20.00	40.00	80.00	175.00
	1886 M	.022	12.50	20.00	50.00	175.00
	1887 M	.032	12.50	20.00	50.00	175.00
	1888 M	.086	7.50	15.00	30.00	175.00
	1889 M	.050	10.00	25.00	50.00	175.00
	1890 M	.091	7.50	17.50	40.00	175.00
	1892/0 M	.016	20.00	40.00	80.00	200.00
	1892 M	Inc. Ab.	20.00	40.00	80.00	200.00

Mint mark: Do

KM#	Date	Mintage	Fine	VF	XF	Unc
406.3	1873 P	892 pcs.	—	—	Rare	—
	1877 P	—	25.00	50.00	100.00	200.00
	1878/7 E	—	250.00	500.00	750.00	—
	1878 B	—	—	—	Rare	—
	1879 B	—	50.00	75.00	125.00	250.00
	1880 B	—	—	—	Rare	—
	1882 C	.017	25.00	50.00	100.00	225.00
	1884/3 C	—	25.00	50.00	100.00	200.00
	1885 C	.015	20.00	40.00	80.00	200.00
	1886 C	.033	15.00	30.00	60.00	200.00
	1887 C	.027	10.00	20.00	50.00	200.00

KM#	Date	Mintage	Fine	VF	XF	Unc
406.3	1888 C	.025	10.00	20.00	50.00	200.00
	1889 C	.029	10.00	20.00	50.00	200.00
	1890 C	.068	7.50	15.00	40.00	200.00

Mint mark: Ga

KM#	Date	Mintage	Fine	VF	XF	Unc
406.4	1880 A	.038	25.00	50.00	100.00	200.00
	1881/0 S	.039	25.00	50.00	100.00	200.00
	1881 S	Inc. Ab.	25.00	50.00	100.00	200.00
	1882 S	.018	25.00	50.00	100.00	200.00
	1883/2 B/S	—	50.00	100.00	150.00	300.00
	1884 B	—	20.00	40.00	80.00	150.00
	1889 S	.030	20.00	40.00	80.00	150.00

Mint mark: Go

KM#	Date	Mintage	Fine	VF	XF	Unc
406.5	1870 S	.128	10.00	20.00	50.00	125.00
	1871 S	.172	10.00	20.00	50.00	125.00
	1872/1 S	.178	10.00	20.00	50.00	125.00
	1872 S	Inc. Ab.	10.00	20.00	50.00	125.00
	1873 S	.120	10.00	20.00	50.00	125.00
406.5	1874 S	—	15.00	30.00	60.00	150.00
	1875/4 S	—	15.00	30.00	60.00	150.00
	1875 S	—	10.00	20.00	50.00	125.00
	1876 S	—	20.00	40.00	80.00	175.00
	1877 S	.124	10.00	20.00	50.00	125.00
	1878 S	.146	10.00	20.00	50.00	125.00
	1879 S	—	10.00	20.00	50.00	125.00
	1880 S	—	20.00	40.00	80.00	175.00
	1881 S	.408	7.50	17.50	45.00	125.00
	1882 S	.204	7.50	17.50	45.00	125.00
	1883 B	.168	7.50	17.50	45.00	125.00
	1884/69 B	—	7.50	17.50	45.00	125.00
	1884/3 B	—	7.50	17.50	45.00	125.00
	1884 B	—	7.50	17.50	45.00	125.00
	1885/65 R	.300	7.50	17.50	45.00	125.00
	1885/69 R	I.A.	7.50	17.50	45.00	125.00
	1885 R	Inc. Ab.	7.50	17.50	45.00	125.00
	1886/66 R	.322	7.50	17.50	45.00	125.00
	1886/69 R/S					
		Inc. Ab.	7.50	17.50	45.00	125.00
	1886/5/69R					
		Inc. Ab.	7.50	15.00	45.00	125.00
	1886 R	Inc. Ab.	7.50	15.00	45.00	125.00
	1887 R	.254	7.50	15.00	45.00	125.00
	1887 Go/Cn R/D					
		Inc. Ab.	7.50	15.00	45.00	125.00
	1888 R	.312	7.50	15.00	45.00	125.00
	1889/8 R	.304	7.50	15.00	45.00	125.00
	1889/8 Go/Cn R/D					
		Inc. Ab.	7.50	15.00	45.00	125.00
	1889 R	Inc. Ab.	7.50	15.00	45.00	125.00
	1890 R	.236	7.50	15.00	45.00	125.00

NOTE: Varieties exist.

Mint mark: Ho

KM#	Date	Mintage	Fine	VF	XF	Unc
406.6	1874 R	.023	10.00	20.00	40.00	125.00
	1874/64 R	I.A.	10.00	20.00	40.00	125.00
	1875 R	—	—	—	Rare	—
	1876/4 F/R					
		.034	10.00	20.00	50.00	150.00
	1876 F/R	I.A.	10.00	25.00	60.00	150.00
	1876 F	Inc. Ab.	10.00	25.00	55.00	135.00
	1877 F	—	10.00	20.00	50.00	125.00
	1878 A	.023	10.00	20.00	50.00	125.00
	1879 A	—	10.00	20.00	50.00	125.00
	1880 A	—	15.00	30.00	60.00	125.00
	1881 A	.019	15.00	30.00	60.00	125.00
	1882 A	8,120	20.00	40.00	80.00	150.00
	1883 M	2,000	100.00	200.00	300.00	600.00
	1884 M	—	12.50	25.00	50.00	150.00
	1885 M	—	10.00	20.00	50.00	125.00
	1886 G	6,400	30.00	60.00	125.00	250.00
	1887 G	.012	10.00	20.00	40.00	125.00
	1888 G	.020	10.00	20.00	40.00	125.00
	1889 G	.028	10.00	20.00	40.00	125.00
	1890/80 G	.018	25.00	50.00	100.00	125.00
	1890 G	Inc. Ab.	25.00	50.00	100.00	125.00

NOTE: Varieties exist.

Mint mark: Mo

KM#	Date	Mintage	Fine	VF	XF	Unc
406.7	1869 C	.076	10.00	25.00	50.00	125.00
	1870/9 C	.136	6.00	12.00	30.00	125.00
	1870 C	Inc. Ab.	6.00	12.00	30.00	125.00
	1871 M	.138	6.00	12.00	30.00	125.00
	1872 M	.220	6.00	12.00	30.00	125.00
	1873/1 M	.048	10.00	25.00	50.00	125.00

KM#	Date	Mintage	Fine	VF	XF	Unc
406.7	1873 M Inc. Ab.		10.00	25.00	50.00	125.00
	1874/69 B/M					
		—	10.00	25.00	50.00	125.00
	1874/3 M	—	10.00	25.00	50.00	125.00
	1874/3 B	—	10.00	25.00	50.00	125.00
	1874 M	—	6.00	12.00	30.00	125.00
	1874 B/M	—	10.00	25.00	50.00	125.00
	1875 B	—	6.00	12.00	30.00	125.00
	1876/5 B	—	7.50	15.00	40.00	125.00
	1876 B	—	6.00	12.00	30.00	125.00
	1877 M	.056	10.00	25.00	50.00	125.00
	1878/1 M	.120	10.00	25.00	50.00	125.00
	1878/7 M I.A.		10.00	25.00	50.00	125.00
	1878 M Inc. Ab.		6.00	12.00	30.00	125.00
	1879 M	—	10.00	20.00	40.00	125.00
	1880 M	—	7.50	15.00	35.00	125.00
	1881/0 M	.300	10.00	25.00	50.00	125.00
	1881 M Inc. Ab.		10.00	25.00	50.00	125.00
	1882 M	.212	7.50	15.00	35.00	125.00
	1883 M	.108	7.50	15.00	35.00	125.00
	1884 M	—	10.00	20.00	40.00	125.00
	1885 M	.216	10.00	20.00	40.00	125.00
	1886/5 M	.436	7.50	15.00	35.00	125.00
	1886 M Inc. Ab.		7.50	15.00	35.00	125.00
	1887 M	.376	7.50	15.00	35.00	125.00
	1888 M	.192	7.50	15.00	35.00	125.00
	1889 M	.132	7.50	15.00	35.00	125.00
	1890 M	.060	10.00	20.00	40.00	125.00

NOTE: Varieties exist.

Mint mark: Pi

KM#	Date	Mintage	Fine	VF	XF	Unc
406.8	1869 S	—	25.00	75.00	150.00	300.00
	1870 G	.050	10.00	30.00	75.00	150.00
	1870 O Inc. Ab.		15.00	35.00	85.00	175.00
	1871 O	.030	10.00	30.00	75.00	150.00
	1872 O	.046	10.00	30.00	75.00	150.00
	1873 O	.013	15.00	40.00	90.00	175.00
	1874 H	—	15.00	40.00	90.00	200.00
	1875 H	—	10.00	20.00	60.00	150.00
	1876/5 H	—	15.00	30.00	80.00	175.00
	1876 H	—	10.00	25.00	65.00	150.00
	1877 H	.019	10.00	25.00	65.00	150.00
	1878 H	—	15.00	30.00	60.00	150.00
	1879/8 H	—	10.00	25.00	60.00	150.00
	1879 H	—	10.00	25.00	60.00	150.00
	1879 E	—	100.00	200.00	300.00	600.00
	1880 H	—	20.00	40.00	100.00	200.00
	1881 H	.050	20.00	40.00	80.00	175.00
	1881 E Inc. Ab.		—	—	Rare	—
	1882 H	.020	10.00	20.00	60.00	150.00
	1883 H	.017	10.00	25.00	65.00	150.00
	1884 H	—	10.00	25.00	65.00	150.00
	1885 H	.043	10.00	25.00	60.00	150.00
	1886 C	.078	10.00	25.00	65.00	150.00
	1886 R Inc. Ab.		7.50	20.00	50.00	150.00
	1886 R 6/inverted 6					
	Inc. Ab.		7.50	20.00	50.00	150.00
	1887 Pi/ZsR	.092	7.50	20.00	50.00	150.00
	1887 Pi/ZsB					
	Inc. Ab.		100.00	150.00	300.00	500.00
	1888 R	.106	7.50	20.00	50.00	150.00
	1888 Pi/ZsR					
	Inc. Ab.		10.00	20.00	50.00	150.00
	1888 R/B I.A.		10.00	20.00	50.00	150.00
	1889 R	.115	7.50	15.00	40.00	150.00
	1889 Pi/ZsR					
	Inc. Ab.		10.00	20.00	50.00	150.00
	1889 R/B I.A.		10.00	20.00	50.00	150.00
	1890 R	.064	10.00	20.00	50.00	150.00
	1890 Pi/ZsR/B					
	Inc. Ab.		7.50	15.00	40.00	150.00
	1890 R/B I.A.		10.00	20.00	50.00	150.00

NOTE: Varieties exist.

Mint mark: Zs

KM#	Date	Mintage	Fine	VF	XF	Unc
406.9	1870 H	.152	6.00	15.00	50.00	125.00
	1871 H	.250	6.00	15.00	50.00	125.00
	1872 H	.260	6.00	15.00	50.00	125.00
	1873 H	.132	6.00	15.00	50.00	125.00
	1874 H	—	10.00	20.00	60.00	125.00
	1874 A	—	10.00	20.00	60.00	125.00
	1875 A	—	7.00	20.00	60.00	125.00
	1876 A	—	6.00	15.00	50.00	125.00
	1876 S	—	6.00	15.00	50.00	125.00
	1877 S	.350	6.00	15.00	50.00	125.00

KM#	Date	Mintage	Fine	VF	XF	Unc
406.9	1878 S	.252	6.00	15.00	50.00	125.00
	1879 S	—	6.00	15.00	50.00	125.00
	1880 S	—	6.00	15.00	50.00	125.00
	1881/0 S	.570	6.00	15.00	50.00	125.00
	1881 S Inc. Ab.		6.00	15.00	50.00	125.00
	1882/1 S	.300	10.00	17.50	55.00	125.00
	1882 S Inc. Ab.		6.00	15.00	50.00	125.00
	1883/2 S	.193	10.00	17.50	55.00	125.00
	1883 S Inc. Ab.		6.00	15.00	50.00	125.00
	1884/3 S	—	10.00	17.50	55.00	125.00
	1884 S	—	6.00	15.00	50.00	125.00
	1885 S	.309	6.00	15.00	50.00	125.00
	1886/5 S	.613	6.00	15.00	50.00	125.00
	1886 S Inc. Ab.		6.00	15.00	50.00	125.00
	1886 Z Inc. Ab.		6.00	15.00	50.00	125.00
	1887 Z	.389	6.00	15.00	50.00	125.00
	1888 Z	.408	6.00	15.00	50.00	125.00
	1889 Z	.400	6.00	15.00	50.00	125.00
	1890 Z	.269	6.00	15.00	50.00	125.00

NOTE: Varieties exist.

50 CENTAVOS

13.5360 g, .903 SILVER, .3930 oz ASW
Mint mark: A,As
Rev: Balance scale.

KM#	Date	Mintage	Fine	VF	XF	Unc
407	1875 L	—	12.00	25.00	60.00	400.00
	1876/5 L	—	25.00	40.00	100.00	450.00
	1876 L	—	12.00	25.00	60.00	400.00
	1876.L	—	—	—	—	—
	1877 L	.026	15.00	30.00	75.00	450.00
	1878 L	—	12.00	25.00	60.00	400.00
	1879 L	—	25.00	50.00	100.00	450.00
	1880 L	.057	12.00	25.00	60.00	400.00
	1881 L	.018	15.00	30.00	75.00	450.00
	1884 L	6,286	75.00	125.00	250.00	650.00
	1885 As/HoL					
		.021	15.00	35.00	80.00	450.00
	1888 L	—	Contemporary counterfeits			

Mint mark: Ca, CHa

KM#	Date	Mintage	Fine	VF	XF	Unc
407.1	1883 M	.012	30.00	60.00	125.00	500.00
	1884 M	—	25.00	50.00	125.00	500.00
	1885 M	.013	15.00	35.00	90.00	400.00
	1886 M	.018	20.00	40.00	100.00	450.00
	1887 M	.026	25.00	65.00	150.00	500.00

Mint mark: Cn

KM#	Date	Mintage	Fine	VF	XF	Unc
407.2	1871 P	—	400.00	550.00	750.00	1500.
	1873 P	—	400.00	550.00	750.00	1500.
	1874 P	—	200.00	300.00	500.00	1000.
	1875/4 P	—	20.00	40.00	75.00	450.00
	1875 P	—	12.00	25.00	50.00	450.00
	1876 P	—	15.00	30.00	60.00	450.00
	1877/6 G	—	15.00	30.00	60.00	450.00
	1877 G	—	12.00	25.00	50.00	450.00
	1878 G	.018	20.00	40.00	75.00	450.00
	1878 D Cn/Mo					
	Inc. Ab.		30.00	60.00	100.00	450.00
	1878 D Inc. Ab.		15.00	35.00	75.00	450.00
	1879 D	—	12.00	25.00	50.00	450.00
	1879 D/G	—	12.00	25.00	50.00	450.00
	1880 D	—	15.00	30.00	60.00	450.00
	1881/0 D	.188	15.00	30.00	60.00	450.00
	1881 D Inc. Ab.		15.00	30.00	60.00	450.00
	1881 G Inc. Ab.		125.00	175.00	275.00	550.00
	1882 D	—	175.00	225.00	325.00	1000.
	1882 G	—	100.00	250.00	300.00	1000.
	1883 D	.019	25.00	50.00	100.00	500.00
	1885/3 CN/Pi M/H					
		9,254	30.00	60.00	100.00	500.00

KM#	Date	Mintage	Fine	VF	XF	Unc
407.2	1886 M/G	7,030	50.00	100.00	150.00	800.00
	1886 M	Inc. Ab.	40.00	80.00	150.00	800.00
	1887 M	.076	20.00	40.00	100.00	450.00
	1888 M	—	Contemporary counterfeits			
	1892 M	8,200	40.00	80.00	150.00	900.00

Mint mark: Do

KM#	Date	Mintage	Fine	VF	XF	Unc
407.3	1871 P	591 pcs.	—	—	Rare	—
	1873 P	4,010	150.00	250.00	500.00	1250.
	1873 M/P	I.A.	150.00	250.00	500.00	1250.
	1874 M	—	20.00	40.00	175.00	750.00
	1875 M	—	20.00	40.00	80.00	350.00
	1875 H	—	150.00	250.00	450.00	1000.
	1876/5 M	—	35.00	70.00	150.00	500.00
	1876 M	—	35.00	70.00	150.00	500.00
	1877 P	2,000	30.00	45.00	150.00	1250.
	1878 B	—	—	—	Rare	—
	1879 B	—	—	—	Rare	—
	1880 P	—	30.00	60.00	125.00	500.00
	1881 P	.010	40.00	80.00	150.00	550.00
	1882 C	8,957	30.00	75.00	200.00	800.00
	1884/2 C	—	20.00	50.00	125.00	600.00
	1884 C	—	—	—	—	—
	1885 B	—	15.00	40.00	100.00	500.00
	1886 C	.016	15.00	40.00	100.00	500.00
	1887 Do/MoC	.028	15.00	40.00	100.00	500.00

Mint mark: Go

KM#	Date	Mintage	Fine	VF	XF	Unc
407.4	1869 S	—	15.00	35.00	75.00	550.00
	1870 S	.166	12.00	25.00	50.00	450.00
	1871 S	.148	12.00	25.00	50.00	450.00
	1872/1 S	.144	15.00	30.00	60.00	500.00
	1872 S	Inc. Ab.	12.00	25.00	50.00	450.00
	1873 S	.050	12.00	25.00	50.00	450.00
	1874 S	—	12.00	25.00	50.00	450.00
	1875 S	—	15.00	35.00	75.00	450.00
	1876/5 S	—	12.00	25.00	50.00	450.00
	1877 S	.076	12.00	25.00	60.00	450.00
	1878 S	.037	15.00	30.00	75.00	550.00
	1879 S	—	12.00	25.00	50.00	450.00
	1880 S	—	12.00	25.00	50.00	450.00
	1881/79 S	.032	15.00	30.00	60.00	500.00
	1881 S	Inc. Ab.	12.00	25.00	50.00	450.00
	1882 S	.018	12.00	25.00	50.00	450.00
	1883/2 B/S	—	15.00	30.00	60.00	500.00
	1883 B	—	12.00	25.00	50.00	450.00
	1883 S	—	—	—	Rare	—
	1884 B/S	—	15.00	30.00	75.00	500.00
	1885 R	.053	12.00	25.00	50.00	450.00
	1886/5 R/B	.059	15.00	30.00	60.00	500.00
	1886/5 R/S	Inc. Ab.	20.00	40.00	75.00	500.00
	1886 R	Inc. Ab.	20.00	40.00	75.00	450.00
	1887 R	.018	20.00	40.00	75.00	550.00
	1888 R	—	Contemporary counterfeits			

NOTE: Varieties exist.

Mint mark: Ho

KM#	Date	Mintage	Fine	VF	XF	Unc
407.5	1874 R	—	20.00	40.00	100.00	600.00
	1875/4 R	—	20.00	50.00	125.00	600.00
	1875 R	—	20.00	50.00	125.00	600.00
	1876/5 F/R	—	15.00	35.00	100.00	550.00
	1876 F	—	15.00	35.00	100.00	550.00
	1877 F	—	50.00	75.00	150.00	650.00
	1880/70 A	—	15.00	35.00	100.00	550.00
	1880 A	—	15.00	35.00	100.00	550.00
	1881 A	.013	15.00	35.00	100.00	550.00
	1882 A	—	75.00	150.00	250.00	750.00
	1888 G	—	Contemporary counterfeits			
	1894 G	.059	15.00	30.00	100.00	450.00
	1895 G	8,000	250.00	350.00	500.00	1250.

NOTE: Varieties exist.

Mint mark: Mo

KM#	Date	Mintage	Fine	VF	XF	Unc
407.6	1869 C	.046	15.00	35.00	95.00	600.00
	1870 C	.052	15.00	30.00	90.00	550.00
	1871 C	.014	40.00	75.00	150.00	650.00
	1871 M/C	I.A.	35.00	75.00	150.00	600.00
	1872/1 M	.060	35.00	75.00	150.00	550.00
	1872 M	Inc. Ab.	35.00	75.00	150.00	550.00
	1873 M	6,000	35.00	75.00	150.00	600.00
	1874/3 M	—	200.00	400.00	600.00	1250.
	1874/2 B	—	15.00	30.00	75.00	500.00
	1874/3 B/M	—	15.00	30.00	75.00	500.00

KM#	Date	Mintage	Fine	VF	XF	Unc
407.6	1874 B	—	15.00	30.00	75.00	500.00
	1875 B	—	15.00	30.00	75.00	550.00
	1876/5 B	—	15.00	30.00	75.00	500.00
	1876 B	—	12.00	25.00	75.00	500.00
	1877/2 M	—	20.00	40.00	100.00	550.00
	1877 M	—	15.00	30.00	90.00	500.00
	1878/7 M	8,000	25.00	50.00	125.00	600.00
	1878 M	Inc. Ab.	15.00	35.00	100.00	550.00
	1879 M	—	25.00	50.00	125.00	550.00
	1880 M	—	100.00	150.00	250.00	750.00
	1881 M	.016	25.00	50.00	125.00	600.00
	1882/1 M	2,000	30.00	60.00	150.00	750.00
	1883/2 M	4,000	150.00	225.00	350.00	1000.
	1884 M	—	150.00	225.00	350.00	1000.
	1885 M	.012	30.00	60.00	150.00	600.00
	1886/5 M	.066	15.00	35.00	90.00	450.00
	1886 M	Inc. Ab.	12.00	25.00	75.00	400.00
	1887/6 M	.088	15.00	35.00	90.00	450.00
	1887 M	Inc. Ab.	15.00	35.00	75.00	450.00
	1888 M	—	Contemporary counterfeits			

Mint mark: Pi

KM#	Date	Mintage	Fine	VF	XF	Unc
407.7	1870/780 G	.050	25.00	45.00	110.00	500.00
	1870 G	Inc. Ab.	20.00	40.00	100.00	450.00
	1870 O	Inc. Ab.	20.00	40.00	100.00	450.00
	1871 O/G	.064	15.00	30.00	80.00	400.00
	1872 O	.052	15.00	30.00	80.00	400.00
	1872 O/G	I.A.	15.00	30.00	80.00	400.00
	1873 O	.032	20.00	40.00	100.00	450.00
	1873 H	Inc. Ab.	25.00	50.00	125.00	550.00
	1874 H/O	—	15.00	30.00	80.00	400.00
	1875 H	—	15.00	30.00	80.00	400.00
	1876 H	—	30.00	60.00	150.00	700.00
	1877 H	.034	20.00	40.00	100.00	450.00
	1878 H	9,700	20.00	40.00	100.00	450.00
	1879/7 H	—	15.00	35.00	90.00	450.00
	1879 H	—	15.00	35.00	90.00	450.00
	1880 H	—	20.00	40.00	100.00	450.00
	1881 H	.028	20.00	40.00	100.00	450.00
	1882 H	.022	15.00	30.00	80.00	400.00
	1883 H 8/8	.029	50.00	100.00	200.00	750.00
	1883 H	Inc. Ab.	15.00	30.00	80.00	400.00
	1884 H	—	50.00	100.00	175.00	600.00
	1885/0 H	.045	20.00	40.00	100.00	450.00
	1885/4 H	I.A.	20.00	40.00	100.00	450.00
	1885 H	Inc. Ab.	25.00	50.00	125.00	450.00
	1886/1 R	.092	50.00	100.00	175.00	600.00
	1886 C	Inc. Ab.	15.00	30.00	80.00	400.00
	1886 R	Inc. Ab.	15.00	30.00	90.00	450.00
	1887 R	.032	15.00	30.00	90.00	500.00
	1888 R	—	Contemporary counterfeits			

Mint mark: Zs

KM#	Date	Mintage	Fine	VF	XF	Unc
407.8	1870 H	.086	12.00	25.00	60.00	450.00
	1871 H	.146	12.00	25.00	50.00	400.00
	1872 H	.132	12.00	25.00	50.00	400.00
	1873 H	.056	12.00	25.00	50.00	400.00
	1874 H	—	12.00	25.00	50.00	400.00
	1874 A	—	—	—	Rare	—
	1875 A	—	12.00	25.00	50.00	400.00
	1876/5 A	—	15.00	30.00	60.00	450.00
	1876 A	—	12.00	25.00	50.00	400.00
	1876 S	—	100.00	200.00	350.00	750.00
	1877 S	.100	12.00	25.00	50.00	400.00
	1878/7 S	.254	15.00	30.00	60.00	450.00
	1878 S	Inc. Ab.	15.00	30.00	60.00	450.00
	1879 S	—	12.00	25.00	50.00	400.00
	1880 S	—	12.00	25.00	50.00	400.00
	1881 S	.201	12.00	25.00	50.00	400.00
	1882/1 S	2,000	50.00	100.00	250.00	650.00
	1882 S	Inc. Ab.	50.00	100.00	250.00	650.00
	1883 Zs/Za S	.031	30.00	60.00	100.00	450.00
	1883 S	Inc. Ab.	25.00	50.00	100.00	450.00
	1884/3 S	—	15.00	30.00	60.00	450.00
	1884 S	—	12.00	25.00	50.00	400.00
	1885/4 S	2,000	25.00	50.00	125.00	450.00
	1885 S	Inc. Ab.	25.00	50.00	125.00	450.00
	1886 Z	2,000	150.00	275.00	400.00	1000.
	1887 Z	.063	30.00	60.00	125.00	450.00

NOTE: Varieties exist.

PESO

27.0730 g, .903 SILVER, .7860 oz ASW
Mint mark: CH
Rev: Balance scale.

KM#	Date	Mintage	Fine	VF	XF	Unc
408	1872 P/M	.747	750.00	1500.	3500.	—
	1872 P	Inc. Ab.	350.00	700.00	1500.	—
	1872/1 M	I.A.	25.00	40.00	75.00	400.00
	1872 M	Inc. Ab.	17.50	25.00	50.00	250.00
	1873 M	.320	20.00	30.00	60.00	250.00
	1873 M/P	I.A.	25.00	40.00	75.00	350.00

Mint mark: Cn

KM#	Date	Mintage	Fine	VF	XF	Unc
408.1	1870 E	—	40.00	80.00	150.00	500.00
	1871/11 P	.478	25.00	45.00	90.00	350.00
	1871 P	Inc. Ab.	20.00	40.00	75.00	300.00
	1872 P	.209	20.00	40.00	75.00	300.00
	1873 P	.527	20.00	40.00	75.00	300.00

Mint mark: Do

KM#	Date	Mintage	Fine	VF	XF	Unc
408.2	1870 P	—	50.00	100.00	175.00	450.00
	1871 P	.427	25.00	50.00	75.00	300.00
	1872 P	.296	20.00	40.00	75.00	350.00
	1872 PT	Inc. Ab.	100.00	175.00	250.00	675.00
	1873 P	.203	25.00	45.00	85.00	350.00

Mint mark: Ga

KM#	Date	Mintage	Fine	VF	XF	Unc
408.3	1870 C	—	650.00	850.00	—	—
	1871 C	.829	25.00	65.00	135.00	600.00
	1872 C	.485	40.00	90.00	175.00	650.00
	1873/2 C	.277	40.00	90.00	175.00	700.00
	1873 C	Inc. Ab.	25.00	65.00	135.00	600.00

Mint mark: Go

KM#	Date	Mintage	Fine	VF	XF	Unc
408.4	1871/0 S	3.946	30.00	50.00	90.00	350.00
	1871/3 S	I.A.	20.00	35.00	70.00	250.00
	1871 S	Inc. Ab.	12.00	20.00	40.00	200.00
	1872 S	4.067	12.00	20.00	40.00	250.00
	1873/2 S	1.560	15.00	25.00	50.00	250.00
	1873 S	Inc. Ab.	12.00	20.00	45.00	200.00
	1873/Go/Mo/S/M					
		Inc. Ab.	12.00	20.00	45.00	250.00

Mint mark: Mo

KM#	Date	Mintage	Fine	VF	XF	Unc
408.5	1869 C	—	35.00	65.00	135.00	450.00
	1870/69 C					
		5.115	15.00	25.00	50.00	275.00
	1870 C	Inc. Ab.	12.00	20.00	40.00	250.00
	1870 M/C	I.A.	18.00	30.00	50.00	275.00
	1870 M	Inc. Ab.	18.00	30.00	50.00	275.00
	1871/0 M					
		6.974	15.00	25.00	50.00	275.00
	1871 M	Inc. Ab.	12.00	20.00	40.00	250.00
	1872/1 M/C					
		4.801	15.00	25.00	50.00	275.00
	1872 M	Inc. Ab.	12.00	20.00	40.00	250.00
	1873 M	1.765	12.00	20.00	40.00	250.00

NOTE: The 1869 C with large LEY on the scroll is a pattern.

Mint mark: Oa

KM#	Date	Mintage	Fine	VF	XF	Unc
408.6	1869 E	—	275.00	400.00	600.00	2000.
	1870 OAE small A					
		Inc. Ab.	15.00	30.00	75.00	400.00
	1870 OA E large A					
		Inc. Ab.	100.00	150.00	300.00	900.00
	1871/69 E	.140	30.00	50.00	125.00	550.00
	1871 OaE small A					
		Inc. Ab.	15.00	30.00	60.00	300.00
	1871 OA E large A					
		Inc. Ab.	15.00	30.00	75.00	400.00
	1872 OaE small A					
		.180	15.00	30.00	75.00	400.00
	1872 OA E large A					
		Inc. Ab.	50.00	100.00	200.00	450.00
	1873 E	.105	15.00	30.00	75.00	350.00

Mint mark: Pi

KM#	Date	Mintage	Fine	VF	XF	Unc
408.7	1870 S	1.967	200.00	350.00	500.00	1000.
	1870 S/A	I.A.	200.00	350.00	500.00	1000.
	1870 G	Inc. Ab.	25.00	50.00	125.00	450.00
	1870 H	Inc. Ab.	Contemporary counterfeit			
	1870 O/G	I.A.	15.00	35.00	125.00	450.00
	1870 O	Inc. Ab.	20.00	30.00	100.00	350.00
	1871/69 O					
		2.103	75.00	150.00	250.00	500.00
	1871 O/G	I.A.	15.00	30.00	60.00	300.00
	1872 O	1.873	15.00	30.00	60.00	300.00
	1873 O	.893	15.00	30.00	60.00	300.00
	1873 H	Inc. Ab.	15.00	30.00	60.00	300.00

NOTE: Varieties exist.

Mint mark: Zs

KM#	Date	Mintage	Fine	VF	XF	Unc
408.8	1870 H	4.519	12.00	30.00	40.00	200.00
	1871 H	4.459	12.00	20.00	40.00	200.00
	1872 H	4.039	12.00	20.00	40.00	200.00
	1873 H	1.782	12.00	20.00	40.00	200.00

NOTE: Varieties exist.

Mint mark: Cn
Liberty cap

KM#	Date	Mintage	Fine	VF	XF	Unc
409	1898 AM	1.720	10.00	15.00	30.00	65.00
	1898 Cn/MoAM					
		Inc. Ab.	15.00	30.00	90.00	150.00
	1899 AM	1.722	10.00	50.00	90.00	175.00
	1899 JQ	Inc. Ab.	10.00	15.00	50.00	125.00
	1900 JQ	1.804	10.00	15.00	30.00	80.00
	1901 JQ	1.473	10.00	15.00	30.00	80.00
	1902 JQ	1.194	10.00	15.00	45.00	125.00
	1903 JQ	1.514	10.00	15.00	30.00	80.00
	1903 FV	Inc. Ab.	25.00	50.00	100.00	225.00
	1904 MH	1.554	10.00	15.00	30.00	80.00
	1904 RP	I.A.	45.00	85.00	125.00	300.00
	1905 RP	.598	20.00	40.00	75.00	225.00

Mint mark: Go

KM#	Date	Mintage	Fine	VF	XF	Unc
409.1	1898 RS	4.256	10.00	15.00	35.00	75.00
	1898 Go/MoRS					
		Inc. Ab.	20.00	30.00	60.00	125.00
	1899 RS	3.207	10.00	15.00	30.00	75.00
	1900 RS	1.489	25.00	50.00	100.00	250.00

NOTE: Varieties exist.

Mint mark: Mo

KM#	Date	Mintage	Fine	VF	XF	Unc
409.2	1898 AM original strike - rev. w/139 Beads					
		10.156	7.50	10.00	17.50	60.00
	1898 AM restrike (1949) - rev. w/134 Beads					
		10.250	7.50	10.00	15.00	40.00
	1899 AM	7.930	10.00	12.50	20.00	70.00

KM#	Date	Mintage	Fine	VF	XF	Unc
409.2	1900 AM	8.226	10.00	12.50	20.00	70.00
	1901 AM	14.505	7.50	10.00	20.00	70.00
	1902/1 AM	16.224	150.00	300.00	500.00	950.00
	1902 AM I.A.		7.50	10.00	20.00	70.00
	1903 AM	22.396	7.50	10.00	20.00	70.00
	1903 MA (error) Inc. Ab.		1500.	2500.	3500.	7500.
	1904 AM	14.935	7.50	10.00	20.00	70.00
	1905 AM	3.557	15.00	25.00	55.00	125.00
	1908 AM	7.575	10.00	12.50	20.00	60.00
	1908 GV I.A.		10.00	12.50	17.50	40.00
	1909 GV	2.924	10.00	12.50	17.50	45.00

NOTE: Varieties exist.

Mint mark: Zs

KM#	Date	Mintage	Fine	VF	XF	Unc
409.3	1898 FZ	5.714	10.00	12.50	20.00	60.00
	1899 FZ	5.618	10.00	12.50	20.00	65.00
	1900 FZ	5.357	10.00	12.50	20.00	65.00
	1901 AZ	5.706	4000.	6500.	10,000.	—
	1901 FZ Inc. Ab.		10.00	12.50	20.00	60.00
	1902 FZ	7.134	10.00	12.50	20.00	60.00
	1903/2 FZ	3.080	12.50	15.00	50.00	125.00
	1903 FZ Inc. Ab.		10.00	12.50	20.00	65.00
	1904 FZ	2.423	10.00	15.00	25.00	70.00
	1904 FM Inc. Ab.		10.00	15.00	25.00	85.00
	1905 FM	.995	20.00	40.00	60.00	150.00

NOTE: Varieties exist.

1.6920 g, .875 GOLD, .0476 oz AGW
Mint mark: As

KM#	Date	Mintage	Fine	VF	XF	Unc
410	1888 L	—	—	—	Rare	—
	1888 AsL/MoM	—	—	—	Rare	—

Mint mark: Ca

KM#	Date	Mintage	Fine	VF	XF	Unc
410.1	1888 Ca/MoM	104 pcs.	—	—	Rare	—

Mint mark: Cn

KM#	Date	Mintage	Fine	VF	XF	Unc
410.2	1873 P	1,221	75.00	100.00	150.00	250.00
	1875 P	—	85.00	125.00	150.00	250.00
	1878 G	248 pcs.	100.00	175.00	225.00	450.00
	1879 D	—	100.00	150.00	175.00	275.00
	1881/0 D	338 pcs.	100.00	150.00	175.00	275.00
	1882 D	340 pcs.	100.00	150.00	175.00	275.00
	1883 D	—	100.00	150.00	175.00	275.00
	1884 M	—	100.00	150.00	175.00	275.00
	1886/4 M	277 pcs.	100.00	150.00	225.00	450.00
	1888/7 M	2,586	100.00	175.00	225.00	450.00
	1888 M Inc. Ab.		65.00	100.00	150.00	250.00
	1889 M	—	—	—	Rare	—
	1891/89 M	969 pcs.	75.00	100.00	150.00	250.00
	1892 M	780 pcs.	75.00	100.00	150.00	250.00
	1893 M	498 pcs.	85.00	125.00	150.00	250.00
	1894 M	493 pcs.	80.00	125.00	150.00	250.00
	1895 M	1,143	65.00	100.00	150.00	250.00
	1896/5 M	1,028	65.00	100.00	150.00	250.00
	1897 M	785 pcs.	65.00	100.00	150.00	250.00
	1898 M	3,521	65.00	100.00	150.00	225.00
	1898 Cn/MoM Inc. Ab.		65.00	100.00	150.00	250.00
	1899 Q	2,000	65.00	100.00	150.00	225.00
	1901/0 Q	2,350	65.00	100.00	150.00	225.00
	1902 Q	2,480	65.00	100.00	150.00	225.00
	1902 Cn/MoQ/C Inc. Ab.		65.00	100.00	150.00	225.00
	1904 H	3,614	65.00	100.00	150.00	225.00
	1904 Cn/Mo/H Inc. Ab.		65.00	100.00	150.00	250.00
	1905 P	1,000	—	Reported, not confirmed		

Mint mark: Go

KM#	Date	Mintage	Fine	VF	XF	Unc
410.3	1870 S	—	100.00	125.00	150.00	250.00
	1871 S	500 pcs.	100.00	175.00	225.00	450.00
	1888 R	210 pcs.	125.00	200.00	250.00	500.00
	1890 R	1,916	75.00	100.00	150.00	250.00
	1892 R	533 pcs.	100.00	150.00	175.00	325.00
	1894 R	180 pcs.	150.00	200.00	250.00	500.00
	1895 R	676 pcs.	100.00	150.00	175.00	300.00
	1896/5 R	4,671	65.00	100.00	150.00	250.00
	1897/6 R	4,280	65.00	100.00	150.00	250.00
	1897 R Inc. Ab.		65.00	100.00	150.00	250.00
	1898 R regular obv.	5,193	65.00	100.00	150.00	250.00
	1898 R mule, 5 Centavos obv., normal rev. Inc. Ab.		75.00	100.00	150.00	250.00
	1899 R	2,748	65.00	100.00	150.00	250.00
	1900/800 R	864 pcs.	75.00	125.00	150.00	275.00

Mint mark: Ho

KM#	Date	Mintage	Fine	VF	XF	Unc
410.4	1875 R	310 pcs.	—	—	Rare	—
	1876 F	—	—	—	Rare	—
	1888 G/MoM	—	—	—	Rare	—

Mint mark: Mo

KM#	Date	Mintage	Fine	VF	XF	Unc
410.5	1870 C	2,540	40.00	60.00	80.00	175.00
	1871 M/C	1,000	50.00	100.00	150.00	225.00
	1872 M/C	3,000	40.00	60.00	80.00	175.00
	1873/1 M	2,900	40.00	60.00	80.00	175.00
	1873 M Inc. Ab.		40.00	60.00	80.00	175.00
	1874 M	—	40.00	60.00	80.00	175.00
	1875 B/M	—	40.00	60.00	80.00	175.00
	1876/5 B/M	—	40.00	60.00	80.00	175.00
	1877 M	—	40.00	60.00	80.00	175.00
	1878 M	2,000	40.00	60.00	80.00	175.00
	1879 M	—	40.00	60.00	80.00	175.00
	1880/70 M	—	40.00	60.00	80.00	175.00
	1881/71 M	1,000	40.00	60.00	80.00	175.00
	1882/72 M	—	40.00	60.00	80.00	175.00
	1883/72 M	1,000	40.00	60.00	80.00	175.00
	1884 M	—	40.00	60.00	80.00	175.00
	1885/71 M	—	40.00	60.00	80.00	175.00
	1885 M	—	40.00	60.00	80.00	175.00
	1886 M	1,700	40.00	60.00	80.00	175.00
	1887 M	2,200	40.00	60.00	80.00	175.00
	1888 M	1,000	40.00	60.00	80.00	175.00
	1889 M	500 pcs.	100.00	150.00	200.00	275.00
	1890 M	570 pcs.	100.00	150.00	200.00	275.00
	1891 M	746 pcs.	100.00	150.00	200.00	275.00
	1892/0 M	2,895	40.00	60.00	80.00	175.00
	1893 M	5,917	40.00	60.00	80.00	175.00
	1894 M	6,244	40.00	60.00	80.00	175.00
	1895 M	8,994	40.00	60.00	80.00	175.00
	1895 B Inc. Ab.		40.00	60.00	80.00	175.00
	1896 B	7,166	40.00	60.00	80.00	175.00
	1896 M Inc. Ab.		40.00	60.00	80.00	175.00
	1897 M	5,131	40.00	60.00	80.00	175.00
	1898/7 M	5,368	40.00	60.00	80.00	175.00
	1899 M	9,515	40.00	60.00	80.00	175.00
	1900/800 M	9,301	40.00	60.00	80.00	175.00
	1900/880 M Inc. Ab.		40.00	60.00	80.00	175.00
	1900/890 M Inc. Ab.		40.00	60.00	80.00	175.00
	1900 M Inc. Ab.		40.00	60.00	80.00	175.00
	1901/801 M large date	8,293	40.00	60.00	80.00	175.00
	1901 M small date Inc. Ab.		40.00	60.00	80.00	175.00
	1902 M large date	.011	40.00	60.00	80.00	175.00
	1902 M small date Inc. Ab.		40.00	60.00	80.00	175.00
	1903 M large date	.010	40.00	60.00	80.00	175.00
	1903 M small date Inc. Ab.		50.00	80.00	120.00	180.00
	1904 M	9,845	40.00	60.00	80.00	175.00
	1905 M	3,429	40.00	60.00	80.00	175.00

Mint mark: Zs

KM#	Date	Mintage	Fine	VF	XF	Unc
410.6	1872 H	2,024	125.00	150.00	175.00	250.00
	1875/3 A	—	125.00	150.00	200.00	300.00
	1878 S	—	125.00	150.00	175.00	250.00
	1888 Z	280 pcs.	175.00	225.00	300.00	650.00
	1889 Z	492 pcs.	150.00	175.00	225.00	425.00
	1890 Z	738 pcs.	150.00	175.00	225.00	425.00

2-1/2 PESOS

4.2300 g, .875 GOLD, .1190 oz AGW

Mint mark: As

KM#	Date	Mintage	Fine	VF	XF	Unc
411	1888 As/MoL	—	—	—	Rare	—

Mint mark: Cn

KM#	Date	Mintage	Fine	VF	XF	Unc
411.1	1893 M	141 pcs.	1500.	2000.	2500.	3500.

Mint mark: Do

KM#	Date	Mintage	Fine	VF	XF	Unc
411.2	1888 C	—	—	—	Rare	—

Mint mark: Go

KM#	Date	Mintage	Fine	VF	XF	Unc
411.3	1871 S	600 pcs.	1250.	2000.	2500.	3250.
	1888 Go/MoR	110 pcs.	1750.	2250.	2750.	3500.

Mint mark: Ho

KM#	Date	Mintage	Fine	VF	XF	Unc
411.4	1874 R	—	—	—	Rare	—
	1888 G	—	—	—	Rare	—

Mint mark: Mo

KM#	Date	Mintage	Fine	VF	XF	Unc
411.5	1870 C	820 pcs.	150.00	250.00	350.00	650.00
	1872 M/C	800 pcs.	150.00	250.00	350.00	650.00
	1873/2 M	—	200.00	350.00	750.00	1250.
	1874 M	—	200.00	350.00	750.00	1250.
	1874 B/M	—	200.00	350.00	750.00	1250.
	1875 B	—	200.00	350.00	750.00	1250.
	1876 B	—	250.00	500.00	1000.	1500.
	1877 M	—	200.00	350.00	750.00	1250.
	1878 M	400 pcs.	200.00	350.00	750.00	1250.
	1879 M	—	200.00	350.00	750.00	1250.
	1880/79 M	—	200.00	350.00	750.00	1250.
	1881 M	400 pcs.	200.00	350.00	750.00	1250.
	1882 M	—	200.00	350.00	750.00	1250.
	1883/73 M	400 pcs.	200.00	350.00	750.00	1250.
	1884 M	—	250.00	500.00	1000.	1500.
	1885 M	—	200.00	350.00	750.00	1250.
	1886 M	400 pcs.	200.00	350.00	750.00	1250.
	1887 M	400 pcs.	200.00	350.00	750.00	1250.
	1888 M	540 pcs.	200.00	350.00	750.00	1250.
	1889 M	240 pcs.	150.00	300.00	525.00	850.00
	1890 M	420 pcs.	200.00	350.00	750.00	1250.
	1891 M	188 pcs.	200.00	350.00	750.00	1250.
	1892 M	240 pcs.	200.00	350.00	750.00	1250.

Mint mark: Zs

KM#	Date	Mintage	Fine	VF	XF	Unc
411.6	1872 H	1,300	200.00	350.00	500.00	1000.
	1873 H	—	175.00	325.00	450.00	700.00
	1875/3 A	—	200.00	350.00	750.00	1250.
	1877 S	—	200.00	350.00	750.00	1250.
	1878 S	300 pcs.	200.00	350.00	750.00	1250.
	1888 Zs/MoS	80 pcs.	300.00	500.00	1000.	1750.
	1889 Zs/MoZ	184 pcs.	250.00	450.00	950.00	1500.
	1890 Z	326 pcs.	200.00	350.00	750.00	1250.

CINCO (5) PESOS

8.4600 g, .875 GOLD, .2380 oz AGW

Mint mark: As

KM#	Date	Mintage	Fine	VF	XF	Unc
412	1875 L	—	—	—	—	—
	1878 L	383 pcs.	900.00	1700.	3000.	4500.

Mint mark: Ca

KM#	Date	Mintage	Fine	VF	XF	Unc
412.1	1888 M	120 pcs.	—	—	Rare	—

Mint mark: Cn

KM#	Date	Mintage	Fine	VF	XF	Unc
412.2	1873 P	—	300.00	600.00	1000.	1500.
	1874 P	—	—	—	—	—
	1875 P	—	300.00	500.00	700.00	1250.
	1876 P	—	300.00	500.00	700.00	1250.
	1877 G	—	300.00	500.00	700.00	1250.
	1882	174 pcs.	—	—	Rare	—
	1888 M	—	500.00	1000.	1350.	2000.
	1890 M	435 pcs.	250.00	500.00	750.00	1250.
	1891 M	1,390	250.00	400.00	500.00	1000.
	1894 M	484 pcs.	250.00	500.00	750.00	1600.
	1895 M	142 pcs.	500.00	750.00	1500.	2500.
	1900 Q	1,536	200.00	300.00	400.00	950.00
	1903 Q	1,000	200.00	300.00	400.00	800.00

Mintmark: Do

KM#	Date	Mintage	Fine	VF	XF	Unc
412.3	1873/2 P	—	700.00	1250.	1800.	3000.
	1877 P	—	700.00	1250.	1800.	3000.
	1878 E	—	700.00	1250.	1800.	3000.
	1879/7 B	—	700.00	1250.	1800.	3000.
	1879 B	—	700.00	1250.	1800.	3000.

Mint mark: Go

KM#	Date	Mintage	Fine	VF	XF	Unc
412.4	1871 S	1,600	400.00	800.00	1250.	2500.
	1887 R	140 pcs.	600.00	1200.	1500.	2750.
	1888 R	65 pcs.	—	—	Rare	—
	1893 R	16 pcs.	—	—	Rare	—

Mint mark: Ho

KM#	Date	Mintage	Fine	VF	XF	Unc
412.5	1874 R	—	1750.	2500.	3000.	4500.
	1877 R	990 pcs.	750.00	1250.	2000.	3000.
	1877 A	Inc. Ab.	650.00	1100.	1750.	2750.
	1888G	—	—	—	Rare	—

Mint mark: Mo

KM#	Date	Mintage	Fine	VF	XF	Unc
412.6	1870 C	550 pcs.	200.00	400.00	550.00	900.00
	1871/69 M	1,600	175.00	350.00	475.00	750.00
	1871 M	Inc. Ab.	175.00	350.00	475.00	750.00
	1872 M	1,600	175.00	350.00	475.00	750.00
	1873/2 M	—	200.00	400.00	550.00	850.00
	1874 M	—	200.00	400.00	550.00	850.00
	1875/3 B/M	—	200.00	400.00	550.00	950.00
	1875 B	—	200.00	400.00	550.00	950.00
	1876/5 B/M	—	200.00	400.00	550.00	1000.
	1877 M	—	250.00	450.00	750.00	1250.
	1878/7 M	400 pcs.	200.00	400.00	550.00	1250.
	1878 M	Inc. Ab.	200.00	400.00	550.00	1250.
	1879/8 M	—	200.00	400.00	550.00	1250.
	1880 M	—	200.00	400.00	550.00	1250.
	1881 M	—	200.00	400.00	550.00	1250.
	1882 M	200 pcs.	250.00	450.00	750.00	1250.
	1883 M	200 pcs.	250.00	450.00	750.00	1250.
	1884 M	—	250.00	450.00	750.00	1250.
	1886 M	200 pcs.	250.00	450.00	750.00	1250.
	1887 M	200 pcs.	250.00	450.00	750.00	1250.
	1888 M	250 pcs.	200.00	400.00	550.00	1250.
	1889 M	190 pcs.	250.00	450.00	750.00	1250.
	1890 M	149 pcs.	250.00	450.00	750.00	1250.
	1891 M	156 pcs.	250.00	450.00	750.00	1250.
	1892 M	214 pcs.	250.00	450.00	750.00	1250.
	1893 M	1,058	200.00	400.00	500.00	800.00
	1897 M	370 pcs.	200.00	400.00	550.00	1000.
	1898 M	376 pcs.	200.00	400.00	550.00	1000.
	1900 M	1,014	175.00	350.00	450.00	750.00
	1901 M	1,071	175.00	350.00	450.00	750.00
	1902 M	1,478	175.00	350.00	450.00	750.00
	1903 M	1,162	175.00	350.00	450.00	750.00
	1904 M	1,415	175.00	350.00	450.00	750.00
	1905 M	563 pcs.	200.00	400.00	550.00	1500.

Mint mark: Zs

KM#	Date	Mintage	Fine	VF	XF	Unc
412.7	1874 A	—	200.00	400.00	500.00	750.00
	1875 A	—	200.00	400.00	500.00	1000.
	1877 S/A	—	200.00	400.00	550.00	1000.
	1878/7 S/A	—	200.00	400.00	550.00	1000.
	1883 S	—	175.00	375.00	500.00	750.00
	1888 Z	70 pcs.	1000.	1500.	2000.	3000.
	1889 Z	373 pcs.	200.00	300.00	500.00	850.00
	1892 Z	1,229	200.00	300.00	450.00	750.00

DIEZ (10) PESOS

16.9200 g, .875 GOLD, .4760 oz AGW
Mint mark: As
Rev: Balance scale.

KM#	Date	Mintage	Fine	VF	XF	Unc
413	1874 DL	—	—	—	Rare	—
	1875 L	642 pcs.	600.00	1250.	2500.	3500.
	1878 L	977 pcs.	500.00	1000.	2000.	3000.
	1879 L	1,078	500.00	1000.	2000.	3000.
	1880 L	2,629	500.00	1000.	2000.	3000.
	1881 L	2,574	500.00	1000.	2000.	3000.
	1882 L	3,403	500.00	1000.	2000.	3000.
	1883 L	3,597	500.00	1000.	2000.	3000.
	1884 L	—	—	—	Rare	—
	1885 L	4,562	500.00	1000.	2000.	3000.
	1886 L	4,643	500.00	1000.	2000.	3000.
	1887 L	3,667	500.00	1000.	2000.	3000.
	1888 L	4,521	500.00	1000.	2000.	3000.
	1889 L	5,615	500.00	1000.	2000.	3000.
	1890 L	4,920	500.00	1000.	2000.	3000.
	1891 L	568 pcs.	500.00	1000.	2000.	3000.
	1892 L	—	—	—	—	—
	1893 L	817 pcs.	500.00	1000.	2000.	3000.
	1894/3 L	1,658	—	—	—	—
	1894 L	Inc. Ab.	500.00	1000.	2000.	3000.
	1895 L	1,237	500.00	1000.	2000.	3000.

Mint mark: Ca

KM#	Date	Mintage	Fine	VF	XF	Unc
413.1	1888 M	175 pcs.	—	—	7500.	—

Mint mark: Cn

KM#	Date	Mintage	Fine	VF	XF	Unc
413.2	1881 D	—	400.00	600.00	1000.	1750.
	1882 D	874 pcs.	400.00	600.00	1000.	1750.
	1882 E	Inc. Ab.	400.00	600.00	1000.	1750.
	1883 D	221 pcs.	—	—	—	—
	1883 M	Inc. Ab.	400.00	600.00	1000.	1750.
	1884 D	—	400.00	600.00	1000.	1750.
	1884 M	—	400.00	600.00	1000.	1750.
	1885 M	1,235	400.00	600.00	1000.	1750.
	1886 M	981 pcs.	400.00	600.00	1000.	1750.
	1887 M	2,289	400.00	600.00	1000.	1750.
	1888 M	767 pcs.	400.00	600.00	1000.	1750.
	1889 M	859 pcs.	400.00	600.00	1000.	1750.
	1890 M	670 pcs.	400.00	600.00	1000.	1750.
	1891 M	1,427	400.00	600.00	1000.	1750.
	1892 M	379 pcs.	400.00	600.00	1000.	1750.
	1893 M	1,806	400.00	600.00	1000.	1750.
	1895 M	179 pcs.	500.00	1000.	1500.	2500.
	1903 Q	774 pcs.	400.00	600.00	1000.	1750.

Mint mark: Do

KM#	Date	Mintage	Fine	VF	XF	Unc
413.3	1872 P	1,755	350.00	550.00	850.00	1250.
	1873/2 P	1,091	350.00	550.00	900.00	1500.
	1873/2 M/P					
		Inc. Ab.	350.00	550.00	900.00	1500.
	1874 M	—	350.00	550.00	900.00	1500.
	1875 M	—	350.00	550.00	900.00	1500.
	1876 M	—	450.00	750.00	1250.	2000.
	1877 P	—	350.00	550.00	900.00	1500.
	1878 E	582 pcs.	350.00	550.00	900.00	1500.
	1879/8 B	—	350.00	550.00	900.00	1500.
	1879 B	—	350.00	550.00	900.00	1500.
	1880 P	2,030	350.00	550.00	900.00	1500.
	1881/79 P					
		2,617	350.00	550.00	900.00	1500.
	1882 P	1,528	—	—	Rare	—
	1882 C	Inc. Ab.	350.00	550.00	900.00	1500.
	1883 C	793 pcs.	450.00	750.00	1250.	2000.
	1884 C	108 pcs.	450.00	750.00	1250.	2000.

Mint mark: Ga

KM#	Date	Mintage	Fine	VF	XF	Unc
413.4	1870 C	490 pcs.	500.00	800.00	1000.	1500.
	1871 C	1,910	400.00	800.00	1500.	2250.
	1872 C	780 pcs.	500.00	1000.	2000.	2500.

Mint mark: Ga

KM#	Date	Mintage	Fine	VF	XF	Unc
413.4	1873 C	422 pcs.	500.00	1000.	2000.	3000.
	1874/3 C					
		477 pcs.	500.00	1000.	2000.	3000.
	1875 C	710 pcs.	500.00	1000.	2000.	3000.
	1878 A	183 pcs.	600.00	1200.	2500.	3500.
	1879 A	200 pcs.	600.00	1200.	2500.	3500.
	1880 S	404 pcs.	500.00	1000.	2000.	3000.
	1881 S	239 pcs.	600.00	1200.	2500.	3500.
	1891 S	196 pcs.	600.00	1200.	2500.	3500.

Mint mark: Go

KM#	Date	Mintage	Fine	VF	XF	Unc
413.5	1872 S	1,400	800.00	1500.	2000.	3000.
	1887 R	80 pcs.	1250.	2000.	2500.	3500.
	1888 R	68 pcs.	1500.	2500.	3000.	4000.

Mint mark: Ho

KM#	Date	Mintage	Fine	VF	XF	Unc
413.6	1874 R	—	—	—	Rare	—
	1876 F	357 pcs.	—	—	Rare	—
	1878 A	814 pcs.	1750.	3000.	3500.	5500.
	1879 A	—	1000.	2000.	2500.	4000.
	1880 A	—	1000.	2000.	2500.	4000.
	1881 A	—	—	—	Rare	—

Mint mark: Mo

KM#	Date	Mintage	Fine	VF	XF	Unc
413.7	1870 C	480 pcs.	500.00	900.00	1200.	2000.
	1872/1 M/C					
		2,100	350.00	550.00	900.00	1400.
	1873 M	—	400.00	600.00	950.00	1500.
	1874/3 M	—	400.00	600.00	950.00	1500.
	1875 B/M	—	400.00	600.00	950.00	1500.
	1876 B	—	—	—	Rare	—
	1878 M	300 pcs.	400.00	600.00	950.00	1500.
	1879 M	—	—	—	—	—
	1881 M	100 pcs.	500.00	1000.	1600.	2500.
	1882 M	—	400.00	600.00	950.00	1500.
	1883 M	100 pcs.	600.00	1000.	1600.	2500.
	1884 M	—	600.00	1000.	1600.	2500.
	1885 M	—	400.00	600.00	950.00	1500.
	1886 M	100 pcs.	600.00	1000.	1600.	2500.
	1887 M	100 pcs.	600.00	1000.	1625.	2750.
	1888 M	144 pcs.	450.00	750.00	1200.	2000.
	1889 M	88 pcs.	600.00	1000.	1600.	2500.
	1890 M	137 pcs.	600.00	1000.	1600.	2500.
	1891 M	133 pcs.	600.00	1000.	1600.	2500.
	1892 M	45 pcs.	600.00	1000.	1600.	2500.
	1893 M	1,361	350.00	550.00	900.00	1400.
	1897 M	239 pcs.	400.00	600.00	950.00	1500.
	1898/7 M					
		244 pcs.	425.00	625.00	1000.	1750.
	1900 M	733 pcs.	400.00	600.00	950.00	1500.
	1901 M	562 pcs.	350.00	500.00	800.00	1400.
	1902 M	719 pcs.	350.00	500.00	800.00	1400.
	1903 M	713 pcs.	350.00	500.00	800.00	1400.
	1904 M	694 pcs.	350.00	500.00	800.00	1400.
	1905 M	401 pcs.	400.00	600.00	950.00	1500.

Mint mark: Oa

KM#	Date	Mintage	Fine	VF	XF	Unc
413.8	1870 E	4,614	400.00	600.00	900.00	1350.
	1871 E	2,705	400.00	600.00	900.00	1350.
	1872 E	5,897	400.00	600.00	900.00	1350.
	1873 E	3,537	400.00	600.00	950.00	1500.
	1874 E	2,205	400.00	600.00	1200.	1800.
	1875 E	312 pcs.	450.00	750.00	1400.	2250.
	1876 E	766 pcs.	450.00	750.00	1400.	2250.
	1877 E	463 pcs.	450.00	750.00	1400.	2250.
	1878 E	229 pcs.	450.00	750.00	1400.	2250.
	1879 E	210 pcs.	450.00	750.00	1400.	2250.
	1880 E	238 pcs.	450.00	750.00	1400.	2250.
	1881 E	961 pcs.	400.00	600.00	1200.	2000.
	1882 E	170 pcs.	600.00	1000.	1500.	2500.
	1883 E	111 pcs.	600.00	1000.	1500.	2500.
	1884 E	325 pcs.	450.00	750.00	1400.	2250.
	1885 E	370 pcs.	450.00	750.00	1400.	2250.
	1886 E	400 pcs.	450.00	750.00	1400.	2250.

KM#	Date	Mintage	Fine	VF	XF	Unc
413.8	1887 E	—	700.00	1250.	2250.	4000.
	1888 E	—	—	—	—	—

Mint mark: Zs

KM#	Date	Mintage	Fine	VF	XF	Unc
413.9	1871 H	2,000	350.00	550.00	850.00	1200.
	1872 H	3,092	300.00	500.00	700.00	1000.
	1873 H 936 pcs.		400.00	600.00	950.00	1500.
	1874 H	—	400.00	600.00	950.00	1500.
	1875/3 A	—	400.00	600.00	1000.	1750.
	1876/5 S	—	400.00	600.00	1000.	1750.
	1877 S/H 506 pcs.		400.00	600.00	1000.	1750.
	1878 S 711 pcs.		400.00	600.00	1000.	1750.
	1879/8 S	—	450.00	750.00	1400.	2250.
	1879 S	—	450.00	750.00	1400.	2250.
	1880 S	2,089	350.00	550.00	950.00	1500.
	1881 S 736 pcs.		400.00	600.00	1000.	1750.
	1882 S	1,599	350.00	550.00	950.00	1500.
	1883/2 S 256 pcs.		400.00	600.00	1000.	1750.
	1884/3 S	—	350.00	550.00	950.00	1600.
	1884 S	—	350.00	550.00	950.00	1600.
	1885 S	1,588	350.00	550.00	950.00	1500.
	1886 S	5,364	350.00	550.00	950.00	1500.
	1887 Z	2,330	350.00	550.00	950.00	1500.
	1888 Z	4,810	350.00	550.00	950.00	1500.
	1889 Z	6,154	300.00	500.00	750.00	1350.
	1890 Z	1,321	350.00	550.00	950.00	1500.
	1891 Z	1,930	350.00	550.00	950.00	1500.
	1892 Z	1,882	350.00	550.00	950.00	1500.
	1893 Z	2,899	350.00	550.00	950.00	1500.
	1894 Z	2,501	350.00	550.00	950.00	1500.
	1895 Z	1,217	350.00	550.00	950.00	1500.

VEINTE (20) PESOS

33.8400 g, .875 GOLD, .9520 oz AGW
Mint mark: As
Rev: Balance scale.

KM#	Date	Mintage	Fine	VF	XF	Unc
414	1876 L 276 pcs.		—	—	Rare	—
	1877 L 166 pcs.		—	—	Rare	—
	1878 L	—	—	—	—	—
	1888 L	—	—	—	Rare	—

Mint mark: CH,Ca

KM#	Date	Mintage	Fine	VF	XF	Unc
414.1	1872 M 995 pcs.		500.00	650.00	950.00	2500.
	1873 M 950 pcs.		500.00	650.00	950.00	2500.
	1874 M	1,116	500.00	650.00	950.00	2500.
	1875 M 750 pcs.		500.00	650.00	950.00	2500.
	1876 M 600 pcs.		500.00	800.00	1250.	2750.
	1877 55 pcs.		—	—	Rare	—
	1882 M	1,758	500.00	650.00	950.00	2500.
	1883 M 161 pcs.		600.00	1000.	1500.	3000.
	1884 M 496 pcs.		500.00	650.00	950.00	2500.
	1885 M 122 pcs.		600.00	1000.	1500.	3000.
	1887 M 550 pcs.		500.00	650.00	950.00	2500.
	1888 M 351 pcs.		500.00	650.00	950.00	2500.
	1889 M 464 pcs.		500.00	650.00	950.00	2500.
	1890 M	1,209	500.00	650.00	950.00	2500.
	1891 M	2,004	500.00	600.00	900.00	2250.
	1893 M 418 pcs.		500.00	650.00	950.00	2500.
	1895 M 133 pcs.		600.00	1000.	1500.	3000.

Mint mark: Cn

KM#	Date	Mintage	Fine	VF	XF	Unc
414.2	1870 E	3,749	500.00	650.00	950.00	2000.
	1871 P	3,046	500.00	650.00	950.00	2000.
	1872 P 972 pcs.		500.00	650.00	950.00	2000.
	1873 P	1,317	500.00	650.00	950.00	2000.
	1874 P	—	500.00	650.00	950.00	2000.
	1875 P	—	600.00	1200.	1800.	2500.

KM#	Date	Mintage	Fine	VF	XF	Unc
	1876 P	—	500.00	650.00	950.00	2000.
	1876 G	—	500.00	650.00	950.00	2000.
	1877 G 167 pcs.		600.00	1000.	1500.	2500.
	1878 842 pcs.		—	—	Rare	—
	1881/0 D 2,039		—	—	—	—
	1881 D Inc. Ab.		500.00	650.00	950.00	2000.
	1882/1 D 736 pcs.		500.00	650.00	950.00	2000.
	1883 M	1,836	500.00	650.00	950.00	2000.
	1884 M	—	500.00	650.00	950.00	2000.
	1885 M 544 pcs.		500.00	650.00	950.00	2000.
	1886 M 882 pcs.		500.00	650.00	950.00	2000.
	1887 M 837 pcs.		500.00	650.00	950.00	2000.
	1888 M 473 pcs.		500.00	650.00	950.00	2000.
	1889 M	1,376	500.00	650.00	950.00	2000.
	1890 M	—	500.00	650.00	950.00	2000.
	1891 M 237 pcs.		500.00	900.00	1200.	2250.
	1892 M 526 pcs.		500.00	650.00	950.00	2000.
	1893 M	2,062	500.00	650.00	950.00	2000.
	1894 M	4,516	500.00	650.00	950.00	2000.
	1895 M	3,193	500.00	650.00	950.00	2000.
	1896 M	4,072	500.00	650.00	950.00	2000.
	1897/6 M 959 pcs.		500.00	650.00	950.00	2000.
	1897 M Inc. Ab.		500.00	650.00	950.00	2000.
	1898 M	1,660	500.00	650.00	950.00	2000.
	1899 M	1,243	500.00	650.00	950.00	2000.
	1899 Q Inc. Ab.		500.00	900.00	1200.	2250.
	1900 Q	1,558	500.00	650.00	950.00	2000.
	1901/0 Q 1,496		—	—	—	—
	1901 Q Inc. Ab.		500.00	650.00	950.00	2000.
	1902 Q	1,059	500.00	650.00	950.00	2000.
	1903 Q	1,121	500.00	650.00	950.00	2000.
	1904 H	4,646	500.00	650.00	950.00	2000.
	1905 P	1,738	500.00	900.00	1200.	2250.

Mint mark: Do

KM#	Date	Mintage	Fine	VF	XF	Unc
414.3	1870 P 416 pcs.		1000.	1500.	2000.	2500.
	1871/0 P 1,073		1000.	1750.	2250.	2750.
	1871 P Inc. Ab.		1000.	1500.	2000.	2500.
	1872/1 PT	—	1500.	3000.	4500.	7000.
	1876 M	—	1000.	1500.	2000.	2500.
	1877 P 94 pcs.		1500.	2250.	2750.	3250.
	1878 258 pcs.		—	—	Rare	—

Mint mark: Go

KM#	Date	Mintage	Fine	VF	XF	Unc
414.4	1870 S	3,250	500.00	650.00	900.00	1250.
	1871 S	.020	500.00	650.00	900.00	1250.
	1872 S	.018	500.00	650.00	900.00	1250.
	1873 S	7,000	500.00	650.00	900.00	1250.
	1874 S	—	500.00	650.00	900.00	1250.
	1875 S	—	500.00	650.00	900.00	1250.
	1876 S	—	500.00	650.00	900.00	1250.
	1876 M/S	—	—	—	—	—
	1877 M/S .015		—	—	Rare	—
	1877 R Inc. Ab.		500.00	650.00	900.00	1250.
	1877 S Inc. Ab.		—	—	Rare	—
	1878/7 M/S .013		650.00	1250.	2000.	2500.
	1878 M Inc. Ab.		650.00	1250.	2000.	2500.
	1878 S Inc. Ab.		500.00	650.00	900.00	1250.
	1879 S	8,202	500.00	800.00	1200.	2250.
	1880 S	7,375	500.00	650.00	900.00	1250.
	1881 S	4,909	500.00	650.00	900.00	1250.
	1882 S	4,020	500.00	650.00	900.00	1250.
	1883/2 B	3,705	550.00	750.00	1150.	2000.
	1883 B Inc. Ab.		500.00	650.00	900.00	1250.
	1884 B	1,798	500.00	650.00	900.00	1250.
	1885 R	2,660	500.00	650.00	900.00	1250.
	1886 R	1,090	500.00	800.00	1200.	2000.
	1887 R	1,009	500.00	800.00	1200.	2000.
	1888 R	1,011	500.00	800.00	1200.	2000.
	1889 R 956 pcs.		500.00	800.00	1200.	2000.
	1890 R 879 pcs.		500.00	800.00	1200.	2000.
	1891 R 818 pcs.		500.00	800.00	1200.	2000.
	1892 R 730 pcs.		500.00	800.00	1200.	2000.
	1893 R	3,343	500.00	650.00	950.00	1600.
	1894/3 R	6,734	500.00	650.00	900.00	1250.
	1894 R Inc. Ab.		500.00	650.00	900.00	1250.
	1895/3 R	7,118	500.00	650.00	900.00	1250.
	1895 R Inc. Ab.		500.00	650.00	900.00	1250.
	1896 R	9,219	500.00	650.00	900.00	1250.
	1897/6 R	6,781	500.00	650.00	900.00	1250.
	1897 R Inc. Ab.		500.00	650.00	900.00	1250.
	1898 R	7,710	500.00	650.00	900.00	1250.

Mint mark: Go

KM#	Date	Mintage	Fine	VF	XF	Unc
414.4	1899 R	8,527	500.00	650.00	900.00	1250.
	1900 R	4,512	500.00	650.00	900.00	1250.

Mint mark: Ho

KM#	Date	Mintage	Fine	VF	XF	Unc
414.5	1874 R	—	—	—	Rare	—
	1875 R	—	—	—	Rare	—
	1876 F	—	—	—	Rare	—
	1888 G	—	—	—	Rare	—

Mint mark: Mo

KM#	Date	Mintage	Fine	VF	XF	Unc
414.6	1870 C	.014	500.00	600.00	800.00	1300.
	1871 M	.021	500.00	600.00	800.00	1300.
	1872/1 M	.011	500.00	600.00	800.00	1600.
	1872 M	Inc. Ab.	500.00	600.00	800.00	1300.
	1873 M	5,600	500.00	600.00	800.00	1300.
	1874/2 M	—	500.00	600.00	800.00	1350.
	1874/2 B	—	500.00	700.00	1000.	1600.
	1875 B	—	500.00	650.00	900.00	1500.
	1876 B	—	500.00	650.00	900.00	1500.
	1876 M	—	—	Reported, not confirmed		
	1877 M	2,000	500.00	700.00	1100.	2000.
	1878 M	7,000	500.00	650.00	900.00	1500.
	1879 M	—	500.00	650.00	900.00	1750.
	1880 M	—	500.00	650.00	900.00	1750.
	1881/0 M	.011	500.00	600.00	800.00	1350.
	1881 M	Inc. Ab.	500.00	600.00	800.00	1350.
	1882/1 M	5,800	500.00	600.00	800.00	1350.
	1882 M	Inc. Ab.	500.00	600.00	800.00	1350.
	1883/1 M	4,000	500.00	600.00	800.00	1350.
	1883 M	Inc. Ab.	500.00	600.00	800.00	1250.
	1884/3 M	—	500.00	650.00	900.00	1400.
	1884 M	—	500.00	650.00	900.00	1400.
	1885 M	6,000	500.00	650.00	900.00	1750.
	1886 M	.010	500.00	600.00	800.00	1500.
	1887 M	.012	500.00	600.00	800.00	1500.

Mint mark: Mo

KM#	Date	Mintage	Fine	VF	XF	Unc
414.6	1888 M	7,300	500.00	600.00	800.00	1500.
	1889 M	6,477	500.00	600.00	900.00	1650.
	1890 M	7,852	500.00	600.00	800.00	1500.
	1891/0 M	8,725	500.00	600.00	800.00	1500.
	1891 M	Inc. Ab.	500.00	600.00	800.00	1500.
	1892 M	.011	500.00	600.00	800.00	1300.
	1893 M	.015	500.00	600.00	800.00	1300.
	1894 M	.014	500.00	600.00	800.00	1300.
	1895 M	.013	500.00	600.00	800.00	1300.
	1896 B	.014	500.00	600.00	800.00	1300.
	1897/6 M	.012	500.00	600.00	800.00	1300.
	1897 M	Inc. Ab.	500.00	600.00	800.00	1300.
	1898 M	.020	500.00	600.00	800.00	1300.
	1899 M	.023	500.00	600.00	800.00	1300.
	1900 M	.021	500.00	600.00	800.00	1300.
	1901 M	.029	500.00	600.00	800.00	1300.
	1902 M	.038	500.00	600.00	800.00	1300.
	1903/2 M	.031	500.00	600.00	800.00	1300.
	1903 M	Inc. Ab.	500.00	600.00	800.00	1300.
	1904 M	.052	500.00	600.00	800.00	1300.
	1905 M	9,757	500.00	600.00	800.00	1300.

Mint mark: Oa

KM#	Date	Mintage	Fine	VF	XF	Unc
414.7	1870 E	1,131	750.00	1500.	2500.	5000.
	1871 E	1,591	750.00	1500.	2500.	5000.
	1872 E	255 pcs.	1000.	1750.	3000.	7000.
	1888 E	170 pcs.	2000.	3000.	5000.	—

Mint mark: Zs

KM#	Date	Mintage	Fine	VF	XF	Unc
414.8	1871 H	1,000	3500.	6500.	7000.	9000.
	1875 A	—	4000.	6000.	7500.	9500.
	1878 S	441 pcs.	4000.	6000.	7500.	9500.
	1888 Z	50 pcs.	—	—	Rare	—
	1889 Z	640 pcs.	3500.	5500.	7000.	9000.

United States of Mexico

CENTAVO

BRONZE, 20mm

KM#	Date	Mintage	Fine	VF	XF	Unc
415	1905	6.040	3.50	6.50	13.50	90.00
	1906 narrow date					
		*67.505	.50	1.00	1.75	12.50
	1906 wide date					
		Inc. Ab.	.60	1.00	2.00	15.00
	1910	8.700	2.00	3.00	7.50	85.00
	1911	16.450	.75	1.25	2.50	20.00
	1912	12.650	.90	1.50	3.50	32.00
	1913	12.850	.85	1.25	3.00	40.00
	1914	17.350	.75	1.00	2.50	12.50
	1915	2.277	5.00	15.00	50.00	150.00
	1916	.500	50.00	80.00	220.00	1150.
	1920	1.433	20.00	50.00	80.00	375.00
	1921	3.470	6.00	15.00	50.00	250.00
	1922	1.880	7.50	15.00	60.00	300.00
	1923	4.800	.75	1.00	2.00	13.50
	1924/3	2.000	50.00	100.00	250.00	475.00
	1924	Inc. Ab.	4.50	7.50	22.50	250.00
	1925	1.550	5.00	10.00	22.50	225.00
	1926	5.000	1.00	2.00	4.00	25.00
	1927/6	6.000	20.00	40.00	60.00	130.00
	1927	Inc. Ab.	.65	1.75	3.50	27.50
	1928	5.000	.50	1.00	2.50	17.50
	1929	4.500	.75	1.00	2.00	18.50
	1930	7.000	.55	1.00	2.25	19.50
	1933	10.000	.25	.35	.75	15.00
	1934	7.500	.40	1.00	2.50	35.00
	1935	12.400	.15	.25	.40	10.00
	1936	20.100	.15	.20	.30	9.00
	1937	20.000	.15	.25	.35	3.50
	1938	10.000	.10	.15	.30	2.50
	1939	30.000	.10	.15	.30	1.25
	1940	10.000	.20	.30	.60	6.50
	1941	15.800	.15	.25	.35	2.50
	1942	30.400	.15	.20	.30	1.25
	1943	4.310	.25	.50	.75	9.00
	1944	5.645	.15	.25	.50	7.50
	1945	26.375	.10	.15	.25	1.00
	1946	42.135	—	.10	.15	.45
	1947	13.445	—	.10	.15	1.00
	1948	20.040	—	.10	.15	1.00
	1949	6.235	.10	.20	.30	1.25

*NOTE: 50,000,000 pcs. were struck at the Birmingham Mint.
NOTE: Varieties exist.

Zapata Issue
Reduced size, 16mm

416	1915	.179	10.00	25.00	42.00	75.00

BRASS, 16mm

KM#	Date	Mintage	VF	XF	Unc	BU
417	1950	12.815	.15	.30	1.40	2.00
	1951	25.740	.15	.25	.75	1.10
	1952	24.610	.10	.15	.40	.75
	1953	21.160	.10	.15	.40	.85
	1954	25.675	.10	.15	.75	1.10
	1955	9.820	.15	.25	.85	1.50
	1956	11.285	.10	.20	.70	1.15
	1957	9.805	.10	.15	.85	1.35
	1958	12.155	.10	.15	.40	.80
	1959	11.875	.10	.20	.70	1.25
	1960	10.360	—	.10	.35	.65
	1961	6.385	—	.10	.50	.85
	1962	4.850	—	.10	.50	.90
	1963	7.775	—	.10	.25	.45
	1964	4.280	—	.10	.15	.35
	1965	2.255	—	.10	.20	.40
	1966	1.760	.10	.15	.40	.70
	1967	1.290	.10	.15	.40	.70
	1968	1.000	.10	.15	.75	1.20
	1969	1.000	.10	.15	.70	1.00

Reduced size, 13mm.

418	1970	1.000	.20	.35	1.25	1.70
	1972	1.000	.25	.40	1.50	1.90
	1973	1.000	1.50	3.00	7.50	12.00

2 CENTAVOS

BRONZE, 25mm

419	1905	.050	150.00	250.00	400.00	1000.
	1906/inverted 6					
		9.998	20.00	40.00	90.00	275.00
419	1906	*Inc. Ab.	6.50	12.50	20.00	80.00
	1920	1.325	7.50	15.00	42.50	260.00
	1921	4.275	2.75	4.50	11.00	95.00
	1922	—	250.00	550.00	1500.	4000.
	1924	.750	10.00	20.00	45.00	400.00
	1925	3.650	1.50	3.25	6.00	40.00
	1926	4.750	1.25	2.75	5.75	35.00
	1927	7.250	.75	1.25	2.25	25.00
	1928	3.250	1.00	1.75	4.25	28.00
	1929	.250	40.00	70.00	375.00	875.00
	1935	1.250	5.00	10.00	25.00	165.00
	1939	5.000	.45	.85	1.50	20.00
	1941	3.550	.40	.50	1.50	20.00

*NOTE: 5,000,000 pcs. were struck at the Birmingham Mint.

Zapata Issue
Reduced size, 20mm

KM#	Date	Mintage	Fine	VF	XF	Unc
420	1915	.487	4.50	7.50	10.00	55.00

5 CENTAVOS

NICKEL

KM#	Date	Mintage	Fine	VF	XF	Unc
421	1905	1.420	5.00	10.00	25.00	250.00
	1906/5	10.615	12.00	20.00	50.00	275.00
	1906	*Inc. Ab.	.75	1.25	3.25	45.00
	1907	4.000	1.00	3.50	12.00	225.00
	1909	2.052	3.50	9.00	55.00	365.00
	1910	6.181	.90	1.25	4.50	75.00
	1911 narrow date					
		4.487	.75	1.50	5.00	80.00
	1911 wide date					
	Inc. Ab.		2.00	3.50	9.00	100.00
	1912 small mint mark					
		.420	60.00	85.00	190.00	700.00
	1912 large mint mark					
	Inc. Ab.	50.00	75.00	175.00	550.00	
	1913	2.035	1.75	4.50	10.00	100.00
	1914	2.000	1.00	2.00	4.00	55.00

NOTE: 5,000,000 pcs. appear to have been struck at the Birmingham Mint in 1914 and all of 1909-1911. The Mexican Mint report does not mention receiving the 1914 dated coins.

NOTE: Varieties exist.

BRONZE

KM#	Date	Mintage	Fine	VF	XF	Unc
422	1914	2.500	7.50	20.00	45.00	225.00
	1915	11.424	1.50	5.00	16.00	150.00
	1916	2.860	15.00	35.00	180.00	675.00
	1917	.800	75.00	175.00	375.00	800.00
	1918	1.332	37.50	90.00	225.00	600.00
	1919	.400	140.00	200.00	375.00	900.00
	1920	5.920	3.50	8.00	45.00	200.00
	1921	2.080	11.00	25.00	75.00	260.00
	1924	.780	40.00	90.00	250.00	600.00
	1925	4.040	5.00	12.00	45.00	160.00
	1926	3.160	6.00	12.00	45.00	175.00
	1927	3.600	4.00	8.00	30.00	150.00
	1928 large date					
		1.740	9.00	18.00	65.00	195.00
	1928 small date					
	Inc. Ab.	25.00	45.00	90.00	350.00	
	1929	2.400	6.00	10.00	35.00	145.00
	1930 large oval 0 in date					
		2.600	5.00	9.00	35.00	180.00
	1930 small square 0 in date					
	Inc. Ab.	45.00	95.00	200.00	550.00	

KM#	Date	Mintage	Fine	VF	XF	Unc
422	1931	—	500.00	700.00	1150.	3000.
	1933	8.000	1.25	2.00	3.00	25.00
	1934	10.000	1.25	1.75	2.50	22.50
	1935	21.980	.75	1.25	3.00	18.50

COPPER-NICKEL

KM#	Date	Mintage	VF	XF	Unc	BU
423	1936	46.700	.50	1.00	6.50	9.00
	1937	49.060	.40	1.00	5.50	8.00
	1938	3.340	4.50	6.25	52.00	—
	1940	22.800	.90	1.50	7.00	10.00
	1942	7.100	1.50	2.00	20.00	30.00

BRONZE
'Josefa' Ortiz de Dominguez

KM#	Date	Mintage	VF	XF	Unc	BU
424	1942	.900	22.50	65.00	350.00	450.00
	1943	54.660	.50	.75	3.00	4.00
	1944	53.463	.15	.20	.75	1.25
	1945	44.262	.25	.35	.90	1.65
	1946	49.054	.50	.90	2.00	2.75
	1951	50.758	.75	1.00	3.00	4.75
	1952	17.674	1.50	2.50	9.00	11.00
	1953	31.568	.50	1.00	2.75	4.00
	1954	58.680	.50	1.00	2.75	4.00
	1955	31.114	1.25	2.00	11.00	15.00

COPPER-NICKEL
'White Josefa'

425	1950	5.700	.75	1.50	6.00	9.00

NOTE: 5,600,000 pieces struck at Connecticut melted.

BRASS

KM#	Date	Mintage	VF	XF	Unc	BU
426	1954 dot	—	9.00	20.00	150.00	200.00
	1954 w/o dot—	8.00	16.00	125.00	175.00	
	1955	12.136	.90	1.75	9.00	12.50
	1956	60.216	.15	.20	.80	1.50
	1957	55.288	.15	.20	.90	1.50
	1958	104.624	.15	.20	.50	1.00
	1959	106.000	.15	.20	.90	1.35
	1960	99.144	.10	.15	.25	.55
	1961	61.136	.10	.15	.40	.75
	1962	47.232	.10	.15	.30	.55
	1963	156.680	—	.10	.15	.35
	1964	71.168	—	.10	.15	.40
	1965	155.720	—	.10	.15	.35
	1966	124.944	—	.10	.30	.50
	1967	118.816	—	.10	.25	.40
	1968	189.588	—	.10	.25	.35
	1969	210.492	—	.10	.25	.35

COPPER-NICKEL

KM#	Date	Mintage	VF	XF	Unc	BU
426a	1962	19 pcs. 300.00	—	—	—	

BRASS
Reduced size, 18mm.

427	1970	163.368	—	.10	.30	.40
	1971	198.844	—	.10	.15	.20
	1972	225.000	—	.10	.15	.20
	1973 flat top 3					
		595.070	—	.10	.25	.35
	1973 round top 3					
		Inc. Ab.	—	.10	.15	.20
	1974	401.584	—	.10	.20	.25
	1975	342.308	—	.10	.20	.25
	1976	367.524	—	.10	.20	.25

NOTE: Due to some minor alloy variations this type is often encountered with a bronze color toning.

10 CENTAVOS

2.5000 g, .800 SILVER, .0643 oz ASW

428	1905	3.920	6.00	7.50	30.00	40.00
	1906	8.410	4.00	6.75	20.00	25.00
	1907/6	5.950	50.00	125.00	250.00	350.00
	1907	Inc. Ab.	6.00	8.25	25.00	32.50
	1909	2.620	9.00	12.00	50.00	65.00
	1910/00	3.450	10.00	18.00	80.00	100.00
	1910	Inc. Ab.	7.50	10.00	20.00	23.50
	1911	2.550	7.50	10.00	35.00	42.50
	1912	1.350	12.00	22.50	110.00	140.00
	1913/2	1.990	10.00	20.00	40.00	65.00
	1913	Inc. Ab.	7.00	10.00	32.50	40.00
	1914	3.110	4.50	6.75	12.00	18.00

1.8125 g, .800 SILVER, .0466 oz ASW
Reduced size, 15mm.

429	1919	8.360	9.50	17.50	65.00	95.00

BRONZE

430	1919	1.232	25.00	60.00	375.00	450.00
	1920	6.612	15.00	45.00	350.00	425.00
	1921	2.255	35.00	75.00	800.00	1000.
	1935	5.970	17.00	30.00	100.00	125.00

1.6600 g, .720 SILVER, .0384 oz ASW

KM#	Date	Mintage	VF	XF	Unc	BU
431	1925/15	5.350	15.00	30.00	100.00	120.00
	1925/3	Inc. Ab.	20.00	35.00	90.00	110.00
	1925	Inc. Ab.	2.50	4.00	25.00	32.00
	1926/16	2.650	30.00	60.00	150.00	170.00
	1926	Inc. Ab.	3.00	7.25	55.00	80.00
	1927	2.810	2.25	3.50	17.50	21.50
	1928	5.270	1.50	2.50	9.00	11.50
	1930	2.000	3.00	6.00	20.00	23.50
	1933	5.000	2.00	3.00	7.50	9.50
	1934	8.000	1.25	2.00	9.50	12.00
	1935	3.500	3.50	6.00	15.00	20.00

COPPER-NICKEL

432	1936	33.030	.40	.90	7.00	8.50
	1937	3.000	5.00	15.00	215.00	235.00
	1938	3.650	1.50	3.00	45.00	65.00
	1939	6.920	1.00	2.00	20.00	30.00
	1940	12.300	.50	1.25	5.00	6.50
	1942	14.380	.75	1.75	7.00	8.50
	1945	9.558	.35	.60	3.50	4.00
	1946	46.230	.25	.50	2.50	3.00

BRONZE
Benito Juarez

433	1955	1.818	1.00	3.50	22.50	28.00
	1956	5.255	.50	2.25	20.00	25.00
	1957	11.925	.20	.50	5.00	6.50
	1959	26.140	.15	.20	.50	.65
	1966	5.873	.10	.15	.45	.60
	1967	32.318	.10	.15	.35	.50

COPPER-NICKEL
Variety I
Rev: 5 full rows of kernels, sharp stem, wide date.

434.1	1974	6.000	—	.10	.35	.45
	1975	5.550	.10	.15	.45	.55
	1976	7.680	.10	.20	.30	.40
	1977	144.650	.50	2.00	2.50	3.50
	1978	271.870	—	2.00	2.50	3.50
	1979	375.660	—	.10	.30	.40
	1980	21.290	1.25	2.00	4.50	5.00
	1980/79	I.A.	2.25	3.75	6.00	7.00

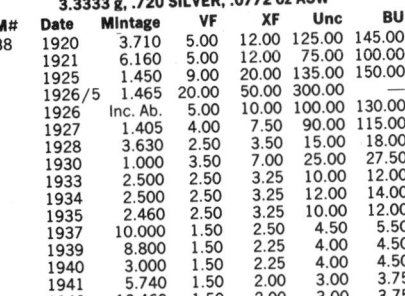

Variety II
Rev: 5 full, plus 1 partial row at left, blunt stem, narrow date.

KM#	Date	Mintage	VF	XF	Unc	BU
434.2	1977	Inc. Ab.	—	.10	.20	.25
	1978	Inc. Ab.	—	.10	.20	.30
	1979	Inc. Ab.	.10	.50	1.00	2.00
	1980	Inc. Ab.	—	.10	.20	.30

20 CENTAVOS

5.0000 g, .800 SILVER, .1286 oz ASW

KM#	Date	Mintage	VF	XF	Unc	BU
435	1905	2.565	10.00	17.50	150.00	175.00
	1906	6.860	7.00	12.00	55.00	70.00
	1907 straight 7	4.000	10.00	15.00	50.00	70.00
	1907 curved 7	5.435	8.00	12.00	50.00	75.00
	1908	.350	65.00	160.00	1500.	—
	1910	1.135	11.00	18.00	75.00	85.00
	1911	1.150	13.00	21.00	125.00	135.00
	1912	.625	35.00	75.00	335.00	375.00
	1913	1.000	14.00	21.00	85.00	100.00
	1914	1.500	10.00	15.00	62.50	75.00

3.6250 g, .800 SILVER, .0932 oz ASW
Reduced size, 19mm.

	Date	Mintage	VF	XF	Unc	BU
436	1919	4.155	30.00	60.00	210.00	250.00

BRONZE

	Date	Mintage	VF	XF	Unc	BU
437	1920	4.835	35.00	90.00	400.00	475.00
	1935	20.000	6.50	9.00	70.00	100.00

3.3333 g, .720 SILVER, .0772 oz ASW

KM#	Date	Mintage	VF	XF	Unc	BU
438	1920	3.710	5.00	12.00	125.00	145.00
	1921	6.160	5.00	12.00	75.00	100.00
	1925	1.450	9.00	20.00	135.00	150.00
	1926/5	1.465	20.00	50.00	300.00	—
	1926	Inc. Ab.	5.00	10.00	100.00	130.00
	1927	1.405	4.00	7.50	90.00	115.00
	1928	3.630	2.50	3.50	15.00	18.00
	1930	1.000	3.50	7.00	25.00	27.50
	1933	2.500	2.50	3.25	10.00	12.00
	1934	2.500	2.50	3.25	12.00	14.00
	1935	2.460	2.50	3.25	10.00	12.00
	1937	10.000	1.50	2.50	4.50	5.50
	1939	8.800	1.50	2.25	4.00	4.50
	1940	3.000	1.50	2.25	4.00	4.50
	1941	5.740	1.50	2.00	3.00	3.75
	1942	12.460	1.50	2.00	3.00	3.75
	1943	3.955	1.50	2.00	3.50	4.25

BRONZE

	Date	Mintage	VF	XF	Unc	BU
439	1943	46.350	.75	3.25	18.00	25.00
	1944	83.650	.50	.75	9.00	11.00
	1945	26.801	.60	2.25	10.00	12.00
	1946	25.695	.45	1.25	6.00	8.25
	1951	11.385	3.00	6.50	85.00	100.00
	1952	6.560	2.00	4.50	25.00	32.50
	1953	26.948	.30	.50	6.50	9.50
	1954	40.108	.30	.50	9.00	12.50
	1955	16.950	3.00	6.50	65.00	80.00

	Date	Mintage	VF	XF	Unc	BU
440	1955	Inc. KM439	.75	1.75	12.00	18.50
	1956	22.431	.25	.35	3.00	4.00
	1957	13.455	.50	1.00	9.00	12.00
	1959	6.017	4.50	9.00	70.00	90.00
	1960	39.756	.15	.20	.75	1.20
	1963	14.869	.20	.30	.90	1.25
	1964	28.654	.10	.15	.50	.90
	1965	74.162	.10	.15	.65	1.00
	1966	43.745	.15	.20	.90	1.30
	1967	46.487	.15	.20	.90	1.20
	1968	15.477	.15	.25	1.10	1.65
	1969	63.647	.15	.25	1.00	1.50
	1970	76.287	.15	.20	.80	1.10
	1971	49.892	.25	.35	1.00	1.40

COPPER-NICKEL
Francisco Madero

KM#	Date	Mintage	VF	XF	Unc	BU
444	1964	20.686	—	.10	.25	.40
	1966 closed beak					
		.180	.50	1.00	2.50	3.00
	1966 open beak					
	Inc. Ab.		1.00	3.50	10.00	14.00

50 CENTAVOS

KM#	Date	Mintage	VF	XF	Unc	BU
441	1971 Inc. KM440		.15	.25	1.00	1.75
	1973	78.398	.10	.15	.90	1.25
	1974	34.200	.20	.30	1.25	1.75

COPPER-NICKEL
Francisco Madero

	Date	Mintage	VF	XF	Unc	BU
442	1974	112.000	—	.10	.25	.30
	1975	611.000	.10	.15	.30	.35
	1976	394.000	.10	.15	.25	.30
	1977	394.350	.10	.15	.40	.45
	1978	527.950	.10	.15	.25	.30
	1979	524.615	—	.10	.25	.35
	1980	326.500	.10	.20	.40	.60
	1981 open 8					
		106.205	.10	.50	1.75	2.25
	1981 closed 8					
		248.500	.10	.50	1.00	1.50
	1981/2	—	30.00	60.00	100.00	—
	1982	286.855	.10	.40	.90	1.10
	1983	100.930	.10	.40	1.75	2.25
	1983	998 pcs.	—	—	Proof	25.00

NOTE: The 1981/2 overdate is often mistaken as 1982/1.

12.5000 g, .800 SILVER, .3215 oz ASW

	Date	Mintage	VF	XF	Unc	BU
445	1905	2.446	15.00	22.50	150.00	175.00
	1906	16.966	6.00	11.00	30.00	50.00
	1907 straight 7					
		18.920	5.75	8.50	25.00	28.50
	1907 curved 7					
		14.841	5.00	7.50	23.00	25.00
	1908	.488	75.00	170.00	525.00	600.00
	1912	3.736	7.50	12.50	45.00	55.00
	1913/07	10.510	35.00	75.00	200.00	250.00
	1913/2	Inc. Ab.	15.00	25.00	55.00	70.00
	1913	Inc. Ab.	6.50	10.00	25.00	30.00
	1914	7.710	6.50	10.00	24.00	28.00
	1916	.480	60.00	90.00	225.00	275.00
	1917	37.112	5.00	7.00	18.00	20.00
	1918	1.320	60.00	100.00	250.00	300.00

BRONZE
Olmec Culture

491	1983	260.000	.10	.25	.90	1.10
	1983	53 pcs.	—	—	Proof	185.00
	1984	180.320	.10	.25	1.50	1.70

25 CENTAVOS

9.0625 g, .800 SILVER, .2331 oz ASW
Reduced size, 27mm.

446	1918/7	2.760	—	625.00	1250.	—
	1918	Inc. Ab.	20.00	55.00	325.00	400.00
	1919	29.670	10.00	20.00	100.00	115.00

3.3330 g, .300 SILVER, .0321 oz ASW

443	1950	77.060	.60	.75	1.75	2.25
	1951	41.172	.60	.75	1.60	2.00
	1952	29.264	.75	1.00	1.80	2.50
	1953	38.144	.60	.75	1.50	2.00

8.3333 g, .720 SILVER, .1929 oz ASW

KM#	Date	Mintage	VF	XF	Unc	BU
447	1919	10.200	8.50	20.00	90.00	110.00
	1920	27.166	6.00	10.00	72.50	80.00
	1921	21.864	6.50	10.50	75.00	90.00
	1925	3.280	10.00	25.00	120.00	145.00
	1937	20.000	4.00	6.00	7.50	8.50
	1938	.100	50.00	100.00	300.00	350.00
	1939	10.440	4.00	6.50	9.00	10.00
	1942	.800	4.00	5.00	8.25	9.50
	1943	41.512	3.50	4.50	5.50	6.50
	1944	55.806	3.50	4.50	5.50	6.50
	1945	56.766	3.50	4.00	5.00	5.75

7.9730 g, .420 SILVER, .1076 oz ASW

448	1935	70.800	1.75	3.25	5.25	6.00

6.6600 g, .300 SILVER, .0642 oz ASW
Cuauhtemoc

449	1950	13.570	1.25	2.25	3.50	4.00
	1951	3.650	1.25	2.75	3.75	4.75

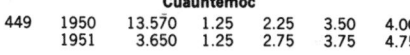

BRONZE

450	1955	3.502	1.00	2.50	25.00	37.50
	1956	34.643	.75	1.25	2.75	3.75
	1957	9.675	.50	.75	4.00	5.00
	1959	4.540	.40	.60	1.50	2.00

COPPER-NICKEL

451	1964	43.806	—	.10	.25	.40
	1965	14.326	—	.10	.30	.45
	1966	1.726	.20	.40	1.30	1.75
	1967	55.144	—	.15	.50	.60
	1968	80.438	—	.15	.50	.60
	1969	87.640	.10	.20	.75	1.00

Obv: Stylized eagle.

KM#	Date	Mintage	VF	XF	Unc	BU
452	1970	76.236	—	.20	1.00	1.20
	1971	125.288	—	.15	.90	1.20
	1972	16.000	1.00	2.00	3.50	4.00
	1975	177.958	.10	.15	.40	.60
	1976	37.480	.10	.20	.50	.65
	1977	12.410	6.00	10.00	32.50	37.50
	1978	85.400	.10	.20	.50	.65
	1979 round 2nd 9 in date					
		229.000	.10	.15	.50	.65
	1979 square 9's in date					
		Inc. Ab.	.10	.35	1.60	2.10
	1980 narrow date					
		89.978	.20	.75	2.00	2.50
	1980 wide date					
		178.188	.10	.25	1.00	1.15
	1981 rectangular 9					
		142.212	.25	1.25	3.50	7.50
	1981 round 9					
		Inc. Ab.	.10	.50	1.25	1.75
	1982	45.474	.10	.35	1.50	2.00
	1983	90.318	.10	.50	2.00	2.50
	1983	998 pcs.	—	—	Proof	25.00

NOTE: Coins dated 1975 and 1976 exist with and without dots in centers of three circles on plumage on reverse.

STAINLESS STEEL
Palenque Culture

492	1983	99.540	—	.25	.75	1.00
	1983	53 pcs.	—	—	Proof	185.00

UN (1) PESO

27.0700 g, .903 SILVER, .7859 oz ASW
'Caballito'

KM#	Date	Mintage	VF	XF	Unc	BU
453	1910	3.814	35.00	50.00	170.00	200.00
	1911 long lower left ray on rev.					
		1.227	40.00	70.00	210.00	275.00
	1911 short lower left ray on rev.					
		Inc. Ab.	140.00	185.00	600.00	800.00
	1912	.322	100.00	225.00	325.00	400.00
	1913/2	2.880	40.00	70.00	275.00	350.00
	1913	Inc. Ab.	40.00	70.00	180.00	210.00
	1914	.120	525.00	950.00	2750.	—

18.1300 g, .800 SILVER, .4663 oz ASW

454	1918	3.050	35.00	100.00	2500.	—
	1919	6.151	22.50	50.00	1200.	1800.

16.6600 g, .720 SILVER, .3856 oz ASW

455	1920/10	8.830	40.00	80.00	300.00	—
	1920	Inc. Ab.	6.00	16.00	160.00	200.00
	1921	5.480	6.00	16.00	160.00	200.00
	1922	33.620	4.00	5.50	22.00	25.00
	1923	35.280	4.00	5.50	22.00	25.00
	1924	33.060	4.00	5.50	22.00	25.00
	1925	9.160	5.00	11.00	37.50	45.00
	1926	28.840	4.00	5.50	20.00	24.00
	1927	5.060	4.50	10.00	60.00	75.00
	1932	50.770	3.50	4.50	6.00	6.75
	1933/2	43.920	15.00	25.00	80.00	—
	1933	Inc. Ab.	3.50	4.50	6.00	6.75
	1934	22.070	3.50	5.00	9.50	11.00
	1935	8.050	3.50	5.50	12.00	13.50
	1938	30.000	3.50	4.00	7.50	8.25
	1940	20.000	3.50	4.00	5.50	6.25
	1943	47.662	3.50	4.00	5.50	6.00
	1944	39.522	3.50	4.00	5.50	6.00
	1945	37.300	3.50	4.00	5.50	6.00

14.0000 g, .500 SILVER, .2250 oz ASW
Jose Morelos y Pavon

KM#	Date	Mintage	VF	XF	Unc	BU
456	1947	61.460	1.50	3.00	5.00	5.50
	1948	22.915	2.00	4.00	6.00	7.00
	1949	*4.000	—	1000.	1850.	2750.
	1949	—	—	—	Proof	4000.

*NOTE: Not released for circulation.

13.3300 g, .300 SILVER, .1285 oz ASW
Jose Morelos y Pavon

457	1950	3.287	3.00	3.75	7.00	8.50

16.0000 g, .100 SILVER, .0514 oz ASW
100th Anniversary of Constitution

458	1957	.500	3.00	4.50	14.00	16.50

Jose Morelos y Pavon

459	1957	28.273	.75	.90	2.50	3.00
	1958	41.899	.70	.85	1.75	2.50
	1959	27.369	1.60	2.00	4.50	6.50
	1960	26.259	.75	.90	3.25	4.00
	1961	52.601	.60	.90	2.25	2.75
	1962	61.094	.60	.90	2.25	2.75
	1963	26.394	BV	.60	1.75	2.00
	1964	15.615	BV	.60	1.75	2.00
	1965	5.004	BV	.60	1.90	2.20
	1966	30.998	BV	.60	2.00	2.50
	1967	9.308	BV	.60	3.00	3.50

COPPER-NICKEL
Jose Morelos y Pavon

KM#	Date	Mintage	VF	XF	Unc	BU
460	1970 narrow date					
		102.715	.15	.35	.65	.85
	1970 wide date					
		Inc. Ab.	.30	.50	1.25	2.75
	1971	426.222	.15	.20	.40	.65
	1972	120.000	.15	.20	.40	.65
	1974	63.700	.20	.25	.65	.90

	1975 tall narrow date					
		205.979	.15	.20	.60	.80

	1975 short wide date					
		Inc. Ab.	.15	.20	.75	1.00
	1976	94.489	.15	.20	.50	.75
	1977 thick date					
		94.364	.15	.40	1.00	1.25
	1977 thin date					
		Inc. Ab.	1.00	2.75	10.00	15.00
	1978 closed 8					
		208.300	.15	.35	.80	1.15
	1978 open 8					
		55.140	.60	1.25	3.50	4.75
	1979 thin date					
		117.884	.15	.30	.65	1.00
	1979 thick date					
		Inc. Ab.	.40	.50	1.00	1.20
	1980 closed 8					
		318.800	.15	.25	.80	.90
	1980 open 8					
		23.865	.50	1.50	6.00	9.75
	1981 closed 8					
		413.349	.20	.30	.75	1.00
	1981 open 8					
		58.616	.50	1.00	7.00	8.50
	1982	235.000	.25	.50	1.75	2.50
	1983 wide date					
		100.000	.20	.30	3.00	3.50
	1983 narrow date					
		Inc. Ab.	.25	.45	1.20	1.50
	1983	1,051	—	—	Proof	25.00

STAINLESS STEEL
Jose Morelos y Pavon

	Date	Mintage		XF	Unc	BU
496	1984	722.802	—	.25	.80	1.00
	1985	985.000	—	.15	.50	.75
	1986	740.000	—	.15	.50	.65
	1987	250.000	—	.15	.50	.80

DOS (2) PESOS

1.6666 g, .900 GOLD, .0482 oz AGW

KM#	Date	Mintage	Fine	VF	XF	Unc
461	1919	1.670	—	BV	30.00	50.00
	1920	4.282	—	BV	30.00	50.00
	1944	.010	27.50	35.00	45.00	70.00
	1945	*.140	—	—	BV + 20%	
	1946	.168	30.00	50.00	55.00	100.00
	1947	.025	27.50	40.00	45.00	65.00
	1948	.045	—	no specimens known		

*NOTE: During 1951-1972 a total of 4,590,493 pieces were restruck, most likely dated 1945.

26.6667 g, .900 SILVER, .7717 oz ASW
Centennial of Independence

KM#	Date	Mintage	VF	XF	Unc	BU
462	1921	1.278	35.00	60.00	325.00	450.00

DOS Y MEDIO (2-1/2) PESOS

2.0833 g, .900 GOLD, .0602 oz AGW

KM#	Date	Mintage	Fine	VF	XF	Unc
463	1918	1.704	—	BV	35.00	60.00
	1919	.984	—	BV	35.00	70.00
	1920/10	.607	—	BV	65.00	120.00
	1920	Inc. Ab.	—	BV	35.00	60.00
	1944	.020	BV	35.00	40.00	70.00
	1945	*.180	—	—	BV + 18%	
	1946	.163	BV	35.00	40.00	65.00
	1947	.024	200.00	250.00	300.00	550.00
	1948	.063	BV	35.00	40.00	65.00

*NOTE: During 1951-1972 a total of 5,025,087 pieces were restruck, most likely dated 1945.

CINCO (5) PESOS

4.1666 g, .900 GOLD, .1205 oz AGW

KM#	Date	Mintage	Fine	VF	XF	Unc
464	1905	.018	100.00	150.00	200.00	600.00
	1906	4.638	—	BV	60.00	90.00
	1907	1.088	—	BV	60.00	90.00
	1910	.100	BV	65.00	75.00	140.00
	1918/7	.609	60.00	65.00	75.00	120.00
	1918	Inc. Ab.	—	BV	60.00	90.00
	1919	.506	—	BV	60.00	90.00
	1920	2.385	—	BV	60.00	80.00
	1955	*.048	—	—		BV + 11%

*NOTE: During 1955-1972 a total of 1,767,645 pieces were restruck, most likely dated 1955.

30.0000 g, .900 SILVER, .8681 oz ASW
Cuauhtemoc

KM#	Date	Mintage	VF	XF	Unc	BU
465	1947	5.110	BV	6.50	9.00	11.00
	1948	26.740	BV	6.00	8.00	10.00

Miguel Hidalgo y Costilla

KM#	Date	Mintage	VF	XF	Unc	BU
467	1951	4.958	BV	5.00	8.00	10.00
	1952	9.595	BV	5.00	8.00	10.00
	1953	20.376	BV	5.50	7.50	9.50
	1954	.030	30.00	60.00	85.00	110.00

Bicentennial of Hidalgo Birth

468	1953	1.000	BV	6.50	9.00	11.00

27.7800 g, .720 SILVER, .6431 oz ASW
Opening of Southern Railroad

466	1950	.200	30.00	40.00	50.00	65.00

NOTE: It is recorded that 100,000 pieces were melted to be used for the 1968 Mexican Olympic 25 Pesos.

18.0500 g, .720 SILVER, .4178 oz ASW
Reduced size, 36mm.

KM#	Date	Mintage	VF	XF	Unc	BU
469	1955	4.271	4.00	5.00	6.00	7.00
	1956	4.596	4.00	5.00	6.00	7.00
	1957	3.464	4.00	5.00	6.00	7.00

KM#	Date	Mintage	VF	XF	Unc	BU
485	1980	266.900	.20	.50	1.75	2.75
	1981	30.500	.20	.50	2.00	3.25
	1982	20.000	.20	.50	3.50	4.75
	1982	1,051	—	—	Proof	30.00
	1983	7 known	—	—	Proof	—
	1984	16.300	1.25	2.00	4.00	6.00
	1985	76.900	1.50	2.25	4.50	6.50

100th Anniversary of Constitution

KM#	Date	Mintage	VF	XF	Unc	BU
470	1957	.200	5.50	9.00	14.00	16.50

BRASS
Circulation Coinage

502	1985	30.000	—	.10	.35	.50
	1987	81.900	—	.10	.35	.50
	1988	76.600	—	.10	.25	.35

DIEZ (10) PESOS

8.3333 g, .900 GOLD, .2411 oz AGW
Miguel Hidalgo

KM#	Date	Mintage	Fine	VF	XF	Unc
473	1905	.039	120.00	135.00	150.00	225.00
	1906	2.949	—	BV	120.00	145.00
	1907	1.589	—	BV	120.00	145.00
	1908	.890	—	BV	120.00	145.00
	1910	.451	—	BV	120.00	145.00
	1916	.026	120.00	135.00	160.00	325.00
	1917	1.967	—	BV	120.00	145.00
	1919	.266	—	BV	120.00	145.00
	1920	.012	175.00	300.00	500.00	750.00
	1959	*.050	—	—		BV + 7%

*NOTE: During 1961-1972 a total of 954,983 pieces were restruck, most likely dated 1959.

Centennial of Carranza Birth

471	1959	1.000	BV	5.00	9.00	11.00

Small date   Large date
COPPER-NICKEL
Vicente Guerrero

472	1971	28.457	.50	.75	2.25	2.75
	1972	75.000	.50	.75	2.00	2.25
	1973	19.405	1.20	1.50	5.50	7.00
	1974	34.500	.20	.50	1.75	2.25
	1976 small date					
		26.121	.75	1.25	3.50	4.25
	1976 large date					
		121.550	.10	.50	1.50	1.75
	1977	102.000	.10	.75	1.50	2.00
	1978	25.700	.50	1.50	5.50	6.75

Quetzalcoatl

28.8800 g, .900 SILVER, .8357 oz ASW
Miguel Hidalgo

KM#	Date	Mintage	VF	XF	Unc	BU
474	1955	.585	BV	6.50	12.50	15.00
	1956	3.535	BV	5.50	10.00	12.50

KM#	Date	Mintage	VF	XF	Unc	BU
477.1	1974	3.900	.50	1.75	3.25	4.00
	1974	—	—	—	Proof	600.00
	1975	1.000	1.00	3.50	10.00	17.50
	1976	74.500	.25	.75	1.75	2.25
	1977	79.620	.50	1.00	2.00	2.50
477.2	1978	124.850	.50	1.00	2.50	2.75
	1979	57.200	.50	1.00	2.25	2.50
	1980	55.200	.50	1.00	2.75	3.50
	1981	222.768	.30	.60	2.00	2.25
	1982	151.770	.40	.75	2.50	3.25
	1982	1,051	—	—	Proof	30.00
	1983	3 known	—	—	Proof	—
	1985	58.000	1.25	1.75	4.75	6.50

Thick flan, 2.3mm.

STAINLESS STEEL
Miguel Hidalgo

	Date	Mintage				
512	1985	257.000	—	.15	.65	.85
	1986	392.000	—	.15	.65	1.50
	1987	305.000	—	.10	.50	.65
	1988	500.300	—	.10	.35	.40
	1989	—	—	.25	.75	1.25
	1990	—	—	.25	.75	1.25

VEINTE (20) PESOS

100th Anniversary of Constitution

KM#	Date	Mintage	VF	XF	Unc	BU
475	1957	.100	15.00	30.00	48.00	55.00

16.6666 g, .900 GOLD, .4823 oz AGW

KM#	Date	Mintage	Fine	VF	XF	Unc
478	1917	.852	—	BV	230.00	265.00
	1918	2.831	—	BV	230.00	275.00
	1919	1.094	—	BV	230.00	265.00
	1920/10	.462	—	BV	235.00	285.00
	1920	Inc. Ab.	—	BV	230.00	275.00
	1921/11	.922	—	BV	240.00	300.00
	1921	Inc. Ab.	—	BV	230.00	265.00
	1959	*.013	—	—		BV+4%

*NOTE: During 1960-1971 a total of 1,158,414 pieces were restruck, most likely dated 1959.

150th Anniversary of War of Independence

476	1960	1.000	BV	7.00	10.00	12.50

COPPER-NICKEL
Miguel Hidalgo
Thin flan, 1.6mm.

COPPER-NICKEL

	Date	Mintage				
486	1980	84.900	.35	.70	2.75	3.50
	1981	250.573	.35	.70	2.50	3.25
	1982	236.892	.35	.70	2.75	3.50
	1982	1,051	—	—	Proof	40.00
	1983	3 known	—	—	Proof	—
	1984	55.000	.50	1.25	4.50	6.50

BRASS
Guadalupe Victoria, First President

KM#	Date	Mintage	VF	XF	Unc	BU
508	1985 wide date					
		25.000	.10	.20	1.00	1.25
	1985 narrow date					
		Inc. Ab.	.10	.25	1.50	2.00
	1986	10.000	—	—	—	5.00
	1988	355.200	—	.10	.40	.50
	1989	—	.15	.30	1.50	2.00
	1990	—	.15	.30	1.50	2.50

VEINTICINCO (25) PESOS

Benito Juarez

KM#	Date	Mintage	VF	XF	Unc	BU
480	1972	2.000	BV	4.00	6.00	7.50

22.5000 g, .720 SILVER, .5209 oz ASW
Summer Olympics - Mexico City
Type I, rings aligned.

KM#	Date	Mintage	VF	XF	Unc	
479.1	1968	27.182	BV	3.50	4.50	5.50

7.7760 g, .720 SILVER, .1800 oz ASW, 24mm
1986 World Cup Soccer Games

497	1985	.354	—	—	—	8.00

8.4060 g, .925 SILVER, .2450 oz ASW
Rev: W/o fineness statement.

497a	1986	—	—	—	Proof	16.00

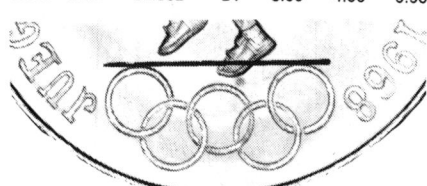

Type II, center ring low.

479.2	1968	Inc. Ab.	BV	5.00	9.00	10.00

1986 World Cup Soccer Games

503	1985	.277	—	—	Proof	16.00

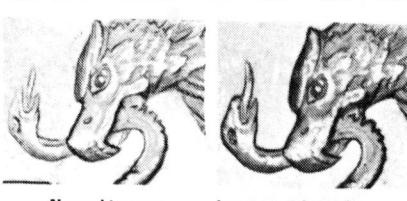

Normal tongue   Long curved tongue
Type III, center rings low.
Snake with long curved tongue.

479.3	1968	Inc. Ab.	BV	6.00	10.00	12.00

1986 World Cup Soccer Games

514	1985	.234	—	—	Proof	16.00

1986 World Cup Soccer Games

KM#	Date	Mintage	VF	XF	Unc	BU
519	1986	—	—	—	Proof	16.00

50 PESOS

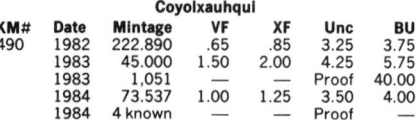

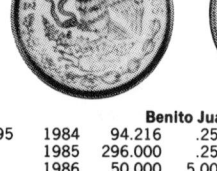

COPPER-NICKEL
Coyolxauhqui

KM#	Date	Mintage	VF	XF	Unc	BU
490	1982	222.890	.65	.85	3.25	3.75
	1983	45.000	1.50	2.00	4.25	5.75
	1983	1,051	—	—	Proof	40.00
	1984	73.537	1.00	1.25	3.50	4.00
	1984	4 known	—	—	Proof	—

Benito Juarez

KM#	Date	Mintage	VF	XF	Unc	BU
495	1984	94.216	.25	1.00	1.50	2.25
	1985	296.000	.25	.75	1.50	2.25
	1986	50.000	5.00	7.00	10.00	12.00
	1987	210.000	—	—	1.00	1.25
	1988	80.200	4.00	6.00	8.00	10.00

STAINLESS STEEL

KM#	Date	Mintage	VF	XF	Unc	BU
495a	1988	353.300	—	.10	.50	.60
	1990	—	—	.25	1.00	2.00
	1992	—	—	.10	.50	.60

41.6666 g, .900 GOLD, 1.2057 oz AGW
Centennial of Independence

KM#	Date	Mintage	Fine	VF	XF	Unc
481	1921	.180	—	—	BV	775.00
	1922	.463	—	—	BV	575.00
	1923	.432	—	—	BV	575.00
	1924	.439	—	—	BV	575.00
	1925	.716	—	—	BV	575.00
	1926	.600	—	—	BV	575.00
	1927	.606	—	—	BV	575.00
	1928	.538	—	—	BV	575.00
	1929	.458	—	—	BV	575.00
	1930	.372	—	—	BV	575.00
	1931	.137	—	—	BV	700.00
	1944	.593	—	—	BV	575.00
	1945	1.012	—	—	BV	575.00
	1946	1.588	—	—	BV	575.00
	1947	.309	—	—	BV + 3%	
	1947	—	—	—	Specimen 6500.	

NOTE: During 1949-1972 a total of 3,975,654 pieces were restruck, most likely dated 1947.

15.5520 g, .720 SILVER, .3601 oz ASW
1986 World Cup Soccer Games

	Date	Mintage	VF	XF	Unc	BU
498	1985	.347	—	—	—	11.00

16.8310 g, .925 SILVER, .5000 oz ASW
Rev: W/o fineness statement.

	Date	Mintage	VF	XF	Unc	BU
498a	1986	.010	—	—	Proof	24.00

1986 World Cup Soccer Games

	Date	Mintage	VF	XF	Unc	BU
504	1985	.347	—	—	Proof	24.00

1986 World Cup Soccer Games

KM#	Date	Mintage	VF	XF	Unc	BU
515	1985	.234	—	—	Proof	24.00

1986 World Cup Soccer Games

523	1986	.190	—	—	Proof	24.00

15.5500 g, .999 SILVER, .5000 oz ASW
50th Anniversary of Nationalization of Oil Industry

532	1988	.030	—	—	12.00	15.00

CIEN (100) PESOS

Low 7's	High 7's

27.7700 g, .720 SILVER, .6429 oz ASW
Jose Morelos y Pavon

KM#	Date	Mintage	VF	XF	Unc	BU
483	1977 low 7's, sloping shoulder					
		5.225	BV	5.00	7.00	10.00
	1977 high 7's, sloping shoulder					
		Inc. Ab.	BV	6.00	10.00	14.50

484	1977 date in line, redesigned higher right shoulder					
		Inc. KM483	BV	4.00	5.00	6.50
	1978	9.879	BV	4.50	6.00	8.50
	1979	.784	BV	5.00	7.00	10.00
	1979	—	—	—	Proof	500.00

ALUMINUM-BRONZE
Venustiano Carranza

493	1984	227.809	.20	.50	2.50	4.00
	1985	377.423	.15	.40	2.00	3.00
	1986	43.000	.75	1.25	4.00	6.00
	1987	165.000	—	.20	1.50	2.00
	1988	433.100	—	.20	.75	1.50
	1989	—	—	.20	1.00	1.75
	1990	—	—	.20	1.00	2.50
	1991	—	—	.20	1.00	2.50
	1992	—	—	.20	1.50	3.00

31.1030 g, .720 SILVER, .7201 oz ASW
1986 World Cup Soccer Games

KM#	Date	Mintage	VF	XF	Unc	BU
499	1985	.302	—	—	—	16.50

1986 World Cup Soccer Games
Rev: W/o fineness statement.

KM#	Date	Mintage	VF	XF	Unc	BU
521	1986	.208	—	—	Proof	35.00

32.6250 g, .925 SILVER, 1.0000 oz ASW
Rev: W/o fineness statement.

499a	1985	9,006	—	—	Proof	35.00

1986 World Cup Soccer Games
Rev: W/o fineness statement.

524	1986	.190	—	—	Proof	35.00

1986 World Cup Soccer Games
Rev: W/o fineness statement.

505	1985	9,006	—	—	Proof	35.00

World Wildlife Fund - Monarch Butterflies

537	1987	*.030	—	—	Proof	50.00

200 PESOS

31.1030 g, .999 SILVER, 1.0000 oz ASW
50th Anniversary of Nationalization of Oil Industry

KM#	Date	Mintage	VF	XF	Unc	BU
533	1988	.010	—	—	22.00	30.00

COPPER-NICKEL
175th Anniversary of Independence

KM#	Date	Mintage	VF	XF	Unc	BU
509	1985	75.000	—	.25	2.50	4.00

75th Anniversary of 1910 Revolution

510	1985	98.590	—	.25	2.25	3.50

33.6250 g, .925 SILVER, 1.0000 oz ASW
Save the Children

539	1991	.030	—	—	—	30.00

1986 World Cup Soccer Games

525	1986	50.000	—	.25	2.75	4.50

27.0000 g, .925 SILVER, .8029 oz ASW
Ibero - American Series - Pillars

540	1991	.075	—	—	Proof	42.50

62.2060 g, .999 SILVER, 2.0000 oz ASW
1986 World Cup Soccer Games

KM#	Date	Mintage	VF	XF	Unc	BU
526	1986	.050	—	—	30.00	50.00

250 PESOS

8.6400 g, .900 GOLD, .2500 oz AGW
1986 World Cup Soccer Games

500.1	1985	.100	—	—	—	110.00
	1986	—	—	—	—	110.00

Rev: W/o fineness statement.

500.2	1985	4,506	—	—	Proof	125.00
	1986	—	—	—	Proof	125.00

1986 World Cup Soccer Games

506.1	1985	.088	—	—	—	115.00

Rev: W/o fineness statement.

506.2	1985	*.080	—	—	Proof	125.00

500 PESOS

17.2800 g, .900 GOLD, .5000 oz AGW
1986 World Cup Soccer Games
Obv: Eagle facing left w/snake in beak.

501.1	1985	.102	—	—	—	210.00
	1986	—	—	—	—	210.00

Rev: W/o fineness statement.

501.2	1985	5,506	—	—	Proof	225.00
	1986	—	—	—	Proof	225.00

1986 World Cup Soccer Games

KM#	Date	Mintage	VF	XF	Unc	BU
507.1	1985	—	—	—	—	215.00

Rev: W/o fineness statement.

507.2	1985	—	—	—	Proof	225.00

33.4500 g, .925 SILVER, 1.0000 oz ASW
75th Anniversary of 1910 Revolution

511	1985	.040	—	—	Proof	40.00

COPPER-NICKEL
Francisco Madero

529	1986	20.000	—	.75	1.75	2.50
	1987	180.000	—	.75	1.75	2.50
	1988	230.000	—	.50	1.50	2.00
	1989	—	—	.50	1.50	2.00
	1990	—	—	.50	1.50	2.00

17.2800 g, .900 GOLD, .5000 oz AGW
50th Anniversary of Nationalization of Oil Industry
Similar to 5000 Pesos, KM#531.

534	1988	—	—	—	—	225.00

1000 PESOS

17.2800 g, .900 GOLD, .5000 oz AGW
175th Anniversary of Independence

KM#	Date	Mintage	VF	XF	Unc	BU
513	1985	—	—	—	Proof	275.00

62.2000 g, .999 GOLD, 2.0000 oz AGW
1986 World Cup Soccer Games

KM#	Date	Mintage	VF	XF	Unc	BU
528	1986	—	—	—	—	1250.

5000 PESOS

31.1030 g, .999 GOLD, 1.0000 oz AGW
1986 World Cup Soccer Games

527	1986	—	—	—	—	675.00

34.5590 g, .900 GOLD, 1.0000 oz AGW
50th Anniversary of Nationalization of Oil Industry
Similar to 5000 Pesos, KM#531.

535	1988	—	—	—	Proof	550.00

COPPER-NICKEL
50th Anniversary of Nationalization of Oil Industry

531	1988	50.000	—	2.75	4.75	6.00

MONETARY REFORM

1 New Peso = 1000 Old Pesos

5 CENTAVOS

STAINLESS STEEL

KM#	Date	Mintage	VF	XF	Unc
546	1992	—	—	—	.10

10 CENTAVOS

STAINLESS STEEL

547	1992	—	—	—	.15

ALUMINUM-BRONZE
Juana de Asbaje

536	1988	229.300	—	1.00	2.00	2.75
	1989	—	—	.75	1.75	2.50
	1990	—	—	1.00	2.00	2.75
	1992	—	—	.75	1.75	2.50

2000 PESOS

20 CENTAVOS

ALUMINUM-BRONZE

548	1992	—	—	—	.25

50 CENTAVOS

ALUMINUM-BRONZE

KM#	Date	Mintage	VF	XF	Unc
549	1992	—	—	—	.50

NEW PESO

STAINLESS STEEL RING, ALUMINUM-BRONZE CENTER

550	1992	—	—	—	1.00

2 NEW PESOS

STAINLESS STEEL RING, ALUMINUM-BRONZE CENTER

551	1992	—	—	—	2.00

5 NEW PESOS

STAINLESS STEEL RING, ALUMINUM-BRONZE CENTER

552	1992	—	—	—	3.75

10 NEW PESOS

ALUMINUM-BRONZE RING, .925 SILVER CENTER

553	1992	—	—	—	5.75

20 NEW PESOS

ALUMINUM-BRONZE RING, .925 SILVER CENTER

KM#	Date	Mintage	VF	XF	Unc
561	1993	—	—	—	7.50

SILVER BULLION ISSUES
25 PESOS

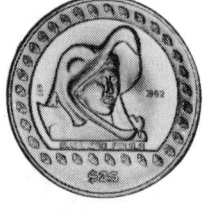

7.7758 g, .999 SILVER, .2500 oz ASW
Eagle Warrior

554	1992	—	—	—	3.50
	1992	—	—	Proof	—

50 PESOS

15.5517 g, .999 SILVER, .5000 oz ASW
Eagle Warrior

555	1992	—	—	—	5.00
	1992	—	—	Proof	—

100 PESOS

Brasero Efigie - The God of Rain

KM#	Date	Mintage	VF	XF	Unc
563	1992	—	—	—	—

31.1035 g, .999 SILVER, 1.0000 oz ASW
Eagle Warrior

KM#	Date	Mintage	VF	XF	Unc
556	1992	—	—	—	10.00
	1992	—	—	Proof	—

Xochipilli - The God of Joy, Music and Dance						**Huehueteotl - The God of Fire**				
562	1992	—	—	—	—	564	1992	—	—	—	—

10000 PESOS

155.5175 g, .999 SILVER, 5.0000 oz ASW
Illustration reduced. Actual size: 65mm.
Native Warriors Taking Female Captive

KM#	Date	Mintage	VF	XF	Unc
557	1992	—	—	—	45.00
	1992	—	—	Proof	—

1/20 ONZA TROY de PLATA
(1/20 Troy Ounce of Silver)

1.5551 g, .999 SILVER, .0500 oz ASW

KM#	Date	Mintage	VF	XF	Unc	BU
542	1991	.054	—	—	—	3.00
	1992	—	—	—	—	2.00

1/10 ONZA TROY de PLATA
(1/10 Troy Ounce of Silver)

3.1103 g, .999 SILVER, .1000 oz ASW

	Date	Mintage	VF	XF	Unc	BU
543	1991	.050	—	—	—	3.00
	1992	—	—	—	—	2.00

1/4 ONZA TROY de PLATA
(1/4 Troy Ounce of Silver)

7.7758 g, .999 SILVER, .2500 oz ASW

	Date	Mintage	VF	XF	Unc	BU
544	1991	.050	—	—	—	4.00
	1992	—	—	—	—	3.00

1/2 ONZA TROY de PLATA
(1/2 Troy Ounce of Silver)

15.5517 g, .999 SILVER, .5000 oz ASW

	Date	Mintage	VF	XF	Unc	BU
545	1991	.051	—	—	—	6.00
	1992	—	—	—	—	5.00

ONZA TROY de PLATA
(Troy Ounce of Silver)

33.6250 g, .925 SILVER, 1.0000 oz ASW
Obv: Mint mark above coin press.

KM#	Date	Mintage	VF	XF	Unc	BU
M49a	1949	1.000	12.50	17.50	25.00	30.00

Type 1. Obv: Wide spacing between DE MONEDA
Rev: Mint mark below balance scale.

| M49b.1 | 1978 | .280 | BV | 8.00 | 16.00 | 20.00 |

Type 2. Obv: Close spacing between DE MONEDA

KM#	Date	Mintage	VF	XF	Unc	BU
M49b.2	1978	Inc. Ab.	—	BV	13.00	18.00

Type 3. Rev: Left scale pan points to U in UNA.

| M49b.3 | 1979 | 4.508 | — | BV | 15.50 | 17.50 |

Type 4. Rev: Left scale pan points between
U and N of UNA.

| M49b.4 | 1979 | Inc. Ab. | — | BV | 13.00 | 15.00 |

Type 5.

| M49b.5 | 1980 | 6.104 | — | BV | 12.00 | 13.50 |
| | 1980/70 | I.A. | — | BV | 15.50 | 17.50 |

LIBERTAD
(Onza Troy de Plata)

31.1000 g, .999 SILVER, 1.0000 oz ASW

			Libertad			
494.1	1982	1.050	—	BV	8.00	10.00
	1983	1.268	—	BV	8.00	10.00
	1983	998 pcs.	—	—	Proof	290.00
	1984	1.014	—	BV	8.00	10.00
	1985	2.017	—	BV	8.00	10.00
	1986	1.699	—	BV	12.50	17.50
	1986	.030	—	—	Proof	25.00
	1987	.500	—	BV	15.00	22.50
	1987	.012	—	—	Proof	45.00
	1988	1.501	—	BV	15.00	25.00
	1989	1.397	—	BV	10.00	12.50
	1989	3,500	—	—	Proof	45.00
		Reeded edge.				
494.2	1990	1.200	—	BV	8.00	10.00
	1990	—	—	—	Proof	20.00
	1991	1.651	—	BV	7.00	9.00
	1991	—	—	—	Proof	25.00
	1992	—	—	BV	7.00	9.00
	1992	—	—	—	Proof	25.00

GOLD BULLION ISSUES
250 PESOS

7.7758 g, .999 GOLD, .2500 oz AGW
Native Culture - Sculpture of Jaguar Head

KM#	Date	Mintage	VF	XF	Unc
558	1992	—	—	—	100.00

KM#	Date	Mintage	VF	XF	Unc	BU
558	1992	—	—	—	Proof	—

500 PESOS

15.5517 g, .999 GOLD, .5000 oz AGW
Native Culture - Sculpture of Jaguar Head

KM#	Date	Mintage	VF	XF	Unc
559	1992	—	—	—	200.00
	1992	—	—	Proof	—

1000 PESOS

31.1035 g, .999 GOLD, 1.0000 oz AGW
Native Culture - Sculpture of Jaguar Head

KM#	Date	Mintage	VF	XF	Unc
560	1992	—	—	—	400.00
	1992	—	—	Proof	—

1/20 ONZA ORO PURO
(1/20 Ounce of Pure Gold)

1.7500 g, .900 GOLD, .0500 oz AGW
Obv: Winged Victory. Rev: Calendar stone.

KM#	Date	Mintage	VF	XF	Unc	BU
530	1987	—	—	—		BV + 30%
	1988	—	—	—		BV + 30%
	1991	.010	—	—		BV + 30%
	1992	—	—	—		BV + 30%

1/10 ONZA ORO PURO
(1/10 Ounce of Pure Gold)

3.5000 g, .900 GOLD, .1000 oz AGW

KM#	Date	Mintage	VF	XF	BU
541	1991	.010	—	—	BV + 20%
	1992	—	—	—	BV + 20%

1/4 ONZA ORO PURO
(1/4 Ounce of Pure Gold)

8.6396 g, .900 GOLD, .2500 oz AGW

KM#	Date	Mintage	VF	XF	BU
487	1981	.313	—	—	BV + 11%
	1991	.010	—	—	BV + 11%
	1992	—	—	—	BV + 11%

1/2 ONZA ORO PURO
(1/2 Ounce of Pure Gold)

17.2792 g, .900 GOLD, .5000 oz AGW

KM#	Date	Mintage	VF	XF	BU
488	1981	.193	—	—	BV + 8%
	1989	3,500	—	—	Proof 400.00
	1991	.010	—	—	BV + 8%
	1992	—	—	—	BV + 8%

ONZA ORO PURO
(1 Ounce of Pure Gold)

KM#	Date	Mintage	VF	XF	Unc	BU
		34.5585 g, .900 GOLD, 1.0000 oz AGW				
489	1981	.596	—	—	BV + 3%
	1985	—	—	—	BV + 3%
	1988	—	—	—	BV + 3%
	1991	.010	—	—	BV + 3%
	1992	—	—	—	BV + 3%

(50 PESOS)

		41.6666 g, .900 GOLD, 1.2057 oz AGW				
482	1943	.089	—	—	BV	525.00

PLATINUM BULLION ISSUES
1/4 ONZA
(1/4 ounce)

		7.7775 g, .999 PLATINUM, .2500 oz APW			
538	1989	3,500	—	—	Proof 200.00

MEDALLIC ISSUES (M)
(10 PESOS)

8.3333 g, .900 GOLD, .2411 oz AGW
200th Anniversary of Birth of Hidalgo

KM#	Date	Mintage	VF	XF	Unc	BU
M91a	1953	—	—	—	BV	135.00

Centennial of Constitution

M123a	1957	*.073	—	—	BV	135.00

*NOTE: Mintage includes #M122a.

(20 PESOS)

16.6666 g, .900 GOLD, .4823 oz AGW
200th Anniversary of Birth of Hidalgo

M92a	1953	—	—	—	BV	240.00

(50 PESOS)

41.6666 g, .900 GOLD, 1.2057 oz AGW
Centennial of Constitution

M122a	1957	Inc. M123a	—	—	BV	575.00

MINT SETS (MS)

KM#	Date	Mintage	Identification	Issue Price	Mkt. Val.
MS1	1977(16)	500	—	—	600.00
MSa2	1977(9)	—	434.1,434.2,442,452, 460 thick date, 460 thin date,472,477.1,484,Type 2 for 3 ring binder	—	125.00
MS2	1978(9)	500	KM434.1,434.2,442,452, 460 open 8, 460 closed 8, 472,477,484,Type 1 flat pack	—	200.00
MS3	1978(9)	—	KM434.1,434.2,442,452, 460 open 8, 460 closed 8, 472,477.2,484,Type 2 for 3 ring binder	—	100.00
MS4	1979(8)	—	KM434.2,442,452 square 9, 452 round 9, 460(2), 472, 477.2,484, Type 1 flat pack	11.00	12.00
MS5	1979(8)	—	KM434.1,434.2,442,452 square 9, 452 round 9, 460,477,484, Type 2 for 3 ring binder	11.00	11.00
MS6	1980(9)	—	KM434.2,442, 452 square 9, 452 round 9, 460 open 8, 460 closed 8, 477.2, 485-486	4.20	15.00
MS7	1981(9)	—	KM442 open 8, 442 closed 8, 452 rectangular 9, 452 round 9, 460 open 8, 460 closed 8, 477.2,485,486	—	17.00
MS8	1982(7)	—	KM442,452,460,477,485,486,490	—	14.00
MS9	1983(11)	—	KM442(2), 452(2), 460(2), 490(1), 491(2), 492(2)	—	15.00
MS10	1983(9)	—	KM442(2),452(2),460(2),490(1), 491(2),492(2) for 3 ring binder	—	13.50
MS11	1984(8)	—	KM485-486,490-491,493,495(2), 496	—	20.00
MS12	1985(12)	—	KM477.2,485,493(2),495(2), 496,502,508,509,510,512	—	22.00

KM#	Date	Mintage	Identification	Issue Price	Mkt. Val.
MS13	1986(7)	—	KM493,495,496,508,512,525,529	—	17.50
MS14	1985/1986(7)	—	KM493,495-496,502,508-509, 512	—	—
MS15	1987(9)	—	KM493,495(2),496,502(2), 512, 529(2)	—	17.50
MS16	1988(8)	—	KM493,495a,502,508,512,529, 531,536	—	25.00

NOTE: The 1978 and 1979 sets were issued in 2 varieties of plastic holders, one of which has holes for insertion in an official 3 ring binder which was sold for $3.30.
NOTE: In 1989 The Banco de Mexico began preparing mint sets by year with coins dated from 1971 thru 1988, MSa2 is such a set.

PROOF SETS (PS)

KM#	Date	Mintage	Identification	Issue Price	Mkt. Val.
PS1	1982/1983(8)	998	KM442,452,460,485,477.2 486,490,494	495.00	485.00
PS2	1982/1983(8)	*2	KM460,477.2,485,486,490 491,492,PnB169(in white box with Mo. in gold)	—	—
PS3	1982/1983(7)	*23	KM460,477.2,485,486,490, 491,492(in white box with Mo in gold)	—	560.00
PS4	1982/1983(7)	*17	KM460,477.2,485,486,490,491, 492(in white box)	—	560.00
PS5	1982/1983(7)	*8	KM460,477.2,485,486,490,491, 492(in blue pouch)	—	560.00
PS6	1983(7)	3	KM460,477.2,485,486,490 491,492	—	—
PS7	1985/1986(12)	—	KM497a-499a,503-505,514- 515,519,521,523-524	—	250.00
PS8	1985(4)	—	KM500.2-501.2,506.2,507.2	—	700.00
PS9	1985(3)	—	KM499a,514,515 (in blue box)	—	75.00
PS10	1985(3)	—	KM503-505 (in blue box)	—	75.00
PS11	1985(2)	—	KM511,513	—	325.00
PS12	1989(3)	3,500	KM488,494,538,Rainbow	730.00	650.00

*NOTE: KM#PS2, PS3, PS4 and PS5 are commonly referred to as pattern proof sets.

Bibliography

Boyd, Julian P. (Editor). *The Papers of Thomas Jefferson.* Vol. 7. New Jersey: Princeton University Press, 1953.

Bowers, Q. David. *The History of United States Coinage as Illustrated by the Garrett Collection.* Los Angeles: Bowers & Ruddy Galleries, 1979.

Breen, Walter. *Walter Breen's Complete Encyclopedia of U.S. and Colonial Coins.* New York: F.C.I. Press, Doubleday, 1988.

Bressett, Ken, and Kosoff, A. *Official A.N.A. Grading Standards for United States Coins,* Fourth Edition. Colorado Springs, Colo.: American Numismatic Association, 1991.

Brown, Martin R., and Dunn, John W. *A Guide to the Grading of United States Coins.* Fourth and Fifth Editions. Racine, Wis.: Whitman Publishing Co., 1964 and 1969.

Bullowa, David M. *Numismatic Notes and Monographs No. 83: The Commemorative Coinage of the United States 1892-1938.* New York, N.Y.: American Numismatic Society, 1938.

Evans, George G. *Illustrated History of the United States Mint.* Revised Edition. Philadelphia: George G. Evans, 1892.

Fitzpatrick, John C. (Editor). *The Writings of George Washington.* Vol. 28. Washington: U.S. Government Printing Office, 1938.

Heath, Dr. George. *The Numismatist,* September 1888 and February 1892.

Hepburn, A. Barton. *A History of Currency in the United States.* Revised Edition. New York: Sentry Press, 1967.

Krueger, Kurt R. "Grading: Bestial Pandemonium Unleashed." *The Numismatist,* January 1976. Colorado Springs, Colo.: American Numismatic Association, 1975.

Ruddy, James F. *Photograde.* Wolfeboro, N.H.: Bowers and Merena Galleries Inc., 1983.

Sheldon, William H. *Early American Cents.* New York: Harper & Row. 1949.

Syrett, Harold C. *The Papers of Alexander Hamilton.* Vol. 7. New York: Columbia University Press, 1963.

Taxay, Don. *The U.S. Mint and Coinage: An Illustrated History From 1776 to the Present.* Second Edition. New York: Arco Publishing Co., 1969.

U.S. Congress. Senate. *International Monetary Conference.* 1878. Senate Ex. Doc., 58. 45th Congress, Third Session. Washington, 1879.

U.S. Congress. Senate. *Coinage Laws of the United States 1792 to 1894 with an Appendix of Statistics Relating to Coins and Currency.* Fourth Edition. Washington, D.C.: Government Printing Office, 1894.

Van Allen, Leroy C., and Mallis, A. George. *Comprehensive Catalog and Encyclopedia of U.S. Morgan and Peace Silver Dollars.* New York: F.C.I. Press, 1976.

Willem, John M. *The United States Trade Dollar: America's Only Unwanted, Unhonored Coin.* New York: By the author, 1959; reprint edition, Racine, Wis.: Western Publishing Co., 1965.

Yeoman, R.S. *A Guidebook of United States Coins.* 45th Edition. Racine, Wis.: Western Publishing Co., 1991.

Featuring U.S. Money

STANDARD CATALOG OF UNITED STATES PAPER MONEY
12th Edition

By Chester Krause and Robert Lemke;
Robert E. Wilhite, Editor
208 pages, 8½" x 11", 550 photos, hardcover
$21.95

More than 175 years of paper money circulated by the Federal Government receives comprehensive treatment here in this new issue. Compares more than 5,000 currency items, punctuated by over 550 original photographs. Market valuations have been totally revised to bring current market value data in the three grades of preservation representing the range of conditions most often encountered.

STRIKING IMPRESSIONS
A Visual Guide to Collecting U.S. Coins

By Robert Van Ryzin
208 pages, 6"x9", $9.95

Based on the popular "Striking Impressions" column appearing regularly in Numismatic News, this book provides type listings and descriptions of all regular-issue U.S. coins from 1792 to date.

Photographs from Krause Publications' extensive photo collection help the collector to readily wade through the sometimes confusing terminology associated with coin collecting, learn to distinguish the differences between major varieties and types, and get a taste of the romance of coin collecting.

AUCTION PRICES REALIZED, U.S. COINS

1993 Edition
Edited by Bob Wilhite and Tom Michael
800 pages, 6"x9", $60.00

Auctions are key market value indicators, providing you with critical information of what buyers have paid for similar coins in a highly competitive market area.

Fingertip availability if recent auction results can mean the difference between profit and a loss in your important coin transactions. When you compare price guide values to actual auction prices, you have the information needed to make the most profitable buy/sell decisions for your coins!

Send check or money order (U.S. funds) for book price plus $2.50 shipping for first book, $1.50 for each additional book (Foreign: add $5.00/book) to:

Return this coupon with payment to:

MasterCard & VISA Cardholders Only call toll-free
1-800-258-0929
6:30 am - 5 pm, Monday thru Friday, 8 am - 2 pm, Saturday, CST

krause publications

WI residents add 5.5% sales tax to total

700 E. State Street, Iola, WI 54990-0001

3 FREE issues of

2 FREE issues of

1 FREE issue of

**To receive your 3 FREE issues of
NUMISMATIC NEWS, fill in the
reverse of this coupon and mail to:**

Numismatic News Circulation Dept.,
700 E. State St.,
Iola, WI 54990-0001

**To receive your 2 FREE issues of
COINS Magazine, fill in the
reverse of this coupon and mail to:**

Coins Magazine Circulation Dept.,
700 E. State St.,
Iola, WI 54990-0001

**To receive your 1 FREE issue of
COIN PRICES, fill in the
reverse of this coupon and mail to:**

Coin Prices Circulation Dept.,
700 E. State St.,
Iola, WI 54990-0001